WYOMING

A Guide to Its History, Highways, and People

A Selection of Wyoming Books Published by the UNP

Bill Nye's Western Humor, by Bill Nye, selected with an introduction
   by T. A. Larson
History of Wyoming, second edition revised, by T. A. Larson
A Lady's Experiences in the Wild West in 1883, by Rose Pender
*South Pass, 1868: James Chisholm's Journal of the Wyoming Gold
   Rush,* by James Chisholm
The War on Powder River, by Helena Huntington Smith

*For a complete list write to the University of Nebraska Press, 901 North
17th Street, Lincoln, Nebraska 68588*

Wyoming

A GUIDE TO ITS HISTORY, HIGHWAYS, AND PEOPLE

Compiled by workers of the Writers'
Program of the Work Projects Administration
in the State of Wyoming
Sponsored by Dr. Lester C. Hunt, Secretary of State

Introduction to the Bison Book Edition
by T. A. Larson

UNIVERSITY OF NEBRASKA PRESS
Lincoln and London

Introduction to the Bison Book edition © 1981
by the University of Nebraska Press
Manufactured in the United States of America

First Bison Book Printing: 1981
Most recent printing indicated by the first digit below:
1   2   3   4   5   6   7   8   9   10

Library of Congress Cataloging in Publication Data

Writers' Program. Wyoming.
   Wyoming, a guide to its history, highways, and people.

   Reprint of the c1941 ed. published by Oxford University Press, New York,
in series: American guide series.
   Bibliography: p.
   Includes index.
   1. Wyoming.   2. Wyoming—Description and travel—Guide—books.   I.
Title.   II. Series: American guide series.
F761.W58 1981   917.87′0433   80–23038
ISBN 0–8032–1958–X
ISBN 0–8032–6854–8 (pbk.)

Contents

INTRODUCTION TO THE BISON BOOK EDITION, by T. A. Larson ix
PREFACE, by Agnes W. Spring xix
GENERAL INFORMATION xxxi
CALENDAR OF ANNUAL EVENTS xxxvii

Part I. Wyoming: Past and Present

CONTEMPORARY SCENE 3
NATURAL SETTING 11
ARCHEOLOGY AND INDIANS 49
HISTORY 58
TRANSPORTATION 79
INDUSTRY, COMMERCE, AND LABOR 90
AGRICULTURE 98
EDUCATION 109
SPORTS AND RECREATION 117
FOLKLORE AND FOLKWAYS 122
LITERATURE 127
THE THEATER 137
MUSIC 147
ART 155
ARCHITECTURE 161

Part II. Cities

CASPER 173
CHEYENNE 183
LARAMIE 195
SHERIDAN 206

Part III. Tours

Tour 1   (Lead, S. Dak.)—Newcastle—Lusk—Torrington—Cheyenne—
(Denver, Colo.) [US 85]   217

Tour 2   (Kimball, Neb.)—Cheyenne—Laramie—Rawlins—Rock Springs
—Junction with US 30S—Kemmerer—(Montpelier, Idaho)
[US 30]   229
Section a. Nebraska Line to Laramie   230
Section b. Laramie to Rawlins   233
Section c. Rawlins to Junction with US 30S   241
Section d. Junction with US 30S to Idaho Line   247

Tour 2A   Cheyenne—Pole Mountain Game Refuge—Junction with US
30 [Happy Jack Road]   251

Tour 2B   Laramie—Saratoga—Junction with US 30 [State 130]   253

Tour 2C   Junction with US 30N—Evanston—(Ogden, Utah) [US 30S]   261

Tour 3   (Billings, Mont.)—Sheridan—Casper—Orin—Cheyenne—(Fort
Collins, Colo.) [US 87]   267
Section a. Montana Line to Buffalo   267
Section b. Buffalo to Junction with US 20   275
Section c. Junction with US 20 to Orin Junction   280
Section d. Orin Junction to Colorado Line   287

Tour 4   (Scottsbluff, Neb.)—Torrington—Junction with US 87 [US 26]   292

Tour 4A   Fort Laramie—Fort Laramie National Monument [Fort Road]   296

Tour 4B   Junction with US 26—Dead Man's Gulch [Guernsey Lake
Drive]   300

Tour 5   South entrance of Yellowstone Park—Junction with US 187—
Dubois—Lander—Rawlins—Laramie—(Fort Collins, Colo.)
[US 287]   302
Section a. Yellowstone Park to Junction with State 287   302
Section b. Junction with State 287 to Lander   307
Section c. Lander to Colorado Line   315

Tour 5A   Junction with US 287—Atlantic City—South Pass City—South
Pass—Junction with US 187 [South Pass Mail Road]   318

Tour 6   (Crawford, Neb.)—Lusk—Casper—Shoshoni—Greybull—
Yellowstone Park (East Entrance) [US 20]   323
Section a. Nebraska Line to Shoshoni   324
Section b. Shoshoni to Greybull   327
Section c. Greybull to Yellowstone Park   334

Tour 6A   Junction with US 14-20—Lovell—Cowley—Frannie—(Billings,
Mont.) [US 310]   339

Tour 7   Junction with US 287—Jackson—Junction with US 189—
          Rock Springs [US 187]   341
          Section a. Junction with US 287 to Junction with State 22   341
          Section b. Junction with State 22 to Rocks Springs   346

Tour 7A   Junction with US 187—Grand Teton National Park Head-
          quarters [Park Drive and US 187]   350

Tour 8   (Custer, S. Dak.)—Newcastle—Gillette—Buffalo—Worland
          [US 16]   356

Tour 9   Junction with US 187—Kemmerer—Junction with US 30S
          [US 189]   366

Tour 10   (Spearfish, S. Dak.)—Beulah—Moorcroft—Ucross—Sheridan—
          Ranchester—Greybull [US 14]   372

Tour 10A Junction with US 14—Kane—Lovell—Byron—Powell—Cody
          [State 14]   380

Tour 11   Casper—Alcova—Three Forks [State 220]   382

Tour 12   Shoshoni—Riverton—Lander [State 320]   388

Tour 13   Wilson—Alpine—Afton—(Montpelier, Idaho) [US 89]   392

Yellowstone National Park   399

     GRAND LOOP TOUR   Mammoth Hot Springs—Norris Junction—Mad-
                        ison Junction—West Thumb—Lake Junction—
                        Canyon Junction—Tower Junction—Mammoth
                        Hot Springs [Grand Loop Road]   409

Part IV. Appendices

Chronology   441

Bibliography   449

Glossary   459

1940 Census Figures   467

Index   469

Introduction

ONE HUNDRED years ago Bill Nye, Wyoming's most famous newspaper editor, complained that the onrush of civilization had "knocked the essential joy out of the life of the pioneer." He observed that "you walk over chaos where the 'hydraulic' has plowed up the valley like a convulsion." Other editors and businessmen were not disturbed by the changes they saw. Indeed, most of them wanted more "civilization."

Recently strip mining and other developments have revived Bill Nye's complaint. In 1980 many citizens took seriously the prophecy that Wyoming, which the *Wall Street Journal* had called the "Lonesome Land" in 1968, was destined to become a "national sacrifice area." It is an appropriate time to bring out a new edition of the long out-of-print Wyoming *Guide* because the book gives us a splendid portrait of Wyoming as it was long before all these modern changes began.

Two Wyoming natives, both graduates of the University of Wyoming, wrote most of the *Guide.* They worked under the auspices of the Works Progress Administration, which supported the preparation of such books in all states. The supervisor and editor-in-chief, Agnes Wright Spring, was born on a ranch on the Little Laramie River near Centennial in 1894. Now retired and living in Fort Collins, Colorado, she can look back on a record of great accomplishments as journalist, state librarian of Wyoming, state historian—first of Wyoming and later of Colorado—editor of the *Colorado Magazine,* and author of many books. Her associate, the senior editor of the *Guide,* Dee Linford (1915–71), was born in western Wyoming's Star Valley. Younger brother of Ernest H. Linford, the well-known newspaper editor and journalism professor, Dee wrote *Man without a Star* (1952), which the distinguished critic and University of Wyoming English professor Ruth Hudson rated as "the most honest and competent fictional treatment of the Wyoming scene yet written and one of the most authentic novels dealing with the history of the cattle country."

Spring and Linford had help from many people. Indeed, they were not the first to work on the book. The first Wyoming Writers' Project supervisor was Mart T. Christensen, Baggs publisher and register of the U.S. Land Office in Cheyenne, 1921–34. Christensen served as supervisor from October 1935 until March 1938, starting out with a staff of ten. Wyoming was permitted to use a 25:75 ratio of nonrelief to relief personnel instead of the preferred 10:90 ratio because the state had so few professional writers.

Christensen submitted much copy to Washington editors, but most of it was rejected. He resigned in March 1938 to run for office and was elected state treasurer in November. Agnes Wright Spring, who had been a member of the project staff since 1936, became supervisor and editor-in-chief in April 1938, and soon employed Linford.

Since Washington stressed the "Tours" portion of the *Guide,* Spring decided to take the road herself. She covered all the main highways and principal secondary roads and byroads, including those of Yellowstone Park. Her husband, an unpaid volunteer, drove while she checked the sites, logged mileages, and jotted down basic notes, which she typed at night. She also visited project field workers and "kept up their morale." The field workers, who numbered as many as forty at one time, provided raw data—interviews, folklore, local anecdotes. Using Spring's logs and notes, and referring to other sources, Linford wrote the two-hundred-page "Tours" part of the *Guide,* except for three pages on Fort Laramie which Spring contributed. Many choice "Tours" vignettes are in fine print, just as Edward Gibbon placed his most delightful comments in the footnotes of *The Decline and Fall of the Roman Empire.*

Spring wrote the "Contemporary Scene" and "Cities" sections. The "Natural Setting" section was assembled by junior editor Richard "Dick" Rossiter, from copy furnished without compensation by three specialists at the University of Wyoming—Professor S. H. Knight, geologist; past president Aven Nelson, botanist; and Professor John W. Scott, zoologist.

Spring, Linford, and Rossiter shared in the preparation of other essays and the Chronology. The Wyoming editors wanted to use an essay on Indians written by the venerable Rev. John Roberts, Episcopal missionary on the Wind River Reservation since 1884, but were overruled. An essay by a young "expert" who was sent out from Washington was substituted. Spring did the index, and affirmed in 1980 that every line of copy for the book "went across my desk before it went to Washington." For readers who would know more about the Wyoming Writers' Project than has been offered here, two articles are recommended: Gordon O. Hendrickson, "The WPA Writers' Project in Wyoming: History and Collections," *Annals of Wyoming* 49, no. 2 (Fall 1977): 175–92; and H. R. Dieterich, "New Deal Cultural Projects in Wyoming: A Survey and an Appraisal," *Annals of Wyoming* 52, no. 2 (October 1980): 30–44.

The Wyoming of the 1930s, which the *Guide* portrays, I remember with affection and a touch of nostalgia. Coming out of Nebraska and Colorado, I worked four summers (1931–34) for the Lodge and Camps Company in Yellowstone Park before I became a permanent resident of Laramie in 1936. The "savages" who worked in the park, with their hiking, fishing, swimming, and dancing, had more fun than the paying guests.

Money was scarce in Wyoming throughout the decade, though more plentiful after 1935 than before. The *Guide* is probably accurate in its report that the cost of a vacation was only $3.66 per person per day. Many vacationers were campers who slept in tents. One could find hotel, "cabin court," and tourist home vacancies at one or two dollars a night. Ten cents would buy a quart of milk, a loaf of bread, or a hamburger. In Jackson Hole there was no Jackson Lake Lodge or Colter Bay Village, but at the dam, a mile south of the present lodge, there was a little two-story hotel that offered no private bath but only "hot and cold water on the floor."

Visitors in Yellowstone Park in the early 1930s numbered no more than 250,000 a year, less than 10 percent of the count recently. With so few visitors there was insufficient garbage for the bear-feeding platforms at Canyon and Old Faithful, so the bears raided campgrounds, lodge cabins, and automobile luggage racks.

Despite the Great Depression, the state's population increased from 225,000 to 250,000 between 1930 and 1940. About one-third lived in cities of 2,500 or more, one-third in towns and villages, and one-third on ranches and farms. Ingrained frugality dictated simple pleasures. Fun was not illegal, yet older people did not laugh very often.

Men over twenty-one outnumbered women five to three in 1930. Perhaps because of the preponderance of men, and their vaunted self-reliance, the state was the last to ask for and to receive (on June 29, 1933) federal assistance for its needy. In the next four years, however, the federal government's nonrecoverable relief expenditures were almost three times as much per capita in Wyoming as in the United

States as a whole, while internal revenue was almost four times as much per capita in the United States as in Wyoming. Seventeen percent of the state's people were on general relief in March 1935. The legislature's general fund appropriations in 1935 totaled only $3,500,000 for the next biennium, and $4,200,000 in 1939.

For a few years rural folks were on relief as much as urban folks because of drought. In 1934 the federal government's emergency cattle and sheep purchase programs revealed the desperate plight of the rural people. Twenty-five percent of the state's cattle and 14 percent of the sheep were purchased from more than nine thousand producers for an average of $14.65 for cattle and $2.00 for sheep. Most of these animals were starving or diseased and had to be put to death.

By 1937 the welfare system and the New Deal in general were under attack from conservative Democrats as well as most Republicans. The legislature, which had almost always been controlled by Republicans, had turned Democratic in 1934 and 1936, then returned to the traditional pattern. Yet the New Deal had caught the fancy of enough Wyoming citizens that Republicans never regained the overwhelming dominance they had enjoyed before 1930.

Economic conditions improved considerably, but there was still no affluence in 1940 when Spring and Linford put the finishing touches on the *Guide*. In 1940–41 lingering concerns about the Great Depression yielded to forebodings about the war in Europe. Americans generally sympathized with Great Britain and France, but they disagreed on how much they should get involved. Japan made the decision for them at Pearl Harbor on December 7, 1941.

Military needs determined construction priorities. Fort Francis E. Warren at Cheyenne was doubled in size in 1941 with the addition of a quartermaster training center. Close to five thousand men, mostly from Wyoming, built the center in six months. A second installation, an army air base, was built eight miles west of Casper in the summer of 1942. Another hurry-up project was the Heart Mountain Relocation Center, built in 1942 between Cody and Powell for Japanese evacuated from the West Coast. Similarly, a prisoner of war camp rose rapidly a mile west of Douglas in 1943. Except for the Fort Warren expansion these installations were dismantled soon after the war.

Two substantial oil refinery expansions occurred in the form of one-hundred-octane plants, one at Cheyenne and the other at Sinclair. Smaller additions were made to five other refineries. Completing the list of major war-connected construction projects were the United Air

Lines Modification Center (for bombers) at Cheyenne, the Interior Department's Bureau of Mines Oil-Shale Experiment Station in Laramie, and a large alumina pilot plant south of Laramie, designed to produce aluminum metal from anorthosite clay. After the war the oil-shale station evolved into the Laramie Energy Technology Center and the alumina plant was placed on a stand-by basis until eventually it was turned over to an adjacent Portland cement plant and modified for cement making. These wartime construction projects entailed no permanent negative consequences.

The federal government furnished most of the capital for wartime industrial expansion. Many chambers of commerce and state leaders who had been seeking manufacturing plants redoubled their efforts in 1941, arguing that new plants should be dispersed for security reasons. Nonetheless expansion occurred mainly in areas already industrialized. Wyoming's employment in manufacturing increased only from 4,500 in 1940 to 5,400 in 1945, and would be only 10,000 in 1980.

Enthusiastic salvage drives gathered much scrap metal, leaving the landscape less cluttered. Another boon was the erosion of parochialism. Almost thirty thousand young men and women left the state for military service, and thousands of others left to take defense jobs. It was good for most of them to be dislodged from their isolation. They returned a few years later with more patriotism, a broader vision of the world and its problems, a more intelligent appreciation of people unlike themselves, and often with marriage partners from far places.

Postwar Wyoming looked much as it did in 1940. The economy, however was definitely improved. Although the state continued to be mainly a producer of raw materials, prices of its products rose substantially. So did profits, wages, and savings. Full employment and good times prevailed into the 1950s as the state shared in the national affluence. The weakest segment of the economy was coal because locomotives converted to diesel fuel and space heating depended almost entirely on natural gas. Coal output fell below two million tons a year in the 1950s.

Considerable out-migration resulted in the 1957–66 period from the depressed coal industry, declining railroad and agricultural employment, and labor-saving practices elsewhere. In the late 1960s, however, growth revived in consequence of developments in two counties, Sweetwater in the southwest and Campbell in the northeast. Expansion of the Jim Bridger power plant and the opening of new trona mines and mills stimulated Sweetwater County. Trona (sodium ses-quicarbonate) had been mined and refined into soda ash there first in 1952. The county had 70 million tons of reserves, which gave it virtually a monopoly of soda ash, a substance in great demand for making glass, soap, and baking soda. Sweetwater County also has oil and gas. Campbell County joined Sweetwater in boosting the state's economy when new oil and gas fields were developed there in the late 1960s. In addition, it began marketing more of its great reserves of strippable coal. When members of the Organization of Petroleum Exporting Countries (OPEC), which supply one-half of U.S. needs, quadrupled their oil prices in 1973–74, they converted Wyoming from a poor state into a rich one. Wyoming had been producing more than 130,000,000 barrels of oil annually for several years at a price of two dollars and fifty cents or less. Although the output leveled off, the rapid rise in price had a strong impact on the economy as profits, wages, exploration, and speculation increased. Natural gas, much of which had been flared for lack of markets, took on great value, causing still more exploration and development. The uranium industry also flourished.

The most spectacular acceleration in production resulting from the energy crisis occurred in coal, the output of which increased from two million tons in 1960 to more than 80 million tons in 1980. Exporting the coal to twenty other states strained the capacity of the Union Pacific and Burlington Northern railroads.

In 1980, Wyoming ranked first among the states in trona produc-tion, second in uranium, fourth in coal, and sixth in both oil and natural gas. Where there had been only 250,000 people in 1940, and only 332,000 in 1970, there were 450,000 in 1980. Two-thirds of the population increase during the forty-year period came in the 1970s. The Cowboy State had become a leading Energy State.

In 1940 the state's largest city had only 22,500 people. That was Cheyenne, the capital. Next came Casper with 18,000, and the next three cities totaled only 30,000. The fabulous 1970s put Cheyenne and Casper close to 50,000 each, Laramie at 25,000, Rock Springs, 20,000, and Sheridan, 15,000. Seven smaller cities doubled in size. Campbell and Sweetwater counties, which had been relatively poor in 1940, had the highest property valuations in 1980. Campbell County tripled its population of 6,000, while Sweetwater doubled its 19,400. On the other hand, the number of farms and ranches fell from 15,000 to fewer than 9,000. As many people live outside of the cities now as in

1940, but many of them are not farming or ranching. These rural nonfarm folks work in the cities or mines and generally are not eager for incorporation.

One of the state's greatest assets continues to be its wildlife, a renewable resource prized for both its aesthetic and its monetary value. Remarkably, there are four times as many big game animals in 1980 as there were in 1940. Doug Crowe of the Game and Fish Department explains that there was a "utopian situation," from 1940 to 1970, with little increase in human population and little habitat-destroying industry. All the department had to do was transplant animals into vacant habitats and restrict harvesting. The situation has changed dramatically with the heavy in-migration of workers who want to hunt and the concurrent reduction of habitats caused by industrial and housing development. Even so, the state still has more big game animals than people—about 275,000 mule deer, 200,000 pronghorn (antelope), 60,000 elk, 45,000 white-tailed deer, 7,000 moose, 3,600 bighorn sheep, 2,200 black bear, and close to 100 grizzly bear and 100 Rocky Mountain goats.

The 200,000 antelope exceed the number present in all the rest of the world. These slender, swift beige and white creatures, about three feet high and four feet long, are the most visible wildlife in the state. They graze close to the highways in hundreds of small herds while sentinels act as lookouts on elevated points. Moving traffic doesn't disturb them, but when automobiles stop and passengers get out, the antelope glide away at speeds up to sixty miles per hour.

The Game and Fish Commission limits the annual harvest to 25 or 30 percent of the game population, sets quotas for nonresidents, and holds lotteries to eliminate most of the applicants who want to hunt. Considering the demand-supply situation and habitat limitations, elk and antelope have reached the state's maximum capacity. Mule deer and moose numbers are declining. A few species, such as white-tailed deer, raccoon, and red fox, can adjust to man and have recently increased in number. Antelope, elk, deer, and moose inevitably encroach on private land (52 percent of the state's area) and eat grass, stacked hay, alfalfa, and grain, making it necessary to recompense landowners in various ways.

Fishing, like hunting, is under pressure of the demand-supply ratio. Much private land is posted, leaving fewer free-access areas outside of the public land reserves. However, reclamation projects have provided several new reservoirs, so lake fishing, mainly from boats, has expanded. And the Game and Fish Commission's active research, stocking, and habitat-enhancing programs continue to furnish widespread opportunities for successful fishing. The favorite fish, as in 1940, are still trout (brook, rainbow, brown, cutthroat, golden, and lake), and there are also grayling, whitefish, perch, walleye, bass, and northern pike. Tourists bent on fishing are wise to get up-to-date information from Travel Commission headquarters at Cheyenne, local chambers of commerce, sporting goods stores, and employees of the Recreation Commission, parks, and forests.

The state's highways were excellent in 1940, thanks to plentiful cheap black oil and heavy federal funding in the 1930s. Even so, the highways are better in 1980. Three federal interstate highways (25, 80, and 90) serve three-quarters of the state very well, leaving only the northwest without a multilane, divided, limited-access highway. The northwest quarter, like the rest of the state, has a network of federal and state two-lane paved highways.

The people of Wyoming, more than those of any other state, are dependent on private automobiles for transportation. They love their pickup trucks and recreation vehicles. Although every city has an airport, airline services change often, and not always for the better. The only railway passenger service is Amtrak's one train a day each way on Union Pacific tracks from Denver to Cheyenne and across southern Wyoming to Ogden, Utah, where there are connections to Los Angeles, San Francisco, and Portland.

If a traveler who had toured Wyoming in 1940 returned for the first time in 1980, he would find much that had changed very little (mountain ranges; lakes; streams; short-grass prairie; sagebrush flats; distant horizons; forests of pine, spruce, and aspen trees; beautiful roads and trails leading through the forests). He would also find many changes: the legislature's biennial general fund appropriations, up from $4 million to $550 million; a tenfold increase in higher education enrollment, with the university quadrupled in size and seven community colleges added, all with beautiful campuses; richer public school programs; more interest in arts, music, and museums; excellent TV stations; a good state newspaper, delivered statewide; Flaming Gorge and Bighorn Canyon National Recreation Areas; many new state parks (Boysen, Buffalo Bill, Curt Gowdy, Glendo, Fort Steele, Guernsey, Keyhole, Seminoe, and Sinks Canyon); a dozen ski resorts with lifts; snowmobiling; many new golf courses, tennis courts, and swimming pools; opulent motor inns; fast-food restaurants; thousands of luxury homes; many more thousands of trailer houses.

In the countryside the returned wanderer would find only one-fourth as many sheep as in 1940; many of the old favorites, Hereford and Angus cattle, and in addition all kinds of crossbreeds; more antelope; more summer fallow and strip farming; sprinkler irrigation; huge, round hay bails; fewer horses and many more pickup trucks; uranium pits; coal strip mines, with some attempts to restore the disturbed surface; four large coal-fired power plants; oil and gas wells in every county; fewer farmsteads; much archeological activity; many more homes in scenic areas; yet much open space still, and very little smog.

My list of favorite places has not changed much in forty years, except for the addition of three (starred below) that were not in existence in 1940. The most powerful magnets for me are Yellowstone and Grand Teton National Parks, Devils Tower, the Buffalo Bill Historical Center* (in Cody), Independence Rock, Devil's Gate, Fort Bridger, the Encampment River above Purgatory Gulch (southwest of Encampment), Deep Lake in the Medicine Bow Mountains (northwest of Centennial), the Laramie Plains Museum* (in Laramie), Robert Russin's statute of Abraham Lincoln* (ten miles east of Laramie), Verauwoo Glen, the capitol and state museum in Cheyenne, Fort Laramie, and the heart of any one of our national forests. It's fortunate that tastes differ. We would not all want to descend on the same place at one time.

Gasoline was so cheap in the spring of 1941 that we drove right past hundreds of less well advertised points of interest to reach a few that were famous. Now that conservation of fuel has become so important, we'll be wise to concentrate on smaller areas. We'll be richly rewarded if we study the *Guide* before we plant foot on the accelerator.

T. A. LARSON
June 1, 1980

Preface

THE *Wyoming Guide* is one of the volumes in the American Guide Series, written by the members of the Writers' Program of the Work Projects Administration. The project primarily was designed to give useful employment to writers and research workers; work on the *Guide* has, in addition, aroused interest in the State and created a desire on the part of many for further research.

With sincerity of purpose and seriousness of effort on the part of the staff, information has been gathered through research, interviews, and personal observation. An effort has been made to select without bias significant and interesting facts about Wyoming and to present them so that the reader may have a picture of the contemporary life of the State against an historic background.

Since April 1938, every main highway, all main side roads, and the important trails in the State, including those in the Yellowstone National Park and Grand Teton National Park, have been logged and checked by the staff, in order that the latest data could be made available to the traveler.

Following the pattern prescribed for the Guide Series covering the forty-eight States, the *Wyoming Guide* is a combination of essays on general subjects and detailed descriptive material on all of the important tours in Wyoming. It therefore should be enjoyed, not only by those touring the State, but by fireside travelers as well.

Grateful acknowledgment is made for the assistance given by numerous consultants, experts in their respective fields. Especially helpful have been Mr. George O. Houser, Executive Secretary, State Planning and Water Conservation Board, Official Sponsor of the Wyoming Writers' Project, Dr. Lester C. Hunt, Secretary of State, sponsor of the *Wyoming Guide,* and John Stahlberg of the Montana Writers' Project.

To name each individual who has assisted in the collection of data and the preparation of material would require many pages, as the Writers' Project is indebted to hundreds of individuals and to many institutions, corporations, and organizations; these include the University of Wyoming, the Wyoming State Library, the National Park Service, the Indian Service, United Air Lines, Inland Air Lines, the Chicago, Burlington, and Quincy Railroad, the Union Pacific Railway, and the Chicago and North Western Railway, the State Department of Commerce and Industry, the State Planning and Water Conservation Board, the Union Pacific Coal Company, the Great Western Sugar Company, editors and owners of Wyoming newspapers, county librarians, postmasters, chambers of commerce, old settlers, and the Frontier Days Committee. We are grateful to the following for supplying the splendid photographs used in the *Wyoming Guide:* F. J. Hiscook, Charles J. Belden, J. E. Haynes, of Haynes Inc., Vern Emmons, E. H. Dagley, Outwest Photo Co., J. E. Stimson, E. Schuler, Stanolind Oil Co., Jerry Brooder, and Dan Healy.

We wish to thank the Delaware Writers' Project for their co-operation in completing the maps used in the *Guide,* and Ross Santee, State Supervisor, and E. S. Upton, of the Arizona Writers' Project, for the art work.

As the Guide went to press before the 1940 census figures were available, the 1930 figures were used throughout the text. There is, however, an alphabetical list of the preliminary 1940 figures in the Appendices.

Since this has been a pioneer work in the field of Wyoming travel books, we realize that errors have crept in. The staff will appreciate the reporting of all inaccuracies, in order that corrections may be made in future editions.

AGNES W. SPRING
State Supervisor

Illustrations

THE SETTING   *Between 34 and 35*

Shoshone Reservoir and Canyon Drive
Devil's Tower
Reservoir Site above Seminoe Dam
Green River Glaciers
Wind River Range (The Continental Divide)
Jackson Lake and the Tetons
Summer Range
Red Cliffs on Gros Ventre River
Independence Rock
Green River, with Gannett Peak and Glacier in Background
In Teton County
Sunset on the Plains

HISTORY   *Between 96 and 97*

Jim Bridger
Graves along the Oregon Trail
Names Carved on Register Cliff, near Guernsey
Jim Baker
Wyoming's Oldest Building, the Post Sutler's Store at Fort Laramie
Fort Supply, Built by the Mormons (1853)
Pony Express Stables, Fort Bridger
The First School House (1860), Fort Bridger
Building Dale Creek Bridge, Union Pacific Route (1869)
Sherman Station, Union Pacific Route (1869)
Indian Attack during Building of Union Pacific
Clearing the Track
Stagecoach at Encampment
Gem City Minstrels, Laramie (1870)

RANGE COUNTRY   *Between* 126 *and* 127

Trailing from the Summer Range
Branding the Calves
The Fine Art of Fore-Footing
Wrangler
Off to the Roundup
Feed Lot
Sheep Wagon
Shearing
At the Crack of Dawn
Jealousy
Cow Country Style
Pot Luck
Bunkhouse Stud

SPORTS AND RECREATION   *Between* 188 *and* 189

Back from the Hunt
Ready for the Trail
Jackson Hole Dude Ranch
Grub Time on the Trail
Setting up for the Night
Frontier Days Celebration, Cheyenne
Bulldogger
Ride 'im, Cowboy!
Ski Run, Casper
Talking It Over
Coming Down!
Riffle Fishing, Gardiner River, Yellowstone Park
Night Swim at Alcova Lake

IN THE CITIES AND TOWNS   *Between* 250 *and* 251

Buffalo Bill Statue, Cody
State Capitol, Cheyenne
University of Wyoming, Laramie
State Supreme Court and Library, Cheyenne
Liberal Arts Building, State University, Laramie
Main Street, Lander
Capitol Avenue, Cheyenne

In the Mormon Town of Afton
Center Street, Casper
The Market, Cheyenne (1874)
Cheyenne (c. 1870)
Early-Day Railroad Town
Sign at Sweetwater
False Fronts, Hartville

AGRICULTURE: INDUSTRY   *Between 312 and 313*
Sheep Range
Whitefaces
Cutting Highland Grain
Threshing Beans, Big Horn Basin
Harvesting Sugar Beets
Beet Dump
Power Transmission Lines Crossing the Desert from Seminoe Dam
Downstream from Alcova Dam
Potato Fields, Shoshone Irrigation Project
Riverton Project Home
Salt Creek Oil Field
Oil Refinery, Casper
Mine Tipple, Superior
Open Pit Coal Mine in the Gillette Area
Airline Hangar and Overhaul Base, Cheyenne
Box Car Construction, Union Pacific Railroad

FLORA AND FAUNA: INDIANS   *Between 374 and 375*
Call of the Wild
Fury of the Storm
Elk Feed Grounds, Jackson Hole
Table d'Hote—Bears in Yellowstone Park
A Big Horn
Buffalo, Yellowstone Park
Wind-Twisted Pine
Sand Lilies
Prickly Pear
Younger Generation
Arapaho Women Tanning Hides, Wind River Reservation
Joint Business Council, Shoshone and Arapaho Indians

Louis Tyler, a Shoshone, and Reverend John Roberts, at Shoshone
    Reservation
Fullblood Shoshone
Arapaho Indian Woman Displaying Her Handicraft
Indian Pictographs, Fremont County

A COLLECTION OF PHOTOGRAPHS BY
    W. H. JACKSON   *Between* 404 *and* 405

Lower Falls of the Yellowstone
Upper Fire Hole, from Old Faithful
Mammoth Hot Springs, Jupiter Terrace, Looking North
Old Faithful
Bad Lands along Wind River
Fremont's Peak
Grand Canyon of the Yellowstone, from Brink of Lower Falls
Photographing in High Places—Scene in Lincoln County
Grand Teton
Chief Washakie of the Shoshone Tribe

Maps

KEY TO WYOMING TOURS	xxvi
HISTORICAL TRAILS OF WYOMING	xxviii
CASPER	178
CHEYENNE	187
LARAMIE	199
SHERIDAN	210

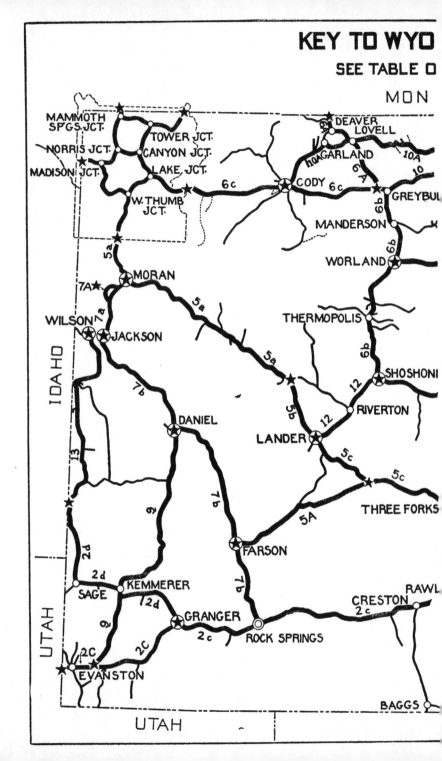

MING TOURS

F CONTENTS

TANA

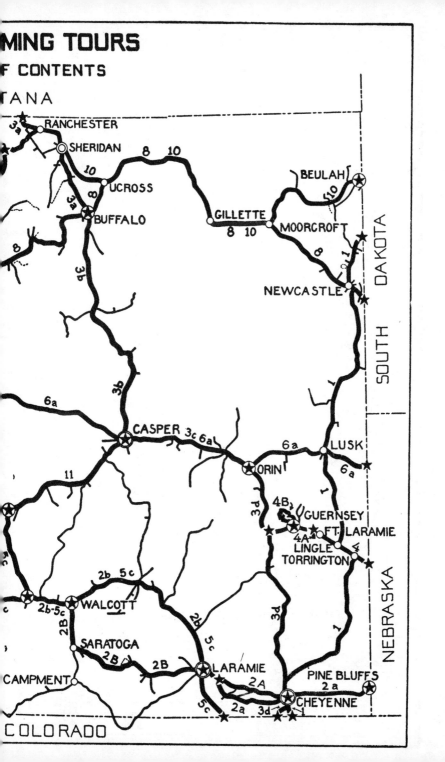

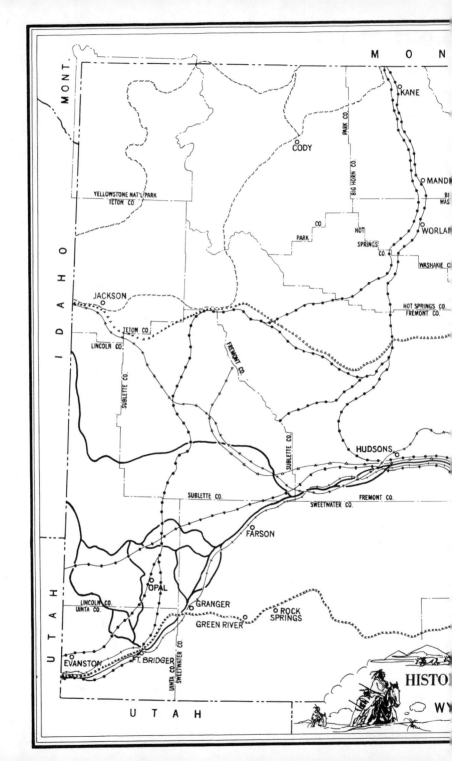

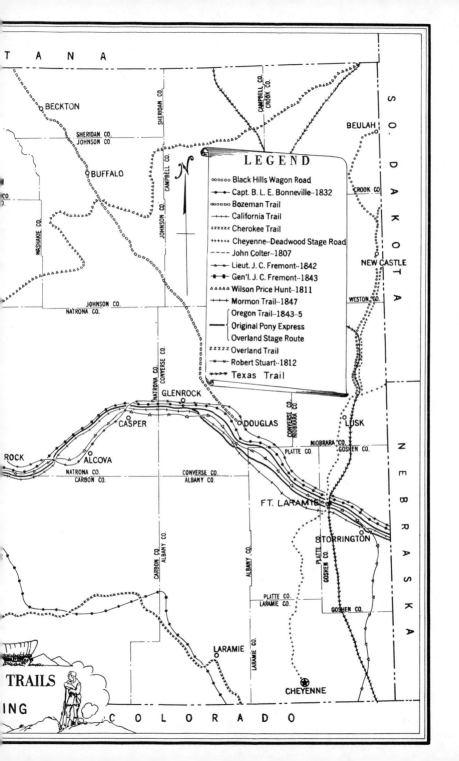

LEGEND

- ∘∘∘∘∘∘ Black Hills Wagon Road
- •—•—• Capt. B. L. E. Bonneville--1832
- ▭▭▭▭▭ Bozeman Trail
- +—+—+ California Trail
- zzzzz Cherokee Trail
- +++++ Cheyenne--Deadwood Stage Road
- ~~~~ John Colter--1807
- •—•—• Lieut. J. C. Fremont--1842
- ■—■—■ Gen'l. J. C. Fremont--1843
- ▵▵▵▵▵ Wilson Price Hunt--1811
- +—+—+ Mormon Trail--1847
- ⎰ Oregon Trail--1843--5
- ⎱ Original Pony Express
- ⎰ Overland Stage Route
- zzzzz Overland Trail
- *—*—* Robert Stuart--1812
- ▸▸▸▸ Texas Trail

TRAILS

ING

General Information

Railroads: Interstate Lines: Union Pacific R.R. (UP); Laramie, North Park & Western R.R. (LNP&W); Chicago & North Western Ry. (Northwestern); Chicago, Burlington & Quincy R.R. (Burlington); Colorado & Southern (C&S) (*see Transportation Map*).

Bus Lines: Interstate Lines: Black Hills Transportation Co., Burlington Transportation Co., Motor Transit Co., Interstate Transit Lines, Wood & Lair, Teton Transportation Co. (Moran-Victor, Idaho via Jackson), Comet Motor Express Co., Inc. (Dixon-Craig, Colo. via Baggs). Intrastate Lines: Salt Creek Transportation Co. (Casper-Sheridan), Hays-Robinson Transportation Co. (Casper-Lander), J. V. Rains (Rock Springs-Pinedale-Jackson), Yellowstone Park Lines (Cody-Yellowstone Park-Moran), Thomas Delgado (Rock Springs-Winton-Dines-Reliance), Rock Springs-Superior Stage Line (Rock Springs-Superior), W. H. Lewis (Rock Springs-Moran), Wyoming Motor Way Co. (Rawlins-Bairoil-Alcova-Casper), Gore & Young (Kemmerer-Gomer Coal Mine).

Airlines: United Air Lines to New York City, Salt Lake City, Seattle, San Francisco, Los Angeles, and Denver; Inland Air Lines (Great Falls, Mont., Lewiston, Mont., Sheridan-Casper-Cheyenne and Scottsbluff, Neb., Rapid City, S.D.-Spearfish-Pierre, Huron). Airports: Cheyenne, Casper, Sheridan, Rock Springs, Laramie; emergency fields along commercial airlines (*see Transportation Map*).

Highways: Wyoming has 25,161 miles of highways open to travel, of which 4,352 miles are improved. Gasoline tax 5¢ (*for highway routes see State Map*).

Motor Vehicle Laws (*digest*): 60 m.p.h. maximum speed on open highways; 20 m.p.h. in business districts; 20 m.p.h. in school zones; 30

m.p.h. in residential districts. Restricted speed indicated by markers. No driver's license required; minimum driver's age, 15 years. Non-resident motorists must purchase Wyoming license plates if the motor vehicle or trailer remains in the State more than 90 days in a calendar year. Drivers must have 500 feet visibility before attempting to pass. No passing on double stripes. It is unlawful to hitchhike or to offer hitchhikers a ride. Driving while intoxicated is a misdemeanor punishable by imprisonment up to one year, or $100 fine, or both. Every motor vehicle must be equipped with a mirror that will give the driver vision to at least 200 feet to his rear. The driver of a vehicle involved in any accident resulting in injury or death of any person, or in property damage, must immediately stop at the scene of the accident and report his name and address to the State Highway Patrol or to other proper police officers.

Climate and Equipment: Wyoming has about 265 clear days each year. The average maximum temperature is 57°. Because of the dry atmosphere and extraordinary amount of sunshine, intense cold spells are short, usually one or two days. The coldest months are December, January, and February. July and August are warmest. Summer nights are cool and the days rarely are warmer than 90°. Precipitation ranges from less than 10 inches on the prairies to 40 inches in the mountains; the average is about 15 inches. Electrical storms are sudden in summer and most severe in the mountains. Sudden winter blizzards blow up on the prairies. Winter travelers thus should inquire about roads and shelter houses before leaving towns. Always take coats on mountain trips. In higher altitudes, beds made on the ground or on pine-bough mattresses are warmer than canvas cots. Sleeping bags are recommended for the 'top country.' Never make camp in dry stream beds or in dry gulches. A cloud burst may wash you out. The standard distress signal in this region is three quickly repeated calls by voice, whistle, or lights. Red Cross stations are available on all main highways.

Accommodations: Best in larger towns. There are 203 hotels in the State with more than 7,300 rooms. Tourist homes and cabins are available summer and winter. One hundred dude ranches accommodate summer guests. Rates vary from $1.50 to $10 a day. Forests and parks have primitive and improved campgrounds.

Liquor Laws: The Wyoming Liquor Commission has the sole right to sell intoxicating liquors at wholesale, not including malt liquor. Incorporated towns and counties within the State regulate the sale of liquor within their boundaries. Railroads are permitted to sell liquors in dining cars, club cars, and Pullman cars. All liquor-dispensing establishments are closed Sundays and from 1 A.M. to 6 A.M. daily.

State Fish and Game Laws (*digest*): Game fish are trout, grayling, pike-perch, bass, crappie, catfish, salmon, perch, whitefish, ling, bluegill. *Open Season for Fishing:* Set by Wyoming Game and Fish Commission usually between the hours of 4 A.M. and 9 P.M. from April 1 to November 30. Closed waters are designated by posted signs. Nonresident or tourist seasonal fishing licenses $3; tourist 7-day fishing license, $1.50. A license for fishing and for big game hunting is required of any person over 14 years of age. A nonresident under 14 years must have a license to fish Wyoming lakes but not Wyoming streams. The fish pole must be held in the hand. Only 15 pounds of fish or no more than 20 fish may be caught in any day or may be in possession at any time. In Teton County the creel limit is 15 fish or 15 pounds. This does not prohibit catching a single fish exceeding 15 pounds.

Hunting: Game animals are elk, deer, mountain sheep, antelope, moose, and bear. Hunting dates are regulated by the Wyoming Game and Fish Commission. Season usually opens in mid-October and closes early in December. Hunting licenses are required for every person more than 14 years old, and persons under 14 are not allowed to hunt big game. A nonresident must have a licensed guide to hunt big game, except antelope. Nonresident hunting and fishing license, $50; nonresident moose permit, $75; nonresident antelope permit, $20; nonresident sheep permit, $75; nonresident bear permit (special), $25. Rifles used in shooting big game must be not less than .23 caliber. Only soft-nosed bullets may be used. Elk, deer, antelope, and bear may be taken with bow and arrow; in addition to the regular hunting license or permit, the hunter must have a special archery permit ($10). The archer's bow must have a pull of not less than 60 pounds, and the cutting head of the arrow shall not be less than 1 inch. Hunters must wear red caps or markings in the field. Game preserves are marked by posted signs on roads or trails. Game birds are dove, grouse, quail, pheasant, partridge, chukar partridge, sage chicken, wild turkey, and prairie chicken. All except pheasants were protected in 1938 and 1939. Migratory birds are sandpiper, plover, tatler, willet, curlew, godwit, avocet, coot, mudhen, duck, goose, and brant. Nonresident bird license, $10. No person less than 12 years of age may hunt game birds in the State unless accompanied by an adult. Hunters of all ages must have license. Bag limit: cock ring-necked pheasants, three a day or in possession; bag limit and seasons on migratory waterfowl usually coincide with Federal regulations. Game, bird, and fish laws and orders of the Wyoming Game and Fish Commission are available in printed form without charge from the Wyoming Game and Fish Commission, Cheyenne, Wyoming.

Poisonous Reptiles, Insects, and Plants: Rattlesnakes are the only poisonous snakes in the State. They are found usually in rocky isolated districts. Rarely do they occur in altitudes above 6,500 feet. They are most common in central and eastern Wyoming. Rocky Mountain spotted fever, sometimes a fatal illness, is caused by an organism carried by the woodtick. The tick season usually starts in March and lasts until late May or early June. Always examine the clothing and body after being in tick-infested areas. The State supplies physicians in tick areas with a special vaccine without cost. Vaccine should be used early in spring. The fever is not contagious. Mosquitoes cause annoyance and are especially vicious in some of the mountain park regions and along mountain streams, usually in July. They disappear in higher altitudes about the middle of August. Deer flies and gnats are prevalent in rural districts in midsummer. Baking soda is a good remedy for the stings. Tularemia, a dreaded fever, is carried by wild rabbits, antelope, sage chickens, coyotes, and deer. Gloves should be worn when handling these animals. Nettles, tall green plants that grow in moist places, cause a stinging skin irritation. Water hemlock, which has a poisonous root, is found in marshes and swamps. Poison ivy is rare; it is found in small quantities in Crook and Sheridan Counties, and in the extreme southern part of Carbon County.

Radio Stations: KWYO, Sheridan, 100-watt station, is a member of the McGregor & Sollie broadcasting system, and a member of the Trans-Radio Press and Radio News Association. KDFN, 1st and Lennox Sts., Casper, is a 500-watt station that covers central Wyoming. KYAN, 1500 E. 5th St., Cheyenne, is a member of the Mutual Broadcasting System and operates a 250-watt station; KFBC, Plains Hotel, Cheyenne, is a member of the National Broadcasting System and operates a 250-watt station. KVRS, a 100- and 250-watt station, broadcasts from Rock Springs.

Recreational Areas (parks, forests, and national monuments): Big Horn National Forest (US 14, US 16); Black Hills National Forest (US 14); Devil's Tower National Monument (US 14); Fort Bridger State Park (US 30S); Fort Laramie National Monument (US 26); Fort Warren Maneuver Reservation and Pole Mountain Game Refuge (US 30); Grand Teton National Park (US 89, US 187); Guernsey Lake Area (US 26); Thermopolis Hot Springs State Park (US 20); Medicine Bow National Forest (State 130, State 230); Saratoga Hot Springs State Park (State 130); Shoshone Indian Reservation (State 287, US 287); Shoshone National Forest (US 20, US 14); Shoshone Cavern National Monument (US 14, US 16); Targhee National Forest (State 22, US 89); Teton National Forest (US 89, US 187, US 287); Washakie National Forest (US 287); Wyoming National Forest (US 89, US 187); Yellowstone National Park (US 14-20, US 89-187-287).

Winter Sports: There are several ski courses in Wyoming mountains. Some popular winter sports areas (skiing, tobogganing, bobsledding, skating, and dogsled racing) are at the A-Bar-A Ranch (State 230); Barrett Ridge (State 130); Casper Mountain (US 20); Cody (US 14-20); Dubois (US 287); Happy Jack (US 30); Jackson (US 89-187); Star Valley (US 89); Snowy Range (State 130); Story (US 87); Tensleep (US 16).

Museums: Buffalo Bill Museum, Cody; Fort Caspar, Casper; State Historical, Cheyenne; Boylan Archeological, Como Bluff; Old Timers' Cabin, Douglas; Fort Bridger, Fort Bridger; Fossil Fish Cliff, Fossil; Guernsey Trailside, Guernsey Lake; Hebard Room, University of Wyoming, Laramie; Paleontological, University of Wyoming, Laramie; The Casino, Newcastle; Hell's Half-Acre, Powder River; Brox Mineral, Rawlins; Smith, Shell; Shoshoni, Shoshoni; Tom Sun's Museum, Sweetwater River; National Park museums at Devil's Tower, Grand Teton and Yellowstone National Parks. Federal art galleries at Casper, Lander, Laramie, Newcastle, Riverton, Rock Springs, Sheridan, and Torrington. Many residents have small collections of arrowheads, spearheads, beads, moss agates, and other relics. Similar artifacts may be found on the plains and in the mountains.

Precautions: Extinguish all cigars and cigarettes before throwing them away. Put out your camp fire. The National Forest Service requires that automobile campers carry a shovel, ax, and pail for this purpose. Do not contaminate any stream or source of water. Ascertain the purity of water before drinking it. Do not chop or cut live trees. Do not pull wild flowers by the roots. Consult the nearest tourist club or chamber of commerce on road and weather information. Do not take shelter under large trees during thunder storms. Do not move persons seriously injured. Let them lie still on the ground. Keep them warm and send someone for help, if possible. Winter drivers should be equipped with shovels, chains, blankets, and food.

What Your Vacation Will Cost: The vacation cost in Wyoming varies with the mode of travel and the type of accommodations. Motor travel in parties of four or more is reported to cost from $1 to $7 per person per day, with a general average of $3.66 per person per day.

Calendar of Annual Events

FEBRUARY

Twenty-sixth	at Cody	William F. Cody Day
No fixed date	at Rawlins	Carbon County Agricultural Meeting

MARCH

No fixed date	at Gillette	Northeastern Wyoming Seed and Poultry Show
No fixed date	at Cody	Trappers' Ball
No fixed date	at Rock Springs	International Night Pageant

APRIL

Sixth	at Fort F. E. Warren	Army Day
No fixed date	at Casper	Poultry Show

MAY

Second week	at Wheatland	Days of '49 Celebration
No fixed date	at Cheyenne	Tri-State Golf Tournament
No fixed date	at Worland	Mardi Gras

JUNE

First week	at Casper	Horse Show
Fifteenth-Sixteenth	at Shoshoni	Rodeo
Third Sunday	at Devil's Tower	Old Settlers' Picnic
No fixed date	at Big Piney	Chuck Wagon Days; Rodeo, Stockmen's Meeting, Barbecue

| No fixed date | at Gillette | Horse Fair |
| No fixed date | at Torrington | Wyoming State Trap Shoot |

JULY

Second-Fourth	at Cody	Cody Stampede
Third-Fourth	at Gillette	Gillette Roundup
Third-Fourth	at Lander	Lander Pioneer Days
Third-Fourth	at Pinedale	Rodeo
Fourth	at Lake De Smet (Buffalo)	Water Carnival
Fourth	at Saratoga	Rodeo
First week	at Jackson	Jackson Hole Frontier Days
Tenth	at Laramie	Equality-Jubilee
Fifteenth-Sixteenth	at Shoshoni	Shoshoni Rodeo
Twenty-fourth	in all Mormon Communities	Mormon Pioneer Days Pageant
Third week	at Sheridan	Sheridan-Wyo-Rodeo
Fourth week	at Cheyenne	Frontier Days
No fixed date	at Ethete	Arapahoe Sun Dance
No fixed date	at Fort Washakie	Shoshone Sun Dance

AUGUST

Seventh	at Lander (Ray Lake)	Water Carnival
Ninth-Eleventh	at Dubois	Rodeo
Ninth-Eleventh	at Jackson	Jackson Hole Rodeo
Eleventh-Thirteenth	at Wheatland	Stone Age Fair
Twenty-first	at Casper (Kendrick Lake)	Regatta and Water Carnival
Third week	at Casper	Wyoming-on-Parade
No fixed date	at Guernsey Lake Park	Water Carnival
No fixed date	at Hyattville	Old Timers' Picnic
No fixed date	at Sundance	Crook County Fair

SEPTEMBER

Labor Day	at Thermopolis	Night Herd Rodeo and Pageant
First week	at Pine Bluffs	Laramie County Fair
First week	at Rawlins	Carbon County Fair
Second week	at Douglas	Wyoming State Fair Pioneer Association Meeting
Second week	at Torrington	Goshen County Fair
No fixed date	at Basin	Bean Festival
No fixed date	at Evanston	Cowboy Days Rodeo
No fixed date	at Powell	Potato Day

NOVEMBER

No fixed date	at Dubois	Elk Barbecue

DECEMBER

Tenth	Statewide	Wyoming Day, anniversary of women's suffrage in Wyoming.
No fixed date	at Afton	Top O' the Rockies Winter Carnival
No fixed date	at Jackson	Winter Carnival

SPECIAL EVENTS

No fixed date	Statewide	Arbor Day: Date set by Governor's Proclamation, usually April or May.

PART I

Wyoming: Past and Present

Contemporary Scene

WYOMING was, and continues to be, the land of the cowboy. Its mountains, plains, and valleys are essentially livestock country. Moreover, the State's citizens take pride in maintaining the traditions of the Old West, while keeping step with the technological progress of the world.

A cowboy astride a bucking broncho greets the visitor from enameled markers at the State boundary lines, and thereafter from automobile license plates, from automobile guest stickers, from newspapers, magazines, and painted signs. The cowboy and the Indian provide decorative motifs for Wyoming stores, hotel stationery, home-woven blankets, rugs, neckerchiefs, shirts, and all sorts of advertising matter. Even the trademark of an important airline is the familiar cowboy on his broncho. At tourist camps whose offices are often replicas of tepees, stuffed horses, posed as bucking, stand ready to be mounted by visitors who wish to be photographed for the folks back home.

Six-gallon hats, leather vests, and high-heeled boots, as well as the latest styles in dress, are seen on the streets of every city, town, and village in Wyoming. Businessmen, ranchmen, and dudes alike wear the habiliments of the old cow country. As a mark of honor or welcome, distinguished guests frequently receive six-gallon hats. A typical Wyoming welcome was accorded to Dr. A. G. Crane in 1923, when he came from Pennsylvania to preside over the University of Wyoming at Laramie. Masked riders waylaid his automobile in a canyon and ushered the Crane family, at the point of guns, into an old Concord stagecoach drawn by six horses. With shots and yells of 'Powder River, let 'er buck,' 500 students, riding cow ponies, escorted the coach to the county fairgrounds at Laramie, about four miles distant. There, with a ten-gallon hat, Dr. Crane was crowned 'King of the Cowboys.'

The rodeo, topped by Frontier Days, the Daddy-of-'em-all, is still the chief tourist entertainment here. Every year at the Frontier Days celebration, at Fourth of July gatherings, at county fairs, and upon other festive occasions, thousands of visitors and residents thrill while cowboys and cowgirls, professional and amateur, jounce across arenas on whirling, frothing, sunfishing, wild-eyed cayuses, or race neck and neck with longhorned steers before leaping through the air to send the critters crashing into the dust. In the ranching areas, the riding of bronchos, the rounding up and branding of cattle, and the trailing to and from summer ranges or to winter markets are still part of the day's routine. But simultaneously with these activities, streamlined engines are being inspected in the big railroad shops, and airplanes are being reconditioned at the largest overhauling base in the country—in Cheyenne.

Wyoming is a land of great open spaces with plenty of elbow room; in 1940 the population density was only 2.1 persons to the square mile. There are sections of the State where it is said you can look farther and see less than any other place in the world. There are places, too, where you can see jagged snow peaks, tumbling waterfalls, multi-colored canyons—spectacular and majestic.

Although Wyoming is called a rural State, only one third of its population of approximately 250,000 people live on ranches or farms. Two thirds of the citizens live in villages, towns, or small cities. In the entire State, which is 78 times the size of Rhode Island, there are only 275 settlements; 151 of these have populations of 100 or less. Only two towns in the State, Cheyenne and Casper, have more than 15,000 population. The towns or settlements are, for the most part, 30 to 50 miles or more apart, usually at junctions of main highways on small creeks or rivers. It is possible in many places in the State to ride 50 miles or more without seeing a dwelling of any kind.

Although Wyoming is a land of great distances, the various sections of the State are not isolated. A network of oiled highways makes it possible to travel from one corner of the State to the other within a day's time. Few of the settlements of 100 or more population are more than ten miles away from an oiled highway. It is possible in only two hours of driving to leave the bustle of a modern city and find the perfect solitude of the great top country above timber line.

The oiled highways have brought modern conveniences and improvements into remote districts. Concrete curbs have supplanted the old-time hitching posts. The recent development of rural electrification has sent the smelly kerosene lamps into the dump heap, and has replaced the washboard and the talking machine with the electric washer and the radio.

The airplane has brought the big game country—Jackson Hole, the Wind River area, the Cody mountains, and the Black Hills—within quick reach of Cheyenne.

Although the State is comparatively new in actual settlement and homebuilding, it has been the theater of many great influxes and migrations. There are still physical remains of many of these movements. Crumbling stumps and logs of old fur presses, ruts worked deep by rumbling wagon wheels, arrow-strewn battle fields, tumbledown shaft houses and rotting sluice boxes, stone abutments of an old railroad trestle, broken aerial tramway cables that whine in the wind, early-day branding irons and roundup camp kettles, ox yokes and rusty beaver traps—all are visible links with the past of Wyoming.

The past presses so closely upon the present that there are men and women in the State today who saw the first Union Pacific train arrive in Cheyenne in 1867. The man who sent the first telegraphic dispatch to the world telling of the death of Custer's men on the Little Big Horn is still alive; a daughter of Jim Baker, the famous scout, makes her home on Snake River; men who trailed longhorns up the Texas Trail and brought sheep and cattle in from Oregon may still be met in Wyoming.

Attics and storerooms house old diaries, ledgers, and letters telling of the days of Jim Bridger, Kit Carson, and John Hunton. Elderly men and women delight in telling of being held up by road agents on the Cheyenne and Black Hills stagecoach. Some of them knew Calamity Jane and Wild Bill Hickok.

Although there are many of these old-time residents and their families, 58 per cent of the present population of Wyoming has come from somewhere else. Many of these people were headed for other horizons and intended merely to pass through Wyoming. Because of various accidents, such as a horse dying, a guide breaking his leg, a car being wrecked, or a blizzard blocking the road, they were delayed in the State. Having once stopped here they lingered and then stayed on and on.

There is a fascination about the vastness of the plains, the ruggedness of the mountains, the uncertainty of the far horizon, the crispness and clearness of the air, the brilliance of the sunshine that holds those who come to the State and that draws them back if they leave.

Wyoming is a land of opportunity. Few questions are asked the newcomer concerning his past or his ancestry. It is not altogether rhetoric to say that a man is accepted for what he is and for what he can do. He must be resourceful and self-reliant to a high degree. Residents are proud of the fact that a man just out of college came into the State with little money and within five years was elected to one of the highest offices in the State government, and in less than ten years was sent to Washington as a member of Congress.

In point of population Wyoming had not qualified for statehood when that honor was conferred on it in 1890, but the influence of certain men succeeded in winning the grant despite the deficiency of population, which was then only 62,500. Owing to the fact that the population was so small, Wyoming for many years resembled a huge family; everyone of importance seemed to be personally known throughout the State. In the earlier days most of the young people attended the University of Wyoming and, since all colleges and schools were concentrated on one campus, they came to know students from every community. With the north-south and east-west railways intersecting at Cheyenne, the capital city for years was, and still is to a large extent, the scene of most of the big business transactions, both public and private. Legislators have always brought their families to Cheyenne during the sessions of the legislature, thus increasing the statewide acquaintanceship. The Cheyenne newspapers, for years the only State dailies, furthered this feeling of friendship between individuals, living as many as 600 miles apart, by carrying statewide personal columns.

Foreign-born citizens, representing nearly 50 nationalities including Greeks, Finns, Slovaks, and Italians, have concentrated near the coal mines at Rock Springs, Sheridan, and Hanna; Russians, German-Russians, and Mexicans are found in the sugar-beet districts of the Big Horn Basin, Sheridan, Riverton, and North Platte valleys. There are many Scandinavians in the dry-farming sections of eastern Wyoming, and in the tie camps along the Wind River, Green River and Laramie and North Platte valleys. English and Scottish residents settled in the big cattle country in the 1880's and 1890's. Many Mormons of English and Danish descent are in the Star Valley, the Big Horn Basin, and in southwestern Wyoming. Just after the close of the Civil War the South contributed its quota of settlers; numbers have come from Iowa, Illinois, Pennsylvania, Ohio, and New York.

Although called the land of the cowboy, Wyoming is by no means solely a man's country. Its great seal bears the words 'Equal Rights.' Here women have shared the adventures, hardships, and accomplishments with men. In 1869, only eight years after the Pony Express was discontinued, the women of the territory were granted equal suffrage;

in 1870 a woman, the first in the United States to fill such an office, was appointed justice of the peace at the rip-roaring mining town of South Pass City; and in 1925 the first woman elected governor of a State, Mrs. Nellie Tayloe Ross of Wyoming, assumed office. Wyoming's women have always given much thought to education and the advancement of things cultural. The State passed one of the first and best county library laws in the Union. Many of the first ranch homes were established by women school teachers who married cattlemen. Education in the State has been liberally financed through the extraction of oil on some of the 3,000,000 acres of land set aside as a permanent endowment for the schools; in 1936 the schools' oil fund totalled $20,000,000. The school system is crowned by the University of Wyoming, whose modern buildings and equipment rival those of much older and larger institutions. The young men and women of the university are equally at home at a country dance in a remote bunkhouse or in the mirrored ballroom of the smart Wyoming Union on the campus at Laramie.

Wyoming's industries are not segregated. Owing to the conglomerate valleys, plains, plateaus, mountains in almost all parts of the State, industries alternate or overlap in many districts.

The oil and mining industries now flourish on an important scale, and agriculture has been added to the once dominant pursuit of stock raising. The oil industry has brought to Wyoming men of a venturesome type who stake their wits and their money on what may or may not exist beneath the earth's surface. During the years immediately following enactment of the oil-leasing law of 1920, Wyoming derived such a large income from oil royalties that many leading editors of the State predicted Wyoming would soon become a taxless State. This dream was dispelled, however, by the universal demand for modern highways and an elaborate system of public schools and buildings.

Wyoming is ideal for recreation. One fourth of the State is given over to national parks, national forests, and an Indian reservation. Here was created the first and the largest of the country's playgrounds —Yellowstone National Park. Annually thousands of visitors walk quietly along trails, wonderstruck by the spouting geysers, the bubbling hot springs, the gurgling mud pots, the vast canyons, and the steaming mountains.

In almost every section of the State, fishermen whip the trout streams or cast from rafts and motorboats on trout-filled lakes; guides pilot big-game hunters along treacherous trails into the land of the moose, elk, big-horn sheep, and grizzly bear. Other outdoor enthusiasts scale mountain peaks or swirl down ski and slalom runs.

The leading industry of the State, livestock raising, has been modified to provide recreation for those who each year leave the hum and grind of cities to follow the trails, breathe the air, and join in the outdoor life of Wyoming. There are dude ranches where the guests eat with the ranchman's family and hired hands, help with the ranch chores, and sleep in simple quarters. On other ranches the guests swim in concrete pools, lounge about luxurious, leather-cushioned club rooms, play badminton and pingpong, and sleep in cabins taken care of by uniformed maids. At all of these ranches, simple or luxurious, horseback riding is the favorite pastime and the hospitality of the Old West is paramount.

In Wyoming men are still exploring and building. Booted engineers with tripods, levels, and transits are running ditch lines, checking section corners, or laying out new highways. The 'rock hound' or geologist, who formerly ran ridges in search of oil-producing structures, has been replaced by crews with delicate seismographs. Every season hundreds of old and young prospectors strike out for the hills, with shovels and grub stakes, to pan the streams for 'colors.'

Scientists are now at work excavating caves and sifting the soil for evidence of the various ancient cultures. They are searching for old campsites, classifying the myriad artifacts, arrowheads, and other relics that have been found in the State, and endeavoring to interpret the chiselings and paintings of prehistoric peoples on the rock walls of caves and canyons. Hundreds of homes here have small collections of Indian relics and stone artifacts.

Artists with easels and photographers with cameras are striving to catch the glamor and mystery of Wyoming's peaks and plains. Writers delve into records, interview pioneers, and gather local color for novels, serials, and historical works. The word 'Cheyenne' produces an electric effect in the world of popular romance and drama.

Here in Wyoming's great spaces, winds blow over prairies and mountains, sending Russian thistle and other tumbleweeds bounding for miles, piling snow in deep drifts or melting it like magic; barbed wire or buck fences stretch for miles; zigzagging snow fences apparently lead nowhere, but actually guard your path; the atmosphere is so clear that mountains far away seem near, and stars shine so brilliantly they look within reach; columns of train smoke rise on far horizons; streamlined trains flash through the sage; mainline ships thunder overhead.

Section gangs along the right of way replace railroad ties or smooth road beds; shining rails stretch for miles with block signals raising or lowering their robot arms; ground blizzards blot out the roads; ties from timber camps plunge down rivers; forest rangers keep vigil from lonely lookouts; cactus, Indian paintbrush, fireweed, lady's-slipper, and phlox spread in great sheets of color; gigantic dams impound flood waters from roaring mountain streams; valleys shelter sheep and cattle; wells spout millions of barrels of oil; mines produce vast quantities of coal; picket-pin gophers sit motionless on road shoulders; large hawks feast on dead bunnies on the highway or sit watchfully on a near-by fence post; prairie dogs scurry to their burrows; tarpaper shacks, with doors hanging open on broken hinges, dot the deserted dry-land sections; snug peeled-log cabins and well-built modern homes stand side by side in prosperous valleys with crudely built pioneer cabins in their shadows; clusters of boxcar houses and small frame dwellings squat near tall water tanks along the railroad right of way; construction camps spread out beside the highway with crude, dirt-roofed dugouts, tents, and streamlined trailer houses. There are sand-washed flats; deeply gouged arroyos; glaciers; snow peaks; hillsides deeply scarred with wavy trenches made by soil erosion experts; shelter belts of pine and Russian olive standing near snow fences or around farm houses; and sheep corrals that look like spilled matchsticks on the desert.

Down the highways rumble big trucks loaded with oil, coal, grain, hay, ties, Christmas trees, sugar beets, cattle, and sheep. Great express trucks and transcontinental busses whiz along. Auto caravans, transporting new cars direct from manufacturer to dealer, appear gigantic around a canyon curve. In hunting season, cars proudly display deer or antelope strapped over the fender and engine. Mexicans in rattletrap cars, loaded high with the family's worldly goods, chug toward the beet fields.

Often there is the smell of fresh oil on the highways, where repairing or re-oiling is in progress; or the pungent odor of greasewood after a cloudburst has struck near by. There is the pervading odor of beet pulp being hauled to feed lots, the scent of pine after rain, the warm fragrance of wild plum and chokecherry blossoms, or of newly cut alfalfa and native hay.

In the early spring and late fall the small streams in the meadows are plainly outlined by the willows, still reddish brown with sap. In autumn yellow sunflowers and rabbit brush fringe the highway shoulders with gold; canyons are splashed with the red and yellow of wild currant and rose bushes; hillsides are splotched with frost-touched golden aspens.

In the ranching country at sundown the heron wings his way up-stream, and great flocks of crows flap to distant rookeries. At dusk cottontails scurry confusedly across the highway, blinded by the lights of cars. The silence of evening is broken by the bleating of sheep, the bawling of cattle, or the piercing cry of flitting nighthawks or screech owls.

The State keeps step with the world, but the sunsets, the peaks, and the old trails that Owen Wister's 'Virginian' knew do not change.

Natural Setting

M IDWAY between the Mississippi River and the Pacific Ocean is the State of Wyoming, a great rectangular plateau of the Rocky Mountain uplift, broken by foothills and mountain ranges, with intervening valleys and extensive stretches of rolling plains. One of the four States that have no boundary lines formed by mountain range, river, or ocean, Wyoming is bounded by Montana on the north, South Dakota and Nebraska on the east, Colorado and Utah on the south, and on the west by Utah, Idaho, and a bit of Montana. The State ranks eighth among the 48 in area, with 97,548 square miles of land surface and 366 square miles of water.

The name Wyoming, it is believed, was derived from the Lenni-Lenape or Delaware Indian language, and was first applied to the Wyoming Valley in Pennsylvania. If the word derives—as according to one interpretation it does—from a compound of the Delaware Indian *maughwau*, meaning 'large,' and *wama*, meaning 'plains,' the name describes the State's outstanding topographic feature, the Great Plains. (Some authorities state that Wyoming comes from two Delaware Indian words signifying 'the end' and 'plains,' therefore 'the end of the plains.')

No definite western boundary marks the merging of the Great Plains with the intermountain region. The Big Horns rise to the northwest and the Laramie and Medicine Bow ranges to the south, breaking the westward flow of the plains over about one third of the State. The three distinguishing characteristics of the Great Plains are the wide expanse of fairly level country, maintaining an average altitude of between 5,000 and 6,000 feet, the absence of forests, and the lack of rainfall sufficient for ordinary agriculture. The altitude of the northern section is half a mile lower than that of the southern, with a low point of 3,100 feet on the Belle Fourche River.

The Laramie Plains and the Cheyenne Plains in the south, primarily grazing country, are divided from the plains of the north by several distinctly agricultural districts; the Wheatland Flats, Platte Valley,

Goshen Hole, the Douglas vicinity, and the Alcova-Casper project among them. The high altitude shortens the growing season, but crops mature rapidly because of the abundant sunshine.

Toward the central part of the State are rolling prairies and stretches of sand, with patches of scrubby pines topping broken hills. Beyond this section are the rock formations of the oil fields, among them Teapot Dome (*see Tour 3b*).

The northern plains, broken east and west by the Cheyenne River and its tributaries, are bounded by the Platte Valley on the south, the Big Horns on the west, and the Black Hills, a low broken, tree-covered area, to the northeast. The most notable physical feature here, visible for many miles, is the Devil's Tower, an extraordinary mass of igneous rock rising 600 feet above the hills at its base, which are in turn 600 feet above the Belle Fourche River (*see Tour 10*). Between Powder River and the Big Horns to the northwest there is land with ample moisture, fertile soil, splendid forage, and a wide range of altitude.

The Big Horn range, one of the largest in the State, with more than a dozen rocky snow peaks that vary in altitude from 9,000 to almost 14,000 feet, stands like a giant wall, covered on the lower levels with pine, fir, and spruce. In the foothills are irrigated farm lands where fine livestock is raised. Many streams have their source in the Big Horns, and lakes of all sizes are scattered along the eastern slope. Cloud Peak, a glacier-sided mountain with an altitude of 13,165 feet, is the highest elevation in the range.

In the northwest corner of the State is Yellowstone Park, whose grandeur and scenic wonders surpass the early explorers' descriptions of smoking valleys, of waterfalls so sheer and high that the water was mist before it reached the bottom, of flaming red canyons, petrified forests, great geysers, and bubbling mud pots.

West of the Great Plains rise the ranges that form the Continental Divide, the lofty ridge of the Rocky Mountains. These mountains, including the Absaroka, the Wind River, the Teton, the Gros Ventre, and the Sierra Madre ranges, extend southeastward from the northwest corner of Yellowstone Park across the southern boundary of Wyoming into Colorado. The high peaks in this chain are crowned with perpetual glacier-forming snows, from which streams cascade down the slopes through timbered woods and flowering meadows, carving canyons and creating waterfalls and lakes. On the crest of the Divide within the borders of the Wyoming National Forest is Gannett Peak, 13,785 feet in altitude, the highest point in Wyoming. Spurs and elevations of the Wind River Range form the Rattlesnake and Seminoe Mountains to the south along the Sweetwater River.

Two distinct breaks are made in the Divide: the first, resembling a plain more than an opening in the mountain, is South Pass, through which hundreds of thousands of emigrants made their way over the old Oregon Trail; the second is the Great Divide Basin, which includes the Red Desert, named from the color of its soil, a vast treeless and unwatered high plateau broken near its southern border by a spur of the Uinta Mountains. The area is not a complete waste, as many sheep forage there during the winter months on the abundant salt sage.

All of Wyoming east of the Continental Divide slopes to the north and east, and all water sources drain in an easterly direction. Here three paralleling mountain ranges extend northward from Colorado into Wyoming: the Sierra Madre, Medicine Bow, and Laramie ranges, with the Upper Platte and Laramie valleys between. West of the Divide, except for a narrow fringe near the State Line, all waters drain to the south.

Three great river systems, the Columbia, the Colorado, and the Missouri, have sources in the mountains of Wyoming. The Snake, with its tributaries, flows to the Columbia; the Green River joins the Colorado; the Yellowstone, Big Horn, and Wind Rivers, which drain the northern part of the State, the Belle Fourche in the northeast corner, and the Laramie, Sweetwater, and North Platte Rivers flowing through central Wyoming, all empty into the Missouri River. The canyons of the Yellowstone, Big Horn, Snake, Shoshone, and Platte Rivers are spectacular gorges cut through the mountains. The falls of the Yellowstone are considered one of the scenic wonders of the country.

Less than 10 per cent of the total area of Wyoming is covered with a mantle of recent (geologically speaking), unconsolidated, water-transported soil. With the exception of the flood plain, sediment, till, and dune areas, the surface of the State has been subjected to active erosion for tens of thousands of years. The fact that there is no mantle of transported soil over most of the State is one very important reason why much of the natural vegetation is confined to such hardy botanical specimens as sagebrush, greasewood, and short grass.

Ranching and farming are distinctly different activities in Wyoming. Ranching is confined to the raising of livestock, and virtually all sections of the State have their herds of cattle and sheep. Farming is limited to sections where there is enough water for irrigation and enough soil to form a root base. The semi-arid foothills are covered with sagebrush, cactus, and grama or buffalo grass, but under irrigation these areas produce bountifully.

There are a number of distinct basin and valley areas in Wyoming, such as Jackson Hole, the Star Valley, Green River Basin, the Upper Platte Valley, the Big Horn Basin, Goshen Hole, Sheridan Valley, and Shirley Basin.

Jackson Hole, a beautiful mountain valley some 6 to 12 miles wide and 60 miles long, has some of the most luxuriant hay meadows of the West. It lies due south of the Yellowstone Park at the foot of the Grand Tetons, the Gros Ventre Mountains, and the Wind River Range. South of Jackson Hole, along the western boundary of Wyoming, is the Star Valley, a long narrow strip of fertile country, hedged in by a succession of rugged mountains, high peaks, and jagged ridges.

Green River Basin covers a large area in southwestern Wyoming, bordered by the Gros Ventre, the Wind River, and the Salt River ranges. Its meadows of natural hay, threaded by tree-lined streams, were in early days the haunt of many fur trappers and traders. One of the best farming regions of the State lies within this basin.

The Saratoga and Encampment Valley, that part of the Upper Platte Valley, which stretches between the Sierra Madre and the Medicine Bow ranges in southern Wyoming, is primarily ranching country. It was a center of activity during one of the big mining booms, and until about 1918 there were many big cattle outfits, now little more than 'ghost' ranches, in the vicinity. The hot springs at Saratoga bring many visitors to the valley, where there are now a number of dude ranches.

Much intensive farming is carried on in the vast fertile area of the Big Horn Basin, the largest division of the kind in the State, approximately 80 miles wide and some 100 miles in length. The Basin is watered by the Big Horn River and its many tributaries, and irrigation projects supplement the regular water supply. The main stream of the Big Horn enters the valley through the precipitous and spectacular Wind River Canyon, in the needlelike Owl Creek Mountains, and flows north through the Big Horn Canyon to Montana.

Edged in some places by chalk bluffs, Goshen Hole, a depression in the great plateau of east-central Wyoming, looks like the scooped-out bed of an ancient lake. Many farms, with now and then a town, lie along the creeks or irrigation ditches of this rich valley; but deserted dry farms in some of the more isolated regions give silent testimony to the lack of moisture.

Shirley Basin, to the east of the Pathfinder Reservoir on the west edge of the Great Plains area, is bordered by breaks and wastelands and extends to the Petrified Forest on the east (*see Tour 2b*).

Among the smaller farming and ranching areas are the Snake River, Wind River, Bear River, and Eden valleys. Excellent honey is produced in the well-irrigated Wind River Valley, and the best fruit grown in the State is said to come from the country around Lander at its western end.

The high elevations exert a noticeable effect on the climate of Wyoming, shifting the direction of the wind and cooling the air that passes over their crests. Since the westerly wind's moisture is condensed and expelled before reaching the plains, the State as a whole has a cool dry climate.

Wyoming had 264 clear days in 1936, a characteristic record that indicates the abundance of sunshine. The average maximum temperature is 57°. The three coldest months are December, January, and February; intensely cold spells are short, usually lasting only one or two days. July and August are the warmest months. In summer the nights are cool and the days rarely register a temperature of more than 90°.

The mountains with their heavy timber afford a storage place for the winter snows that, in summer, feed the lakes and streams, which in turn supply numerous irrigation projects.

Electrical storms, cloudbursts, whirlwinds, and terrific hail storms occur during the summer; cyclones are rare. Although the prevailing winds blow from the west, the presence of mountains and hills influences their direction in different sections. In southern Wyoming the prevailing winds, from the southwest during the winter and from the southeast during the summer, sometimes attain a velocity of 60 miles per hour and often of 40 miles. Not all of Wyoming, however, is windy. The wind velocity in the Lander district, according to record, is the lowest in the United States, with that of Sheridan second.

The Chinook, a drying wind from over the Rockies, is often the salvation of the Wyoming stockman. When feed for the cattle and game is covered with hard-packed snow on the range, it is not unusual for a Chinook wind to melt snowbanks two and three feet deep almost as quickly as if a blast from a furnace had been turned on them. These winds change conditions in a few hours from biting cold to mild spring weather. The mirage is another phenomenon that often appears on the plains of Wyoming.

Visitors should be warned against the danger of blizzards. Because of the character of the country, a small amount of snow can be driven with such force and fury by a 40 to 60 mile gale that any living thing caught in it will perish. A blizzard is caused sometimes by a high wind whipping apart old drifts in sub-zero weather, sometimes by a combination of old and new snow carried by a high-speed wind.

Among the outstanding points of interest in the State are the Devil's Playground, Vedauwoo Glen, and other eroded sandstone formations (*see Tour 2A*); the Petrified Forest (*see Tour 2b*); Register Cliff (*see Tour 4*); The Sinks (*see Tour 5b*); Chimney Rock (*see Tour 5c*); Thermopolis Hot Springs, Ayers' Natural Bridge (*see Tour 6b*); Shoshone National Monument (*see Tour 6c*); Natural Bridge and Cave, Devil's Tower (*see Tour 10*); Red Buttes, Independence Rock, Devil's Gate (*see Tour 11*).

GEOLOGY AND PALEONTOLOGY

In its mountains and plateaus, Wyoming keeps a record of many events in the geological and paleontological history of the world during the past billion years: a record of the advances and retreats of the sea, of the deposition of great alluvial flood plains, of the birth and destruction of lofty mountain ranges, of volcanic outbursts, and of the invasion of the earth's own shell by liquid rock-forming material. A wealth of fossils entombed in the rocks exhibits eloquently the evolution of life upon the earth. For the past 60 years, groups of scientists representing the larger natural history museums and institutions of higher learning have been searching and excavating to bring to light these treasures. Various Federal and private agencies have assisted in geological research. The pioneer surveys made from 1869 to 1879, by Dr. F. V. Hayden and Clarence King, under the direction of the Department of the Interior, were followed in later years by those of the United States Geological Survey. Several of the larger museums and universities of the East have made important contributions to knowledge of Wyoming fossils. The Geological Survey of Wyoming and the Department of Geology, University of Wyoming, have shared in a small way in the investigations.

Wyoming affords exceptionally favorable conditions for geological observations. First, the relief pattern of the State is one of deeply eroded mountain ranges separated by large basinlike depressions; second, the semi-arid climate that prevails, except in the higher mountains, prevents the growth of dense vegetation, the presence of which would obscure the rocks; third, the sedimentary formations are unusually rich in fossil remains of past life, especially the skeletal remains of vertebrate animals; fourth, evidences of volcanic activity in the Yellowstone Plateau area and associated hot-water phenomena are exceptional. This combination of factors offers an unusual opportunity to see and to understand geological processes and their results.

The backbone of several of the larger mountain ranges, notably the Laramie, Medicine Bow, Sierra Madre, Wind River, and Big Horn Mountains, are composed of an ancient complex aggregate of metamorphic (*meta*, change; *morph*, form) and igneous (*ignis*, fire) rocks. These constitute the oldest known rocks and, as all younger rocks were laid down upon them, they are collectively spoken of as the Basement Complex.

The metamorphic rocks of the Basement Complex were originally a succession of sediments, such as sandstones, mudstones, and limestones, interbedded with extensive accumulations of lava. This succession of rocks, with an aggregate thickness of many thousands of feet, are known to have been laid down not less than 500 million years ago, and the oldest may have been laid down a billion years ago. The character of these ancient sediments tells us that they were derived from still more ancient rocks and that they were originally formed under conditions very similar to those that prevail upon the earth today. During the lapse of time since the sediments were laid down, they have been greatly affected by physical and chemical change. The sandstones have been changed into quartzites, the mudstones into a variety of schists, and the limestones into dolomites and marble. The upturned and truncated edges of the metamorphic derivations of the ancient sediments and associated lavas are admirably exposed in the Medicine Bow Mountains along the Centennial-Saratoga Highway (*see Tour 2B*).

Intermixed with the metamorphic rocks of the Basement Complex are igneous rocks of many types that were intruded into the older sediments and lavas in the form of liquid rock-forming material (magma). Repeated intrusions of various kinds of magma gave rise to complex associations of rock types. Granites, syenites, anorthosites, and other intrusive rocks cut and invade the quartzites, schists, dolomites, and ancient lavas in great profusion.

It is believed that the Basement Complex was a half billion or more years in the making. Then there ensued a long period during which erosion planed off the then-existing mountains and bit deeply into the Basement Complex, which at that time composed the crust of the earth. Many millions of years must have elapsed to permit erosion to plane off all relief and to leave a monotonously flat surface. This period of erosion is one of the great lost intervals in the history of the earth.

Lying (unconformably) upon the deeply eroded surface of the Basement Complex is a thick succession of sandstones, shales, and limestones, which were, for the most part, deposited beneath the sea during the Paleozoic Era. This succession is much thicker and more nearly complete in the northwest portion of the State, where formations deposited during the Cambrian, Ordovician, Devonian, Mississippian, Pennsylvanian, and Permian periods are found. These formations gradually thin out and, in part, disappear as they are traced into southeastern Wyoming. The high conspicuous hogbacks along the flanks of mountain ranges are made up of these old sediments. The oldest (the Cambrian formations) were deposited beneath a sea that covered much of the present North American Continent 500 million years ago. The youngest (the Permian formations) were deposited some 300 million years later. During these ages the sea advanced and retreated many times, so that the record preserved by the rocks is a very disconnected one.

Near the base of this older succession of sedimentary rocks are found fragments of the oldest known vertebrate animal, a primitive fish.

Upon the older sedimentary rocks rests (disconformably) a vast succession of sandstones and shales, having a total thickness of more than 20,000 feet, which were deposited between 200 million and 600 million years ago. For the most part, the rock fragments making up this succession were derived from a mountainous area that occupied a position 100 miles or so to the west of the western boundary of the State. Rivers flowing eastward from these mountains transported vast amounts of sediments and deposited them on broad alluvial flood plains and on shallow-sea deltas. Representative formations of Triassic, Jurassic, and Cretaceous systems were deposited during this time.

The Triassic rocks (Chugwater and Jelm) are made conspicuous by their brilliant red color. These Red Beds can be traced for miles along the foothills of the mountain ranges. Interbedded with the red shales are numerous seams of white gypsum, which stand out in strong contrast to the enclosing red rock. Remains of semiaquatic crocodile-like reptiles have been discovered in these rocks in the vicinity of Lander and elsewhere (*see Tour* 5).

Resting upon the red Triassic rocks is a succession of brown- and green-colored sandstones and shale (Sundance formation), which was deposited in a shallow sea during part of the Jurassic period. The skeletal remains of giant marine reptiles and the shells of many types of sea animals buried in the rocks illustrate the life that inhabited the world at this time. Recent discoveries have demonstrated that, in certain localities, these rocks contain valuable accumulations of oil.

Lying directly above the Jurassic rocks is a relatively thin succession of variously colored shales and sandstones (Morrison formation), deposited early in Cretaceous time. This formation is one of the most interesting in the entire rock column, for in it are found the skeletons of the giant dinosaurs. When the bones of these animals were first discovered in Como Bluff in Albany and Carbon Counties during the 1870's (*see Tour* 2*b*), their great size astonished their discoverers. When the vast host of giant land-living reptiles first arrived, Wyoming was a great low-lying flood plain, devoid of marked relief, and upon this flood plain the mighty creatures lived, fought, and died. Many years of arduous toil and many thousands of dollars have been spent in exhuming and reconstructing these fantastic reptiles.

Resting upon the variegated shales of the Morrison formation is a thick succession of sandstones and shales deposited during Upper Cretaceous time. Repeated advances and retreats of the Cretaceous sea left in their wake an alternating sequence of marine and continental formations. The shore line of the sea advanced from the east toward the west. When the sea retreated, the shore line shifted from the west toward the east. During times of maximum flooding most, if not all, of the State was beneath the sea, while during times of minimum flooding most of its surface was exposed. The periodic advances and retreats of the sea can readily be traced in the sediments deposited during this period. Rocks laid down on the floor of the sea contain the fossil remains of marine organisms, while conversely, rocks deposited on flood plains contain the fossil remains of land-living animals and plants.

During the latter part of Upper Cretaceous time the sea withdrew from the Rocky Mountain region for the last time, leaving the marine rocks buried under several thousand feet of fresh-water deposits. At the time the sediments were being deposited, great forests of semitropical trees covered much of the State. These forests contained a mixture of medieval and modern flora; elms, oaks, maples, and magnolias had made their appearance. Luxurious semitropical forests gave rise to extensive deposits of coal. In the Green River Basin area alone the estimated supply of coal within 3,000 feet of the surface is more than 600 billion tons, the second greatest quantity of coal contained in any single area of continuous coal-bearing rocks in the United States. In the marine rocks of Upper Cretaceous age are many valuable oil-producing horizons, while the overlying continental rocks contain extensive reserves of coal.

At the conclusion of Upper Cretaceous time all of the existing rock of the earth's crust, throughout the Rocky Mountain region, was thrown by mountain-making movements into a succession of folds. The larger upwarped areas formed the mountainous areas and the intervening larger downwarps produced the basins. In many instances the strains produced by folding caused the rocks to break and mountainous masses of rock were shoved over adjacent masses. No part of Wyoming escaped these movements, although some areas were affected more intensely than others.

When the mountains began to form, their newly uplifted crests were attacked by the forces of erosion and their destruction began. No one knows just how long the mountain-making movements lasted, but we know that the time is to be estimated in hundreds of thousands of years. While we can measure the thousands of feet of rock that have been removed from the crest of the mountains, we shall probably never know their maximum heights, for they were being reduced by erosion at the same time that they were being elevated.

Resting (unconformably) upon all the older rocks is a thick succession of sandstones and shales (Fort Union and Hanna formations), which were derived from the mountainous areas and deposited in the adjacent basins by rivers. This erosion of the mountains and deposition in the basins continued until the mountains were virtually buried in their own rock debris. The formations laid down during this interval contain numerous coal seams and the fossil skeletal parts of the diminutive ancestors of the present great mammalian class of vertebrates.

Following the deposition of the early Cenozoic (Paleocene) sediments, Wyoming was again subjected to mountain-making movements that re-elevated the buried mountains and depressed the filled basins. This action was followed by another prolonged period of erosion. Gradually the gradients of the streams were reduced and their burden of sand and silt brought from the mountains was deposited as a succession of beds.

This period of time (Eocene) also marks the beginning of great outpourings of lava and volcanic ash from active volcanoes, notably in the Yellowstone Plateau-Absaroka Mountain region. Many large freshwater lakes partially filled the basins. The perfectly preserved fossil fish found in the Green River shale in Lincoln County once lived in one of the larger of these lakes (*see Tour 2d*). In the flood plain deposits, laid down at this time, are found the early ancestors of many of the modern mammals. The diminutive four-toed horse browsed along the banks of the river.

Gradually through millions of years the mountains wasted away and the basins filled with rock debris from the mountains and volcanic ash. The Yellowstone Plateau and Absaroka Mountains were built up by an alternating sequence of lava flows and ash beds. The filling of the basins was frequently interrupted. Erosion stripped some of the accumulated layers and they were transported down the rivers, to be deposited elsewhere. Finally, after a lapse of some 30,000,000 years the mountains lay buried under flanking sediments. A few resistant remnants, the last vestiges of their former grandeur, remained.

The next to the last chapter in the geological history of Wyoming was characterized by a regional uplift, which rejuvenated the streams and put them to work re-excavating the basins. Gradually the mountains emerged as the blanketing sediments were stripped from their flanks. Because of their greater resistance to erosion, the Basement Complex and older sediments did not succumb as rapidly as the younger sediments.

During the last half million years, great continental ice sheets formed in northerly latitudes and pushed gradually southward. None of these great ice sheets penetrated into Wyoming, but when finally they covered much of North America, extensive ice caps formed on the higher mountain ranges. Valley glaciers fed from the ice caps moved down the existing river valleys to the basin floors. On their way, they sculptured the higher portions of the mountains into alpine peaks and U-shaped valleys, and left numerous morainal deposits scattered along the valley floors and impounding beautiful mountain lakes.

FLORA

The winds that carry the seed and pollen of Wyoming's trees and grass sweep from the mountains across an ever-changing landscape of gulch and rolling plain, of sun-baked plateau and cloud-freshened valley.

From the flatlands of the Upper Sonoran life zone to the treeless Arctic-Alpine, the serried hills mount 10,700 feet; between the northern and southern borders of the State there is a difference of 4° in latitude. Records of the Rocky Mountain Herbarium at the University of Wyoming show that the State has more than 2,500 distinct species of seed-bearing plants and about the same number of ferns, mosses, algae, and fungi. Of the seven North American continental life zones, only the warm Lower Sonoran and the Tropical are not represented in the State. Within Wyoming are an Upper Sonoran zone in the valley and plain levels; a Transition zone of the high plains, the lower mountain slopes, and all except the highest foothills; a Canadian level, covering the middle slopes of the mountains and highest foothill ranges; the narrow Hudsonian belt at timber line; and the Arctic-Alpine, a zone bare of trees along the crests above timber line.

The arid Upper Sonoran zone stretches over nearly a third of the State's total area, covering all of the lowest levels. Warm climate, a long growing season, and rich soils make this the chief zone of crop production and grazing.

Several species of cottonwood border the creeks and rivers and afford shade to cattle and horses on the range. In early summer, as the trees drop their cottony tufts, the winds blow the white bits for long distances, covering the shallow ponds and prairie hollows. Balsam poplars bloom in April and May, and with the fall of their red blossoms shining olive-yellow leaves appear, filling the air with a sweet resinous scent. Ranging in size from small shrubs to moderately large trees the willows are found wherever a spring, bog, or rivulet saturates the sand and grass-grown soil. Their graceful silhouettes, in varying shades of green, standing out against the drying prairie, make the meandering pattern of the stream beds visible for many miles. Low-growing ash clustered with red buds, spreading elms, and low green-blossomed box elders are occasionally seen along the highways.

The more familiar shrubs and low trees of the Upper Sonoran are the alder, birch, hawthorn, serviceberry, and mountain mahogany. Cactus and rabbit brush alternate with black and gray sage. Throughout the semidesert regions, the fleshy-stemmed and usually leafless cactus draws a meager life from the baked sands and shales. Its thick leathery rind, covering an inner tissue of thick-walled, water-storing cells, retards the loss of moisture by evaporation. Sweet cactus, a native of the plains, is a small plant that rests close to the soil. Its flowers are yellow, tinged with red. Purple cactus, named for the bright hue of its flowers, spreads in bunches over the prairies and dry hills to altitudes of 4,000 and 5,000 feet. Greasewood, a low erect shrub, freely branched and thorny, keeps to the moist salt flats close to the mountains. For sheep-herders and solitary campers on the plains, greasewood provides a ready source of quick-burning fuel. The common sagebrush, also known as black sage, a heavily branched small tree or shrub, is one of the most widely distributed types of sagebrush, celebrated in stories of the cattle country. During the winter, sheep that feed over desert areas eat the leaves. Dark-green aromatic sagebrush with tufted stems is common to mountain valleys and plains. Eaton sagebrush is a spiny plant grow-ing in alkali desert regions; young plants are covered with gray wool; the older stems bear a gray shreddy bark. As late as mid-September, when most other flowers have dried, the sage blossoms still flourish in yellow spikes above the sprawling gray plants. Throughout their sea-son, wild flowers appear in great variety and vivid profusion and, dur-ing the months when rains are frequent, their small blossoms are bright against the brown sod and jagged rocks. Tucked into crevices and sun-warmed pockets on the high slopes, or bent by the wind on the drying prairie, are saxifrage, five-fingers, sour dock, windflower, flax, evening star, fireweed, kinnikinnick, wintergreen, miner's candle, beardtongue, arnica, and the gregarious dandelion.

About half of Wyoming lies in the Transition zone of the high plains, an area for the greater part open and treeless, characterized by ex-tensive grass plains, sagebrush flats, high watersheds, plateaus, and pine-clad foothills. Along the streams near the base of the mountains, white-flowered hawthorn, diamond willow, black and red haws, wild gooseberry, currant, and serviceberry huddle in the thickets near the life-giving water. Over the eastern foothills spread Rocky Mountain cedars, angular and twisted on the upper ridges, upright and tall on the shady northern slopes and in the stream valleys. Utah junipers, moderate in height and bushy in shape, with erect and contorted branches forming a broad open head, are scattered through the hills and arroyos of the western section. Smaller scrubby junipers grow in many parts of the State in large matlike clusters that lend a vivid green to the hillsides and the forest floor.

Within the Transition zone the vast grazing lands, foundation of the stockman's wealth, are overspread by more than 150 types of grass and an almost equal number of sedges and rushes. The majority of the grasses are unimportant economically, because of their scarcity, small size, and inaccessibility; but some of the blue grasses, wheat grasses, fescues, and redtops have real value as stock forage. Along the Powder River, blue grass is the staple range plant; its high nutritive value allows a restriction of range acreage without a corresponding weight loss in the cattle grazed. Wheat grass, growing in clumps that sometimes reach a height of three feet, is the typical range grass throughout the rest of the State, because of its bulk and prevalence on most of the cattle lands. Tufted fescues and redtops, the latter native to meadows and wet banks, make up the balance of the range grasses. Several other grasses in the region, of less value as forage, by their color and gracefulness of form justify classification as ornamentals. In the spring and early summer the retreating snows uncover the tender green blades that soften the harsh brown of dry plain or rock-strewn bluff and ridge.

The largest area of the Canadian zone lies in the mountainous northwest and includes most of the forested plateau of Yellowstone National Park, the mixed forest and open country near Jackson Hole and along the Hoback River, the southern end of Wyoming range, and the wooded slopes of the Wind River, Absaroka, Teton, Gros Ventre, Salt River, Snake River, and Wyoming ranges. The zone stretches from the base of the mountains to an elevation of 9,000 or 10,000 feet.

Of the plants common to the Canadian level, the trees have the greatest economic importance. Six national forests lie entirely within Wyoming, and six others are partly within its borders. Their trees are primarily evergreens, including four distinct species of pine—lodgepole, white, yellow, and whitebark. The first three of these occur, not only in the national forests, but in many areas not under Government supervision; but the whitebark is rare in the State, having spread into the northwest corner from Montana and Idaho.

Lodgepole pines, whose name suggests their tall stature and gradually tapering trunk, are plentiful in the Canadian belt. At altitudes from 7,000 to 10,000 feet, the trees in dense stands allow little sunlight to filter through to the forest floor. Over the ruggedness of mountain and canyon the lodgepoles spread in soft yellow-green waves of feathery tops.

Rocky Mountain white pine is distributed through most of the mountainous sections except in the northeast corner of the State, and frequently grows in conjunction with the Douglas fir along ridges and dry slopes. Tall specimens of Rocky Mountain white pine are rare in Wyoming. It occurs typically in patches or scattered stands, except in deep-soiled mountain sections where groves develop more readily.

Along the eastern slopes of the Big Horns and in the region of the

Upper Platte the yellow pine stands in heavy open forest, scattered pockets, and fringe. The widely separated limbs give the tree a rugged, unsymmetrical appearance, and the irregularly plated brown bark indicates the species' resistance to fire and insect attack. Yellowish-green needles, four to six inches long, cluster at the ends of the twigs. After a rain, the accumulated moisture on the long leaves collects in pearls, and the entire forest is shrouded in a gray mist.

Douglas firs, the towering lumber trees of the Northwest, extend from the eastern base of the Rocky Mountains to the Pacific in dense groves or as scattered specimens. Their thick bark, which becomes deeply furrowed with age, provides efficient fire protection, allowing the trees to withstand fires that completely destroy near-by forests of lodgepole and other pine. On the northern slopes the Douglas firs are often covered with green lichen known as 'old man's beard,' and with black, hanging lichen. The new leaves of the Douglas fir are light yellow, deepening to green with maturity. In May the yellow leaves, the bright red pistillate spikes at the ends of the limbs, and the orange-red blossoms give the tree the appearance of a flaming spire.

True spruces form a large part of Wyoming's forests. In the sheltered basins of the mountain areas where snow lies deep, the Engelmann spruce crowds out the alpine fir and lodgepole pines. The leaves of this spruce remain eight to fifteen years, making the branches heavy and causing them to droop with the weight of snows like a great umbrella. The bark of the adult tree is thin and flakes easily. During the spring, scarlet cylindrical cones and dark purple clusters of staminate flowers cover the upper third of the trees. The oval-shaped, papery cones become chestnut brown in August and September. Blue spruce is less common in Wyoming and is usually found at lower altitudes than the Engelmann. It is a handsome tree, used extensively for ornamental planting throughout the United States and frequently in Europe. Its leaves are denser and darker than the Engelmann and make a deeper bed of needles than any other conifer. White spruce, also an ornamental, is found sparingly in Crook County, into which it has spread from the Black Hills of South Dakota.

The most common broad-leaved tree in Yellowstone National Park, and one of the most representative trees of Wyoming's highlands, is the quaking aspen, a variety of poplar. During spring and summer, the leaves are dark green on their upper surface, and a lighter grayish green below. These small leaves, suspended on slender heart-shaped flattened stems, are set in quivering motion by the slightest breeze.

In autumn the foliage turns a bright yellow intermixed with red. Groves of aspens enliven the mountain sides, in spring their bright green foliage and graceful, silvery trunks mingling with the less vivid spring-time hues of spruce and pine, or later with flame-dipped leaves dancing in the autumn wind.

Many shrubs flourish along the watercourses and in the sheltered dips of the mountains. The hardy mountain alder is found in growths of varying density near cold mountain streams; stream-bank birch grows near creeks and ponds, sometimes attaining a height of 25 feet. The first to blossom in spring, this birch drops its purple flowers in March or April. It frequently grows within the shade of cottonwoods where water is close to the surface. Mountain yellow rose, puffed clematis, antelope brush, and beaked hazelnut, crowded in dense underbrush in aspen thickets, grow in profusion over hills and plains and along the highways.

Fringing the upper edge of the Canadian belt along timber line, a narrow Hudsonian zone girdles the peaks of the northwestern ranges. The division varies in breadth with slope and soil condition from a few hundred to a thousand feet, broadest in cold gulches and narrowest on unsheltered ridges. Heavy snow and drifts that withstand the summer sun prevail in the near-Arctic atmosphere. Some spruce reach into the zone, as do the white-barked pines, which become ragged, dwarfed, and lopsided in the high, gale-swept reaches. Engelmann spruce, bowed by the snows, grows with the prostrate juniper in great impenetrable mats over which the mountain climber can walk. Small flowering plants carpet the slopes for a short season. With the mountain grasses the globeflower, mountain cowslip, shooting star, spurred columbine, Jacob's ladder, forget-me-not, buttercup, saxifrage, and Drabas nod and bend with the gales.

One true fir, the alpine, occurs on the upper slopes. Of less commercial value than many of the other trees in Wyoming, it is nevertheless notable for the shade it gives in the mountain forests near the 7,000- to 10,000-foot levels. The thin bark is silvery white to light brown in color, smooth on the young trees and roughened on the mature. In June, luxuriant violet-purple and indigo-blue blossoms cover the upper parts of the trees. Near timber line the alpine fir diminishes to a small shrub that clings to the rock crevices; near the meadows at low altitudes these firs grow high in symmetrical spires.

Corresponding in climate and vegetation to the barren wastes of the Arctic, the Arctic-Alpine zone lies above timber line in small, broken areas interrupted by intrusions of the Canadian-zone valleys. Over the shoulders of the Wind River range extend the most continuous of the Arctic-Alpine areas in Wyoming. Restricted portions of the zone cap the highest points of the Absaroka, Gros Ventre, Teton, Big Horn, Medicine Bow, and Snowy ranges. Deep snow, intermittent rain, sleet storms, and arctic temperatures are common in all seasons. Extensive snow and ice fields last through the entire year in the canyons and gorges scoured out among the high peaks. Tree growth ceases at the lower border of this zone.

During the short growing season, lasting from the middle of May until August, the usually barren slopes are covered with brightly tinted buttercups, saxifrage, lupine, dwarfed gentians, alpine forget-me-not, and goldenrod. Alpine grasses and sedge spread at random where the soil can support their growth, giving forage for the mountain sheep and the few other mammals who venture into this inclement region. Plant growth diminishes in size above the 12,000-foot level, and the small matted vegetation consists for the most part of willow thickets and copses of shrubby cinquefoil near the moisture-retaining basins. On the stony ridges the mountain heath and alpine avens edge in tangled masses toward the summits. Over the slide-rock and talus the spiny red currant and dwarfed raspberry struggle upward with the dwarf alpine willows that mat the ground above timber line, and occasionally, with the mosses and lichens, attain the highest summits.

FAUNA

The distribution of fauna follows roughly the occurrence of continental life zones, although zone limits cannot be defined with exactness. Local conditions often produce climatic changes within a zone, permitting the intrusion of plant and animal life from a higher or a lower level. Slope exposures may support life typical of a higher or lower elevation depending upon their relation to sunlight and prevailing winds. Because of these changing local conditions, animals, especially birds, are likely to range from one altitude to another rather than directionally.

Wyoming's lowest elevations are covered by the arid Upper Sonoran level, a grass-plain and desert land. The American antelope or prong-horn, the only representative of the antelope goat family (a family distinct from the tree antelope), wanders the dry open plains seeking grass and sage. He is about four and a half feet long and three feet high. The upper parts, sides, and legs are yellowish brown; underparts and rump are white. Bucks gather their harems in September and October and join other herds in large winter migrations determined by weather and the presence of abundant food and water. Winter usually finds them in the sheltered hill valleys, from which they journey to the open plains and low foothills in spring.

Ground squirrels, grasshopper mice, bushy-tailed wood rats, yellow pocket gophers, Wyoming kangaroo rats, ferrets, and moles live in bushes and burrows on the sagebrush and greasewood flats. Buff cottontails range over the open prairies.

High above the broad plains, blue-winged and cinnamon teals cut the air with powerful wing strokes. Far over the marsh lands the booming of the bittern is a familiar call, uttered as the bird, often unseen because of its protective coloring, stands in the high grass. Brown mourning doves travel swiftly for long distances, using their strong wings with skill. Fighting noisily and soaring to great heights, the Arkansas kingbird, gray over his upper parts and lemon-yellow beneath, seeks the open country. Bullock orioles, orange-breasted and black-winged, nest in sunny cottonwood groves along irrigation ditches and streams. In grassy meadows, perched atop a tall weed, the buff and gray western grasshopper sparrow is often seen and heard. Bronzed grackles, with purple necks and heads and uniformly bronze bodies, spend much of their time on the ground, the sunlight burnishing their plumage as they turn their heads from side to side. In the treetops their gossip is a cheerful clatter. Less demonstrative are the lark buntings, shy black and white plainsmen that occasionally send a wave of chorused melody over the prairie. One of the most familiar of western birds is the brownish-gray lark sparrow, whose purring phrase identifies his long and varied song. Glimpses of the yellow warbler's bright tail patches are caught among the willow stream thickets where its leisurely insect hunting is often interrupted by loud and cheery singing. Another resident of the plains is the brown thrasher, reddish brown in coat with white-barred wings. Buffoon of the lowlands, the long-tailed chat announces his spring arrival by a fanfare of song. His upper parts are olive gray; throat and breast are bright yellow. Briery thickets are his home, from which mocking, derisive cries and whistlings are broadcast. In the open he prances and sways along the ground or balances in the air with legs adangle. Almost as impulsive is the western mockingbird, drab and gray with blackish, white-striped wings. His bursts of song are accompanied by a lifting of the wings in gesture and an occasional pirouetting into the air. Not always so pleasing to the hunters are his mimicries of almost every other bird song, sweet or raucous.

Few reptiles live on the eastern Wyoming plains. The list includes the plains rattlesnake, prairie bull snake, hog-nosed snake, blue racer, garter snake, desert horned lizard, sand swift, scaly lizard, six-lined lizard, and many-lined skink.

The Transition zone of the high plains extends over half of the State. Open and treeless, it comprises the interior sagebrush plains and watersheds, plateaus and high-altitude basins, and elevated grassy plains; it also includes pine-clad foothill ranges in the eastern part of the State and the sagebrush slopes of the high western mountain ranges.

Mule deer are inhabitants of the mountains and foothills. In summer they move to the higher elevations and timber until winter drives them back to warmer levels. The strongest characteristics of the mule deer are: large double-branched pronged antlers, large broad ears, and rounded whitish tail with brushlike black tip. Their summer coat is a rich rusty red that becomes grayish brown in winter. As summer wanes and rutting season draws near, the bucks don their best: coats take on a gloss and antlers shine in the sunlight, their velvet rubbed off. Unlike the whitetails, mule deer have little protective caution and, when frightened, bound high into the air, facing this way and that until, as the disturbance continues, they dash off with bounding leaps that cover rough terrain quickly.

White-tailed jackrabbits and Wyoming cottontails are prairie types. The former is yellow buff, gray, and white. Because of his size and speed the white-tailed jack has little cause for fear and is a common sight along the highways. The cottontail is pale pinkish buff in color, with gray and black shadings. He is a wanderer of the open country, living in abandoned prairie-dog holes or about rabbit brush, sagebrush, and greasewood.

The white-tailed prairie dog is a small burrowing rodent, notable for his sociability in living with his fellows in 'dog towns' that sometimes cover miles of prairie. Each burrow entrance is ringed by a mound of earth, and as the 'towns' are approached, the prairie dogs may be seen sitting atop the mounds, barking alarm in a voice like that of a young puppy. Other burrowing animals in the upper plains regions are: Wyoming and Uinta ground squirrels, field and pocket mice, prairie jumping mice, and pygmy pocket gophers.

The northern plains skunk is a small stocky animal, sharp nosed, bushy tailed, and black and white in color. Usually nocturnal in his hunting, the skunk is sometimes seen in daylight, looking for grubs and other insects. Another night hunter is the long-legged bat, who flies in erratic twists and turns in search of night insects.

Over the high alkali and dry sagebrush stretches, sometimes at altitudes of more than 7,000 feet, sage hens (also known as sage cocks and sage grouse) travel in packs in search of food. Strong wings carry the sage hens beyond the reach of natural enemies, but although since 1936 it has been illegal to kill these birds, their numbers have been depleted. About 25 inches long, their upper parts are black, brown, and yellowish white; beneath, they are brownish yellow.

The mating season of the sage hen furnishes an unusual prairie scene. It is begun by a drumming or croaking song at dawn, voiced by the males as they gather on the mating ground—conspicuous barren flats where 100 or more males flock together in February and March. In the early morning and at sunset the females also gather. Standing erect, the males lift their wings away from their sides, raise and spread the tail, as the air sacs on the sides of the neck are inflated to a great size, and the feathers surrounding them bristle out in all directions. The skin between the sacs is drawn in by a sucking motion, and the air is expelled from the throat with a grunting or croaking. Sounding their love call, the cocks strut about, tail feathers erect, dancing or fighting. Sometimes they lower the breast to the ground and push it along in the dust.

Bushwhacker of the plains is the sharp-shinned hawk. His upper parts are bluish gray; under parts are white, barred and spotted with reddish brown. The hawk compensates for a small stature by an amazing audacity and belligerence. A light body, short wings, and long tail enable him to turn and pivot among the bushes and to pounce upon smaller birds or even barnyard fowls many times his own size and weight.

The saw-whet owl is a small species, usually found in pine forests or in rock clefts. It is dark grayish brown, spotted with white. In daylight the saw-whet stays close to the tree trunks; during the night his noiseless wings carry him along the edges of open parks and meadows in search of mice. At the first signs of spring, his love song echoes through the wood—a monotonous, low, scraping note sung in quick succession like the sound of a saw being filed. Near the foothills and lower ranges the Lewis woodpecker thrums a sharp staccato as he drills the tree trunks for insects. At higher levels the white-throated swift flashes with startling velocity through the trees and around rocks in search of food. Its nest, placed high on inaccessible cliffs, is seldom reached by man. The Wright flycatcher, gray and white in dress, is at home in the sagebrush or in mountain parks where insects are plentiful. Garrulous magpies raise a clamor over the plains as they hunt in groups for small life. Near the pines of the foothills and the short junipers of the plains grayish blue piñon jays flap along, cawing much as crows do. Other birds found in the Transition zone are: McGown longspur, white-winged junco, mountain song sparrow, arctic and green-tailed towhee, western tanager, plumbeous vireo, Macgillivray warbler, Rocky Mountain and pygmy nuthatches, and willow thrush.

Garter snakes, toads, and frogs are numerous in the upper plains regions, and rocky hillsides provide shelter for horned and scaly rock lizards. Along the streams and swampy hollows salamanders and smooth green snakes live in the lush grass.

The Canadian zone stretches through the mountainous northwest corner of Wyoming, over most of the forested plateau of Yellowstone National Park, the Jackson Hole, and Hoback basin, and parts of most of the mountain ranges in the State. Forests of spruce, fir, lodgepole pine, and aspen cover most of this level, which presents a cool, humid climate during summer, and low winter temperatures that sometimes reach to 40° below zero. Animals in this zone, with the exception of many breeding birds that make a short summer stay, are species adapted to a region of long cold winters and short cool summers.

Among these animals are elk (wapiti) and moose, largest of the deer family in America. Bull elk weigh as much as 800 pounds; their head, neck, and under parts are dark brown, sometimes nearly black; the sides, back, and thighs are yellowish gray, shading to a tan patch on the rump and to white between the legs. Antlers attain their full size— about five feet in length from tip to burr—in late July or August, when the velvet dries and peels off or is rubbed off against tree trunks and branches. Rutting season is heralded by the bugling of the bulls, a sonorous call, first heard as a guttural roaring. It passes through trumpet pitches to a shrill, screaming whistle that modulates abruptly to the guttural again, then breaks off to a grunt. A challenge as well as a love call, the bugling is a frequent prelude to battle in which sharp antlers flash savagely at the charge. Occasionally antlers interlock during the attack, and the rivals die together.

Before settlers brought fences to the upland ranges, elk wintered in the lower altitudes where snow was not too deep to prevent foraging. When spring brought herds into the hills, the cows paused in the lower aspen groves for calving, and the bulls continued high into the heavier pine and spruce timber, where the growth of their antlers was completed by August. In the next month the bulls began to seek out the cows, then, with snowfall, they drifted down to winter range to browse on grass, brush, and twigs until spring. In Jackson Hole, winter ground of the largest bands, fencing changed the yearly trek: elk still came to the lower levels for winter, but, finding their winter range fenced in, broke down the barriers to get at the haystacks. To aid the remnants of Wyoming elk herds the State furnishes food to 15,000 on the 24,000-acre Teton Forest Game Sanctuary in Jackson Hole. Throughout the State there are 33,000 elk in bands designated as the Jackson or Yellowstone herd, the Wind River, Grey's River, Big Horn Mountains, Green River, Shoshone, Medicine Bow, Laramie Peak, and Black Hills herds.

Moose are usually seen near the mountain lakes and valley swamps, not far from the heavy forests. The bulls are giants, standing seven feet to the shoulder line and ten feet to the antler tips. Weight varies from 1,200 to 1,400 pounds. Antlers are thick, curved bone slabs with as many as ten points on each; strong forelegs are equipped with sharp hoofs. Thus armed, the moose will strike back at any rival.

Hermit of the mountains is the grizzly bear. A lumbering brute with low swinging head, the grizzly slouches through the forest, stopping now and then to gorge himself with berries or to warm his shaggy brownish-yellow coat in the open sunlight. The grizzly can kill anything in his domain, and his fighting supremacy is unquestioned among the crags, yet his common fare is usually limited to mice, insects, berries, wild plums, and green plants. Winters are passed in hibernation, for which the grizzly, like the black bear, prepares himself by fattening. Shelter varies: sometimes it is a cave among the rocks or a hole beneath the roots of an upturned tree. Winter snows cover the openings and make the den weathertight. Before the long winter is over, warm days may bring the big bear out for a short ramble in the sun.

The black (or brown) bear is a fat, lazy wanderer, coming down out of the mountains to kill sheep and small cattle or to shuffle through the hills for leisurely hunting and fishing as inclination leads. Because his ceaseless roving takes him over miles of mountain and valley, he is more often seen by motorists than is the grizzly, who usually stays in the upper hills. On the hunt the black bear is noiseless, but his crashing among the bushes at berry time is bold and loud.

Best known of the big predators in Wyoming is the mountain lion, also called puma, cougar, and panther. A flesh eater, the mountain lion prefers the meat of its own kill—horseflesh, venison, and beef—rather than carrion. This great brown and gray cat will lie in wait for hours on cliffs and shelves above the game trails, ready to leap on the unwary deer, elk, or calf that passes below. Its wild screaming cry often sounds through the forest from the high ledges, as he wanders tirelessly on his night hunt. A foe of game and livestock, the mountain lion is gradually disappearing from the ranges because of the endless campaign against him.

Bobcats, known also as wildcats or bay lynx, are scarce in the State, because they have been hunted as enemies of livestock. From his covert in rocky and creviced ledges, the buff and white bobcat forays at dusk to prey upon small stock, rabbits, birds, or any other quarry not too large for his strength.

Coyotes, most cunning of all predators, are numerous in Wyoming, in spite of the relentless campaign against their destruction of calves, sheep, elk, deer, and game birds. Adaptable to all living conditions, the coyote thrives in all the life zones, from the Sonoran to the mountain heights, and will live in any lair, either that made by himself or one borrowed from other animals. The coyote, averaging about four feet in length, is grizzled above, shaded with gray, black, and tan. To ranchers and homesteaders on the sagebrush plains the dismal quaver of the coyote pack is a familiar warning of thieving bands.

Canada lynx are natives of the high mountain forests. With strong body, long legs, and large feet, the lynx is a formidable enemy. The long, dense fur is light gray, tinged with red at the base of the hairs.

One of the most vicious and destructive animals in the West is the wolverine, a low-built, powerful animal, known to the French voyageurs as the carcajou. A marauder, strong and ferocious, the wolverine is a foe of all but the largest animals in its domain and has been known to follow trap lines to eat and destroy the catch.

Most important of the fur-bearing animals are the beavers, some 6,000 of which were taken in the State during 1938 under provisions of the Wyoming Game and Fish Commission, which allows trapping when beavers are damaging property. A semiaquatic animal, the beaver is the craftsman of the woodland. His dams are a familiar sight along the streams where he fells trees to block the current and to create small still lakes for his lodge. Over the cut trunks he packs willow branches and mud, far enough above water level to form a dry cavity—a large enough home—in which a grass bed is laid. Entrance to the chamber is gained through a tunnel opening below the water surface. The beaver, largest of the rodents, is well adapted to his environment. Warmly dressed in close, thick fur, he is completely at home in the water. He is strong muscled and able to fell and bring trees to the water's edge and tow them against strong currents. Large strong teeth aid in tree cutting; webbed feet drive the sleek body through swift streams.

Frequenting streams and lakes where fish are plentiful, the otter is an admirable swimmer. Too short-legged to cover ground quickly, he is agile in the water and will follow streams for miles or cross from one creek to another to find food. Four or five feet long, he has a prized dusky-brown fur touched with gray. The marten, also hunted for its brown and yellow coat, roams the inaccessible forest wilderness. A clever hunter, it can climb trees swiftly and jump from branch to branch in pursuit of squirrels, chipmunks, and wood rats. Fierce in battle, the marten often attacks its own kind, squalling and shrieking, or hissing and barking. Raccoons, classed as predacious, protected animals, are most common in the Black Hills. The raccoon is short and stocky, with dark grizzled coat. Its club-shaped tail is ringed and tipped with black, brown, and gray. A broad black stripe, merging to white near the muzzle, takes in the eye and extends back almost to the ear. Raccoons are seldom seen in the daytime, as most of their foraging is done at night along the streams and lakes and through cornfields.

The whistling marmot is the largest and most handsome of American marmots. Similar in appearance to the woodchuck, the marmot is about twice as heavy, and has a thicker, grayish-brown fur. It usually selects a home high in the mountains, in the broken rock masses of glacial moraines or stony ledges. In summer the marmot, keen of sight and hearing, often suns himself atop a large boulder and surveys the surrounding country. He fattens quickly in autumn, and before the approach of icy weather retires to his den to sleep the winter through.

Smaller animals found among the rocks and talus slopes of the mountain flanks are familiar to motorists and campers. Chipmunks, here surprisingly tame, are busy foragers—handfuls of black and white, striped in brown. Rocky Mountain jumping mice range to altitudes of 10,000 feet. Their long hind legs and slender bodies are well made for leaps of eight feet or more. Another burrower on the high slopes is the shrew, a tiny animal, living among tree roots and searching the forest floor constantly for food.

The red squirrel, known also as the pine squirrel, has little of the shyness common to most forest animals. Rust-colored and small, it is

The Setting

Photograph by courtesy of C. B. & Q. R. R. Co.

SHOSHONE RESERVOIR AND CANYON DRIVE

DEVIL'S TOWER

Photograph by courtesy of Wyoming Department of Commerce and Industry

RESERVOIR SITE ABOVE SEMINOE DAM

GREEN RIVER GLACIERS

Photograph by Carl Blaurock

JACKSON LAKE AND THE TETONS

Photograph by courtesy of Union Pacific Railroad Company

WIND RIVER RANGE (The Continental Divide)

SUMMER RANGE

Photograph by courtesy of U. S. Forest Service

RED CLIFFS ON GROS VENTRE RIVER

INDEPENDENCE ROCK

Photograph by courtesy of Wonderful Wyoming Society

Photograph by courtesy of J. E. Stimson

GREEN RIVER, WITH GANNETT PEAK AND GLACIER IN BACKGROUND

Photograph by Rothstein; courtesy of Farm Security Administration

IN TETON COUNTY

SUNSET ON THE PLAINS

Photograph by Rothstein; courtesy of Farm Security Administration

easily identified by its scolding bravado. Besides his chatter, the red squirrel has a song—a long-drawn churring, varied with ventriloqual cadences.

Among the birds in the Canadian zone are two varieties interesting for their size and habitat. On Molly Island, sequestered in the southern arm of Yellowstone Lake, white pelicans, ungainly on land and superb in flight, thrive in undisturbed sanctuary. These birds have formed the only white-pelican breeding colony within the confines of a national park. Nearly five feet long and weighing about seventeen pounds, the pelican has a majestic wingspread of nine feet. A large pouch or bag hangs beneath the long bill. When contracted the pouch is small, but it is distended as a scoop for fishing or for feeding the young. Lake shores are the pelican's breeding grounds; eggs are laid in nests built on the sand, where the youngsters waddle around on their large webbed feet, their wings dragging like new crutches, and their great mouths hopefully agape.

Largest of North American waterfowl, the trumpeter swan is vanishing slowly from America and is seen rarely even in the wilder regions. A bird of the fresh waters, it travels far inland to the isolated lakes, winging in unswerving V flights, loud in its clarion. Pure white in plumage, the swan is masterful in flight and stately on the water.

In the tall pines near mountain streams or on the rocky ledge of bold, inaccessible cliffs, the bald eagle builds his nest, a flat structure of sticks and other rough material. Snowy white covers the eagle's head, neck, and tail; the rest of the body is black or dark brown. Total length of the body is about 30 inches. This eagle has been popularly termed 'bald' because of the gleaming whiteness of his head, but the only parts of his body lacking feathers are the lower parts of the legs. The bald eagle's likeness appears on the great seal of the United States as the symbol of supremacy, but he has a contrary reputation as a thieving parasite. His superior strength serves him well in his piracy of other nests and in the courageous defense of his own.

Canada geese nest on the low marsh ground of the broad valleys between the long migratory flights of spring and fall. Large, noisy birds, they sail high over grain fields, prairie, and lakes. Their feathers are gray and white, trimmed with black over head, neck, rump, and tail. A white band covers the throat and cheeks.

Unpopular for his insolence and thievery, the Canada jay, known also as Whiskey Jack, moose bird, meat hawk, and grease bird, is a native of the evergreen forests, where his whistlings, chucks, squalls, and screams are a familiar nuisance to still-hunters. A gray bird about 11 inches long, he flies among the conifers to a bulky, high-walled nest built near the pine trunks, or to near-by campsites where unguarded bacon and potatoes are his for the pillaging.

The water ouzel, or American dipper, builds his nest beside or behind a waterfall so that the spray may keep the moss lining green and fresh. His body is chunky and about as large as the robin's. His dull slate color is sometimes difficult to distinguish against the canyon rocks or in the foaming rapids, where he makes frequent plunges for underwater insects. Completely at home under water, he walks on the gravelly creek bottoms, fearless of the swift current, protected from the cold by soft thick plumage, sure-footed on slippery rocks.

Frequently to be heard in the high pine forests is the bright whistle of the mountain chickadee on his short fluttering flight. Like the woodpecker, the chickadee searches the tree bark thoroughly for insects and larvae, often clinging to the underside of twigs and branch tips.

Another mountaineer is the junco, known also as the snowbird, a hardy member of the sparrow family that remains near its nest until late in the fall before descending to warmer levels. Nearly 20 varieties of the junco have been counted in the Rocky Mountain region. All show differences in color, but their habits of nesting, feeding, and singing are similar. Nests are built under grass or weeds and occasionally in rock crevices or upturned tree roots.

In high, wooded mountains the Richardson dusky grouse may be seen, bluish slate in color, finely mottled with gray and brown. Large wings carry him onto the crags and ridges from which a call of 'whoo! whoo! whoo!' echoes loudly in the dusk. To produce his call the grouse sits with tail spread and wings hanging, filling his neck pouches with air until they are greatly enlarged; then, with a pumping motion of the head, he deflates them with hollow, muffled hoots.

Smaller birds in the mountain forests are the crested buffle-head, red-breasted sapsucker, Barrow golden-eye, broad-tailed hummingbird, purple finch, crossbill, winter wren, red-breasted nuthatch, and Audubon hermit thrush.

Above the Canadian forest belt on the high mountain ranges the Hudsonian zone forms a narrow division that blends into the Arctic-Alpine. Dwarf forest and depauperate vegetation give way to timber line and bare rock. An arctic climate characterizes these levels; deep snows fill the canyons in winter, and in summer, snowdrifts linger in the shaded hollows. Stunted trees, blown by high winds, take strange shapes.

In summer, mountain sheep browse in small flocks to the summits above timber line until winter drives them down through the open timber and foothills. Rough ground is the typical range of these traditionally sure-footed sheep. They have thick, sharply curving horns, and are brownish gray above, with a dark line along the middle of the back, and white over the under parts, buttocks, inside of legs, and upper throat. About five feet long, the mountain sheep moves quickly and easily for its size and weight, and will bound from ledges 20 feet or more in height.

Smaller animals in the Hudsonian and Alpine zones are also typical of the Canadian level just below. Summer brings many of them up into timber line limits and along the crests. Coyotes, red foxes, snowshoe rabbits, ground and red squirrels, marmots, shrews, and chipmunks make a brief warm weather sojourn along the rocky ledges.

At timber line and along the crests the cony, a member of the pika family, makes his home among the shale and broken rock masses. The cony resembles the hare, except that it is tailless and has smaller ears, which lie closer to the head. Its legs are shorter and incapable of the hare's swiftness. Known also as Little Chief Hare, rock rabbit, tailless hare, and whistling hare, the cony is a whiskered rodent about seven or eight inches long. His thickset body is covered with soft grayish fur. Between the rocks near his home small piles of 'hay'—stems and leaves of various shrubs and grasses—are garnered by him during the fall and allowed to dry in the sun. His familiar call is a series of sharp, squealing notes or cries, deceptive as to distance or locality.

In the fire-blackened timber the Alpine three-toed woodpecker nests in the tall conifers. His upper parts are black, barred with white. A yellow patch crowns his blue-glossed head. Under parts are white and black, with black on the sides and flanks.

Near the snowbanks the carmine grosbeak gathers insects and conifer seeds, and builds a platform rest high in the pines. The small brown Rocky Mountain creeper, like the woodpeckers and chickadees, clings to dark-shaded pine trunks to examine them thoroughly for insects. Golden-crowned kinglets, rosy finches, pipits, and titlarks are natives of the forests and high clearings.

Of the 83 species of fish in Wyoming waters, 15 are game fish; all the varieties of nongame fish are native to the State. These include the minnows, of which shiners, chubs, and dace are subspecies. There are also 11 species of sucker, three of which are edible. Killifish, darters, and sculpans are smaller types, valuable as food for the larger varieties.

Wyoming's only native trout is the cutthroat, known also as native or black-spotted trout. It is found throughout the State, and can be distinguished from other trout by a bright-red mark on each side of the throat along the inner edge of the lower jaw.

Rocky Mountain whitefish, called 'grayling' in some localities, is native to Wyoming and the only member of the whitefish family found in the State. A small, slightly ventral mouth distinguishes it. The only real grayling in the State is the Montana grayling, found only in the Madison River in Yellowstone National Park. Its high, broad dorsal fin is brilliantly colored.

Slow, deep streams are the usual haunts of the fork-tailed channel catfish and the sand pike or sauger, found only in the North Platte and Wind Rivers and their tributaries.

Many fish have been introduced into the State for stocking game streams. Most important of these are: Loch Leven, golden, rainbow, lake, and eastern brook trout, black crappie, yellow or ringed perch, black bullhead, and bluegill sunfish.

NATURAL RESOURCES

Abundant and various natural resources, including valuable minerals and the materials necessary to their processing, are potential bases for a vast regional industrial expansion in Wyoming, but up to this time this development has been impeded by scarcity of power and problems of transportation.

Soil: Elevations vary in Wyoming from 3,125 feet to 13,785 feet. The climate is arid, and in many regions precipitation is sufficient to maintain only the hardiest desert flora.

Even while the earliest stock raisers were exploiting the grass bonanza of the open range, there were natural setbacks—droughts, floods, wind erosion, and gradual destruction of grass-supporting soil. The cattlemen blamed the sheepmen; the sheepmen accused the cattle growers of overstocking; and both expounded the folly of breaking the thin topsoil with plows.

But early Government conservation programs did much to restrain the exploitation. Yellowstone National Park, a 2,199,680-acre reserve, was closed to private utilization in 1876, while the open range was still a constant factor in large-scale ranching. In 1891 President Benjamin

Harrison set aside more than a million acres of forest land adjoining the park in northwestern Wyoming as the Yellowstone Timber Land Reserve. This was the first Federal timber reserve in the United States. Other similar reservations were made later, and in 1939 less than half of Wyoming's 62,485,640 acres were privately owned. The State had title to about 6 per cent, and the United States owned 48 per cent as public grazing domain, national forests, parks, and monuments, and in Indian reservation lands.

More than two-thirds of the State's soil is thin and arid; its only possible economic use is for grazing. And so sparse is the cover that, according to stockmen, a cow or horse requires 50 average Wyoming acres annually for pasture.

About 7,515,000 acres are under farming and of these about 2,000,-000 are irrigated. The prairies are level for wide stretches, and their potential productive use is limited only by the availability of water. Thus other millions of acres may be reclaimed as more water is impounded. Lack of water, however, will always prevent such large areas as the Red Desert and Great Divide basins in southern central Wyoming from becoming productive.

Until recent years livestock raising and farming were the most reliable sources of income in Wyoming, but repeated drouth, soil erosion and to some extent over-grazing have proved to be extremely detrimental to both industries. Cattle and sheep growers have not always overstocked, but naturally herds have been concentrated in areas where water was available.

The transient homesteaders who stopped long enough on the prairies to break the shallow grass roots with their plows left thousands of acres to blow into sand and dust. Those who stayed to become dry farmers broke many more thousands of acres; these acres lay bare in winter, perennial winds whipped the soil from around the dead grain roots, and each year the dry farmer's soil was thinner.

Others, in the watered valleys, built irrigation systems and used their water too generously, causing seepage and eventual alkalization of their ground. Some of the settlers farmed ground that was too steep, and the soil was blown away.

Ten years ago few recognized the destructive power of erosion or realized it was costing farmers of the United States at least $400,000,-000 a year in the removal of soil fertility alone; and Wyoming was contributing its portion to this staggering figure of soil losses.

Although a number of erosion experiment stations were established by the Department of Agriculture in representative agriculture sections of the country in 1929, to carry on basic investigations, it was not until the fall of 1933 that direct attempts to deal with the erosion problem on any comprehensive scale was started. At that time, the Soil Erosion Service was established as an emergency agency in the Department of the Interior; and in April 1935, the Erosion Service was transferred to the Department of Agriculture under congressional declaration, authorizing the Secretary of Agriculture to establish an agency to be known as the Soil Conservation Service.

In August 1935, a demonstration project of 2,300,000 acres was established at Lander, Wyoming, in co-operation with the Indian Service, local farmers and ranchers; and in November 1936, a soil conservation demonstration project was established at Torrington, Wyoming.

These demonstration projects were carried on on the premise that farmers, over a considerable area surrounding each project, were able to observe the demonstration of soil and moisture conservation practices and profit by the practical experiences of farmers solving soil erosion problems, and adopt those practices adaptable to their land.

Previous experiments had shown that no single erosion-control measure provided effective erosion control on range and agricultural land, and, therefore, all adaptable measures should be utilized and co-ordinated to obtain the maximum possible degree of conservation. This new program included, in a co-ordinated approach of range management, agronomy, woodland management, crop rotation, wildlife conservation, and all other available vegetational and mechanical measures that would help prevent and control erosion.

In November 1934 the Land Utilization project at Douglas, Wyoming, embracing 2,410,000 acres in Weston, Campbell, Crook, and Converse Counties, was established by the Resettlement Administration, and in 1938 transferred to the Soil Conservation Service. Much of the 2,410,000 acres of land was unsuited to farming, and a part of this was purchased as the first step in developing a co-ordinated land use program that could be managed conservatively for the use of the greatest number of local operators. Land purchase consisted primarily of three types: small, dry-land farms, unsuited for cultivation and too small to produce a satisfactory living, owned by families who wished to find other locations; abandoned homesteads over which no satisfactory management could be exercised without Government purchase; and selected tracts located at strategic points throughout the project area on which water facilities could be developed for the improvement of the range.

Local operators, seeing their advantage in a program of land management, organized co-operative grazing associations, and proceeded to lease privately owned land, State land, and public domain in addition to tracts purchased in the land-use program.

Thus, with two Soil Conservation Service demonstration projects, a Land-Utilization project with a land purchase and management division, co-operative Extension Service and Soil Conservation Service demonstration farms in 17 counties, and a water-facilities program, in co-operation with the Farm Security Administration, Agricultural Conservation Program, Extension Service, Division of Grazing, Forest Service, Indian Service, together with local operators and other Federal, State, and county agencies, it is possible to develop a constructive range management and soil and moisture conservation program. These agencies have co-operated in making it possible to develop a program that takes into consideration the basic physical principle of soil and moisture conservation; that the use of every acre, of every field, pasture, and of every farm, according to its individual adaptabilities, and the treatment of every acre, of every field, pasture, and woodlot of every farm should be according to its individual needs. And for every farm included in the demonstration program of the Soil Conservation Service a farm plan has been developed that endeavors, on the basis of all available information, to plot the course toward maximum conservation of soil and water resources consistent with an adequate economic return from the farm or ranch.

Water: Precipitation varies greatly in seasonal distribution both between the plains and basins, and from year to year. In 1938 the statewide average rain- and snowfall was about 15 inches. In 1923 it was more than 19 inches. In 1904 it was less than 10. The statewide average annual from 1892 to 1937 was 14.8 inches.

From 50 inches in the higher mountain ranges, where snowfall is heavy, this precipitation decreases to less than 6 inches on the arid sagebrush steppes of the lower Big Horn Basin. In the Great Divide Basin and surrounding areas, precipitation averages less than 10 inches; on the prairies of eastern and central Wyoming it exceeds 15 inches. In both latter areas, about 73 per cent of the total is furnished by rainfall between April and September.

Seasonal snowfall, included in the annual precipitation computations, averages 51 inches over the plains and lower valleys, and about 150 inches in mountain areas above 8,000 feet.

Snow and rain provide an average of nearly 18,000,000 acre-feet of water a year over the entire State. Of this 14.9 per cent, or less than 3,000,000 acre-feet, is used by Wyoming irrigators; the remaining 15,000,000 acre-feet drain down the three major rivers that head in Wyoming, and much of it is used in surrounding States. But developments of potential water resources are expected to double the amount used for irrigation in Wyoming.

The State has an important problem to solve in its use of water. Since Wyoming was settled late, and since priority right has long governed the use of water, much of the annual run-off is claimed by priorities in neighboring States. This condition was recognized when Wyoming became a State in 1890, and an attempt was made to remedy it. Although the constitutional convention in 1889 had no alternative but to recognize priority as the basic right to water for irrigation, a 'joker' clause was embodied in the statutes. This provided that 'priorities for beneficial uses shall be given the better right,' and that 'no appropriation shall be denied except where such denial is demanded by the public interests.' The State has since been the defendant in suits brought by States that object to the qualification 'beneficial uses' in the Wyoming laws and to Wyoming's interpretation of the words.

Mormon colonists experimented with small reclamation projects in the southwestern corner of the State near Fort Bridger as early as 1853, and in 1855 Spanish farmers were taking water from the Platte for irrigation near Fort Laramie. But the first legal Wyoming water entries were made in 1862 by the Meyers Land and Livestock Company on the Bear River, and by E. N. Carter on Black's Fork of the Green (at Fort Bridger).

Later settlers developed small-scale but efficient irrigation systems in stream valleys where simple structural forms were sufficient; and larger systems were undertaken on arid benchlands and plains by the United States Bureau of Reclamation, the Wyoming Development Company, and smaller private companies under Carey Act provisions. Now the North Platte, Snake, Big Horn, Powder, Tongue, and Green Rivers and their tributaries are furnishing water to reclaim arid lands; and 2,608,000 acres of Wyoming land are under constructed irrigation systems.

Most large-scale reclamation work has been undertaken since 1900, and progress has been rapid. In 1940 there were 39 storage reservoirs that had been completed, impounding 4,650,896 acre-feet of water, and 34 other reservoirs, with an aggregate capacity of 1,746,811 acre-feet, had been proposed.

But more than three-fourths of the State's reclaimed acres are irrigated by small private systems that take water directly from streams and have limited storage facilities. Thus in wet years these 1,980,000 acres are well watered and productive; when precipitation and run-off is low, there is unrelieved drought.

Whereas the aim of this type of irrigation is primarily one of exploitation, the Government and Government-supervised projects are essentially conservational. They impound flood waters for irrigation, thereby preventing water erosion, as well as supplying water for irrigation during dry seasons.

Bureau of Reclamation projects impound more than 3,000,000 acre-feet of water in 8 storage reservoirs, and this water irrigates 339,621 acres in Wyoming. The North Platte Project, largest in the State, impounds water in Pathfinder Reservoir (1,070,000 acre-feet capacity) in Carbon and Natrona Counties (*see Tour 11*), and in Guernsey Lake (72,700 acre-feet capacity) in Platte County (*see Tour 4B*). Only 58,-621 Wyoming acres are watered from the North Platte Project; the remainder of the water goes into Nebraska.

The Wind River Project impounds water in Pilot Butte Reservoir (30,000 acre-feet capacity) and in Bull Lake (115,000 acre-feet capacity) in Fremont County (*see Tour 12*). When completed it will reclaim 100,000 acres in the Wind River Basin.

The 155,581-acre Shoshone Project (*see Tour 6c*) is served by water from the Shoshone Reservoir (456,600 acre-feet capacity) and the Ralston Reservoir (2,100 acre-feet capacity). The Kendrick Project (formerly Casper-Alcova) has two storage units, the Seminoe Reservoir (1,360,000 acre-feet capacity) and the Alcova Reservoir (170,000 acre-feet capacity) (*see Tour 11*). This project will reclaim about 66,000 acres in Natrona County. Jackson Lake stores 380,000 acre-feet of water for use in Idaho.

Twenty-eight completed irrigation projects, administered by the Commissioner of Public Lands under Carey Act provisions, water about 220,000 acres of arid land in widespread parts of the State.

The high gradient of river channels along the Continental Divide gives Wyoming streams a vast potential electrical energy and the development of hydroelectric power in the State has paralleled the other water developments. The earlier plants were privately owned hydroelectric generators, and, despite the abundance of cheap coal, water power is still of major importance in generating electricity in Wyoming. The expansion of Government or Government-financed plants has been rapid in recent years, however, and their total output in 1939 was much greater than that produced by privately owned plants. Of the estimated 284,000,000 k.w.h. generated by all Wyoming plants during 1939, only about 100,000,000 k.w.h. were produced by private companies. Approximately 182,544,070 k.w.h. or 65 per cent of the total was produced by four Bureau of Reclamation plants. The largest of these, the Seminoe Power Plant (see Tour 11), generated 140,000,000 k.w.h. Three-fourths of the output is used in Wyoming; the rest is transmitted to Colorado and Nebraska. The Guernsey Plant (see Tour 4B) generated 17,763,000 k.w.h.; the Lingle Plant (see Tour 4), 8,901,-000 k.w.h.; the Shoshone Plant (see Tour 6c) produced 12,618,600 k.w.h.; and the Pilot Butte Plant on the Riverton Project (see Tour 12) generated 3,261,470 k.w.h.

This large-scale development of electrical energy has supplied power to widespread rural areas that could not be served by the smaller private plants. In 1939 ten co-operative electricity-dispensing companies, financed by the Rural Electrification Administration, were serving 4,000 consumers. Of these only one project, Lower Star Valley Power and Light Inc., was producing its own power (600 k.w. capacity). The others were purchasing electricity wholesale from other plants, largely from the Bureau of Reclamation, and were distributing it over their own lines at reduced rates.

Minerals: The energy-producing minerals are paramount in Wyoming. Coal, petroleum, and gas sales accounted for 96 per cent of the $472,734,000 in minerals marketed from Wyoming between 1925 and 1934.

Dr. S. H. Knight, Wyoming State Geologist, has estimated coal deposits in the State within 2,000 feet of the surface at 700 billion tons; deposits within 3,000 feet of the surface he estimated at more than a trillion tons. Coal is mined in varying amounts in every Wyoming county except Laramie. Bituminous beds underlie the Rock Springs and Kemmerer areas, and subbituminous deposits occur in the Sheridan, Basin, Glenrock, Gillette, Hudson, Hanna, and Evanston districts. Some subbituminous beds are at Kemmerer.

Near Gillette, where the strip-mine process of shoveling coal from the open seam is employed at the Wyodak Mine, construction of a large steam electric power plant is contemplated to take advantage of the cheap fuel.

Petroleum produced in Wyoming has exceeded coal in market value. The output from 1925 to 1934 was 187,000 barrels valued at $248,-

464,000. More than 200 oil-bearing structures have been recognized officially in Wyoming, and it is estimated that other major structures underlie the Tertiary mantle that extends over much of the State and has not yet been penetrated.

Petroleum recovered in Wyoming has been of two general types: light green and brown oils, of high Baumé gravity and paraffin base, and heavy black oils of asphaltum base. More of the lighter types have been produced, and high extractions of gasoline and lubricating fluids have been obtained from these. The heavier oils have been exploited less, but they are valuable as reserves; their principal use has been for surfacing highways.

From 1925 to 1934 Wyoming's natural gas production was 388,731,-000,000 cubic feet, valued at $38,260,000. Natural gasoline produced totaled 401,519,000 gallons, valued at $25,000,000.

The more important metals occurring in Wyoming are iron, gold, copper, silver, lead, and aluminum. The most common nonmetallic minerals are Bentonite clays, phosphate, and sodium salts. There are large quantities of bauxite in the western portion of the State and of alumina in the southeastern portion; both of these are leading sources of aluminum elsewhere, but they have not been developed in Wyoming.

Production of iron ore has been slow because of the decreasing demand for steel. The output from 1925 to 1929 averaged 510,630 tons annually. The ore is of high iron content, ranging from 52.8 to 56.7 per cent. The Sunrise Mine at Hartville is one of the 20 largest iron producers in the United States.

Bentonite clays, which are becoming increasingly important in the manufacture of paper and cosmetics, occur in large deposits in northeastern Wyoming.

Immense phosphate deposits occur in Fremont, Lincoln, Sublette, and Teton Counties. Some deposits contain 50 per cent tricalcium phosphate, although the average content is lower. Potash, derived from mountain lava flows, borders the phosphate beds. Thus, two important ingredients of commercial fertilizer lie near large coal deposits and near proposed hydroelectric developments, two energies necessary to their processing.

Calcium silica and alumina are abundant in the Niobrara formation that covers a large area in southeastern Wyoming. These minerals occur in the correct proportions for the manufacture of cement and require only grinding or calcining to form a natural mix known commonly as Portland. A cement plant is operated at Laramie (*see Tour 5c*).

Building stone, gypsum, graphite, clays, limestone, sand, gravel, and other building materials occur in sufficient quantities to promise lowered building costs. Such minerals as asbestos, chromite, vermiculite, cyanite, sulphur, mica, and feldspar have been discovered, but their extent and purity have not been investigated.

Forests: Nearly one-seventh of Wyoming is forest land. Twelve national forests within or partly within the State, exclusive of Yellowstone and Grand Teton national parks, cover 8,864,000 acres. Six lie entirely within the State's borders: the Big Horn, the Medicine Bow, the Shoshone, the Teton, the Washakie, and the Wyoming. The Black Hills and Harney forests extend into northeastern Wyoming from South Dakota; the Ashley, Caribou, and Wasatch flank the southwestern border, and the Targhee Forest follows the western watershed of the Teton Range south of Yellowstone Park.

The timber stand in these forests is estimated at 15 billion board feet. No important stands are privately owned. About 40,500,000 board feet, valued at $125,000, are harvested annually under supervision of forest service officials. The harvest is conducted on a sustained-yield basis, and the volume is governed by the estimated replacement power of the forest. Other conservational forest service activities include suppression of insect invasions, fire prevention and control, and supervision of cutting to preserve watershed.

Activity of the Civilian Conservation Corps since 1933 has been important in forest conservation in the Rocky Mountain region. In addition to 'chasing smoke,' the youthful corps workers have constructed roads, campgrounds, and fire-trails; exterminated destructive insects; built ranger stations and fire lookouts; and reforested depleted areas under Forest Service supervision.

An estimated total of 766,000 domestic and game animals graze on national forests and preserves within Wyoming, and this grazing is closely supervised. An annual game census is taken, and recommendations are made to the Wyoming Game and Fish Department for diminishing the number of game animals in over-grazed sectors. The number of domestic animals per acre in summer is regulated strictly by permit, and the dates for their admission and expulsion are determined by climatic and range conditions.

Wild Life: Because altitudes vary more than 10,000 feet in Wyoming, and because the area was settled late and wild animals came from four directions to its borders driven by hunters and the presence of wire fences elsewhere, Wyoming has an unusually diversified fauna.

More than 90 per cent of the State's fish and game animals are on Federal land, either in the national forests and parks or on the public domain.

All game animals are the property of the State, and the wild life program is administered by the Wyoming Game and Fish Commission, in co-operation with Forest Service and Taylor Grazing Act officials. Migratory birds and predatory animals are controlled by the United States Biological Survey.

Thirty-eight species of mammals are represented in Wyoming; the more important game species or varieties include 33,000 elk, 30,000 Rocky Mountain mule and white-tailed deer, 2,500 moose, 25,000 pronghorn antelope, 3,300 Rocky Mountain and Audubon bighorn sheep, and 2,200 black and grizzly bears. (These figures are exclusive of Yellowstone National Park.)

About 800 Plains bison graze in Yellowstone Park, and two smaller wild herds range in the Big Horn Mountains and on the plains west of Medicine Bow. Small herds or zoo specimens are kept at Careyhurst, Cheyenne, Thermopolis, Sheridan, and near Gillette.

Bison and beaver are the protected mammals in Wyoming. Protected birds include the ptarmigan, swan, seagull, bittern, and all insectivorous and songbirds except the English sparrow, magpie, sharpshinned hawk, Cooper hawk, goshawk, duck hawk, golden eagle, brown eagle, bald eagle, kingfisher, blue heron, great horned owl, and crow.

Wild life conservation in Wyoming dates back to the first territorial legislative assembly in 1869. Settlements then were limited to a few mushroom towns along the Union Pacific and near South Pass, and many settlers still were depending on wild game for subsistence. But the first legislators made it unlawful to sell or offer for sale any wild meat between February 1 and August 15, declared a short closed season on game birds, and forbade the taking of trout by any means other than with hook and line.

In 1939, 18 game preserves had been established in Wyoming, and 42 sportsmen's organizations were functioning: moose, antelope, and mountain-sheep killing is regulated by permit limitations. Hunting seasons on the various game birds (nonmigratory) have been closed for several years to permit their restocking.

In addition to its conservation program, the State is developing an efficient wild-life propagation project. Nine State and four Federal hatcheries produced 26,373,731 game fish for Wyoming streams in 1937 and 1938, and ten State hatcheries were operating in 1939. A game-bird propagation farm was established at Big Horn in 1937, and 4,972 pheasants were released in 1938. This number was doubled in 1939. Other exotic species of game birds are raised in smaller numbers.

The first provision for supplying winter feed to the larger game animals was made in 1909. In 1937–8 the State Game and Fish Commission spent $770,142 to feed 20,000 elk, deer, and moose. About 15,000 elk are fed in one herd at Jackson Hole (*see Tour 7a*) at the Federal Elk Refuge.

A different type of conservation is carried on by the United States Bureau of Biological Survey, which, during the fiscal year ending in June 1938, had killed 10,727 predators within the State. Classified as predatory mammals are the bobcat, lynx, wolf, mountain lion, coyote, skunk, badger, civet cat, weasel, porcupine, jackrabbit, raccoon, and stray domestic cat. The damage they do to property and domestic and game animals is estimated at more than $500,000 annually.

Archeology and Indians

ARCHEOLOGICAL investigations in the State have not yet reached a point where it is possible to trace the development of Wyoming's prehistoric cultures or to determine their relation to those of the adjacent areas. Certain rock quarries, boulder lodge circles, rock carvings and paintings, and numerous places containing evidence of former human habitation have been surveyed, but the material has not yet been dated or related in a historical sequence.

Aboriginal quarries at the Spanish Diggings, one of the more important sites, cover an area of 10 x 40 miles extending from the southwest corner of Niobrara County into the northeast corner of Platte County. Some of the larger quarries are reasonably accessible and can be reached by following US 20 westward out of Lusk. At a point 22 miles west, a large sign pointing south directs travelers to the diggings at a distance of 11 miles. Here the quarries and shop sites begin, many of them named for scientists who have made repeated explorations in the region (*see Tour* 6).

Expeditions to explore the sites have been conducted by Harlan Ingers Smith of the Canadian Geological Expedition; Dr. George A. Dorsey (1868–1931), late curator of anthropology of the Field Museum; Dr. Erwin Barbour, of the University of Nebraska; Professor Richard Lull, of Yale University; C. H. Robinson, representing Illinois State Museum; William Henry Holmes (1846–1933), author of *Handbook of Aboriginal American Antiquities,* for the Smithsonian Institution; and Dr. Etienne B. Renaud, of the University of Denver. The Smithsonian Institution sent out a party of scientists in 1915, and since then many of the larger colleges have done likewise. Reports of these various investigations disclose, among other things, that material quarried for implements was obtained from a peculiar stratum of quartzite lying in sandstone, probably selected because its conchoidal fracture left sharp edges. It is noted, also, that rock mining was done entirely with rock tools, such as wedges and hammers. In some instances wedges were found set in the rock seams ready to be driven. Nowhere is there any evidence that metal tools were used.

In addition to the site of the Spanish Diggings, large and typical sites are in southwestern Wyoming, five miles east of Lyman, in Uinta County. Several more have been discovered in southern Wyoming further east. The principal materials found in them all are chert, quartzite, jasper and moss agate, and chalcedony, from which were fashioned such tools as hand axes, bifaced cleavers, and scrapers, side choppers, knives, hammers, hoes, grinding mills, wedges, mauls, and what appear to have been agricultural implements. Nearly all the output of the quarries was of a characteristic type of quartzite so distinctive that, in the surrounding country and in the neighboring State of Nebraska, the tools can be easily recognized as coming from the Wyoming quarries. The character of the stone at once establishes an almost perfect trade-mark. The Indians of today show no knowledge whatever of the system employed in mining these huge quarries.

Picture writing, of both the carved and painted varieties, is found at numerous sites: 20 miles southeast of Lander in Fremont County, near US 287, are pictographs (painted); upon the high cliffs of Castle Gardens, about 20 miles south of Moneta, are many petroglyphs (carved); in the southwest part of Converse County in central Wyoming some rare red-painted pictographs have been found well preserved in a cave. Other groups are found in Albany County, south central Wyoming, and in the extreme northeastern part of the State. Although found widely distributed in the western regions of North America, no satisfactory interpretation of their significance has been made, nor has it been possible to link them definitely with the culture of any particular people.

Extensive collections of the well-known Folsom and Yuma types of arrowheads from Colorado and New Mexico, characteristic of the early Southwestern culture, are often on display in museums and in many Wyoming towns and villages. Although their discovery associated with remains of extinct animal species in Colorado and New Mexico gives them an early date in the history of the New World, there is no proof of the antiquity of the surface finds in Wyoming. Points of a similar type have since been reported from the Atlantic Coast and from the Canadian border to the Gulf of Mexico.

Surveys of the area have disclosed numerous remains of nomadic groups, such as the Plains Indians, who occupied the region during historic times. Articles of stone used to weight down the edges of their skin tents are found in many parts of the State, and also the so-called game blinds. These structures are generally stone breastworks occupying the crests of ridges overlooking valleys and game trails: curved stone fences, evidently erected to hide hunters spying upon game and to enable them to shoot at closer range with their crude weapons. In the northern part of Platte County several such game blinds are still intact; by their selected location, they indicate their builders' hunting tactics.

Cooking pots—globular vessels, wider than they are high, with flattish bottoms—and other specimens of coiled black and white pottery have been found in eastern Wyoming. Pottery makers working in Wyoming did not follow well-established traditions nor did they strive for beauty; they seemed to be more interested in fashioning practical utensils. In the Wind River district of central Wyoming, huge pestles have been discovered, about five feet in length, consisting of a ball eight or nine inches in diameter and a stem tapering to about four inches. They were discovered by Indians who suggest that they were probably used for grinding grain, grass seeds, and dry berries. In neither case have these artifacts been linked with a particular people, nor with the cultures to the East or the Southwest.

Wyoming Indians of today disclaim any knowledge of how to make pottery, baskets, or arrowheads. If their forebears had such a culture it is a lost art among their descendants. The same is true of pictography. Present day Indians are as much puzzled as their white brethren regarding picture writing on cliffs and how it was accomplished at elevations that can be reached today only with the aid of ladders. Neither have they any legends or knowledge concerning the builders of the famous Medicine Wheel on top of the Big Horn Mountains west of Sheridan. They refer to it only as a prehistoric Indian shrine, beyond the reach of tradition or history (*see Tour* 10A). The oldest Indian leaders in Wyoming quite uniformly declare it was built 'before the light came' by people 'who had no iron.'

The Wheel, built of stone, has a circumference of 245 feet. The rocks laid in the formation have never been removed or disturbed. The center cairn of stone, about three feet high, is the largest and probably represented the sun. From this center, corresponding to the hub of a wheel, there radiate 28 rock spokes, the number supposedly corresponding to the 28 lunar days. Around the edges of the wheel are six medicine tepees (so called by the Crow) for the planets. There is a seventh medicine tepee approximately 15 feet from the Wheel.

These shelters, which were very low with a slab of rock across the top, were evidently the shelters for the chiefs or medicine men of the different tribes in time of worship. They must have been propped up by heavy pine logs such as those now found mixed with the piles of stone. On the projecting slabs within the central structure rests a perfectly bleached buffalo skull, which was so placed that it looks toward the rising sun.

INDIANS

Old camp sites and caves used as living quarters, with heaps of bones, fireplaces, tools made of stone and bone, ornaments, weapons, burial cairns, and mining shafts close by, prove that Wyoming was early the abode of man. Rock paintings and carvings near these sites or along trails record visits, battles, hunts, ceremonies, dreams, warnings, beliefs, and information about water or trails. At what period the aborigines disappeared and the present tribes took their place remains unknown.

With its vast grassy plains and deep mountain valleys, Wyoming was the hunting ground of 12 great Indian tribes: Crow, Blackfeet, Sioux, Ute, Bannock, Flathead, Cheyenne, Arapaho, Shoshone, Modoc, Nez Percé, and Kiowa. Some of these tribes established themselves here and bitterly contested the white man's progress westward. But though thousands of red men at one time wandered over Wyoming, the 1939 population of the State included only 1,184 Shoshone and 1,198 Arapaho, all living on the Shoshone Reservation at the base of the Wind River Mountains (*see Tour 5b*).

Members of the Crow Nation were the first known Indian inhabitants of Wyoming. They found the Big Horn country a rich hunting ground and a pleasant place in which to live. Later the Sioux, Cheyenne, and Arapaho pushed in from the east and southeast; Blackfeet and Flathead came in from the north; Shoshone and Nez Percé, from the west; Ute and Gros Ventre, from the south. Many bloody battles were fought before the Crow relinquished their homes, and like the tribes that displaced them, they continued sending war and hunting parties through the region long after white occupation began.

Certain warlike Plains tribes, Sioux, Cheyenne, and Arapaho chiefly, controlled eastern Wyoming for generations before white men came. Not content with holding the plains and fighting one another, they continually raided the mountain tribes. When homeseekers and prospectors started their mass movement toward Oregon, California, and Utah in the 1840's, these Indians opposed them most bitterly and consistently. And in the end it was the Plains Indians who were driven out of Wyoming by the white advance, leaving the Shoshone for a time the only remaining tribe in the whole vast area. Later, by a fluke, the northern Arapaho were returned to Wyoming.

The history of the Shoshone, most northerly of the great Shoshonean tribes, which all belong to the extensive Uto-Aztecan linguistic stock, is full of paradox. They occupied western Wyoming, central and southern Idaho, northeastern Nevada, and northwestern Utah. The Snake River country in Idaho was their stronghold, but their expeditions sometimes reached the Columbia. Holding somewhat in contempt their less vigorous cousins to the south—the root-eating Ute, Hopi, and Paiute—they themselves seem to have been almost equally despised by the Plains tribes. Originally plains rangers, they were driven to the mountains by the Atsina and Siksika before the coming of white men. Even the peaceable Crow singled them out to raid when they wished to compensate themselves for their losses to the Sioux. The Shoshone therefore welcomed the whites as allies. When the tribe was reduced to scarcely more than 1,000 men, women, and children, Washakie, its chief, requested a reservation and Government protection.

Nevertheless, the Shoshone were good fighters. The warlike Ogallala who often raided them for scalps, wives, and horses, found a warm reception among them. Red Cloud's son was killed in a raid in the early 1860's, and Red Cloud was not too successful in a foray he led against the Shoshone just before he resigned himself to reservation life (*see Tour 3a*). When the Shoshone chose to fight the whites, they did almost overnight what the combined Plains tribes had attempted to do for months: they closed every stage and mail station for 200 miles (*see Tour 5*).

'Shoshoni' (in the valley, or valley dwellers) is apparently not a Shoshonean word, although the people of the tribe recognize it as their name. The Cheyenne call the Comanche, who speak a Shoshonean language, Shishi-noats-hitaneo (snake people), and they have a different name for the Shoshone. But the name, Snake, has been adopted for the Shoshone, especially those of Oregon, probably because the sign for these Indians is a serpentine motion of the hand with the index finger extended. Actually the sign is believed to refer to the weaving of grass lodges by the Shoshone, who are known as 'grass-house people' among several tribes.

The northern and eastern Shoshone were riding and buffalo-hunting

Indians, but those to the west along Snake River and to the south in Nevada were of a wholly different type. Much of this country was so barren and so lacking in large game that the inhabitants depended for food largely on fish, rabbits, roots, nuts, and seeds. They were frequently called Diggers, and sometimes Walkers, which simply meant that they did not have horses. The same name was applied to horseless Shoshone elsewhere. None of the Shoshone were agriculturists.

In the north and east they lived in tepees, but in the sagebrush country to the west they used roofless half circles of brush, which afforded inadequate protection from wind and snow. They spoke many mutually intelligible dialects. Clothing among the Wyoming groups consisted of a knee-length shirt, a breechcloth, a headdress, and thigh leggings for men, and a long shirt-dress with ample cape sleeves, a belt, leggings, and moccasins for women. A buffalo robe served as a bed.

As late as the 1880's members of a group of Shoshone called Sheep Eaters (*see Yellowstone National Park*) lived in Wyoming. Their Shoshonean name was Doog-oo-riga. In primitive times they hunted mountain sheep with flint-pointed arrows, surrounding them on a crag to shoot them. As a rule they were intelligent, self-reliant people.

The Shoshone divisions, so far as known, were: Hohandika, Shoberboobeer, Shohoaigadika, Shonivikidika, Tazaaigadika, Towahnahiooks, Tukuarika, Tussawehe, Washakie, Wahinasht, and Yahandika.

The Shoshone claim the land beyond the setting sun, 'our father's abode,' as their original home. They believe in a future life free from want and care; in ghosts and supernatural powers, personal and impersonal; and in a personified bad luck who pursues them and shoots an invisible flint-pointed arrow into them. Their traditions are full of references to a period when they had no horses, when small game took the place of the buffalo, and people had no skin tepees in which to live. They venerate the chickadee as the little bird that discovered the world. They dread the gopher. If one of them finds a dead gopher near his camp, he immediately leaves, believing that the gopher died to spite him. Like the Arapaho, they are expert weather forecasters.

Shoshone mythology, like that of many tribes of the Great Basin, shows little trace of cosmological ideas. It is limited to tales of animals whose actions long ago are responsible for the present state of the world and for Shoshone customs.

A favorite legend is that of the cottontail and the sun. Long ago, the story runs, the sun was so near the ground that it burned the Indians. In their extremity they held a council and appointed the cottontail rabbit to shoot the sun. The cottontail went toward the sunrise and dug a deep pit from which he shot arrow after arrow, but each fell burned and harmless to the ground. At last he took the stick he had used for a fire drill in the old Indian fashion and discharged it from his bow. At once the sun fell into the pit. The new sun that arose from the old one has always kept a respectful distance from the earth. The cottontail carried away marks on his body where the falling sun struck him.

The legend of the origin of the Shoshone tells that a great flood once covered the land. A water bird swam about the surface with tufts of grass in its bill. The Creator breathed life into the tufts, which became people, white as snow. After several children were born to them, the woman ate some fruit given to her by Coyote, the Trickster. When the fruit turned her flesh brown, she induced her family to eat it as well.

The Shoshone believe that infinitesimal people called Nin-am-bea inhabit the recesses of the mountains, and that some of the medicine men can see them and talk with them. The Nin-am-bea are deadly enemies of the eagle. Now and then they shoot a Shoshone if they find he has ridiculed their existence, but on the whole they are friendly.

The Arapaho, an important branch of the great Algonquian family, recognize among themselves five main divisions, speaking as many dialects. They originally called themselves *Inuanaina* (our people, or chosen people). The name Arapaho may possibly be derived from the Pawnee *tirapihu* or *larapihu* (trader). By the Sioux and Cheyenne the Arapaho were called 'blue sky men,' or 'cloud men.' No reason for this is known.

The origin myth of the Arapaho is told in full during ceremonies involving the tribal palladium, the Flat Pipe; parts of it are told on other occasions. One part relates: 'In the beginning there was nothing but water, with Father (Flat Pipe) floating on four sticks. Father told the waterfowl to dive down and find clay. Duck brought some, but it was not enough. Turtle dived down and came up with clay in his four feet. Father added it to the other and stretched it out to dry. He blew pieces to the northeast, southeast, northwest, and southwest. He swung the rest to make the earth. With a rod he made the rivers, and where the dirt was thickest he made mountains. He then made the sun and moon, and a clay man and woman.'

Another legend has it that the primal waters covered everything except the top of a high mountain. There the first Arapaho sat weeping with loneliness. Looking up he saw Je-sa-ne-au-thau (Creator) walking toward him on the water. Je-sa-ne-au-thau commanded a dove to find a country for the man. Returning from fruitless search, the dove said, 'The water is over all.' Je-sa-ne-au-thau then sent the turtle, which dived into the water and came up with some earth in its mouth and reported that there was more of the substance under the water. The Creator said, 'Let the waters flow away to the big seas and let the dry land appear.' Immediately, mountains, valleys, hills, and plains appeared before them, fresh and green as in the spring. He turned to the Arapaho and gave him the land. Then he gave him the flat pipe and told him that it would serve 'as a guide and a blessing.'

The Arapaho preserved this pipe with utmost care. Where the pipe led, the tribe followed; where it stopped, they camped. It was too sacred to be carried on horseback, so the custodian had to carry it afoot in his arms. It led the tribe to battle and victory. A dying Arapaho gazing on it was always led safely 'to our home.'

The Arapaho say that they were once a sedentary, agricultural people, living far to the northeast, apparently near the Red River Valley. They moved southwestward across the Missouri about the time when the Cheyenne moved out of Minnesota. The northern Arapaho made lodges at the edge of the mountains about the head of the North Platte; the southern, near the Arkansas. They made peace with the Sioux, Kiowa, and Comanche about 1840, but continued fighting the Shoshone, Ute, and Pawnee until confined to reservations. The northern Arapaho is regarded as the mother tribe and retains the sacred tribal possessions: a tubular pipe, an ear of corn, and a turtle figurine, all of stone. Tribesmen use the sign for 'mother' when speaking of the tribe, tapping the left breast with the fingertips.

In 1868, by a treaty concluded at Fort Laramie, the Cheyenne and Arapaho relinquished their claim to lands in Wyoming and agreed to accept a home in Dakota. There the Sioux had reserved so large a proportion of the hunting rights that the Arapaho asked for a new region. In 1876 they agreed to move to Indian Territory. At the Platte River in eastern Wyoming, some of them stopped, determined that they would go no farther until they had communicated to the President at Washington their desire for a reservation where they were. When the agent sent in answer to their request reached Wyoming, the tribe was starving, with winter upon them. The Bureau of Indian

Affairs obtained the reluctant consent of Chief Washakie to place them on the Shoshone Reservation for the winter. There, over Washakie's protests, the Government left them. The two tribes were constrained to live as neighbors, but never intermingled; both were mortified when one of Washakie's sons married an Arapaho maiden. During the half-century that followed, only four intertribal marriages were recorded.

On March 3, 1937, Congress granted the Shoshone permission to sue the Government for the value of the land and natural resources used by the Arapaho. The suit resulted in an award of more than $4,000,000 to the Shoshone and legalization of the Arapaho's claim to homes in Wyoming.

The solution of other problems of the Shoshone and Arapaho lies to a certain extent with the Indians themselves. Administration of Indian affairs tends to be based more and more on recognition of the Indian as an individual and an integral part of the Nation's life. Changes are constantly taking place; and these the Indians are accepting to their own advantage and the advantage of their white neighbors, who now at length realize that they have everything to gain by understanding the Indians and helping to preserve their rich culture.

History

INTO the region that is now the State of Wyoming came explorers, daring fur traders and trappers, friendly and hostile Indians, travel-weary emigrants, and missionaries; scientists, gold-seekers, frontier soldiers, pony express riders, telegraph operators, and stage-coach drivers; English and French nobility bent on big game hunts, railroad builders, cattle barons and cowboys, sheep owners and herders, bandits and rustlers, diamond swindlers, courageous homeseekers, and settlers.

Wyoming is the only State composed of territory acquired from all four of the principal annexations to the original United States. Parts of the state have been claimed at times by five nations, and some 30 changes of boundary have resulted in the present rectangle now on the map.

Although little or nothing was known of the vast territory beyond the Mississippi Valley and Wyoming remained untenanted by white men, Spain, after Columbus's discovery of America, claimed the continent under the papal 'bull' in 1493 as part of the 'countries inhabited by infidels'; her claim being given greater force by De Soto's discovery of the Mississippi River in 1541. The Spanish claim to the country east of the Rocky Mountains was superseded by that of France following the 1682 expedition of La Salle, who gave the territory the name of Louisiana.

France ceded to Spain the western part of this basin in 1762, but in 1792 Lieutenant W. R. Broughton of the Vancouver Expedition claimed the basin of the Columbia River for Great Britain, though Captain Robert Gray of Boston was the first to discover the river in the same year. In 1800 France regained the region that had been relinquished to Spain. This was purchased by the United States in 1803 and was formed into the District of Louisiana in 1804, and then into the Territory of Louisiana in 1805. In 1812 it was organized into Missouri Territory, and in 1834 was made into the Indian Country.

When the Republic of Texas was organized in 1836 the territory claimed by it included a part of southwestern Wyoming and in 1845, when Texas was annexed by the United States, parts of what later became Carbon, Albany, and Laramie Counties, Wyoming came into the Union. The following year the treaty with Great Britain established the right of the United States to the 'Oregon Country,' including parts of western and north-central Wyoming. The undisputed right to all of Wyoming came to the United States with the cession of territory by Mexico, through the treaty of Guadalupe Hidalgo in 1848. During the next 20 years Wyoming was, in whole or in part, under the jurisdiction of Dakota Territory, Nebraska Territory, Utah Territory, Idaho Territory, and again Dakota Territory. In 1868 it was made an organized territory of the United States, and the territorial officers took office early in 1869. Twenty-one years later Wyoming became a State.

The history of Wyoming may be divided into five periods: exploration and fur trading; emigration along the Oregon-California and Overland trails; Indian campaigns; territorial days; and statehood.

According to some authorities, one of the numerous Spanish expeditions that left Old Mexico during the latter part of the sixteenth or early part of the seventeenth century penetrated as far north as the Missouri River and reached the Yellowstone country. Available historical facts make it seem not unlikely that some of these expeditions came into Wyoming. A map prepared by the Jesuits as early as 1792, preserved in the archives of Paris, contains a correct topographical sketch of the Black Hills and the Big Horn Mountains, but the source of the information used in making the map cannot be definitely ascertained. Ruins of stone houses and fortifications, traces of iron tools, and old mine workings in the Big Horn Basin are also considered by some authorities as strong evidence of early Spanish explorations in the State.

According to some historians the first white men to set foot in Wyoming were the Verendryes—François and Louis Joseph—French Canadians, sons of Pierre Gaultier de Varrenes, Sieur de la Verendrye. Recent research, however, would have it that they merely sighted the Big Horns of Wyoming. Orin G. Libby in his *Some Verendrye Enigmas* published in 1916 says: 'From their journal we know that they left this Mantanne village on the Missouri July 23, 1742. . . . Their route lay between the Yellowstone and the Little Missouri in a general southwest direction . . . Finally in company with a war party of the Gens de L'Arc, they reach a village of the Serpent tribe, which Parkman identifies as the Snake or Shoshone. At this point a wooded range of mountains is observed, which represents the point farthest west attained by the party. Whether the mountains seen were the Big Horn range of the Rocky mountains may still be a matter of doubt but it is certain they can not be identified as the Black Hills, since the route of the party along the upper waters of the Yellowstone and Powder rivers was obviously far to the west of this region.'

While the United States was completing the purchase of the Louisiana Territory in 1803, the Lewis and Clark Expedition was organized for the purpose of exploring for a route to the Pacific. Although the Lewis and Clark Expedition of 1804–6 did not cross Wyoming, two of the members of the party later were in the Wyoming area: John Colter, trapper and woodsman, and Sacajawea, the Shoshone woman who acted as guide and interpreter for the Expedition. She died on the Wind River Reservation (*see Tour 5b*).

On the return trip from the coast, when near the Mandan villages, Colter asked for a discharge from the expedition and turned back into the wilderness to trap. In 1807 he passed through the Pryor Gap of the Big Horn Mountains, wandered about on Clark's Fork, then on the Stinking Water (now the Shoshone River in the Big Horn Basin), and from there it is believed he reached the headwaters of the Green River. Later he discovered the wonders of the Yellowstone Region. In 1810 he returned to St. Louis where he related stories of burning mountains and steaming, spouting geysers. His accounts of nature's wonders were not accepted by the public, but Captain Clark did outline Colter's course on the map of the Lewis and Clark Expedition, marking it 'Colter's Route in 1807.'

John Colter's trapping expedition into Wyoming marks the beginning of the fur-trading period in Wyoming's history. From 1807 until the close of the war of 1812, a large number of trappers from the Great Lakes region transferred their enterprise to the headwaters of the Missouri. One party, led by Ezekiel Williams in 1807, spent some time trapping on the tributaries of the Yellowstone. Later, on account of the hostility of the Indians, these men took a southerly course, presumably up the Big Horn River, and must have crossed the Wind River Valley. One of their number, Edward Rose, remained in the Crow country and is credited with being the first permanent American resident in the Big Horn Basin. It is said that he was in this vicinity until 1823; afterward he became a guide for Thomas Fitzpatrick and William Sublette.

John Jacob Astor's preliminary enterprise, the American Fur Company, and the Missouri Fur Company of the picturesque Lisa, Henry, and others of St. Louis were formed in 1808. As a consequence, by the following year there were many white trappers in what is now eastern Wyoming.

In June 1810 John Jacob Astor organized the Pacific Fur Company, which was to include the China trade as well as supply the northern Russian establishments in America. He immediately planned two expeditions to meet on the Pacific Coast. One of these in the ship *Tonquin* went around Cape Horn and entered the Columbia in the spring of 1811. Later most of the crew were massacred by the Indians and the ship was blown to pieces. By the end of May of that year a fort had been built 12 miles upstream, and named Astoria. The land expedition, under Wilson Price Hunt, crossed the northern boundary into the present State of Wyoming about August 1, 1811, and, moving westward, left the State by way of a canyon (to which he gave the name of Hoback for John Hoback, a trapper) and over Teton Pass. Hoback River and basin are now visited annually by thousands of tourists, who take the south entrance into Yellowstone Park (*see Tours 5, 7*). The mountains, subsequently named by French trappers *les Trois Tetons* (the three breasts), were christened by Hunt the Pilot Knobs.

Hunt's expedition was remarkable in that it followed a route through a wilderness never before taken by white men and that it blazed the way across the continent from St. Louis to the Pacific Coast in 340 days. This first effort, made to discover a central land route from the Missouri River to the Oregon region, brought Wyoming definitely into American history.

On June 29, 1812, six months after Hunt's arrival at Astoria, Robert Stuart with a small party started back across the mountains, bearing dispatches to John Jacob Astor in New York—an event of great importance in the annals of Wyoming. In nine months of travel the party made a new route, which was, in large part, what was later known to thousands as the Oregon Trail. On this trip Robert Stuart journeyed through South Pass, for years the most important gateway between the Atlantic slope and the Pacific. His party crossed the Continental Divide on October 22, 1812, and was the first group of explorers to trace out a river flowing to the east directly from the mountains. Stuart made a winter camp near Bessemer Bend in Wyoming and also camped near the present site of Torrington. This venturesome Astorian expedition practically opened up the Oregon Trail and blazed the way for more than 300,000 persons who, from 1840 to 1869, traveled across Wyoming on their way to claim a new country and to build an empire.

Scant written record remains of operations in Wyoming during the decade following Stuart's trip, though little doubt exists that the country, at least the Jackson Hole and the Big Horn Basin regions, was visited by many trappers and traders. In 1822 General William H. Ashley of St. Louis, with a company of able men, went up the Missouri, established a trading post on the Yellowstone, and from there covered the country with his trappers for a considerable distance to the south. Ashley returned to St. Louis in the fall of 1823 and in the following year made another trip, during which he did considerable exploring and named the Sweetwater River. He also changed the name of the Spanish River to Green River in honor of one of his St. Louis partners.

In his party of 43 men were many who afterwards became famous in the Rocky Mountain country, and whose names are closely associated with Wyoming's early history—Robert Campbell, Jim Bridger, William Sublette, Thomas Fitzpatrick, Jim Beckwourth, and Moses Harris.

Ashley revolutionized the methods of trapping, mounting his men on horseback and employing none but expert riders and those who could handle a rifle with deadly effect. Because of the vastness and roughness of the wilderness over which these solitary men worked and the hostility of the western Indians, the forts and trading posts of earlier American trapping history were impracticable in the Rocky Mountain area. Ashley abandoned efforts to conduct trade from fixed trading posts and relied on itinerant parties, who met other trappers and Indians at the annual rendezvous where the trappers traded furs to the company for ammunition, whisky, and various supplies. The Indians were always eager for powdered vermilion, beads, and other trinkets. The rendezvous was noted for its mixture of business, mirth, gambling, and brawls.

The first gathering of the trappers was an experiment conducted by Thomas Fitzpatrick on the Green River in 1824 for General Ashley's fur company. Fitzpatrick was known to the Indians as 'Broken Hand, Chief of the Mountain Men.' The assemblage was small, with only

Ashley's men participating. The next year Ashley himself selected a spot on Henry's Fork of the Green River and posted signs inviting all trappers to attend. From that date until the end of free trapping in the 1840's, the rendezvous was an annual event.

Trappers trekked in singly, in pairs, and in groups, from far, hidden valleys and nameless streams, to swap their catch for powder, traps, guns, knives and even cash. Long trains of pack mules or carts and wagons labored 1,000 miles over dim trails to bring commodities. The loads included such things as salt and a few luxuries—sugar, coffee, and clothing—and mirrors, beads, and bright bits of cloth, which, together with whisky, guns, and ammunition, were staples for the Indian trade. Bands of Shoshone, Crow, Nez Percé, Flathead, and Bannock came with their tepees, squaws, children, horses, and dogs. The camps of rival companies were segregated and each competed, with gusto and few scruples, for pelts and for the services of trappers during the year to follow. Sometimes more than 1,500 trappers took part in the rendezvous.

In 1826 General Ashley retired, selling out his interests in Wyoming to Sublette, David E. Jackson, and Jedediah S. Smith, who in turn sold in 1829 to a group that operated under the firm name of Rocky Mountain Fur Company.

It is reported that three-fifths of all the men who served under Ashley, Sublette, Campbell, Bridger, and Fitzpatrick were killed by Indians, and yet the fascination of the life kept the ranks full and the fur-trapping business active until the supply of fur-bearing animals was depleted.

Trading posts were soon established in various parts of the country; the first in Wyoming, on Middle Fork of Powder River 12 miles east of Kaycee, was known as the 'Portuguese Houses.' These houses of heavy hewn logs were erected by Antonio Mateo, a free trader, in 1828, and some of them were still standing in the 1860's. Little is known of the early history of the post. The Hudson's Bay Company is said to have stored a large shipment of furs there one winter.

Wagons could travel with comparative ease in the territory covered by General Ashley's men, but the country to the west was in many places almost impassable. The first wheeled vehicle to cross the mountains, going through South Pass and out to Great Salt Lake, is said to have been taken by an expedition that left St. Louis in March 1827. It was a rude carriage, on which was mounted a cannon, drawn by a team of mules.

In the spring of 1829 William Sublette left St. Louis with a large party of men, and arrived on July 10 at the rendezvous in the Wind River country near the mouth of the Popo Agie. This was said to be the first time that wagons came to the Rocky Mountains. The unusual feature of this expedition was its equipment, consisting of ten wagons, two Dearborn buggies, four head of cattle, and a milch cow. At this rendezvous Smith, Jackson, and Sublette sold their interests in the fur business to Thomas Fitzpatrick, Milton Sublette, James Bridger, Henry Fraeb, and Baptiste Gervais. When the retiring partners went home with their furs they took with them the cattle and wagons, but the two buggies were left in the mountains. The new partners continued their operations until 1834 as the Rocky Mountain Fur Company.

Accounts of the profits made in the fur business spread rapidly, and on May 1, 1832, Captain B. L. E. Bonneville, an American soldier born in France, took leave from the Seventh United States Infantry and started west from Fort Osage on the Missouri River with 110 men and a train of 20 wagons. These wagons, each drawn by four mules, four horses, and four oxen were loaded with ammunition, provisions, and merchandise. The expedition was well organized and was conducted with military precision.

Bonneville followed the usual route taken at that time—northwest across the Plains, up the Platte to Laramie's Fork (where Fort Laramie was later established), up the Sweetwater, past Independence Rock and Devil's Gate, and through South Pass to Green River. Bonneville's wagons traced the first outlines of a wagon road over the western slope beyond the Wind River in Wyoming, and from Laramie's Fork west met with great difficulty.

Late in 1832 Bonneville built a post about five miles above the mouth of Horse Creek, which was called 'Fort Nonsense' or 'Bonneville's Folly' (see Tour 9). Its situation had no reference to the fur trade. Bonneville was interested in discovering what the British were doing beyond the mountains. As the hostility of the Indians near the fort compelled Bonneville to evacuate it almost as soon as it was completed, he went over to the headwaters of the Salmon River where he established his winter quarters. The rendezvous of 1832 was held at what later became the principal crossing of the Green River.

Closely following the fur men came the missionaries, and one of the first was the Reverend Samuel Parker. Accompanied by Dr. Marcus Whitman, Parker reached the Green River rendezvous on August 12,

1835, traveling through South Pass with an expedition of the American Fur Company. There the two missionaries had interviews with the chiefs of the Flathead and the Nez Percé Indians. Whitman returned to the East in order to try to interest missionaries in working among the Indian tribes, but Parker continued westward. On August 23, 1835, he delivered what is believed to have been the first Protestant sermon in the Rocky Mountain area, at the head of the Hoback Canyon in Wyoming.

The following year Whitman came West again with the Reverend Henry H. Spalding; both were accompanied by their brides, the first white women to make this journey over the trail. The little party reached South Pass on the night of July 3, 1836, and observed the Fourth of July with a fitting ceremony.

By this time many began to push their way across the Plains, and in the opening of the new country there was need of a trading post both for the purpose of barter and for protection against hostile Indians. Therefore, in 1834 Robert Campbell and William Sublette built the first structure on the Laramie River, about a mile and a half above its junction with the North Platte River. This fort, at first named Fort William and later Fort John and then Fort Laramie, was the first permanent fur-trading post to be established in what is now the State of Wyoming, and is historically the most interesting site in the State. In 1849 the Government purchased Fort Laramie and established a garrison there to protect emigrants and others entering the country (*see Tour 4A*).

Second in importance to Fort Laramie was Fort Bridger, built by James Bridger in 1842 and opened for trade by Bridger and Louis Vasquez in 1843. This fort, the second permanent settlement in Wyoming, was purchased in 1853 by a Mormon named Lewis Robinson, quartermaster general of the Utah Militia and presumably an agent of Brigham Young. For a time it was the center of Mormon activity, as members of that church began to settle along the near-by Green River and its tributaries. With the crises in the struggle between the local government and the United States officials in Utah in 1857, the Mormons, fleeing before Johnston's army, burned their homes and the buildings at Fort Supply and Fort Bridger. The latter was rebuilt and became a military base in the fall of 1857 and housed troops until 1878. During 1867 and 1868 five companies of regulars were stationed at Fort Bridger to protect the surveyors and construction crews of the Union Pacific Railway.

Jim Bridger, the first owner of the fort, was perhaps the most picturesque figure in early Wyoming. He was often called the 'Daniel Boone of the Rockies.' Fort Bridger, which he built; Bridger's Pass, which he discovered; his explorations in the Yellowstone National Park; and his life services in Wyoming are all monuments to his memory (*see Tour 2C*). Contemporaries of Jim Bridger were Jim Beckwourth and Jim Baker, both expert as trappers, guides, and scouts.

Among the outstanding pathbreakers of Wyoming was Father Pierre Jean De Smet, who came West in 1840 with an American Fur Company party bound for the Northwest. He reached Green River on June 30 and on the following Sunday, July 5, celebrated Mass before a motley crowd of trappers and Indians. This is believed to be the first Mass celebrated in what is now the State of Wyoming. While on one of his journeys through the mountains, Father De Smet discovered and named Lake De Smet, in the northern part of Johnson County.

The decline of the fur trade in Wyoming left many trappers and traders in the mountains ready to take up new occupations. The majority of frontiersmen settled along the emigrant trail; some became guides to trains going across the country, others furnished supplies of various kinds, including horses and cattle, which they traded to the emigrants for their broken-down horses and cattle and a certain additional consideration. This stock, after being turned out to feed and rest, was soon in prime condition to exchange for other disabled stock, becoming thus a source of great profit to the traders.

Although hundreds of thousands of emigrants passed through the State, few settled here until the Mormon emigrants began to come in 1847. A number of these people settled, for a time at least, in western and southwestern Wyoming. One of the most tragic pages of Wyoming's history is that which records the journey in 1856 of a group of Mormon recruits, many of whom were caught in a blizzard and perished along the trail (*see Tour 5A*).

A new era in the life and settlement of the Rocky Mountain West began with the discovery of gold in California in 1848. To the dull routine of ox-team travel over the Oregon Trail was added the zest of fortune hunting and adventure. In the early season of 1850 some 60,000 gold seekers and 90,000 animals went over the California Trail. The high tide of emigration was reached about 1850–51. The eagerness of the travelers to push on to the coast was so great that they threw away much of the freight that impeded their progress. Thus the trail, especially through Wyoming, was strewn with anvils, crowbars, drills, axes, grindstones, trunks, clothing, and furniture. It has been estimated that 34,000 died along the trail from 1840 to 1870—some through sickness, others by accident, many at the hands of Indians. They were buried in unmarked graves.

Landmarks of the old Oregon and California Trails, which paralleled or overlapped in many places, probably are more numerous in Wyoming than elsewhere along the 2,000-mile route. The emigrants had trekked 667 miles when they reached Fort Laramie, and the remainder of the distance was the most difficult part of the journey. Along the route where the pioneers camped for a day or a night many inscribed their names upon the granite or sandstone cliffs. Some names inscribed more than 80 years ago are still visible, reminders of the hardships endured by these sturdy people.

Of the various expeditions organized to explore the western territory, two under Lieutenant John C. Frémont came into Wyoming. The 1842 Frémont expedition traversed central Wyoming; the 1843 expedition crossed the Laramie Plains to the south. In 1845 General Stephen W. Kearny, with several companies of dragoons, marched from Fort Leavenworth to Fort Laramie, whence he sent part of his command on an exploring expedition to the Sweetwater.

In 1849 Captain Howard Stansbury was commissioned by the United States Government to explore the Great Salt Lake Valley and to make a report on its topography. After performing that duty he made a reconnaissance for a railway route from Salt Lake City to Fort Bridger, and from Fort Bridger eastward to some point in the Platte Valley. When the Union Pacific Railway was built some years later, it followed in general the route outlined by Captain Stansbury.

Lieutenant G. K. Warren, United States topographical engineer, made an exploration of Wyoming from Fort Laramie to the western slope of the Black Hills in northeastern Wyoming in 1857, and was followed two years later by Captain W. F. Raynolds, who explored the Black Hills and then pushed westward through the valleys of the Powder and Big Horn Rivers.

Captain Walter W. De Lacy in 1863 led a prospecting party from Virginia City, Montana, into Idaho and up the Snake River in Wyoming. The men followed the stream through Jackson Hole and discovered what is now known as Shoshone Lake; then they passed through Yellowstone Park, noting many hot springs and geysers, but directing most of their energies toward the search for gold. Following De Lacy's party were others, all in search of the precious metal.

A party headed by David E. Folsom, C. W. Cook, and William Peterson penetrated the Yellowstone Region six years later and were so impressed by its wonders that their reports led to the organization of the Yellowstone Expedition of 1870, headed by Washburn and Doane. These expeditions, followed by that of Dr. F. V. Hayden under the Department of the Interior, led in 1872 to the establishment by Congress of the Yellowstone National Park.

One of the great handicaps of the early days on the frontier was the lack of communication with the East. Letters intended for various posts were usually sent to Fort Leavenworth and then forwarded whenever possible. John M. Hockaday and William Liggett took advantage of the situation and in 1851 established a semimonthly stage line for carrying mail and packages from St. Louis to Salt Lake City. By 1859 the Central, Overland, California and Pikes Peak Express Company was well established. In April 1860 the company established the Pony Express, which followed in general the Oregon Trail (*see Transportation*).

A subsidy of $40,000 a year for ten years was offered by the United States Government to the builder of the first telegraph line across the Plains. Edward Creighton was the successful competitor, and on October 24, 1861, his line was completed and in working order. This, of course, meant the downfall of the Pony Express, the operation of which had proved to be almost prohibitive in cost.

Telegraph stations were built at Fort Laramie, Horse Shoe Creek, Deer Creek, Platte Bridge, Three Crossings, Rocky Ridge, Sweetwater Bridge, South Pass, Upper Crossing, Sand Creek, Fort Bridger, and several other points within the present State of Wyoming, then known as Idaho Territory. Later, when the stage route was moved to the southern part of the State, Creighton constructed a telegraph line to follow the new route across the Laramie Plains and through Bridger's Pass.

There had been early troubles with the Indians in Wyoming—including the slaughter of Grattan's men in 1854 near Fort Laramie (*see Tour* 4); the expedition of General William S. Harney, with 1,500 men against the Sioux in the summer of 1855, during which an attack was made on the camp of Little Thunder at Ash Hollow just across the Nebraska line; and an expedition in 1857 against the Cheyenne Indians under the direction of Colonel E. V. Sumner—but the period of the most active and continued military operations in Wyoming was between 1862 and 1868.

Tribes previously peaceful became hostile, and when regular soldiers stationed through the West were called away to fight in the Civil War, the Indians were quick to take advantage of the situation. After harassing the emigrants and settlers by means of small attacking parties, they began to organize into large bands.

Early in 1862 the first division of the Eleventh Ohio Volunteer Cavalry, with Colonel William O. Collins in command, reached Fort Laramie and was at once sent out to guard the stage and telegraph lines west as far as Pacific Springs. The troops were scattered in small detachments and did escort duty, accompanying stages and emigrant trains.

After the Indians attacked the station at Sweetwater, General P. E. Connor early in 1863 was ordered into Wyoming to assist in protecting the Overland Stage Route from Fort Kearny, Nebraska, to Salt Lake City, Utah. An expedition under his direction clashed with the Indians on Bear River near the present site of Franklin, Idaho, with the result that 224 Indians were killed, while Connor's command suffered the loss of 14 men and had 53 wounded.

Owing to the determination of General Connor to suppress further attack and because the troops were stationed all along the stage route, the Indians as far west as South Pass discontinued their depredations, and for a time peace prevailed. The Indians, seeing the formidable force, adopted a system of harassing the troops until the officers found it dangerous even to send out men to repair the telegraph line without giving them strong escort.

After several trips through eastern Wyoming, J. M. Bozeman of Montana laid out a road in 1863 from the Platte River, up Powder River to the Three Forks on the Missouri River, intending that it should be used by miners going to Montana. The Bozeman Road was open by 1864, and the Indians at once objected to the passage of emigrant trains through their country, and fought to protect their hunting grounds.

In addition to numerous battles came the Sand Creek Massacre of the Cheyenne in Colorado in November 1864, in which Colonel Chivington directed the troops. Chivington's report said: 'I have captured no prisoners; between 500 and 600 Indians were left dead on the ground.' As a direct result of this massacre, the Indians in all directions declared war and very soon began to raid along the Platte into the heart of Wyoming.

The year 1865 was known as the 'Bloody Year on the Plains,' as there were constant attacks by Indians on emigrant trains and stage stations. In the spring of that year came attacks on Julesburg, Colorado; the Mud Springs Ranch, Nebraska, just 105 miles east of Fort Laramie; and at Deer Creek Station, Wyoming. These were followed in July by the Platte Bridge fight near the site of the present town of Casper, so named for the heroic Lieutenant Caspar Collins, who met his death in that fight. (The spelling of the town's name has been accepted through long usage.)

In that same year two expeditions into the Indian country were planned by the Government: one was to ascend the Missouri and approach the Black Hills from the east; the other, commanded by General Connor, was scheduled to attack the Indians on Powder River. Connor's expedition assisted in establishing a line of forts along the so-called Bozeman Trail, including Forts Reno and Phil Kearny. Along this trail many skirmishes and battles took place, two of the most historic being the Fetterman Massacre near Fort Phil Kearny on December 21, 1866, and the Wagon Box Fight in 1867 (*see Tour 3a*).

During these years several forts were built in the State, including Fort Sanders in 1866, three miles south of the present site of Laramie (*see Tour 5c*); Fort Fetterman, 1867 (*see Tour 3c*); Fort D. A. Russell (Fort F. E. Warren) on Crow Creek, 1867, three miles northwest of Cheyenne (*see Cheyenne*); and Fort Steele, 1868 (*see Tour 2b*). Fort Russell and Fort Steele were established primarily as headquarters for troops to be used in protecting the builders of the new railway.

Among the outstanding treaties made with the Indians relative to land now within the confines of Wyoming were those at Fort Laramie in 1851, 1865, 1868, and in 1876; and at Fort Bridger in 1863 and 1868.

The earlier treaties were broken by both the whites and the Indians, and in 1868 a Peace Commission was sent West by the Government, members of which signed treaties with the Sioux, Crow, Cheyenne, and Arapaho at Fort Laramie, and with the Bannock and Eastern Shoshone at Fort Bridger.

By the 1868 treaty at Fort Bridger, Chief Washakie and his Shoshone tribe and the Bannock were allotted the Shoshone Reservation in the Wind River Valley. In 1877, upon an appeal from the Government, Washakie permitted the Arapaho to winter on his reservation, and here they have remained ever since. Despite these later treaties, however, the mining settlements in the South Pass District suffered several raids in 1869, with the result that Camp Brown (Augur) and Camp Stambaugh were established (*see Tour 5b*).

By the Fort Laramie Treaty of 1868 the white men were forbidden to go into the Powder River country. Nevertheless prospectors made their way into the Black Hills, and the Indians attempted to protect their rights by continued raids upon the settlements. These Indian depredations and the protests of territorial officials, however, comprised only a small part of the activities that centered around the Black Hills, and out of which came the last general Indian war in the Northwest. The climax of Indian fighting came in 1876 when the names of Generals Crook, Custer, and Mackenzie, and of Sitting Bull, Dull Knife, Red Cloud, and other Indian chiefs were indelibly written into American history.

From this time on the settlers of Wyoming enjoyed comparative security. Early population was grouped around mining communities, army posts, and along the railway. Gold mining in Wyoming antedated the coming of the railway. A mining stampede that brought many enterprises, including various kinds of commercial business, agriculture, and stock raising, followed the discovery of the Carissa lode in 1867 at South Pass. Some 15 mining camps were opened in rapid succession in the South Pass district. The miners, miles away from the nearest established local government and feeling the need of some authority to enforce law and order, created a county called 'Carter' (in honor of W. A. Carter of Fort Bridger), extending eastward for a distance of about 130 miles from what is the present western boundary of Sweetwater County. The Dakota Legislature legalized this action in a bill approved on December 27, 1867; the county was organized on January 3, 1868, with John Murphy as the first sheriff.

News of the important gold discoveries in the Sweetwater Valley through which the emigrants were journeying on the western trail, the finding of huge coal deposits in the southwestern corner of the State, and knowledge that Wyoming's range grasses offered excellent grazing for cattle began luring people in considerable numbers to this virgin territory.

By 1867 and 1868 the Union Pacific Railroad was pushing its way across the southern part of Wyoming. The settlement of Cheyenne, the first railway terminal town in the State, began in July 1867. Within a month a temporary government had been formed. A string of settlements, including speculative townsites, hastily erected stores, saloons and gambling halls, coal mines, lumber and tie camps, were filled with a restless and shifting population. Coal mining—one of the State's foundation industries—quickly developed, with the construction of the railway.

The first proposal to establish a temporary government for the territory of Wyoming was made on January 5, 1865, by James M. Ashley of Ohio, who for a short time served as Governor of the Territory of Montana, and later became chairman of the House Committee on Territories. Politicians in Dakota Territory, to which Wyoming belonged, also favored a subdivision, since they realized that the large population following the new railway could swing an election, regardless of what the older citizens of Dakota wished.

The Wyoming Organic Act, creating the Territory of Wyoming out of parts of Dakota, Utah, and Idaho, was approved July 25, 1868; the Territorial Government of Wyoming was formally inaugurated when the Governor and Secretary took the oaths of office on April 15, 1869. Cheyenne was designated the territorial capital, and on May 25 the first territorial court was held there.

By an act approved December 10, 1869, the first territorial legislature, which had convened on October 12, 1869, granted equal rights to women for the first time in the history of America; and, in keeping with this privilege, women served on juries at Laramie, Wyoming, in 1870. In the same year Mrs. Esther M. Morris of South Pass City was appointed the first woman justice of the peace in the world.

By 1870 Wyoming was credited with 34 manufacturing establishments, representing an invested capital of more than $1,000,000. These included lumber mills, blacksmiths' establishments, quartz mills, and plants for the making of railroad ties, posts, and lumber.

Cattlemen of Texas, learning of the great open ranges to the north, began trailing their herds up from the South, and the Texas drives were soon a spectacular feature of the cattle industry. Many buyers invested in thousands of head of Texas longhorns, and drove them up the trail to their Wyoming ranches. In 1884 it was estimated that 800,000 head of cattle were moved north from Texas over the trail. The Texas Trail, or Long Trail, became second only to the Oregon Trail in point of adventure, tragedy, and romance. With the available free open range and the excessive profits to be made from the range herds, the Wyoming cattle business was considered a bonanza.

With the development of the cattle industry, the demand for horses increased. At first the horses were brought from Texas and Mexico, but it was soon found that Wyoming was as well adapted to the raising of horses as to that of cattle, and a large industry in that line developed.

The eight years following the Civil War were marked by intense activity throughout the West. Then came the panic of 1873, and Wyoming in general felt its effect along with other sections of the West. About this time Governor Campbell called attention to the use of artificial irrigation, pointing to the supply of water from running streams and to the Union Pacific Railway's success in sinking artesian wells. Vast areas of arid land in Wyoming and many other parts of the West, he said, might be made remarkably productive by irrigation. Adequate water supply was needed also for the development of the mining interests. It was apparent that irrigation systems as proposed could not be undertaken by private enterprise; Government aid was necessary. A memorial to Congress proposed that the Government should grant to the western States and territories one-half of the arid lands, not mineral, within their borders, the proceeds from the sale of which should be devoted to the construction of irrigating canals and reservoirs.

Wyoming was materially affected by Congressional action that followed the memorial; yet three-fourths of all the irrigation works constructed before the passage of the Carey Act in 1894 were built by cattlemen or from proceeds of the range business. Ditches constructed primarily to furnish water for the homes of the ranchmen were essential aids to the grazing interests.

From these irrigation systems, used at first for the raising of native hay, came a rapid and important development in agricultural operations, especially in Johnson, Sheridan, Crook, and Weston Counties. Towns sprang up in likely locations, transportation facilities were provided for the more thickly settled areas; soon the livestock and agricultural industries spread to every corner of Wyoming.

The rule of the cattle barons, powerful while it lasted, began to wane with the terrific losses during the winter of 1886–7 and with the coming of the settlers in the 1880's, many of whom availed themselves of the privileges of the pre-emption and homestead laws. On any public land to which the Indian title had been extinguished, a settler might pre-empt and undertake improvements on acreage not to exceed a quarter section, though in the case of unsurveyed lands the title could not be completed until the surveys had been finished.

Many homesteaders were cowboys who bought a few head of cattle and started 160-acre ranches of their own. In the early days it was the unwritten law of the cattle range that any unbranded animal over a year old—a maverick—could be branded and claimed by the person who found it. From the beginning of the cattle industry there was much trouble with cattle thieves, or rustlers, who changed the brands or killed the animals for beef. This stealing was doubly hard to curb, with mavericks available on the range that could be used as the basis of a new herd. During the early 1890's the term 'rustler' came also to be applied indiscriminately to settlers and homeseekers who resisted the large owners. Gradually bands of rustlers were organized, who preyed on herds of the large cattlemen; the courts were appealed to, but gave no redress, and the illegal traffic grew to such an extent that the cattle owners formed vigilance committees and even imported gunmen from Texas. Several killings resulted. The bitterness engendered from the rustling led to the so-called Johnson County Cattle War of 1892 (see *Tour 3a*).

Peace soon was restored between the cattle factions, aided perhaps by the permanent establishment of sheepmen on the public ranges during the closing years of the 1890's. The cattlemen, both large and small owners, held a common grievance against the sheepmen because they claimed that the cattle refused to graze on land overrun and closely cropped by sheep. Feeling became so bitter in some sections that 'dead lines' were established, over which sheep could cross only 'on pain of death.' In the ensuing controversies lives were lost on both sides. The famous case of Tom Horn, who was hanged in Cheyenne in November 1903 as the murderer of little Willie Nickell, was undoubtedly the result of a cattleman-sheepman range feud (see *Cheyenne*). While cattlemen held their own for a while, sheep interests eventually won a place and brought much wealth in the State.

An era of settlement beginning in the 1880's resulted in a 300 per cent increase in population in Wyoming within ten years. Between 1870 and 1900 the State's population increased tenfold—from 9,118 to 92,531—and during the next 30 years it rose to 225,565, of which 70,097 persons were classified as urban dwellers and 155,468 as rural. Of the total residents, 58.5 per cent were born in other States, a figure exceeded only by Arizona.

The rush for land in the middle 1880's was stimulated not so much by a desire to farm as by the need to supplement ranch and livestock holdings. Within two years more than 3,000,000 acres of land passed from railway or Government ownership into private hands.

Up to this time the problem of transportation had retarded settlement, owing to the great distances and the inadequate roads. Freight lines and stages were the only means of transportation for passengers and supplies north of the Union Pacific Railroad to the Montana Line.

As Wyoming developed, attention was turned towards railway building. The Chicago and Northwestern Railway financed an extension into central Wyoming, and the Chicago, Burlington & Quincy crossed the northeastern corner into the Sheridan Valley on its way to Montana. Later this same company built up the Big Horn River to Cody and Thermopolis.

An influx of settlers followed the railways, and various laws were passed that gave increased impetus to the settlement and agricultural development of the State, including the 320-acre and 640-acre acts.

About 1905, as the population began to push westward from Nebraska, land companies brought into southeastern and eastern Wyoming hundreds of settlers who attempted dry farming—that is, farming without irrigation. In many districts this form of agriculture proved satisfactory; in others the farmers have been driven out by drought and excessive erosion. Many who have remained have been assisted by Federal farm loans and rehabilitation help.

In the early 1900's came a period of conservation of natural resources, including the setting aside of forest reserves (later called national forests), the building of dams, and the protection of fish and game. The Yellowstone Forest Reserve, created in 1902, was the first of the reserves now known as national forests.

Substantial settlement has come in a number of localities as the result of large reclamation projects, such as the Pathfinder Dam for the irrigation of the North Platte Valley; the Wind River Project; the Shoshone Project; and the Kendrick or Alcova-Casper Project.

In 1915 the State legislature accepted the terms of the Smith-Lever Act of 1914 and authorized the University of Wyoming to accept the grants of money appropriated by the Federal Government for agricultural or farm demonstrations or field work. Counties were thus enabled to hire agricultural experts or county agents and county home demonstrators to supervise experimental and demonstration work. From this beginning there has developed throughout the State splendid extension service, which assists in the agricultural work in every district, with special stress placed upon 4-H Club work and all phases of farm improvement.

Up to about 1910 the highways of the State had been under the control of the local county commissioners. With the increase in population and the coming of the automobile, better roads were in demand. Good roads organizations were formed in almost every community and through the efforts of 'good roads boosters' a transcontinental route—the Lincoln Highway—became a reality across southern Wyoming. Then followed the Yellowstone Highway and the Park-to-Park Highway.

In 1917 the State Highway Department was created by the legislature, and a system of highway construction was launched, which has developed 23,000 miles of roads at an expenditure in excess of $80,000,000. Wyoming with its supply of crude oil became a pioneer in the surfacing of highways with oil. During the last several years the highway department has been keeping pace with the development of high-speed automobile travel through the improvement of alignment, grades, and visibility, and the construction of wider roadbeds on new projects.

There has been statewide development of emergency landing fields for airplanes, and two airlines operate east to west and north to south across the State. Wyoming citizens have been air enthusiasts since the establishment of regular air service across the State in 1920.

With the development of highways and motor travel came the creation of new counties. From 1890 to 1909 the number of counties—13—had remained unchanged. In the succeeding 12 years, the number was increased to 23.

The industrial development of Wyoming has been greatly augmented by the discovery of oil in large quantities, especially in the Salt Creek field. Although oil had been discovered in commercial quantities in this field as early as 1888, the entire petroleum production for the State in 1911 was less than 200,000 barrels. With the bringing in of a 1,200-barrel gusher in Salt Creek, in 1912, a boom was precipitated. By 1918 the State's annual production of crude oil had reached 12,500,000 barrels. Refineries were erected at Casper and at various other places in the State. Hundreds of newcomers swarmed into Wyoming in search of work or business opportunities, as the result of the oil activities. Oil royalties enriched the school funds and made possible the construction of the State's network of highways.

Through the years coal mining has continued to be a leading industry of the State, with the refining of sugar, the refining of oil, the milling of flour, and the manufacture of dairy products holding places of importance. Copper mining and iron mining, too, are substantial industries.

Within the past decade there has been extensive development of rural electrification. The most recent source of electrical power is the newly constructed Seminoe Dam in Carbon County.

With the decline of petroleum production attention is again being directed to the improvement of livestock and farming interests, including extensive dude ranching.

Much stress at present is being placed upon the State's recreational features. In Wyoming are Yellowstone National Park, the first and largest of the Nation's playgrounds, established in 1872; the Grand Teton National Park, established in 1929, one of the last and finest of the national park areas; and the Nation's first national monument—Devil's Tower. Facilities are available and are being increased for the enjoyment of both summer and winter sports.

Cognizant of the motto on the great seal of the Territory of Wyoming—'Cedant Arma Togae' (Let Arms Yield to the Gown)—Wyoming residents have always fostered education and cultural development; they have erected substantial public buildings, good schools, and a splendid State university. Through an excellent county library law, library facilities are made available to every citizen. When Wyoming was admitted to the Union as the forty-fourth state on July 10, 1890, the constitution provided political equality for women, a privilege which the women had enjoyed during territorial days.

Wyoming's military record is outstanding. In both the Spanish-American War and the World War the State's percentage of men serving, compared with the number of residents, was high.

As early as 1871, because of Indian attacks along the Sweetwater, the territorial governor created three militia districts in Wyoming and authorized the commanding officer in each to organize a regiment from among the citizens. In that same year the second legislative assembly passed a militia act authorizing the formation of volunteer companies.

In the Spanish-American War Wyoming was the first State to respond to the call for volunteers with a full quota—furnishing, in fact, four and one-half times its quota.

In 1916 two battalions of the Wyoming National Guard did duty on the Mexican border. Wyoming sent 11,393 soldiers into the World War—7 per cent of its population—and according to a report on the selective draft made in January 1918, out of 2,733 men called for examination 1,376 were accepted. This proportion of 50.02 per cent was said to be the highest among the States.

In 1938 an important decision was made by the Court of Claims in Washington in a suit brought by the Shoshone Indians, who claimed the Arapaho had occupied their reservation for 60 years without reimbursement to them. The decision cleared the title to 2,343,540 acres of Wyoming land; gave legal status to the homes of more than 1,000 Wyoming people, the Arapaho; and brought to the Shoshone about $4,000,000.

With its immense area and its great diversity of resources the Wyoming of tomorrow promises even greater changes than those that have taken place in the comparatively short period between the early settlement of the State and the present decade.

Transportation

OWING to the extremely rugged topography of many parts of Wyoming, the important transportation lines parallel each other along three main routes, spreading fanshape from Cheyenne, in the southeastern corner of the State, across the southern, central, central-to-northern, and northeastern parts.

Twenty-five numbered highways, 13 of them Federal, spread a network over the State which penetrates the more remote regions, including the national forests and Grand Teton and Yellowstone National Parks. Although the highways skirt or cross the national forests, there is much virgin territory in these areas that can be reached only by pack horse or on foot. Main highways parallel all important railway systems.

For many years Wyoming was merely a link in a transcontinental route over which hundreds of thousands passed on their way to the Oregon country, to California, or to Salt Lake Valley. Therefore, whatever of importance occurred in the early days relative to transportation in the area that later became Wyoming was due in some way to forces outside of the present boundaries of the State. The State's history has been colored by every major transportation movement of the central West. In fact, the formation of the Wyoming Territory came as the direct result of the construction of the first transcontinental railway.

From 1841 to 1845 the Oregon emigration was extremely heavy through central Wyoming. The Mormon migration followed in 1847. At one time, approximately 16,000 Mormons plodded across Wyoming in the largest single migration in the history of the country. Early in 1850, following the discovery of gold in California, some 60,000 gold seekers feverishly pushed their way over the Government Trail spanning Wyoming.

One of the chief problems of the first explorers and the early trappers and traders in Wyoming was that of transportation. It was with great difficulty that they brought their equipment into the mountains and with even greater difficulty took their packs of furs out to the far-distant settlements and market places. Two-wheeled carts, pack animals, and men's backs were used chiefly; Indian and animal trails were followed whenever possible.

In the early days political influence kept the mail route through central Wyoming in a subsidiary position to the southern route across Arizona, which was controlled by the Butterfield Line. The influence, however, shifted during the winter of 1848–9, and the Government authorized a bimonthly mail between Council Bluffs and Salt Lake City. This first Government-contract mail service to cross Wyoming was begun on July 1, 1850, by Judge Samuel H. Woodson, who used either a team and wagon or a set of pack animals once a month to cover the distance. The route followed the Oregon Trail by way of Fort Laramie to Fort Bridger, then along the Salt Lake Trail to Salt Lake City.

In 1851 John M. Hockaday and William Liggett established a stage line to carry mail and express from Independence, Missouri, to Salt Lake City, where a connection was made with a line to the western coast. The trip schedule was 21 days.

Although various individuals intermittently hauled supplies across the Plains, the first organized effort at freighting was that of Alexander Majors and William H. Russell, who hauled some 500,000 pounds of supplies for Johnston's army in 1857. The next spring they contracted with the War Department for the hauling of an immense amount of supplies for the troops at Fort Laramie, Fort Bridger, Fort Hall, and Salt Lake. Another partner was added to the firm and the name became Russell, Majors, and Waddell. At one period in its business the firm was using 75,000 oxen and 6,250 canvas covered wagons of the Conestoga type. These wagons, capable of carrying from two to six tons of freight, were equipped with boxes or beds about 16 feet long and from four to five feet deep.

This freighting service and the occupation of Fort Bridger by the United States Government prepared the way for the development of a commercial business in the transportation of mail, passengers, and supplies over the great central route to the Pacific. In 1858 Russell, Majors, and Waddell bought out Hockaday and Liggett and put on a daily service, making the trip from Atchison, Kansas, to Salt Lake City in ten days with Concord coaches. Stage stations were built in Wyoming, as elsewhere, and were equipped with horses and provisions.

The line was called the Central Overland, California, and Pikes Peak Express Company.

This great firm practically controlled the freight and passenger traffic across the Plains. Perhaps the greatest achievement of the company was the establishment and operation of the Pony Express, which made its first trip in April 1860 from St. Joseph, Missouri, to Sacramento, California. Some of the most harrowing escapes of the riders during the 18-months' brief existence of the Pony Express were made along the Wyoming section of the route, where the Indians were especially troublesome. The Pony Express, however, so impoverished the stage company that the firm failed, and on March 21, 1862, the equipment was sold at public sale to Ben Holladay.

Because of the increasing Indian troubles, Holladay in 1862 moved the stage route from central Wyoming to the southern part across the Laramie Plains and west through Bridger's Pass. Gradually the tide of transportation turned to this new road called the Overland Route. This was the general line later paralleled by the first railroad across Wyoming. It was Holladay's boast that no transportation company ever owned a better lot of horses. The six horses of each Holladay team were matched in color and size as nearly as possible.

A 'cross country' railway, to run from the headwaters of inland navigation over a direct route to the Pacific, was proposed as early as 1819 by Robert Mills of Virginia, but little attention was paid to his theories until years later when the great movement to Oregon began.

In 1849 the Government sent out an expedition under Captain Howard Stansbury to make a survey for the construction of a post route, or the building of a railway communication across the continent, and appropriated $150,000 for additional surveys. Various sectional controversies and the slavery issue, however, submerged the early railway proposals and nothing definite was done for years, until private industry became active. Although for a time the promotion of a Pacific railroad was blocked by the Civil War, in the long run the war was responsible for the actual construction of the transcontinental system. The cutting off of supplies from the South and the Nation's difficulty with Great Britain at that time made the public realize the urgent need of a direct connection with far-away California and Oregon.

Early in 1862 a bill was passed by Congress, and signed on July 1 by President Lincoln, creating the Union Pacific Railway Company, which was authorized and empowered to build a system westward across the Territory of Nebraska to the western boundary of Nevada Territory. This, of course, included Wyoming.

Up to about 1859, it had been the general idea that a central railroad would follow the beaten track of the Oregon and California emigrants, since there was no outstanding commercial reason for such a line to be located elsewhere, but with the Pikes Peak gold rush and the consequent influx of population into Colorado, attention immediately centered upon the possibility of extending the main line through Denver.

Ground was broken by the Union Pacific Railroad in the North Omaha Bottoms on December 2, 1863, and actual construction began. While the rails were being laid to Fort Kearny, Nebraska, surveying parties spread out over a large area of northern Colorado and eastern Wyoming in an effort to determine the best place for crossing the Rocky Mountains, as near to Denver as possible.

On his return from a military expedition in the Powder River country in 1865, General Grenville M. Dodge discovered a pass across the Black Hills, or Laramie Mountains, that determined the final location of the Union Pacific route. The finding of this pass over what is now called Sherman Hill and the final location of the railway route were of supreme importance since it was apparent that a road using this pass would be 40 miles shorter than the Oregon Trail and would run through districts where coal could easily be mined. The coal supply was an extremely important consideration, since before 1868 coal used in the building of the railway had to be obtained in Illinois, Missouri, and Iowa, and transported from 500 to 1,000 miles at a cost of from $28 to $42 a ton.

Nearly nine months previous to the beginning of the actual construction work by the Union Pacific Railroad, the Central Pacific had broken ground at Sacramento, California, as a link in the transcontinental line. The original act chartering the Union Pacific authorized the company to build to the western boundary of Nevada. Later in 1866 this was changed and the Central Pacific received authority to build eastward until a connection with the Union Pacific was formed. The bill gave the Union Pacific the privilege of extending beyond the western border of Nevada unless the junction with the Central Pacific should be made sooner. The construction therefore became a great race as each railway hoped to push as far as possible in order to acquire the tempting subsidies promised by the Government. These subsidies granted to the companies a right of way 400 feet wide through the public lands, and every alternate or odd-numbered section of land to the amount of ten alternate sections per mile on each side of the road within the limit of 10 miles, not sold or otherwise disposed of, mineral lands excepted.

In the spring of 1867, General Dodge located a division point of the Union Pacific Railway on Crow Creek as the 6th base and called it Cheyenne. Immediately a military post called Fort D. A. Russell (now Fort Francis E. Warren) was established about two miles north of the townsite. The line moved westward under the protection of soldiers at Fort Sanders and Fort Fred Steele.

The actual building of the railway across Wyoming, done at top speed, was practically completed in 1867-8.

Every foot was built under military escort, as the Indians constantly harassed the surveying parties and the construction crews, running off horses, stealing equipment, and, whenever possible, killing the men. Many of the workers were Civil War veterans accustomed to discipline, and they performed their duties with military precision. All were armed and were under orders to be ready at all times to fight and never to run when attacked. The encounters with the Indians were said to have been most frequent and sanguinary between Fort Kearny, Nebraska, and Bitter Creek, Wyoming.

The townsite of Cheyenne was laid out in July 1867 by the Union Pacific Railroad and by November 13 the first contingent of 'Hell on Wheels,' as the track headquarters was known, arrived at the town. Citizens swarmed along the grade and watched with keen interest and enthusiasm the magic work of the track laying.

In describing the arrival of the railway, the Cheyenne *Leader* of November 16, 1867, gave credit to General J. S. Casement, who with his brother did most of the construction work on the Wyoming division.

A vast assemblage of citizens and railroad men convened to celebrate the occasion of the advent of the U.P.R.R. and organized with E. Brown, acting Chairman in the absence of Mayor Hook. Eddy Street and the City Hall were splendidly illuminated. The large transparency near the speakers' stand bore the mottoes: 'The Magic City greets the continental railway.' 'Honor to whom honor is due.' 'Old Casement, we welcome you'; which last, if relating to the General's years, is certainly a misrepresentation; but if to the accomplishments of a life time, few men have ever done so much. Judge Miller presented the resolutions, on the part of the committee, which were unanimously adopted . . .

The history of early Cheyenne was similar to that of the other terminal towns along the line through Wyoming, and it was possibly the greatest gambling place ever established on the Plains. At this

division point many miles of sidings were put in for switching purposes and unloading tracks. It was a not uncommon sight to see as
many as 1,000 teams waiting at the base for the loads to haul forward
to the end of the track.

The progress of the railway through Wyoming was so fast that towns
moved every few weeks. The 'town' would simply be packed on a
freight train and would be transported some 50 or 60 miles to the
end of the track. In turn, Cheyenne, Laramie, Benton, Green River,
and Bear River City, more commonly known as Beartown, became
headquarters. Often, with the advance of the railway, the townsite
became deserted prairie with only the street lines and debris left
behind.

When the railway base was moved westward to Laramie in the
spring of 1868, although the bulk of the 10,000 population followed
as usual, some 1,500 remained behind in Cheyenne. The Denver Pacific
branched off at this point and these citizens visualized the town as
a future metropolis.

With the great movement of workers there came the camp followers,
who were for the most part as dangerous as the Indians. They were
the dregs of society who existed by robbing and plundering. In these
towns of tents and portable houses, murders were of daily occurrence;
gambling dens, saloons, and dance halls thrived. Many times the Vigilance Committee took matters in its hands, usually with good effect
(see Laramie).

Across Wyoming in 1867–8, 10,000 men and 10,000 animals were
pushing their strength to the last reserve in the race with the men
from the Coast who were building the western railway up the slopes
of the Sierras. Out in front were the surveyors running grades and
staking out the route. Next came the graders, who with good luck
could construct about 100 miles of roadbed in 30 days. As soon as
the grade was finished the bridge gangs took up their work and kept
about 26 miles ahead of the tracklayers.

From April 1868 to May 1869, the engineers covered 726 miles of
road and the contractors built 55 miles of roadbed and laid 589 miles
of track, bringing most of the material, with the exception of some
ties, from the Missouri River. The average distance made by the tracklayers was from one to three miles a day. One day a record of eight
and a half miles was made. All of the work, however, did not go as
fast as it did across the Plains country. Between Cheyenne and Laramie a trestle more than 130 feet high had to be constructed over

Dale Creek, a chasm between 600 and 700 feet wide. Material for this bridge was hauled out ahead of the track. From Dale Creek down to the Laramie Plains, much of the work was through solid rock. It was often necessary to haul water in trains to the end of the track and then to carry it, sometimes 50 or 60 miles to the 'front' in wagons. Provisions and supplies were transported from the end of the track by mule teams at a cost, it is said, of $25 per day for each team. It is interesting to note that although the road was pushed at top speed, few changes were made in it after its completion.

After leaving the boundary of Wyoming the railroad pushed on toward Ogden and Salt Lake City. The last spike, known as the 'golden spike,' which welded the East and the West together with a great transcontinental railway, was driven on May 10, 1869, at Promontory, Utah, where the Union Pacific and the Central Pacific met. The road was opened immediately to traffic.

In addition to the difficulties the builders of the Union Pacific had with weather, Indians, desperadoes, and many other hindrances, there was the gigantic and continual problem of insufficient finances. To complete the undertaking it took the courage of men like Oliver and Oakes Ames, who sacrificed their personal fortunes in order to save the credit of the railway. A monument was erected later, at the highest point on the right-of-way, in honor of these great builders (*see Tour 2a*).

For a time the buffalo continued to roam the Plains in such numbers that trains were sometimes delayed for hours while a herd crossed the tracks. The first winter of the road's operation, 1869–70, the blizzards were so many and so fierce that six Union Pacific trains were blockaded west of Laramie near Cooper Lake for some weeks.

Up to the time that the railroad was built across Wyoming, the population of the State was grouped in the Sweetwater mining communities and around the army posts. Although there had been some talk of forming a new territory, nothing was done until the railroad arrived, bringing with it a larger population than existed at that time in the entire Dakota Territory. After the completion of the railway, the people living between Cheyenne and Green River had more convenient access to the capitals of Nebraska and Utah, and even of Nevada, than to Yankton in Dakota Territory.

Owing to the fact that the railway population could vote, Wyoming, then a part of Dakota Territory, played a conspicuous part in the territorial campaign of 1868. Realizing that this railway element could rule the whole territory, both the governor and the legislature recommended the organization of a new territory out of the southern part of Dakota. The creation of the Territory of Wyoming left Dakota without a railway.

Although the railway was responsible for the first political organization of Wyoming, since that time the only outstanding political fight in which the Union Pacific has taken an open stand and in which, it is said, it endeavored to control the State legislature was in 1915, when a utilities commission was proposed by some of the legislators in keeping with the general trend of the times. This was one of the most bitter fights in the history of Wyoming politics and ended in the defeat of the railway interests.

For many years the Union Pacific was the only railway in Wyoming. The Oregon Short Line branch of the Union Pacific from Granger is a consolidation of a Union Pacific extension started in 1882 and the Utah and Northern, a railroad launched in 1873 by John W. Young, a son of Brigham Young. The latter road, starting at Hamsfork, Wyoming, ran along the line of the old Oregon Trail westward to connect with the Northern Pacific. In 1889 these two companies and six others under Union Pacific control, identified with Utah and southern Idaho branch and connecting lines, were consolidated under the name Oregon Short Line and Utah Northern Railway Company. In 1897, through reorganization, the present corporate name of Oregon Short Line Railroad Company was taken.

The Colorado, Wyoming, & Eastern Railroad in Albany County and the Saratoga & Encampment Railroad in Carbon County, both branches of the Union Pacific, run through valleys of historic and economic interest.

From 1876 to 1887 the Cheyenne and Black Hills Stage Line operated a daily schedule between Cheyenne and the Black Hills country of Dakota, transporting passengers and express to the gold mines near Deadwood and Custer City. This line also was used by many cattlemen, who had established large ranches in eastern and central Wyoming.

As the herds increased and settlers moved into the State, the freight lines spread in every direction, but even then, owing to the lack of good roads, many of the settlers were isolated for long periods. Some of the freighters in the 1870's used ox teams, others used mules, and a few, horses. Poor roads that became impassable because of mud and drifts were all in the day's work for the 'bullwhackers' or 'mule skinners,' as the drivers of the freight outfits were called. Often these men had to camp on the prairie at night, cooking their meal over a camp fire, or sometimes eating a cold supper in the rain.

As the population of the State increased, a network of star routes was established by the Government. The rural carriers usually carried freight and passengers in addition to mail.

With the steady economic growth of Wyoming, railroad financiers turned their attention to various parts of the State. In 1886 the Colorado & Southern, originally called the Cheyenne & Northern, was built from Denver to Cheyenne and north to Wendover, paralleling from Cheyenne the old Black Hills stage route. Later the road connected with the Chicago & Northwestern at Orin Junction.

The Chicago & Northwestern line came into Wyoming in 1888, with its acquisition of the Wyoming Central Railway Company, a small railway built in 1886 between Douglas and the eastern boundary of the State, where it joined the Fremont, Elkhorn & Missouri Valley Railroad. The Chicago & Northwestern extended the road to Casper in 1888 and, after several years, built the line to Lander, the present western terminus. This railroad brought many grangers into the State.

With the agricultural developments and the increase in population in central Wyoming, the Chicago, Burlington & Quincy extended its line from Alliance, Nebraska, into Wyoming in 1891, running up the north fork of the Platte to Douglas, from which point it paralleled the Chicago & Northwestern to the old east boundary of the Shoshone Indian Reservation. Upon acquiring the charter of the Big Horn Valley Railroad, the Chicago, Burlington & Quincy built from Billings, Montana, to Cody in 1901 in order to take care of the Yellowstone Park tourist travel and also to make accessible the big-game country near Cody. In 1906 the railroad built from Frannie up the Big Horn River to Thermopolis and then on to Shoshoni. Another branch of the Burlington system was constructed in the early 1890's across the northeastern part of Wyoming, through extensive cattle territory to the agricultural and ranching districts near Sheridan.

In many instances the old stage routes have been converted into modern highways. In 1916 Wyoming adopted a constitutional amendment that made it possible for the State to participate in the Federal aid for post roads. A State highway commission was created the next year, which has since carried on an extensive building program. The production of oil on State-owned lands has been responsible in large measure for the network of more than 3,000 miles of excellent oiled roads spreading over the State.

A project initiated by the State highway department in 1935 involves the collection of wild-flower seeds in order to replace the weed-covered highway borders with plants native to the State. While the primary object is roadside beautification, the prevention of shoulder erosion by the use of mat-forming plants, the elimination of weeds, and the reduction of snow hazards are also given consideration.

Wyoming's 16 bus lines have done much to counteract the isolation of some of the more remote regions. According to a recent estimate 80 per cent of the passengers who ride on busses in Wyoming are local passengers. Motor trucks transporting State and interstate freight increased in number from 400 in 1934 to 4,000 in 1936.

Two major airlines operate in Wyoming: United Air Lines and the Inland Air Lines. Within Wyoming there are 48 airports, including those municipally and those privately owned. Since September 8, 1920, daily transcontinental mail service has been maintained across Wyoming through the Cheyenne airport. At first this mail route followed very closely the line of the Union Pacific Railroad. Later, with the rapid development of radio, the building of larger and better airplanes, and the establishment of beacon lights, the airway across Wyoming was laid out with regular airports at Cheyenne, Laramie, Parco, Rawlins, and Rock Springs, with intermediate landing fields and radio-beam stations at Medicine Bow, Cherokee, Rock Springs, Le Roy, Knight, and Bitter Creek.

Airway beacons are stationed every 10 to 20 miles, depending upon the contour of the country, east and west across Wyoming along the United Air Lines route, and north and south along Inland Air routes. Weather and wind-velocity reports are broadcast regularly to the pilots by radiophone from the Department of Commerce weather-bureau observations made at Cheyenne, Rock Springs, and Knight.

From Cheyenne the air mileage to Salt Lake City is 392 miles, with an average flying time of 2¾ hours; to Chicago it is 887 miles, with 5½ hours' flying time. Airmail service from Cheyenne to Billings, Montana, was inaugurated in May 1934; and to Rapid City, South Dakota, in 1938.

Wyoming has no navigable waterways, though a steamboat called the *El Paso* once, in 1851, navigated the Platte River from the Missouri to the site of the Guernsey Dam. Because of the strong current, the *El Paso* could not proceed farther than the mouth of the Platte Canyon, but to have reached that point was considered quite a feat.

Industry, Commerce and Labor

WYOMING has no congested industrial centers. Its oil refineries, coal and iron mines, sugar-beet factories, flour mills, and small enterprises are scattered about the State. Since no navigable rivers link the sources of supply, these have had to wait the extension of railway and truck lines for commercial exploitation. Widely distributed natural resources remain unproved, not only because of their inaccessibility to present markets, but because their location and proportions have not been generally known. Wyoming has always been an agricultural State, and until the oil boom of the 1920's investment depended largely upon livestock, ranching, and farming for its returns.

Except for the petroleum and beet-sugar industries, manufacturing enterprises are not large, but the State has great potentialities of hydroelectric energy, and fuel reserves in crude oil, natural gas, and coal. The increasing development of these and other resources is inevitably hastening the process of industrialization.

The first white men to enter the Wyoming region in the early 1800's traded in furs and by 1860 had built up a flourishing business. Many of the big fur companies of the United States maintained large crews of trappers, who worked the streams of this territory for beaver and other pelts. The first posts of importance established in the State, Forts Laramie and Bridger, were built for trading purposes, as were the Portuguese Houses, built about 1828 by a free trader (see Tour 3).

After the fur trappers came professional hunters, mostly frontier settlers who commercialized their marksmanship and disposed of thousands of buffalo robes and tons of buffalo and antelope meat. With the depletion of natural resources, trapping and hunting declined. For many years there was little commercial activity beyond that connected with the livestock industry.

As early as 1842 gold was discovered in the South Pass district in the Wind River Mountains, but actual prospecting did not begin until the 1850's. In 1861 the prospectors abandoned their claims when they found it more profitable to put up hay and deliver telegraph poles to the Overland Stage Company. Indian troubles curbed mining activity near the Pass for several years, but in the late 1860's the gulches and valleys hummed with the sound of men at work panning the streams or operating their claims. Approximately $3,000,000 in gold were taken out of the vicinity between 1869 and 1871, before miners and promoters were attracted to more promising fields in Montana and Nevada. For many years the South Pass country lay idle. In 1934 activity was revived and dredges began to take out placer gold in paying quantities.

'Ghost' towns or fragments of them still exist in various localities that once roared with activity. Among them are Atlantic City, Battle, Cambria, Cumming's City, Fairbanks, and Eadsville.

A gold strike was reported in 1937 near Encampment in southern Wyoming. In the summer of 1937 miners resumed activity in the Centennial and Albany districts of the Medicine Bow Mountains. The Rambler and Keystone mines in this vicinity were formerly good producers of copper and gold. Some gold mining is carried on each summer in the Big Horn Mountains near the old Fortunatus area (*see Tour* 10).

Discovered and classified in Wyoming are 157 distinct metals, non-metallic minerals, and clays that have present commercial value or potential uses. Exploration and geological research have revealed a great abundance and variety of mineral deposits. Platinum, gold, silver, copper, mercury, iron, and asbestos, worth millions of dollars, have been discovered, often half-exposed, in the mountains and slopes.

In northeastern Wyoming, especially near the town of Newcastle, vast deposits of bentonite clay have been uncovered and are supplying a considerable market in the Middle West. Quantities of bentonite are available in the Cheyenne district in Natrona County and in various other sections. In several localities, including Laramie, Rawlins, and Islay, fine building rock and limestone are quarried.

From the great soda deposits in Natrona County, shipments have been made to Eastern markets for several years. Valuable potash beds and extensive deposits of oil shale in Sweetwater and Carbon Counties have not yet been worked (1939). Some of the world's largest deposits of asbestos rock and fiber exist in several parts of the State, notably on Casper Mountain in Natrona County, where large chromite deposits are also found.

Beet-sugar factories in Sheridan, Lovell, Worland, Wheatland, and

Torrington annually refine hundreds of thousands of bags of table and preserving sugar. Wyoming beets average a high yield per acre and rank at the top in sugar content.

In the farming regions, especially around Sheridan, Wheatland, and Powell, flour mills utilize the high-quality wheat and other grains of Wyoming in the manufacture of flour, cereals, and feeds.

The Portland cement business of the State centers in the new $2,500,000 plant at Laramie. Plaster mills also are operated there.

At Sheridan, Lovell, and other points, brick and tile are manufactured from abundant deposits of native clays.

While there is at present no copper-mining industry in Wyoming, during the World War nearly $1,000,000 worth of copper ore was shipped from the famous Sunrise mines district near Guernsey in Platte County. This district now produces only iron ore, supplying by far the greater bulk of the high-grade ore for the huge smelters at Pueblo, Colorado. The glory hole of the Sunrise mine is one of the spectacles of Wyoming (*see Tour* 4).

More iron ore is mined in Wyoming than in all the other Rocky Mountain States together, and there are huge deposits still untouched. It is estimated that in the Sunrise district alone at least half a billion tons remain. In the Seminoe Mountains, 100 miles west of Sunrise in the northern part of Carbon County, are huge iron deposits that may equal or exceed those that made the Sunrise mines famous.

Wyoming is said to contain the largest coal reserves in the United States, estimated to a depth of 3,000 feet from the surface. Only a small fraction of the coal available has been mined. A number of mines owned by the Union Pacific Coal Company are being worked in southern Wyoming. There is a large open-pit, electrically operated coal mine near Gillette.

One of the State's largest industries has developed from oil. Crude petroleum is produced from 61 oil fields in 15 of the 23 counties. Gas is found in some 27 areas, 17 of which are considered important. The first recorded discovery of oil occurred in 1832, when Captain B. L. E. Bonneville explored the region. In his book, *The Adventures of Captain Bonneville, U. S. A.,* Washington Irving wrote '. . . the captain made search for the "Great Tar Springs," one of the wonders of the mountains; the medicinal properties of which he had heard extravagantly lauded by the trappers. After a toilsome search, he found it at the foot of a sand-bluff, a little to the east of the Wind River Mountains, where it exuded in a small stream of the color and consistency of tar. The men immediately hastened to collect a quantity of it to use as an ointment for the galled backs of their horses, and as a balsam for their own pains and aches. From the description given of it, it is evidently the bituminous oil, called petroleum or naphtha, which forms a principal ingredient in the patent medicine called British Oil.'

In the 1850's the crude oil from natural springs in southwestern Wyoming was traded by Indians to emigrants going over the Mormon Trail. It was used for axles and harness.

Bonneville's discovery was reported to the War Department, but no attention was paid to the Wyoming oil springs until after the Civil War, when the Government sent a man to Fort Bridger to investigate. The first oil well in Wyoming was drilled near Fort Bridger in the late 1860's and its small production sold unrefined at $20 to $25 a barrel.

Other oil seepages were found and irregularly developed in the next few years. In his 1878 report, Governor John W. Hoyt referred to White's Oil Springs near Evanston, and stated that borings had been made to a depth of 175 feet, with a view toward practical operations. For many years oil prospectors worked in the State, especially in the central part. In 1880 three test wells were drilled in the Lander district, and in 1889 the first well was completed in the Shannon field adjoining the Salt Creek wells on the north. Lack of funds prevented most of the earlier oil prospectors from profiting by the exploitation of the wells.

Many claims were filed on oil lands in Natrona County as early as 1885, but nothing was done toward the actual drilling of oil, except for assessment purposes, until 1888. Drillers began about three miles northwest of Casper, producing a 'duster' or dry hole, that was abandoned the next year.

Drilling in the Salt Creek Field was started in 1880 in what is now known as the 'Shannon Field.' The first well, completed in 1889, was a good producer of lubricating oil which sold at $10 a barrel. From 1893 to 1896, eight wells were brought in, but development was retarded by transportation difficulties. The oil had to be hauled 50 miles to Casper by team. These teams, made up of 16 to 20 head of horses and four wagons coupled together, hauled supplies to the field and returned with a load of oil. In 1895 a small refinery was built in Casper.

For about 30 years oil development in Wyoming continued on a small scale. The oil boom began in 1910. The men who made vast fortunes for themselves in the oil fields were very different from the original prospectors. Many were amateurs in the oil game—lawyers, doctors, merchants, ministers, men in all walks of life. They pooled what money they could raise for the drilling of a well and shared in the profits.

With the development of the billion-dollar Salt Creek oil field near Casper, thousands of men and women rushed into central Wyoming. From 1915 to 1918 the population of Casper, in the grip of a frenzied oil boom, grew from 2,000 to 20,000 in a few months. The Muddy Field, Poison Spider, Iron Creek, Lost Soldier, and other fields were rapidly developed. Refineries were built and constantly added new units. The excitement over oil matched the uproar of the California, Montana, and Colorado gold rushes.

Since its intensive development the Salt Creek light-oil field, lying adjacent to Teapot Dome, 50 miles north of Casper (*see Tour* 3), has been immensely productive. The daily average flow is 25,000 barrels of crude oil, which makes it one of the greatest light-oil fields in the world. Teapot Dome, a front-page subject in newspapers throughout the country for several years, was for a time leased to the Sinclair Crude Oil Purchasing Company.

Following a decision by the United States Supreme Court in 1927 canceling the leases on the Dome, after evidence that fraud and irregularities had entered into their negotiation, control and operating rights were returned to the Navy Department. The property is now known as United States Naval Petroleum Reserve No. 3. With the transfer went all of the improvements made by the Mammoth Oil Company, including elaborate camp buildings, derricks, and other equipment at the wells; machine shops, pumping station, 17 steel storage tanks with an aggregate capacity of 1,150,000 barrels, and four tanks of 80,000-barrel capacity each. The litigation over the leasing of Teapot Dome attracted worldwide attention.

The subsequent trials for bribery and conspiracy ended with a fine of $100,000 and the sentence of a year in prison for Albert B. Fall, Secretary of the Interior under President Harding; a jail sentence amounting to six-and-a-half months for Harry F. Sinclair, oil operator and lessor, for his refusal to testify before the Senate investigating committee; and receivership for the Richfield Oil Company and the Pan American Petroleum Company (the latter a property of Edward L. Doheny, another operator and lessor), as a result of judgments obtained against the companies for the oil they had appropriated.

The Rocky Mountain region obtains most of its gasoline, lubricating oils and greases, fuel and road oils, asphalt and other refined petroleum products from the extensive oil refineries as Casper and smaller plants at Greybull, Parco, Glenrock, and Thermopolis. In 1925 nearly 30,000,000 barrels of crude oil, with an approximate value of $50,000,000, were produced in Wyoming; in 1938 the production was 19,022,141 barrels.

Three huge pipelines originate in Wyoming, carrying oil to refineries at Cheyenne, Denver, and Salt Lake City. The largest line has a maximum daily capacity of 10,000 barrels. In 1937 oil activity was renewed all over the State, especially near Lusk and Douglas, where in a formation considered unproductive, new pools have been tapped. Wyoming converts much oil and gas into heat and light. Plants supplying carbon black, to be used as a base for paints and for printing inks and in the manufacture of automobile tires, operate near Lusk in Niobrara County.

A meat-packing plant at Casper offers the State's largest local market for hogs, and supplies the trade territory of this centrally located city. Packing plants are also located in Cheyenne, Rock Springs, Sheridan, and other cities.

Wyoming timber is favored especially for railroad ties. Treating plants at Riverton, Laramie, and Sheridan annually turn out quantities of ties for railways that traverse this and adjoining States. The spectacular tie drives, especially on the Wind, Green, and Laramie Rivers, are of particular interest to visitors. The cutting of railroad ties, mine props and timbers, and common lumber from several of the 12 national forests, lying wholly or in part within the State, affords employment to large crews of men and provides an annual output constantly increasing in value.

Distant from the larger centers of population, Wyoming has built up a flourishing wholesale industry. From Casper, Cheyenne, and Sheridan, commodities in general use are supplied to retail merchants and consumers throughout the State.

Early commerce depended upon freight outfits and stage lines and the hauling of freight and supplies was expensive. Railways and highways now stimulate trade. The splendid system of oiled highways that reaches into every section of the State has increased hauling by motor truck at an almost unbelievable rate.

The State of Wyoming engages in the following industries: road building and upkeep, manufacture of woolen goods at the state penitentiary, the raising of trout for stocking streams and lakes, the whole-saling of liquor, and the maintenance of health resorts at Thermopolis and Saratoga.

Dude ranching, with its sidelines of guiding, hunting, and pack trips into the high country, is a well-established industry, especially in Sheridan, Park, Fremont, Johnson, Carbon, and Teton Counties. In 1938 approximately 11,000 guests at these ranches spent $2,197,000 in Wyoming. In the same year one and one-half million tourists passed through the State.

With the development of farming, attention was turned to dairying, and by 1917 more than 1,000 dairies were doing business in Wyoming. The Star Valley was found to be especially adapted, and the large cheese factories there utilize the produce of the country about them.

More than 100 types of articles are manufactured in Wyoming in-cluding expensive leather goods, tick powders, toy pistols, high grade violins, artificial ice, head gates for irrigation ditches, fertilizer, sage-brush incense, sage candles, cigars, scrubbing soap, and sheep wagons. Stone and gem cutting is becoming one of the thriving home industries.

The commercial canning of truck crops holds promise of future growth in the irrigated areas. Such crops as peas, corn, pumpkins, and asparagus are being canned in abundance, especially in the Big Horn Basin. The town of Cowley has a cannery that specializes in vegetables. A large pea-sorting plant is located at Douglas.

In the last nine years assessed property valuation in the State has increased from $188,560,000 to $327,000,000. In 1930 Wyoming's population was estimated at 225,565. Of this number 92,451 were gainfully employed. Estimates of 1940 show that approximately 101,145 State residents were employed in all industries, including 17,000 in agriculture.

Labor: Wyoming's labor organizations, having the largest member-ship in proportion to industrial population of any State, play an impor-tant role in local government. Through representation in State legisla-tures, labor groups have given valuable aid in obtaining the passage of numerous laws, equitable in purpose, such as the Workmen's Com-pensation Act, the act governing hours for female labor, the Unem-ployment Compensation Act, and an act creating a child-labor com-mission. According to the secretary of the Wyoming State Federation of Labor, this legislation and the co-operative spirit of employers friendly to the participation of labor in industrial relations have aided materially in the establishment of satisfactory labor conditions. The

History

Photograph by courtesy of Wyoming Historical Department

JIM BRIDGER

GRAVES ALONG THE OREGON TRAIL

NAMES CARVED ON REGISTER CLIFF, NEAR GUERNSEY

Photograph by courtesy of *Wyoming Historical Department*

JIM BAKER

WYOMING'S OLDEST BUILDING, THE POST SUTLER'S STORE AT FORT LARAMIE
The doorway (left) is a remnant of the American Fur Company's store (1836); the main section was built in 1852

FORT SUPPLY, BUILT BY THE MORMONS (1853)
Drawing by Merritt D. Houghton; courtesy of Wyoming Historical Department

PONY EXPRESS STABLES, FORT BRIDGER

THE FIRST SCHOOL HOUSE (1860), FORT BRIDGER

BUILDING DALE CREEK BRIDGE, UNION PACIFIC ROUTE (1869)

SHERMAN STATION, UNION PACIFIC ROUTE (1869)

**SOLDIERS AND CONSTRUCTION WORKERS FIGHTING OFF INDIAN ATTACK
DURING BUILDING OF UNION PACIFIC**

CLEARING THE TRACK

Buffalo were often so numerous it was necessary to frighten them
off the track by ejecting a jet of steam from the locomotive

Photograph by courtesy of Rocky Mountain Studio, Encampment

STAGECOACH AT ENCAMPMENT

GEM CITY MINSTRELS, LARAMIE (1870)

Wyoming Workmen's Compensation Law of 1915, as amended, is considered a model law by both workers and employers.

Statutes provide an eight-hour day on all public works—State, county, and municipal. Hours for mine workers are prescribed by Federal law under the Guffey Act. Hours of work for women are limited to eight per day and forty-eight per week in designated occupations.

Local unions of shop, maintenance, and clerical employees in railway service, affiliated with the American Federation of Labor and the United Mine Workers of America, make up the largest organized groups in the State. The Railway Brotherhoods, unaffiliated with either the American Federation of Labor or the Congress for Industrial Organization, have some 8,000 members.

In addition to mining and railway employee organizations, there are unions for oil workers, caterers, barbers, building craftsmen, lumber and sawmill workers, laundry workers, automobile workers, teamsters and chauffeurs, printers, and Federal Government employees.

Only three serious strikes have occurred in Wyoming. The Rock Springs 'riot' of 1885 was the worst and resulted in fatalities. After the importation of Chinese coolies to the Pacific Coast, anti-Chinese agitation spread from San Francisco over the entire West. Chinese laborers first came to Rock Springs in 1875, just after coal production had been interrupted by a strike in the Union mines. The new labor hired to operate the mines was a mixed force, one-third white, two-thirds Chinese. An equal wage was paid both. Anti-Chinese feeling grew steadily and culminated in a riot on September 2, 1885, when many resident Chinese were killed, and the rest warned to leave the town immediately. Some of the Chinese returned to Rock Springs later and began small business enterprises.

Wyoming labor took part in the nationwide strike of bituminous coal miners, called in 1922 in protest against a proposed decrease in the wages that prevailed during the World War. During the national railroad shop-crafts strike in the same year, also against wage reductions, stockades were built around the railway shops in Cheyenne as protection for those who remained at work.

There are practically no so-called 'seasonal' occupations in Wyoming in any of the trades. Employment is comparatively steady with a constant demand for skilled craftsmen in the building trades.

The *Wyoming Labor Journal,* owned by the State Federation of Labor, is published weekly in Cheyenne from a modern printing plant belonging to the federation.

Agriculture

EARLY in the nineteenth century, Wyoming was marked on the map as part of the Great American Desert. According to Daniel Webster, it 'was not worth a cent,' being, as he declared in 1844, 'a region of savages, wild beasts, shifting sands, whirlwinds of dust, cactus, and prairie dogs.'

For a time many shared his opinion. During the 1840's and 1850's hundreds of thousands of emigrants pushed their way over the Oregon and California Trails in search of homes on the Pacific Coast, unmindful of the agricultural possibilities of the territory they traversed. Perhaps this was because the old trails crossed some of the most barren, desolate, and unpromising parts of what later became Wyoming.

It is now a great rural State, where three kinds of agriculture—stock raising, farming by irrigation, and dry farming—are practiced. Although the values of land and livestock have diminished in relation to the corporate property of the State, stock raising is still about six times as important as crop farming. Hay is the foremost crop, both in acreage and value, and alfalfa is first among the varieties cultivated. Wheat, corn, potatoes, beets of unusually high sugar content, barley, rye, beans, and apples are among the crops raised.

The great range in altitudes affords a wide variety in soil and climatic conditions, and the small amount of rainfall during the harvest season permits produce to ripen or cure in fine condition. Forage and cereal crops excel in nutritive value; vegetables develop to unusual sizes in the higher altitudes and are especially solid, crisp, and full of flavor.

The greatest agricultural development, since pioneer times, has been in the livestock industry. The proportion of good farming lands in the State is small compared with the great ranch areas that are, and probably always will be, best adapted to grazing. Agricultural experts recommend the merging of small areas of submarginal land, such as have been farmed in parts of northeastern and eastern Wyoming, into ranching tracts of about 4,000 acres.

The story is that the wealth that lies in the wild native grasses of Wyoming was discovered in 1864, when a Government trader with a wagon train of supplies drawn by oxen was caught on the Laramie Plains in a December blizzard. He had to turn his animals loose, although fearing that they would perish. To his astonishment they came through the winter in excellent condition by grazing. When the war had ended, cattlemen began to trail their great herds up from Texas in search of better grazing lands, since Texas ranges had become overstocked. Because of the highly nutritive quality of native vegetation along the Texas and Bozeman Trails, the cattle were fat and sleek when they reached the northern shipping points.

The establishment of military posts and the advent of new mining communities provided a local market for beef, and the completion of the Union Pacific Railroad in 1868 made Eastern cattle markets accessible to Western growers. Cattlemen were quick to see the possibilities for the cattle industry of this high plateau of vast rolling grasslands, broken by foothills and lofty mountain ranges, with a network of rivers and small streams bordered by brush that afforded ample shelter for stock.

News of the first successful attempts to raise cattle in Wyoming soon reached the East, and the Western cattle boom began. Here was a new untenanted land with room for all. Newcomers selected the ranges they wanted, using natural boundaries for their holdings, and built ranch headquarters, barns, and corrals. The unwritten law of possession held sway. As soon as each outfit was established the company usually issued a statement in the advertising columns of a well-circulated newspaper in such terms as these: 'The X Bar K Cattle Company; home ranch on Poison Spider. Our range extends from Muddy Creek, north to Elk Buttes, east to Sawtooth Mountain and west to Rattlesnake River.'

In the spring and fall, great roundups were held to brand and sort cattle and to cut them out for market. Each outfit had a foreman who did the actual overseeing; the owners in many instances lived in Cheyenne or even in New York City or London.

The Wyoming Stock Growers Association, organized (as the Laramie County Stock Growers Association) in Cheyenne in 1873, with the primary purpose of regulating the industry and protecting the livestock interests, has been from the first one of the foremost organizations of its kind in the United States. By 1885 it had 400 members who

owned some 2,000,000 head of cattle, which with other ranch invest-
ments represented $100,000,000. This organization was influential in
the formation of the American Livestock Association and of the United
States Bureau of Animal Industry. It is a significant fact that four
members of the association represented Wyoming in Congress from its
territorial days until January 1937. These men, Senators Joseph M.
Carey, Francis E. Warren, John B. Kendrick, and Robert D. Carey,
also served the State as Governors.

From 1870 to the middle 1880's the cattle industry rapidly expanded.
European capital invested heavily in the new cattle country, and companies were formed with large capitalization. Cattle were bought sight-
unseen and on the 'book-count' of the seller. The book-count, however,
was a poor system of estimate, since it assumed that when so many
cows under a certain brand had been turned out on the range, they
remained there without death loss, each cow producing a calf.

Investment in the cattle bonanza reached its peak in 1883–4. Favorable rains all over the West made excellent pasturage, and cattle speculation ran wild. By 1886 the tally of Wyoming stock stood at 8,000,000
head. The free and easy methods of turning cattle onto the range
and forgetting about them until roundup time appealed to the new
owners.

Several important factors, however, had been overlooked by the
cattle companies. Winter losses were heavier than they had expected.
Prices paid for cattle were often far out of proportion to true value;
much grazing land was overstocked and rapidly becoming depleted
of forage. Little more was needed to prick the bubble of speculation.
A severe winter followed the exceptionally dry spring and summer
of 1886, and the final blow came in the spring of 1887. Cattle died
by the thousands, the losses in herds ranging from 30 to 100 per cent.
Crops were poor that year in the Corn Belt and there was little
demand for feeder cattle. Western cattlemen failed, and many of the
big outfits never recovered from the blows of 1886–7.

Although the first homestead entry in Wyoming was completed in
1870, it was not until the late 1880's and the early 1890's that a tide
of settlement came into Wyoming under homestead laws. Many newcomers took up land and began to build wire fences, abominated by
the large cattle owner who used the open range, since they prevented
his herds from drifting to natural shelter in storms and blocked the
way to water holes. Much ill feeling developed against the so-called
'nester.' Cattle rustling, especially in the 'Hole-in-the-Wall' country (in

central Wyoming near the headwaters of the Powder River), became prevalent and even forced some cattlemen to quit business. Matters came to a head in 1892 with the cattlemen's so-called 'Invasion of Johnson County' (*see Tour* 3). The armed expedition of cattlemen that penetrated the rustlers' stronghold in central Wyoming accomplished little of apparent consequence beyond putting a decided curb on the practice. Today, however (1940), rustlers have streamlined their tactics and still prey upon the herds by whisking away stolen cattle in fast trucks. The Wyoming Stock Growers Association leads the fight against the rustlers.

Gradually range methods improved and the cattle industry settled to a steady growth. When large holdings were broken up, small owners took control. After the experiences of 1886–7, stockmen had more respect for the vagaries of western climate and made provision for shelter and feeding against the hard winters. By 1906 the market for feeder cattle had so improved that the estimated valuation of Wyoming stock was $7,283,000, and in 1916 the World War raised the figure to $26,241,000.

Ranching has felt the lean years of drought and depression that began in 1929, and many outfits have never regained solvency. Rains in 1938 helped to restore the range, and in 1939 the estimate of Wyoming cattle was 836,000 head, valued at $30,967,000.

The range-beef production outfit of today is vastly different from that of early days. In general the size of ranches has been materially reduced; many outfits have been converted into 'dude ranches.' No longer is it possible in the cattle business in Wyoming to profit through sheer magnitude of operation. The number of cattle run on a given grazing area must have a definite relation to the feed furnished by that area over a long period. The greatest change is in the animals themselves. Economy has ordained that modern cattle must be, not only more efficient converters of feed into beef, but also of a type to yield a maximum of the higher-priced cuts of meat. Hence both the big rugged steer and the earlier-maturing type, which can be finished into good beef at an early age, are now found on Wyoming ranches. The Hereford is the most popular breed at present.

Closely allied to the cattle industry in Wyoming is that of horse-raising. Every big outfit that trailed cattle into the State employed from 15 to 20 cowboys, each with a string or 'cavvy' of from six to ten ponies. Later, highbred horses were introduced. As a result of the invigorating air, the altitude that expands the lungs, and the minerals in the soil, water, and foods that make strong hard bone and hoof, Wyoming-raised horses are highly regarded by military experts for their endurance, muscle, energy, and tenacity. Thousands of Wyoming horses were sold for service in the Spanish-American, the Boer, and the World Wars. Several ranches raise exceptionally fine polo ponies; two ranches breed draft horses; and at least two ranches are now raising fine race horses. Comparatively few wild horses wander over the ranges today; hundreds have been rounded up and sold to canning factories and to fox farms and for shipment to Europe.

A few sheep were in Wyoming as early as 1845 at Fort Bridger. Later herds were brought in about 1869. It was soon found that the State's contour and native flora in many sections were suited to their raising. Vast ranges in arid or semi-arid sections, that had been found unfit for grazing other livestock, proved well adapted to sheep. The dry climate makes healthy sheep and the dry cold is conducive to a heavy growth of fine, long wool. By 1886 the territory had more than 500,000 sheep. By 1890 sheep had begun to crowd out cattle on many of the ranges. The State enumeration in 1906 showed that 4,312,030 head were thriving upon Wyoming grazing lands.

In the early days of the industry the sheep owner usually hired a herder, who took out an average flock of 2,000 sheep on a free range and wandered from place to place as the sheep grazed. A tent or canvas, a couple of sheep dogs, a little grub, and a rifle made up the herder's equipment. His was purely a nomadic life and he had to contend with the opposition of cattle owners and cowboys, inclement weather in the lambing or shearing season, predatory animals, and range disputes.

Since the close grazing of sheep was said to spoil much of the range for cattle, the sheep industry was actively opposed by cattlemen. Sheep were killed, wagons burned, herders driven off, and some of them killed. Deadlines were drawn and sheepmen were notified not to cross them. Such troubles were numerous in the 1890's and early 1900's, with tragedies resulting in the Jackson Hole, the Tensleep area, and in Crook County.

At last, however, sheepmen were protected in their rights, and today they work side by side with cattlemen for the best interests of the entire livestock industry. With improved methods of handling sheep, establishment of ranches with extensive corrals, sheds, and sheep-feeding stations, and with community shearing-pens, dipping-pens, and lambing-sheds, the sheep business has attained permanence and security. The modern sheepherder has a wagon equipped with spring bed, stove, table, and modern appliances; sometimes he even has a radio. Usually the bands vary from 1,500 to 2,000 head. Each is usually handled by one herder, who lives in a covered wagon and stays with the sheep day and night throughout the season. A camp tender or camp-jack moves the herder's wagon and brings supplies to him. Sometimes the camp-jack stays a while to cook meals, gather fuel, and do camp chores, but usually the herder works alone and sleeps 'with one eye open.' At night with his dogs, he brings the sheep to the bedground, around which he places flags several feet apart, forming a sort of corral to scare away coyotes, bobcats, and bears. By day he moves slowly about with the band, listening to the continual bleating, watching the sheep in woolly waves feeding on the slopes. The loneliness and the deadly monotony have been known to drive herders insane.

The time of leaving summer range depends on the weather and on range and market conditions; it is usually early September. Lambs which have attained the desired finish and weight (75 to 85 pounds) are trailed to shipping points. Some sheepmen fatten lambs on beet by-products, corn, barley, and wheat, with alfalfa hay for roughage. Others ship them to feed lots in adjoining States. They examine the teeth of the older sheep and send only those in good condition to the salt sage winter ranges.

The sheep industry in the State has had fluctuations, but in 1939 Wyoming stood second among the States in production of wool and mutton, ranking next to Texas. More than 1,500,000 head of sheep and lambs grazed under permit in 1939 in Wyoming's national forests; an equal number fed on the prairies and on ranches and farms, bringing the total, including imported feeders, to 3,647,000 head. Nearly 25,000,000 pounds of wool yearly go from Wyoming into the clothing supply of the Nation. Sheep from the famous King Brothers' Ranch near Laramie and from the University of Wyoming flock are shipped all over the world, especially to Japan, China, and Russia, for breeding purposes. The Wyoming Wool Growers Association, the leading organization of its kind in the State, conducts wool sales and an annual ram sale at Casper that attract many breeders and buyers. Lamb fattening has become an important branch of the sheep business, and many thousands of lambs are now fed in the districts where grain, alfalfa, and beet pulp are available.

The sale of cattle, calves, beef, and veal brought the Wyoming ranchers a cash income of $12,669,000 in 1938, with a gross income of $13,103,000. Through the sale of hogs, pork, and lard, the farmers realized in the same year a gross income of $723,000 and a cash income of $511,000. Wyoming sheep growers received for the same period $9,038,000 in cash incomes from the sale of sheep, lambs, and mutton and a gross income of $9,157,000.

For more than 20 years livestock interests have waged war on predatory animals through the joint co-operation of the United States Bureau of Biological Survey, the State and county governments, and livestock associations. From 1916 up to the close of the 1939 fiscal year, 122,052 animals, including bears, bobcats, coyotes, mountain lions, lynxes, and wolves, had been killed. Private hunters and trappers have also taken a large number of these animals.

The average cattlemen and their families live in well-built, spacious ranch homes. They are hospitable and cling to many of the early day traditions. Often they move into a neighboring town during the winter in order to send the children to high school or to the State university. Many attend stock shows in Denver, Kansas City, and Chicago, and they visit Cheyenne during the sessions of the legislature. They are well informed on current topics and keep abreast of the times. Because they are vitally concerned in matters pertaining to grazing on public lands, soil erosion, permits on the national forests, and the development of reclamation projects, they are often more interested in national politics and policies than in those of the State.

Since 1933 much work has been done by Civilian Conservation Corps forces and others engaged under relief programs, to improve forage conditions and to facilitate the management of livestock on the ranges. Areas only partially utilized heretofore, because of lack of water, have been made suitable for sheep and cattle by construction of livestock watering ponds and reservoirs. Range fences have been constructed to separate range allotments and to reduce drift of cattle. Stock drive-ways, trails and bridges, corrals, and cattle guards that have been built will facilitate the use of approximately 5,000,000 acres of live-stock ranges in the national forests in Wyoming.

A total of 1,611,476 head of livestock grazed in districts in Wyoming during 1938, including 152,278 cattle, 14,104 horses, 1,444,480 sheep, and 254 goats.

Diversified agriculture has been practiced in Wyoming from the time of the Indians, when the Crow grew corn, beans, and pumpkins in the rich soils along the Powder River and its tributaries. The early army posts along the Oregon Trail ordered garden seeds and imple-ments through the sutler at Fort Laramie as early as 1867, as his records show. During the drought and depression of the 1930's, many Wyoming farmers who were unable to finance the farming of their large acreages made a living by maintaining a small flock of sheep, some turkeys and chickens, and a few milk cows, and cultivated only sufficient land to raise feed for the stock and for a small garden.

Because of its numerous rivers and the great accumulations of snow in the mountain ranges, Wyoming is one of the most favorably situated of all arid States for the development of large areas by irrigation. White men first began to farm by this means in 1853, when a group of Mormons settled at Fort Supply near Fort Bridger. In the same year some Mormons began to farm near Deer Creek, upon order of Brigham Young (*see Tour 3c*), to raise vegetables for converts bound for Utah. The remnants of the old irrigation ditches may still be seen in Mormon Canyon. This farming was abandoned in the 1860's.

Spaniards at Fort Laramie irrigated gardens with water from the Laramie River as early as 1855, but the first legal water rights in the State were filed in 1862 by the Myers Land and Livestock Company on Bear River.

The present irrigated agricultural lands of the State may be divided roughly into three sections: the north-central, southeastern, and western. In addition to native forages the main crops include alfalfa, sugar beets, potatoes, the small cereals, beans, peas, clover seed, vegetables, and fruits. Most of these crops are utilized in livestock feeding.

Under the territorial system there were neither restrictions nor supervision of water distribution. Anyone who wanted water took it. As a result there was a haphazard building of ditches, chiefly for the purpose of irrigating hay meadows, and the builders took as much water as their ditches would hold. A new era opened in 1889 with the creation of the office of territorial engineer. At first the mere diversion of water from its natural channel by means of an irrigation ditch gave priority rights to the persons diverting it, regardless of the use. Later water allotments were restricted in proportion to the actual acreage reclaimed. It was soon found that crops of high quality could be raised in Wyoming almost anywhere that water could be put on the land. At the World's Fair in Chicago in 1893, Wyoming wheat scored highest in its class, despite the fact that at that time the wheat acreage in the State was less than 100 acres.

Under the Carey Act, providing for reclamation and settlement of land, large arid tracts throughout the State have been placed under cultivation. Owners who have built ditches individually, in partnership, or through co-operative organization have taken the greatest part in this reclamation. In most cases their lands are in the stream valleys where ditches and canals have been easy to construct. Larger areas being reclaimed under the Carey Act and the United States Bureau of Reclamation lie, for the most part, upon the benchlands where long and expensive canals with large storage reservoirs have been necessary.

Farmers and their families living in the irrigated farming districts have neat, modernized homes equipped with labor-saving devices and electricity. They co-operate enthusiastically with agricultural extension workers, sponsor such organizations as 4-H clubs, own modern machinery, and run their farms along modern lines. They devote a great deal of attention to the raising of purebred stock and certified seed crops.

Many of the farmers have taken advantage of the Federal-State co-operative plan provided by the Clarke-McNary Law and, during 1939 alone, planted 66,200 trees for windbreaks and shelterbelts.

In addition to the irrigated areas in Wyoming there are large tracts of fertile soils especially adapted to the production of crops under natural rainfall. This system of agriculture, known as dry farming, was first introduced into Wyoming in 1878, some 40 miles northeast of Cheyenne, by a group of Swedes. Towards the close of the 1890's dry farming became popular throughout a section 20 to 100 miles wide, extending from south to north in the eastern part of the State. In the early 1900's, as the result of such experiments in the vicinity of Cheyenne, an experimental station was established at Archer, and hundreds of families moved into Wyoming from Iowa, Nebraska, and Missouri.

Dry farmers have prospered in certain districts, especially where the raising of certified potatoes has been successful. They have built thriving villages with schools, churches, elevators, and banks; they own automobiles, good homes, and purebred stock; and they hold institutes and fairs.

In other districts, because of the lack of rainfall and the invasion of crickets during the past few years, dry farming has been a complete failure. Deserted shacks with doors gaping on broken hinges and yards overgrown with tumbleweeds and littered with remnants of household furniture are silent testimony to years of fruitless struggle. In many localities, especially in the ten counties in northeastern and eastern Wyoming, the topsoil, which was plowed up on dry farms, has blown away. In these ten counties farm poverty has been caused, not only by wind and water erosion, but by the practice of holding land in units too small for successful operation. Most of the area was settled in 640-acre tracts; but this land is more suited to ranching than to farming, and, in order to be profitable, operation would have to be on a scale of about 3,840 acres to the ranch. Realizing that this land, either overgrazed or plowed up, must be converted into good pasture if it is to become profitable, the Department of Agriculture has undertaken a land-purchase project in Campbell, Converse, Weston, and Crook Counties, buying 275,000 acres to be developed into grazing range.

Ranchers in that vicinity have organized a co-operative grazing association to utilize this large area in addition to about 65,000 acres of public domain adjoining the purchased land. Stock dams to provide water for cattle and sheep have been built and a large area has been reseeded to grass, under the development program of the Farm Security Administration.

Wyoming's nine well-equipped experiment stations have been of great service to farmers and ranchmen in problems concerning crops, livestock, and horticulture. Especially valuable assistance has been given in combating crop enemies, among them the noxious weeds that become an acute problem in irrigated country. These stations have developed certain agricultural specialties that make possible the maximum use of the unique conditions found in Wyoming. One of these, the Cheyenne Horticultural Field Station, maintained by the Government for the purpose of experimenting with shrubs and trees suitable for growth in the plains area, was established in 1928.

Fruit growing in Wyoming is limited by altitude and short growing seasons. Excellent apples, however, are grown in the Lander Valley, and the experimental station maintained about seven miles from Lander produces some splendid varieties of hardy fruit. Apples also grow in the Sheridan and North Platte Valleys. Pears and cherries are sometimes produced near Egbert, but are not a reliable crop because of early frosts.

Wyoming's sunshiny climate is exceptionally favorable to turkey raising. This agricultural side line developed very rapidly within a few years, especially in the Big Horn Basin and the North Platte Valley. In 1935 growers reported a profit of more than $1,000,000. The National Poultry Improvement Plan was adopted by the State during the early part of 1936, and the 1939 crop of turkeys was estimated at 270,000 birds, or a 20 per cent increase over 1938.

The honey bee is a money-maker for the Wyoming farmer because of the many wild flowers and the many fields of alfalfa. More than 4,000,000 pounds of honey, uniform in color, of fine texture and flavor, are produced annually from 26,000 colonies of bees. Many carloads of honey are shipped abroad, especially to England, from Wyoming producers. In this field, co-operative production and marketing have been developed.

Domesticated fur farming is now well established as a branch of Wyoming agriculture. Cold winters and cool summer nights develop a high quality of fur. Twenty-nine silver fox farms reported a total of 4,712 animals in 1939. Mink farming is increasing. White breeds of rabbits are raised extensively in some areas and Wyoming has one of the 30 chinchilla farms in the world. The silver badger industry, too, is still profitable. Muskrat farms, however, have almost disappeared, owing to the influx of nutria to the market from South America.

Dairying is important in several areas of the State; some 15 butter-making plants are scattered in 11 counties. The old-time canned milk has given way to the cream separator. The center of the dairy industry in Wyoming is the Star Valley, known locally as 'the little Switzerland of America,' where nine mountain streams supply pure irrigation water. More than 3,000,000 pounds of cheese are manufactured annually in modern factories here, and transported by motor over the mountains to the railway in Idaho for shipment to the West Coast and even to Hawaii and the Philippine Islands. The varieties of cheese produced in Star Valley have excellent flavor and texture and are highly nutritious. Approximately 17,000 Wyoming farmers and ranchers produce and sell dairy products.

With much nontillable land and great areas valuable only for grazing purposes, Wyoming continues to be primarily a livestock State with hay its most remunerative farm market crop. In 1938 the gross farm income amounted to $9,493,000 from crops and $34,858,000 from livestock. The total gross farm income, including Government payment, was $47,123,000.

The tame hay crop for 1939 was estimated at 849,000 tons; alfalfa hay, 532,000 tons; sugar beets, 648,000 tons; and beans, 448,000 bags. Potatoes were estimated at 1,730,000 bushels; wheat, 3,337,000 bushels; corn, 2,034,000 bushels; oats, 2,350,000 bushels; and barley, 1,488,000 bushels.

Education

THE Reverend William Vaux, post chaplain, established a school at Fort Laramie in 1852, long before the territory was organized. A decade later a private school was conducted at Fort Bridger for the family of the post sutler, Judge William A. Carter. At that time there were only three permanent settlements in southwestern Dakota—in what later became Wyoming. Including the two forts and a few ranches along the North Platte River, these settlements had a total population of only about 400, chiefly adults.

With the coming of the Union Pacific Railroad, however, towns sprang up across southern Wyoming, and by 1867 Judge Kuykendall reported to the Dakota superintendent of public instruction that there were in Cheyenne some 200 children between the ages of 5 and 21, but no school facilities. On January 5, 1868, with the thermometer registering 23° below zero, the citizens of Cheyenne dedicated the first school building.

The first school law in Wyoming Territory, which became effective on December 10, 1869, was considered an important step in the general system of education, not only in the immediate vicinity but in other parts of the United States. This law provided that schools should be maintained by general taxation instead of by the customary system of voluntary contributions or subscriptions prevalent before the Civil War.

Under this law the entire matter of education was placed in the hands of the territorial auditor, who was made ex-officio superintendent of public instruction. The chief duties of the superintendent were to distribute the funds among the several counties, to keep the school records, to put the school system into uniform operation, to create and supervise all of the district schools, and to recommend uniform textbooks. School taxes, to be levied by the county commissioners, were to be distributed by the county superintendents.

Provision also was made in this first law that when there were 15 or more Negro children within a specified district, the school board with the approval of the county superintendent might provide a separate school. The only segregated school recorded in the State was the one in Laramie. According to the *Cheyenne Daily Leader* of March 12, 1875: 'The colored population are to have a school in Laramie. They have rented a building, hired a teacher, and school will be commenced at once.' No statistics are available on the duration of the school.

In the early days the private schools exceeded the public schools in importance, the census of 1870 showing four public schools with four teachers and five day and boarding schools with eleven teachers. There is record of a private school started in Laramie in 1869 by George Lancaster, and of an Episcopal school opened a short time later by the Right Reverend Joseph (Holy Joe) Cornell. Neither remained open long. More important among the early private schools were two established at Laramie in 1870: the Wyoming Institute, a Baptist school, which continued four years; and St. Mary's, a Roman Catholic institution established by the Sisters of Charity, which survived until 1885.

In 1875, 25 pupils were enrolled in the private school of a Miss Ellis in Cheyenne, and in 1876 Miss Annie B. DeLany opened a 'select day school' at the Rectory School House in Cheyenne, for children between 6 and 12 years, and announced that on Saturdays she would conduct a 'class for little girls in sewing, embroidery, miniature dress making, and general deportment.' Lessons in French and music were promised for the future. How long the school existed is not known.

Miss Doloph taught a private kindergarten in Cheyenne in the early 1880's, and in 1886 Mrs. F. D. M. Bratten established the Magic City Kindergarten there. Subsequently other similar kindergartens were established and public kindergartens were authorized in 1895.

Occasionally new private schools opened their doors but few withstood the difficulties created by shifting populations and restricted budgets.

The largest private school in Wyoming, the Academy of the Holy Child Jesus, was founded in Cheyenne in 1885 by the Roman Catholic church and is still (1940) a substantial institution. At the time of its founding there were also two branches of St. John's parochial school in Cheyenne, with an enrollment of about 250 pupils. The Sisters of St. Joseph conducted a school in Laramie from some time in the 1890's until about 1904.

Among the few other private schools opened in more recent times is the Valley Ranch School for Boys at Valley, which was begun in 1922 as a college preparatory school. The classwork is carried on in a ranch environment near the Absaroka Mountains, and the enrollment is limited to 40. Sherwood Hall, the Cathedral School for Boys at Laramie, was established by the Episcopal church in 1924. Originally planned to provide typical preparatory instruction, the curriculum was altered in 1938 to include training and recreational activities patterned after those of the military academy.

Public schools along the Union Pacific Railroad, in Cheyenne, Laramie, Rawlins, and Evanston, were established in the late 1860's, and their growth kept steady pace with the thriving new localities. The district schools, however, varied in character according to the facilities at hand and the personnel of the district school boards. One of the earliest district schools was established at Fort Laramie, the citizens of that precinct taking preliminary steps for the organization of a school district in December 1875.

Since the district school boards determined the site of the school house, the length of term, the expenditures for erection or rental, and the curriculum to be followed in the lower grades, they became important factors in the educational development of the territory and State. Bitter feuds verging on small wars were sometimes waged by these local school boards. To families living in isolated districts the hiring or firing of the 'schoolma'am,' the question whether the children should ride to Rawhide Creek or to Muskrat, whether they should attend school three months or six months each year, have been of paramount importance, temporarily overshadowing everything else. Nor was concern over school matters limited to parents. It is related that a ballot box at a school election was stuffed outrageously by the miners of a camp called New Rambler, who wished to keep the good-looking teacher on their side of Poverty Gulch.

The residents of Wyoming's pioneer communities were so eager for schools that they made use of any and all materials at hand when standard equipment was not available. One school in the Shell Creek country opened in an abandoned stable where the children sat on the manger. A pair of old rubber boots was split open and tacked on the wall for a blackboard. In Evanston a school was opened in 1871 above a saloon, with an outside wooden stairway for an entrance; the equipment consisted of a blackboard, a small table, and some common chairs.

In some communities the schools were taught first on one ranch and then on another, sometimes changing several times a year. In the Jackson Hole area distances were so great and population so sparse that one mother begged the use of a room for a home for the children of her neighborhood, and three mothers took turns keeping house there for the eleven youngsters while they attended school. The housemother cared for the children, washed and mended their clothes, and cooked the food brought from the home cupboards.

It was the rule, rather than the exception, that the country school teachers, many of whom had come from eastern States, married ranchmen or cowboys and settled permanently in the communities where they had been teaching. Their interest in school matters naturally continued, and they were instrumental in promoting every movement for better education. Not all of the teachers, of course, were women. The second teacher at Cokeville was a man known as Ike McVay, later reported to have had an eventful career as a quack doctor and a horse thief.

The State superintendent's reports of the 1870's and 1880's list schools held in diverse places: a log building with a dirt roof; the upper room of a railroad section house; a rented building; the spare room of a ranch; an abandoned chicken house; the vacant office of a mining company; a blacksmith's shop; the basement of the town hall; and a sheep wagon.

Secondary or high school education in the districts was left to the county superintendents, acting in conjunction with the district boards. Cheyenne had the first high school in 1875, and Buffalo the second in 1881.

The failure on the part of district clerks and county superintendents to make reports in the early days resulted in a lack of statistics for many sections of the State. It was generally known, though, that wherever possible education was being fostered, and the available reports state that the 'teachers are an industrious, well-trained group.'

In his report in 1878 to the Commissioner of Education at Washington, D. C., Territorial Governor John W. Hoyt said:

> It is worthy of note that the public at large feels a great pride in the public schools of the Territory and is ever ready with liberal means, as well as with active moral influence to promote their advancement. In fact, I have never known a community, whether in this country or in Europe, more zealously devoted to the cause of popular education than the people of this new Territory.

The governor noted also that a need would soon be felt for a territorial college. Colonel Stephen W. Downey, one of the earliest residents of the Territory of Wyoming, had already taken the lead in advocating the establishment of a university. As a member of the territorial legislature in 1871, 1875, and 1877 and as Delegate to Congress in 1878, he was thoroughly versed in the needs of the territory, and in 1886 he sponsored the bill by which the University of Wyoming was created.

On September 6, 1887, the university was opened at Laramie with ex-Governor Hoyt as its first president. Dr. Hoyt, who had been offered the appointment as minister to Spain just previous to his accepting the governorship of Wyoming Territory, was widely traveled and had exceptional qualifications as publicist, educator, and writer. With his guidance the university had a most favorable beginning. The first building erected on the campus was the Liberal Arts College, known now as 'Old Main.' All departments and schools of the university have been kept on one campus, centralizing the State's higher education and making possible the utilization of funds for the employment of outstanding instructors and the purchase of the finest equipment. The university is governed by a board of trustees, appointed by the governor, distinct from the State board of education.

President Hoyt organized the Wyoming Academy of Arts, Sciences, and Letters, and under its auspices many literary and historical meetings were held in which residents of the State, as well as members of the university faculty, participated. This academy was the beginning of university extension work in the State, and through its efforts a State teachers' association was founded in 1891. It existed until 1902 and published a monthly called *The Wyoming School Journal.* The association was revived and reorganized in 1904 and again took up the publication of the magazine.

From time to time short-lived private colleges have been organized. The Wyoming Collegiate Institute at Big Horn was established in 1894 by the Congregational church, and the Sheridan College came into being in 1898. Neither existed long. Jireh College at Jireh, Niobrara County, was maintained by the Christian church from 1909 until 1918. The Big Horn Academy was opened at Lovell in 1909 with 41 students. Organized by the church board of education of the Latter-day Saints, the school held its first term in Lovell and its succeeding sessions in Cowley. Maximum enrollment reached 175 before the academy was converted into a county high school in 1924. The Cheyenne Business College, founded in 1905, filled a special local need and continued for 29 years.

The foundation of the present system of education in the State really dates from 1873, when the legislature reviewed the whole system as provided by the law of 1869 and laid a new groundwork. The territorial librarian was made ex-officio superintendent of public instruction, annual teachers' institutes were provided for, and uniform courses of study were sponsored. Teachers' institutes, either State or county, have been held annually since that time. Uniform textbooks, courses of study for the elementary and secondary schools, and the certification of teachers have been the chief concern of these institutes.

In 1890 the constitutional convention and the first State legislature adopted virtually the same system of education that had been developed during territorial times. Various changes occurred during the ensuing years, but nothing unusual took place until 1915, when the State legislature provided funds for a commission to study the Wyoming public school system, with the aid of experts from the U. S. Bureau of Education. The report of this commission led in 1917 to the enactment of a law creating the office of commissioner of education. This commissioner and the superintendent of public instruction jointly supervised the public school system until about 1919, when the State board of education and the commissioner of education were placed under the supervision of the State superintendent of public instruction. This arrangement now prevails (1940).

The State board of education, composed of seven members appointed by the State superintendent of public instruction, includes the commissioner as secretary. Two of the members are required to be engaged actively in educational work. The State superintendent is a member of the board ex-officio, and, in addition to duties in connection with supervision of schools, serves on numerous other State boards.

The State department of public instruction exercises general supervision of the public school system; assists and directs the work of the schools, particularly in the rural districts; gathers statistics and prepares courses of study, forms, and blanks; supervises certification of teachers; sets up standards for high and elementary schools, for rural school buildings, and for transportation of school children; interprets school laws and assists with school budgets and other school matters; helps county superintendents with rural school problems; and holds conferences with school officials for improving school conditions and promoting an understanding of good school practices.

The department has a well-established vocational educational program in many communities; practical courses are given in agriculture, home economics, trade and industry, rehabilitation, and Americanization. Perhaps the outstanding course is vocational agriculture, planned to teach farmers modern methods and to give them a progressive point of view. Through this latter course three groups are reached: farm boys of school age who attend regular day-school classes; adult farmers who want additional training and who enroll in evening classes; and out-of-school farm boys of school age who want some specialized training. From the supervised farming carried on as a part of the regular vocational program by 883 boys enrolled in classes for 1934–5, the total income was $60,852.60 as against the cost of the training amounting to $29,354.35.

The Union Pacific Railroad recognizes the value of this work, and since 1926 has granted University of Wyoming scholarships to the vocational agriculture students completing the best supervised-farming programs in each county traversed by the railroad. The Work Projects Administration, also, has recognized the need for this type of work and has provided trained men to assist in conducting the courses.

Wyoming holds the enviable position of receiving a larger proportion of its school support from nontaxation sources than any State in the Union. Originally direct taxation provided liberal support to schools in Wyoming; then, through the discovery of oil on State lands, Wyoming began to accumulate the largest financial endowment for public schools, per capita, of any State in the Nation. These State school lands, comprising some 3,500,000 acres, have provided immense returns from sales and royalties to the Permanent School Fund, which in 1936 passed the $20,000,000 mark. One area, referred to as 'Section 36,' in the Salt Creek oil field, Natrona County, became famous at its peak of production as the richest 640 acres in the world. Up to 1936 it paid the State $10,775,000 in royalties, of which 50 per cent went to the school funds and 9 per cent to the university. With this rich endowment supporting its educational system, Wyoming ranked among the 12 States having the lowest percentage of illiteracy, according to a 1932 report of the National Educational Association. In comparison with other western States during a normal year, Wyoming spent as much on education as the average, with 37.93 cents per day per pupil.

The rural schools far outnumber the urban ones in the State. In 1936 there were 1,093 rural schools with an average enrollment per teacher of 11.7 pupils. Out of the 532 routes maintained to transport approximately 10,583 pupils to these schools, 480 were supported by the State.

As no public school facilities are available in Yellowstone Park, the parents of school children there maintain and operate an elementary school, purchasing all schoolroom equipment and supplies as well as paying the salaries of the two teachers. The necessary funds are derived by holding dances or other profit-making entertainments, and all the park operators contribute toward the maintenance of the school.

Much attention is given in Wyoming to the special education of all classes of handicapped children, including the blind, deaf, crippled, and mentally retarded. Before 1911 it was the practice to send juvenile delinquents out of the State: the boys going to the Colorado State Industrial School at Golden and the girls to the House of the Good Shepherd at Denver. Now the boys are sent to the Wyoming Industrial Institute at Worland, the girls to the Girls' Industrial Institute at Sheridan. The Wyoming State Training School is at Lander. A field agent under the State department of education supervises the work with the deaf and blind who are not of school age.

Education of the Indians on the Wind River Reservation began as early as 1870 with the establishment by the Protestant Episcopal church of a school among the Shoshone. This was followed by mission schools. At present (1940) the head community worker in charge of the reservation's educational program endeavors to utilize all teaching aids in the community. Public schools, three mission schools, and a Government day school are in operation. The Government day school is not of the regular academic type, but is organized along practical lines adapted to daily living. About one-eighth of the children attend public school, a few are in local high schools, and several attend the university. The Government pays all tuition. Most of the Arapaho children attend St. Michael's or St. Stephen's missions, both boarding schools on the reservation. A small mission boarding school for Shoshone children is maintained by the Reverend Mr. Roberts near Wind River.

Wyoming was one of the first States to maintain at its own expense a service for the placement of teachers. Authorized by the legislature of 1917, this service provides for registering certificates at the office of the State board of education in Cheyenne. It was also the first State to adopt the system of high school military training devised by Major Edgar Z. Steever. Since 1901 the State has provided free textbooks in the schools.

Education, fostered so eagerly by the pioneers of Wyoming Territory, loyally endorsed by the citizens, and generously supported by the lawmakers, has kept pace with the development of the State.

Sports and Recreation

WYOMING'S first recreational appeal is one of natural setting, the contrast of mountain and plain, of forest and lake and sagebrush waste. Outdoor sports are emphasized, and they are still individual and recreational. There are no professional baseball or football leagues, and no 'booked' horse racing. Although prize fighting was legalized in 1921, no important matches have been held. But Wyoming has 15,000,000 acres of mountain country, with steep game trails in summer and ski slopes in winter. Half of the mountain area is forest; and in the forests are 33,000 elk, 30,000 deer, 2,500 moose, 3,300 mountain sheep, and 2,200 black and grizzly bears. There are 14,846 miles of fishing streams, exclusive of those in national parks, and 107,410 acres of lake water for boating, swimming, and fishing. There are 25,000 antelope on the plains.

Since the times of Bridger and Buffalo Bill, sportsmen have come to the Wyoming plains and mountains to hunt. Many of the bird species that Bridger recommended for the table are gone; others are protected. The ring-necked pheasant today is the only widely hunted nonmigratory game bird, and it is not native to the State.

But all the game mammals, except the buffalo, may be hunted. The only restrictions are on antelope, moose, and mountain sheep; these are hunted with special permit. In 1939, 3,000 antelope permits were authorized, 60 sheep permits, and 50 moose permits.

The best elk hunting is in the green forest area that extends east and south of Yellowstone Park in the western quarter of the State. Here also moose, sheep, and bear are hunted. But antelope, deer, ducks, and geese may be taken within a few miles of arterial highways from Cheyenne to Yellowstone.

For unparalleled natural phenomena there is Yellowstone Park. For sheer grandeur there are the Teton and Wind River peaks. Both of these are approached by arterial highways, but each is penetrated only by winding game trails. Horses and guides are available for short or extended pack trips into these ranges.

Less spectacular but more easily accessible are the Medicine Bow (Snowy Range), Big Horn, Laramie, and Absaroka ranges; all are crossed or skirted by transcontinental highways, and all have lodges and camps to accommodate tourists who have only a day or so to hike or hunt or fish.

Wyoming's most distinctive tourist attractions are the dude ranches. These are of two kinds: the bona-fide cow ranch that keeps an extra bunkhouse or row of cabins for summer visitors, and the lodge that offers the visitor most of the comforts of his urban home and, in addition, a saddle horse and guide in summer or a pair of skis and guide in winter.

More than 100 dude ranches now operate in Wyoming. Most often they are near mountains, close to hunting, fishing, and forests. But wherever there is a tourist highway, there will be dude ranches. Accommodations vary from modern resort hotels to cramped ranch houses with kerosene illumination and outside plumbing. At one extreme, the well-paying guest may order his breakfast in bed, and select his food and drink from menus only half translated from French. At the other, he may sleep in a built-in bunk, bathe in the creek, eat in the kitchen with the family and the hired man, and lend a hand at chores. At both places the hospitality, even if paid for by the hour, has a genuine and spontaneous air.

The living arrangements at most dude ranches are in informal family style, and references are usually required of guests. The conventional dress is Western—blue denim jeans, bright shirts, high-heeled boots, and big hats. The guest's time is his own, but since some planned routine is necessary to entertain the heterogeneous crowd the dude ranch attracts, the mornings are usually devoted to riding, either in guided groups or short rides alone. In afternoons there is more riding, swimming in lakes or streams, or in the ranch pool if it is a large-scale place. At night there are games, dancing, and amateur entertainments around campfires or in recreation halls. Every ranch has at least one banjo and one harmonica 'on the staff,' and old and modern Western music is made at night.

Eating is a major activity on the dude ranch. There are ranch-grown vegetables, beef, mutton, and chicken and, in season, venison, elk, and wild fowl. Usually there is fresh milk from the ranch dairy herd and, consequently, fresh butter and cheese and buttermilk in the cooler. If the ranch is a regular spread, the hands will have done three or four hours' work before breakfast, and there will be fried meats, potatoes, hot cakes, eggs, coffee, and fruit.

At spring and fall roundups on the cow ranches, guests may see from the 'opera boxes' on the corral fence the original rodeo activity— roping and tying for branding or marking. When mornings are cool and every horse has a knot in his back, there are extempore bucking expositions in the wrangling corral. The larger commercial places stage regular small-scale rodeos with stock kept for that purpose. But this 'fair grounding' is scowled at on the regular cow ranch; it is bad for the stock.

Many of the ranches are open the year round, and winter activity varies from skiing and snowshoeing to hauling hay, logging, trapping, skating, sleighing, and tending stock.

Skis have been used in Wyoming ever since the Creightons' Scandinavian linemen used them to maintain the first transcontinental telegraph line in the 1860's. Settlers used them later to get around in the deep snow, and many snow-locked Wyoming communities have been supplied with food by strong men who skied as far as 100 miles with heavy packs strapped to their backs.

Skiing as a sport dates almost as far back, especially among the rural populations of Scandinavian extraction. Often these skiers are pulled by ropes behind saddle horses, sleighs, or automobiles. It is only in recent years that skiing areas have been developed as tourist attractions (see General Information). Hans Teichner, Austrian ski expert and former coach of the Spanish Olympic team, laid out many of the courses in the State and aroused enthusiasm for the sport. Tobogganing, bobsledding, skating, and dogsled racing are other popular winter sports.

Nearly every community in the State has developed municipal ice rinks, usually maintained in co-operation with the Work Projects Administration.

The great community sport in Wyoming is rodeo. When two or more ranch youths get together on a Sunday afternoon, it is inevitable that they will 'ride calves' and call it rodeo. The very term, with the accent on the first syllable, is synonymous with celebration. No Independence Day or Labor Day is considered properly observed without cowboys and bucking animals. No county fair is complete without them. And rodeo is a matter of civic pride. A community that cannot sponsor at least one each season is not progressive.

The smaller shows are more sincere than spectacular. Livestock is contributed from surrounding farms and ranches, prizes are modest, and the riding talent is local. Since capable-looking estrays are frequently impounded for rodeo service, the rodeo committee has opportunity once each year to discipline those among their neighbors who are inclined to pasture their stock on the highways and streets.

The larger shows, Frontier Days (*see Cheyenne*), Sheridan-Wyo Rodeo (*see Sheridan*), Cody Stampede (*see Tour 6c*), and a few others, are well-organized outdoor entertainments that feature all the acts in modern rodeo repertoire, and feature them well: bucking horses and steers, roping, bulldogging, wild-horse races, wild-cow milking, cowboy and cowgirl races. Purses are large enough to attract the best talent in the country.

Even these larger shows are community ventures; the box-office surplus reverts to a permanent rodeo fund and goes to make the next year's show bigger and better. But the crowds bring money to town and business booms; stores and hotels hire extra help, and families sleep in their basements and rent their rooms.

The athletic sports are still amateur. A statewide semiprofessional baseball league exists, and almost every town has its 'semipro' basketball and softball leagues, with teams competing in the names of business houses. But the sponsoring businessman seldom incurs expense beyond the cost of suits and equipment for his athletes. Some district or regional competition goes on between leagues or towns.

There are statewide high school football and basketball leagues and track tournaments. All collegiate athletic competition is either intramural or interstate, since Wyoming University combines all its five colleges on one campus at Laramie. Like the high schools, the State university prescribes at least two years' physical education for all its students and has facilities for fencing, boxing, wrestling, golf, and tennis.

Few Wyoming towns of 1,000 inhabitants are without a golf course and half a dozen tennis courts, and statewide tennis and golf associations have annual tournaments in Casper. Badminton and polo are played, and some fine polo ponies are bred at Big Horn and near Cheyenne. The Big Horn Polo Club is a member of the United States Polo Association, and games are played with teams from surrounding ranches on the Gallatin and Moncreiffe Fields. Casper also has polo clubs, and United States Army teams compete on the Fort Francis E. Warren field at Cheyenne.

Trapshooting clubs, rifle clubs, and pistol clubs over the State continue a Wyoming tradition that there is honor in knowing guns and how to work them. Torrington, Casper, Laramie, Evanston, Sheridan, and Burns have annual trapshooting meets; the Wyoming Rifle Association encourages its members to shoot for trophies in national competition, and State rifle and pistol meets are conducted by the National Guard.

Nearly every community has its little-theater groups, and various town hall organizations promote lyceum lectures, minor concerts, theatrical productions, and other amusements. Laramie, where the university subsidizes entertainment, takes the lead. But the schools, churches, cinemas, and the Saturday night dance are universals in Wyoming social life. Their importance varies inversely with the size of the community, but few Wyoming towns are large enough to be unaffected by the pattern they impose.

Folklore and Folkways

THE cowboy is the most important figure in Wyoming folklore. In this country of strong wills and tastes, there is a local fondness for the tradition of the cowpuncher's regalia and his feats at corral and bar. Less commonly understood is the fact that calf-roping and bronco-busting are chores that the ranch hand may be called on to perform a dozen times a day in the course of earning his 'forty dollars and found.' Common apparel also has been a source of wonderment to visitors, who usually do not know that the big hat, the loose shirt, the leather chaps, and the high-heeled boots are strictly utilitarian in purpose; that the jaunty effect of the costume is a by-product albeit a prized one. However, familiar tests of strength and endurance and the stories that spread the cowboy's fame through bunkhouse and parlor represent a type of American folklore that is still in the making. Yarn-spinning is inspired by hours in the saddle. The tales 'traded' give life and currency to such expressions as 'cow sense,' 'chew it finer,' 'maverick,' 'raking a horse,' 'rustler,' 'hog tie,' and 'running iron.' And in the glow of roundup fires, tales of fearless men and horses, blazing suns and congealing winters, still make the rounds and grow better with telling.

Sometimes the cowboy sang with his fellows or alone on the night ride. Typical themes were the cowman's life and loves, and the beauty of prairies and mountains. Many of the songs followed the longhorns up from the Southwest; others originated in the State. They were usually melancholy, full of pathos and love of mother and home. Most often they were quiet and in contrast to the accepted notion of the carefree, roving cowboy (*see Music*).

Throughout the Rocky Mountain and Plains region, and especially in Wyoming, ghosts and restless spirits are rare. A few phantom riders have been known, especially where unexplained killings have occurred. Above one famous hot spring in the Big Horn Basin a pale man on a white horse floats in the mist. Ghost lights appear in a small area south of Newcastle on the old Morrisey Road; some say they emanate as fox fire from the soil. There are haunted tunnels on the old Cross Anchor Ranch where murders were once committed. Here at night moans and groans and angry voices rise above the rustle of shuffled cards and the clack of poker chips.

There are tales of buried loot in the mountain country. Many lost mines—Lost Cabin, Lost Soldier, Lost Shovel, and Lost Dutchman— are still being sought. Slade's Canyon near Guernsey Lake and Cache Creek in Jackson Hole are two of many places believed to conceal the ill-gotten gain of early freebooters—Jack Slade, the Jameses, Butch Cassidy, Big Nose George, Teton Jackson—whose names now are folklore.

Social life in Wyoming has centered in the ranch. At first diversion was limited to poker, song, and narrative; but as families and community life developed, gayer entertainment helped fill long winter evenings. There were country dances attended by families from 50 miles away, who brought with them their contributions to the midnight lunch. After refreshments the dancing continued usually until day. Similar parties are still frequent in the range country. Some of them combine the older dance measures with the new; in other cases, dancing is limited to the quadrille, the sylvan glide, and other old and graceful steps.

Evidence of the cattle and Indian frontiers' influence on the popular mind is seen in the many Wild West shows, rodeos, and parades held throughout the State in the summer.

During the period of free land and migration, Wyoming became the home of many nationalities—Italians and Greeks in mining, Scandinavians in logging, Mexicans and Russian-Germans in the beet-raising centers, Basques in the north-central part of the State, Chinese along the Union Pacific Railroad, together with Hungarians, Czechs, Slovaks, Danes, Englishmen, Irishmen, Esthonians, and Japanese. These have helped settle and build up the State, and have become an integral part of Wyoming life, past and present.

Several ethnic groups have preserved Old-World cultural traits in the new environment. At the beginning of the century Hartville was populated almost exclusively by Italian and Greek mine laborers who had no intention of becoming American citizens. They had come to this country to earn as much as they might and to return to their original homes. There was no community consciousness, and spare pennies were sent back to 'the old country' to be invested or held by relatives until the day of returning. These immigrants spoke the mother tongue, followed old-country customs, and learned only such English as their work required.

Not all, however, returned to the old country, and their native-born children attended American schools and demanded American clothing and food. Many of them spoke nothing but English in their homes and, as they matured, scoffed at the idea of going to a foreign land. When America entered the World War, the sons fought in the United States army. Today Hartville is typical of many American communities in which Old-World traits are being assimilated or discarded by succeeding generations.

Greek-Americans at the funeral services of a countryman follow the traditional and impressive rite of their homeland. Each person is given a taper to hold during the reading of the service and the responses. The priest lights the first taper and the rest are lighted one from the other. Incense is burned and tiny bells are rung. If the deceased is unmarried, a bridal wreath is placed upon the head and a wedding ring on the finger to symbolize a wedding with death. Formerly the coffin was carried to the little Hartville cemetery on the shoulders of the men, with priest and mourners following on foot. At present modern conveyances are used.

The Dante Alighieri Society, a fraternal organization of Hartville Italians, holds an annual August celebration at which the chief attractions are Italian food and wines and singing from such operas as *Il Trovatore* and *Carmen*. At night there is dancing for the younger people, and older couples perform the tarantella, a brilliant measure from old Italy.

Rock Springs is known as the 'melting pot' of Wyoming. Into this coal-mining community have poured Italians, Greeks, Russians, Finns, Irish, Chinese, and Negroes. As fellow workers, with common needs and interests, they have mingled with good will for half a century.

Many of the Chinese came to the United States to work as section hands on the Union Pacific Railroad and as miners in the coal fields. During the labor riots of 1885 (*see Tour 2c*), they left the mines to open laundries and cafes. Once intensely patriotic, they were widely known for their parades and celebrations. Their Joss House at Evanston was one of three in the United States and one of the city's most important buildings. On Chinese New Year, about February 10, thousands came to worship there and to celebrate with firecrackers. The design of the building was elaborate. Carved panels flanked the door, and within were banners and richly embroidered draperies. Behind gates of carved teakwood was an altar, delicately fashioned of the same wood, on which a joss stick burned before an idol. Shortly after the labor trouble of 1885, the Chinese were driven from the neighborhood. The Joss House burned to the ground in 1922.

There have been comparatively few Negroes in Wyoming, and most of these have remained in the southern part of the State because of early resentment against them in other districts. Cheyenne has two Negro churches. The Searchlight Club in that city devotes itself to the preservation of old Negro hymns and to the poetry of Paul Laurence Dunbar.

In Cheyenne and Casper a few Filipinos work in the hotels. A small number have prospered through their interests in petroleum developments.

Another important unit in the social structure of Wyoming is the Mormon population in Star Valley, Big Horn Basin, and the fertile ranching areas in the southwestern corner of the State. The dynamic personalities of the early leaders of the Church of Jesus Christ of Latter-day Saints left their mark on the outlook of present day Mormons, and institutions designed half a century ago to meet the needs of a frontier society still function. Church-sponsored socioreligious organizations are dominant in isolated communities. Beginning with 'Primary classes' at four or five years, the Mormon child's life is taken up with an array of organizations and duties, both social and religious, planned to provide him with leisure-time activities that are both recreational and instructive. From Primary, Mormon girls graduate into Beehive, Campfire, Seagull, and Gleaner Girls organizations; boys become Cubs, Trailbuilders, Boy Scouts, and 'M' Men. The Mutual Improvement Association ('M' Men and 'M' Women) performs a function similar to the Y.M.C.A. and the Y.W.C.A. in other communities. It sponsors regional programs in dancing, reading, drama, rhetoric, debating, religious education, and athletics. The Relief Society, whose name suggests its original function in a pioneer background, is a sort of official sewing circle. The quaintest holdover from the pioneer social order is the 'Old Folks' Party,' a gathering comparable to quilting or log-rolling bees of an older tradition, except that work is not the reason for the gathering. These co-operative functions are held once each year in all Mormon communities whose populations are not so large as to hinder their success. They are usually held during winter months when chores are less confining, and they are open to all married members of the ward. Refreshments are important: meats, cakes, jellies, and pies are prepared in the home and contributed by those who will attend, according to assignments made by the committee in charge. Early on the day appointed, the church custodian 'fires up' the chapel and the 'old folks' come—in automobiles, bobsleds, on horseback, afoot. A few of the benches are reserved as baby depositories, and the others are stacked against the walls to make room for eating, visiting, and dancing. All activities are suspended at nightfall and resumed after chores are done.

Pioneer Day (July 24) is observed in Mormon communities to retell the story of the Great Trek to Salt Lake Valley in 1847. A parade displays handcarts, ox teams and covered wagons; men and women don the clothes their ancestors wore, and carry the guns and cooking utensils their grandparents carried 2,000 miles across mountains and plains. A terrific whoop announces an Indian attack. Wagons are corralled at this signal and a grand sham battle reminds onlookers of the dangers and terrors their forefathers knew three-quarters of a century ago. Details are realistic and accurate, arranged by old-timers who either 'were there' themselves or remember the tales of others. There is usually a rodeo and, at night, dancing and singing.

The story of the Three Nephites, survivors of the original Church of Mormon who cannot die, is a variant of the legend of the Wandering Jew. Christ himself exempted the trio from death as a reward for faithfulness, and they commune freely between heaven and earth, bearing messages, warnings, and advice from deceased relatives and friends. Most often they wear white flowing robes, and always they appear together. Their favorite manifestation is to appear simultaneously in widely separated parts of Mormondom, then drop from sight as suddenly. More common are the 'Evil Spirits' that attack a body with the idea of taking possession; prayer is the only effective weapon against them.

Range Country

Photograph by Charles J. Belden

TRAILING FROM THE SUMMER RANGE

Photograph by Charles J. Belden

BRANDING THE CALVES

THE FINE ART OF FORE-FOOTING

Photograph by Charles J. Belden

Photograph by Charles J. Belden

WRANGLER

OFF TO THE ROUNDUP

Photograph by Charles J. Belden

FEED LOT

Photograph by Dan Healy

Photograph by Rothstein; courtesy of Farm Security Administration

SHEEP WAGON

SHEARING

Photograph by Rothstein; courtesy of Farm Security Administration

Photograph by Charles J. Belden

AT THE CRACK OF DAWN

Photograph by Charles J. Belden

COW COUNTRY STYLE Photograph by Charles J. Belden

Photograph by Charles J. Belden **POT LUCK**

Photograph by Charles J. Belden

BUNKHOUSE STUD

Literature

IF ALL that has been written in or concerning Wyoming were taken collectively as Wyoming literature, the State would have a century-old literary tradition. It would be necessary, however, to distinguish between works written about Wyoming by people outside the State and those written by Wyoming authors. And Wyoming writers would have to be subdivided into those who came to the State as mere visitors and those who have remained permanently.

Trappers, explorers, missionaries, and soldiers started writing about Wyoming when what is now the State was a vast semidesert, a place to cross as quickly as possible and to tell about later. These adventurers wrote copiously of the physical environment and of the rigors of life on the frontier. Few of the diaries or journals were written with literary intent. It remained for more skillful writers to draw from the maze of details, compass readings, and colloquial observations a picture of the Wyoming of that day.

The most attractive early account, if not the most fully documented, is included in the volumes written by Washington Irving as chronicler of John Jacob Astor's American Fur Company. Irving's *Astoria; or Anecdotes of an Enterprise beyond the Rocky Mountains* (1836) weaves into narrative a vast amount of material, letters, journals, and descriptions by travelers, trappers, and commercial agents, including the diaries of Wilson Price Hunt and Robert Stuart, Astor associates. Hunt's party, on the way from St. Louis to the mouth of the Columbia River, crossed Wyoming in 1811; and Stuart led a return party in 1811–13 (*see History*). The original diaries were not published until 1935, when Philip Ashton Rollins edited them with interpretive notes as *The Discovery of the Oregon Trail.*

The Rocky Mountains: or, Scenes, Incidents and Adventures in the Far West (1837), which Irving based upon the unpublished journals of Captain B. L. E. Bonneville, described the Wind River Mountains and the Green River area in western Wyoming; it testifies that the

Wind Rivers are 20,000 feet high. The book has been reprinted as *The Adventures of Captain Bonneville*.

The immediate success of Irving's books interested others in the Western scene, and during the century that followed, numerous writers reported their own and others' experiences on the Indian frontier.

Of these the most notable, perhaps, were General John C. Frémont's *Memoirs* (1845–56); Francis Parkman's *California and Oregon Trail,* which appeared in 1849 when the romance of the Oregon road was growing; T. D. Bonner's *Life and Adventures of James P. Beckwourth* (1856), a saga of the most celebrated liar on the early frontier (*see Tour* 9); Mark Twain's *Roughing It* (1872), which chronicled Clemens's stagecoach journey from Missouri to Carson City, Nevada, in 1861; General Hiram M. Chittenden's *The American Fur Trade in the Far West* (1902) and *Life, Letters and Travels of Father Pierre Jean De Smet* (1905); Le Roy R. Hafen's *The Overland Mail* (1926), *Broken Hand* (1931), written in collaboration with W. J. Ghent, and *Fort Laramie and the Pageant of the West* (1938), of which Francis Marion Young is coauthor. None of these writers lived in Wyoming. Harrison C. Dale, author of *Ashley-Smith Explorations* (1918), wrote his account while a professor of political science at the University of Wyoming, using the original diaries of Major General William H. Ashley and Jedediah S. Smith, who traveled during the early days in Wyoming and the West.

Since R. E. Strahorn brought out his *Handbook of Wyoming* in 1877, there have been numerous excursions into the general history of the State. *The History of Nevada, Colorado, and Wyoming* (1890) was one of the famous series of studies of the West issued by Hubert Howe Bancroft. C. G. Coutant, State historian for many years, was the first to attempt a comprehensive study, but his work was stopped by financial difficulties. The first volume of his *History of Wyoming* (1899), the only volume printed, went as far as the organization of Wyoming Territory in 1869.

Exhaustive surveys of Wyoming history were conducted by Dr. Grace Raymond Hebard (1861–1936), for 40 years librarian and professor of history at the University of Wyoming. She published 14 volumes and numerous articles, often drawing upon previously untouched sources. Outstanding among her works are *Pathbreakers from River to Ocean* (1911), *The Bozeman Trail* (1922), *Washakie* (1930), and *Sacajawea* (1933); the latter was the result of 30 years' research into the life of 'the Boat Woman' who piloted Lewis and Clark's expedition across the continent (*see Tour 5b*).

A post-war movement to identify pioneer landmarks and rechart trails has kindled a new interest in regional history, and several works of local importance have been printed. I. S. Bartlett's *History of Wyoming* (1918) is a forerunner of this trend, and Frances Birkhead Beard's *Wyoming from Territorial Days to the Present* (1933) is an outstanding contribution. Historical monographs have been published by Alfred J. Mokler, Robert B. David, Dan Greenburg, Agnes Wright Spring, Tacetta Walker, W. C. Deming, Elsa Spear Edwards, Doris Garst, and others.

The first nationally known writer to whom Wyoming has claim is Edgar Wilson (Bill) Nye (1850–96) (*see Laramie*). Nye was in Wyoming only seven years, and most of his best-known works were produced after he returned East. But it was on the Wyoming frontier that he found the material. for the characteristic subject matter and style of his humor.

There was a world of marvels west of the Mississippi in the 1870's and 1880's. Towns appeared in a day and were gone the next. Paupers became millionaires and paupers again in an evening. The wife of Leadville Johnny Brown burned $300,000 in paper money her husband had hidden in their cook stove, and Brown consoled her with the promise that he would make her a million the next day. He did. So did Tabor, Bonfils, Quealy, and a hundred others. Prospectors 'salted' a Wyoming mesa with tooled diamonds, pearls, rubies, and sapphires, and bilked the Rothschilds, Tiffany, and Horace Greeley out of half a million dollars. Men hid gold fortunes in tin cans and paupers found them; 'long riders' robbed mines and pay-roll trains and spent their money freely over hand-carved bars. And all the while the Englishmen were paying thousands of dollars for mythical cattle, and Colter's Hell was steaming.

There was credulity, extravagance, burlesque, and a taste for contrast. There were hardships and disappointments, but always optimism. Music, books, art, and theaters were rare; but men could laugh, and they rewarded those who furnished something to laugh at.

It was to this frontier that Nye came as a young man in 1876, and the story of his career sums up one side of the 'Gilded Age' in which he matured. Arriving in Wyoming with 35¢ in his pocket, he became justice of the peace, United States commissioner, postmaster, editor, correspondent for regional newspapers, staff writer for the New York

World, and a platform lecturer with James Whitcomb Riley. When he died at 46, Nye left his family nearly half a million dollars.

Nye's early work, published in the hand-set columns of the Laramie *Daily Sentinel* and the Laramie *Boomerang,* often suffered by the casual way it was produced. His humor relies almost entirely on irreverence, gross exaggeration, unexpected comparisons, and verbal contrast. It rarely reaches the level of the social comment or satire of Mark Twain or Josh Billings. He was best when laughing at conventionality or snobbery.

'The . . . ball was disposed of last evening,' Nye reported on his society page in 1880. 'Edward Ivinson was resplendent in demi-skirt and California undershirt, held in place with imported suspenders . . . Henry Wagner wore an organdie paletot, with inlaid burlaps, looped back with moire antique, hair done up in pampador wads . . . C. W. Spaulding wore a gross grain Russia iron applique, with corsage of tin roofing held in place with buckskin strings. J. H. Hayford [Nye's employer] wore his usual thoughtful expression and gold-bowed eye glasses. This costume was set off to good effect by a chew of fine cut tobacco, wore plain.' When Jesse James was reported killed for the tenth time, Nye observed, 'Another terrible mortality has broken out among the James boys.' His most widely read volumes are *Bill Nye and the Boomerang* (1881), *Forty Liars and Other Lies* (1882), and *Baled Hay* (1884).

Merris Clark Barrow, Nye's disciple and associate who wrote under the name 'Bill Barlow,' also won an audience for his humor and philosophy. From the middle 1890's until his death in 1910, Barlow published *Sagebrush Philosophy,* whose title is suggestive of its content.

Perhaps the most brilliant and unaffected expression, however, of the later frontier was by word of mouth. The cowboy was the creative genius here, and the native ranchman, the speculator, and the yeoman communicated in a language rich in vigorous similes and anecdotes deeply rooted in Western experience. In his own language, the cowboy was a 'man with guts and a horse.' When a companion met sudden death, which usually happened at night, it was 'no breakfast, forever' for him. And if he were trampled to death by a thousand hoofs, those who found him might feel their guts 'turn to fiddlestrings.'

On the long trail to market or to better grass, or riding the summer range, or during the long hours on the 'graveyard stretch,' Wyoming men recited poems and songs heard in childhood, in dance halls, road houses, brothels, or around trail fires. When his repertoire was limited, the range rider improvised new verses to old melodies (*see Music*) and retold and modified stories he had heard.

The cowboy's manner of living did not last long enough to crystallize into literature. When the big ranches broke up, he lost his distinctive social position and became a farmer; the pitchfork and shovel replaced *la reata* and the single-action Colt. But his idiom is important today in the Western vernacular, and some day it may produce important effects in a regional literature.

The flowering of romantic and historical fiction during the 1890's and early 1900's brought a boom in Western romances, done mostly by casual visitors from the East who exploited the Wyoming scene for its color. These were attracted quite naturally to the cowboy as a picturesque type, rather than to the actual social life of the ranch country. A few of these visiting writers came in time to find the cowboy as he was; fewer succeeded in portraying him as they found him. Ranch life was, however, described in several works by men who knew the subject at first hand. Frank Wilkeson's 'Cattle-raising on the Plains' ran in *Harper's* in 1888. Moreton Frewen, director of the vast Powder River Cattle Company and father of Claire Sheridan (English author and sculptor), returned to England and set down his memoirs during his old age in *Melton Mowbray* (1924). John Clay, the Scottish gentleman who managed the Swan or Two-Bar Outfit, largest cattle outfit Wyoming ever had, published *My Life on the Range* (1924).

In the van of the romancers was Emerson Hough, whose *Story of the Cowboy* (1897), *Story of the Outlaw* (1906), and *The Passing of the Frontier* (1918) dealt at length with the Wyoming environment. A year before his death in 1923, Hough published his most popular work, *The Covered Wagon,* a romantic rehearsal of the fact and legend of America's most famous pioneer highway, the Oregon Trail.

The most popular raconteur of Western ranch tales contemporary with Hough was Owen Wister. Wister's *Lin McLean* (1898) and *The Virginian* (1902) drew heavily from the cow-country locale and assured the cowboy a place in American fiction. Russell Blankenship describes the 'Virginian' as the respectable ancestor of the whole flock of tawdry descendants done by later hack writers, of which Wyoming produced its share.

General Charles King, stationed at Fort Laramie for a few years, was a prolific writer of action novels from 1890 until 1915. Many of his stories were laid in the West he had known as a soldier. *Laramie, Queen of Bedlam* (1909) was set in Fort Laramie. In a different vein is Elinore Pruitt Stewart's *Letters of a Woman Homesteader,* written from Burntfork, which ran in *The Atlantic Monthly* and in 1914 appeared in volume form.

Zane Grey paused in Wyoming and found attractive material in the early scene. His *U. P. Trail* (1918) fictionized the building of the Union Pacific Railroad across Wyoming in the late 1860's.

Mary Roberts Rinehart's *Breaking Point* (1924) and *Lost Ecstasy* (1927) emphasize the rigors of Wyoming ranch life. She has a summer home at Wolf. Elizabeth Page, whose historical novels are careful records of changes taking place in American thought and culture, spent five years at Basin collecting material for *Wagons West* (1930) and *Wild Horses and Gold* (1936). The former was based on the letters that an ancestor, Henry Page, wrote to his wife while traveling over the Oregon Trail in 1849. *Wild Horses and Gold* tells the experience of Sheriff F. B. Wickwire of Big Horn County, who drove a herd of 70 horses from the Big Horn Basin to the Klondike during the gold rush of 1899. *The Tree of Liberty* (1939), Mrs. Page's most ambitious and widely known novel, gives a fictional account of half a century of American Colonial and Revolutionary history.

Anticipating the muckraking era, Asa Shinn Mercer, Cheyenne newspaperman, issued in 1894 his *Banditti of the Plains, or The Cattlemen's Invasion of Wyoming—'The Crowning Infamy of the Ages,'* a partisan exposé of the 'feudal system' imposed on the Western range country by powerful cattle magnates, and of the big ranchers' part in the Johnson County War (*see Tour 3a, b*).

Wyoming's first native novelist was Charles E. Winter of Casper, attorney, promoter, and congressman. His *Grandon of Sierra* (1907) and *Ben Warman* (1917) utilize the Saratoga-Encampment background, where Winter helped develop a mining industry (*see Tour 2B*). In 1932 he published *Four Hundred Million Acres,* a documentary discussion of public land uses.

Perhaps the best-known writers of modern Wyoming are Struthers and Katherine Newlin Burt, who since 1908 have spent their summers writing at their ranch in Jackson Hole. Burt, former Princeton University professor, is a poet and novelist. Of his 13 published volumes, *In the High Hills* (1914) and *The Diary of a Dude Wrangler* (1924) represent an Easterner's reaction to the West. *Powder River* (1938), a story of the stream that has come to symbolize Wyoming and the cow country, is refreshing in its perspective and style. Critics have acclaimed it the best volume ever written about Wyoming.

Mrs. Burt, fiction editor of the *Ladies' Home Journal* (1939), has written 14 novels since coming to Wyoming, including *The Branding Iron* (1919) and *When Beggars Choose* (1937).

Allied to the work of Struthers Burt in setting and treatment are the novels and short stories of Caroline Lockhart and Hal Evarts, occasional Wyoming residents. Miss Lockhart for several years owned and published the *Cody Enterprise,* a weekly newspaper, and in 1939 was president of the Cody Stampede Association. On her Circle Slash Heart Ranch near Yellowstone Park, Miss Lockhart has written several novels of the Wyoming scene. *The Lady Doc* (1912) retold the experiences of a woman medical practitioner in early Wyoming. Her portrayal of Cody background and characters was more spirited than flattering. Other Lockhart volumes that have to do with the Western locale are *The Fighting Shepherdess* (1919) and *Old West and New* (1933).

In 1919 Evarts was snowbound on a ranch in western Wyoming. To while away the winter months he wrote a story. It was immediately successful, and until his death in 1935 he published numerous action stories and novels; several were reproduced on the screen. One popular Evarts creation, *Silent Call* (1920), was filmed as *Strongheart*. In 1923 he was elected president of the Western Writers Association at Cody, an organization dedicated to the 'preservation of the romance and fascination of the West,' and he became the champion of a movement to extend the areas of national parks and game preserves in Wyoming.

Wyoming poets have written of the rugged scenery, of the romantic cowboy, of Indian lore, and of life on the ranch and in the mining camps. Some of their verse is reflective and in minor key, but much of it attempts to evoke a romantic frontier of melodrama and pageantry. The ballads and rhymed homilies of Captain Jack Crawford (1847–1917) are in simple meter, but keen and authentic in the use of dialect. In contrast, *The Heavenly Dykes* (1904), the only published volume of Dr. June E. Downey, late professor of psychology at the University of Wyoming, contains sensitive and introspective verses that their author composed for her own enjoyment. Agnes Mathilde Wergeland, member of a distinguished Norwegian family of poets, artists, and statesmen, and a pupil of Edvard Grieg, with whom she made several public appearances as pianist in Bergen and Stockholm, came to Wyoming in 1902 as chairman of the State university's department of history. She wrote several notable historical monographs dealing with European politics, which were published after her death in 1914, and also issued two volumes of verse in her native tongue, *Amerika 'og Andre Digte* (1912) and *Efertadle Digte* (1914).

E. Richard Shipp, Casper attorney, aroused local interest with his books of verse in praise of Wyoming, published privately between 1916 and his death in 1932. Porter Coolidge of Lander, also a lawyer, has published verses with Indian themes. Sara Trousdale Mallory, wife of a university professor at Laramie, published a single volume, *Mnemonic and Other Verses* (1935). Three privately published books by C. P. Arnold, Laramie attorney, contain vigorous, thoughtful verse.

The poet Ted Olson, who is also a journalist and short-story writer, is a native of Wyoming (Laramie). In 1928 Olson was awarded the Younger Poets' prize by *Poetry* and published a slender volume, *A Stranger and Afraid*, in the Yale Series of Younger Poets. His poems have also appeared in *Voices, Saturday Review of Literature, Harper's, New Republic, American Mercury*, and *Frontier and Midland*. Olson edited the Laramie *Republican-Boomerang* for a decade, and in 1938 returned to a position he had formerly occupied on the editorial staff of the New York *Herald Tribune*. While Olson can hardly be classified as a regional writer, his titles, landscapes, and moods often reflect the geography and thinking of his locality; and his short-stories in *Story, Frontier and Midland, Harper's*, and other magazines reveal an understanding of the people whose roots are in the soil of the western plains.

The single novel of Olga Moore (Arnold), *Windswept* (1937), especially in its opening chapters, has something of the flavor of the author's native north-central Wyoming. Since 1922 Mrs. Bonnie Hunter of Thermopolis has written short stories for the popular magazines; other short-story writers are Dell Deloe Orndorff of Casper, Floribel Muir Morrison of Rock Springs (now of New York), Ida McPherson of Sheridan, Lucy Terrill Keller of Sheridan and Hollywood, William F. Bragg of Thermopolis, and Dee Linford (Langford) of Cheyenne. The stories of Lorene Pearson of Laramie are reflective studies, concerned with intellectual currents in a land that is losing its agrarian character.

Names linked to Wyoming are those of George Abbott, New York playwright, who for several years was a Federal employee in Cheyenne; Harold G. Merriam, Wyoming's first Rhodes scholar, editor in Missoula, Montana, of the literary magazine, *Frontier and Midland;* and G. Edward Pendray, former science editor of the *Literary Digest*, whose novels of science, *Earth Tubes* (1929) and *Men, Mirrors and Stars* (1935), were published over the pseudonym 'Gawain Edwards.'

Formerly Dean of the University of West Virginia Law School and professor of law at Harvard, Thurman Arnold, Assistant United States Attorney General, was born and received his early education in Laramie. There is a trace of Bill Nye in his two widely read books, in which he pokes solemn fun at American folkways. In his first published volume, *The Symbols of Government* (1935), Arnold made an ingenious examination of the symbolic patterns underlying legal and social institutions. His *Folklore of Capitalism* (1937), which continued his analysis of the prejudices, contradictions, and ceremonial functions inherent in public behavior, has aroused much controversy. Some critics hailed it as the 'rallying post of long-lost left wing liberals' and as the 'work of an anatomist of social behavior'; while Henry Hazlitt, writing in the *Saturday Review of Literature,* and thinking perhaps of Arnold's tendency to justify as 'human' a great many abusive practives, appraised it as the work of an academic Ed Wynn who would have us laugh our way into fascism.

For a small institution (52 years old, 2,000 enrollment), the University of Wyoming has contributed liberally to scholarship and scientific literature. Dr. Aven Nelson, botanist and president emeritus of the State university (former president of the Botanical Society of America), is an international authority on Rocky Mountain flora. The late June Etta Downey published seven books and more than 70 articles in the field of psychology, showing a special interest in the psychology of literary creation. Dr. F. L. Nussbaum, professor of history, is an international authority on the economics of pre-revolutionary France. His *History of the Economic Institutions of Europe* (1933) won wide critical attention, and in 1939 he was working on a volume for the *Harper Series on the Rise of Modern Europe*. Clarence Morris of the law faculty published a little volume, *How Lawyers Think,* in 1937, and W. O. Clough of the English department wrote the *History of the University of Wyoming* for the school's golden jubilee in 1937. He also was literary editor of Ted Olson's *Republican-Boomerang* for ten years, and has contributed verse and articles to regional literary magazines.

Ann Winslow (Verna Elizabeth Grubbs) and Dr. Clara F. McIntyre of the State university have done much to stimulate new writers to expression. Dr. McIntyre, associated with the department of English since 1913, has published short stories and articles, and is editor of *Parchment,* National Quill Club magazine. Miss Winslow, founder and present editor of *College Verse,* publication of the College Poetry Society of America, has been at Laramie since 1936. Her *Trial Balances* (1935) is an anthology of younger American poets. In 1938 she inspired the establishment of a Robert Frost Library of Poetry at the university; Frost himself contributed 19 volumes of poetry and several unpublished manuscripts. A statewide association has been formed to promote the growth of the library.

Wyoming student poets and writers have been contributors to both *Parchment* and *College Verse*. Of these, the most conspicuous is Alan Swallow of Powell. In 1937 the College Poetry Society named Swallow one of the three outstanding college poets in the United States. His poems have appeared in *College Verse, Voices, Poetry, Frontier and Midland, Kleidograph,* and in smaller regional magazines and journals of verse. He has also experimented with criticism and the short story.

No Cather or Sandoz has yet told the story of Wyoming—of the brutality of the frontier, of the feudal land system, the grass and wire wars, the graft and political maneuvering, the hardy folk who killed and plundered in their passion for land, the vast sage areas and forested mountains that supply life to hundreds of thousands of cattle and sheep, of the life of farm folk, and the harshness and tragedy of the dry years. Wyoming literature is still at the beginning of its career. But in the work of the younger writers, including the *émigrés* to eastern cities and colleges, there is promise of a literary understanding of the past of the State that will give this region an important place in American literature.

The Theater

THE Julesburg Theatrical Troupe, Wyoming's first dramatic performers, reached Cheyenne by stagecoach, wheels rumbling and
harness jingling, in September 1867, preceding the coming of the Union
Pacific Railroad by approximately 60 days. The town itself was then
only three months old. The first issue of the city's pioneer newspaper,
the *Cheyenne Leader,* announced the troupe with the comment, 'A
general desire to witness theatrical performances renders their arrival
very welcome just now.' Eleven days later the *Leader* reported: 'A
Mr. King and a Mr. Metcalf from the theatre at Julesburg, Colo.,
are making preparations to offer Cheyenneites first-class entertainment
in the histrionic art.'

Accordingly a building some 80 by 26 feet was thrown together in
less than a week, with 'parquet, dress circle, private boxes and all modern improvement.' This was called the King Theatre, and its career
began with a variety entertainment, popular at that time, consisting
of dramatic, minstrel, acrobatic, and vocal numbers.

In rapid succession came the Variety Theatre, Melodeon Hall, Beevaise Hall, the Theatre Comique, and other entertainment halls, which
usually combined, under one roof, saloon, gambling house, and theater.
In some instances all three were in one room.

From 1867 to 1882 Cheyenne supported six theaters that offered
legitimate productions and at least 17 variety halls. There were undoubtedly more than 17 of the latter, but no record remains except
of those that used newspaper advertising.

Although these early theaters were frequented chiefly by a conglomerate group of rough, restless, railroad workers, frontiersmen, gamblers, demimondaines, and outlaws, an effort was made by some of
the theater managers to cater to all the citizens of the town. On December 7, 1867, the Melodeon announced that 'Ladies may now attend
this place of amusement with impunity. The management is determined
to preserve strict order and will allow no disreputable characters admis-

sion to the hall.' The Theatre Comique advertised: 'On Tuesday and Friday. Entertainment designed especially for ladies. No smoking or drinking permitted. On other nights of the week cigars and beer may be had during the performance.' In one edition of the *Leader* the editor warned: 'We respectfully advise the manager of the Melodeon to "shut down" on a certain class of comic songs, if he would desire a remunerative business.'

Responding to the rapid shifts of population in the path and wake of the railroad as it was extended across Wyoming, the Cheyenne theaters changed hands, names, and managers almost overnight. Among the early theater managers, Jim McDaniels was outstanding. The 'professor,' as he called himself, was a born showman, trained under P. T. Barnum. He was exceedingly resourceful and could arrange elaborate programs in short order. Although small in stature, he was courageous, and on one occasion stopped a fight among 100 armed men. A number of times he was roughly handled during melees in his theater and twice (once in Cheyenne and once in Leadville, Colorado) was thrown from the gallery to the pit, sustaining serious injuries.

Arriving in Cheyenne in 1867, McDaniels converted the Planter's House, a hotel formerly called Beevaise Hall, into a museum where he exhibited stereoscopic views. Quickly the place grew into McDaniels Variety Theatre.

One of the hundreds of humorous advertisements written by Mc-Daniels for the newspapers, reads as follows:

> Astronomical eclipses are of infrequent occurrence, but there is an eclipse taking place on Eddy St., daily and nightly. It is Professor McDaniels' Museum, which eclipses every other place of amusement in Cheyenne . . . Ye Gods! What nectar the Professor concocts in those China mugs. Better than the dew on a Damsel's lips. Speaking of damsels just step into the Museum and you'll see 'em, large as life, besides 1,000 other sciences, embracing every known subject. It is an awe-inspiring view.
> The dogmatical and surreptitiously concentrated stultification of extraneous baboons may be heterogeneous hypothesis, all of which, we politely assert has nothing to do with Mac's cigars, T. & Js., elevated ornithological tails made of gin, 'or any other man.'

During the first eight months of 1868, McDaniels added to his stock of museum pieces various stuffed animals, including American and Egyptian porcupines, white parrots, anacondas, monkeys, and apes. Later in the year he took the collection to Denver, where he exhibited it at the Territorial Fair, and in the 1870's he made regular annual trips to Colorado. One of his prize exhibits was Miss Charlotte Temple, the 'English Giantess.'

In 1871 the McDaniels building contained a spacious saloon, which took up all the large central section; at the sides were a business office, rooms and parlors for guests, an auditorium, and a museum. After the building had been damaged by fire in 1875 and by a cave-in of the roof after the historic storm of 1876, McDaniels took over the New Dramatic Theatre, originally called the Gold Room, a two-story structure hastily thrown together from lumber that had been transported by bull teams from Omaha. During its earliest years such well-known characters as Wild Bill Hickok, Calamity Jane, Buffalo Bill, and Kit Carson had been patrons of the Gold Room. McDaniels renovated and changed it into a structure 132 feet deep and 48 feet wide with a 'dozen elegantly fitted private boxes and four commodious parlors, in addition to a dress circle and parquet with seating facilities for 800.' One of the highly popular entertainers in the new theater the first season was Mlle Cerito, a danseuse and vocalist. During the Black Hills gold rush in the late 1870's, when daily stages ran north from Cheyenne to Deadwood, McDaniels's net income was said to have been at least $500 a day.

In the early 1880's he moved to Leadville, Colorado, then to Denver, where in 1888 he was connected with the Olympia Theatre, and in the following year returned to Cheyenne with a combination museum and menagerie. It is reported that he died penniless in a park in El Paso, Texas, in 1907.

Another extraordinary figure in Wyoming's theatrical history was Chris Fletcher, saloonman of Hartville, who during the copper boom of the 1880's built his well-known variety theater. Performers were recruited from Denver and near-by cities, and though their talents were often mediocre, there were among them some actors and singers of ability who had been forced to take any sort of work that would provide them with food. And the food was excellent, for Fletcher gave his actors board and room, knowing that they would be more content if they were comfortable.

During the show, which was run on the lines of ordinary burlesque, women sold drinks in the private boxes on the balcony and at tables on the floor. Only men were allowed at these performances, with the exception of those given on Sunday night, known as 'Ladies' Night,' when the acts were the best that the players could give and no liquor was sold.

For a number of years this theater prospered, although Fletcher, who had once been a cowman, often complained bitterly that as soon as his artists 'got the wrinkles out of their bellies' they went temperamental on him and were worse to handle than a milling herd.

The Blue Front Theatre at Laramie, erected on A Street in the late 1860's, was a one-story structure with its board front painted bright blue. It was originally run by the Union Pacific freight agent, M. Shannessy, who sold out to Mr. Fuhr, the operator of his gambling tables. Shannessy went on to Deadwood and was fatally shot there.

Vaudeville stunts for men only were the main attraction at the Blue Front Theatre, but people outside could enjoy the music of the band that played on the roof of the building. In 1869 August Trabing purchased the theater and used it as headquarters for his mercantile company. It was in this building that the first trial ever held in Laramie took place, when two horse thieves were brought to justice for stealing a team of mules. The first grand jury in the world to have women members is said to have convened in the old Blue Front.

A traveling minstrel troupe and a circus came to Cheyenne in 1869, and after the completion of the railroad to the Pacific Coast many traveling companies made regular stops in Wyoming. Among these were the Satsuma Acrobatic Troupe, Alf Burnett's Specialty Troupe, the company of General Tom Thumb, the Swiss Bell Ringers, and magicians and operatic singers. Companies similar to the Selden Irwin Troupe, which had a varied repertoire of 'superior quality,' often played in Cheyenne for three or four months. The plays they presented —the *Lady of Lyons, The Drunkard, Romeo and Juliet, Othello, The Stranger*—were followed by 'afterpieces.' The audiences, representing many divergent types, seemed to appreciate Shakespearean plays and always gave them respectful attention.

In 1872 a corporation was formed to build the Cheyenne Opera House, later called Recreation Hall, which seated 600. The scenery was painted by one Monsieur La Harte. This hall was used for professional plays, church benefits, lectures, concerts, and home-talent productions, and for three years was a competitor of the McDaniels Variety Theatre. Then in 1876 the hall came under the management of McDaniels. Later it was run as a roller-skating rink and in 1881 became a meat market.

The Richings-Bernard Opera Company was the first major operatic group to visit Cheyenne. It gave five performances in 1877, including *Martha, The Bohemian Girl, Il Trovatore, Maritana,* and *Fra Diavolo.* This company was the forerunner of many similar ones.

The period 1882–1902 in Wyoming's theatrical history may rightly be designated as the 'opera house era.' A number of prominent citizens, including Joseph M. Carey and Francis E. Warren, both of whom later served the State as Governor and United States senator, incorporated in 1882 and built the Opera House in Cheyenne. The Comly-Barton Opera Company gave the opening performances, which were attended by the elite of Wyoming and Colorado. A special train brought guests from Laramie, almost 60 miles over the mountains; and more than 50 persons came from Denver and Fort Collins, Colorado. Each lady in the audience received a satin program, and after the first performance the Opera House management entertained at a complimentary ball in Library Hall.

Up to this time few of the nationally prominent theatrical companies had stopped in Wyoming, but with splendid new facilities and the prestige given the theater by the State's leading citizens, Cheyenne became a regular stop on the coast-to-coast tours of outstanding companies from Broadway. During the next 20 years leading actors, singers, and musicians who toured over the Union Pacific System appeared in the Opera House in Cheyenne, including such notables as Lily Langtry, Sarah Bernhardt, Helena Modjeska, Otis Skinner, Valeska Suratt, and Paderewski. Most of the best road shows stopped in Cheyenne and often in Laramie, Evanston, and other Wyoming towns along the Union Pacific.

On June 28, 1875, Montgomery Queen's circus exhibited in Laramie. Later the Wyoming Legislature passed a law requiring that a circus pay a $250 license before being permitted to show in the State. Edgar Wilson (Bill) Nye, who became editor of the *Laramie Boomerang* in 1881 and wrote amusing dramatic criticisms, vigorously attacked this circus-licensing law:

> The history of that law is a history of repeated injury and usurpation. Our people were bowed down to the earth with the iron heel of an unjust legislature and forced to drag out the weary years without the pleasures which come to the other states and other territories.

Commenting upon *The Bohemian Girl,* Nye wrote:

> Most every one thinks that I don't know much about music and the opera, but this is not the case. I am very enthusiastic over this class of entertainment and I will take the liberty to trespass upon the time and patience of my readers for a few moments while I speak briefly but graphically on this subject.
> A few evenings ago I had the pleasure of listening to the rendition of the *Bohemian Girl* by Emma Abbott and her troupe at the Grand Opera House. The plot of the play seems to be that 'Arline,' a nice little chunk of a girl, is stolen by a band of gypsies, owned and operated by 'Devilshoof,' who looks some like 'Othello' and some like Sitting Bull. 'Arline' grows up among the gypsies and

falls in love with 'Thaddeus.' 'Thaddeus' was played by Brignoli. Brignoli was named after a thoroughbred horse.

'Arline' falls asleep in the gypsy camp and dreams a large majolica dream, which she tells to 'Thaddeus.' She says that she dreamed she dwelt in marble halls and kept a girl and had a pretty fly time generally, but after all she said it tickled her more to know that 'Thaddeus' loved her still the same, and she kept saying this to him in G, and up on the upper register, and down on the second added line below, and crescendo and diminuendo and duodecimo, forward and back and swing opposite lady to place, till I would have given 1,000 shares paid-up assessable stock in the *Boomerang* if I could have been 'Thad.'

Brignoli, however, did not enter into the spirit of the thing. He made me mad, and if it hadn't been for Em, I would have put on my hat and gone home. He looked like the man who first discovered and introduced Bock beer into the country. She would come and put her sunny head up against his cardigan jacket and put one white arm on each shoulder and sing like a bobolink, and tell him how all-fired glad she was that he was still solid. I couldn't help thinking how small a salary I would be willing to play 'Thaddeus' for, but he stood there like a basswood man with Tobias movement, and stuck his arms out like a sore toe, and told her in F that he felt greatly honored by her attention, and hoped some day to be able to retaliate, or words to that effect . . .

There is a good deal of singing in this opera. Most everybody sings. I like good singing myself . . . Emma Abbott certainly warbles first-rate, and her love-making takes me back to the halcyon days when I cared more for the forbidding future of my mustache, and less for meal-time than I do now. But Brignoli is no singer according to my aesthetic taste. He sings like a man who hasn't taken out his second papers yet, and his stomach is too large. It gets in the way and Arline has to go around it and lean up on his flank when she wants to put her head on his breast.

During this period, Laramie also was developing into a show town. The Blue Front Theatre was followed by other amusement places, including the National Theatre (1870), the Blackburn Hall, Ivinson Hall, and Mannerchor Hall. The W. H. Holliday Company built an opera house in the third story of its store building in 1887. It was planned to open the Opera House with Wagner's opera *Die Walküre,* to be produced by home talent accompanied by a 40-piece orchestra. After the singers had been practicing for some time, however, acoustics proved so poor that the opera had to be postponed, and it was not produced until the following year in Ivinson Hall. This opera was repeated in 1895 in Mannerchor Hall. After a few entertainments the Holliday Opera House was condemned and closed because of inadequate beaming.

Soon after the completion of the Holliday, the Mannerchor Society built a stage at the back of its big hall and became a rival show company. Under the managership of Professor William Marquardt, instructor of music in the Laramie city schools, the society presented Lily Langtry, members of the Drew family, John Philip Sousa on a continental band tour, and other famous men and women.

In the 1890's Bill Root bought the Blackburn Hall, which had been used as an assembling place for native wild animals—deer, elk, bear, and antelope that were being held for sale to estates in England and other foreign countries. After Root's death, his widow, Mrs. Helen Root, leased the building to a traveling medicine show, and the venture proved such a success that the building was remodeled for a theater with Mrs. Root as manager. Many of the seats in the new Root's Opera House were purchased from the old Tabor Grand Opera House of Denver. Mrs. Root, known to the residents of Laramie as 'Sissy' Root, learned every phase of theater management, and hers was a familiar figure, with long brush and paste bucket, atop a ladder and plank as she helped post the bills. She was known to theatrical folk all over the country as the first 'Woman Bill Poster.' One-week engagements were played at Root's Opera House by many touring companies in *Uncle Tom's Cabin, East Lynne,* and other popular plays.

Evanston, on the main line of the Union Pacific in the southwestern corner of Wyoming, participated in the 'opera era' and drew its share of good stock and opera on their way to San Francisco. In 1885 Peter J. Downs built the Opera House on Front Street at a cost of about $12,000. The building was said to be fireproof and had a full basement with cement floor, which was used as a skating rink. George Statler of Johnstown, Pennsylvania, a brother-in-law of Downs, painted the three curtains: the outer butterfly curtain, the scenic curtain, and the advertising curtain. This last curtain was the outstanding feature, with a painting of A. B. Beckwith's barn and racetrack in the center, edged by advertisements. The seats on the main floor of the Opera House were movable in order to permit dancing. Two lavishly decorated boxes flanked the graduated gallery seats. At the rear of the gallery was a long row of lockers, each bearing the name of a prominent local family. These lockers were retained permanently by each family so that wraps and valuables could be stored during entertainments.

The Theodore Lorch troupe, the Armin stock players, the Arlington Comedians, the Spooner Dramatic Company, and various other road companies played in Evanston during the next 15 years. An announcement of the Spooner Dramatic Company, on June 4, 1898, read in part (after a description of the cast):

> The above excellent company will begin a week's engagement at the Opera House on Monday night, June 6th. A new play each night mounted superbly with scenery and costumed exquisitely with elegant and handsome wardrobe. New and up to date specialties and the latest improved moving

picture machine. The Cinneograph, giving life like news of scenes in and about Cuba with Admiral Dewey's Victorious Fleet . . .

The first shows to reach northeastern Wyoming were put on by traveling medicine show men who set up their small stands in the streets and attracted an audience by their line of ballyhoo, augmented by singing and the banjo. In the mining camp called Cambria (*see Tour* 1), these men carried on a lively business by the light of gasoline torches at night, as the miners were then free to watch the shows. The many antics attracted large crowds of shouting men, who exchanged good-natured banter with the glib-tongued salesmen until a brawl or a riot broke up the show. Soapy Smith, a famous medicine man and early-day character, had a neat trick of pretending to wrap a five-dollar bill around a cake of soap just before selling it. Not only was the soap very 'super,' but a greenback went with it all—all for the measly sum of 25¢. The bills though had a way of disappearing, leaving the disillusioned buyer with only a bar of very inferior soap.

When Cambria was first established, the coal company built a large bunkhouse for the miners, with a hall and gymnasium in the basement. In 'Crummy Junction,' as the building was called, many fine entertainments and socials were held. In 1898 the Opera House was erected in the town and was opened for the first time to welcome home the boys who had served in the Philippines during the Spanish-American War. Among the first performers to play at the Opera House were Johnnie and Della Pringle, who returned year after year for one-week stands. The Georgia Minstrels with Billy Kersands also played there. One of the most popular productions given in the Opera House was *Faust,* which was read, not sung.

Sometimes the traveling troupes used home talent to complete their cast and thus became well acquainted with the local residents. One time, while a company was playing in Cambria, a daughter was born to the wife of the manager. She was at once named Cambria and was treated by the residents as a royal princess.

The first circus to make its way into the Black Hills section reached Newcastle in 1891. It was known as Van Amburg Shows, Greatest-on-Earth, and consisted of one elephant, a lion, a cage of sleepy snakes, and a few dogs and ponies. Packed into three or four wagons the circus bumped its way across the rough mountain and prairie roads from Sundance.

The only three-ring circus that ever visited Crook County was the

Barnum and Bailey's big circus that stopped at Moorcroft in 1913 to feed the livestock. The circus management decided to spread the tent and to put on the circus with all the frills. The natives came from far and near, on foot, on horseback, in wagons, and in cars. The parade was so long and the main street so short that the turn was made a mile and half out of town.

Buffalo Bill's circus visited many Wyoming towns in the 1890's. Usually there would be a play enacting some famous battle of the whites and the Indians, a few trick riders, a herd of buffalo, 'saddle' clowns, and exhibition shooting and riding by Buffalo Bill.

The first nonprofessional dramatic group in the State of which there is record was the California Minstrels, a soldier troupe, who gave a concert at Fort Bridger in 1863, charging an admission of 50¢. In 1869 the Cheyenne Dramatic Club held occasional meetings. Some four years later the club gave two stage productions, *On His Last Legs* and *Box and Cox.*

In Evanston, as early as 1882, the Evanston Dramatic Club gave a successful performance of *The Last Leaf,* followed by a farce, *Smith and Brown, or My Neighbor's Wife.* The club was so successful that another group was formed, the Home Town Play Club, which gave plays at various holiday seasons. Its members patterned their acting after that of many visiting road companies.

Since its establishment in 1887 the University of Wyoming has fostered dramatic work. It now has a thriving theater group, the University Players, organized in 1921, which usually gives four long plays of dramatic significance each season. For several years the university sponsored pageants at Vedauwoo Glen in the Pole Mountain division of the Medicine Bow National Forest, where one of the finest natural amphitheaters in the country furnished a background for historical spectacles.

Under the extension division of the department of agriculture of the university, dramatics have been a feature at a number of summer camps for farm women; an experienced dramatist instructs the women in the technique of play production.

In Cheyenne two well-organized groups, the Cheyenne Little Theatre Players and the 12th Nite Dramatic Club, regularly produce plays of good quality. The Cheyenne Little Theatre Players, organized in 1927, has a membership of 500 and a board of 12 directors, selected from several of the city's service clubs. Four full-length plays are given during each season at the exceptionally fine theater in the Consistory

Temple. The membership fee of $2 admits members to all perform-
ances. Seats not used by members are available to the public at 50¢
each. In addition to the regular plays a number of one-act studio or
workshop plays, most of them original, are given by the members at
the club's regular weekly meetings. The 12th Nite Dramatic Club,
organized in 1930, is a branch of the national organization with
headquarters in New York City. There are no membership dues or
entrance fees; necessary funds are raised by special assessment. Two
to four plays are given annually, and it is a rule of the organization to
produce one play written by local talent every five years. The local
branch is sponsored by the Knights of Pythias, B'nai B'rith, and
other prominent groups, and proceeds are used to provide lunches for
undernourished children attending the junior high school.

Music

LONG before the coming of the cowboy, the Plains Indians of the West sang of the vast prairies, their hunting grounds for centuries. Often their songs had no words but were sung with vocables set to a rhythm beaten out on tom-toms, drums, or baskets. Similarity and repetition of syllables can readily be recognized in these Arapaho words for the Ghost Dance:

Ni ni ni tu bi . , na hu — hu
Ni ni ni tu bi . , na hu — hu
Ba ta hi . . na . . ni hu . . hu
Ba ta hi . , na . . ni hu . , hu
Na hi na . . ni ha thi na
Na hi na . , ni ha thi na

In specific religious ceremonies great care was exercised by older men of the tribe to make certain that the words sung by an individual conformed to the ritual, else, they said, the offering would be harmful, and the worshiper would not travel a 'straight path.' Most of their songs were simple, and during the ceremonial dances the performers were sometimes so engrossed in portraying their emotions that music became incidental. In general the drum beats governed the action and movements of the body, while the song, frequently sung in different time, voiced the emotion of the appeal.

The tradition and conventions of Western music are a part of the heritage brought up along the cattle trails by Texas riders, whose professed and constantly restated melancholy and longing for the ranges 'back home' became the adopted and accepted themes of northern rangeland songs. The exact locations of 'home' varied widely, but the cowhand's desire to be 'somewhere else' was constant.

The State of Wyoming typifies the Old West, and here are found many of the original cowboy songs—the folk music of the Plains. The songs the cowboys sang while herding or at the roundup and their favorite 'lonesome' songs, which they sang around the campfire or in the bunkhouse in the evenings, form the bases of many popular contemporary Western songs. Themes for the ballads were taken from actual experiences of the daily or nightly range routine.

From Natrona County comes the 'Old Cowman's Appeal,' a song written by an old Wyoming cowhand:

> I rode across a valley range
>   I had not seen for years,
> The trail was all so spoiled and strange,
>   It nearly fetched the tears.
>
> I had to let the fences down;
>   The fussy lanes ran wrong,
> And each new line would make me swear,
>   And hum this little song.
>
> With skyline bounds from east to west;
>   And room to go and come,
> I loved my fellows best . . . best
>   When they were scattered some.
>
> When my old soul hunts range and rest
>   Beyond the Great Divide,
> Just plant me in some stretch out West
>   That's sunny, lonely and wide.
>
> Let cattle rub my tombstone round,
>   And coyotes mourn their kin;
> Let horses come and paw my mound,
>   *But don't you fence me in!*

A favorite with night herders in the Hartville region, 'Go Slow, Dogies, Slow' is a typical prairie lament. Dogies are the motherless or weakling calves that because of their faltering gait hinder the progress of the trail herds.

> Go slow, little dogies, why don't you slow down?
> You've wandered and trampled all over the ground.
> Oh, graze along dogies. Go slow, kinda slow
> And don't be always on the go.
> Move slow, dogies, move slow.
>
> Oh say, little dogies, why don't you lay down?
> And quit this forever siftin' around?
> My arms are weary, my seat is sore.
> Oh, lay down, don't be on the go.
> Lay down, dogies, lay down.

'Pitch, You Old Piebally, Pitch,' a variation of E. A. Brininstool's 'A Corral Soliloquy,' is a favorite in the Jackson Hole country:

> You've been roped and saddled, bridled and straddled;
>   I've spurred and I've quirted you, too;
> You've squealed and cavorted, you sunfished and snorted,
>   As 'round the corral you flew.
> Your eyes all afire with one mad desire,
>   To pound me down there in the dirt;
> But to do it, old fellow, there's no streak of yellow
>   Beneath this old blue flannel shirt.

When I met you and matched you, I raked you and scratched you,
   You'd like to pound me in the ditch;
But I swore I would bust you, so that I could trust you,
   So pitch, you old Piebally, pitch.
With your squealing and lunging and plunging,
   And corkscrewing 'round like a top,
You'd sure like to beat me, but you can't unseat me;
   I'll ride you, ole hoss, till you drop.

You are a Jim dandy, you're tuff and you're sandy,
   But the way you go at it is rich;
So keep on a humpin' your back up and jumpin',
   And pitch, you ole Piebally, pitch.
You're snaky and greasy but you won't find it easy
   To shake this ole whoopin' cowpunch;
For spite of your kickin' you'll still find me stickin',
   And just let me hand you this hunch.

You ain't the first disgusted cayuse
   I've busted and rode to a frazzle to stick,
And if you only knew it, you've got to come to it,
   I'll match you for every damned trick.
Well, who would have thunk it, you piled me at last,
   And you landed me square in the ditch;
And you busted my jaw, you damned ornery outlaw,
   So pitch, you Piebally 'son of a maverick.'

A member of the Garner outfit in Fort Worth, Texas, wrote a ballad that has been sung in Wyoming, especially the northern part, for years, 'Joe Garner's Trail Herd':

Come, all you old-timers, and listen to my song;
I'll make it short as possible and I'll not keep you long!
I'll relate to you about the time you all remember well
When we with old Joe Garner drove a beef herd up the trail.

When we left the ranch it was early in the spring,
We had as good a corporal as ever a rope did swing;
Good hands and good horses, good outfit through and through,
We went well equipped, we were a jolly crew.

We had no little herd—two thousand head or more—
And some as wild brush beeves as you ever saw before.
We swung to them all the way and sometimes by the tail,
Oh, you know we had a circus as we all went up the trail.

Till we reached the open plains everything went well,
And then them cattle turned in and dealt us merry hell.
They stampeded every night that came and did it without fail—
Oh, you know we had a circus as we all went up the trail.

We would round them up at morning and the boss would make a count,
And say, 'Look here, old punchers, we are out quite an amount;
You must make all losses good and do it without fail,
Or you'll never get another job driving up the trail.'

When we reached Red River we gave the Inspector the dodge,
He swore by God Almighty in jail old Joe should lodge.
We told him if he'd taken our boss and had him locked in jail,
We would shore get his scalp as we all came down the trail.

When we reached the Reservation how squirmish we did feel,
Although we had tried old Garner and knew him true as steel.
And if we would follow him and do as he said to,
That old bald-headed cow-thief would surely take us through.

When we reached Dodge City we drew our four months' pay;
Times were better then, boys, than they are today.
The way we drank and gambled and threw the girls around—
'Say, a crowd of Texas cowboys had come to take our town.'

The cowboy sees many hardships, although he takes them well;
The fun we had upon that trip no human tongue can tell.
The cowboy's life is a dreary life, though his mind it is no load,
And he always spends his money like he found it in the road.

If you ever meet old Garner, you must meet him on the square
For he's the biggest cow-thief that ever tramped out there.
But if you want to hear him roar and spin a lively tale,
Just ask him about the time we all went up the trail.

An old refrain heard in many parts of the West as a dance song, often taking the place of 'Home, Sweet Home' at Wyoming cowboy balls, is 'Old Paint.' Usually the fiddle is silenced and the entire company at the dance sings this refrain:

Goodbye, Old Paint, I'm a-leavin' Cheyenne;
Goodbye, Old Paint, I'm a-leavin' Cheyenne.

My foot in the stirrup, my pony won't stand;
Goodbye, Old Paint, I'm a-leavin' Cheyenne.

I'm a-leavin' Cheyenne, I'm off for Montan';
Goodbye, Old Paint, I'm a-leavin' Cheyenne.

Old Paint's a good pony, he paces when he can;
Goodbye, Little Annie, I'm off for Cheyenne.

Oh, hitch up your horses and feed 'em some hay,
And seat yourself by me so long as you stay.

My horses ain't hungry, they'll not eat your hay;
My wagon is loaded and rolling away.

My foot in my stirrup, my reins in my hand;
Good-morning, young lady, my horses won't stand.

Goodbye, Old Paint, I'm a-leavin' Cheyenne,
Goodbye, Old Paint, I'm a-leavin' Cheyenne.

In northern Platte County a lively tune called the 'Hartville Rag' is still heard at country dances. It is played on one fiddle string, much to the delight of the dancers. The song originated some years ago when a group of neighbors held a series of dances, moving from one ranch to the other each night for a week. On the last night it was discovered at Hartville that the fiddler, named Reagan, had worn out all of the strings on his violin except one, but he managed to evoke a lively tune which he played over and over. It was dubbed the 'Hartville Rag.'

'The Promised Land,' a song popular in the East about 1859, was brought over the Oregon Trail some years later. Its lively air distinguished it from the mournful hymns and ballads of the time, and although it was originally a religious song, the term 'promised land' undoubtedly described the destination of the travelers, when it was sung along the trail by the emigrants.

> I have a father, in the Promised Land;
> I have a father, in the Promised Land;
> When my father calls me, I must go
> To meet him in the Promised Land.
>
> *Refrain*
> I'll away, I'll away, I'll away to the Promised Land;
> I'll away, I'll away, I'll away to the Promised Land;
> When my father calls me, I must go
> To meet him in the Promised Land.

In the Jackson Hole country a favorite song is 'Home in the West':

> I love the broad plains and the cowboy domains,
>   Horizons of silver and gold,
> To the hills of white chalk, where the antelope flock,
>   Where love's story never grows old.
>
> *Chorus:*
> A home, a home, a home in the west,
>   Where the deer and the antelope play;
> Where there never is heard a discouraging word,
>   And the skies are not clouded all day.
> Where the air is so pure and the zephyrs so free,
>   And the breezes so balmy and light;
> There's more peace and rest in a home in the west,
>   Than in all of your cities so bright.
>
> I love the wild flowers in this dear land of ours,
>   The curlew I love to hear scream;
> I love the white rocks where the antelope flock,
>   To graze on the mountain so green.
>
> Where the rugged peaks rise and kissing the skies,
>   With their mantles of glistening snow;
> Such a glorious scene and the forests so green,
>   On the slopes and the valley below.
>
> Oh, give me a land where the bright diamond sand,
>   Flows leisurely down the stream;
> And the graceful white swan goes gliding along,
>   Like a maid in a heavenly dream.
>
> The red man was pressed from his home in the west,
>   And no more he'll ever return
> To the banks of the Red River where seldom, if ever,
>   His flickering campfires burn.

How oft-time at night when the heavens are bright,
    With light from the flickering stars;
Have I layed there amazed and thought as I gazed,
    That their glory exceeds that of ours.

I long for the range and the mountains and plains,
    Where the friends and companions are best;
I'm returning once more to the Red River shore,
    To my little ranch home in the west.

European traditions are reflected to some extent in the local music of the State. Native-born workers in the coal camps in northern Wyoming often join their foreign-born companions in singing 'Where Is the German Fatherland?' It has been translated as follows:

Where is the German Fatherland? In Prussia bold? In Swabia old?
Or where the Rhine grapes purple bloom? Or seagulls haunt the northern gloom?
Oh, no, no, no, no! The Fatherland is greater yet, the Fatherland is greater yet.

Chorus:
Where is the German Fatherland? O, let me know its glorious name!
Where e'er the German has poured its love in song, to God our Lord,
There shall it be, There shall it be, There, comrades brave,
There shall it be.
There, comrades brave, there shall it be.
That is the German Fatherland, O God above, stretch forth Thy hand,
Protect Thy sons so brave and bold, Their country with Thy love enfold,
That is thy land, that is thy land, that, comrades brave, that is thy land.
      That, comrades brave, that is thy land.
      That, comrades brave, that is thy land.

John L. Hunton of Laramie is the only Wyoming composer whose work is known to any extent outside the State. In his piano and violin studies, which describe the roundups, cattle stampedes, blizzards, the beauty of hazy prairies, and similar Western scenes, he has woven original versions of some of the oldest cowboy songs. For the piano Hunton wrote 'Sagebrush,' 'Prairie Dogs,' 'Indian Paintbrush,' 'Jackrabbits,' 'Autumn Aspen,' and 'Blizzards'; for the violin and piano and male chorus: 'The Tetons' (words by Porter Coolidge and Frederick Boothroyd of Lander), 'Sacajawea,' and a group of ten songs (words by Coolidge). Two Hunton compositions for voice are 'Wyoming' (words anonymous) and 'Cowboy Sonata.'

Hugh Mackinnon, organist of St. Matthew's Cathedral at Laramie since 1929, is the composer of sacred and secular music that has been played extensively in churches of the East.

Permanent musical organizations in Cheyenne are: the Cheyenne Little Symphony; Philomelian Club male chorus; the Mothersingers of the Parent-Teacher Association; Sons of the American Legion Drum and Bugle Corps; American Legion Drum Corps; Music Study

Club; Staff and Clef Club; B Sharp Music Club; Madrigal Trio; Silver Leaf Club; Boys' Band; and Cheyenne City Band.

Casper has several musical organizations, including the Philharmonic Orchestra and the Treble Clef Chorus. The State Music Festival, an annual event held at Casper during April, is designed, not as a contest, but to aid amateur musicians with constructive criticism offered by experienced critics and teachers. School bands, orchestras, vocal ensembles, and soloists make up the program. Most of the participants are students from Wyoming schools. A similar festival is conducted at Greybull.

The University Orchestra and University Glee Club appear in annual concerts at Laramie under the direction of the department of music at the University of Wyoming. Community singing and methods of teaching folk songs to children are part of the music instruction program offered by the University Extension Division at the vacation camps attended by Wyoming farm women each summer. The Musical Arts Club of Laramie, whose membership of 40 includes accomplished musicians, has sponsored the appearance in Laramie of some of the country's finest concert artists.

The Young Women's and Young Men's Mutual Improvement Association of the Mormon Church in the Big Horn Basin sponsors both secular and religious concerts. At one time nearly 200 young people between the ages of 14 and 24 met each week and often traveled long distances to keep engagements. Home music is popular in the Mormon towns of Wyoming, and each evening at dusk singing may be heard along many streets; sometimes it is a folk song, such as 'My Old Kentucky Home'; another time it may be the 'Soldier's Chorus'; or again, a simple church hymn.

'Heritage,' a prize song in a contest held in Big Horn Basin, is sung in many communities of the district.

> We're sons of the men who founded the town,
> We carry the torch they bore
> While wielding the axe and guiding the plow
> Which conquered this western moor.
>
> The grounds where they camped we've made into lawns
> And gardens of flowers fair,
> A school house now stands out there where they fought,
> A church where they bowed in prayer.
>
> It thrills us to breathe the air they breathed;
> We'll oil their old trails with care.
> We'll cherish their dreams, their hopes and their faith;
> We're proud of the names we bear!

The composition 'Wyoming,' with words by the Honorable Charles E. Winter of Casper and music by G. E. Knapp of Laramie and Mrs. Harold Vaughan of Cheyenne, is accepted as the State song, although Wyoming has never officially adopted it or any other. The first verse and chorus are as follows:

> In the far and mighty West,
> Where the crimson sun seeks rest,
> There's a growing, splendid state that lies above
> On the breast of this great land;
> Where the massive Rockies stand,
> That's Wyoming young and strong, the state I love!
>
> *Chorus:*
> Wyoming, Wyoming! Land of the sunlight clear!
> Wyoming, Wyoming! Land that we hold so dear!
> Wyoming, Wyoming! Precious art thou and thine!
> Wyoming, Wyoming! Beloved state of mine!

The official song of the University of Wyoming, 'The Brown and Yellow,' was composed by the late Dr. June E. Downey:

> Where the western lights long shadows
> Over boundless prairies fling,
> And the mountain winds are vocal
> With thy dear name, Wyoming.
>
> There it is, the brown and yellow
> Floats in loving loyalty,
> While the college throws its portals
> Open wide to all men free.
>
> *Chorus:*
> And so our songs we bring,
> Our Alma Mater sing,
> To her our hearts shall cling,
> Shall cling forever more.

Art

THE art left by the prehistoric tribesmen, who covered many cliff and cave walls in Wyoming with pictographs and petroglyphs, is generally classified under two main headings: those composed of conventionalized signs and symbols, and those that attempt a more realistic representation of natural objects, such as bear tracks, trees, deer, elk, and tepees. In many places these designs are tinted with red, black, brown, yellow, green, pale orange, purplish red, and white, the pigments being obtained from vegetable, animal, and mineral sources. In these drawings there is no indication of any conscious artistic or symbolic intention.

The Plains Indians who later roamed over the State practiced more advanced crafts and learned to make rawhide shields, war bonnets, clothing, skin cradles, ornaments, and parfleches.

The shield, usually made by an old warrior or recognized medicine man, always took its design from a dream in which the dreamer was instructed by the spirit concerning the number of shields he might make and how they should be painted. Those who acquired the shields compensated the makers with horses, blankets, or other valuable property. Hide, obtained from the neck of a bull buffalo, was toughened by shrinking while wet over a fire. The cutting, painting, and decorating with feathers and pendants were accompanied by great ceremony.

Ceremony and song were also part of the making of war bonnets by the warriors of the tribe. A battle honor was recounted upon each feather before it was placed in position. Previous to the use of horses by the Indians, the flap at the back of the war bonnet rarely extended below the wearer's waist. After the warriors began to ride horseback, the 'spine' with its bright feather ruff was lengthened to equal the owner's height.

Each tribe had its own peculiar cut and decoration for tepee, moccasin, and other personal effects. In the buffalo country the women seldom decorated their own robes, but often embroidered those worn by the men. Sometimes a man painted his robe in accordance with a dream, sometimes with a yearly pictorial record of his own deeds or of prominent tribal events.

Skill was displayed in the making of skin cradles, which were usually finished with intricate bead work, and in the fashioning of ornaments from claws, horn, bones, teeth, shells, feathers, quills, and beads.

The parfleche, a skin bag or box made in varying sizes and shapes, was commonly used for carrying food and clothing. Dried meat, pounded into a powder called pemmican, was often carried in a parfleche by the Indians and early trappers. This skin bag offered ample opportunity for embellishment and was often painted with figures and abstract designs. Some excellent parfleches are now on display in the Wyoming State Historical Museum, Supreme Court Building, Cheyenne.

From the ceramic fragments discovered in the State it appears that pottery making by the Wyoming Indians was neither extensively practiced nor perfected as a craft. Pottery has been found at only 6 per cent of the campsites recorded in the State as against 19 per cent for Colorado sites. The lack of standardization in any phase of their work is an indication, in the opinion of Dr. E. B. Renaud, Professor of Anthropology of the University of Denver, that the Wyoming potters did not follow any established tradition or strive for beauty in their work. They seemed interested merely in fashioning a useful cooking vessel—which might be either plain or decorated with the usual cord imprint, grass mark, or tooling done with a stick or bone awl. Only one piece of painted pottery has been found in the State, and that was evidently of foreign origin.

Early white settlers in Wyoming devoted little time to handicrafts other than those demanded by necessity. Beds, called 'bunks,' were built from rough lumber and were fitted with 'springs' made of rawhide. Chairs, tables, cradles, churns, and other household equipment were made from materials at hand. Buffalo, horse, and cow hides often were used for chair seats. Lamps or lanterns, commonly called 'Happy Jacks,' were rudely fashioned from tin syrup cans and lit by candles.

In the hayfields most of the equipment was handmade. The go-devil, sweep, and pusher were typical of early ranch implements. Early ranches had their blacksmith shops in which were forged many implements, including horseshoes, branding irons, wagon tires, and ranch tools. One of the most skilled blacksmiths in the West was the late

Harry P. Hynds, who built and for many years owned the Plains Hotel in Cheyenne. Another expert blacksmith and wagon-maker was Robert Hall of Laramie, who made some of the finest tallyhos, wagons, and carryalls used in Wyoming.

Two other pioneers known throughout the Rocky Mountain region for their craftsmanship were Frank Menea and Ernest A. Logan of Cheyenne. Menea became widely known for his hand-tooled saddles, bridles, cuffs, harness, chaps, and other leather equipment. Logan worked chiefly in silver ornamentation for bridles and other cowboy paraphernalia. Many early-day cowboys and stage drivers were skilled in making horsehair bridles, hat bands, and fine whips.

Best known of Wyoming's contemporary craftsmen is Tom Molesworth of Cody, who designs and builds furniture from native cedar and pine, incorporating grotesque knots and gnarled branches in the finished pieces. Molesworth's leather work has also become widely known. Thomas McKinley Wood of Big Horn has been very successful in reviving the sturdy romance of old ranch life in his iron silhouettes of cowboys, roundup wagons, bucking horses, Texas steers and the like. In the tie camps of the State, there are a number of expert Swedish wood carvers who learned their art in their native land. They carve portrait figures, miniature animals, and toys. Of those who acquired their training and skill in this country, Earl Mark Spade, the cowboy artist, is one of the best known. P. V. O'Kelly of Cheyenne whittles totem poles that are sent all over the country. He is said to be one of the few who recreate the true Alaskan totem pole.

Many towns and villages of Wyoming have art shops where native handicraft objects are displayed. Woodwork, in which gnarled pine is used extensively, is designed and finished by residents of Esterbrook in northern Albany County. In and near Jackson furniture is made from elk horns and small decorative pieces are made from elk teeth (*see Tour* 7). Near Sheridan, sagebrush is deftly converted into candles, pillows, and incense. Worthy of mention is the leather clothing especially designed by a Sheridan manufacturer for dude-ranch wear. This clothing follows, in general, the designs of early-day cowmen.

Wyoming artists, stimulated by frequent association with visiting professional painters, have formed a number of art clubs, societies, and classes for the study and encouragement of the arts in the State. The leading organization of this kind is the Wyoming Artists Association, of which Stanley P. Hunt of Laramie is the president. Principal work of this group since 1932 has been the sponsorship of an annual no-jury exhibit of professional and amateur painting in the State. This exhibit is first shown in Laramie and then sent to various points in Wyoming.

The University of Wyoming summer school offers art courses especially planned for teachers and prospective teachers. Informal discussion and sketching clubs have been organized at Laramie, Casper, and Cheyenne.

The artist's colony established near Cody in 1937 was first suggested by Gertrude Vanderbilt Whitney of New York, whose memorial to Colonel W. F. (Buffalo Bill) Cody is an outstanding landmark near Cody. This colony is under the supervision of Edward T. Grigware and Stan Kershaw, formerly of Chicago. At the present time it consists of a group of peeled-log cabins, which form a nucleus for the future growth of the venture. The residents of the colony are especially interested in depicting the Buffalo Bill country. Tenny Stevens of Cody, sculptor, was awarded a $2,500 prize at the 1938 Los Angeles County Fair held at Pomona, California, for his model, *Harvest*.

Under the Federal Art Project of the Work Projects Administration, an experimental gallery has been established at Laramie, with extension galleries in Sheridan, Newcastle, Lander, Casper, Torrington, Rock Springs, and Riverton; here the work of WPA artists and others has been shown. By 1937 the galleries indicated a significant growth in professional skill on the part of local artists. Murals, pictures, etchings, block prints, and other work by WPA artists have been contributed to the university and to many schools and libraries in Wyoming.

In Casper classes have been formed for training in wood carving, metal and leather work, weaving, clay modeling, and pottery. Further activity in this field has been inaugurated by the art department of the Parent-Teacher Association, which sponsors the 'More Beautiful Wyoming' movement and arranges annually a week of programs devoted to art and to home and city beautification. The State Department of Education joins in this work by encouraging art programs in the schools during this week and by offering prizes for the best posters based on the 'More Beautiful Wyoming' topic.

Thomas Moran, a native of England who did some of his best work in Wyoming, accompanied the U. S. Geological Survey expedition under F. V. Hayden to the Yellowstone Park region in 1871 and from his sketches painted the large panoramic study entitled *The Grand Canyon of the Yellowstone*. Two years later he made a second Western exploration to the Grand Canyon of the Colorado, the subject for his *Chasm of the Colorado*. These two pictures were purchased by Congress for $10,000 each, as additions to the Capitol galleries in Washington. A collection of Moran's paintings was recently presented by his daughter to the National Park Service, for display in park museums. In recognition of his great contribution to the Western tradition, the painter's name has been given to Mount Moran of the Teton Range.

In addition to his work in color Moran did many etchings and illustrations of genuine merit. His work, grandiose and romantic in style, nevertheless captures the color and feeling of the rugged Western scene.

Moran's friend and coworker on many western journeys was William H. Jackson, photographer of distinction and a skilled worker with pencil and brush. As photographer for the Union Pacific Railroad in the late 1860's and for the Hayden party in the 1870's, Jackson did remarkable work. In 1892 he was commissioned by the State to make a series of photographs for a proposed exhibit of Wyoming scenery at the Columbian Exposition of 1893 in Chicago. Jackson has done more than anyone else to make a record with camera, brush, and pencil of pioneer times in Wyoming. Although more than 94 years old, he is still active, and for a number of years has been secretary of the Oregon Trail Memorial Association, New York City. Jackson's entire collection of early-day photographic plates is now owned by the Dearborn Institute of Flint, Michigan.

E. W. Gollings, called the 'Cowboy Artist,' who died in 1932, was internationally known for his Western paintings. Gollings punched cows for big outfits in South Dakota, Montana, and Wyoming. In the summer he worked from a roundup wagon and in the winter fed cattle at ranches. During his spare time he drew. Later he won a scholarship at the Chicago Academy of Fine Arts and quickly combined the technical training he received there with his natural artistic ability. By 1909 he had established a studio in Sheridan, Wyoming, and was winning favor with his Western paintings, not only in America, but also in Europe. Four of his pictures hang in the State capitol at Cheyenne: *The Smoke Signal, The Indian Attack on Overland Stage, Emigrants on the Platte,* and *The Wagon Box Fight.*

Charles Belden, owner of the Pitchfork Ranch, has gained wide recognition for his rangeland photographs. Joseph Stimson of Cheyenne has won honors for his colored photographs of the Tetons and other regions in Wyoming.

Hans Kleiber has celebrated the beauty of Wyoming in distinctive etchings of wild life and Western landscapes, many of which are in public and private collections throughout the country. A forest ranger who taught himself the difficult technique of etching, Kleiber has successfully exhibited in most of the larger cities in the United States and London. His workshop is a log studio in the foothills of the Big Horn Mountains near Dayton, 25 miles northwest of Sheridan (*see Tour* 10). Among Kleiber's best prints are: *Geese Crossing Wyoming, Snow in the Rockies,* and *Leaving the High Country.* The latter is an elk print that won the silver medal at the 1931 Print Maker's International Exhibit in Los Angeles. In addition to etching Kleiber paints oils and watercolors.

Perhaps the most notorious painting in the State is *Paul Potter's Bull,* finished by Nesker in 1885. This painting, which hangs in a reception room of the Cheyenne Chamber of Commerce, is said to have been the cause of the dismissal of one of the prominent members of the old Cheyenne Club. The member, a wealthy cattle owner and an admirer of fine stock, objected strenuously to the painting, on the grounds that it was a travesty on Wyoming livestock. In a derisive moment he pulled out his gun and shot a hole through the painted bull's front leg. The gentleman was summarily dropped from the rolls of the club.

Small art collections on exhibit in Wyoming include those of Ruth Joy Hopkins, Lin Hopkins, Charles Anda, and Mrs. F. C. Nicolaysen of Casper; Elizabeth Neal Forsling of Casper Mountain; the Haynes Studio and Crandall's Studio at Moran and in Yellowstone Park; the Lusk Indian Collection at the State Historical Museum, Supreme Court Building, Cheyenne; and the Olive Fell Collection of etchings, Buffalo Bill Museum, Cody. An especially good collection of paintings by Wyoming artists is in the capitol, Cheyenne.

Throughout the State along the old historical trails and at the sites of historic battles, stage stations, and old forts, there are markers, usually made of native granite, bearing descriptive bronze plaques. Among these the Oregon Trail markers at Guernsey and the town of Fort Laramie are the most unusual. Embedded in the granite of these monuments are such relics of the old trail as ox and mule shoes, bullets, wagon irons, and guns.

Architecture

SWEEPING winds and a rigorous climate, a great diversity of settings, and the availability in some localities of native building materials, lacking in others—all these factors have played a part in determining the architecture of the State. It is generally characterized by utilitarianism.

Early inhabitants of the region left many evidences of the use of rock caves as shelters. The best known of these are in Dinwoodie Canyon, now the center of intensive archeological investigation. Natural caves, with smoke-stained walls and floors strewn with charcoal scraps and flint chippings, are found at the bottom of the limestone cliffs in a gorge in Whalen Canyon, Platte County. A great part of the State served only as a summer camp or hunting ground for the later migrant tribes of Indians, including the Shoshone, Crow, Sioux, and Blackfoot. Their shelters were brush huts or movable skin tepees.

The first cabin in Wyoming of which there is a record was a crude structure erected by Robert Stuart and his Astorians at Bessemer Bend in 1812, on their return trip from the Pacific Coast to St. Louis. It was 8 feet wide and 18 feet long. Its walls, 6 feet high, were hung within with buffalo skins, and a hole in the roof served as chimney for the fireplace in the center of the dwelling.

Most of the early trappers and traders moved about according to the seasons or the game supply, and their temporary shelter was usually a one-room log hut on the bank of a stream. Jack Robertson, a trapper known as 'Uncle Jack Robinson,' is said to have established a permanent cabin on Black's Fork in 1834.

With the development of the fur business, trading posts were erected; the first one, built about 1828 by Antonio Mateo, stood near the forks of Powder River. Mateo's buildings, constructed of hewn logs, mortised to a heavy sill, were surrounded by a bastioned log stockade about 200 feet square and 8 to 10 feet high. These stockades, called Portuguese Houses, were used for trading. On the river bank, a few hundred yards from the post, was a press built of hewn cottonwood, in which beaver hides were compressed into bales.

The early forts of the State were of no settled pattern, and were constructed of the materials nearest at hand. In 1832 Captain B. L. E. Bonneville built of logs and pickets a temporary winter shelter for his men in the Upper Green River Valley. Two years later Fort Laramie was established as a trading post. This structure, as it appeared in the early 1840's, was built of adobe, according to the methods of the Mexicans, who evidently had come up from the Southwest by way of the St. Vrain and had assisted in the building of the fort. Parkman wrote of the fort that it was 'built of bricks dried in the sun, and externally is of an oblong form with bastions of clay, in the form of ordinary block houses at two of the corners.' Frémont said that its 'lofty walls, whitewashed and picketed, with the large bastions at the angles, gave it quite an imposing appearance . . . a quadrangular structure, built of clay . . . with walls fifteen feet high, surmounted with a wooden palisade.' The houses or living quarters adjoined each other around a yard about 130 feet square. Each apartment had a door and window opening on the inner court. The two entrances to the court itself were placed in the center of two opposing walls. Over the main entrance was a square tower built of earth, with loopholes. Large square bastions, so arranged as to sweep the four faces of the wall, were placed diagonally opposite each other at two of the angles. 'The great entrance,' wrote Frémont, '. . . which was floored, and about fifteen feet long, made a pleasant, shaded seat through which the breeze swept constantly.'

The oldest known building now standing in Wyoming, the post sutler's store at old Fort Laramie, looks as though it were built of modern concrete; actually it is constructed of a mixture similar to concrete, composed of sand and cement from gypsum beds in the near-by Guernsey district.

Fort Laramie was sold to the Government as a military post in 1849, and new buildings were constructed, including a clubhouse or bachelor officers' quarters called 'Old Bedlam.' The lumber for this two-story building was hauled 800 miles by wagon from Fort Leavenworth, at a cost estimated at between $60,000 and $85,000. Large two-story gallery porches shaded the entire front of the building.

There was nothing distinctive in the architecture of the original (1842) Fort Bridger. In 1847 it was said to consist of 'two adjoining log houses, dirt roofs, and a small picket yard of logs set in the ground, about eight feet high.' Some time after 1853 the Mormons built a stone wall around it. In 1855 the fort, rebuilt of boulderstone, was 100 feet square and 14 feet high. Pickets were placed on the top of the walls, and bastions were located on diagonal corners, similar to those at Fort Laramie. A corral 52 feet wide was built against the fort. In 1858 United States troops built barracks and quarters of stone, log, and lumber.

Later forts built along the Bozeman, the Oregon, and Overland Trails were of the same general type—log houses or apartments surrounded by high stockades.

The buffalo and antelope hunters on the Wyoming plains, and the early cattle men who trailed herds up from Texas, often found the country lacking in timber and, unable to build, made their winter quarters in excavations in a bank or hillside near a spring or stream. These shelters were called dugouts, and buffalo or cow hides were used to cover their entrances. Early settlers in the State sometimes used similar shelters. One of these dugouts that housed a pioneer family was built near Oil Creek in Weston County. It is described as an excavation, 16 feet square, made in the southern slope of a hill; it was roofed with boards and earth and had a window in the upper half of the door. The dirt floor was covered with cattails as a padding for the carpet; the walls were lined with muslin.

Although the log cabin belongs to every pioneer era, the first log houses built by the early Wyoming settlers differed in some respects from those of other regions, especially from those in the Southern mountains; these differences were mainly due to the type of materials at hand and the later date of construction. The logs used for Wyoming cabins were seldom dressed down, and stone fireplaces were rarely constructed. Most of these early cabins were one-room, rectangular buildings about 12 by 15 feet, built by notching the logs and fitting them one above the other at the corners so that some six inches or more of each log projected. The joints between the logs were battened with large chips, over which a chinking of mud, clay, dung, or plaster was daubed. Some cabins were chinked first with mud, or plaster, and then stripped with lathes or lengths of crude lumber. There were no foundations, and earth was banked around the base to keep out the cold and wind. In some of the cabins of later construction, the walls were built by cutting a groove in one log, filling the groove with oakum, and then laying over it a peeled log smoothed to fit the groove. With this arrangement no further chinking was necessary.

Most of the cabins had roofs made of small poles, brush, or rough slabs covered with about six inches of dirt, from which plants or weeds grew in season. Some of these roofs extended over the front of the houses, forming a porch. The porch roofs varied, some projecting in the form of a gable, others sloping over the door in the manner of a lean-to.

The cabins for the most part were low-ceiled and had a door in the center of the front wall and a small window on each side. The windows were usually of the barn-sash type (a single sash with four small panes), hung on hinges to open either in or out; or, if two sashes were used, they were so constructed that the sashes could be pushed back into a groove in the wall when the windows were opened. Windows and doors facing north were avoided, especially in the windswept open country and in areas where snowfall was heavy and slow to melt in spring.

Since Wyoming was not settled until after the coming of the railway, stoves were usually cheaper and more convenient than stone fireplaces and flues. The stovepipe, collared by a piece of sheet iron or tin, projected above the roof.

The first cabins were built by trappers, hunters, or cattlemen without families, who worked singly or in pairs and hence, being out in the mountains or on the range much of the time, did not need large living quarters. Later, when settlers arrived, their cabins grew with their families, the added rooms forming a rambling structure of no particular design. These paintless, weather-beaten dwellings of natural logs gradually assumed the brown color of the hills and prairies.

A few of the early cabins had two compartments under one roof with a runway between, similar to the 'dogtrot' houses of the Atlantic States. One half of the building was living quarters, and the other half served as a barn. A hewn-log building of this type, said to be one of the oldest cabins in Wyoming, is still standing on the Goose Egg Ranch in Natrona County.

It was characteristic of many of the earliest ranches that the living quarters and bunkhouses were comparatively small, while the barns, cattle sheds, outbuildings, and pole corrals for the livestock were extensive. As the ranchman's holdings increased he built a larger and better house for his family. Since there was always plenty of space, he did not tear down the original cabin but merely built another one near it, using the first one for a bunkhouse or storehouse. Many ranches today have a group of cabins of various ages, sizes, and shapes clustered together with a modern home near by. In some areas the roofs of the outbuildings are thatched with brush and straw, and where the loft is absent, hay for winter feeding is often stacked on top of the one-story barn.

Probably the best known cabin in the State is the Jim Baker cabin, now in Frontier Park, Cheyenne. Originally it stood near Snake River in Carbon County, where it was built in 1873 by Jim Baker, noted scout and frontiersman. The State appropriated money to have the cabin moved to its present site. Made of hewn logs, dovetailed at the corners, it was at first a three-story structure of the blockhouse type, with a cupola and loopholes. Later the cupola was removed, leaving two stories, the upper one smaller than the lower.

In Wyoming's frontier towns the 'false front' building was typical. It was a structure with a square front extending beyond the ridge of the roof to give the effect of another story. The first dwellings in these small communities were erected with whatever materials were at hand and in any fashion suited to the builder's craftsmanship.

As early as 1869 a brick business house was erected in Cheyenne, and in the 1870's many two-story brick buildings appeared in the business district, particularly in 1874, when a number of disastrous fires destroyed much property in the town. During that year more than $66,000 was expended in brick buildings in the new town, including many one-story brick dwellings.

The business buildings were constructed of so-called 'fireproof brick,' and often had eight- or ten-foot cellars. Usually the lower story was used for a store, bank, or other business purpose, while the upstairs was arranged for offices, lodge rooms, or living quarters. When livery stables flourished, various types of business were carried on in their upper stories in space not required to store hay and other feed. Bill Nye's *Boomerang* was first published in a room over a Laramie livery stable, which was entered by an outside wooden stair. At the bottom of the stair was the sign 'Twist the Grey Mule's Tail and Take the Elevator.'

The Drug Emporium of Addoms & Glover at Cheyenne was described in 1874 as a 'two story fire proof brick with an iron and Frear stone front.' The walls and ceilings were said to 'present a beautiful cream-colored appearance, with imitation frescoe in dark brown color, just beneath where the walls and ceiling meet. The room is divided forty-six feet from the door by a partition and architrave, on top of which stands a bust of the American eagle with poised wings and gilded plumage. In front is a handsome dispensing counter of black walnut, elaborately carved. The shelving is set off by copiously carved mouldings and brackets, and heavy cornices, richly painted and refinished in gloss.' The establishment of Pease & Taylor in 1875 was 'two-story, firepoof brick, 28 by 96 feet, with a 10-foot cellar underneath the whole. The door columns, caps, sills, window caps and sills, and corner trimmings are of polished Manitou marble, and make an elegant and attractive front.'

In the 1880's and 1890's many English and Scotch cattle owners established permanent town houses in Wyoming, a number of them building substantial frame structures in Cheyenne. These were designed in the manner of medieval English rural architecture with low roof lines and half-timbering. Some of these houses still stand in Cheyenne, including those now owned by Mrs. Harry P. Hynds, 118 East Eighteenth Street, Mrs. R. S. Van Tassell, 1622 Morrie Avenue, the Charles D. Carey family, 821 East Seventeenth Street, the Potter Apartments, Warren Avenue and Eighteenth Street, and the house formerely owned by Percy Hoyt at the corner of Eighteenth and House Streets. The old Laramie Club at Fifth Street and University Avenue in Laramie, once the headquarters of a group of wealthy Albany County cattlemen (now owned by the Woodmen of the World Lodge), is also of this old English rural type. Several such houses were designed by W. S. Rainsford, an architect who practiced for many years in New York City and who owned and operated the Diamond Ranch near Chugwater.

Some of the English ranchmen constructed substantial stone residences that reflected the more formal type of English country house popular in the reign of Queen Anne. Others built ranch houses of hewn logs, carefully dovetailed and chinked with white plaster.

Many of the miners who settled in the Rock Springs area made use of native stone to construct houses along the sheltered hillsides. They discovered that the alkali mud from Killpecker Creek made a perfect chinking. One house built more than 60 years ago still retains its original mud mortar. In the Burntfork district in southwestern Wyoming, native clay has been used unchanged as plaster for inside walls. A few buildings of a coarse kind of cement, called 'grout,' have been built in various sections.

The influence of Sir Charles L. Eastlake, a late nineteenth-century English architect, spread through Wyoming during the 1880's and 1890's. It shows itself in many small houses, in queer windows of 'bull's-eye' glass, turned spindles, fringes and frills around porch pillars, an effusion of sunflowers and rosettes, and myriad jigsaw curlicues dripping from the eaves.

About this time a number of pretentious three-story red-brick homes were erected in the State, especially in Cheyenne. The luxuriously appointed interiors have hardwood floors inlaid in intricate patterns, hand-carved stairways, and elaborate ceilings. Typical examples in Cheyenne are the homes of the late Senator Joseph M. Carey, Twenty-second Street and Carey Avenue, and the late Judge John W. Lacey, 300 East Seventeenth Street, the Idleman residence, 2323 Carey Avenue, and in Newcastle the home of former U. S. Representative Frank W. Mondell.

The homesteaders and dry farmers who swarmed into Wyoming in the late 1890's and early 1900's built many one-room shacks, approximately 10 by 14 feet. These were, for the most part, constructed of slabs of rough-hewn lumber, covered with a thickness of tar paper that was held down with laths fastened by shingle nails in tin discs; sometimes they were covered by a second wall of slabs. Since an all-year residence was not required on the homesteads, these shacks were often built for use only in the warmer months. Many, however, were lined with heavy building paper inside and banked on the outside with dirt, which insulated them against cold weather. The slabs used in many of the shacks of this type were called 'winnie edge,' the term applied to the first cut after the main slab was removed from the log. The roofs of rough lumber, covered with tar paper, had a one-third to one-fourth pitch. A lean-to of slabs was often built on a shack to provide space for storage or for fuel. Since the shack was not accredited to 'improvements' on the homestead, the barn was often a much more substantial structure. In the more prosperous communities the tar-paper shacks have given way to trim farmhouses of the modern frame bungalow type.

Another frame dwelling seen in various parts of the State is known as the Mormon 'box house,' a perfectly square house with a four-sided roof. The dude ranches in Wyoming are not outstandingly different from those in other areas. They usually include a large community building of peeled and polished logs, used as a dining and recreation hall. Easily accessible to this main building are individual cabins, replicas of those of frontier days, where the guests are housed.

The use of heavy timber and native stone is especially favored for construction in national parks and in recreational areas. The new

Guernsey Lake Museum at Guernsey Lake Park, designed by the architect of the National Park Service, is massive in appearance, with weather-faced sandstone walls, thick at the base and tapering upward. The roof is of open rafter construction covered with cedar shakes, laid apparently at random in keeping with the rustic architecture. The hardware is of heavy hand-hammered iron, made by camp workers. The picnic shelters in the park are also of massive native rock and timber construction.

Peeled-log construction is now used widely over the State, not only in summer homes and permanent residences, but in churches, hospitals, museums, and even airplane hangars. In Yellowstone Park peeled-log buildings predominate. Old Faithful Inn, designed by R. C. Reamer of Seattle, is said to be one of the largest and finest log structures in the United States. The Canyon Hotel, celebrated for its huge lounge, is built on bold structural lines entirely in keeping with its grand primeval setting.

The rural schools of the State have been standardized in design and are usually constructed of lumber, painted white. In the northeastern part of the State the newer schools are constructed of poured concrete, tinted by the red sand used in the mixture. These country schools usually have 20 square feet of floor space per person and ample window areas. Because of the sparse settlement in the country districts, the small school is usually located on a section equidistant from a number of ranch houses—frequently the only building in sight.

The public libraries, most of which were built through Carnegie aid, are designed largely in the classical mode. One of the most notable of these is the Carnegie Library in Cheyenne. Of the other public buildings, it can not be said that any particular style is represented, although they are generally similar in design. Many of them were designed by William A. Dubois of Cheyenne in neoclassic and modified Romanesque style, making use whenever possible of native stone. Frederick H. Porter, another architect of Cheyenne, usually designs his public buildings in the neoclassic style.

In 1923 the University of Wyoming began to develop an architectural program through the work of Wilbur Hitchcock, professor of engineering and architecture. His most successful works in the State are the Albany County Courthouse in Laramie and the Engineering Building at the University of Wyoming, both of Neo-Gothic design. The Ivinson Home for Aged Women in Laramie, also designed by Hitchcock, follows the English half-timbered style.

Since the death of Mr. Hitchcock in 1930 other architects have continued to adopt the Gothic to the University of Wyoming buildings. The university owns its own quarries of sandstone, which varies in tints from a delicate buff to deep rose. 'Old Main,' the first building erected on the campus, is an example of Romanesque revival architecture, with thick walls, round arch construction, and small openings.

The Cathedral Close, on the edge of Laramie's business district, has the atmosphere of Old-World cloister. St. Matthew's Episcopal Cathedral, of Tudor Gothic design, built of native stone, dominates the square. It was designed by William Halsey Wood of New York City and was completed in 1916. The ten stained-glass windows in the edifice were made by Heaton, Butler, and Bayne of London and New York. The Sherwood School for Boys and the Deanery are of the same style. The Bishop's Home, directly north of the Cathedral, is of Georgian Colonial architecture in red brick. The cathedral tower was designed by Frederick H. Porter.

Parco Hotel at Parco is another notable example of stylistic architecture. The style of this hotel is in the Spanish tradition. The design of the ceiling in the lobby is based upon the famous wooden ceiling in the cloister of the former Monastery of Montesion, Barcelona, by Agostin Regalt.

A new type of construction has been attempted in Cheyenne with the erection of an all-steel residence. Because of the cost of importing the material and the necessity of having skilled workmen, this structural innovation is not yet practicable for housing.

Perhaps the most streamlined modern buildings are the numerous filling stations, tourist camps, and small hotels along the main highways of the State.

Bridge construction emphasizes again the characteristic aspect of the State as a whole: the presence of the primitive and the modern, side by side. It is possible to find simple arrangements of poles laid across stringers that are set on cribs filled with rocks; but there are also fine structures of concrete and steel.

Barns, bridges, fences, and hayfield equipment in Wyoming vary in design in different sections of the State. There are low-built cattle sheds with open fronts facing the south, huge hip-roof barns for storing tons of hay and accommodating dairy stock, and, in areas where winters are severe, the snugly built log barns with thatched roofs. Fences are of varying types: pole, buck, and barbwire. Stackers, go-devils, sweeps, and other hayfield equipment are for the most part constructed along the same lines whether in the ranching country of the Saratoga Valley or in the Jackson Hole.

The miles and miles of open country in southern Wyoming are broken now and then by clusters of yellow frame section houses and black water tanks along the Union Pacific. Tall, slender block signals and telegraph poles occasionally break the monotony of broad spaces. In the dry farming country, windmills are scattered along the skyline, and in the beet country and rich farming areas silos tower above the farmhouses and outbuildings. But here and there, throughout the State, a cabin or dugout reminds the traveler of the still-present pioneer.

PART II

Cities

Casper

Railroad Stations: Burlington Station, N. Wolcott and E. C Sts., for Chicago, Burlington & Quincy R.R.; Chicago and North Western Station, Railroad Ave. and Center St., for Chicago & North Western Ry.
Bus Stations: Burlington Station, 152 N. Center St., for Burlington Transportation Co., Salt Creek Transportation Co., Wyoming Motorways, and Hays-Robinson Transportation Co.
Airport: Wardwell Field, 6 m. N. on US 87, for Inland Air Service; taxi 50¢.
Taxis: 25¢ upward according to distance and number of passengers.
City Bus Line: Fare 5¢.

Accommodations: 13 hotels, 11 tourist camps.

Information Service: Chamber of Commerce, 328 E. 2nd St.

Radio Station: KDFN (1440 kc.).
Motion-Picture Houses: 3.
Swimming: V. F. W. Pool, Washington Memorial Park, Jefferson St. between 10th and 6th Sts., 8 a.m. to 8 p.m.
Golf: Community Course, 4.5 blocks E. of intersection of Wolcott and 15th Sts. and 2 blocks S. on County road, 18 holes, greens fee 75¢.
Baseball and Softball: Burlington Park, Center and E. F Sts., and High School Athletic Field, 8th St. between Oak and Elm Sts. and extending to Railroad Ave., for Wyoming Semi-Professional League baseball and Casper Civic League softball.
Polo: Municipal Polo Ground, 1.2 m. W. on Carey Lane, local and regional meets during summer.

Annual Events: Boot and Spur Horse Show, in late May or early June; Caspar Collins Day, July 26; picnics of Natrona· County Pioneer Association, Aug.; Wyoming-on-Parade, Aug. (third week); Natrona County Pioneer Association Reunion, Nov. 12; poultry show, no definite date; Wyoming State High School Music Festival, variable date in spring.

CASPER (5,123 alt., 16,619 pop.), seat of Natrona County and second largest city in Wyoming, lies in a great bend on the south side of the North Platte River; south of the town the pine-studded slopes of Casper Mountain rise to an altitude of more than 8,000 feet.

An industrialized cow-town, Casper retains many characteristics of its youth. Ranch hands of the old C Y outfit, whose pastures once included present Casper, still work cattle and make hay almost within the shadows of oil refineries and storage tanks. Sage chickens scuttle between clumps of sage and rabbit brush on the outskirts of the city, and residents drive out to the flats to watch the cocks parade during the mating season in the spring.

Log cabins and derelict frame buildings still shoulder against newer brick structures. Residential additions extend Old Casper on the south, east, and north, and unimproved plots within the additions suggest the tempestuous nature of Casper's growth. Its streets are wide, and many are bordered with sentinel rows of cottonwoods and poplars. Newer residences in the southern sector are of Georgian colonial style, with brick walls, circular porticoes, and wrought-iron balconies. The Standard Addition, southwest of the original townsite, has several hundred houses of modified Spanish mission design.

Casper's central location in Wyoming has contributed much to its development as an industrial and commercial center. Its basic industry is oil, but its geographic location at the juncture of four national highways and two mainline railroads has made it the distribution point for a wide trade area. Trucks loaded with casing and cables lumber through the city to near-by oil fields. Freight is piled high at the depot yards for transportation to rural areas or reclamation projects in the Casper trade zone. The silver Mainliners of Inland Air Lines fly north and south from their Casper headquarters; the drone of their motors rises above the hum of city activity as they gain altitude or circle into the landing headwind.

Casper's outstanding annual event is Wyoming-on-Parade, during the third week in August. The feature is a parade that reproduces scenes from the city's and State's frontier days, and the subsequent progress and development. Of unusual interest is the jerkline freight team of 16 horses harnessed to three old freight wagons and driven by bona-fide 'mule skinners.' Legendary frontier characters are revived and uniformed bands, National Guard cavalry units, and gaudily clad cowboys and cowgirls complete the procession.

The Platte River Valley provided the most satisfactory wagon route westward during the 1840's and 1850's, and an estimated 300,000 persons followed the Oregon Trail across what is now the townsite of Casper before wagon traffic was rerouted over the southern Overland Trail in the 1860's. The first white men known to pass through the region were Robert Stuart's Astorians, who trekked through central Wyoming in 1812, en route to St. Louis from Astor's Pacific Coast trading post. The exploring parties of Bonneville and Frémont followed, and in 1842 Elijah White's prairie schooners were rolling along the Platte.

In June 1847 Brigham Young's first company of Mormon emigrants camped about three miles east of present Casper, where John Richaud (Reshaw) later built his toll bridge. Here the Saints constructed a sole-leather skiff to transport their wagons across the Platte, but a train of Oregon-bound Missourians arrived before the Mormons were boated across. The Saints, with an unwavering eye for business, rented their ferry to the gentiles and crossed their own wagons on pole rafts about five miles up the river. Young charged the Missourians $1.50 per wagon transported; pay was in flour, bacon, and meal at Missouri prices, and the proceeds were divided equally among those of the Mormon train. 'It looked as much of a miracle to me,' wrote Apostle Wilford Woodruff, 'to see our flour and meal bags replenished in the

Black Hills, as it did to have the children of Israel fed with manna in the wilderness.' When the train resumed its journey toward the Utah Canaan, Young left several men to ferry oncoming Mormons across the Platte, and also instructed them to assist gentile trains 'in the hope of earning enough to supply the later Mormon trains with badly needed provisions.'

When migration to Oregon increased in the early 1850's, Louis Guinard built a substantial toll bridge near present Fort Caspar (*see Tour* 11), for which the city was named. The difference in spelling is attributed to a careless railway clerk's mistake.

The Treaty of 1868 confined the Cheyenne, Arapaho, and Sioux to the north side of the Platte, but not until the tribes were herded onto reservations in 1877 was the Platte Valley considered safe for ranching. The first major outfit to move north of the Platte was the J. M. Carey Company, which trailed a herd of 15,000 cattle to the Platte Valley in the autumn of 1876. Cattle did well on the buffalo grass and other ranchers followed Carey into the region.

In 1885 the Chicago & North Western Railroad, which controlled the Fremont, Elkhorn, & Missouri Valley Railroad, then operating between Omaha and Chadron, Nebraska, announced plans to extend its line west into the rich central-Wyoming cattle country. In 1888 Judge Carey designated part of the C Y meadowland as the site for a new town. Settlers filtered in, and when the first passenger train arrived on June 15, nearly 100 persons had located on the townsite. Here they lived in tents, shacks, wagon boxes, and dugouts until November, when the town was platted and lots sold by the Pioneer Townsite Company for about $250 each. Lumber was provided for new buildings by a sawmill on Casper Mountain, seven miles away.

Casper was the terminus of the branch railroad until 1905, when the line was extended to Lander, but the railroad was not then a main line, and the city's growth did not parallel that of the earlier Union Pacific terminals. In 1889 when the population numbered only a few hundred, eight saloons stood along Main Street, a geographical abstraction 500 feet long. The town's best customers were Indians and cowboys. When the cowboys came to town, usually once a month, they spent cash freely on '40 rod' whisky and other available entertainment. Businessmen tolerated the cowboys' strenuous relaxation, for their stay was limited to two or three days a month and the cash drawers of the bartenders and shopkeepers were heavier when they left.

The town was incorporated in April 1889, and an ordinance adopted at the first meeting of the new council made it unlawful to discharge firearms within the town's limits. But it is recorded that within a year the mayor beat his man to the draw in a personal duel on Main Street, while disinterested citizens ducked for cover. A civic decree also made it unlawful for any woman to 'use any vile, profane, or indecent language, or to act in a boisterous or lewd manner, or to smoke any cigar, cigarette or pipe on Casper's streets,' and a similar law forbade any woman, on pain of fine, to 'frequent or remain in the barroom of any saloon in the town of Casper between the hours of 7 A.M. and 10 P.M.'

Until the spring of 1898, when a reform government was voted in on a promise to whitewash the town, woman's emancipation in Casper was complete between ten in the evening and seven in the morning. But the reformers revoked the privilege and banned all women from saloons; they also practiced a mild form of vigilante authority in ridding downtown Casper of its less desirable citizenry.

Until the underground water and sewage system was completed in 1896, drinking water was supplied by a series of civic wells. These were equipped with hand pumps in 1891, but well water was in such demand that saloons purchased river water 'chasers' at 35¢ a barrel. The first firemen's organization assessed volunteer members a fee in 1895, and purchased a complete outfit: hose-cart, 150 feet of hose, nozzle, and a trumpet for the chief. Although it was a year before the civic water system was installed, the bright-red equipment was displayed with pride at every fire, while bucket brigades extinguished the blaze.

Casper's first school, a private one, was established in March 1889 with 19 pupils attending. In July, School District No. 33 of Carbon County was organized, and a public school was opened that autumn in the Congregational Church, first religious sect in Casper.

The organization of the northern third of Carbon County into Natrona County was authorized in the same unprecedented bill that created Sheridan County in 1888, but, owing to financial inability, the new county did not function until 1890. In April of that year there was an election to select the new county seat. Casper and Bessemer, a village several miles southwest, competed for the distinction. Bessemer piled up a vote of 731 to Casper's 353; but since all votes for Bessemer were cast in its own precincts, and since its population was less than 100, the election commissioners ruled that the Bessemer ballots were 'irregular,' and the vote was not considered. The county seat was awarded to Casper.

The usual gold strike was made near Casper in the early 1890's. Businessmen, laborers, cowboys, and shopkeepers shouldered miners' tools and looked for yellow metal on Casper Mountain. Excitement became intense as rumors of rich ore deposits persisted. Then, as suddenly as it had arisen, the fever was over. But gold is where you find it, and prospectors looked for it on Casper Mountain until 1895, when exhaustive tests showed the 'rich' veins were only asbestos.

The first oil well in the Casper area was brought in on the Salt Creek Field in 1890 (see Tour 3b). A gaping world soon heard of the rich Wyoming oil pockets. The fine texture of the 'liquid gold' amazed analytic chemists in the East, who declared solemnly that such oil did not exist in a natural state. They suspected the samples had been compounded with animal oils, and direct investigations were made before prospective financiers were convinced the Casper strike was not a hoax.

The Pennsylvania Oil and Gas Company, owners of six producing wells on the Salt Creek Field, erected the first refinery in Wyoming at Casper in 1895. Crude oil was hauled 50 miles from the wells in tanks attached to the running gears of specially built wagons. Oil was carried one way and supplies for oil workers the other. Freighting became an industry. An outfit, usually comprising four wagons pulled by 28 mules, was piloted by two drivers or 'mule skinners.' When the weather was good, the freighter averaged ten or twelve miles a day. When the roads were impassable, loaded wagons might be abandoned for several days, while the drivers drafted stray horses into service or went for repairs. Although Casper harbored rustlers, thieves, and bandits, a freighter's wagon was seldom molested. Like sheep stealing, robbing abandoned freight wagons was below even a horse thief's dignity.

For 25 years Casper had only one railroad. The Chicago & North Western Railroad hauled all freight, mail, express, and passengers to and from the city until October 20, 1913, when the Chicago, Burlington & Quincy Railroad service was established. The Burlington had an 'accommodation passenger run' before the regular service was started. The crews frequently left the train standing between stations while they hunted sage chickens or jack rabbits on the prairies. The passengers had the choice of joining the chase or amusing themselves until the trainmen returned.

The World War oil market and the construction of two pipe lines from Salt Creek to Casper in 1916 precipitated the oil boom era, whose peak was reached late in 1917.

A building boom accompanied the expansion of the oil industry. Temporary shacks, reminiscent of the earlier frontier, were erected of scrap lumber and metal in the city and in the oil camps. Living quarters in garages, basements, sheds, and tents brought enormous rentals; many could find no place to sleep and walked Casper's streets all night. Trucks and wagons crowded the unimproved roads between Casper and the oil fields. Stocks were sold at auction and local companies organized to share in the profits. Businessmen closed their shops and doctors and lawyers left their offices to buy, sell, and rebuy stocks. Ministers in black frock coats haggled with faro dealers over leases and margins. Aproned housewives supported babies on one arm and waved greenback bills at auctioneers with the other. The poor were rich and the rich were richer—or broke.

Most trading was in the lobby of the Midwest (Henning) Hotel. Brokers operated in small rooms off the lobby, for which they paid fabulous rentals. Auctioneers shouted themselves hoarse from the tops of desks, and when trading became too heavy, business was conducted in the streets. New oil companies were organized every day, and their stocks placed on the block. Some companies had rich holdings and others sold claims on worthless waste lands. Buyers purchased indiscriminately; brokers complained of a slump if no more than half a million dollars in stocks changed hands in a day.

Land-grabbers and claim-jumpers were there, and hardy line riders, successors to the solitary line riders of the cattle-sheep range feud, were engaged to patrol lease boundaries. Titles to valuable lands were acquired by strong-arm or extralegal methods, and national cabinet

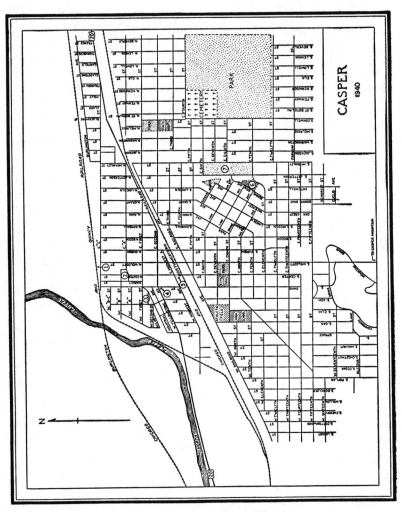

KEY FOR CASPER MAP

1. Old Freight Wagon and Concord Stagecoach   2. Natrona County Courthouse
3. The Sanbar   4. Site of the Old Town Hall   5. Pioneer Monument   6. Little
House   7. Washington Memorial Park

members were embroiled with hijackers, fakers, and shyster lawyers
in the eventual exposé. The most notorious case was that of the Teapot
Dome, investigation of which sent a Secretary of the Interior to Federal
prison (*see Tour* 3).

During the conflicts, contests, and litigations, the Midwest Oil Company in ten years grew from a small local corporation to a $50,000,000
concern before it was in turn swallowed by the Standard Oil Company.
The Standard refinery, built in 1914, was one of the largest in the

United States. The Producers' and Refiners' Corporation plant, with a capacity to handle 40,000,000 cubic feet of natural gas, was classed as the largest absorptive plant in the world. In 1923 the Texas Company erected a third large refinery three miles east of the city. A year later the White Eagle Company also established its refinery east of the city.

The boom pushed Casper into prominence. Its population increased until a local census in 1925 showed 30,000 persons within the city limits and 2,000 in the suburban refinery camps. During the period of growth and free spending, the sky was the limit in Casper, and astounded residents of the former cow-town could see no limit to the rising value of waste lands and the free flow of capital. Hundreds of thousands of dollars were spent on luxurious hotels and office buildings. A million dollars was spent to build and equip a high school, and the municipal government launched a sweeping program of civic improvements. Residents saw Casper as the financial and industrial center of the Rocky Mountain region. They resented Denver and were chagrined that their city was not the seat of the State government. Pointing to its more central geographic location, its superior population, its money and industries, Casper newspapers conducted a vigorous drive for removal of the capital from Cheyenne to Casper, and civic organizations flooded the State with a series of 'Casper the Capital' folders and pamphlets.

But the boom ended in the late 1920's. The steadily producing wells were connected to feeder lines, and their rigs were dismantled. Several hundred miles of pipe line connected the fields with Casper refineries, and the need for extensive field equipment was over. A small branch railroad was built from Illco, near the edge of Casper, to the town of Salt Creek, thus eliminating the truckers. The financial crisis and crash of 1930 completed the retrenchment, and within a few years Casper's population was little more than half its total during the boom years.

POINTS OF INTEREST

1. OLD FREIGHT WAGON AND CONCORD STAGECOACH, W. end of Chicago, Burlington and Quincy Railroad Station on E. C St., at N. Wolcott St., are covered by a frame canopy with screened-in sides. Both were used on the Overland Trail route across the Laramie Plains in the late 1860's.

2. The NATRONA COUNTY COURTHOUSE, N. Center St. at intersection with A St., a brick and sandstone structure erected in 1907, houses the county offices. In the sheriff's quarters in the basement is an OLD GUN COLLECTION (*may be seen upon arrangement*), the property of Sheriff R. John Allen, who came west from New York in the late 1880's. During his subsequent career as cowhand, Rough Rider in the Spanish-American War, member of Buffalo Bill Cody's Wild West Show, World War soldier, State law-enforcement officer, and sheriff, he collected old guns and other historical relics.

Included in the collection is a long-barreled, delicately balanced single-action Colt .45 pistol, in whose yellow ivory grips eight notches have been filed. The gun, once the property of a Hole-in-the-Wall outlaw, is known to have taken the lives of two United States marshals. An old Spencer rifle, dated 1860, has a long barrel and a singular magazine attachment in the stock, resembling the clip in an automatic pistol. An old Sharps single-shot buffalo gun was picked up on the site of the Wounded Knee Battle on the Sioux reservation in South Dakota, in which battle Chief Sitting Bull was killed. The gun has several notches in its stock, and other marks indicate it was carried for some time in a boot; an old Springfield was used by Troop B of the Seventh Cavalry in the Battle of the Little Big Horn in Montana; its regulation leather sheath is still in good condition. A muzzle-loading handmade flintlock dates back to the 1700's; a colonial squirrel rifle, beautifully inlaid and carved, is complete even to the ramrod. An old matchlock rifle, manufactured in China, is typical of those used in South Sea trade, and a cap and ball Remington used in the Civil War is complete with tallow box and ramrod.

Also displayed are several old coins dating back to the Puritan colonization in New England, a 175-year-old snuff box, a French inkwell used at Brandywine, a gun-knife that functions in either capacity, the peace pipe of old Chief Spoon Hunter, and many Indian arrowheads.

3. The SITE OF OLD TOWN HALL, 200 S. David St., is occupied by a row of business houses. The old hall, 140 by 30 feet, was erected in 1890 at a cost of $1,985. Public buildings were rare in Casper, and in 1895, when the ground floor was equipped with a stage, lighting effects, dressing rooms, scenery, and a drop curtain adorned with a mountain landscape bordered by business advertising signs, the hall was Casper's social center. Here, when the council was not in session, stock companies and home-talent organizations presented shows and opera; political parties rented the auditorium for rallies; school and church classes convened in the foyer; and on Saturday nights the benches were pushed back against the walls for public dances. In 1910 the first moving picture in Casper was shown in the old hall. Two years later the structure was nearly destroyed by fire and was restored to serve as a firehouse. In 1917 the building and grounds were traded to private individuals for a site on which to erect a new city building.

The old city jail occupied a wing of the hall. Here Red Cloud, fallen war lord of the Big Horns, was imprisoned. In June 1894 the former generalissimo of the Sioux and Cheyenne passed through Casper en route to the Shoshone Reservation to visit Arapaho friends. The old chieftain, who had passed his seventieth birthday, was accompanied by his son Jack Red Cloud, his chief counsellor Dreaming Bear, and about 300 braves and women. When the troupe returned from the mountains, searchers found fresh antelope in the wagons. The chief, his son, and Dreaming Bear were promptly placed under arrest and confined to the city jail. To the charge of hunting antelope out of season was added the ironical charge that the chief and his people were nonresidents of the State. Fines of $20 each were imposed on the three leaders and, as they could not pay, they were held in jail several days. At last authorities agreed to accept Red Cloud's team, wagon, and harness in payment of the fine and costs. They demanded a bill of sale for the property, then escorted the tribesmen to the city limits and ordered them to leave Wyoming.

4. PIONEER MONUMENT, S. Center St. between Midwest Ave. and the North Western Railroad tracks, in a small grassed area with encircling drive, is a limestone obelisk 40 feet high, erected in 1911 by women of the Natrona County Pioneer Association, at a cost of $3,000. The monument, which marks the Oregon Trail, is constructed in three sections, tapering at the top into a four-square point. It bears a bronze tablet commemorating the pioneers of the Oregon Trail and Fort Caspar, U. S. military post.

5. The LITTLE HOUSE, Girl Scouts' Casper Clubhouse, 1011 Bonnie Brae Ave., is a one-story California-style stucco house with living room and large demonstration rooms. Here also are craft rooms and shops, where the girls make rugs, weave, do leather work, and make tincraft objects that resemble beaten silver. In the yard at the rear is a large outdoor fireplace for steak fries and outdoor picnics.

6. WASHINGTON MEMORIAL PARK, Jefferson St. between E. 10th and E. 6th Sts. and extending to McKinley St., covers 26 acres of landscaped ground, overlooking the greater part of the city. The park contains the Veterans of Foreign Wars' swimming pool (*open in summer, lifeguard*), tennis courts, baseball diamond, horseshoe courts, and ice-skating pond.

MOUNTAIN DRIVE TOUR

Left from Casper on S. Wolcott St. which becomes a graveled road; on this road to MONTGOMERY HILL, 0.2 *m.*, which commands a splendid view of the city, the outlying tank 'farms,' refineries, and other industrial plants. The highway parallels an equestrian path (R) to the high plateau at the crest of the hill, then proceeds southward over rolling hills and begins a steep climb at 4.6 *m.* In the distance R. along the base of Casper Mountain are a number of summer homes scattered along Upper Garden Creek. At BESSEMER TURN, 5.3 *m.*, there is a turnout with a view of the valley and plains far below through which the tree-bordered Platte River makes a huge S. Continuing, the road narrows and climbs very rapidly up steep grades and around blind curves. Drive carefully. There are no guard rails. The HAIRPIN TURN, beginning at 5.7 *m.*, attains an altitude of 6,800 feet. Paralleling a rushing mountain stream with a deep, timbered canyon (R), the road crosses the STATE GAME PRESERVE BOUNDARY, 7.1 *m.* Here is BROOKSIDE INN (R), 7,200 alt. DIXIE LODGE, 7.4 *m.*, is at the base of Thunder Bolt Ski Course, two-and-one-half miles in length. High up on the mountainside to the R. is the shafthouse of an old asbestos mine. ASBESTOS SPRING, 7.7 *m.* (R), has good drinking water. WA-WA LODGE, 8 *m.*, serves meals in season and has a dance floor. At 8.2 *m.* is the junction with a dirt road; L. here .25 *m.* to the CCC CAMP, LIONS CLUB LODGE and CAMP FOR GIRL SCOUTS. At 8.3 *m.* is an excellent view of the NURSERY SKI COURSE, along which are many cabins owned by Casper residents. As many as 2,500 people attend the winter sports events on the mountain.

Continuing, the road becomes the City Park Loop and Circle Drive, which crosses the top of the mountain and intersects State 220 (*see Tour* 11). At 10 *m.* is the SITE OF OLD EADSVILLE, consisting of 20 acres of land on top of the mountain, which was filed on in 1890 by Charles W. Eads. The tract was surveyed and platted for a stamp mill, and although it had only three log cabins was called a town early in 1891. During the years 1891 and 1892 a dozen cabins were built. In the center of the town was a large spring of pure, ice-cold water, of sufficient flow to supply several hundred people. Gold, silver, galena, copper, lead, and asbestos mines were opened up on the mountains in all directions from the town. The first real mining excitement in this camp occurred in January 1891, when S. S. (Jack) Currier received the certificate of an assay from Omaha on some ore he sent in, which showed 33 ounces of silver and 82 per cent lead. In February of this same year, upon the strength of this assay, a telegram was received from Deadwood, South Dakota, requesting that six carloads of ore per day be shipped to the mills there. Because snow in the canyons was from 6 to 10 feet deep, and since the mines had not yet been properly opened, the shipments could not be made. Many inquiries were made about the vicinity and many men were ready to go into the new camp in the spring. A report made by an expert from a Denver mining syndicate led to the belief that Casper Mountain held copper ore enough to supply a smelter. The excitement grew intense, and the samples of ore continued to run rich in copper and silver. Hundreds of claims were located on the mountain during the spring and early summer. New mines were found and many deals were made. Some of the miners became millionaires over night, on paper. Eadsville continued to grow in population and wealth. When the excitement was at its peak, a report was received from the smelter to the effect that the returns were not sufficient to justify the work and the cash outlay for the production and transportation of ore. Like the rush of an avalanche from the mountainside this news fell upon the community. An exodus followed immediately. Today only the drone of the wind through the logs of a few tumble-down cabins recalls the whine of the windlass.

OTHER POINTS OF INTEREST IN ENVIRONS

Salt Creek Oil Field, 44.6 *m.* (*see Tour* 3*b*); Hell's Half Acre, 42.8 *m.* (*see Tour* 6*a*); Casper Mountain Recreational Area, 10 *m.*, Fort Caspar, 1.3 *m.* Izaak Walton Park and Lodge, 1.4 *m.*, Goose Egg Ranch, 13.8 *m.*, Alcova Dam, 31.7 *m.*, Pathfinder Dam and Reservoir, 43.3 *m.*, Independence Rock, 54.7 *m.*, Devil's Gate, 60.9 *m.*, Seminoe Dam, 71.3 *m.* (*see Tour* 11), Teapot Dome 38.6 *m.* (*see Tour* 3).

Cheyenne

Railroad Stations: Union Pacific Depot, 15th St. and Capitol Ave., for Union Pacific R.R.; Burlington Depot, Capitol Ave. between 15th and 16th Sts., for Chicago, Burlington and Quincy R.R. and Colorado and Southern Ry.

Bus Stations: Union Bus Terminal, 1503 Capitol Ave., for Interstate Transit Lines System (Union Pacific) and Union Pacific Stages; Burlington Depot, Capitol Ave. between 15th and 16th Sts., and the Normandie Hotel, 1516 Capitol Ave., for National Trailways System (Burlington).

Airport: Municipal Airport, NE. boundary of city on US 85–87, for United Air Lines (east-west) and Inland Air Lines (north-south).

Taxis: 25¢ upward, according to number of passengers and distance.

Busses: Cheyenne Motor Bus, 7¢ anywhere in city, 10¢ to Fort Warren.

Traffic Regulations: Stop streets, Randall Ave., Carey Ave. from 20th St. to 26th St., and Central Ave. from 16th St. to 26th St.

Accommodations: 21 hotels, 14 automobile tourist camps. Rates higher during Frontier Days Celebration in July.

Information Service: Chamber of Commerce, 17th St. and Warren Ave.; Rocky Mountain Motorists (AAA), 17th St. and Warren Ave.

Hospital: Frances Warren Pershing Memorial Hospital, 23rd St. between Evans Ave. and House Ave.

Radio Stations: KYAN (1370 kc.), KFBC (1420 kc.).

Theaters and Motion-Picture Houses: Little Theater in Consistory Temple, 20th St. and Capitol Ave., local productions; The Lincoln, 1619 Central Ave., occasional road shows and vaudeville; 3 motion-picture houses.

Tennis: Pioneer Park, 1401 Cosgriff Court.

Swimming: Kiwanis Beach, Lake Terry, on Carey Ave.; bathhouse, free.

Golf: Airport Golf Course, 1 m. N. on US 85–87, 18 holes, greens fee 50¢ a day. Cheyenne Country Club, Carey Ave., 18 holes, greens fee 50¢ a day, 75¢ on Saturdays, Sundays, and holidays.

Fishing: Cheyenne Lakes, May 15 to October 15.

Softball: Pioneer Park, 1401 Cosgriff Court, admission 10¢.

Annual Events: Army Day, Fort F. E. Warren, April 6; Cheyenne Frontier Days, last 5 days in last full week in July.

CHEYENNE (6,062 alt., 17,361 pop.), pronounced *shi-an*, capital and metropolis of Wyoming, is on a broad plain where the gradual slope of the prairie meets the steepening grades of the Laramie Mountains.

Older Cheyenne was laid out parallel with the Union Pacific Railroad tracks, and its streets are diagonal to the main compass points. Recent residential additions were platted with regular compass directions; and where these additions join the original townsite, streets are a maze of pointed intersections, short courts, and blind avenues. Residents and visitors alike are uncertain of compass directions.

Cheyenne is old enough to have crabbed, corroded tenement districts downtown, but the prevalence of green lawns, paved streets, and new pressed-brick and steel houses in all parts of the city give it an atmosphere of 'wet paint' freshness. Old brick and stone mansions in the 1890 style, many with extensive stables converted into garages, are canopied by tall cottonwoods and poplars and surrounded by clusters of modern homes and solid commercial houses. Newer homes in the residential additions are prim and correct on their treeless, terraced lawns. Trees grow slowly on the high plains, and only the earlier-settled parts of the town are old enough to have trees of any size.

Cheyenne's location as a focal point for transcontinental travel has made it a commercial city, with railroad division shops and United Air Lines' repair depot. The cow-town where Tom Horn was hanged in 1903 for the murder of a sheepman's son has changed its ways and its appearance, but stockmen in Stetson hats and high-heeled boots still come to town for supplies, and several thousand market steers are shipped from the Cheyenne ranching area each year. Polo horses raised in the vicinity are sold in far-distant parts of the country.

Persons afflicted with asthma and tuberculosis find relief in Cheyenne's altitude and in the 290 days of sunshine weather experts record each year. Wyoming's 60-day divorce law brings other temporary residents to the State capital.

Once each year during its Frontier Days Celebration, Cheyenne revives its cattleman tradition with hobbles, hackamores, and professional 'bucking strings.' This rodeo, held annually since 1897, was first held on the prairies north of town. Spectators came equipped with umbrellas in case of rain. A bucking horse or steer could be shooed away by suddenly opening the parasol. The show has grown to a five-day celebration that attracts amateur and professional rodeo performers from many parts of the West, and 30,000 spectators from a wider orbit. For several weeks preceding the celebration, Cheyenne citizens dress up in big hats, high-heeled boots, and bright shirts; and the Sioux come in from their Dakota reservation to dance. The bucking strings arrive on special railroad cars.

Headlining Frontier Days is the annual parade at 10 A.M. on Wednesday and Friday. The pageant features the development of transportation facilities in America since 1860 and displays Indian travois, ox-drawn prairie schooners, stagecoaches, freight wagons, lumber wagons, carryalls, surreys, hacks, express wagons, tallyhos, phaetons, tandems, hansoms, single buggies, racing gigs, dogcarts, high-wheeled bicycles, a miniature freight and passenger train, and a replica of a streamliner.

Daily events at the show are the grand entry of contestants; calf roping, bulldogging, bronco, and steer-riding contests; cowgirls' relay race; Indian squaw race; cowboys' pony race; potato race; Indian war dances; wild horse races; Frontier Derby; old-timers' calf-roping contest; and military maneuvers by artillery units from Fort Francis E. Warren, third-largest military post in the United States.

Cheyenne bears the name of an Algonquian tribe of Plains Indians, warlike and skilled horsemen. Major General Grenville M. Dodge, later chief engineer for the Union Pacific, came upon the site of the town while investigating a feasible railroad route over the Laramie Mountains. Dodge and his troops camped on Crow Creek late in the summer of 1865, and two years later as U.P. chief engineer he chose his old campsite as the location of a terminal town. He named it Cheyenne. His pronunciation of the word is not known, but on July 3, 1869, the editor of the *Montana Post* gave its true pronunciation as 'shai-en-na, with a prolonged breathing accent on the second syllable.' The journalist lamented that in condensing the three syllables into two, the whites were 'losing their beauty as no doubt their meaning.'

As soon as Dodge had selected the site of the U.P. terminus, General C. C. Augur and Colonel J. D. Stevenson established Fort D. A. Russell adjoining the town on the northwest. Word soon got around that Cheyenne would be made a division point, and a heterogeneous population began to drift in while the end of track or 'Hell on Wheels' was still at Julesburg, Colorado, 100 miles away.

One commentator of the time divided the population of the frontier into two major groups—those who came West and those who drifted West. Both types stampeded to Cheyenne ahead of the rails. Real-estate speculators, gamblers, shopkeepers, freighters, craftsmen, all saw a bonanza in the future division point. Union Pacific as usual claimed the townsite and laid out building plots to sell. No one was allowed to settle until titles could be furnished. This policy caused unrest; and, at a mass meeting, the citizens denounced the railroad's legal right to the land. They began to settle where they chose and as there was no court to adjust the dispute, they held their claims with guns. But the army's major assignment on the Plains at the time was to protect railroad property, and a troop of bluecoats from the near-by fort immediately drove the land-jumpers from the town. They were not permitted to return until they agreed to respect company ownership.

On August 8, 1867, a charter was adopted; two days later H. M. Hook, owner of the Pilgrim House Hotel and the Great Western Stables, was elected mayor. Four months later the charter was accepted by the Dakota Territorial Legislature and Cheyenne was incorporated.

The first issue of N. A. Baker's *Daily Leader* appeared on September 16, 1867, and on October 25 the telegraph line came in from Laporte, Colorado. Difficulties encountered by the telegraph line crews have a place in Wyoming folklore. Indolent buffalo still roamed the treeless prairie between Omaha and the Laramie Mountains in great herds. They regarded the newly set poles as scratching posts, and several bison could rub a pole out of the ground in a few hours. The line boss decided to spike the poles, points out, to discourage them. This, from the buffalo's point of view, added greatly to their value. Within a few hours, according to the legend, a waiting line of 30 buffalo had formed at every telegraph pole between Cheyenne and Omaha. And when a lone bison lumbered east from Cheyenne, oldsters allowed he had heard of a vacant pole 'somewhere this side of Omaha.'

By November 1867 Cheyenne's population had reached 4,000, and lots that sold originally for $150 were bringing speculators $2,500. Citizens lived in anything that would shed rain and sun: covered wagon boxes, dugouts, tents, shacks. More than 3,000 such dwellings had been erected within six months. A wag described the houses of Cheyenne as 'standing insults to every wind that blows.'

On November 9 John Hardy and John Shaughnessy fought a 126-round prizefight in a makeshift ring downtown; on the same day Cheyenne's first public school was planned.

The rails came in November 13, and Cheyenne 'blew the lid' in observance of the occasion. The first train was piled high with frame shacks, boards, furniture, poles, tents, and all the rubbish of a mushroom city. When the locomotive came to a wheezing stop, a guard jumped off his van and shouted, 'Gentlemen, here's Julesburg.'

By January 1, 1868, 300 business houses were operating, supported by trappers, hunters, laborers, trainmen, engineers, lawyers, artists, Sioux, Cheyenne, Pawnee, railway clerks, gamblers, soldiers, promoters, and professional gunmen.

Commentators invariably associated the terminal town with Hell, and Cheyenne's reputation ranked with that of Julesburg. General Dodge said in 1868 that it was the gambling center of the world, and its reputation grew with its population. When the Reverend J. W. Cook organized an Episcopal congregation in 1868, he received a letter from Pennsylvania addressed merely 'Cheyenne.'

The seditious nature of the frontier is generally overdrawn, but Cheyenne inherited all the lawlessness of the Hell-on-Wheels, in addition to its own soldiery and flotsam. Liquor was cheap, pay was good, and stakes were high for gamblers, confidence men, promoters, and robbers. Soldiers and workers alike were just out of a four-year war where they had been schooled at length in the strategy of quick decision and action. Deaths were frequent, often violent; the cemetery was as essential as the post office. Both came second to the saloon. Enraged Indians and white ruffians were not the worker's only potential enemies. A drunken friend or straying bullets from someone else's quarrel could be as dangerous. Many workers became as callous and excitable as the bad folk. 'Hell must have been raked to furnish them,' one early Cheyenne visitor said, 'and to Hell must they naturally return after graduating here.'

The provisional government was timid and prudent. The only effective law was of the vigilante brand, and the distinction between the lawless and the 'committee' was one of motive, rather than of function or tactics. Of many similar homicides, it was not always determined which were murders and which were executions.

The Dakota Legislature incorporated the city on December 24, 1867, and buttressed the civic government with what authority could be loaned from far-away Yankton. But town officials continued to rely on vigilante support to preserve peace and property.

A log cabin on Thomes Avenue was converted into a jail for tramps and other petty offenders. When the one-room structure became full,

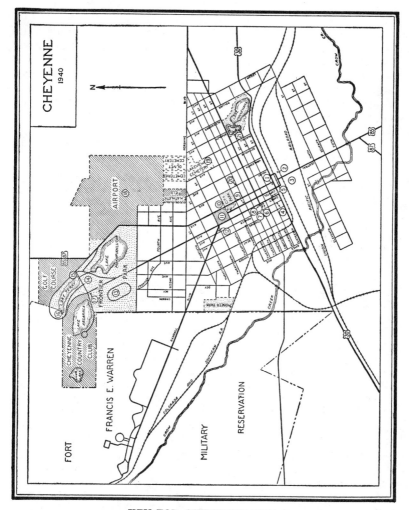

KEY FOR CHEYENNE MAP

1. Plains Hotel 2. Old Stagecoach 3. Union Pacific Railroad Shops and Yards
4. Old McDaniels Block 5. Site of the Old Territorial Legislative Hall
6. Wyoming Stock Growers Association Headquarters 7. Site of the First Public
School in Wyoming 8. City and County Building 9. St. Mary's Cathedral
10. Supreme Court Building 11. Capitol Building 12. Robert Burns Statue
13. Frontier Park 14. Lions Park 15. Kiwanis Beach 16. American Legion Park
17. Old Fort Laramie Trail Marker 18. Airport 19. Lakeview Cemetery
20. Governor's Mansion 21. Holliday Park

a semiofficial mob would take the occupants out, one at a time, ask
each where he wished to go, face him in the named direction, and
suggest that he 'git.' Offenders who didn't get fast enough were hurried
with a whip or with a six-gun kicking dirt at their heels.

W. F. Bailey, in his *Story of the First Transcontinental Railroad* (1906) relates that Colonel Luke Murrin, first mayor of incorporated Cheyenne, added 25¢ to each fine he imposed, explaining that his was dry work and that the extra quarter was to cover the expense of stimulants necessary to efficient administration of justice. Citizens also complained that Murrin advanced the city's script 18¢ on the dollar during his regime, because he fined all persons $10 who shot at someone else in the city limits, whether they hit their target or not.

Louis L. Simonin, a French mineralogist who visited Cheyenne late in 1867, was impressed. He wrote:

> This little city, the youngest, if not the least populated of all cities in the world, which no geography yet mentions, proud of its hotels, its newspapers, its marvelous growth, and its topographic situation, already dreams of the title of capital. It does not wish to be annexed to Colorado. It wishes to annex Colorado. As it is the only city in Dakota, and as this territory is still entirely deserted, it does not wish to be a part of Dakota. It dreams of detaching a fragment from this territory and from Colorado and Utah, of which it will be the center. So local patriotism is born, and so local questions arise, even in the midst of a great desert.

Early in 1868 the churches engineered a civic ordinance that closed all saloons on Sundays from 10 A.M. to 2 P.M. Another statute, poorly enforced, required all visitors to 'check' their guns when entering town. But in January 1868 a reorganized vigilance committee took a firmer stand. The undesirables were known, witnesses were not required, and the committee's judgment was final. No one kept account but 12 men were known to have been executed before the organization was a year old, and numerous others received less severe judgments.

When the railhead was moved west toward Sherman Pass early in 1868, much of the transient population went along. But plans were already drawn for the division point shops, and within a year the grade of a spur railroad to Denver was being completed. Red Cloud was fighting the first Sioux War north of the Platte, and Camp Carlin at Fort Russell was quartermaster depot for widespread armies and a dozen military posts in the Rocky Mountain region.

In January 1868 Laramie County was reorganized and the county seat transferred from Fort Sanders to Cheyenne. The Wyoming Organic Act was approved by Congress in July 1868, but the new territory did not function until its officials were sworn in on April 15, 1869. Brigadier General John A. Campbell, assistant secretary of war in President Grant's cabinet, was named governor. Cheyenne was the largest town in the new territory, and Governor Campbell promptly designated it as his capital. When the territory became a State in 1890, it was still the largest city, and its $150,000 capitol building had just been completed. So it continued as the capital city, in spite of murmurs from other growing Wyoming towns.

By 1869 cattle were coming north from Texas, and in 1870 the first Wyoming-finished cattle were loaded at Cheyenne for a European mar-

Sports and Recreation

Photograph by Lawrence Harshbarger

BACK FROM THE HUNT

Photograph by courtesy of Crandall Studios

READY FOR THE TRAIL

JACKSON HOLE DUDE RANCH

Photograph by courtesy of Crandall Studios

GRUB TIME ON THE TRAIL

SETTING UP FOR THE NIGHT

FRONTIER DAYS CELEBRATION, CHEYENNE

BULLDOGGER

RIDE 'IM, COWBOY!

SKI RUN, CASPER

Photograph by courtesy of Casper Chamber of Commerce

TALKING IT OVER

Photograph by J. A. Shaw

Photograph by J. Frank McDaniel

COMING DOWN!

RIFFLE FISHING, GARDINER RIVER, YELLOWSTONE PARK

Photograph by courtesy of Hayne Inc.

NIGHT SWIM AT ALCOVA LAKE
Spray from a hot spring provides a contrast to the cool lake waters

ket. By the middle 1870's the Cheyenne Plains were stocked; the Wyoming Stock Growers Association had been founded; and Cheyenne was the capital of a vast cattle-ranching area. The Englishmen came and the 'foreign' and local aristocracy established the Cheyenne Club. Here the cattlemen sat in winter, sipping rich wines, playing Boston, and determining policies that affected the cattle industry throughout the West. Deals were made 'by the book' and range detectives were hired and sent to safeguard the cowman's interests in far parts of the cattle empire.

When the Black Hills (Dakota) gold fields were unofficially opened in 1875, Cheyenne did a good business outfitting prospectors and miners; long string teams hauled provisions, mining machinery, and a few passengers north from the Cheyenne railhead. Soon the Cheyenne and Black Hills Stage Company began transporting thousands of passengers and much treasure between the railroad and the mines, and the city advanced rapidly.

In 1880 the Union Pacific Railroad installed a system of pumps to bring water from Crow Creek into large tanks, from which it was sent through mains to the railroad shops and the business section. The residential section continued to depend on wells. Two years later water was brought to the city by the force of gravity from Lake Makhplahlutah, a mile and a half away. The population in 1880 according to the census was 3,456, and by 1897 was estimated to be about 10,000. In 1886 the legislature passed an act appropriating $150,000 to begin building a capitol, which was to cost $300,000 when completed. In 1887 the post office here was doing such a large business—$20,000 a year—that city delivery service was established. The next year an additional $125,000 was voted for the capitol. Electric lights were installed here in 1882 and the sidewalks and streets were paved before 1897.

In addition to being the State capital, Cheyenne, with its cattle industry, three railroads, transcontinental airline and highways, Federal and county offices, and wide trade area, is still the most important city in Wyoming. The larger manufactories include an oil refinery, window-sash factory, five bakeries, and four creameries. Two newspapers, *The Wyoming Eagle* and the *Wyoming State Tribune-Leader,* both with state-wide circulation, are published daily and the *Wyoming Stockman-Farmer* and *Cow Country* are issued monthly.

POINTS OF INTEREST

1. The PLAINS HOTEL, NW. corner 16th St. and Central Ave., contains highly polished cedar furniture and picture frames made by Tom Molesworth of Cody. On the colored leather upholstery are hand-painted Western scenes. Leather picture frames on the walls are woven from strips of leather cut in the shape of early Wyoming cattle brands.

2. The OLD STAGE COACH, in SE. corner of Union Pacific Park, 15th St. and Warren Ave., is housed in a small shelter cabin with large

plate-glass windows. The old coach is typical of those used on the Overland and Black Hills stage routes during the 1860's and 1870's.

3. The UNION PACIFIC RAILROAD SHOPS AND YARDS (*open by permission of shop superintendent*), Capitol Ave. between 12th and 15th Sts., occupy a 470-acre tract in downtown Cheyenne. Many of the buildings date back to 1889. The machine shop built in 1919 houses the 250-ton crane that hoists 140-ton locomotives for overhauling.

4. The OLD McDANIELS BLOCK, 1615 Pioneer Ave., a large, rectangular, red brick structure with green frame trim, was built in 1877 on the site of the old McDaniels Variety Theater. The theater, destroyed by fire, was a popular resort in early Cheyenne. Traveling troupes gave dramatic and vaudeville productions; girls served drinks during the performance, and when the performance was pleasing, applause was heard several blocks away.

5. The SITE OF THE OLD TERRITORIAL LEGISLATIVE HALL, SE. corner Carey Ave. and 17th St., is designated by a tablet on the north wall of the Bank Building, a white brick two-story structure. In the small frame building that stood on the site, the first Wyoming Territorial Legislature passed the first woman-suffrage law in the United States. The bill was approved by Governor Campbell and became a law on December 10, 1869.

6. The WYOMING STOCK GROWERS ASSOCIATION HEADQUARTERS (*open weekdays*), 1816 Carey Ave., displays a collection of rangeland relics, including an old stagecoach treasure-box, Dutch ovens, branding irons, maverick irons, saddles, and guns. After its organization in 1873, the association became one of the most powerful and effective of its kind.

7. The SITE OF THE FIRST PUBLIC SCHOOL in Wyoming, SW. corner Carey Ave. and 19th St., is marked by a bronze tablet on the north wall of a small frame building. Here Cheyenne's first school was dedicated January 5, 1868, in a 20-by-40-foot one-room frame building. One hundred pupils reported the first day—with two teachers.

8. The CITY AND COUNTY BUILDING, NW. corner Carey and 19th St., a three-story red-brick building of neoclassic design, stands on the site of the old courthouse where Tom Horn was hanged November 20, 1903. Horn, a 'range detective' hired by cattlemen to combat rustlers and others unfriendly to the big cattle owners, was suspected of killing at least a dozen offenders before he was convicted of killing 13-year-old Willie Nickell. The elder Nickell, an Iron Mountain rancher, was running sheep in cow country, and according to a purported confession Horn was paid $500 to kill the rancher, but shot the son by mistake. Horn was held in jail several weeks before his execution and, as the hanging day neared, feeling was high in Cheyenne between the cattlemen and the sheepman-granger coalition. Horn escaped the jail once, and rumors persisted that the cattlemen had 'fixed things' so that Horn would escape secretly at the final moment. After the hanging Nickell demanded to see the body. The county attorney refused permission, saying he feared a riot. Many persons took this as proof that

the law had been 'bought' and, like most celebrated American bad-man heroes, Tom Horn has been 'seen' in various parts of Wyoming since his hanging. The OLD FIRE BELL, cast in 1879, stands on a concrete block at the northwest corner of the courthouse. From 1880 until 1910 it warned of fires within the city.

9. ST. MARY'S CATHEDRAL, NE. corner of Capitol Ave. and 21st St., of modified English Gothic architecture, constructed of Wyoming sandstone in 1917, is 135 feet long and 70 feet wide, the largest church in Wyoming. The floor slopes toward the altar, and no columns obstruct the view.

10. The SUPREME COURT BUILDING, Capitol Ave. between 23rd and 24th Sts., is a three-story Bedford limestone building of neoclassic design, striking in its simplicity. It was built in 1937 to house the Wyoming Supreme Court, the State Miscellaneous and Law Library, the State Historical Department (museum and library), and several State departmental offices. The walls of the first floor lobby are of dull Colorado travertine. Window and door cases are of brass, and all the halls are trimmed with varicolored marble.

The STATE HISTORICAL MUSEUM (*open 8–4 weekdays*), in the basement, contains the Lusk Indian Collection, the Pennewill Collection of World War Trophies, and various relics of the early Wyoming frontier. The assortment of Indian artifacts and paraphernalia, donated by Frank S. Lusk of Wyoming, was started by the donor's mother while Wyoming was still a territory. It contains specimens from all representative western American tribes. The World War trophies, collected in Europe during the war by Sergeant Robert Pennewill, were presented to the museum by William R. Coe of New York, who owns Wyoming ranch property. It is one of the most complete collections of German military articles in the United States; it includes rifles, pistols, trench and plumed helmets, uniforms, insignia, blankets, and other items, dating back to the Franco-Prussian War. Paintings, photographs, manuscripts, rare maps, books, and other relics significant of life in the early West are also exhibited.

The STATE LIBRARY (*open 8–4 weekdays*), a law and miscellaneous library, was established to accommodate supreme court justices, but its facilities have been made available to the public.

11. The CAPITOL BUILDING (*open 8–5 weekdays*), Capitol Ave. between Carey and Central Aves., and 24th and 25th Sts., houses the offices of State officials and the State legislative chambers and committee rooms. The three-and-a-half-story sandstone building, designed in 1887 by D. W. Gibbs, is of neoclassic design. The dome, rising 145 feet above the ground, is 50 feet in diameter. It is surmounted by a classic lantern cupola and rests on a colonnaded octagonal drum; the drum is pierced by arched windows on each face. The main entrance is in the rusticated base of a porticoed central pavilion. A broad hall, 18 feet wide, opens into the central rotunda, and halls of similar width lead east and west to the main wings. The floors are tile and the wood-

work is carved cherry. A mellow light flows into the rotunda through yellow cathedral glass in the dome.

Legislative halls contain portraits of early Wyoming statesmen and murals that take their themes from the Wyoming pioneer tradition.

12. ROBERT BURNS STATUE, in a small triangular park bounded by Randall Ave., Pioneer Ave., and 26th St., was sculptured by Henry Snell Gomly of Edinburgh, Scotland. It was erected by the Scottish residents of Cheyenne in 1929.

13. FRONTIER PARK (*open all year*), Frontier Ave. between Hynds and Reed Sts., is the scene of the annual Frontier Days Celebration. Surrounded by high mesh wire, the park contains a race track, bucking arena, grandstands, bleachers, the site of the annual Indian encampment, and the stables and corrals for race horses, bucking horses, and steers. At the south end of the park is the BUFFALO PASTURE, which is best approached by the Frontier Ave. or Carey Ave. entrances. Half a dozen American bison have their home in this two-acre area. JIM BAKER'S CABIN (*not open*), SE. corner of the park, near the Carey Ave. entrance, is a small, two-story log structure that resembles the blockhouse of early American Colonial history. This home of a noted scout was moved here from its original site by the State (*see Tour 2B*).

14. LIONS PARK, between Carey Ave. and US 85–87, adjoins Frontier Park on the east. On the north shore of Lake Makhplahlutah, largest of five lakes in the Cheyenne vicinity, are sunken gardens, picnic tables, and a community house. Southwest of the lake, paralleling Carey Avenue, is a fenced pasture containing a small herd of Rocky Mountain mule deer.

15. KIWANIS BEACH (*admission free*) is a summer bathing resort on Terry Lake, northwest of Lions Park.

16. AMERICAN LEGION PARK, at the northwest tip of Terry Lake, is a small recreation area.

17. The OLD FORT LARAMIE TRAIL is designated by a stone marker west of Lake Terry where Carey Avenue is intersected by an unnamed gravel road connecting Lake Absarraca with US 85–87. Old grass-grown wheel tracks indicate the route of the road, established in the early 1870's as a military road from Camp Carlin to Fort Laramie and other posts north. It was later used by freighters and by the Cheyenne and Black Hills Stage.

18. CHEYENNE MUNICIPAL AIRPORT (6,140 alt.) (*hangars and shops open on arrangement*) is in the extreme northeastern section of the city, along US 85–87. The 400-acre landing field has oiled runways and its mechanical shops house one of the largest unsubsidized commercial airplane overhaul bases in the country. Lighted airways running east, west, and south are supplemented by a radio blind-landing system, which is available to private pilots. All flying equipment of United Air Lines is inspected and serviced in the Cheyenne shops after each 600 miles of flight duty. U. S. Department of Commerce weather station reports weather conditions daily. Observations are made each day from a plane at 18,000 feet.

19. In LAKE VIEW CEMETERY, Seymour Ave. between 23rd and 28th Sts. and extending to Morrie Ave., are the graves of Senator Francis E. Warren, Senator Joseph M. Carey, Senator Robert D. Carey, John (Portugee) Phillips, and Mrs. John J. Pershing and her three daughters. Frances Warren, daughter of Francis E. Warren of Cheyenne, married Captain John J. (Black Jack) Pershing while he was stationed at Fort D. A. Russell in the early 1900's. She and her three small daughters were burned to death in army quarters at the Presidio of San Francisco in 1915.

20. The GOVERNOR'S MANSION (*private*), 300 E. 21st St., of red brick in Georgian Colonial style, was completed in 1905. The interior was renovated and completely refurnished in 1937.

21. HOLLIDAY PARK, bordering Lake Minnehaha at the end of E. 18th St., affords a pleasant lake-shore drive. In the northeast corner is a picnic ground with roughhewn log tables and benches.

POINTS OF INTEREST IN ENVIRONS

FORT FRANCIS E. WARREN (6,294 alt., 5,000 pop.), entrance at end of Randall Avenue, one mile from the capitol, is the third largest military post in the United States. Randall Avenue runs through the reservation between rectangular barracks (L) and parade grounds (R), named for World War battlefields. (*Drive slowly and await signal at small guardhouse (L): signs on driveways indicate enforced speed limits.*) The slate-roofed, red brick buildings of the post, surrounded by spacious lawns, are spread over flat prairies north of Crow Creek. The fully equipped post, on a reserve of more than 5,000 acres, has cavalry, infantry, ordnance, signal, and medical detachments. The 52,000-acre maneuver reservation (*see below*) is the largest in the Nation.

Major General Grenville M. Dodge selected the site of Cheyenne for a construction camp in the summer of 1867; and General C. C. Augur and Colonel J. D. Stevenson established a military post northwest of the railroad terminal, to protect graders and citizens of the new town. Log barracks, officers' quarters, and a hospital were built. The post was named in honor of Brigadier General David A. Russell, who was killed, at Opequon, Virginia, September 19, 1864. When other forts in the Rocky Mountain region were being abandoned in the early 1880's, Fort D. A. Russell's frame and log buildings were replaced with brick structures. It was gradually enlarged until, at the time of the First World War, it was one of the largest military posts in the United States. In 1930 it was renamed in honor of Francis E. Warren (1844–1929), Civil War veteran, first governor of the State, and United States senator from 1890 until 1929. Its personnel has included such men as General John J. Pershing, whose wife was a daughter of Senator Warren.

On Randall Avenue is the junction with First Street; L. here to the CIVILIAN COMPONENT SUMMER CAMP, which has several rows of steel tent frames. Here each summer 500 members of Western and Southwestern R.O.T.C. and C.M.T.C. units encamp for several weeks of tactical training, under direction of fort officials. Left from the camp on a graveled road to WARREN BOWL (1930), largest stadium in Wyoming, where inter-brigade athletic contests and outdoor games of the Cheyenne High School are played. The U-shaped stadium seats 4,000 and is capable of expansion to seat 12,000. The wooden seats are mounted on concrete steps; concrete tunnels through the sides of the bowl form gateways to the turfed, lighted field, which is surrounded by a quarter-mile cinder track.

First Street crosses the Chicago, Burlington & Quincy tracks; L. here to the SITE OF CAMP CARLIN, which is marked with a granite monument near an old cottonwood tree. Here, in August 1867, Captain E. B. Carling established a quartermaster's depot. Supplies reached the depot over a spur from the Union Pacific two miles away, and were carried to 14 military posts within a 400-mile radius by long wagon trains. The post employed 500 men and kept 24,000 head of stock; 100 wagons and 5 pack trains were in use regularly. The stables accommodated 1,000 mules. During the 1870's, the post came within the enlarged Fort Russell reservation. Named for Captain Carling, with the name misspelled, it was also known as Cheyenne Depot. It was abandoned in 1888, its buildings dismantled or moved to Cheyenne or Fort Russell.

On Randall Avenue are the FORT EXCHANGE, the POST OFFICE and GUARDHOUSE; R. is a MOTION PICTURE THEATER. L. at the junction with Sixth Street to RIDING HALL, where indoor cavalry drills and horse shows are held.

At the junction with Warren Avenue, which, with Randall Avenue and First Street, forms a circle, drive L. on Randall Avenue, which becomes an oiled road, to the U. S. HORTICULTURAL FIELD STATION, one of three stations maintained by the Department of Agriculture for variety testing and cultural experiments with fruits, ornamental plants, vegetables, and shelter-belt trees. The circle drive goes R. on Warren Avenue. Officers' quarters with well-kept lawns are L., enlisted men's quarters R., across the parade grounds.

On Warren Avenue is the junction with Seventh Street, which becomes Hospital Drive; L. here to the POST HOSPITAL. On Staff Circle are the residences of the general staff; L. here to a junction with Headquarters Drive; L. on Headquarters Drive to POST HEADQUARTERS.

Warren Avenue continues past officers' two- and three-story duplex brick houses, with white frame porches. The COMMANDING OFFICER'S QUARTERS (L), red brick with massive white columns, supporting a frame portico, is Colonial in style. Winding northeast, then veering south, Warren Avenue borders Wyoming Park (R). On the POLO FIELD (L), local clubs play in summer. The PRACTICE ATHLETIC FIELD (R) is in a corner of the Argonne Parade Ground.

Veterans' Administration Hospital, 3.7 *m.*, Wyoming Hereford Ranch, 9.5 *m.* (*see Tour 2a*); U. S. Horticultural Field Station, 5.2 *m.*, Pole Mountain Game Refuge, 28.6 *m.*, Vedauwoo Glen, 36 *m.*, Happy Jack Winter Sports Area, 38.5 *m.* (*see Tour 2A*).

Laramie

Railroad Stations: Union Pacific Station, 1st and Kearney Sts., for Union Pacific R.R.; North Park and Western Station, W. end of Fremont St., NW. limits of city, for Laramie, North Park and Western R.R. (Union Pacific).
Bus Stations: Connor Hotel, 3rd St. and Grand Ave., for Interstate Transit Lines (Union Pacific); Johnson Hotel, 217 S. 1st St., for Burlington Trailways; Kuster Hotel, 108 Ivinson Ave., for Fort Collins and Walden (Colorado) Stage Line.
Airport: Laramie Municipal, 3.5 m. W. on State 130; no scheduled service.
Taxis: 10¢ upward according to distance and number of passengers. One taxi maintains sightseeing service.
Traffic Regulations: No U turns in business district or on through streets. Speed limit, 25 m.p.h. on through streets, 20 m.p.h. on other streets, strictly enforced. Stop streets: Grand Ave., 2nd St., and University Ave. at 2nd and 3rd Sts.

Accommodations: 6 hotels, 15 tourist camps.

Information Service: Chamber of Commerce, 116 S. 2nd St.

Hospital: Ivinson Memorial, Ivinson Ave. and 10th St.
Theaters and Motion Picture Houses: University of Wyoming Auditorium, Liberal Arts Building, occasional local and professional dramatic, operatic, and musical productions; 2 motion-picture houses.
Swimming: Municipal Pool (outdoor), city limits, West Laramie, open 10–4:30; supervised, free.
Tennis: Municipal Court, 7th and Steele Sts., free.
Golf: Laramie Country Club, 3 m. S. on US 287, 18 holes, greens fee, 50¢ a day. Union Pacific Athletic Club, 2 m. E. on US 30, 18 holes, greens fee 50¢ a day.
Softball: Rainbow Ave. and 18th St., games played regularly during summer, fee 10¢.
Hockey: Municipal Rink, Park Ave. and 5th St., adults 25¢, children free.

LARAMIE (7,145 alt., 8,609 pop.), seat of the University of Wyoming, is on the east bank of the Laramie River at the southeastern edge of the Laramie Plains. Rows of cottonwoods and poplars bordering the streets are conspicuous against the barren prairie background. Spacious lawns and yards, low-built houses, and wide streets continue within the city the impression of the prairie's wideness. East of the city the Laramie Mountains reach an elevation of approximately 9,000 feet, and day and night temperatures vary from an average high of 77° in summer to an average low of 48°.

A cement factory, an ice-storing plant, a brick and tile kiln, a gypsum refinery, and a timber creosoting plant operate in suburban Laramie, but perennial winds break up the thin wisps of smoke that rise from great jutting smokestacks. There is no hint of industrial activity in downtown Laramie.

One of Wyoming's oldest cities, Laramie is no older than some of its residents. Among modern pressed-brick houses and business buildings stand many huge square Southern Colonial structures. Two rambling frame barracks, which housed United States Army officers at Fort Sanders during the Indian wars of the 1860's and 1870's, now serve as a college sorority chapter house and as a clubhouse for a young people's religious organization.

Jack McCall's arrest in Laramie on August 30, 1876, for shooting Wild Bill Hickok in the back of the head in a Deadwood (South Dakota) saloon is still remembered by Laramie citizens. One year after McCall's arrest, Jesse James, with several companions, was lodged in the Laramie jail as a suspect in a near-by stagecoach holdup, but was freed before his identity was known. The University of Wyoming, three years older than the State of Wyoming, celebrated its fiftieth anniversary in the spring of 1937, and two members of its original faculty were present.

In a region not far removed from the mood and severity of the frontier, interests are limited and directed toward immediate problems; but Bill Nye's contribution to American local-color literature of the 1880's made Laramie self-conscious and somewhat aware of literary currents, while Wyoming was yet a territory. The establishment of Wyoming's only college there in 1887 stimulated interest in the humanist tradition, and the college provided inspiration and opportunity for disinterested thought that could not be paralleled in another Wyoming community.

Here, while citizens elsewhere in Wyoming disputed range and water rights or mined valuable minerals, Grace Raymond Hebard and June Etta Downey were writing volumes on Wyoming history and experimental psychology, and Agnes M. Wergeland was composing music or eulogizing the Wyoming scene in delicate Norwegian verse. Here, too, Ted Olson experimented with verse forms and journalism in school newspapers; G. Edward Pendray observed chemical reactions in test tubes to get authentic data for his novels and articles on mechanized science; and Olga Moore (Arnold) wrote her first sketches and short stories for campus publications.

Laramie has several art and humanist societies that developed from campus organizations, and townspeople enjoy college-sponsored dramatic and operatic productions and lecture lyceums. The university's extension and lecture services are spreading over the State.

The town was named for the legendary French-Canadian trapper, Jacques La Ramie, whose name was also given to a military post, a mountain range, a peak, a river, a county, and a section of the Wyoming Plains. About 1820 La Ramie, a free trapper, worked the tributaries of the North Platte in what became southeastern Wyoming. According to Coutant, he was killed by Indians somewhere along the river that bears his name.

The first settlements near Laramie were the road ranches on the Laramie Plains, along the Overland Trail, in the 1860's. Operators of these ranch stations lived by supplying hay and emergency provisions to stage companies, freighters, and emigrants.

When the steel tracks of the Union Pacific Railroad glistened along the west slope of the Laramie Mountains in the spring of 1868, Fort John Buford (Fort Sanders) had already been established near the Laramie River to protect tie workers and grading crews building west of Cheyenne (*see Tour* 5c).

Several weeks before the tracks arrived, a tent town appeared on the river bank. The railroad company had platted a townsite, but allowed no one to settle until lots could be officially sold and recorded. The date of sale was fixed early in April, and land speculators who had done well in Cheyenne were on hand to get choice titles. Within a week 400 plots had been sold at prices ranging from $25 to $260. Ten days later 500 shacks had been erected of logs, canvas, condemned railroad ties, and dismantled wagon boxes. The first train slid down the steep grade into town on May 9, 1868, and with the train came all the population and paraphernalia of 'Hell-on-Wheels.' The first freight carried iron rails, crossties, plows, scrapers, tents, portable shanties, lumber, groceries, cookstoves, crockery, tinware, liquors, and the transient population of the terminal town: gamblers, workers, harlots, hunters, migratory shop and saloonkeepers, peddlers with their packs, and straggling settlers' families.

Work was pushed, and Laramie was not long the end of track. But the steep grade over Sherman Hill and the barren desert land to the west forecast the need of railroad shops and warehouses at Laramie. Additional settlers came to the new town, and the gamblers and keepers of brothels and saloons quickly saw their business opportunity.

Early in May a provisional government was formed and a mayor and trustees elected. But the lawless element had learned from vigilantes in other terminal settlements the value of union, and in Laramie it organized first. After bucking the outlaw organization three weeks, the government resigned. The period of anarchy that followed was something more than casual outlawry. Brawls and shootings were commonplace. In August a hesitant vigilance committee of 20 shopkeepers and railroad workers lynched a desperado, who called himself 'The Kid.' Other members of the loosely organized gang regarded the incident as a challenge and terrorized the town.

By autumn Laramie had a more stable population, and war was declared on the ruffians and bullies. Five hundred armed vigilantes planned simultaneous raids on several outlaw strongholds on the evening of October 29. Although plans miscarried, the group concentrated on the dance hall 'Belle of the West.' In the gun battle that followed, in which most of the town participated, five men were killed and fifteen wounded. Four outlaws surrendered and were hanged to telegraph poles downtown.

This demonstration of vigilante strength cowed many of the lawless and they followed the rails west. Others joined the vigilantes, became the most militant advocates of law and order, and eventually controlled the organization. Out of this committee grew the second provisional government, which was chartered in December 1868 by the Dakota Legislature when it created Albany County and made Laramie its seat.

Under legal guise, the outlaws again intimidated the citizenry, but the Dakota Legislature revoked the charter, dissolved the government, and placed the town under jurisdiction of the Federal courts. It remained so until January 1874, when it was reincorporated by the Wyoming Territorial Legislature.

During the period of court rule in Laramie women were first empaneled for service on a grand jury in Wyoming. The act of enfranchising women also included the right to hold office, and several months before the voting right could be exercised, Judge J. H. Howe summoned several women to serve on the grand and petit juries in the second district court in Laramie during March 1870. Wyoming's woman suffrage law had attracted attention, but the territory received its widest publicity when news of its 'mixed' grand jury got around.

King William of Prussia cabled congratulations to President Grant on this evidence of 'progress, enlightenment and civil liberty in America.' Newspaper correspondents came to the frontier to watch the feminine jurors at work. Heavy veils masked the women jurors, and annoyed photographers reproduced them in caricature. The most popular cartoons showed ladies of severe mien jouncing fretting babes while hearing evidence. These were generally captioned with jingles or couplets, as:

> Baby, Baby, don't get in a fury;
> Your mamma's gone to sit on the jury.

In the little one-story shack that did duty for store, post office, and courthouse, the six women on the petit jury heard all cases on the court docket. They found one man guilty of manslaughter, in a trial following a duel in a hotel lobby, and convicted others of misdemeanors and felonies ranging from disturbance of the peace to cattle stealing.

The first public school was founded February 15, 1869. By summer of that year congregations of the Episcopal, Methodist, Roman Catholic, and Baptist churches organized. The city's first newspaper was the *Frontier Index,* a tramp publication issued at Fort Sanders early in 1868; later it followed the tracks west and the presses were destroyed by a mob at Beartown. The *Laramie Sentinel* was published from 1869 to 1895, and several other dailies appeared spasmodically. The *Boomerang* founded by Bill Nye in 1881 and the *Republican* established by W. E. Chaplin in 1890 were combined in 1924 and have been published since as the *Republican and Boomerang.*

A few scrub cattle brought in by road ranchers along the Overland Trail grazed on the Laramie Plains in scattered herds by 1868. By 1870 the railroad had absorbed most of the overland traffic, and the road ranchers left the country or turned their full attention to breeding the cattle they had collected by barter or accident from the wagon trains. This turned out to be good business, and by 1871 the long queues of

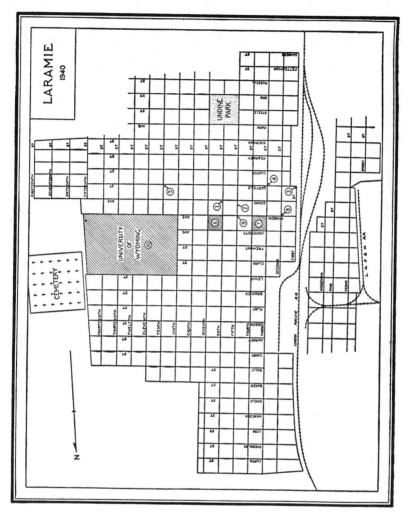

KEY FOR LARAMIE MAP

1. Kappa Kappa Gamma House   2. John Wesley Clubhouse   3. Site of Wyoming's
First 'Mixed' Jury Trial   4. Bill Nye's Boomerang Office   5. Hebard House
6. Ivinson School   7. Cathedral Close   8. Site of the Den of the Forty Liars
9. Woodmen Hall   10. University of Wyoming

longhorns from Texas were stringing onto the plains. Both the re-
habilitated work cattle and the longhorns did well on the grass prairies,
and within a decade stories of the grass bonanza had reached the Atlantic Seaboard and Europe. Eastern and European capital came to
Laramie. English gentlemen came, acquired choice ranching areas, built
mansions in town, and organized their clubs. After the crash in the
1880's the 'foreigners' closed their clubs and mansions and returned

to their brokerage offices in London or Edinburgh. But those who had seen hard times as road ranchers stayed on and stocked a better grade of cattle. Sheep were introduced a few years later, and Laramie grew with the livestock industry on the surrounding plains.

Mineral outcroppings in the vicinity gave Laramie a brick and tile factory, plaster mills, an iron foundry and roller mill (destroyed by fire), a soda refinery, a cement factory, and an oil refinery. Small veins of gold were discovered in near-by mountains, and for a time Laramie threatened to eclipse the territorial capital on the other side of the Laramie Mountains. Rivalry with Cheyenne became sharper. Newspapers came to the defense of their communities, and editorial broadsides were exchanged.

A Cheyenne journalist saw Laramie in 1873 as 'an example of how much better it is to walk with humble livers in content than to attempt to build a town on no more enduring foundation than a hundred western towns have had (as Bunyan says of *Vanity Fair*) "laid by juggling cheats, games, plays, fools, apes, rogues, and that of every kind, together with that to be seen with murderers, adulterers, false-swearers and that for nothing." ' Ten years later J. H. Hayford, bellicose editor of the *Laramie Sentinel*, complained that 'Cheyenne gets first chance at everybody who comes to the country, and takes great pains to decry and run down the resources and advantages of our city.' It was this same Hayford who referred to President Grant as 'the most consummate ass that ever disgraced the presidential chair,' when the President removed the editor's friend from the Laramie Post Office.

Shack towns and camps appeared along the mountain gulches west and south of Laramie, where yellow metal was found. Laramie, the promotion center, was optimistic. But the deposits were too slight for intensive development, and the veins petered out. Bonded companies went into bankruptcy, and melancholy ghost towns now dot an area within a 100-mile radius of the city. Solitary prospectors who still haunt the area are dogmatic in defending the region's mining possibilities and are short-tempered with unbelievers.

POINTS OF INTEREST

1. KAPPA KAPPA GAMMA HOUSE (*private*), NE. corner Grand Ave. and 6th St., a three-story rambling frame building, was moved to Laramie in the middle 1880's from Fort Sanders, where it had served for several years as officers' quarters.

2. JOHN WESLEY CLUBHOUSE (*private*), 206 S. 5th St., a one-story frame building, was a barracks for army officers at Fort Sanders during the Indian Wars.

3. The SITE OF WYOMING'S FIRST 'MIXED' JURY TRIAL is on the NE. corner of Garfield and First Sts. Wyoming women, serving on a mixed petit jury, heard and decided cases before the district court in 1870. Five women served on the grand jury, six on the petit.

4. BILL NYE'S BOOMERANG OFFICE, SW. corner Garfield and

3rd Sts., is on the second floor of an old brick building, now a ware-house. The first floor was a livery stable in the 1880's, and callers at the newspaper office were greeted by a sign at the bottom of an outside stairs, 'Twist the Grey Mule's Tail and Take the Elevator.' Edgar Wilson (Bill) Nye was born in Shirley, Maine, August 25, 1850, and died February 22, 1896, in Asheville, North Carolina. Coming to Wyoming from Wisconsin in May 1876, Nye was admitted to the bar in that year, served a term in the territorial legislature, and was postmaster and justice of the peace in Laramie. He was news editor of Hayford's *Sentinel* for a time, and when the *Boomerang* (named for Nye's pet mule) was established as a Republican party mouthpiece in 1881, Nye was made editor. His humorous writings attracted nationwide attention, and in 1883 he left Laramie to accept a position on the *New York World*. He later wrote and lectured in collaboration with James Whitcomb Riley.

In resigning the Laramie postmastership, Nye wrote:

> Post Office Divan
> Laramie City, W. T.
> Oct. 1, 1883

To the President of the United States:

Sir: I beg leave at this time to officially tender my resignation as postmaster of this place, and in due form to deliver the great seal and key to the front door of this office. The safe combination is set on the numbers 33, 66, and 99, though I do not remember at this moment which comes first, or how many times you revolve the knob, or which direction you turn it at first in order to make it operate . . .

You will find the postal cards that have not been used under the distributing table, and the coal down in the cellar. If the stove draws too hard, close the damper in the pipe and shut the general delivery window . . .

Acting under the advice of General Hatton, a year ago, I removed the feather-bed with which my predecessor, Deacon Hayford, had bolstered up his administration by stuffing the window, and substituted glass. Finding nothing in the book of instructions which made the featherbed a part of my official duties, I filed it away in an obscure place and burned it in effigy, also in the gloaming . . .

I need not say that I herewith transmit my resignation with great sorrow and genuine regret. We have toiled together month after month, asking no reward except the innate consciousness of rectitude and the salary as fixed by law. Now we are to separate. Here the roads seem to fork, as it were, and you and I, and the cabinet, must leave each other . . .

You will find the key under the door-mat and you had better turn the cat out at night when you close the office. If she does not go readily, you can make it clearer to her mind by throwing the canceling stamp at her. If Deacon Hayford does not pay his box rent, you might as well put his mail in the general delivery, and when Bob Head gets drunk and insists on a letter from one of his wives every day in the week, you can salute him through the box delivery with an Old Queen Ann tomahawk, which you will find near the Etruscan water pail . . .

Mr. President, as an official of this government, I now retire . . .

> *Bill Nye.*

5. The HEBARD HOUSE (*private*), NW. corner Garfield and 10th Sts., is the house shared in the early 1900's by Grace Raymond Hebard and the poet, Agnes Wergeland. Since the death of both educator-authors, the gray two-story frame house has been a family dwelling.

Dr. Hebard came to Wyoming soon after graduating from the University of Iowa, was connected with the University of Wyoming as librarian and teacher, and was active in having the provision for equal suffrage incorporated in the State constitution. She wrote several volumes of Wyoming and other Western history, including *Sacajawea,* an account of the Indian woman who accompanied Lewis and Clark, the explorers, to the West Coast.

6. The IVINSON SCHOOL, Ivinson Ave. between 6th and 7th Sts., and extending to University Ave., is a private Episcopal school for girls. The house, a huge, square, three-story structure with gables and a tower, was the residence of Edward Ivinson, who willed the house and spacious grounds to the church. The combined stable and coachhouse has been converted into a small social room and nursery.

7. CATHEDRAL CLOSE, Ivinson Ave. between 3rd and 4th Sts. and extending to University Ave., is an iron-fenced block, charming in its Old-World atmosphere. St. Matthew's Cathedral, Tudor Gothic in design, is built of native sandstone. This congregation is the outgrowth of the first religious services held in 1868 by the Reverend J. C. Cook of Cheyenne. Other buildings in the block are Sherwood Hall, a private dormitory and military school for boys, and the Deanery, both English in design; and the Bishop's House, home of the bishop of Wyoming, designed in Early Colonial style. In the center of the square is a white stone Gothic cross, 25 feet high, dedicated to the memory of Wyoming's Episcopalians killed in the First World War.

8. The SITE OF THE DEN OF THE FORTY LIARS, SW. corner Ivinson Ave. and 2nd Sts., is occupied by a brick sporting-goods store. On dull afternoons, Bill Nye was accustomed to hobnobbing with friends in the back room of a hardware store that stood on the site. The proportions of the attendance and of the stories exchanged caused the group to become known as the Forty Liars Club, and the building as the Den of the Forty Liars. The organization inspired one of Nye's books, *Forty Liars and Other Lies* (1882).

9. The WOODMEN HALL (*admission by arrangement with attendant in basement*), NW. corner University Ave. and 5th St., a squat one-story frame building, was built and maintained as a clubhouse by English and Scottish ranchers in the Laramie vicinity during the 1880's. Here the gentlemen ranchers swung cattle deals, sipped burgundy, and danced with ladies in hoops and brocades.

10. The UNIVERSITY OF WYOMING, 9th St. between Ivinson Ave. and Lewis St. and extending to 16th St., occupies a 96-acre landscaped campus on the northeast edge of Laramie. Its 20 buildings are for the most part of native sandstone from a quarry north of the campus. Modified Gothic is the dominant architectural scheme, particularly in the newer buildings. Broken perpendicular lines predominate, and the whole gives an impression of mass, suggestive of the natural rock and cliff formations in the area.

A land-grant institution, the University of Wyoming was founded by a bill championed in the Wyoming Legislature in 1886 by Colonel

Stephen W. Downey, father of Sheridan Downey, U. S. senator from California. The university is supported by State and Federal funds. Until 1933, its State funds came from a direct three-eighths mill property tax. In that year, however, the legislature repealed all university tax laws and substituted direct legislative appropriation. Its colleges are: liberal arts, education, engineering, agriculture, and law. Master degrees are awarded in the liberal arts, education, and agricultural colleges, and work leading to the degree of doctor of philosophy is offered in the liberal arts college.

A science summer camp is maintained in collaboration with Columbia University in the Medicine Bow Mountains, 38 miles west of Laramie (*see Tour 2B*). The extension service of the college of agriculture is the official carrier of experimental and research information from the Federal Department of Agriculture and the university to Wyoming's rural population. The *Branding Iron*, weekly campus newspaper, is sponsored by the Associated Students organization. Responsible offices are filled by administrative appointment.

One of the school's traditions is the annual Senior Swingout, a ceremony performed by junior and senior students during Commencement Week. Flanked by their classmates, the junior and senior class presidents in cowboy regalia meet on horseback in front of a log gate and ride through together. The bridle and spurs, symbolic of the college tradition, are passed from the senior president to the junior leader, as classmates and spectators sing *Alma Mater*.

CAMPUS TOUR

Buildings on the campus are listed, as far as practicable, in accordance with their geographical sequence from the main entrance on Fremont St. Unless otherwise stated all buildings are open during school sessions.

1. The UNIVERSITY LIBRARY (R), a modern three-story brick building erected in 1923, contains 87,000 volumes and has 500 magazines on file. Also a United States depository, it contains all reports distributed by the Government Printing Office, the reports of State experiment stations, and allied material. The HEBARD ROOM (*open by permission*) on the second floor, contains rare old manuscripts, maps, books, photographs, and other relics of the early West, including the first piano brought to Wyoming over the Oregon Trail. The collection was willed to the university by Dr. Grace Raymond Hebard. The LAW SCHOOL, with its library and moot court room, is on the third floor. Thurman W. Arnold, author of *The Folklore of Capitalism*, taught in the law school from 1921 to 1926.

2. UNIVERSITY HALL (Old Main), oldest building on the campus, was erected of native sandstone and limestone in 1887. For more than a decade this building housed all classrooms and laboratories. Its tower, a landmark until 1916, was removed after it had been condemned as unsafe. Remodeled in 1938-9, the building is now used as administration headquarters.

3. The LIBERAL ARTS BUILDING, most imposing structure on the campus, borders the west end of the large parade ground and faces toward the Laramie Mountains. It was constructed of native sandstone in 1936 and conforms to the design of the newer buildings. In addition to the administrative offices and most classrooms of the college of liberal arts, the building has an auditorium seating 2,000 persons. The stage is 80 by 30 feet, equipped with modern lighting and sound devices. The LARAMIE-FEDERAL ART GALLERY, sponsored by the Work Projects Administration, is in the second-floor lobby. Here paintings, etchings, charcoals, and unusual photographs of local and nationally known artists are displayed. The exhibits change twice monthly.

4. The WYOMING UNION BUILDING, an impressive sandstone structure completed in 1939, conforms to the architectural plan of the other native stone buildings. It is the social center for the university community, with student offices, campus post office, alumni offices, ballroom, student and faculty lounge, reading rooms, and the like.

5. ENGINEERING HALL, a modern fireproof sandstone structure completed in 1927, houses the classrooms, laboratories, and shops of the civil-, electrical-, and mechanical-engineering departments. On the third floor is the ROCKY MOUNTAIN HERBARIUM (*open to botanical research workers*), containing one of the largest collections of plant specimens west of the Mississippi River, with about 142,000 sheets of specimens. The collection is growing at an average rate of 5,000 a year, under the direction of its founder and curator, Dr. Aven Nelson, president emeritus of the university and former president of the Botanical Society of America.

6. SCIENCE HALL, built of sandstone in 1902, third-oldest building on the campus, is headquarters of the department of geology. In the basement is the PALEONTOLOGICAL MUSEUM (*open weekdays during the university session*) containing fossil remains of dinosaurs, prehistoric fish, and other forms of ancient life, collected largely from Wyoming fossil beds. AGRICULTURAL HALL (L), built of native limestone in 1914, houses research laboratories of the home economics, wool, agronomy, animal production, chemistry, and zoology departments, the office of the State chemist, and a Federal weather station. On the main floor is the WOOL EXHIBIT, a gift to the university from the King Brothers Sheep Company of Laramie.

Other buildings on the campus are: The MECHANICAL ARTS BUILDING, of native sandstone, finished in 1893, which houses divisions of the college of education, including the art studios; the NORMAL SCHOOL, completed in 1910, of white limestone, headquarters of the college of education; the GREENHOUSE, used as a laboratory for the department of agriculture; the COMMONS, established in 1917 as a mess hall for the ROTC unit on the campus, now used as the college dining hall; the ENGINEERING SHOPS, which house a laboratory for farm mechanics; the OIL EXPERIMENTAL LABORATORY, conducted in conjunction with the Federal Government; the MEN'S RESIDENCE HALL, built in 1928 of native sandstone; the GYMNASIUM, built in 1925; the ATHLETIC

FIELD, comprising the stadium, running track, football field, bleachers, and field house; the HOME MANAGEMENT HOUSE, a seven-room cottage used as a laboratory for practical work in home management classes; HOYT HALL, named after the university's first president, John W. Hoyt; the MUSIC HALL, a pressed-brick structure, built in 1920; and MERICA HALL, bearing the name of a former university president, Charles O. Merica.

POINTS OF INTEREST IN ENVIRONS

Ames Monument, 20 *m.* (*see Tour 2a*) ; Vedauwoo Glen, 19.4 *m.* (*see Tour 2A*) ; Wyoming Agricultural Experiment Station, 1.1 *m.,* Migratory Bird Refuge, 9.8 *m.,* Overland Trail Marker, 11.8 *m.,* Sheep Mountain Game Refuge, 22.9 *m.,* Medicine Bow National Forest, 30 *m.* (*see Tour 2B*). Tie Plant, 1.1 *m.,* Fort Sanders, 2 *m.,* Cement Factory, 3.1 *m.* (*see Tour 5c*), Sand Creek Area, 19 *m.*

Sheridan

Railroad Stations: Burlington Depot, N. end of Broadway, for Chicago, Burlington & Quincy R.R.

Bus Stations: Salt Creek Terminal, 334 Broadway, for Salt Creek Transportation Co.; Western Hotel, 104 S. Main St., for Sheridan-Billings Bus Line, which connects with Greyhound Lines at Billings and with Burlington Bus Line at Casper.

Airport: Municipal Airport, 2 m. S. on county road, for Inland Air Lines Inc., north-south route; taxi fare 50¢.

Taxis: 15¢ anywhere in city.

Traffic Regulations: No U turn on Main St. between Whitney and Dow Sts. Stop Streets: Main and Loucks Sts. and Coffeen Ave.

Accommodations: 4 hotels, 6 tourist camps.

Information Service: Chamber of Commerce, Whitney Trust Bldg., SW. corner Main and Loucks Sts.; map service.

Hospital: Sheridan County Memorial Hospital, Saberton St. between 6th and 7th Sts.

Radio Station: KWYO (1350 kc.).

Motion-Picture Houses: 2.

Swimming: Municipal Pool, Kendrick Park, Badger St. and Clarendon Ave.; open 10–9 daily, in summer; dressing rooms and showers; adults 20¢, children 10¢. Dean Gravel Pit Pool at W. edge of city, free.

Golf: Municipal Golf Course, 2.5 m. W. on Big Goose Highway, 18 holes, greens fee 35¢ for 9 holes, 50¢ all day.

Tennis: Kendrick Park, Badger St. and Clarendon Ave.

Annual Events: Sheridan-Wyo Rodeo in July, usually third week; Big Hat Day, precedes rodeo; Flower Show, usually in September.

SHERIDAN (3,737 alt., 8,536 pop.), largest town in northern Wyoming, is a shaded community of cottonwoods and hedges at the confluence of Goose and Little Goose Creeks, in saucerlike Sheridan Valley. Fifteen miles west are the black, wooded humps of the Big Horn Mountains; to the east, the valley ends in the rolling Powder River pampas and waste lands.

Low altitudes and plenty of water give the area an exuberant flora. Gardens and parks are masses of bloom in summer; citizens compete for honors at the Sheridan Flower Show, sponsored each September by the Sheridan Garden Club, and seasonal blooms are shown informally.

Meandering Goose Creek traces an irregular dark-green line across the town, breaking the streets into short oblique avenues. Jutting smokestacks mark industrial plants among the trees; cows low in the distance at milking time. There is rarely any wind; the average velocity is the second lowest in the United States.

A division point on the Chicago, Burlington & Quincy Railroad, and connected by regular plane service to a transcontinental airline, Sheridan serves a wide trade area. Vast veins of sub-bituminous coal within a few miles of the city have been important in developing its manufacturing establishments: flour, livestock-feed, and cereal mills; a sugar-beet refinery, a brewery, an artificial-ice plant, an iron foundry, a brick and tile kiln, and several creameries. Two newspapers are published: the *Sheridan Press* (daily except Saturday) and the *Sheridan News* (bi-weekly).

The business houses, in good cow-town fashion, are clustered along Main Street. Saloons still function as employment bureaus for the surrounding range. The rancher or farmer who needs a rider or hay hand writes a notice in chalk on the blackboard behind the bar; transients and others wishing work first consult these 'call boards.'

Conventional summer styles here vary from wide, studded leather belts and high-heeled boots to soft-tanned leather outfits. On Big Hat Day, which opens the rodeo season in July, residents appear in high-crowned felt hats. These are worn the rest of the season.

Crow and Cheyenne Indians, who come to Sheridan from near-by reservations to trade, add to the 'Old West' atmosphere. Like the cowboy, the Indians have been brought up to date; instead of skins and hand-tanned robes, they wear bright blankets of modern design and bits of calico and rayon milled in New England. The headgear of the men is the somber Indian hat—always black—with wide brim and tapering crown. White canvas tents, successors to the skin tepees, are pitched on Goose Creek near the city limits during these trips, and children watch the innumerable dogs and horses while adults visit in town.

Many Polish families, who immigrated to the Sheridan Valley in the 1890's and early 1900's to develop the coal mines, have moved to Sheridan in recent years. They have entered enthusiastically into the life of the community and are leaders in civic musical organizations. Their native folk customs are preserved in periodic dances privately sponsored, patterned after Old-World festivals. Many of the dances originally had religious or nationalistic significance, but in Sheridan their main purpose is to provide diversion and recreation. The costumes worn on these occasions are modeled after native Polish dress. Men wear leather moccasins, leggings, bright-colored knee breeches, and shirts with long full sleeves. Women are charming in their white veils, numerous petticoats, blouses, flare skirts, and checkered aprons. The beer is free. The music is joyous and brassy.

Sheridan Valley was part of the last unreserved Indian land in the United States, set aside for the Sioux, Cheyenne, and Arapaho in 1868. Here Dull Knife, Old David, Man-Afraid-of-His-Horses, Red Cloud, and his son-in-law, Crazy Horse, fought it out with the bluecoat volunteers and regulars before accepting confinement on reservations.

During the summer of 1868, immediately after the close of the war over the Bozeman Road, Father Pierre Jean De Smet preached the first Catholic sermon in the vicinity of Sheridan, before a large gathering of the Crow Nation. A legend of a miracle the 'Black Robe' (as Father De Smet was called by the Indians) performed to illustrate the potency of the white man's God is still repeated in the valley. Because white men had brought war and pestilence with them into the West, the Indians regarded their God with suspicion and mistrust. When De Smet arrived in the Crow camp, a chieftain pointed out an aged buffalo bull near by and commanded the priest to approach him and place his hand on the head of the enraged animal. De Smet, the legend says, approached the bison warily, expecting to be gored. But the sun glistened on the silver crucifix that hung from the Black Robe's throat, and the bull was hypnotized by the reflection; he stood very quiet while the priest reached out and scratched his head. Then De Smet returned to accept the homage of the tribesmen.

According to her own account it was on the site of Sheridan that Martha Canary was dubbed Calamity Jane. The story is told in the *Life and Adventures of Calamity Jane, by Herself,* edited by Paul C. Phillips (*Frontier and Midland,* 1931), which the frontierswoman published and peddled during her hungry old age.

> It was during this campaign [Big Horn, 1872] that I was christened Calamity Jane. It was on Goose creek, Wyoming, where the town of Sheridan is now located, Captain Egan was in command of the post. We were ordered out to quell an uprising of the Indians, and were out for several days, had numerous skirmishes during which six of the soldiers were killed and several severely wounded. When on returning to the post we were ambushed about a mile and a half from our destination. When fired upon Captain Egan was shot. I was riding in advance and on hearing the firing turned in my saddle and saw the captain reeling in his saddle as though about to fall. I turned my horse and galloped back with all haste to his side and got there in time to catch him as he was falling. I lifted him onto my horse in front of me and succeeded in getting him in safely to the post. Captain, on recovering, laughingly said, 'I name you Calamity Jane, the heroine of the plains.'

At the close of the Second Sioux War (*see History*) the tribes were removed from northern Wyoming, and the area was opened to white settlement in 1877. In that year the Wyoming-Dakota Boundary Line was surveyed, and all the former Wyoming Indian territory between the latitude 43° 30′ and the Montana Line was divided into two counties, Pease and Crook. The counties were not organized immediately, however, because the governor reported he 'could not even learn the names of a sufficient number of residents to fill the offices necessary to organization.' In December 1879, the legislature changed the name of Pease County to Johnson County, and provided that the county might be organized on the initiative of 300 electors, rather than the usually required 500. Even with this concession, Johnson County was not organized until March 1881.

The first settlers in Sheridan Valley found a log house on Little Goose Creek with stables large enough for 20 horses. This was believed to be the hideout station of a loose confederation of outlaws and road agents, led by Big Nose George Parrot, that robbed stages and settlers along the Cheyenne-Deadwood route. Jesse and Frank James also were supposed to have used the hideout when chased into Indian land by the law.

A trapper named Jim Mason seems to have erected the first building at present Sheridan in 1878. Other settlers came in, and long trail herds followed them to the fertile ranching area. In 1881 Harry Mandel converted the one-room, dirt-roofed Mason cabin into a store and post office and named it Mandel. A year later J. D. Loucks purchased the Mandel holdings, drew the plat of a town on a piece of brown wrapping paper from his store, prepared a petition for incorporation, and scoured the valley for signatures. Free building plots were offered to first signers, and the three-dollar registration fee accompanied the wrapping-paper plat and petition to Cheyenne.

The town was staked out on a 40-acre plot on May 10, 1882, and Loucks named it in honor of his Civil War commander, General Philip H. Sheridan. Lots sold for $2.50, but a special rate of 50¢ was made on all lots over one. On March 6, 1883, Sheridan was incorporated by the Wyoming Territorial Assembly, and Loucks was chosen mayor.

Sheridan was a ranchers' town; its growth was quiet and slow. One smithy and two general stores were operating before a saloon was opened. The charter provided for a constable and a justice of the peace, but the court operated on a part-time basis. Mayor Loucks recorded that only one person was arrested in Sheridan during its first two years, and Justice George Brundage set a precedent in simple and efficient legal procedure when he handed down his first decision. The offender, arrested for some petty rupture of the peace, was conducted firmly by the constable toward the justice court in Brundage's two-room cabin on the bank of Goose Creek. It was spring, however, and the Big Goose was a formidable stream to cross on foot. As the constable considered the situation, he saw Justice Brundage spading in his garden. Attracting the judge's attention, the constable presented the prisoner and explained the nature of his crime. The prisoner admitted his guilt, and the justice shouted back above the roar of the stream the first legal decision in the Sheridan Municipal Court: 'Men, the verdict of this court is that the prisoner pay into the hands of the constable five dollars, and when it is paid, the prisoner is at liberty.'

Sheridan's first school was opened in one room of a dirt-roofed cabin during the winter of 1882–3; 13 pupils attended. By the end of 1883, more than 50 buildings had been erected, including a schoolhouse, hotel, several stores, three smithies, two saloons, two livery stables, a barber shop, a law office, a butcher shop, and a harness and shoe shop. The first newspapers, the *Sheridan Post* and the *Sheridan Enterprise*, started printing in 1887, and congregations of the Baptist and Methodist churches were established.

Cattlemen and homesteaders on the overstocked plains south of the Sioux land had looked speculatively north of the Platte; finally, with

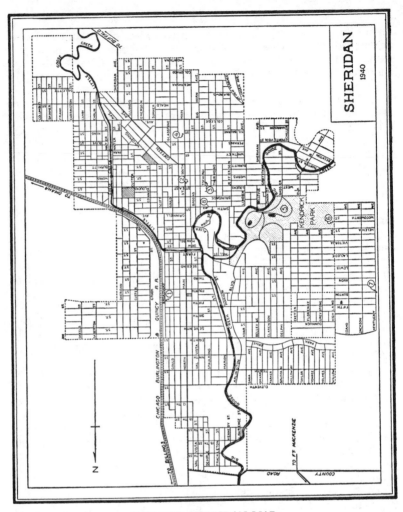

KEY FOR SHERIDAN MAP

1. Sheridan Inn   2. Edelman Drugstore   3. Sheridan Women's Clubhouse
4. United States Weather Bureau Building   5. Kendrick Park   6. Trail End
7. Fair Grounds   8. Site of Sheridan's First Cabin

the help of the Government, they forced the Indians to move. Then
cattle poured into the unpastured ranges, and million-dollar corporations were organized to get in on the grass bonanza. One of the first
ranches was stocked with 25,000 head of cattle; its range extended 100
miles along the Powder River.

The homesteaders and 'little men' came also, and the valley shared
in the struggle against the powerful cattlemen that flared to open warfare at Buffalo a few miles south (*see Tour 3a, b, and History*). 'Cattle

barons' came to town surrounded by their legions of armed riders, and homesteaders traveled the range in armed groups; men swung wide when they passed on the streets, keeping both hands in sight; the county sheriff's pay check was boosted to $750 a month.

During the 1880's the residents of the town were still afraid of Indian attacks, for, although the main tribes had been confined to reservations, small hunting parties haunted the mountains. Also, Sheridan's nearness to the Crow Reservation in Montana made the townspeople uneasy.

On the night of November 4, 1887, a drunken man was run out of Dayton, a small village 20 miles northwest of Sheridan. The autumn night was chilly, and the disturber ignited a straw stack to keep himself warm. A party en route to Sheridan from Dayton saw the red flames against the sky and concluded that the Crow were attacking and burning Dayton. An alarm was spread, and ranching families raced toward Sheridan from the outlying districts. In the town the larger public buildings were barricaded, and throughout the night the populace, many in night clothes, listened for the war cry of the Crow. When dawn came, scouts sent to Dayton returned with the report that no massacre had occurred. That night, however, Indian police killed a chief, Sword Bearer, in a skirmish near the reservation agency, and the attitude of the settlers is reflected in an item which appeared in the *Post* a few days later:

> A number of our settlers have laid in a heavy supply of ammunition. Sackett bought 500 rounds. He has a large cellar under his new house, and thinks that with his force of work hands he can stand off quite a bunch of the noble red . . . It seems to be the general impression if they [the Indians] get down here amongst the settlers, they will never get back.

Sheridan grew with the country, but Big Horn City, 10 miles to the southwest, made its bid for the trade of the wide ranching valley. However, when Sheridan County was created in a stormy session of the territorial legislature in 1888, Loucks, representative from Johnson County, saw to it that Sheridan was made the county seat.

At this session Loucks sponsored a bill that proposed the organization of four new counties, including Sheridan. The bill passed the council (senate) without opposition but was rejected by the house and sent back to a conference committee, where it was amended to provide for the formation of only three counties. Before the bill could be reintroduced, it was stolen by a member of the opposition group. This happened on the last day of the session, when there was still unfinished business. The only 'must' legislation left when the clock was stopped at midnight was the appropriations bill; and Loucks, with a bloc of supporters, had a clause providing for the formation of the counties tacked in unprecedented fashion onto the end of this. Debate was heated, but the Loucks bloc served notice that the bill would not be passed without the rider. At four o'clock in the morning, the weary legislators passed the bill. Governor Thomas Moonlight, who received the bill an hour later, promptly vetoed it and sent it back. At six o'clock the sleepy lawmakers passed the bill again over the governor's veto and went home to bed.

In 1892 the Chicago, Burlington & Quincy's northern Wyoming branch reached Sheridan, making it possible to develop the rich coal fields in the vicinity.

In 1939 there was a change in the political control of Wyoming's government. A number of Sheridan residents, dissatisfied with the new patronage system, called upon northern Wyoming to secede from the rest of the State and form a forty-ninth sovereign State, Absaroka. Sheridan's street commissioner appointed himself governor and chose a small staff. The forty-ninth State was declared to include Yellowstone National Park and most of Wyoming north of the Platte. No petition was ever submitted from the new State, but discontented residents in this northern section appealed to the 'governor of Absaroka' for redress when not pleased by action of the Wyoming government. The ensuing publicity was generally regarded as bad for the State government, and most claims were adjusted to the satisfaction of the Absarokians.

POINTS OF INTEREST

1. SHERIDAN INN, SW. corner Broadway and 5th St., erected in 1892, is a large rambling, smoke-stained structure, 130 feet long and 50 feet wide, set on an acre-and-a-half lot. A wide porch extends the full length of the front and along the south side. Here, and in the spacious lobby, oldsters trade astounding stories of early Sheridan.

The idea of constructing a lavish hotel at Sheridan was conceived by George Holdredge, general manager of the Chicago, Burlington & Quincy Railroad Company. The road was then building toward Sheridan, and the hotel's completion was to be coincident with the arrival of the rails. Holdredge organized a company and engaged Thomas R. Kimball of Omaha, Nebraska, as architect. Kimball, who had just returned from Scotland, designed the hotel from his impression of an old Scottish country inn.

Established while Buffalo Bill was at the height of his show career, the hotel was the Sheridan home of the famed huntsman. Other distinguished names on the old hotel register are General Nelson A. Miles, Charles Russell, Captain John J. Pershing, William Jennings Bryan, William Howard Taft, Mary Roberts Rinehart, Calamity Jane, General O. O. Howard, General Leonard Wood, and Senator Joseph Taylor Robinson.

At the rear of the inn stood the elaborate barns and livery stable of the Cody Transportation Company, operated jointly by Colonel Cody and the hotel management. Here, guests' horses were accommodated and mounts were supplied for horseless guests. A special coach and span was maintained by the hostelry to conduct paying guests on a tour of the city and its environs.

For two decades the Sheridan Inn was the social center of the valley; in its dining room the cow-country aristocracy danced the schottische and the Virginia reel. These occasions filled the inn to capacity: women in evening gowns, men in 'bally-faced, board shirts' and tails. Women usually came early to shop, and the men to see their neighbors, who often lived 100 miles away.

2. The EDELMAN DRUG STORE, 22 S. Main St., has on its walls a number of original Gollings paintings. E. W. Gollings, whose portrayal of ranch scenes brought him modest fame as a 'cowboy artist,' was born in an Idaho mining camp in 1878. He studied painting irregularly in Chicago, and, when he was 18 years old, hired out as a cowboy in South Dakota. For several years he rode the Dakota prairies and painted what he saw. One painting won him a scholarship to the Chicago Academy of Fine Arts. In 1909 he established a studio in Sheridan. Gollings died in 1932. Among his best-known works are *Smoke Signal, Indian Attack on an Overland Stage, Emigrants on the Platte,* and *The Wagon Box Fight.*

3. The SHERIDAN WOMEN'S CLUBHOUSE, 20 S. Tschirgi St., is a low, concrete building, one of the few in Sheridan of modified Spanish design. The club is the outgrowth of a music club that was organized in 1895. Early members drove their own buckboards 10 and 20 miles to attend meetings. Among these was Mrs. John B. Kendrick, wife of Senator Kendrick and at one time president of the Ladies of the Senate Club in Washington, D. C.

4. The UNITED STATES WEATHER BUREAU BUILDING (*open by arrangement*), 447 S. Main St., is a three-story building of brick and Vermont sandstone. Its observation platform on the roof affords a good view of the Sheridan Valley and the Big Horn Mountains.

5. KENDRICK PARK (Formerly Pioneer Park), entrance on Badger St. and Clarendon Ave., is a landscaped area of 80 acres, bordered on the east by Big Goose Creek. The area was given to the city by John B. Kendrick, a Texas trail hand who became a prominent rancher, governor, and United States senator. The Corinthian Column was erected by friends to the memory of Senator Kendrick in the center of the park.

The park's Zoo contains one of the most complete collections in Wyoming, including buffalo, deer, elk, antelope, wolves, coyotes, bobcats, golden pheasants, and monkeys. Except for the monkeys, all the animals are native. At the west end of the park is a heated, outdoor SWIMMING POOL (*open 10–9, summer*), and beyond it, a shallow pool for children. Near by are tennis courts, swings, slides, bars, and other playground equipment.

6. TRAIL END (*private*), Neilson Heights, overlooking Kendrick Park, is the palatial stone residence of the Kendrick family, completed in 1914. The large evergreen trees on the grounds were transplanted from near-by mountains.

7. The FAIR GROUNDS, entrances on W. Burton St. and Kentucky Ave., has a RODEO ARENA and grandstands to seat 7,000. Here, the Sheridan-Wyo Rodeo is held, usually during the third week in July. This show, rated Class A by the major-league rodeo circuit, offers

$10,000 in prize money and attracts many of the big names in rodeo. For days preceding the rodeo, roads leading to Sheridan are crowded with top hands, Indians, tourists, dudes, and cowboys from local ranches. At night the Indians perform their tribal dances around blinking campfires.

8. The SITE OF SHERIDAN'S FIRST CABIN, vacant lot on Smith St. between Thurmond and Brooks Sts., is marked by a granite boulder. The cabin was erected in 1878 by Jim Mason, a trapper, and was later sold to two cattlemen, Frank Yates and Bean Belly Brown. Brown and Yates sold the house to Harry Mandel, who resold it for $50 to John D. Loucks. The first school in the settlement was opened here during the winter of 1882–3.

POINTS OF INTEREST IN ENVIRONS

Holly Sugar Factory, 1.3 *m.*, Sheridan Flour Mills, 1.9 *m.*, Veteran's Administration (Fort Mackenzie), 3.2 *m.*, Girl's Industrial Institute, 3.9 *m.*, Observation Tower, 18.9 *m.*, Site of Fetterman Fight, 19.1 *m.*, Site of the Wagon Box Fight, 21 *m.*, Moncreiffe Polo Grounds, 23 *m.*, Fort Phil Kearny, 23.5 *m.* (*see Tour 3a*); Connor Battlefield, 18.8 *m.*, Big Horn National Forest, 30 *m.*, Eaton Dude Ranch, 33.1 *m.* (*see Tour 10*).

PART III

Tours

Tour 1

(Lead, S. Dak.)—Newcastle—Lusk—Torrington—Cheyenne—(Denver, Colo.); US 85.
South Dakota Line to Colorado Line, 270.6 *m.*

Graveled and oil-surfaced roadbed; open all seasons.
Route touches Chicago, Burlington & Quincy R.R. and Union Pacific R.R. briefly.
Accommodations adequate.

Running along the eastern edge of Wyoming, US 85 winds for a short distance between timbered mountains, then among fields, meadows, and grazing lands. For approximately 165 miles (to the junction with US 26), it parallels closely the general route of the old Cheyenne and Black Hills Stage Line, through a territory rich in the lore of Indian and pioneer, in tales of stagecoach holdups, of pursuit and capture and escape, and of fighting and gunplay. This territory was for many years the hunting ground of the Sioux and other tribesmen, who camped along the creeks and hunted the vast herds of buffalo and antelope that grazed on the plains near by.

By the treaty signed at Fort Laramie in 1868, this territory was set aside for the Sioux, to whom it was a sacred land, an abode of spirits, and the strategic center of their nation. They made expeditions here, not only to hunt and fish, but to obtain lodge poles and medicinal herbs. For many years the Government tried to keep white men out of this territory, but they could not be held back, and many skirmishes took place as the Sioux, under Sitting Bull, fought to hold their land. After the discovery in 1874 of gold on French Creek near the present site of Custer, South Dakota, gold seekers, evading the military, penetrated the Black Hills, using Cheyenne as one of the main gateways. After the Custer and Crook military expeditions and the geological expedition under Professor Walter P. Jenney had made reports on the country, a treaty was effected with the Indians late in 1876, by which the territory between the Platte and Powder Rivers was ceded to the white men.

Immediately thousands of gold seekers, bound for the Black Hills, headed north from Cheyenne, Rawlins, and other points, on foot, on horseback, or in any sort of available conveyance. Great strings of oxen and mules pulled overloaded freight wagons through mud and sand, across vast plains, and up and down the hills. By the spring of

1877 stage and freight lines were operating on regular schedules between Cheyenne and Deadwood.

Adventurous characters of the western border, including Wild Bill Hickok, Buffalo Bill, Calamity Jane, Jack Langrishe and his theatrical troupers, and various 'Deadwood Dicks,' were travelers along this route. In the late 1870's and early 1880's great herds of cattle were trailed from Texas and Oregon to fatten on the knee-deep grass of the eastern Wyoming range. Large cattle ranches were established along the main route of travel. Thousands of sheep soon followed over the same route. Today, in a few localities, farming is carried on. Oil, coal, and wood are available.

US 85 crosses the SOUTH DAKOTA LINE, 0 *m.*, 29 miles southwest of Lead, South Dakota. At 0.3 *m.* is a deserted sawmill (R) and a lumber camp (L) on the edge of a mountain meadow. The road winds southward to SOLDIER CREEK, 6.6 *m.*, so named because General George A. Custer and his men camped here in 1874, with what was said to be the largest and best-equipped expedition up to that time to enter the Northwest. This expedition, comprising 10 companies of the Seventh Cavalry, one each of the Twentieth and Seventeenth Infantry, a detachment of nearly 100 Indian scouts, with guides, interpreters, and teamsters, numbered about 1,000 men. One hundred ten wagons (each drawn by six mules), several ambulances, 1,000 cavalry horses, and 300 beeves were part of the equipment. Too, there were civilian teamsters with wagons, herders, blacksmiths, saddlers, and others, and also a military band. Because of the persistent rumors of the presence of valuable minerals, the U. S. Government had sent General Custer into the Black Hills 'to ascertain the feasibility of the possible location of a military post to command the region between Ft. Laramie and Montana forts and to learn about mineral resources.' Horatio N. Ross, one of the two practical miners with the expedition, is credited with having made the first gold discovery on French Creek, South Dakota, July 30, 1874.

News of the discovery was released by Custer and carried to Cheyenne by Scout Charlie Reynolds, where it was sent out to the entire country. From that time on it was next to impossible to hold back the gold seekers.

Custer's expedition made various camps in northeastern Wyoming (*see Tour* 10).

US 85 parallels Soldier Creek for about two miles, then curves uphill through pines and aspens to grazing country.

At 10.8 *m.* is the junction with State 585 (*see Tour* 10).

PRAIRIE STORE, 10.9 *m.* is a rural trade center.

Left from Prairie Store on a winding graded road to the Ross ALLEN RANCH (R), 4.2 *m.*, near the head of Stockade Beaver Creek. This ranch once known as Canyon Springs Station was on the main route of the Cheyenne and Black Hills Stage Line. Here on September 29, 1878, four road agents overpowered the crew of the Cheyenne and Black Hills stage, killed one man, and took $37,000 in gold dust, bars, and currency from the safe in the treasure coach. Two were captured and later convicted; the others escaped. Most of the gold was recovered, but $3,000 in currency was lost.

STOCKADE BEAVER RECREATION CAMP, 5.4 m., of the Veterans of Foreign Wars and other groups, is in a sheltered valley. The gabled main building of peeled and varnished logs has a fireplace of varicolored stones; the roomy sunporch is floored with flagstones. (*Cabins, tennis courts, 9-hole golf course, baseball diamond. Trout in Stockade Beaver Creek.*)

South of Prairie Store, grain fields and red fallow lands border the highway. RED BUTTE, 15.4 m., a lookout for cattlemen, stands (L) at the head of a small valley. Its brick-colored sides are deeply eroded, and only its cap of white stone prevents its crumbling. A belt of red earth surrounds the butte.

The small BLACK HILLS GOLD EAGLE REFINERY (L), 18.4 m., receives oil from near-by Mule Creek Field.

At 18.9 m. is the junction with a dirt road.

Left on this road through Rainey's Ranch to MOUNT PISGAH, 1.5 m., the highest point (6,000 alt.) in Weston County. A steep trail leads to the summit. The view embraces a 50-mile radius, with the Black Hills to the east and prairies to the west. The mountain resembles a huge molar, roots and all. Vapor rising from a deep hole in the summit keeps the surrounding grass green. Crevices in the cliffs on one side retain snow and ice until midsummer, and in a pocket near the summit is a little lake that once supplied water to Cambria (now deserted) in the valley (*see below*).

At 21 m. on US 85 is a junction with a dirt road.

Right on this road, which ascends through a valley of pine, cedar, and aspen, to SWEETWATER LAKE (*campground, good fishing*), 5 m., which is fringed with pine, spruce, and white birch. A wall of rock on the west is mirrored in the water on still days. Numerous muskrats and beavers live here; and raspberries, strawberries, and sour, slow-ripening gooseberries grow abundantly near the lake.

The FLYING V RANCH, 21.4 m., with headquarters in Salt Creek Canyon, comprises 18,000 acres. The main building, the Casino, built as a memorial to those who discovered and developed the anthracite coal beds at Cambria, is composed of several granite units, Old English in style, joined in the shape of an L. The interior is semirustic: great beams, many of them mine timbers, support the ceilings. The north wing houses a collection of pioneer relics, fossils, and mineralogical specimens. The ranch maintains a nine-hole golf course and has a natural salt-water swimming pool, adjoining a fresh-water pool.

Right from the Flying V on a foot or bridle trail to the ghost city of CAMBRIA, 2 m., at the head of Coal Creek Canyon. Frank W. Mondell, then employed by the Chicago, Burlington & Quincy Railroad, discovered the coal in the late eighties; the railroad was routed to take advantage of the discovery. For 39 years Cambria flourished. The mines, on a hill overlooking the town, the only hard-coal producers in the vast western region, yielded 12,000,000 tons of anthracite. Mine cars of coal were dumped at the tipple with deafening clatter, and then transported along a high trestle to the loading station on the railroad. Much of the early coal mined was converted into coke and shipped to the reduction plants of the Homestake Mine at Lead, South Dakota. In Cambria's palmy days its general store had almost anything commonly found in city department stores. Cambria had a population made up chiefly of Austrians, Italians, and Swedes, with a small proportion of native-born Americans. Because the coal company opposed the sale of liquor, Cambria was known as a saloonless town, something of a distinction in those days. Beer wagons came up frequently, however, from Newcastle. On one such occasion Giacchino, a saloon keeper, and his driver, Peter Nora, who had been to Cambria to dispose of a load of beer, were robbed and murdered on their homeward trip, supposedly by members of the Black Hand. There were other robberies and killings both earlier and later, and Cambria, like Western frontier towns in general, defended itself by lynching a few of its 'bad men.'

When the mines closed in 1928, Cambria's population moved out almost overnight. Stores were abandoned with goods on the shelves; dwellings were left with all their furnishings. Later, the buildings were dismantled by prowlers; rain warped and stained expensive inlaid hardwood floors. The tracks that connected the mine with the railroad were removed, leaving great scars in the canyon. In the cemetery north of town, grass and weeds hide leveled graves. The town's only inhabitants are owls and pack rats; an occasional wind stirs the dust of its forgotten streets. Cliffs and gnarled trees provide a fit setting for the desolate remnants.

From Salt Creek, whose banks are white with salt deposits, US 85 winds upward to a plateau.

At 24.4 *m.* is a junction with an unimproved dirt road.

Right on this road, which doubles back due north along the plateau for about three miles and then drops through a steep canyon, is old CAMBRIA, 3.5 *m.* (*see above*).

OBSERVATION POINT, 27.7 *m.* (4,750 alt.), commands a view that on clear days embraces LARAMIE PEAK and the BIG HORN MOUNTAINS, far to the west. FANNY'S PEAK (L) was named according to legend in honor of a pioneer girl who, true to the story-books, threw herself from its summit rather than be captured by Indians.

The highway follows hairpin loops through pine-edged arroyos (*keep car in gear*).

NEWCASTLE, 28.8 *m.* (4,334 alt., 1,600 pop.), the seat of Weston County, named for the great English coal port, Newcastle-upon-Tyne, proudly calls itself the 'Western Gateway to the Black Hills.' Many of its houses cling to the sides of steep hills several hundred feet above the main street. On the east and north the slopes rise to piny crests; to the south and west, sage-covered prairies slant gently downward, then rise again toward the dim Black Hills. The wide, sheltered streets are lined with modern buildings. Newcastle is a shipping point for lumber, oil, and bentonite, a colloidal clay prepared chiefly in Weston County mills. Sheep, cattle, hogs, turkeys, and dairy foods are produced in the vicinity. Near-by lakes and creeks offer good trout fishing; old wagon roads provide opportunity for pleasant hikes and horseback trips. On Saturday, Newcastle's busy day, fashionably dressed people rub elbows with cowpunchers in broad-brimmed hats and high-heeled boots and long-haired sheepherders just in from the range.

JENNEY'S STOCKADE, courthouse yard on Warren Ave., is an old-time log cabin (1875), moved in 1933 from its original site on Stockade Beaver Creek (*see Tour* 8) and rebuilt in Newcastle as a pioneer museum.

HENDERSON MUSEUM (*open by arrangement*), four blocks north of Antlers Hotel on Warren Ave., contains Indian and pioneer relics and specimens of all important Black Hills minerals.

1. Right from Newcastle on a dirt road to the unoccupied FRANK W. MONDELL HOUSE (*caretaker acts as guide*), 0.1 *m.*, set in tree-shaded grounds on a hill overlooking the town. This green-painted frame house, tall and rather narrow, with elaborate scrollwork, red roof, and several chimneys, was built in 1892. A flight of stone steps ascends to the main entrance. The original carpets and furniture, upholstered in green, are intact; the large-windowed reception and drawing rooms are decorated in ivory; crystal chandeliers, still fitted with old carbon-filament bulbs, hang from the lavishly decorated ceilings. A piano stands in one corner of the drawing room. There are several tiled fireplaces with marble-topped mantels and one of semitransparent stone, whose color harmonizes with the walls. Frank W. Mondell, mayor of Newcastle from 1890–95, later served in Congress and, as chairman of the Committee on Public Lands, was especially active in sponsoring land laws, including one providing for the retention of mineral rights by the Government on agricultural lands, and another for the creation of the 640-acre grazing homestead. For a time he was Republican floor leader of the House.

2. Right from Newcastle on the unimproved Morrissey Road to the GHOST LIGHT AREA, 3 *m.* Strange vivid lights are said to roll over the ground here like tumbleweeds. Some motorists have reported driving their cars off the road to avoid hitting them.

3. Right from Newcastle on a rough dirt road along a ridge north of town. The road winds to a tableland dotted with varicolored rocks, resembling haystacks, tepees, and stairways, and deeply gashed with arroyos. Rows of treetops extend above the rims of these slashes. At sunset, the taller monoliths cast long fingers of shadow that deepen the impression of fantastic unreality. At 3 *m.* is CAVE SPRINGS, a picnic ground near the arched mouth of a cool, shallow, white-limestone cave at the head of a canyon. A pool reflects the arch 40 feet above. Ice-cold water flows from the lower level, where a sandstone layer covers deeper shales. Velvet-green mosses and lichens pad the walls; graceful ferns find root-hold in the crevices. Sandstone boulders and heaps of fine white sand are piled before the entrance.

a. Left from Cave Springs on a dim trail to shallow GOTHIC CAVE, 2 *m.*, cut in slate-blue, rust, and brown rock. The walls are carved with niches.

b. Left from Cave Springs on a foot trail to the mouth of small ALUM CREEK, 2 *m.*, which rises in the springs and winds through a canyon, sculpturing the stone walls into thrones, shrines, and queer shapes. The narrow stream glides over great flat rocks, drops into a crevice, trickles into emerald pools 40 feet below; then rushes noisily over large boulders, where moss and lichen cling. Pine, cedar, and aspen line the steep banks; in their branches live birds and squirrels. Rocky Mountain fern, rare in this region, grows near by. Short coal-mine tunnels mark the hillsides.

At Newcastle is the junction with US 16 (*see Tour* 8), which unites with US 85 to a junction at 31.2 *m.* Here US 85 turns R.

At 43.2 *m.* is a junction with a dirt road.

Left on this dirt road to CLIFTON, 0.5 *m.*, a Burlington Railroad siding. On cliffs in this vicinity are a number of Indian pictographs, which may be reached by following official signboards. At Clifton, the old stage route diverged; one branch wound through the foothills in a southeasterly direction to Robbers' Roost, Indian Creek, and the Hat Creek Station (*see below*); the other, which went almost due south through more open country along Old Woman's Creek to Hat Creek Station, is overlain in many sections by US 85.

Of the many shipments hauled over the old stage route, perhaps the load of cats taken from Cheyenne to Deadwood in 1877 by Phatty Thompson was one of the most unusual. According to old-timers, Thompson, a 'shotgun' freighter who bought, hauled, and sold his freight himself, decided to take a load of pets to the dance-hall girls at Deadwood. By paying Cheyenne youngsters 25¢ a head, he succeeded in rounding up a huge crate of cats at the Elephant Corral in Cheyenne. En route to Dakota the wagon tipped over and the cargo was scattered to the four winds. After much cajoling with tasty morsels, Phatty enticed his charges back into the crate and at last reached his destination, where he disposed of the cats at sums ranging from $10 to $25.

In 1876 Mrs. Thomas Durbin, a pioneer Cheyenne resident, carried $10,000 in currency to Deadwood in a handbag, in order that her brother-in-law and others might open a bank. The coach in which Mrs. Durbin was a passenger was the first one over the route after the killing of the Metz family in Red Canyon, South Dakota, thought to have been the work of Persimmons Bill and his gang. Persimmons Bill, a native of South Carolina, whose real name was William F. Chambers, was one of the most notorious outlaws in the hills.

Various bands, or gangs, of road agents operated in different sections along the stage route. Tom Price was known as the captain of a gang that held up the stage on numerous occasions in the area just south of Clifton. At least two of his lieutenants, McLaughlin and Mansfield, were captured and taken to Cheyenne. When it was found that the court had adjourned and that the prisoners would have to be kept in jail for six months, the officers decided to take them back to Deadwood for trial. Heading north from Fort Laramie, on the return trip, the stage was stopped by masked men, and the two prisoners were whisked off and away to a cottonwood grove along the North Platte River, where the hangman's noose awaited them. The stage proceeded without further molestation.

South of the wooded hills that close in around WHOOPUP CREEK, 44.1 m. (see Tour 8), the highway runs through a valley of hay meadows. At 50.4 m., a flat-roofed, one-room log cabin, typical of an earlier day, stands in ruins (L). On the plains that slope toward the Cheyenne River grow patches of blue flax, wild rose, aster, and mallow, and near the stream are solitary wind-twisted cottonwoods. Road agents in the early days often held up the Cheyenne and Black Hills stage at the crossing of CHEYENNE RIVER, 61.7 m., because they could make quick get-away into the neighboring brakes.

Pumps and pipe lines mark the MULE CREEK OIL FIELD, 66.7 m., which supplies oil for surfacing State highways.

US 85 veers southward over hills crisscrossed by cattle trails, with occasional water holes, familiar to readers of Western fiction. Meadowlarks trill from fences along the road. Rabbits often get in the way of cars on these long stretches; instead of escaping to one side or the other as they could easily do, they bound frantically down the road until overtaken and crushed under the wheels. Then stately hawks and gossipy magpies feast on their mangled bodies.

The RED BIRD STORE, 79.6 m. (cabins), is in the heart of a vast, sparsely settled territory. The road crosses OLD WOMAN CREEK, 79.8 m., so named for an Indian squaw, whose spirit was said to dance nightly on a neighboring rimrock. Hogbacks (long, narrow, and somewhat steep hills) jut across lower ground (R). Fields in the vicinity flaunt red grasses, as bright as the flowers that grow among them. To the north, the Black Hills sink into blue distance. Pine-clad slopes rise on the right.

At 91 *m.* is the junction with a dirt road.

Right on this road to LANCE CREEK OIL FIELD, 14 *m.* During the peak years (1919–28), the oil from this field was carried by pipe line to Lusk (*see below*) and transported by rail to Wyoming, Montana, and Canadian refineries. From 1928 to 1934, the field was shut in, except for about 200 barrels a day that were refined locally. With the discovery of oil in the upper Sundance level in 1930, the work of development was resumed. Fifty-four wells were completed in 1939, and the Lance Creek field promises to become second only to Salt Creek in production. The oil is now carried hundreds of miles by pipe line to reach markets in Sugar Creek, Missouri; Denver, Colorado; Scottsbluff, Nebraska; Salt Lake City, Utah; and Cheyenne, Casper, Glenrock, Douglas, Lusk, Newcastle, and Parco, Wyoming.

Due north of the Lance Creek Oil Field are the LIMESTONE FOSSIL BEDS, which have yielded some of the best Triceratops fossils found in America. Paleontologists agree that one of the greatest herds of reptiles on the continent made its home here, in the days when swamps and lakes covered the land.

At 102.3 *m.* on US 85 is the junction with a graveled road.

Left on this road to an improved dirt side road, 1 *m.*; R. here to the SITE OF THE HAT CREEK STAGE STATION, 3 *m.*, marked with a stone bearing a bronze frieze of a stagecoach and horses. A small cemetery is adjacent. In 1868 soldiers were ordered to establish a post on Hat Creek in western Nebraska, but by mistake they came on to Sage Creek. For several years a small detachment was stationed here to turn back settlers or prospectors trying to enter Indian country. When Indian troubles ended, the soldiers' quarters were used for a post office and stage and telegraph station on the Cheyenne and Black Hills line.

Many of the holdups staged near this station were directed by Dunc Blackburn and his confederates, among whom were Lane Bradley, Wall, Lame Johnny Webster, and Hartwell. It was to Hat Creek Station that 'Stuttering Brown' was taken in 1875, after being fatally shot by Persimmons Bill Chambers during an altercation over stolen horses. Brown, an expert stage man, had been transferred into Wyoming from Utah by Gilmer and Saulsbury, stage owners, to stop the depredations of horse thieves.

In 1876 some Black Hills freighters, heading north from Hat Creek, were attacked by 500 Indians. They were saved from annihilation by the arrival of Captain Eagan and his white horse troop, who had been summoned from their encampment at Rawhide Buttes.

One night in August 1877, Boone May and John Zimmerman, 'shotgun' messengers, who were guarding a passenger coach on a trip to Hat Creek Station, engaged in a fight with road agents near Robbers' Roost. May shot and killed one of the bandits, whom he recognized as Frank Towle. Upon his arrival in Cheyenne a day or so later, May learned that a reward of several thousand dollars had been offered by the county commissioners there for the capture of Towle, dead or alive. The next day he returned to the scene of the fight, located Towle's body, which had been partially hidden in a plum thicket, cut off the head and put it in a gunnysack. When he delivered his grisly trophy to the commissioners, he was told that the reward had been withdrawn. His efforts to collect were in vain.

US 85 winds between spectacular sandstone and chalk cliffs and along piny arroyos to windswept, rolling grassland, then descends to the NIOBRARA (Ind., flat or broad) RIVER, 116.1 *m.*

LUSK, 116.3 *m.* (5,015 alt., 1,218 pop.), seat of Niobrara County and a brisk, modern town, was named for Frank Lusk, an early settler. It is a trading center for one of Wyoming's best dry-farming and live-stock-growing regions. Bordering it on the west are red cliffs, from which the Indians took material for paint. The site was selected for its advantages as a cattle-shipping point. The surrounding region was well grassed and well stocked, and a good trail, with water at convenient intervals, ran through it from the Powder River country. Established in 1886, Lusk had 200 inhabitants before any building was far enough along for painting. On August 1 of that year, a violent storm wrecked most of the town, but building was soon begun again.

Discovery of oil in 1918 in the Buck Creek Dome, 18 miles north, gave Lusk a boom population of 10,000. For a time, men worked throughout the day, hiring women to wait in line at the post office for their mail. Lots sold quickly, and additions were created to supply the demand. When oil production shrank, the town settled into the doldrums, until new discoveries in the Lance Creek district somewhat revived activity.

The LUSK MUSEUM (*caretaker at near-by filling station*), on Main St., is housed in a well-built, peeled-log structure. Old-time Wyoming cattle brands are burned into the ends of the logs. The pioneer collection includes a coach once used on the Cheyenne and Black Hills Stage Line.

In Lusk is the junction with US 20 (*see Tour 6a*).

Right from Lusk on a dirt road to the SITE OF THE SILVER CLIFF MINES and the RUNNING WATER STAGE STATION, 1 *m.*, in Bradley's Meadow. Only the foundation of an old rock barn remains. The CARDINAL'S CHAIR, an eroded sandstone formation, is on the north edge of the meadow.

US 85 runs due south, with heavily wooded hills on the right. Houses appear rarely on the broad plain, and occasionally an abandoned ranch. At 130 *m.* are the timbered RAWHIDE BUTTES (R). According to legend, an Easterner asserted he would kill the first Indian he saw, and, although the first one was a woman, he kept his word. The angry Indians stretched his skin on these blue-black buttes.

The highway runs parallel with Rawhide Creek, through meadows of native hay that stretch toward the foothills. In summer the shoulders of the road are covered with waxy sandflowers, which can be picked and kept in good condition for months. Ranch buildings in this region follow a familiar pattern: large barns, usually red, overshadow the small white houses.

At 139.4 *m.* is the junction with an improved road.

Right on this road is JAY EM, 0.1 *m.*, a village on Rawhide Creek. The name is made of the spelled-out letters of an old cattle brand. Here is one of the largest gem stone cutting works in the State, where trained workers make various useful and ornamental articles from local agate, marble, jasper, and petrified wood. Many similar establishments have been organized in the State during the past four years, in response to the traveling mineralogy school sponsored by the State department of vocational education.

At 149.1 *m*. is a SILVER FOX FARM (L) (*see below*).

US 85 runs through a small valley walled with chalk cliffs. Grazing lands give way to dry farms, on which kafir-corn and some small grains are raised. From these, the road winds into a region of rich fields irrigated by the INTERSTATE CANAL, 160.5 *m*., which carries water impounded by the Pathfinder Dam (*see Tour 11*).

Fine sugar beets are raised in this area. Here, Russian-German and Mexican families work in the fields, planting, thinning, irrigating, pulling, or topping beets, according to season. A few years ago all sugar-beet seed was imported from Central Europe, chiefly from Germany, Czechoslovakia, and Denmark, but now most of the seed used in Wyoming is produced in Arizona and New Mexico. Experimental work, however, is being carried on in various sections of the State by the Holly Sugar Company, with small plots of sugar beets called 'isolations,' where the 'mother beets' are raised and tested for shape, size, uniformity, and sugar content. These beets are then planted in greenhouses, with powerful electric lights taking the place of the sun. It requires two years to produce beet seed. Many varieties, from common table beets to wild sugar beets from the Mediterranean countries, are being grown in these experimental plots. Thousands of paper sacks are tied over the seed stalks, even before the buds are open, to prevent the pollen from becoming mixed. Experiments in crossing varieties are being carried on in an effort to find a beet especially adapted to this country.

The beet seed for the regular crop is planted as early in the spring as weather conditions permit. The quantity of seed required per acre varies greatly, but it is generally conceded that each acre of land requires from 12 to 20 pounds. A uniform stand can be obtained only if the seed is sown on a well-fitted seed bed and proper attention given to thinning and cultivation. When the plants have sprouted about two inches above the ground, they are blocked out with a sharp four-inch hoe, and small bunches of beets, from six to eight inches apart, are left for the thinners, who pull out all except the healthiest beets. During thinning, the workers crawl slowly down the long rows on hands and knees. A space of 8 to 12 inches is left between the plants. Intensive cultivation, with careful attention to weeds, is necessary to a good crop, and, to avoid laceration of the leaves, most of the weeding must be done by hand. Tests show that the time of irrigation has a greater effect on the sugar content of beets than does any other factor.

At harvest time the beets are loosened in the ground by a plow or harvester. Then heavy knives rise and fall mechanically, as the workers slash off the green tops and toss the gray-white beets into heaps, to be removed from the field to beet dumps for transportation to the factory, either by motor or rail. Usually the beet tops are piled in the field for livestock feed.

The large amount of hand labor required in the sugar-beet industry brings into the State annually large numbers of itinerant Spanish-American and Mexican workers. Each laborer and his family tend about ten acres of beets from the planting to the harvesting. They live in small houses, usually one or two rooms, and their main food is beans with chili peppers. In some localities, the sugar companies maintain houses or 'colonies' for the workers.

LINGLE, 164.8 *m.* (4,165 alt., 415 pop.) (*see Tour* 4), is at the junction with US 26 (*see Tour* 4), which unites eastward with US 85 to Torrington, following the Laramie River. Pioneer trails ran along both banks of the Laramie, the Mormon on the north, and the Oregon on the south.

TORRINGTON, 174.9 *m.* (4,104 alt., 1,811 pop.), seat of Goshen County, has a busy business center, trim houses, and gardens. Torrington proper is on the north side of the North Platte River, in the midst of sugar-beet, potato, and alfalfa fields. Certified seed crops are grown here, under contract to various commercial firms. The county has no bonded indebtedness; royalties from oil, coal, and other mineral products provide much of its revenue. In Torrington is a large cold-storage plant, with individual locker boxes for rent by the month. Customers bring in their cattle or hogs to be butchered. The meat is pre-cooled, carved into steaks, roasts, and other cuts, and stored in the lockers.

St. Joseph's Orphanage (L), 175 *m.*, under Catholic supervision, has accommodations for 50 children and maintains its own farm.

The Holly Sugar Company's Factory (R), 175.4 *m.*, is on a branch of the Union Pacific, in South Torrington. The large, many-windowed, concrete structure, with great flues and landscaped yard, is a center of activity from September to late November, while trucks and wagons loaded with beets come in to be weighed and unloaded. The great steel arms of the piler move the beets into mountainous heaps, alongside the piles of limerock and coke used in the refining. All factory machinery is driven by electricity generated by steam turbines. The daily slicing capacity of the factory is 2,000 tons.

Beets enter the factory through washing flumes, in which rapidly moving warm water carries off adhering soil and bits of leaves, and are then run to a picking table or moving platform, where rocks and other materials that might injure cutting knives are removed. Carried by elevator to 20-ton capacity hoppers, the beets are weighed and dumped into cutters. After being sliced into strips called cossettes, they are fed by 'noodle punchers' into a 'diffusion' battery of cylindrical tanks where the sugar is extracted, and 'raw,' or 'diffusion,' juice and pulp are produced. The pulp is either stored in a wet-pulp silo or is brought to a dryer, where it is dried and sacked for use as livestock feed.

Raw juice is first treated with milk of lime, a suspension of slaked lime in water, which coagulates and renders insoluble some of the non-sugars; carbon dioxide is next bubbled through the mixture to render the lime insoluble; there the insoluble lime and non-sugars are separated by filtration from the sugar in solution, leaving 'first press' juice and lime cake. After further filtering and processing a clear, sparkling liquor is obtained, which is pumped into vacuum pans and boiled under pressure, until crystallization begins. A thick crystal and syrup mixture known as 'massecuite' is formed and run into centrifuges, where the sugar crystals separate from the mother liquor and cling to a metal screen or basket; the syrup flies through the screen, leaving a brown mass of wet sugar, which is dried in granulators—revolving drums 60 feet long—and then screened, sacked, and stored. Syrup taken from the centrifuge is of two grades and may be reworked for further sugar recovery.

A 'campaign,' the period during which the beets are run through the factory, usually lasts from 60 to 90 days, depending upon the size of the crop. Previous to the World War of 1914-18, the expert work of sugar boiling was usually done by itinerant workers, referred to as 'sugar tramps,' who moved from factory to factory according to the seasons—from Jamaica to Wyoming and on to California. Then the sugar companies began to train their own factory men and to build up maintenance crews, who stay at the plants the year around. The name 'sugar tramps,' however, still clings.

US 20 crosses the OREGON TRAIL (see Tour 4), 176 m., and proceeds through a region of irrigated farms, where, in autumn, yellow and silvery strawstacks dot the fields. A tall water tower and a smokestack rise above the trees of Torrington to the north.

At 178.1 m. is the junction with a dirt road.

Right on this road, 10 m., to a desolate 'dust bowl' region of more than 109,000 acres, most of it in Goshen County. Formerly 149 families lived in this area, a prolific wheat-growing section, before its soil was worn away by erosion; of these only 64 families remain. Since 1936, the Goshen Hole Project of the United States Soil Conservation Service, with headquarters in Torrington, has made notable progress toward checking further erosion, by means of contour cultivation, restoration of grass, and other conservation techniques. Dams and innumerable shallow contour furrows divert the runoff after rains from the arroyos to the bordering land, where it is absorbed. The region may never be brought back as 'farming country,' but the work of the service has progressed sufficiently to indicate that it can be restored to the status of good grazing lands. The project is a co-operative one, operating under five-year contracts, between the landowners and the Government, on a 50-50 basis.

At 179.3 m. is the junction with a dirt road.

Right on this road to the HARVARD FOSSIL BEDS, 1.1 m., believed to contain thousands of fossils, including many of the three-toed horse. Since the beds were purchased by Harvard University in 1930, extensive exploratory work has been done here under the direction of Dr. Erich Schlaikjer. Except when expeditions are encamped in the summer season, there is little for the visitor to see, as the excavations are carefully covered when not being worked.

For a stretch of more than 60 miles, HAWK SPRINGS, 196.4 m. (4,394 alt., 135 pop.), is the only wayside settlement offering accommodations.

At 198.2 m. is the junction with a dirt road.

Right on this road (steep; sharp turns) to LONETREE CANYON, 11 m., scooped out from the flat prairie. The CHUGWATER FLATS, 13 m., were settled in 1910 by many Iowa farmers, who built substantial homes and cultivated dry farms. For several years there was sufficient rainfall for good crops; then came years of drought and hail. Now dozens of farms are deserted; windows are boarded up, and machinery stands rusting in the barnyards.

US 85 runs smoothly for miles across GOSHEN HOLE, a basin said to have been named for the French trapper Gosche, who frequented the region in the 1840's. In the distance, on either side of the highway, are eroded bluffs—gigantic fortresses, steeples, and towers of chalk. Arroyos among the cliffs are filled with vines, red, yellow, and orange in autumn, against the white background. One draw is fragrant with wild roses in June.

The road swings southwest and crosses several streams, including the Bear, Horse, and Little Horse Creeks. Near Horse Creek is MERIDEN, 215.5 m. (post office, store, gas station). Narrow shelter belts of pine, Russian olive, and Chinese elm, planted by the State highway department to serve as windbreaks, grow along the road. These hardy trees obtain sufficient moisture from drifted snow and occasional summer rains. A ridge of pine-clad hills (L) rises beyond broad acres of rolling grassland. As the road curves southwestward, the Laramie Mountains lift on the horizon, and Colorado snowpeaks are outlined dimly in the distance (L).

Along LODGEPOLE CREEK, 246.1 m., is the LODGEPOLE RANCH of the Warren Livestock Company, one of the largest cattle outfits in Wyoming. Sheep-grazing country lies to the south.

At 252.5 m. is the junction with US 87 (see Tour 3), which unites southward with US 85 for 13 miles.

In CHEYENNE, 260.2 m. (6,062 alt., 17,361 pop.) (see Cheyenne), is the junction with US 30 (see Tour 2a).

At 261.3 m. is the junction with an oiled road.

Left on this road to a SILVER FOX FARM, 1 m., surrounded by a high board fence. Fur primes early in the Rocky Mountain and High Plains areas, and its production has become a million-dollar industry in Wyoming. From 50 to 300 pairs are maintained at each farm. Mating is usually for life, and each pair has its individual pen, usually about 25 by 50 feet in dimensions, surrounded by 10-foot, mesh-wire fences. Cleats project at right angles from the top of the posts, carrying the mesh-wire over in a 90° bend, to prevent the lithe animals from scaling the fence. Each pen is equipped with a kennel, concrete cave, and summer drinking pan. (Foxes eat snow in winter.) The concrete-lined cave is warm in winter and cool in summer.

Silver foxes mate once each year, usually in January and February, and the young are born in April and May. The litters range in number from one to ten; four is considered average. Foxes are among the world's most efficient diggers, and their main toe tendons are clipped soon after birth, to prevent their digging under the fences. The vixen weans her young at about eight weeks, and, by the time the fur has primed in October and November, the pups have attained their full growth. They measure about three and one-half feet from nose to tip of tail, and weigh from 12 to 15 pounds.

In December, the harvest is carefully graded and culled, and the best stock is kept for breeding. The others are killed with carbon monoxide gas, and their pelts sold to commercial furriers. The average pelt in 1940 brought about $25, but exceptional skins sold for as high as $80. Five years is considered to be the maximum period that brood stock can reproduce efficiently, and the fox farmer has no fear of inbreeding.

From birth to death, silver foxes are kept on a strict diet. The staple dish is a hash made up of ground meat, malted grains, dried buttermilk and skim milk, wheat germ, wheat-germ oil, liver meal, blood meal, linseed-oil meal, sea kelp, soya beans, charcoal, molasses, mineral salt, alfalfa-leaf meal, dehydrated fruit and vegetables, and brewers' yeast. Meat makes up 75 per cent of the diet; each fox is fed about a pound and a quarter a day. Jack rabbit is the main meat ingredient for fox diet in Wyoming. It has been estimated that more than 1,500,000 pounds of jack rabbit meat is fed to foxes annually in the Rocky Mountain region. Regular dealers, who maintain hunters and skinners, market the rabbit fur in the East and deliver the carcasses upon order to fox farmers.

Most of the fox fur produced in Wyoming goes into dress and coat trimming. Each grower markets independently, although most have membership in the Rocky Mountain National Fur Growers' Association.

At 265.6 *m.* US 87 branches R. (*see Tour 3d*). US 85 continues across grassy hills to the COLORADO LINE, 270.6 *m.*, 93 miles north of Denver, Colorado.

Tour 2

(Kimball, Nebraska)—Cheyenne—Laramie—Rawlins—Rock Springs—Junction with US 30S—Kemmerer—(Montpelier, Idaho); US 30. Nebraska Line to Idaho Line, 465.9 *m.*

Concrete- or asphalt-paved roadbed throughout, open all seasons; no mainline railway crossings; snow at higher elevations in winter.
Route paralleled by Union Pacific R.R.
Plentiful accommodations in eastern section; many camps and hotels. Towns far apart on western half of route; stops should be planned carefully.
Excellent route for trailers.

US 30, locally known as the Lincoln Highway, crosses the rolling prairies and deserts of southern Wyoming, with heavily timbered, snow-capped mountains in view nearly all the way. Although it reaches its greatest altitude (8,835 feet) near Laramie and crosses the Continental Divide at Creston, it offers easy grades, with little mountain driving. The route connects several of the largest towns in Wyoming, yet has vast stretches where no dwelling is seen for many miles. Long freight trains chuff over glistening rails near the highway, and streamlined expresses slither swiftly through the sage, making bright orange streaks across the dead brown and gray-green plain, which sometimes sweeps unbroken from one blue barrier to another. At intervals along the road, shelter belts of Russian olive, Chinese elm, and pine have been planted under the direction of the State highway commission, to supplement the older buck and picket types of snow fence.

The first dim lines of this route were traced by the travois poles of Indians, on their way to obtain mountain birch for bows and arrows or to participate in hunting encampments. Fur brigades, with heavily laden carts, made the first wheel tracks; emigrants, with ox-drawn wagons and loose stock, wore these tracks deeper. After an Indian uprising in 1862, the frothing horses and swaying coaches of the Overland stage used this route instead of the Oregon Trail through central Wyoming. Remains of stage stations and military posts are still to be seen along US 30. In the late 1860's, engineers and contractors laid the track of the first transcontinental railroad beside the old trail. Today the planes of great airlines hum overhead; at night, beacons flash their lights across the sky.

Feeder roads reach the main route from fertile valleys, in which are some of the finest ranches in the State. Trails lead into mountain areas that offer facilities for winter and summer sports.

Section a. NEBRASKA LINE to LARAMIE; 93.8 m. US 30.

This section of the route lies almost straight across the plain between the Nebraska Line and the feet of the Laramie Mountains. West of Cheyenne, it crosses these mountains, rising 1,772 feet in 40 miles.

US 30 crosses the NEBRASKA LINE, 0 m., 22 miles west of Kimball, Nebraska. The 'Entering Wyoming' sign bears the silhouettes of two cowboys on bucking broncos, the motif of many posters and commercial designs in the State.

PINE BLUFFS, 0.5 m. (5,047 alt., 700 pop.), with its storage tanks, smudged coal chute, and houses grouped in a neat grove of trees, is set against a background of yellow-gray bluffs, bristling with the stubby green spires of small pines. This was once the center of a vast hunting area, over which wandered the Arapaho, Cheyenne, Ute, Sioux, Blackfeet, and other Indian tribes. Many skirmishes between hunting parties took place in this vicinity.

Fields of grain and certified seed potatoes alternate in summer with wide reaches of dry, dust-gray, short grass, flecked with small islands of yellow rabbit brush and vivid green weeds. On most of the farms are frame dwellings and weathered outbuildings, and nearly every place is marked by the steel tower and whirling wings of a windmill. A typical box house (R) is at 30.8 m. (see Architecture).

The ARCHER FIELD STATION (6,000 alt.), 32.6 m., an 880-acre experiment farm, specializes in dry farming and highland grain growing. The average precipitation is 11.97 inches, and the average frost-free period lasts 127 days. The program, carried on co-operatively by the State and the U. S. Department of Agriculture, includes crop rotations and cultural practices, varietal tests of cereals and forages, tests with shelter belts and fruits, experiments with livestock, and the collection of weather data. In the eccentric one-way plow, developed by the station, every other disk is two inches larger in diameter than the disks generally used. With this plow the land is pit fallowed; that is, pits are left on the surface to catch all moisture and prevent loss by runoff. This pitting of the ground also tends to check wind erosion.

At 34.4 *m.* is the junction with a dirt road.

> Left on this road to the WYOMING HEREFORD RANCH, 2 *m.*, 6,000 acres of prairie and meadow, where range 3,000 head of pure-bred cattle and a dairy herd of 40 cows. Animals from this herd have been sent to several foreign countries.

The highway overpasses the tracks of the Union Pacific. At night, streamliners flash through, their rows of lights blended into a single flame against the darkness. Soon the dome of the State capitol and the chimneys of Cheyenne rise ahead, against a horizon banked with deep-blue mountains.

At 39.2 *m.* is the junction with a graveled road.

> Right on this road to the VETERANS ADMINISTRATION FACILITY (*open 2–4 and 7–8 daily*), 1 *m.*, spacious red-brick buildings of modified Spanish design, erected in 1933. The regional office and hospital (108 *beds*) are here.

CHEYENNE, 41.9 *m.* (6,062 alt., 17,361 pop.) (*see Cheyenne*).

In Cheyenne, US 30 intersects US 85 (*see Tour 1*) and US 87 (*see Tour 3d*). At the western edge of town is a junction with a dirt road, which connects with the Happy Jack Road (*see Tour 2A*), an alternate route.

Between Cheyenne and the top of Sherman Hill, a distance of 33 miles, US 30 follows the old roadbed of the Union Pacific, which crossed the Laramie Mountains on a relatively flat summit. The route was discovered by General Grenville M. Dodge and a party of surveyors, who were endeavoring to escape an Indian attack. Along the road are strangely eroded rock masses. The snowy peaks of Colorado, about 60 miles to the south, are plainly visible, and to the north are rugged pine-topped ridges. Herds of fine beef cattle are sometimes met along the road. The punchers who drive them are usually dressed in ordinary working clothes; most of them do not even wear that trademark of the West, the ten-gallon hat. Their yells, however, have the old-time quality.

Because of difficulties of construction on a 150-mile stretch, the Union Pacific Railroad was allowed double payment for each mile. The wooden Dale Creek bridge, 650 feet long and 135 feet high, spanning a chasm, was at the time of building (1868–9) the highest railway bridge in the world. It was rendered unnecessary later by a new grade and a long tunnel. The new grade lies about two miles south of the original road-bed and 237 feet lower.

The Indians, realizing that the roadbuilders were a threat to their way of life, were especially hostile. Every mile of the railway was surveyed and built under military escort. Workers were subject to military drill and had orders to stand and fight if attacked.

A limestone quarry in INGLESIDE, 60.8 *m.*, provides material used in sugar refineries in Wyoming and Colorado (*see Tour 1*).

GRANITE CANYON, 61.5 *m.* (7,315 alt.), a railway station with a store, a gasoline pump, and springs of pure water, was named for the heaps and ridges of stone that marked the countryside.

At 69.8 *m.* is the junction with a graveled road.

Left on this road is BUFORD, 0.3 *m.* (7,862 alt.), a loading point for the red Sherman Hill gravel used by the Union Pacific in making roadbeds.

The OLD PINE TREE, 72.3 *m.*, which appears to grow out of a large granite boulder, was kept alive in early days by Union Pacific firemen, who daily drenched its roots. The trunk grows through a great crack in the rock, while the roots are in the soil beneath the boulder. The tree is possibly the most-photographed object in Wyoming. An iron fence protects it from souvenir hunters.

At 74.6 *m.* is the junction with a dirt road.

Left on this road to AMES MONUMENT, 1 *m.*, a granite pyramid erected in 1881–2 in honor of Oliver and Oakes Ames, important figures in the financial history of the Union Pacific Railroad. The Ames brothers were heavy subscribers to the Crédit Mobilier, formed to finance the Union Pacific's construction. Oliver became president of the road, and Oakes assumed virtual control of construction. The monument is 60 feet square at the base and 60 feet high. In the center of the east side is a likeness of Oliver Ames in low relief; on the west side is one of Oakes Ames. These medallions were cut in Quincy granite in Boston. The monument was erected about 600 feet from the original roadbed and marked the greatest elevation on the old Union Pacific (8,235 alt.).

Some years after the completion of the monument, a Laramie justice of the peace named Murphy discovered that it was on public land. He immediately claimed the property for a homestead and notified the railroad to take the pile of stone off his 'farm.' To bring Murphy to terms, railroad attorneys were compelled to threaten him with impeachment for conspiracy.

At 1.1 *m.* is an old CEMETERY, all that remains of the Old Sherman station, on the Union Pacific. The station was moved two miles south when the line was changed.

At 75.5 *m.* is a STORM SHELTER HOUSE (R). (*Sudden blizzards, Oct.-April, often make immediate shelter necessary.*)

At 76.1 *m.* is the junction with a graveled road.

Right on this road to VEDAUWOO GLEN, 2.2 *m.*, a picnicking place (*see Tour 2A*).

US 30 crosses a boundary of the Pole Mountain District of the MEDICINE BOW NATIONAL FOREST, 78.8 *m.* Here is a junction with a graveled road.

Right on this road to BLAIRS MEADOW, 2 *m.*, and NATIONAL GUARD CAMP, 4 *m.* (*see Tour 2A*).

The highway tops the Laramie Mountains (8,835 alt.) and reaches SUMMIT TAVERN (*parking space; short drives and bridle trips*), 82.3 *m.*

1. Left from Summit Tavern on a foot trail to the summit of CROW CREEK HILL, 300 *yds.* To the east lies a deep wooded valley, bounded by the rugged Pole Mountain and Ragged Top; beyond are the rolling Great Plains. To the south is the ridge followed by the Union Pacific, bordering a wide valley, purple toward its farther edge. Westward are the snow-capped Mummy Range, the Never Summer Range, and the snowy Rabbit Ear Peaks of Colorado.

Nearer on the west rise Jelm (9,000 alt.), Sheep (9,583 alt.), Centennial (9,700 alt.), and Corner Mountains (9,582 alt.), topped by snow-capped Medicine Bow Peak (12,005 alt.). Toward their feet stretch the lake-dotted, stream-traced Laramie Plains, with Laramie in the middle distance. Elk Mountain (11,162 alt.) is more than 100 miles to the north.

2. Right from Summit Tavern on an improved road to a U. S. FOREST SERVICE NURSERY, where pine trees are grown from seed.

US 30 drops quickly down the west slope of the range; through TELEPHONE CANYON, it descends 1,669 feet in 9 miles, one of the steepest stretches on the Lincoln Highway (*blind curves; keep car in gear; speed limit in canyon*, 35 m.p.h.).

In Telephone Canyon and on the sides of the Laramie Mountains, aspen leaves in early autumn flame golden and copper-colored against the dark green of lodgepole pines. As the leaves fall, the trees on the high wind-swept slopes stand out gnarled and deformed. In cold weather, frequent fogs glaze the pines in the lower canyon with ice that shimmers in the sunlight.

At 84.2 *m.* is a junction with the Happy Jack Road (*see Tour 2A*).

At 84.7 *m.* is KIWANIS SPRING (*drinking water; picnic facilities*).

West of the canyon the highway runs across a stretch of dun and lavender sagebrush prairie. Approaching Laramie, it passes for some distance between red gravel knolls (L) and cutbanks of white clay (R).

SPRING CREEK CAMP, 91.6 *m.*, with tourist cabins of local red sandstone, is owned and operated by Bill Carlisle, one-time train robber. On three occasions, Carlisle sardonically notified the Union Pacific that he intended to rob a train. He would board the train as a passenger, feigning illness; a little later, he would force the brakeman or conductor to collect the cash from the male passengers; and then, with his loot, he would jump from the train, while it was taking a hill. Carlisle's prison term was reduced for good behavior.

The IVINSON HOME FOR AGED WOMEN (R), 92.3 *m.*, is a large rambling structure, built of limestone on the lines of an English manor.

The CATHEDRAL HOME (R), 92.8 *m.*, a three-story, pressed-brick building, with third-floor dormers, is an orphanage maintained by the Protestant Episcopal church.

In LARAMIE, 93.8 *m.* (7,165 alt., 8,609 pop.) (*see Laramie*), are the junctions with State 130 (*see Tour 2b*) and US 287 (*see Tour 5c*). Between Laramie and Rawlins, US 30 and US 287 unite.

Section b. LARAMIE to RAWLINS; 118.1 m. US 30-287.

Following a northerly course for nearly 50 miles, US 30 edges gradually away from the Laramie Mountains; then it veers westward through rugged hill country and emerges on dry plains near Walcott.

North of LARAMIE, 0 *m.*, a wide view may be had of the countryside. The Medicine Bow Range stands out in distinct units to the west. Laramie Peak (10,274 alt.), 85 miles to the northeast, lifts, very blue, above the horizon. Pine-covered Pilot Knob (9,000 alt.), topping the

Laramie Mountains east of the city, was a landmark in the days of the Overland Trail.

The STATE TOURIST BUREAU (R), 1.9 *m.*, in a peeled-log building, distributes tourist information.

At 2.1 *m.* is the junction with a graveled road.

Left on this road to the UNION PACIFIC ICING PLANT, 0.3 *m.* Strings of refrigerator cars are usually on the sidings here, taking on tons of ice cakes.

US 30 runs northward over level grassland. The ranching country along the Laramie River was settled chiefly by wealthy Englishmen and Scots in the 1880's. Many of the fields of hay (R) belong to the King Brothers, known throughout the world for their purebred sheep. Small antelope herds, unafraid because they have been so long protected, are sometimes silhouetted along distant ridges.

At 18 *m.* is the junction with State 26 (*see Tour 3d*).

BOSLER, 19.6 *m.* (7,074 alt., 264 pop.), on the Laramie Plains, bears the name of the former owner of the Diamond Ranch (R). The Diamond for some time was headquarters of Tom Horn (*see Cheyenne*), who was charged with being paid by the big cattle interests to keep the range clear of sheep.

US 30 crosses the Laramie River at Bosler and passes Cooper Lake (L). The plain (L) billows away to distant mountains; sage flats (R) alternate with pine-tipped rocky ledges and pastures where white-faced cattle feed.

The road crosses ROCK CREEK, 38.6 *m.*, and climbs to the plain above. At 38.9 *m.* a weather-beaten stagecoach, originally used by the Cheyenne and Black Hills Stage Line, stands under a small shelter. For many years after the line was sold, the coach was used in parades in Laramie and was then purchased by Sam White of Rock River. It played an important part in the festivities of the town, always being used in charivaris. It ultimately became the property of the cashier of Rock River's First National Bank, and when that institution closed its doors the old coach was about to be sold with other bank property. When the residents of Rock River discovered that the coach was to be shipped to a buyer in Brunswick, New Jersey, they took up a subscription and purchased it for the school children of the town.

ROCK RIVER, 39.8 *m.* (6,892 alt., 260 pop.), a town made up of false-front stores and scattered houses, is a livestock and oil-shipping point and a center for outlying ranches. Great concrete snowsheds were built over the railroad tracks here and also north of the town, after a 1916 blizzard had tied up overland trains for more than a week.

1. Left from Rock River on a graded road to McFADDEN (7,200 alt., 300 pop.), 12.5 *m.*, an oil camp, with rows of trim white houses, stores, and modern equipment. The west edge of the settlement slopes to the beautiful hay meadows along Rock Creek, which are dotted with black oil rigs.

ARLINGTON, 21.5 *m.*, a post office on the ranch of Alvy Dickson, an old-time ranchman, is at the SITE OF THE OLD ROCK CREEK CROSSING on the Overland Trail, used in the 1860's.

Here, in 1865, the Cheyenne attacked a train of 75 wagons and surrounded a family named Fletcher. They killed the mother, wounded the father (who hid in a ditch and escaped), and captured the two daughters, Mary, thirteen, and Lizzie, two. Three sons escaped. Mary was struck with several arrows but pulled them out with her own hands. The marauders fled to the mountains; there Mary, separated from Lizzie, watched the wagons burning in the valley. For weeks Mary tramped with the squaws, while the braves led the way on ponies. She dressed and painted like an Indian, cared for 14 ponies and helped gather firewood, waded and swam streams, and struggled through deep snows. In the spring of 1866, aided by jealous squaws who wanted to get rid of her, she got in touch with a white trader named Hanger, who paid a horse, a gun, and $1,600 for her release. A year later she found her father in Salt Lake City.

Thirty-five years after the raid, a white woman, who spoke only Arapaho, visited Casper with some Indians from the Wind River Reservation. Mary Fletcher read about her in a newspaper, returned to Wyoming, and identified the woman as her sister. Lizzie remembered nothing about her capture, and refused to go back with Mary. The proof that she was white, however, gave her a sense of superiority to the Indian women among whom she lived. It also elevated her Arapaho husband, John Brokenhorn. When lands were allotted the tribe in 1908, Brokenhorn refused his share, contending that the white men's Government had no right to confine Indians to a part of the land which was wholly their own.

2. Right from Rock River on a dirt road to the FLAKE HALL RANCH, 11 *m.*, SITE OF OLD ROCK CREEK, a station on the Union Pacific with section house, pump house, and a water tank. In 1878, freighters from Medicine Bow, who desired to establish a new route that would avoid numerous river crossings between the Union Pacific Railroad and Fort Fetterman, established a new station on the bank of Rock Creek. A few old buildings remain, including the old warehouse and general store. William Taylor, quartermaster's agent, had charge of the Government warehouse; C. D. Thayer, son of the territorial governor, opened the first general merchandise store; Harry Holloway started a blacksmith shop; and William Baker opened an 'eating house.' Three saloons were started, large stockyards were built, and two hotels soon were erected. By 1883 Rock Creek was one of the liveliest little towns in Wyoming. At that time there were 175 teams freighting out of Rock Creek, and, according to the railroad agent at the station, the average shipment of cattle from August to November was 100 cars every 24 hours. A stage line was established from Rock Creek to Junction City, Montana, spanning a distance of 400 miles. In 1884 T. S. Garrett was appointed postmaster of the town. Last names were seldom used among the cowboys here, but everyone knew Slim, Shorty, Dollar Bill, Winchester Bill, Nebraska, and the Kid—all of them fun lovers and known for their jokes. Rock Creek was abandoned as a railroad station on April 1, 1900, with the establishment of Rock River, at the time that the main line of the Union Pacific was changed between the Laramie River crossing and Medicine Bow.

In 1916 two cowboys in Rock Creek, excavating a caved-in cellarway on property owned by William Taylor, unearthed several thousand dollars in old gold coins stored in glass jars. Taylor claimed the money; the Supreme Court of Wyoming upheld his claim. Some said the coins had been hidden by a German innkeeper, who had lived on the place and had disappeared after setting out to visit Germany. Others believed the coins had been stolen from a stagecoach.

Approximately six miles west of old Rock Creek, near the abandoned railroad line, is the SITE OF OLD WILCOX STATION. Here, on June 2, 1899, two men flagged a Union Pacific Railroad train and, with revolvers drawn, ordered the engineer to cut the engine and express and baggage cars loose and to pull across the bridge beyond Wilcox and stop. They dynamited the bridge to prevent arrival of the second section of the train, due in ten minutes; forced the engineer to run the train two miles west; then looted the express cars and escaped with $60,000 in unsigned bank notes. More than 100 pounds of dynamite were found near the scene of the robbery the next day. The robbers rode northward and escaped to Montana. Butch Cassidy and Flat Nose George Currie are credited with planning the robbery.

At 41.3 *m.* is a junction with a dirt road.

Right on this road (the La Bonte Road) through an area of bleak hills and sheep camps to hillside ranches, timber lands, and fishing and hunting grounds in the LARAMIE PEAK DISTRICT, 50 *m.* (*few accommodations*).

An OLD CABIN, 41.4 *m.*, on US 30, made of rough dovetailed logs and roofed with slabs and dirt, stands as it was when some hardy settler built it. Fields of alfalfa and clover spread away toward sagebrush flats, and the highway is fringed with sunflower, yellow gumweed, and Russian thistle, which turns bright red in the fall, then dun, and sometimes blackish-brown. With the establishment of irrigation here after 1900, many farmers sold their holdings in Iowa and Illinois and moved to the Laramie Plains. Some attempted to transplant peach and apple trees from their home orchards, but found that the altitude and the short seasons were not conducive to the growth of fruit.

US 30 runs through rolling short-grass country, where great herds of buffalo once roamed. Some of the old buffalo wallows can be seen from the highway. Cattle and horses ramble at will over the unfenced prairie.

CREATION MUSEUM, 50.6 *m.* (6,786 alt.), which contains many fossils, artifacts, and relics, is made chiefly of dinosaur bones set in concrete.

Right from the museum on a dirt road to COMO BLUFF FOSSIL BEDS, 1.3 *m.*, from which was taken the first complete dinosaur fossil discovered in the Rocky Mountain region. Fourteen others, taken from the beds since 1880, are in important museums of natural history.

At intervals, on a sandstone ledge beginning at 51.1 *m.*, are SHEEP-HERDERS' MONUMENTS, slender shafts, six to ten feet high, composed of rocks piled up by sheepherders, when time hung heavily upon their hands. A few look like men silhouetted against the horizon.

US 30 crosses the MEDICINE BOW RIVER, 55.1 *m.*, so named, according to tradition, because the Indians found mountain birch, a wood suited to the making of bows, along the stream. Terrific battles were fought when hostile tribes met here.

MEDICINE BOW, 58 *m.* (6,563 alt., 264 pop.), huddled on a broad prairie, is a supply center for livestock-raising and oil-drilling interests. Its buildings include false-front stores, log cabins, and a hip-roof hotel. The town was headquarters of the hero of Owen Wister's novel, *The Virginian*. Before writing the book, the author rode for the Two Bar outfit.

The VIRGINIAN HOTEL, a three-story, stone-block building with pagodalike roof, stands in the center of town. It has an old-time bar. Opposite the hotel is a monument, chiefly of agatized wood, erected in 1939 in honor of Wister.

1. Left from Medicine Bow on a dirt road to a MAGNESIUM SULPHATE AND BENTONITE DEPOSIT, 12 *m.*

2. Left from Medicine Bow on a dirt road to an OIL WELL, 10 *m.*, which produces daily 6,000 barrels of oil of such high gravity (63° A.P.I.) that it can be used, without refining, in automobile motors. It also produces daily 80,000,000 cubic feet of gas.

3. Right from Medicine Bow on a dirt road to the PETRIFIED FOREST, 30 *m.*, which covers 2,560 acres (in Sections 11, 12 and 13, T27N, R78W). It is judged by paleontologists to be 50,000,000 years old. This is the simplest kind of petrified wood, in which silica has replaced the tree tissues. Only a little of the wood is agatized.

4. Right from Medicine Bow is a dirt road to EPSOM SALT BEDS, 11 *m.*

US 30 runs through hilly country, dotted with sheep and sheepherders' wagons. Long stretches have no other sign of human occupation.

A little lake (L), 67.5 *m.*, is a haven for migrant ducks. West of it the hills close in.

HANNA, 78.8 *m.* (6,777 alt., 1,500 pop.), a Union Pacific R.R. coal camp, is identified by its shaft houses, mine dumps, and mine machinery. Great water tanks, a smudged coal chute, and begrimed frame houses edge the tracks, which divide the town. Up on the brown hillsides are rows of white houses, with green-tiled roofs. On a tall concrete monument, honoring local men who served in the First World War, five names are starred. The names on the bronze plaque—Nick Zakis, Kagas Kappas, and the others—are familiar ones in the community.

Left from Hanna on an oiled road 12.2 *m.* to a rough, unimproved road; R. here to the SITE OF FT. HALLECK, 6.6 *m.*, on the Quealey Ranch. Established in 1862 and named for Major General H. W. Halleck, the fort was a strategic post and station on the Overland stage route. Company A, 11th Ohio Volunteer Cavalry, selected the site and built the post, when the stage route was moved southward from the Oregon Trail. Joseph Slade (*see Tour 4B*) was a frequent visitor here, as a superintendent on the stage line.

In February 1864, a party of Fort Halleck soldiers was caught in one of the worst blizzards of early Wyoming history. Colonel William O. Collins reported: 'The air was so filled with snow that it was often impossible to see ten yards . . . any track was obliterated in a very few minutes . . . Some of the men became much benumbed . . . About ten men stopped and I remained with them . . . but it was impossible to kindle a fire on account of the violence of the wind . . . and the march was resumed. When within about two miles of the fort, Private Frank W. Courtright . . . fell from his horse . . . Private Joseph Hudnell . . . could sit upon his horse by holding to the mane but could not guide him . . . We determined to go forward and save Hudnell if possible and to send back for Courtright . . . who was brought in in a very short time, but . . . died in about fifteen minutes . . . When I dismounted . . . I could not walk [and] had no feeling until being rubbed with snow for some time . . . I began to suffer intensely. The thumbs and fingers of both hands were frozen . . . also my ears, eyelids and nose . . . It is difficult to form an idea of the storm . . . The snow, moving horizontally, struck the face like shot, perfectly blinding the eyes . . .'

On the oiled road is the village of ELK MOUNTAIN, 16 *m.* (7,000 alt., 54 pop.), on the Medicine Bow River (*trout*) at the base of Elk Mountain, a landmark in covered-wagon days. One of the first bands of sheep in Wyoming was trailed in from California by Louis Sederlin of Elk Mountain.

Left from Elk Mountain on a rough, unimproved road, which ends near the CABIN AND GRAVE OF JOHN SUBLETTE, Wyoming pioneer. The handmade furniture of the Sublette family remains in the cabin. (*Exact directions for reaching the cabin may be obtained in Elk Mountain.*)

The highway winds through broken hills marked with the burrows of prairie dogs. These little creatures rise on their haunches, hold their forepaws together across their breasts, rolling little balls of grass between them, then bark shrilly and scamper away. An occasional gray jack rabbit breaks from cover and speeds over a hilltop in great rocking leaps.

At 84.1 *m.* is the junction with a dirt road.

Right on this road to DANA SECTION HOUSE, 0.5 *m.* Near Dana, in 1934, an ex-convict named Lovett tried to rob the Portland Rose, the overland limited train. He derailed the engine, a baggage car, and one coach—but the coach was filled with marines, and Lovett retreated in some haste. The fireman was almost buried by coal, only one hand remaining in view; he was extricated by passengers and recovered. Lovett was soon captured.

At 85.1 *m.* on US 30 is the junction with a dirt road.

Left on this road to the SITE OF CARBON, 2 *m.*, once a coal-mining town. Six mines were opened here and, in the 1880's, they employed up to 600 men. During the Indian-fighting era the people of Carbon sometimes stayed in the mines at night, while guards kept watch at the surface. Mining ended here in 1902, three years after the Hanna cutoff threw Carbon off the main line of the Union Pacific.

At 85.4 *m.* on US 30 is the junction with an oiled and gravel-surfaced road.

Left on this road is the village of ELK MOUNTAIN, 18 *m.* (*see above*).

The orange and white posts of an emergency landing field are R. at 86.6 *m.* Far ahead appear five typically shadowed ridges, one above another.

At COYOTE SPRINGS, 92.7 *m.*, is a filling station and store. Ridges topped with rock ledges rise R. and L. Snow fences, sometimes in double and triple rows, line the road.

At 96.1 *m.* is the junction with State 130 (*see Tour 2B*).

At 96.2 *m.* is the junction with a graveled road.

Right on this road is WALCOTT, 0.5 *m.* (6,650 alt., 10 pop.), where the Union Pacific branch to Encampment Valley joins the main line. During the development of the Encampment mining district in the early 1900's, more freight was handled at Walcott than at any other Union Pacific station between Omaha and Ogden. Mine and smelter machinery, coal, coke, and building material came in; ore and smelter products went out.

The tops of the oil tanks at the Parco tank farm are seen ahead. When the sun is right, the tanks gleam in the distance like polished steel.

The NORTH PLATTE RIVER, 102.6 *m.*, is crowded with logs from Saratoga in summer. In the fall its banks are aflame with the deep orange of frosted cottonwood leaves.

Just west of the river is the junction with a dirt road.

Right on this rough road is FORT FRED STEELE, 2.5 *m.* (6,480 alt., 30 pop.), a post established to protect the overland route in 1868. A few weather-beaten log and frame buildings remain, and a bullet-riddled marker displays the red, white, and blue sign of the old Lincoln Highway. On a hilltop just south of the settlement, broken headstones lie about inside and outside the picket-fenced burial ground.

In 1843, when Lieutenant John C. Frémont camped near this spot, he had a large number of buffalo killed. Scaffolds were erected, fires made, and the meat was cut into thin slices for drying. Suddenly the camp was attacked by 70 mounted Cheyenne and Arapaho. Frémont's men rushed into a grove and brought the Indians to a halt. The warriors then approached saying they had thought they were charging enemy Indians. The peace pipe was smoked, and gifts were exchanged.

Fort Steele was occupied as an army post from June 20, 1868, to August 7, 1886. From it in mid-September 1879 Major Thomas F. Thornburg led a soldier troop to the aid of Nathan C. Meeker, agent to the White River Ute in northwestern Colorado. The Ute objected to the Government's efforts to establish a farming economy for them, and when Agent Meeker attempted to enforce his agricultural policy, they revolted and killed him. Ambushed by about 250 Indians, Thornburg and 12 men were killed; 47 were wounded. The Ute set fire to the brush along Milk River and destroyed the wagons and supplies. Jo Rankin, a scout, escaped at night, obtained a horse, and carried the news to Rawlins, 164 miles away, in 24 hours. Troops were rushed from Fort Douglas, Utah, and Fort Russell, Wyoming; those from Utah arrived within 36 hours, but found that the Ute had taken Meeker's agency, killed the white men, burned most of the buildings, and carried away the women and children. In 1880, J. W. Hugus, post-trader at Fort Steele, operated a ferryboat on the North Platte River. When the river was at flood from melting snow in the mountains, A. J. Frayer, who with his wife and two children were westward bound by covered wagon, were being ferried over the river. In midstream, the cable broke, the boat capsized, and the ferryman, Joe Barger, Frayer's wife, children, and the team drowned. Frayer drifted down stream half a mile, clinging to the upturned boat. Four soldiers who saw the mishap dragged the imperiled man to shore with a rope. The bodies of the wife and children were never found. Hugus furnished Frayer with a team, a wagon, and a supply of provisions, that he might continue his journey.

PARCO, 111.6 *m.* (6,592 alt., 727 pop.), is modern from its water-works to its hotel. Dominating the town is an oil refinery, its shiny tanks twined about with spiral stairways and weblike steel ladders: great stacks, tubes, and stills rise about it, and the water-cooling plant sends volumes of spray into the air. Oil is piped to the refinery from the Lost Soldier Field (*see Tour* 5).

The modernity of Parco is emphasized by its isolation on miles and miles of awe-inspiring, but sometimes monotonous, sagebrush plain. Many dwellings, of stucco, are of the California bungalow type. The principal buildings are grouped around three sides of a grassy plaza. An 80-room hotel, with Spanish motifs, occupies a whole block; the ceiling with open beams was modeled after one in the Monastery of Montesion in Barcelona.

Left from Parco on an unimproved road to a 20-MILE POST, 3.2 *m.*, surrounded by a white fence, one of the few 20-mile railroad section markers still in existence. The Government accepted the Union Pacific R.R. in sections marked with such posts. Near this one is the SITE OF BENTON, one of the towns that mushroomed along the U.P. in 1868. The first one established west of Laramie, Benton, within two weeks, had a population of 3,000. According to J. H. Beadle's *Undeveloped West:* 'There were . . . squares arranged into five yards, a city government . . . a daily paper, and a volume of ordinances for the public health. It was the end of the freight and passenger, and the beginning of the construction division; twice every day immense trains arrived and departed, and stages left for Utah, Montana, and Idaho; all goods formerly hauled across the plains came here by rail and were reshipped, and for ten hours daily the streets were filled with Indians, gamblers, "cappers," saloon-keepers, merchants, miners, and mulewhackers. The streets were eight inches deep in white dust as I entered the city of canvas tents and polehouses; the suburbs appeared as banks of dirty white lime, and a new arrival with black clothes looked like nothing so much as a cockroach struggling through a flour barrel; the great institution of Benton was the "Big Tent" . . . a nice frame building 100 feet long and 40 feet wide, covered with canvas and conveniently floored for dancing, to which and gambling it was entirely devoted.'

RAWLINS, 118.1 *m*. (6,755 alt., 4,868 pop.), seat of Carbon County, is a distribution and supply point for extensive oil and gas fields, sheep and cattle ranches, coal mines, and quarries. Near by are the 'Rawlins Red' paint mines, from which, in 1874, John C. Friend shipped a car-load of pigment for use on Brooklyn Bridge.

Rawlins has wide streets, laid at right angles; tree-bordered lawns around neat, comfortable dwellings; fine churches, schools, and business houses; and excellent water piped from the Medicine Bow Range. A rodeo and county fair are held here annually in September.

When, in 1867, General John A. Rawlins discovered a spring in a draw near this point, he called it 'the most gracious and acceptable of anything' he found in this area; he told General Grenville M. Dodge that if anything were ever named for him, he should prefer it to be a spring. Both the spring and the town established near it the following year were named Rawlins. General Rawlins, said to have been the only officer who could influence General U. S. Grant, is believed to have planned some important moves of the Union armies during the Civil War.

Like most towns in southern Wyoming, Rawlins grew up swiftly as the railway pushed westward. The first settlement was south of the railroad tracks near Rawlins Spring, which was a godsend to construction crews in this otherwise desert country. About a year later, settlement began on the north side, where most of the present city stands. Some 2,000 people built houses there, using any materials from cloth and railroad ties to logs.

The stabler citizens of Rawlins were at first beset by the usual lawless frontier elements. In June 1878, 'Big Nose George' Parrot and 'Dutch Charlie' Burris, with two accomplices, tried to derail the westbound Union Pacific pay car by drawing the spikes that held the rails. The bandits fled when a section boss, who noticed the loose rails, flagged the train and notified the sheriff. Tip Vincent and Ed Widdowfield, leading a posse, followed the trail of the bandits to a cove of willows and, while stooping to examine the ashes of a campfire, were shot dead by the men they were trailing. The bandits seized their horses and fled. About a year later word came from Miles City, Montana, that the bandits had been arrested there. Both were brought back to Wyoming for trial, but at Carbon, Dutch Charlie was taken off the train by local citizens and hanged from a telegraph pole; Big Nose was tried before Judge Jesse Knight at Rawlins and sentenced to hanging. His legs were kept shackled. One evening, having managed to file through one of the bolts with a case knife, he swung the shackles upon Bob Rankin, the jailer; Mrs. Rankin, however, closed the cell door and gave the alarm. That night a crowd took Big Nose from jail and hanged him. The Vigilantes then sent warnings to 24 other bad men, and next morning the Rawlins ticket office of the Union Pacific sold 24 tickets.

The STATE PENITENTIARY, on the northern edge of town, has two-story wings and a four-story central unit, topped by two guard towers, all built of granite from local quarries. A high wall, with a tower at each corner, surrounds the recreation grounds back of the main building. Landscaped grounds, with gardens, shrubbery, trees, and flower beds, contradict the somberness of high walls and barred windows. Inmates manufacture woolen goods, such as blankets and rugs; Rawlins is in an important wool-growing region, but with few manufacturing plants.

At Rawlins is the western junction with US 287 (see Tour 5).

Section c. RAWLINS to JUNCTION WITH US 30S; 155.1 m. US 30

This section of US 30 crosses the Continental Divide on a nearly level plain and runs westward along the southern rim of the Red Desert. Only the desert colors and the occasional buttes and rocky walls beside the road relieve the monotony of a region that is bleak and almost wholly undeveloped.

West of RAWLINS, 0 m., the road runs through a gap to sage flats used for sheep grazing. A long line of broken hills (R) is marked with outcrops of gray sandstone. At 3.4 m. are pens and sheds used for sheep shearing. The highway runs upward to a broad plateau, on which slender white Union Pacific block signals stand like robots, silently raising and lowering their yellow, red, and black striped arms.

PIKER SPRINGS, 20.9 m., a filling station, maintains a small museum of archeological specimens and Indian relics.

At 23.8 m., across a grassy valley, is a large emergency landing field.

At 27 m. is the junction with State 330.

Left on this oil-surfaced road across the southern Great Divide Basin, a wide sheep-grazing region of sage, cactus, and alkali. It is largely unfenced and very sparsely populated.

At 28.5 m. is the junction with a dirt road; R. here 0.2 m. to DAD, a sheepmen's post office. Sheds and shearing pens are near by. Lambing season here is late March to mid-April, when new grass comes up. On some ranches, lambing sheds are prepared; on others, small tents are used to protect ewes and lambs from bad weather.

Shearing usually begins in May; snowstorms and late cold sometimes cause heavy losses among newly sheared sheep. Both hand shears and machine shears are used. The shearing crew, which travels from outfit to outfit, is composed of shearers, wranglers, herders, and a 'tromper.'

Enough sheep are penned up at one time to last the shearers half a day; from the large pen, shouting wranglers haze them through a chute to 6-by-12-foot shearing pens. One or two shearers work in each pen, with cans of cold water handy in which to plunge the shears. Each man catches a hindleg and pulls his sheep to a sitting position. With his legs he holds the squirming animal, while he slips his shears into the wool near its ear. Cutting downward and around, he peels the fleece off in one piece. A flunky rolls it, tail to neck, ties it into a neat bundle with a glazed tally string, and tosses it to the tromper on the work tower. Since the strings used are a record of the day's work, the shearer starts the day with a definite number. For a ram's fleece, the shearer receives double credit. An experienced shearer can finish a sheep every five minutes, and earn from $12 to $18 a day.

In a tower framework near the pens, a burlap sack is held by an iron ring. The sack, 7 to 8 feet long and 4 feet wide, hangs with its bottom just off the ground. The tromper, his head usually below the rim of the sack, tromps five 9-pound fleeces into it at a time. A well-tromped sack will hold 40 to 50 fleeces. When filled, it is sewed at the top and marked with the owner's brand and the weight of the wool.

The sheared sheep are run through a vat containing a hot solution of coal, tar, sulphur, or lime, to prevent scab, tick infestation, and eye diseases. The lambs are docked, the sheep branded with paint, and all are trailed to summer range, usually in a national forest. Owners select feeding grounds carefully, to avoid areas infested with death camas, larkspur, and other plants toxic to sheep.

State 330 crosses Muddy Creek, 33.8 m. An occasional rattlesnake on, or beside, the road, the eroded cliffs (R), and vast stretches of desert create a feeling of isolation here. The sage is bluish-green, like heather.

BAGGS, 50.9 m. (6,245 alt., 192 pop.), named for Maggie and George Baggs, early settlers, is in the Little Snake Valley. Made up partly of false-front and rough log buildings, partly of modern concrete, pressed-brick, and peeled-log structures, it has a homelike, comfortable air.

Because of its isolation, Baggs in the 1880's and 1890's was a rendezvous of bad men. Tom Horn and Bob Meldrum, quick-triggered livestock detectives, frequented the vicinity. Tom had a rock fortress on the Seven-Mile Ranch below Baggs; Bob killed his last man here when Chick Bowan, a popular cowpuncher, resisted arrest. The Powder Springs gang, led by Butch Cassidy (see Tour 3b), came here to celebrate holdups in surrounding States. After one $35,000 haul in Winnemucca, Nevada, they took possession of Baggs and threw money and bullets about with abandon. The inhabitants, though not exactly at ease during the celebration, knew the gang intended no harm. Financially, they profited by the visits, for no outlaw destroyed property without paying generously for it. When absent from headquarters, which was on a mountain 40 miles west, the gang kept its swift, sturdy horses under guard and ready, its arms and ammunition stacked in military fashion.

Citizens of Baggs strove for years to have a good highway built from Rawlins to the Little Snake Valley, to bring business to the community. When the road at length came through in 1929, it achieved the opposite purpose: it provided a fast and easy exit for citizens, who preferred to shop at distant points.

At Baggs is the junction with the Encampment Road (see Tour 2B).

At 53.9 m. the highway crosses the Colorado Line, 43 miles north of Craig, Colorado.

The CONTINENTAL DIVIDE (7,178 alt.), 30.4 m., is approached so gradually that it is difficult to recognize the highest point. West of it, the road runs through barren and mostly uninhabited country, with few accommodations. Here and there a bridge over a dry streambed indicates that this is cloudburst country—a land where provision must be made for draining off the water of rare torrential rains, which otherwise would wash out, in a few minutes, roads that took months to build, endangering the lives of those who use them.

Across the sage ahead, the beacon equipment of the Bitter Creek landing field resembles a steel-gray battleship riding a green-gray sea. At 41.2 *m.* is the junction with a dirt road.

Left on this road is WAMSUTTER, 0.2 *m.* (6,709 alt., 50 pop.), one of the oldest wool-shipping centers in the State. Derricks top wooden buildings over the wells, from which the town obtains its water. On summer nights, this lonely place is merely a small group of lights set in blackness and silence. Over the immense darkness, stars shine brilliantly, neither dimmed by other lights nor hidden by smoke and dust in the air. A meteor flames against the winking stars; an aeroplane, winging toward Cheyenne or Salt Lake City, seems trying to imitate it. Wamsutter is on the edge of the RED DESERT, where colors change hourly, according to the brilliance and direction of the sunlight. Although the region seems barren, hundreds of thousands of sheep winter there.

US 30 passes 'Wamsutter-on-the-Highway,' a cluster of cabins, filling stations, and other buildings, erected when the new highway left the old town some distance off the route.

The road runs straight, broad, and nearly level for 20 miles. Relics of early days, remnants of wagons, human and animal skeletons, and Indian trophies lie along dim trails (L). (*Smooth highway and monotonous surroundings often make drivers drowsy in this region.*)

At 60.5 *m.* is the junction with an old trail.

Left on this trail to the SITE OF BARREL SPRINGS STATION, 15 *m.*, on the Overland route. In a vast expanse of sagebrush and greasewood is a crystal-clear spring, almost ice-cold, very different from the vile streams of this Bitter Creek country. The station keeper here knocked the ends out of a 50-gallon whisky barrel and set it in the ground around the spring.

TABLE ROCK STATION (*store, gas pump*), 64.6 *m.*, was named for the butte not far away.

Left on another vague trail to TABLE ROCK, 8 *m.* (6,840 alt.), a sandstone formation, sometimes called Diamond Mesa, at the head of Ruby Gulch. In 1876 two old prospectors salted the mesa with precious stones procured in Holland; then they took interested persons to the place, blindfolded, to see their great discovery. They managed to fleece such men as Horace Greeley, the Rothschilds, and Tiffany, out of more than $500,000 for a promotion company. The fraud was discovered when a cook, with a geological survey party, kicked up from an ant hill a diamond that showed traces of a lapidary's tool.

An official report, made after the scandal was discovered, said: 'Upon raised domelike portions of Table Rock, rubies and diamonds lay . . . where the storms of one or two winters must inevitably have dislodged them . . . unaccompanied by quartz or iron concretions. In the ravines and upon the mesa near by are numerous ant hills which were found to bear rubies on their surfaces. A still closer examination showed artificial holes, broken horizontally with some stick or small implement through the natural crust of the mound; holes easily distinguished from the natural avenues made by the insects themselves. When traced to its end, each artificial hole held one or two rubies . . . This rock has produced four distinct types of diamonds, oriental rubies, garnets, spinels, sapphires, emeralds and amethysts, an association . . . impossible in nature.'

Antelope graze on the flats in the Red Desert, where, it is said, cowboys in 1888 captured six buffalo calves at a roundup, but strangled two with their lariats. For 20 miles there is not a sign of human habitation.

Several buttes stand out (R): one, flat-topped, with sloping sides; another, irregular in form; a third, pyramidal; and a fourth, a broad wedge. All are blue-gray in shadow, with yellowish tints under sunlight. The waste of sage and desert weeds extends to them and beyond them —a taut coverlet of red, yellow, burnt umber, and gray-green, patched with deeper green—as far as vision reaches. An occasional Union Pacific train (L) raises a column of smoke that is instantly bent backward into a cloudy horizontal bar, then diffused to a dirty gray mist blotched with black. The long-drawn call of the locomotive pierces the distance.

Breaks, with sheer fronts and flat tops, appear (R), each face edged at the top with a stratum of burnt-looking rock. The sides of the buttes and the flat, with its deep-cut gullies, are water-washed. It is a land of torrential rains and long dry seasons. The yellow flowers of rabbit brush make bright channels through the sage.

ROCKY POINT, 84.3 *m.*, is a tourist camp (*filling stations*).

At 85.4 *m.* is the junction with a side road.

Left on this road to the ALMOND STAGE STATION, 0.5 *m.*, a relay point after 1862 for the Ben Holladay Overland Stages. Two rough stone cabins and a frame shed remain.

POINT OF ROCKS, 85.5 *m.* (6,509 alt., 100 pop.), is named for the great gray sandstone ledges that rise 1,100 feet above the railroad. Near by are sulphur springs and small canyons. Winds here are hot and dry.

In the early 1870's Point of Rocks was the railway station nearest the South Pass and Sweetwater districts (*see Tour 5A*). Most of the buildings were of adobe. The Wells-Fargo Company maintained offices here and ran daily stages to South Pass.

Gray cliffs form a mile-long wall beside the road. They have a strange moth-eaten appearance. Holes and small caves in the stone have apparently been scoured out by wind and rain. Farther west are rusty brown, grayish-yellow, and red rimrocks. West of these, the buttes are less spectacular. The distant hills look like monstrous sand piles, their sides ribbed wtih light-gray material and dented with darker hollows.

US 30 parallels Bitter Creek (L).

At THAYER JUNCTION on the U.P., 92.9 *m.*, is an old stone-front dugout, a common form of dwelling during the railroad-building era. North of the junction rise the Leucite Hills; to the south, the scalloped edges of dark-gray cliffs lift beyond sand and clay flats, streaked and splotched with vivid green greasewood and yellow rabbit brush. After a rain, the pungent smell of greasewood fills the air.

The canyon of HORSE THIEF CREEK, 93.1 *m.*, is said to have been a rendezvous for early-day outlaws.

At 94 *m.* is the junction with an oiled road.

Right on this road to SUPERIOR, 8 *m.* (7,100 alt., 1,150 pop.), a coal-mining town.

Right from Superior on a trail to THE CORRALS, 6 *m.*, composed of rocks half a mile long and a quarter-mile wide. Subterranean passages here contain ice throughout the year.

US 30 runs through desert, in which greasewood forms light-green islands in a gray sea of salt sage. The view to the left is not unlike certain views in the Grand Canyon of Colorado, except that its coloring is less brilliant.

The burned, barren hillsides, especially near Rock Springs, are relieved only by the strip of green weeds along the railroad tracks. Rough dirt roads lead to coal and oil developments. High rocky ledges, resembling ancient ruins, hedge the road as the valley narrows.

ROCK SPRINGS, 111.3 *m.* (6,271 alt., 8,440 pop.), is a city of large gray shafthouses and black smokestacks, spur tracks and crooked streets, fine homes and tiny shacks, modern business houses and old, tumble-down, false-front frame structures. The air pulsates with the sounds of machinery. The Rock Springs coal mines, owned by the Union Pacific, are among the largest west of the Mississippi. Like many mining communities, Rock Springs is cosmopolitan, with a population including 47 nationalities. On winding K Street are French bakeries, Greek candy shops, a Chinese restaurant, a Jewish market. International Night, first celebrated about 1924, usually comes in May, with exhibits by all resident nationalities. Members of each group, dressed in national costume, sing and dance as in the country of their origin.

Rock Springs is an outfitting point for big-game hunting and fishing in the Wind River Mountains, Hoback Canyon, Jackson Hole, and the Yellowstone country.

A Pony Express rider in 1861, detouring to avoid Indians, came upon the spring for which the town was named, flowing from a rock northwest of the present town. A stage station was established, and in 1866 Archie and Duncan Blair built a stone bridge and stone cabin opposite the station (*see Tour 7b*). When the town was settled, houses were built anywhere and in any position that suited the builders' tastes; the aggregation looked as if scattered from a huge pepperbox. Miners trudged to work over winding paths. Some families lived in dugouts along Bitter Creek. As the town grew, it spread out from the haphazard early streets, but retained the intricate bends and turns that puzzle strangers today.

To defeat a miners' strike in 1875, the railroad hired Chinese workmen. By 1885 Chinatown had nearly 1,200 inhabitants—more than the white settlement. That year, a mob suddenly attacked Chinatown, burned it, killed 30 Chinese, and attempted to drive the others out. Troops rushed to the scene by the Governor were kept there until 1898.

According to a witness of the riot:

The mob set fire to every building . . . Two thousand or more shots were fired while the burning houses roared in the night. The houses . . . were connected by underground . . . passageways . . . Men . . . engaged to dig into the tunnels . . . were paid $20 for each dead Oriental that they found . . .

Chinatown was rebuilt, larger than ever . . . The Chinese displayed their dragon frequently. Since the dragon was nearly 100 feet long, from 30 to 40 men were required to carry it through the streets. The covering of its long back and sides was silk. The frame was made of bows similar to those of the covered sheep wagon . . . The head . . . was like that of a long-horned Texas steer, curved. The mouth was that of a mad bull, with tongue pronged like that of a viper. Its eyes were red and green, bulging out. Each time the procession reached a Chinese place of business, the dragon halted with head turned toward the house and made several bows, while the band played to the accompaniment of . . . thousands of firecrackers.

At Rock Springs is the junction with US 187 (*see Tour 7b*).

US 30 skirts rocky ledges through a region of scrubby sage and lowgrowing greasewood. Far ahead, a prominent butte shows through a gap; emigrants used it as a landmark.

An occasional small chicken ranch, with weather-beaten buildings, appears along the highway, and a cluster of bright-yellow section houses stands by the railroad. The road runs on between eroded red and white sandstone hills, where receding prehistoric seas left their sediments in great wavelike deposits; then it winds out of a bowl, up through Bitter Creek Valley, and curves down a steep hill. Running along a shelf, it commands a view of the Green River, which in flood times is jammed with ties. Smoke from many trains and from railroad shops hangs over the valley.

GREEN RIVER, 126.7 *m.* (6,100 alt., 2,589 pop.), seat of Sweetwater County, division point on the Union Pacific and eastern terminus of the Oregon Short Line, is built on the north bank of the Green River. During tie drives, when more than 300,000 ties are floated down river, daring youngsters amuse themselves by walking up the bank a mile or so and riding the ties down the swollen stream.

Green River, with trim houses, lawns, and gardens and tree-lined streets, is bordered (R) by sandstone cliffs, of which the most prominent, CASTLE ROCK, rises 1,000 feet above the river. A path leads to the crest, circling the rock on the east. Across the valley (L) is a curiously eroded formation, known as the OLD MAN'S FACE.

In 1862, the Overland stage route crossed the Green River a little to the south. Settlement did not begin until July 1868, when some men, who hoped to profit by the boom the railroad was likely to bring, laid out a town; by September 2,000 people occupied the site. When the Union Pacific arrived, however, its builders gave the speculators no attention, but bridged the river and moved on as fast as possible.

The small HUTTON MUSEUM (*adm. by appointment*), 185 N. 2nd St. contains fossils, Indian relics, and pioneer mementos.

Running sharply uphill through a cut, US 30 follows the river. The Union Pacific roadbed (L) is cut from the mountainside high above the stream. At TOLLGATE ROCK, 128.2 *m.*, Mormons cut a passage and charged a toll of those who passed. Brigham Young, on the way to Salt Lake Valley in 1847, is said to have delivered a sermon from PULPIT ROCK (R). For more than a mile the highway skirts the PALISADES, sheer buff sandstone cliffs, tinted pink and rose by late afternoon sunglow.

Though the GREEN RIVER, 131.2 *m.*, takes the color of the shale over which it flows, it was named for a business associate of the trader, William H. Ashley. The Indians called it the Seeds-ke-dee-agie (Ind., prairie hen). It was also known as Spanish River. The valley, which has many small truck farms and sheep ranches, extends more than 125 miles north and south. Protected by mountain ranges on the western slope of the Continental Divide, it has relatively mild winters, with only brief cold snaps. Summer heat, too, is moderate. The valley was for many years a trappers' rendezvous (*see Tour 9*). Wild flowers are numerous here, especially red Indian paintbrush (the State flower), white rock and sand lilies, and bluebells. Wild currants grow abundantly along the riverbanks. Cactus, greasewood, sagebrush, mesquite, and grama grass are found on the hills and in the canyons. Cottontail and jack rabbits, prairie dogs, gophers, chipmunks, coyotes, badgers, weasels, beavers, deer, and antelope are native to the region. Sage hens, sparrows, magpies, hawks, bluebirds, and robins are common. Rattlesnakes and scorpions are seen occasionally.

West of the valley, the highway veers across low sage-covered hills and flood-washed sand flats. An occasional large truck carrying ties, with axes crossed atop the load, rumbles past.

At 139.7 *m.* is the junction with a dimly marked trail.

Right on this trail to the SITE OF BRYAN, 0.2 *m.*, where in 1868 the Union Pacific built machine shops and a 12-stall roundhouse; from the Government freight depot here, shipments were taken by wagon and stage to other places. Beginning in 1869, a daily stage ran to the Sweetwater gold district, and considerable freighting was done to the gold camps. When the railroad straightened its tracks, the freighting business shifted to Point of Rocks, and Bryan became a ghost town. The cemetery remains.

An old concrete Lincoln Highway marker (R), 144.2 *m.*, recalls the early days of the first transcontinental highway. On December 13, 1913, a string of bonfires, nearly 450 miles long, lighted the route across southern Wyoming, heralding the opening of the pioneer transcontinental route.

At 155.1 *m.* US 30 divides: US 30N branches northwest; US 30S, southwest (*see Tour 2C*).

Section d. JUNCTION WITH US 30S to IDAHO LINE; 98.9 m.
US 30N

US 30N traces an irregular northwesterly course across ranching and coal-mining areas, where gray sage flats extend to horizons of low hills, broken occasionally by eroded peaks. Sage is interspersed with rabbit brush and smaller dry-land plants, so gray and wizened they blend with the complexion of the soil and become all but invisible. Infrequent streams have ribbons of meadows along their banks, but in many places the growth is too thin to support cattle. Snow provides moisture in winter, and thousands of hardy sheep then pick a living from the desert plants.

US 30N, now the route, swings R. from the junction with 30S, 0 *m.*

BLACK'S FORK, 2.4 *m.*, a tributary of Green River, heads in the distant Uinta Mountains (L). General Ashley named it in 1825 for Daniel Black, one of his St. Louis associates. Once a stream of some volume, much of its flow has been diverted for irrigation in the Lyman area (*see Tour 2C*).

At 2.6 *m.* is a junction with a graveled road.

Left on this road is GRANGER, 0.3 *m.* (6,240 alt., 135 pop.), a lonely hamlet set amid drab sagebrush. Founded in 1868, it was first a rail's end camp, or 'hell on wheels,' but endured as a stock-shipping depot.

In 1880 the Union Pacific started building a branch line northwestward to join the Utah Northern and the Oregon Short Line, and in 1884, when the latter was completed to the Pacific Coast, Granger became an important division point. Three boxcars on a siding provided a station; the center car was the ticket and baggage office, and the other two were used as freight depot and waiting room; a chalk line divided the waiting room into men's and women's lounges, and men could smoke only on their own side. Soon Granger had a hotel, several stores, cafés, railroad shops, and a saloon. In 1899 the Union Pacific bought the Short Line and moved the division point to Green River; and in the middle 1930's the route of US 30N was changed, leaving the town, which had been on a main highway since the days of Elijah White's wagon train (1842), a quarter-mile off side. It is now chiefly a winter headquarters of sheepmen.

At 0.4 *m.* is a junction with an old oil-surfaced road (the former US 30N); L. here 0.1 *m.* to SOUTH BEND STAGE STATION. Built of stone in 1850, and later covered with adobe mortar, with a frame lean-to stock shed, the station was on the first transcontinental stage line until the stage was superseded by the railroad in 1869. It was also a Pony Express and, later, a telegraph station.

Running over barren, rolling plains, in contrast to the green valley of Ham's Fork (L), the highway drops into a valley enclosed by low chalk hills. Willows and cottonwoods border the river meadows; the higher treeless pastures have rude brush livestock shelters. Buildings here illustrate the evolution of ranch architecture. Early log cabins and weather-beaten frame houses, many overshadowed by large new frame dwellings, serve as barns or storehouses.

OPAL, 28.3 *m.* (6,668 alt., 65 pop.), a shipping point for wool and sheep, was named for the jewel, but is pronounced O-pál.

The highway climbs to an almost level plateau, where black scars on gray sage hillsides mark coal mines on both sides.

At 42.1 *m.* is the east junction with US 189 (*see Tour 9*), which unites briefly westward with US 30.

DIAMONDVILLE, 42.5 *m.* (6,885 alt., 812 pop.), once a prosperous mining community, is a somber, partly deserted village of uniform company houses. In 1868 Harrison Church, a prospector, found a vein of coal about a mile to the north; in the early 1870's a company, organized with Eastern capital, acquired extensive holdings; but the veins were not worked until 1894. They lasted nearly 40 years; and then, when the miners moved to other camps, Diamondville almost became a ghost town. Low rents, however, kept it alive as a suburb of Kemmerer.

KEMMERER, 43.8 *m.* (6,927 alt., 1,884 pop.), seat of Lincoln County, has attractive houses, with large shade trees and lawns; its business section faces a triangular, landscaped park. Railroaders, ranchers, truckers, and tourists give Kemmerer a large transient population, but the town is essentially a polyglot mining community. Residents boast that 'each time the school bell rings, a league of nations convenes.'

When in 1897 P. J. Quealy, coal inspector for Wyoming, recognized the value of coal veins being opened near Diamondville, he got the backing of Mahlon S. Kemmerer of Mauch Chunk, Pennsylvania, and organized a mining company. During the boom that followed, he laid out a town here. An outstanding institution of early Kemmerer was the saloon of 'Preaching Lime' Huggins, who claimed that he never served a drink to a man already 'under the influence.' Over the mirror behind the bar hung mottoes: 'Don't buy a drink before seeing that your baby has shoes'; 'Whatever you are, be a good one'; 'Fill the mouths of the children first.' One patron remarked that he liked Preaching Lime's place because he could repent while sinning and 'get the whole thing over at once.'

J. C. Penney, founder of one of the largest chain-store systems in the United States, was once a clerk in Kemmerer and opened his first store there.

In Kemmerer is the western junction with US 189 (*see Tour 9*).

Several old stone houses, 47.3 *m.*, mark the SITE OF ADERVILLE (L), an early mining camp.

FOSSIL, 54.4 *m.* (7,400 alt., 151 pop.), named for the Fossil Cliffs near by (*see below*), stands in a desolate setting. A museum (R) displays remains of early sea and jungle life.

Anna Richey, only woman ever convicted of cattle rustling in Wyoming, had a ranch near Fossil. The divorced wife of a Kemmerer teacher and the daughter of a wealthy rancher and railroad contractor, she was regarded by her neighbors as a woman of culture—until she donned overalls and boots and did the work of a range hand. Some described her as 'thirty, purty, and full of life.' In July 1919, she drove 32 head of cattle to Fossil, loaded them alone, and shipped them to Omaha. She was accused of rustling and, on the way to her trial, was shot by a masked rider. She survived, however, and was convicted of altering eight brands. Sentenced to six years in the penitentiary, she was freed on bond to wind up her ranch business. While thus occupied, she died, supposedly poisoned; ranchers along Ham's Fork describe a tall stranger who talked with her on the day of her death.

At 54.8 *m.* is a junction with a dirt road.

Right on this rough, rutted road to FOSSIL FISH BEDS, 1.8 *m.* In low cliffs, about a mile long, are preserved creatures that lived in or about a great inland lake 50,000,000 years ago. The fossils lie buried under 35 feet of slate and calcite, but fossil hunters since 1890 have blasted away the protecting layer over parts of the hill. Specimens found include a 13-foot alligator; garfishes 4 to 6 feet long; a bird resembling a chicken; and small fishes and plants.

US 30N crosses shaly hills and goes through canyons to SAGE, 67.1 *m*. (6,332 alt., 40 pop.), a sheepmen's shipping point.

At 68.5 *m*. is the junction with State 89 (*see Tour 2C*).

In Bear River Valley, a sheep and cattle ranching area, meadows and fields alternate with sage-covered hills and flats. Ranches seem prosperous but old, with spacious weather-beaten buildings. Great brown haystacks dot the meadows. Much hay is baled and trucked to winter sheep stations on the Red Desert.

COKEVILLE, 88.4 *m*. (6,191 alt., 431 pop.), a ranching center by the Oregon Trail, was once a multimillion-dollar sheep-shipping point. All its business places are on one street, facing a small landscaped park, and its dwellings are set among gardens, lawns, and large shade trees.

Tilford Kutz, a squaw man, built a one-room cabin on Smith's Fork of Bear River in 1873 and operated a ferry and trading post that served the diminishing numbers of emigrants. His best customers, however, were the Bannock and Shoshone; several hundred lodges often stood around the tiny store. Then, when the Oregon Short Line laid its tracks through the valley, Coe and Carter, who supplied most of the ties, set up an office here. The settlement grew gradually, as huge cattle ranches sprawled across the valley; later, sheep occupied the desert to the east, which was useless to cattlemen. During the First World War, boom residents of Cokeville boasted that their town was the richest per capita in Wyoming.

North of Smith's Fork, 89.9 *m*., the valley is hemmed in by barren, humped mountains. Log houses and barns alternate with modern brick and concrete structures on the ranches. Open-front, straw-roofed, slab shelters stand in extensive pole corrals. The highway swings (L) toward the mountains.

At BORDER JUNCTION, 98.8 *m*. (6,100 alt., 80 pop.), a filling station and inn on the Idaho Line, is the junction with State 89 (*see Tour 2C*). During the Volstead era, Border was a rumrunning station, whose potent and relatively safe whisky was known from Cheyenne to Los Angeles. One dispenser operated a fleet of sleek yellow Packard coupés, with cargoes stowed in special compartments; one of these, with compartment securely locked, would be parked in a convenient spot at Kemmerer or Border Junction, a driver would be told to take it to some assigned point on the road, where he would deliver it to another driver, who in turn surrendered the wheel farther on. No driver saw what the special compartment contained. On rare occasions, a Federal raid would upset the routine, but usually 'protection' was available.

At 98.9 *m*. US 30N crosses the IDAHO LINE, 23 miles southeast of Montpelier, Idaho.

In the Cities and Towns

BUFFALO BILL STATUE, CODY

STATE CAPITOL, CHEYENNE

UNIVERSITY OF WYOMING, LARAMIE

STATE SUPREME COURT AND LIBRARY, CHEYENNE

Photograph by courtesy of Federal Works Agency

LIBERAL ARTS BUILDING, STATE UNIVERSITY, LARAMIE

MAIN STREET, LANDER

CAPITOL AVENUE, CHEYENNE

IN THE MORMON TOWN OF AFTON

Photograph by courtesy of Casper Herald-Tribune

CENTER STREET, CASPER

Photograph by courtesy of Wyoming Historical Society

THE MARKET, CHEYENNE (1874)

CHEYENNE (c. 1870)

EARLY-DAY RAILROAD TOWN

SIGN AT SWEETWATER

FALSE FRONTS, HARTVILLE

Tour 2A

Cheyenne—Pole Mountain Game Refuge—Junction with US 30; 40.6 *m.*, Happy Jack Road.

Dirt road, partly graveled.
No accommodations.

The Happy Jack Road is an alternate route between Cheyenne and Laramie, with side roads to the Fort Warren Military Reservation and to picnic areas. It was named for 'Happy Jack' Hollingsworth, who took up a ranch near the foothills of the Laramie Range in 1884. Hollingsworth built a small adobe house and, for many years, hauled wood from the mountains to sell in Cheyenne. He always sang at his work. Later, he left Cheyenne for the San Juan country, where he was killed by Mexicans during a brawl. This route through Cheyenne Pass was much used in the early days.

The Happy Jack Road goes north from US 30 (*see Tour 2a*) in CHEYENNE, 0 *m.*, then swings L. on 19th Street. It crosses Crow Creek, 0.9 *m.*, and underpasses the Chicago, Burlington & Quincy Railroad, 1.2 *m.*

The Happy Jack Road curves westward over grassy hills. The webbed steel radio towers of Fort Warren are outlined (R) against the sky. Small, not too prosperous, farm tracts are scattered along the road.

The Cox RANCH (R), 5 *m.*, with large barns and neat sheds and dwelling, is one of the largest race-horse breeding ranches west of the Mississippi Valley. The horses are especially well known in racing circles on the Pacific Coast. Meadows of native hay are carpets of color in spring, when shooting stars, lady's-slippers, yellow sweet peas, bluebells, wild mustard, and other wild flowers bloom.

At 13.1 *m.* is the junction with a dirt road.

Right on this road to the SILVER CROWN HILLS, 1 *m.*, where a gold-mining boom in 1885 set men to digging prospect holes. When Professor Aughey announced that a prospect called Carbonate Belle was possibly the greatest bonanza since the Comstock lode, Cheyenne businessmen agreed to put $500,000 into development work, if the assays were satisfactory. The professor managed to salt the assays, but another professor, Wilbur C. Knight of the University of Wyoming, exposed the fraud.

On October 7, 1935, a major air disaster occurred here, when 12 persons were killed in the crash of a transport plane. The cause of the accident was never determined.

At 15.9 *m.* is the junction with a graveled road.

Straight ahead on this road to HECLA, 4.8 *m.*, a mining district on Middle Crow Creek, which has been worked at intervals since the late 1880's. Men still prospect here for copper, silver, and gold. Ruins of a brickkiln, a copper smelter, log cabins, and adobe houses are scattered near ranch buildings and corrals, surrounded by gnarled, nearly dead apple trees.

The highway veers sharply R., passes a large stone ranch house (L), 16.3 *m.*, and at 16.6 *m.* turns L. across a tableland. Far to the south, puffs of smoke rise from trains laboring up Sherman Hill, the highest point on the Union Pacific system. The road winds upward into hills, with sandstone outcrops R. and L. At 23.2 *m.* it gains a broad view of the rock-tipped Laramie Mountains. A strong wind usually blows here; parts of the road are whipped and worn into small bumpy ridges or washboard formations.

At 24.6 *m.* CRYSTAL LAKE (*excellent trout fishing*) is visible far to the L. in a small valley, an important reservoir in the Cheyenne water system. Rocks, pines, peaks, and open spaces alternate in the view along this stretch. Deep purple larkspur and yellow rabbit brush border the highway. Many pines and aspens, in the grove at 27.7 *m.*, are dwarfed by winds and heavy snows. Tall grass covers the spaces between them.

The road crosses the boundary of FORT WARREN MANEUVER RESERVATION, 28.5 *m.* From mid-July to mid-August, this is the scene of field-artillery and small-arms target practice (*guards keep visitors out of danger areas*). The Army chose this site for maneuvers because of the varied terrain.

Kaibab deer, imported in 1927, range in the POLE MOUNTAIN GAME REFUGE, a division of the MEDICINE BOW NATIONAL FOREST, 28.6 *m.* In early days, much timber was cut here; most of it was marketed in the form of railroad ties and fuel.

At the refuge boundary is the junction with a dirt road.

Left on this rough, narrow road, which winds between pine-studded hills to a small valley of shrubs and aspens and then climbs to primitive, hilltop picnic grounds. At 3.7 *m.* it crosses a boundary of the Medicine Bow National Forest. From the crest of a hill, 5.4 *m.*, the snow-capped Colorado mountains are visible 60 miles to the south.

At 6.6 *m.* is another dirt road; R. here 0.8 *m.* to VEDAUWOO GLEN (*shelters, fireplaces, other facilities*), a natural amphitheater and picnic spot. Sheltered by masses of eroded rock, the glen is cool in summer. Excellent drinking water is piped from a spring in a grove of aspens and pines. Sudden brief showers that turn to hail are frequent here in summer and early fall.

The main side road joins US 30 at 8 *m.* (*see Tour 2a*).

At 33.6 *m.* on the Happy Jack Road is the junction with a graveled road.

Left on this road to the MILITARY CAMP, 1.9 *m.*, a cluster of frame buildings used as summer headquarters for troops engaged in maneuvers. Pine-covered hills, seamed with aspen-filled draws, shield the camp from severe northwesterly winds. BLAIR'S MEADOWS, 3.5 *m.*, primitive picnic grounds used by organizations in Cheyenne and Laramie, were named for Dave Blair, pioneer ranchman who formerly owned the land.

The Happy Jack Road winds westward through aspen groves called the JUNGLES. After early autumn frosts, they are a mass of gold splashed with red.

The HAPPY JACK WINTER SPORTS AREA (8,500 alt.) offers a ski run (L), 38.5 m., and a shelter cabin, 39.3 m., equipped with a large stone fireplace. A Forest Service caretaker regulates the use of slides and runs. There is a 1,400-foot, iced-trough toboggan run; a 1,500-foot slalom run, with 15 to 30 per cent slopes; and a practice ski area, with slopes of 10 to 20 per cent. Ascending through Cheyenne Pass to the head of Telephone Canyon, the road joins US 30 (*see Tour 2a*) at 40.6 m., at a point 9.4 miles east of Laramie. Many emigrants used the road through Cheyenne Pass in the 1860's, as a cutoff from Fort Laramie to the Laramie Plains by the way of Camp Walbach on Lodgepole Creek.

Tour 2B

Laramie—Saratoga—Junction with US 30; 99.5 m., State 130.

Route paralleled by Laramie, North Park & Western R.R. between Laramie and Centennial; Saratoga and Encampment R.R., north of Saratoga.
Oil-surfaced and graveled roadbed; closed by deep snow between Brooklyn Lake and Saratoga in winter; always open between Centennial and Snowy Range Sports Area.
Resorts and lodges.

State 130, the Snowy Range Road, is an alternate route over the Medicine Bow Mountains between Laramie and Walcott (Rawlins). It winds through timbered canyons to altitudes of 10,000 feet, skirts timber-line lakes at the base of perpetual snowbanks, then descends the west slope of the range to the Saratoga-Encampment Valley, one of Wyoming's oldest cattle-ranching areas. Here it veers north over salt sage wastes to the Lincoln Highway.

Branching west from US 30-287 (*see Tours 2 and 5*) in LARAMIE, 0 m., State 130 overpasses the Union Pacific and crosses the Laramie River, 0.8 m., which at high water carries railroad ties from Medicine Bow National Forest to the creosote-treating plant at Laramie (*see Tour 5c*).

UNIVERSITY OF WYOMING EXPERIMENT STATION (R), 1.1 *m.*, specializes in livestock and highland grains. The formidable stone dairy barn, with gabled roof and heavily barred windows, was Wyoming's first penitentiary. Completed in 1876 as a Federal prison, it accepted territorial prisoners at one dollar a day. Later the territory found cheaper quarters for its criminals, first in Detroit, Michigan, and then at Joliet, Illinois. But as it approached statehood, Wyoming became self-conscious; 'Wyoming prisons for Wyoming prisoners,' the legislators said. In 1888 they appropriated funds for the State prison at Rawlins (*see Tour 2b*), and until 1900, when the Government closed the Laramie prison, the two institutions competed for prisoners. The Federal prison became too expensive to maintain for the number of prisoners it received.

At 1.8 *m.* is the junction with State 230.

Left on this oil-surfaced and graveled road up the Laramie River toward Jelm Mountain (9,665 alt.), dominant peak on the east slope of the Medicine Bow Mountains. South of Jelm is Red Mountain, part of a horizontal outcrop of the strata known as the Rocky Mountain Red Beds. The ranching district along the Laramie River is old country, by Wyoming criteria. Log and frame buildings, surrounded by alfalfa fields and meadows laced with willow-fringed ditches, are weather-beaten and gray. Around them lie bits of harness, worn tools and utensils, broken machinery. White-faced cattle and a few sheep graze on the higher lands.

At 6.1 *m.* is the junction with a dirt road; R. here 15 *m.* through Pahloe Lane to LAKE HATTIE (*excellent fishing*).

WOODS LANDING, 23.8 *m.* (7,462 alt., 10 pop.), ranchers' trade center, was named for Sam S. Woods, a pioneer who operated a sawmill near by. Saturday night dances at the community hall attract cowhands, lumberjacks, and Laramie college students.

State 230 winds upward along a canyon shelf above Woods Creek. Hills on both sides are rock-strewn and covered with gray and purple sage. At the boundary of the MEDICINE BOW NATIONAL FOREST, 24 *m.*, glades among the thick stands of jackpine, aspen, and ponderosa pine provide good camping and picnic grounds. Timbers for ties or mine props are trimmed here in winter and stacked near the highway for transportation in spring.

At 31.1 *m.* is a graded dirt road; L. here 7 *m.* to JELM (7,550 alt., 9 pop.), post office on the SITE OF CUMMINS CITY. On the grassy bottoms here, a city of 170 blocks was laid out in the 1870's, when John Cummins displayed ore samples, which he asserted he had found near by. A Denver company paid $10,000 for rights in the vicinity, only to find that Cummins had salted the area.

Climbing along Woods Creek, State 230 traverses the Chimney Park forest area, named for its jutting rock formations.

At 33 *m.* is the Foxpark Road; R. here 0.8 *m.* to EVANS PICNIC GROUND. At 1.2 *m.* on the Foxpark Road is a dirt road; L. here 3.4 *m.* up wooded slopes to SOMBER HILL LOOKOUT (9,430 alt.). From the crow's-nest atop the tower (*open to the public*), reached by a perpendicular ladder, the timbered slopes and ridges of the southern Medicine Bow National Forest resemble a gigantic green relief map. Snowy Colorado peaks are blue and white to the south. At 1.4 *m.* on the Foxpark Road is FOXPARK (9,100 alt., 101 pop.), a supply point for woodsmen. Several hundred 'tie hacks,' mostly of Swedish descent, live in timber camps near here. Off duty, the lumbermen swap yarns over coffee or sing Swedish folk songs to an accordion accompaniment.

Left from Foxpark on a gravel-surfaced road through dense timber and occasional glades to an abandoned mining area. Rusting dredges, cabins flattened by heavy snows, and great holes gouged in streambeds are all that remain. The road winds through thinned lodgepole pine to KEYSTONE, 13 *m.*, a mining and timber-cutting region, with sawmill, lumbersheds, log houses, and stamp mill; then, west of this point, it plunges down long avenues of silver spruce and dark pine (*campgrounds*), where tracks of deer are fresh in the soft earth beside streams. In clearings and on hillsides are old mine dumps, ruined shaft houses, windlasses, and cabins. Where the forest thins, sage and lupine grow tall. The road joins State 230, 50.4 *m.*, 4 miles south of Riverside (*see below*).

North of Foxpark, the Foxpark Road crosses wooded hills and ridges. At 14.1 *m.* is the junction with a dirt road; L. here 3 *m.* to ALBANY (8,391 alt., 101 pop.), a summer-home community. Lodgepole pine grows tall and straight around the village; wild flowers bloom during the short growing season. At RICHARDS' GARDEN (*open in August*) are rare varieties of tulips, gladioli, peonies, and pansies. Skirting the base of Sheep Mountain, the Foxpark Road joins State 130, 23.7 *m.*, about one-quarter mile east of Centennial (*see below*).

State 230 runs southwest toward the white peaks of the Medicine Bow Range, topped with waves of blue-black pine and spruce. It passes through MOUNTAIN HOME, 37.4 *m.* (6,815 alt., 70 pop.), and crosses the Colorado Line at 39.2 *m.* There it joins Colo. 127, curves southward to the junction with Colo. 125, and then swings back across the State Line to a junction with State 130 at Saratoga (*see below*).

LARAMIE AIRPORT (L), 4.6 *m.*, with four steel radio towers and beacons, is on the transcontinental route of United Air Lines. When dense fog hampers vision over the Laramie Mountains, transport planes land here rather than at Cheyenne, the regular stop.

Heading westward toward the Medicine Bow Mountains, State 130 rises and falls with the undulating plain, where tough native grasses provide winter and summer feed for large cattle herds. In the rare air, the snow-backed mountains, 20 miles away, seem within easy walking distance. When afternoon shadows slide down the eastern slopes, the blue-green pines high up become purple and black. In summer the vast, treeless Laramie Plains are carpeted with bluebell, primrose, prickly pear, and wild verbena. Cattle, horses, prairie dogs, coyotes, and jack rabbits are the only inhabitants. Paralleling the route of the Laramie-Centennial-Rambler Mine Stage, which operated in the early 1900's, the highway rims a basin (L) known as BIG HOLLOW, where oil wells are drilled. Cattle trails pattern the basin floor with swirling lines like those of a horoscope.

At 6.8 *m.* is the junction with a graveled road.

Right on this road to the Little Laramie ranching area and to BAMFORTH LAKE, 3 *m.*, a 1,166-acre Federal migratory bird refuge, administered by the United States Bureau of Biological Survey. Here, at various seasons, are found ducks, geese, curlew, brant, and sandpiper.

Small markers at 11.8 *m.* indicate the Overland Trail. In spring and early summer, the old wagon tracks are plainly outlined by grass along the ruts.

Pinched between SHEEP MOUNTAIN (9,583 alt.), on whose dark, timbered slopes elk, deer, and bighorn sheep are protected, and CORNER MOUNTAIN (9,582 alt.), is Centennial Valley. Here in the meadows in summer, men mow, rake, sweep, haul, and stack wild hay. High slab fences protect the finished stacks from elk that come down from the mountains after heavy snows. CENTENNIAL MOUNTAIN

(9,600 alt.) is dotted with aspen groves, silver in summer and bright yellow and orange in autumn; heavy timber tips the crest.

Despite a short growing season, this area produces abundant carrots, parsnips, turnips, rutabagas, and potatoes. Stout log houses, built by early cattlemen, are partly concealed by trees along the Little Laramie. On the rocky slopes above the river (R) are tepee rings—circles of bleached stones used by Indians to hold down the edges of their skin lodges.

At 29.9 m. is the junction with the Foxpark Road (see above).

CENTENNIAL, 30.1 m. (8,076 alt., 30 pop.), a trading point for ranches and mines in the Centennial Valley, is on a rocky wind-swept hillside. In the 1870's, Colonel Stephen W. Downey refused $100,000 for a rich gold lode, uncovered along the North Fork, and opened a mine here; but the vein pinched out. The adjacent ledges and slopes are scarred with the gopherings of prospectors, who refused to believe that it was exhausted.

Left from Centennial on a dirt road to the SITE OF PLATINUM CITY, 2 m., where only a brick powerhouse and one or two small buildings in a hay meadow remain. In the late 1920's prospectors, searching the Centennial Mountain district for the lost Downey Lode, found traces of platinum among the fine grains of gold, copper, and silver. Promoters imported mining machinery and bought the meadows at the foot of Centennial Ridge, as the site for a city. The site was platted, and the building lots were offered for sale, but the mine did not meet operating expenses. In 1938, the Government confiscated the property for taxes. Meadowland, machinery, camp equipment, and household articles, once valued at more than $100,000, were sold at public auction for $7,000.

The highway parallels the North Fork (L) toward bald, snow-mantled peaks. At 32.2 m. it crosses the eastern boundary of MEDICINE BOW NATIONAL FOREST (camps and summer lodges), created in 1902, which contains an estimated 4,852,000,000 board feet in trees ten inches or more in diameter. Eighty per cent is lodgepole pine. On distant slopes the dense timber resembles heavy bluegrass lawns. Milky glacial streams feed more than 100 forest lakes, within a radius of 50 miles; larger streams cascade to the valley. Circling BARBER LAKE (R), 34 m., the highway curves up a mountain side.

The SNOWY RANGE WINTER SPORTS AREA (8,500 to 11,500 alt.) is sheltered by sharp timbered ridges. (Powder snow Dec.-June; ski and toboggan runs; slalom courses 0.3 mile long, gradients 20–40 per cent; ski-tow; 20-by-24-foot rustic log shelters.)

The UNIVERSITY SCIENCE SUMMER CAMP (co-educational), 38 m., is in a small clearing. Blue-black spruce trees partly conceal the brown varnished-log buildings, which include lecture halls, laboratories, and cabins to accommodate 100 persons. The camp, started in 1922 and administered by the University of Wyoming in collaboration with Columbia University, is self-supporting. It offers field classes in botany, geology, and zoology. The adjoining SNOWY RANGE NATURAL AREA, a 771-acre spruce forest, is preserved in its natural state for research. Gentian, Indian paintbrush, and rare blue and white columbine bloom along the streambanks.

At 38.8 *m.* is the junction with a graded dirt road.

Right on this road to a junction with a side road, 1 *m;* L. here 1.8 *m.* to BROOKLYN LAKE (*good bank fishing*). Summer cabins stand among the pines on the shore.

The highway cuts through ice-crusted snowbanks, near whose edges, in late June and July, tiny orchids, buttercups, and snowdrops push through the soft earth. The summits here rise in grim, bare scarps and rough granite pyramids and pinnacles. Near timber line the pines are 'winged': because of icy winds from the north, limbs grow only on the south side of the trunks. Seen from a distance, the trees resemble Indians in feathered headdress. Dirt-roofed cabins, their untrimmed logs crumbling and brown, mark the claims of early prospectors.

MIRROR LAKE (R), 44.6 *m.*, is light green under sunlight, its glassy surface reflecting the scrub pines and mossy rocks along its shore. The highway skirts LAKE MARIE (R), 44.9 *m.*, in a mountain recess among granite cliffs that rise sheer from the water's edge; then it winds over shoulders of rock beside snow-crested peaks. Woodchucks may be seen, standing erect on protruding ledges or waddling through the sparse brush, as an automobile approaches. Bristling porcupines gnaw at the trees. SILVER LAKE, below (L), 47.8 *m.*, is silver-black, with reflections of the wooded slopes that surround it.

At 49.8 *m.* is the junction with a bridle trail.

Right on this trail to MEDICINE BOW PEAK LOOKOUT TOWER, 5 *m.* (12,005 alt.), which stands at the edge of a sheer quartzite cliff.

State 130 descends rapidly through heavy timber. Unimproved side roads lead to small lumber camps. At 60.3 *m.* the highway crosses the western boundary of the MEDICINE BOW NATIONAL FOREST. Here is the BARRETT RIDGE WINTER SPORTS AREA (*ski and slalom runs; average gradients* 60°; *shelter cabin*).

The highway descends over sagebrush foothills to the long, narrow, Saratoga-Encampment Valley, between the Sierra Madre Mountains (L) and the Medicine Bow Range (R), drained by the North Platte River and its tributaries. Ranches here vary from 6,000 to 10,000 acres; annual hay crops run between 700 to 1,500 tons. The benchlands around the river meadows produce grains, potatoes, and garden vegetables. Ranch buildings are large, with well-kept yards and gardens. Some ranches take paying guests. Near-by mountains provide good hunting and fishing; winter-sports areas are being developed throughout the valley.

The first white men in this region were trappers. After them came restless prospectors, searching for the rich gold veins described in Indian legends. They found ruins of placer shafts and tunnels of unknown age, but little gold. Some, however, found rich deposits of copper and other metals (*see below*). Sometime after the middle 1800's, the region was entered by permanent settlers, chiefly those who turned southward from the Overland Trail and the Union Pacific.

SARATOGA HOT SPRINGS STATE RESERVE (L), 77.2 *m.*, a landscaped area with hot mineral springs, was set aside by the State for treatment of rheumatism and similar ills.

SARATOGA, 77.6 *m.* (6,786 alt., 567 pop.), is a supply point for hunters, fishermen, and ranchers. Its first building (1878) was a trading post. Early settlers called the place the Springs, Warm Springs, or Hot Springs, but it was named later for the big Saratoga Hot Springs, in New York. The building of the railroad and the Sierra Madre mining boom of the 1890's and early 1900's greatly aided its development.

Left from Saratoga on graveled State 230 up the green, narrow valley. Rubber-booted ranchers ride slowly through the meadows in irrigating season, shovels balanced on their shoulders. Fishermen, with colored bandannas under their hats for protection against gnats, appear and disappear along willowed streambanks.

In RIVERSIDE, 18.6 *m.* (7,200 alt., 34 pop.), a wayside supply point, is the junction with the graded Encampment-Baggs Road; R. here 0.9 *m.* is ENCAMPMENT (7,323 alt., 809 pop.), former mining boom town, where the Encampment River issues from the Sierra Madre Mountains. Vacant false-front frame buildings are being replaced with brick business and residential structures; abandoned log cabins and shanties, with paneless or boarded-up windows, squat on knolls at the edge of town. The site was originally called Grand Encampment, for a trappers' rendezvous held here in 1851.

In 1896 Ed Haggarty, prospector, found outcrops of copper ore near Bridger Peak. The mine, developed here by Haggarty and the partners who had grubstaked him, was called Rudefeha, a name composed of the first and second letters of the partners' names: Rumsey, Deal, Ferris, and Haggarty. Encampment was founded the next year by Willis George Emerson, novelist, lawyer, politician, and promoter, who formed the North American Copper Company, bought the Rudefeha, and renamed it the Ferris-Haggarty. Emerson built a smelter on the banks of Encampment River, organized a coal company to supply fuel, and erected a 16-mile aerial tramway to bring ore to the smelter from the mine. Another company was organized to build a spur railroad between Encampment and the Union Pacific at Walcott. Soon miners' and prospectors' tent and shack towns—Battle, Copperton, Doane-Rambler, Rudefeha, Dillon—scarred the slopes near timber line.

Newspapers at Encampment, Copperton, and Dillon proclaimed the country's riches; new settlers hurried in to share the wealth. By 1901 more than 260 companies were operating in the valley, and Encampment was a city of 2,000. Literature was invoked to spread the good word; Emerson himself and Charles E. Winter, an attorney, together wrote six novels, using the Encampment locale. The bubble burst in 1908. Despite the $2,000,000 worth of ore taken out after 1900, it became clear that the value of the metal in a falling market was not sufficient to meet costs. Speculators dumped their holdings; within a year the transient population was gone. Encampment survives, but the other towns are trash heaps in mountain parks. The smelter was dismantled and shipped to South America. To retain the transportation service they needed, valley ranchers bought the spur railroad and gave it to the Union Pacific, on the agreement that it would be kept in operation.

The Encampment-Baggs Road, here a graveled highway, climbs the Sierra Madre Mountains along pine-bordered shelves and crosses the range at the BATTLE CAMPGROUND, 14 *m.* (9,916 alt.), near the site of Old Battle. Caved-in shafts, crumbling dugouts, and odd bits of trash mark the place where the town once stood, on the barren, windswept summit of the Continental Divide. Battle Lake, unusually blue in its alpine setting, is visible in a small sheltered valley 1,000 feet below.

The road winds sharply downward over twisting switchbacks.

At 14.5 *m.* is a junction with an unimproved, rock-strewn road; R. here 4 *m.*

to BRIDGER PEAK (11,007 alt.), named for the frontiersman. A foot trail leads to a fire lookout on the summit.

At 15.9 m. is a junction with a dirt road; L. here to RAMBLER (Doane-Rambler), a ghost town on the shore of Battle Lake. A sheep outfit uses some of the old cabins as summer headquarters; the others are deserted and falling down. The old mine tunnel has caved in; but the dump, complete with a 50-yard car track and shelter shed, is still intact.

While a member of the Henry Draper Astronomical Expedition, which came to Rawlins to witness a solar eclipse, Thomas A. Edison made a fishing trip to Battle Lake in 1878. Doubtful tradition holds that Edison as he sat here stripping the tough, pliable strands of bamboo from a fishing rod, conceived the idea of the durable, nonconducting filament that made possible the incandescent electric lamp. Bamboo was used later in his first experimental lamps.

One log building marks the SITE OF COPPERTON (L), 23.5 m., near Haggarty Creek. At Copperton is a junction with an unimproved wagon road; R. here on this old freight road, which becomes a foot trail, up Haggarty Gulch, scene of the biggest mining boom in Wyoming. The road, used now by sheep wagons and forest service pack outfits, follows the tracks worn deep in the mountain soil by long string teams, as they hauled freight between Rudefeha and Encampment during the boom. Timbers, laid close together to form corduroy roadbeds across the swamps, are gray and crumbling.

Old tumbledown log cabins and the weathered debris of a dead mushroom town are all that remain of DILLON, 4 m. Roofless cabins, old iron bedsteads and stoves, cans, innumerable bottles, broken wagon parts, used machinery, part of an old printing press, and innumerable odds and ends, too heavy for the pack rats to salvage, are scattered over 40 acres in a grassy mountain park. An old safe, its thick door sagging, sits alone in the center of the flat.

Snow must have lain deep in Dillon; the houses were built on the ground, but the outside toilets were ingeniously designed to overcome the difficulties presented by deep winter drifts. They were sturdy structures, and many of them still stand; most of them are in better condition than the log houses. Some are frame shacks perched upon cribbed log bases, eight feet high; others are towering silo-like structures, with doors opening halfway up their fronts. Rotting wooden steps lead up ten feet to railed platforms in front of the doors. One, with shingled outside walls, in an excellent state of preservation, is visible at a far greater distance than any other object in Dillon.

Dillon, a miner's town, was founded when the mining company banned saloons in Rudefeha. The saloonkeepers moved down the gulch, and Rudefeha's population followed. The new town was named for Millica Dillon, a former soldier with Major General George Crook, who also was at the Milk River Fight (see Tour 2b). Dillon opened a boarding house and saloon in the new town, and legend has it that he operated his boarding house entirely free of charge the first year, depending on his liquor receipts to run the place. In 1903, Dillon erected a hotel, and levied a charge for his accommodations.

Grant Jones, graduate of Northwestern University and a star reporter on metropolitan newspapers, published the Dillon *Doublejack*. Jones who had lost many jobs because of drinking, spent his last years in this wilderness area, free of the pressure of big-city journalism, did his best writing. His yarns of the Cogly Woo, Backaboar, and One-eyed Screaming Emu, strange fauna that haunted the Sierra Madre Mountains, were reprinted in various parts of the country. Grant died at Dillon in June 1903.

The Cogly Woo was a six-legged creature with a sharp, broad tail; when closely pursued, he stood up on his tail and whirled rapidly around, thereby boring into the ground. Into his hole the Cogly Woo disappeared, and the hole disappeared after him. The deathly Backaboar was a four-legged beast, with short legs on the left side and long ones on the right—admirably adjusted for mountain climbing. It could be captured only by turning it from its course, so that the short legs were on the downhill side; in this case, the Backaboar invariably fell off into space and was lost. The One-eyed Screaming Emu was a terrible bird inhabiting the highest crags. To avoid capture, this bird could swallow itself in one gulp, casting back on his pursuers, as he did so, a look of mingled scorn and derision.

RUDEFEHA was built on the steep side of the gulch above the ore mill, 5 *m.* The old mill still stands on Haggarty Creek, a sprawling mass of huge rough lumber sheds, rusted machinery and boilers, and tailing dumps. When it was closed, the cost of transporting the machinery down from the isolated gulch exceeded its market worth, so it was left to crumble eventually under the heavy winter snows. Shacks and the ruins of cabins scar the hills for half a mile in every direction, and the old wooden towers, once a part of the 16-mile tramway, still stand, with rusted cables sagging from their cross-arms. Dead timber, cut and left to rot, litters the steep north slope of the gulch; and high on this slope are sturdy rough-board houses, still propped by heavy timbers on the downhill side. Around these houses are ruins of extensive log stables and old hay piles that have settled and decayed. Sheep rest in the shade of the ruins at midday, and timid deer start from the tangled thickets that have grown up inside the roofless cabins.

Old-time residents of the Saratoga and Encampment Valley bite on their pipes and look away when the Rudefeha is mentioned. They say they were betrayed by the promoters and that mining in the area will 'come back.' In summer, the mountains echo again with the ring of picks on rock, and the hills, within a 50-mile radius of Rudefeha, are scarred with prospect diggings.

The road crosses a boundary of the BATTLE MOUNTAIN STATE GAME PRESERVE, 32.2 *m.* Near the confluence of Battle Creek and Little Snake River, south of Battle Mountain, a party of American Fur Company trappers, including Henry Fraeb (Frapp) and Jim Baker, was attacked by Cheyenne and Sioux in 1841. Several trappers were killed.

Crossing the western boundary of the MEDICINE BOW NATIONAL FOREST, 36.9 *m.,* the road drops into upper Little Snake Valley, a sheltered farming and ranching area on the west face of the Sierra Madres. It follows the stream across the Colorado Line to Slater, Colorado, 44.8 *m.,* and swings back to SAVERY, 49 *m.* (6,500 alt., 50 pop.), a ranching settlement that was for many years the headquarters of Jim Baker. In a field (L), 50.2 *m.,* is the SITE OF BAKER'S CABIN (1873), which was moved to Frontier Park in Cheyenne in 1917; R. from the field on a foot trail 300 *yds.* to BAKER'S GRAVE. Baker was born in Belleville, Illinois, on December 18, 1818, and came West at the age of 13. He freighted, trapped with Jim Bridger, operated a ferry over Green River on the Oregon Trail, traded and prospected in the Sierra Madre region, and acted as guide and scout. In 1873 he settled down with his two Indian wives in the Little Snake country, where he built a three-story blockhouse for a dwelling. Baker adopted certain Indian tribal customs: in particular, that of having his womenfolk tend his trap line on the Little Snake River. He liked to sit and smoke in the clearing before his blockhouse, while his wives combed and curled his flowing light hair and beard. He died in 1898.

DIXON, 54.7 *m.* (6,324 alt., 100 pop.), grew around a trading post for Indians and settlers. The Encampment-Baggs Road crosses the LITTLE SNAKE, 55.7 *m.,* and skirts hayfields and potato patches to the junction with US 187 at BAGGS, 62.5 *m.* (6,245 alt., 192 pop.) (*see Tour 2b*).

South of Riverside, State 230 swings southeastward up the North Platte Valley, with the Sierra Madre and Medicine Bow Mountains converging ahead. At 46.3 *m.* it crosses the Colorado Line, 24 miles northwest of Walden, Colorado, and then loops back into Wyoming (*see above*).

North of Saratoga, State 130 runs along a sheltered valley floor, which gives way to bleak sage wastes. Huge bands of sheep graze here in summer, tended by Mexican herders and their dogs. Vegetation becomes scant; drifting sand dunes appear. On both sides, the plain rises in wide, slow swells to distant conical peaks, northern termini of the Medicine Bow and Sierra Madre ranges.

At 89.7 *m.* is the junction with a dirt road.

Left on this road, paralleling the Overland Trail, to the SITE OF THE OLD PLATTE RIVER CROSSING, 5 *m.* Twisted buffalo hides were used as cables to tow the first ferry over the Platte at this point.

At 99.5 *m.* is the western junction with US 30-287 (*see Tours 2b and 5*), at a point 17.3 miles west of Hanna.

Tour 2C

Junction with US 30N—Evanston—(Ogden, Utah); US 30S.
Junction with US 30N to Utah Line, 75.6 *m.*

Route paralleled by Union Pacific R.R.
Asphalt-paved roadbed.
Accommodations adequate.

US 30S, the branch of the Lincoln Highway which swings down through northeastern Utah, crosses a corner of Wyoming. As in most of the southwestern part of the State, the route follows a succession of dry hills and equally dry flats, where the population, as well as the vegetation, is gathered into limited valley areas beside flowing water. The region is known historically as the locale of Jim Bridger's trading activities (1842–55).

Branching south from the junction with US 30N, 0 *m.* (*See Tour 2d*) at a point 28 miles west of Green River, the highway crosses a barren flat. In LITTLE AMERICA, 1.3 *m.*, a hotel of modern design, with straight lines, rounded corners, and large windows, appears unexpectedly in a vast waste. Between Little America and Fort Bridger, the road parallels the Oregon, Mormon, California, and Overland trails. The Pony Express also followed this route.

CHURCH BUTTES (L), 12.5 *m.*, eroded blue and black sandstone cliffs, in a mass resembling a cathedral, rise 75 feet above the surrounding hills. Similar buttes thrust up near by. The flats west of Church Buttes are marked with patches of greenish shale and clumps of greasewood.

US 30S twice crosses Black's Fork of Green River, winding between deep-cut banks.

The MORMON CAMP SITE, 21.6 *m.*, used by Brigham Young's first party, July 7, 1847, is marked with a ten-foot concrete shaft (L), topped with the beehive symbol of the Latter-day Saint church.

At 22.7 *m.*, extending southward to the tops of high stony bluffs is a PREHISTORIC CAMP SITE, explored in 1935 under the leadership of Dr. E. B. Renaud, anthropologist of the University of Denver. Many artifacts from the site, including *coups de poing* or handstones, choppers, scrapers, points, and blades of chert, quartzite, and moss agate, were pronounced identical with paleoliths from Europe and Africa. Dr. Renaud described the site as 'extensive and very rich . . . entirely treeless, and the ground barren, except for a short, dry grass in places, and bushes here and there holding the sandy surface from water and wind erosion . . . On the top of the bluffs, on their slopes when they are not too abrupt or too deeply cut by erosion, and especially over the undulating floor . . . the ground is littered with stones and pebbles . . . rounded by the ancient rolling action of water, patinated to . . . buff or yellow, light to dark brown, sometimes orange red, often blackish, by very long exposure to hot sun and the elements . . . Implements of chert [were] so much like the unworked stones . . . that [they were] hard to distinguish . . . for collection purposes.'

Across the road is another site, equally rich. Dr. Renaud reported 69 such areas in southwestern Wyoming. 'The weird landscape,' he wrote, 'seems to be made of gray or yellowish dried-up mud and gravel, strangely eroded by water and wind . . . Poplars grow along the streams, spruce on the highlands; elsewhere only short grass, bushes and scrub vegetation . . . Trails [are] sometimes cut by dry washes and gulches, broken by rains and erosion . . . Maps are . . . uncertain . . . bench marks are difficult to find.'

The road continues over bare hills and greasewood flats. Snow fences slant beside it.

The UNIVERSITY OF WYOMING EXPERIMENTAL FARM, 27.3 *m.*, develops dairy cattle, grains, hays, garden truck, and trees adapted to western Wyoming.

The highway runs between well-kept farms and groves of poplar, cottonwood, and willow, into thickly settled territory.

LYMAN, 28.9 *m.* (6,695 alt., 869 pop.), a poultry center in a good fishing and hunting area, has a successful co-operative marketing association. The residents are mostly Mormons. A small MUSEUM (*open by arrangement*), in the high school building, contains fossil fish, shells, wood, and bones, mounted animal heads, samples of ore, and Indian artifacts.

Left from Lyman on a dirt road to BURNTFORK, 30.9 *m.* Here, in 1825, General William H. Ashley held his first rendezvous with trappers, free traders, and Indians (*see Tour 9*).

West of Lyman, US 30S curves across flat ranching country. Many of the ranch buildings are of logs. The road descends into a broad, level valley, where shady groves and meadows lie between barren sweeps of hill and flat. Thousands of emigrants stopped to rest in this pleasant valley.

The village of FORT BRIDGER, 34.8 *m.* (6,657 alt., 381 pop.), consists of a few dwellings and small business houses. The SITE OF FORT BRIDGER, 34.9 *m.*, which was established in 1842 by Jim Bridger, guide, mountain man, and trader, is now a State park, administered by the Wyoming Historical Landmarks Commission. Sheltered under tall cottonwoods, poplars, and willows, along Black's Fork of Green River, are the simple, slant-roofed buildings, mostly one-story, of rough lumber, logs, or stone. In 1937, canopies were erected over several of them, and some were reroofed. Primitive paths, bordered by knee-deep grass and wild flowers, meander through the grounds. A large stone gate flanks the entrance, with commemorative markers L. and R. At the picket gate near the museum is a directory of points of interest; numbered signs identify buildings and sites.

The museum now occupies the POST TRADER'S STORE (*open* 8–6 *daily*) on the east side of Black's Fork. The collection includes pioneer relics, such as gold scales, a bear trap, ox yokes, parts of wagons, guns, saddles, trunks, maps, manuscripts, a sand blotter, extract of logwood (used for ink), a gold pan, a butter worker, a letter press, and numerous Indian trophies.

Part of the MORMON WALL, built of cobblestones in 1855 to replace Bridger's stockade, still stands west of the museum. In the CEMETERY, south side of the reservation, are the graves of Judge W. A. Carter, long-time post sutler, and of Mary Bridger Hahn, daughter of Jim Bridger.

The vicinity was a rendezvous as early as 1834, when John Robertson ('Uncle Jack Robinson'), trapper, trader, and friend of Bridger, built a dwelling here. Robertson encouraged Bridger to start a trading post on Black's Fork; and Bridger, knowing the changing conditions, concluded that this rich valley was indeed the place to establish a way station for westbound travelers. He began the erection of a post in 1842 and, after a trip to St. Louis for equipment, opened the fort to trade in 1843. It consisted of two houses joined together, surrounded by a fence eight feet high. Louis Vasquez, Bridger's partner, attended, somewhat irregularly, to trade, which was good at first and boomed when heavy migration began. Trails forked here; the north fork led to Fort Hall, Idaho, and the south to Salt Lake Valley.

In his Oregon Trail journal, Joel Palmer wrote on July 25, 1845: 'Traveled about 16 miles, crossed the creek several times, and encamped near Fort Bridger . . . It is built of poles and daubed with mud . . . a shabby concern. Here are about 25 lodges of Indians, or rather white trappers' lodges occupied by their Indian wives. They have a good supply of robes, dressed deer, elk and antelope skins, coats, pants, moccasins, and other Indian fixens, which they trade low for flour, pork, powder, lead, blankets, butcher-knives, spirits, hats, ready-made clothes, coffee, sugar, etc. They ask for a horse from twenty-five to fifty dollars in trade . . . At this place the bottoms are wide, and covered with good grass. Cotton-wood timber in plenty. The stream abounds with trout.'

Brigham Young, in 1847, stopped at the fort on his way to Salt Lake

Valley. In 1853 a few Mormons were sent up to Willow Creek, 12 miles south of Fort Bridger, to farm in the region and to establish a rival trading post. This first agricultural settlement in Wyoming was called Fort Supply. Shortly after its establishment, Bridger and Vasquez left Fort Bridger, and Lewis Robinson, quartermaster of the Utah Militia, took it over. Bridger said the Mormons drove him out; the Mormons insisted they had bought the fort. Robinson built several stone houses at the site and enclosed them with a stone wall 400 feet long and 14 feet high, with a corral 82 feet wide.

The Mormons burned Forts Bridger and Supply and fled in 1857, when Colonel Albert S. Johnston advanced westward with a military force (*see History*). While his men rebuilt the post, Colonel Johnston established temporary Camp Scott, about two miles south of Fort Bridger. Troops subsequently stationed at Fort Bridger guarded the Overland stage route and the engineers who built the Union Pacific, and in the late 1860's the fort was a base for troops at the Wind River agency and in the Sweetwater mining district. From May 23, 1878, to June 1880, it had no garrison; then it was reoccupied because of the uprising on the Uinta Reservation and the Meeker massacre in Colorado (*see Tour 2b*). It was abandoned as a military post November 6, 1890.

Jim Bridger (1804–81), who came West with General William H. Ashley's men in 1822, followed the trails for about 50 years; the whole central and northern Rocky Mountain area was his range. Men who came to the frontier convinced of their own superiority often had to be led through the wilderness like children by Bridger. To compensate himself for any annoyance, Jim poked elaborate fun at their ignorance and credulity. The 'flora and fauna of Jim Bridger's country' became legendary lore. One of his favorite yarns involved a petrified forest, in which he tried to jump across a gorge and found it too wide; had not his weight been supported by petrified air, he would have been killed.

During military operations against the Indians, Bridger was indispensable. Frances C. Carrington, wife of Colonel H. B. Carrington, in *My Army Life and the Fort Phil Kearney Massacre*, wrote of him: 'There was one faithful and simple-minded man at the post, the colonel's confidential guide at all times, who seemed instinctively to know the visible as well as the invisible operations of the Indians, good Jim Bridger.' When Carrington was ordered to dismiss Bridger, in order to save the cost of a scout, he returned the order to headquarters with the notation: 'Impossible of execution.'

Bridger married three times. His first wife, the daughter of a Flathead chief (d. 1846) and the second, a Ute woman (d. 1849), are said to be buried on a hill north of the fort. His third wife was a Shoshone.

US 30S crosses two small bridges over Black's Fork, then climbs to a plateau. The LEROY EMERGENCY LANDING FIELD, 42.8 *m.*, is a splash of orange and white on the dun plain (R). The road winds down from the highland, and pine-tipped hills close in. To the east, at 53.3 *m.*, the pavement traces a gigantic S among the hills.

At 57 *m.* is the junction with US 189 (*see Tour 9*).

US 30S curves through breaks, runs by a rock ledge, and winds between grassy slopes. At 60.9 *m.* is a spring of drinking water (L). At 65.7 *m.* the Bear River Valley and Evanston are glimpsed through a gap ahead. Flocks of migrant Canadian geese and ducks float on valley ponds and streams in spring and autumn.

At 70.2 *m.* is the junction with State 89.

Right on this oil-surfaced highway down the wide Bear River Valley. Ranches here are prosperous and neat, with luxuriant gardens and typical Mormon box houses. Where the hills meet the irrigated valley, sage often grows three or four feet tall.

The SITE OF ALMY (R), 5.5 *m.*, is indicated by the gray-black coal dumps of abandoned mines. The Uinta County deposits were shown on Captain Howard Stansbury's Great Coal Basin map in 1852. In 1868, the Union Pacific prospected the Almy district for coal; completion of the railroad in 1869 sent prices soaring, and Almy prospered. Water, explosive dust, and firedamp were present in the mines here, however, and in 1895 in one blast 67 miners were killed. Workers became reluctant to enter the mines; costs rose; and, little by little, activity ceased; mine buildings were destroyed or moved to other camps. One mine still supplies coal to a local market.

The road crosses BEAR RIVER, 7.9 *m.*, then skirts a rim of red hills along the edge of the valley, a continuous meadow bordered by fields of alfalfa and grain. State 89 crosses the Utah Line, 11.6 *m.*, and becomes Utah 3, which joins Utah 51 at 38.6 *m.* This section of the highway is known as the Randolph Road, because it passes through Randolph, Utah, where eager Wyoming couples take advantage of Utah's no-wait marriage laws. Utah 51 crosses the Wyoming Line, 43.6 *m.*, and becomes the central link of State 89. Ahead is the drab wasteland that borders Bear River Valley.

At 48.5 *m.* is the junction with US 30N (*see Tour 2d*), with which State 89 unites to BORDER JUNCTION, 78.8 *m.* (6,100 alt., 80 pop.) (*see Tour 2d*).

State 89, here a graveled highway, follows the State Line down a wide hay-growing and cattle-ranching valley, watered by Thomas Fork of Bear River. In the upper end of the valley are some of the oldest and largest sheep outfits in Wyoming. White shale faults, crested with gnarled pine, their flat surfaces toward the highway, run parallel (R) with barren and austere mountains. At 85.5 *m.* towering white cliffs thrust out on both sides of a canyon (R), forming a narrow gateway. Through the canyon mouth, the high back country looms up, a series of jagged scarps. In this canyon, in 1925, three bank bandits took refuge after a robbery at Afton. A few shots were exchanged; then a posse, under the direction of Federal officers, surrounded the trio and laid siege. One by one, as hunger became intense, the robbers surrendered.

At 89.1 *m.* is the junction with US 89 (*see Tour 13*).

EVANSTON, 70.6 *m.* (6,748 alt., 7,000 pop.), is the center of a farming and dairying area. It has comfortable houses, well-kept lawns, parks, and gardens, and many shade trees. Most of its business places are along the south side of Front Street, facing the Union Pacific station and tracks.

In winter, farmers from the upper Bear River Valley put away their wheeled rigs and drive into Evanston in bobsleds. At Christmas time, the Three Wise Men, their camels, and the Star of Bethlehem are outlined in electric lights on a snowy hill east of the city.

Harvey Booth, first settler, pitched a tent on the site of Evanston, November 23, 1868, and opened a restaurant, saloon, and hotel. In December the railroad arrived and with it came more than 600 people.

'Raghouses' of canvas and wood were hurriedly built, but soon the railroad decided to move division headquarters to Wasatch, Utah, 12 miles west; 24 hours later only two persons remained in Evanston. Headquarters came back the following June, and the town settled down. The first public school was opened in 1870; on September 6, 1870, Uinta County voted to make Evanston its seat.

Soon after the establishment of Evanston, a huddle of shanties appeared north of the railroad tracks. Built of odds and ends of lumber, packing boxes, tar paper, and flattened tin oilcans, they looked more like children's playhouses than the homes of men. Here lived Chinese merchants and laundrymen, vegetable peddlers who cultivated gardens near the river, and about 600 Almy coal miners and railroad section hands. Some of the shanties were opium dens and gambling houses. While white men doubted the productivity of the land, the Chinese lifted water from the stream with wheels like those of their native land and raised a crop that supplied the town. They built a joss house, one of three in the United States. Carved panels flanked the door, and banners and richly embroidered draperies hung inside. Behind gates of carved teakwood, fragrant joss sticks burned before a placid idol. Chinese came long distances to worship in the ornate two-story building. But the Oriental population soon dwindled; the joss house burned in 1922.

China Mary, one of the earliest residents of Chinatown, was found dead in her shack on January 13, 1939. She was believed to be then between 104 and 110 years old. Few knew her real name, but the county welfare department had her listed as Ah Yuen. She was buried in garments she had kept ready for years—pajamas and jacket of fine purple material and a black head scarf.

During the 1870's a familiar figure in Evanston was Washakie, chief of the Shoshone (*see Tour 5b*). The treaty by which the Shoshone Reservation was created is in the Evanston courthouse.

1. Left from Evanston on Front Street, which becomes a graveled road, to the WYOMING STATE HOSPITAL (*open 2–4 Sun., Tues., Thurs.*), 0.2 *m.*, for the mentally ill. Five buildings house patients and attendants; auxiliary buildings include a modern dairy barn. All are of red pressed brick.

2. Left from Evanston on a dirt road beside the old Union Pacific grade to the SITE OF BEARTOWN, 15 *m.* Gamblers, confidence men, and toughs flocked to this grading camp in early days. On November 20, 1868, several were jailed by a vigilance committee. Next morning, the *Frontier Index,* the transient news sheet that followed the rails, expressed approval of the action and warned against further lawlessness. Incited by the remaining lawbreakers, the graders marched into town, armed with picks and shovels. Editor Freeman climbed on a horse and 'made a dust'; a spectator said he traveled 'so fast you could have played checkers on his coattails.' His dust still was in the air when the mob arrived, ransacked his office, destroyed furniture, presses, and records, and burned the building.

US 30S climbs out of the valley, goes westward through ranching country, and veers L. across a bleak countryside to the UTAH LINE, 75.6 *m.,* at a point 35 miles northeast of Echo, Utah.

Tour 3

(Billings, Mont.)—Sheridan—Casper—Orin—Cheyenne—(Fort Collins, Colo.); US 87.
Montana Line to Colorado Line, 398.9 *m.*

Oil-surfaced roadbed, open all seasons; occasional cloudbursts, especially in Chugwater district. Excellent for trailers.
Route paralleled by Chicago, Burlington & Quincy R.R. and Chicago & Northwestern Ry. between Casper and Orin; by C.B. & Q.R.R. and Colorado & Southern R.R. between Orin and Colorado Line.
All types of accommodations.

US 87, Wyoming's principal north-south highway, passes through an area rich in frontier lore and representative of Wyoming in its industries and scenery. It crosses the Sheridan ranching and coal-mining areas and broad Johnson County, with its outlaw and cattleman traditions. It climbs the arid Casper prairie, cuts through the Salt Creek oil field, and turns eastward down the North Platte River, along whose clay banks in the middle 1800's half a million westbound emigrants trudged patiently or jolted in springless prairie schooners. Then it swings southward again among farms and ranches to the Cheyenne plains.

Section a. MONTANA LINE to BUFFALO; 68.7 m. US 87-14.

Between the Montana Line and Buffalo, US 87 runs close to the majestic Big Horns. On the east, the plain spreads its tremendous billows toward muddy Powder River, whose name is perhaps better known to Americans than that of any other Western river of comparable size. This unhurried alkaline stream, which washes its first salty mud off the cankerous deserts of Natrona County, is put to little use, but seems to typify something Western. The description, 'a mile wide, an inch deep, and runs uphill,' and the cry, 'Powder River, let 'er buck!' once adopted by American soldiers, have been repeated from Maine to California.

The Big Horn country was first the home of the Crow; but the Sioux, a proud forest folk who came West and became the most formidable mounted warriors in America, conquered it and ruled it for half a century. At first the Sioux, whose lands lay north of emigrant routes, kept aloof when the white man came; but, when their own land was threatened by cattlemen and miners, they resisted. There was pathos as well as horror in their fighting code. To them a battle was a war; when it ended, the war was over. Only when final defeat was at hand, did they begin to understand the white man's dogged and merciless campaign warfare. When homesteaders and small ranchers challenged the cattleman's right to the conquered territory, and another war followed the Indian wars, the defeated Sioux must have felt profound satisfaction.

Altitudes along the Powder average slightly more than half those of the plains to the south, and the growing season is longer. Wind velocity in the Sheridan Valley is second lowest in the United States. Ranches sprawl on the highlands; grain, sugar beets, and hay make deep green borders along the streams.

US 87 crosses the MONTANA LINE, 0 *m.*, 58 miles south of Hardin, Montana.

PARKMAN, 3.1 *m.* (4,300 alt., 50 pop.), is a supply point for ranchers.

The BIG HORN MOUNTAINS (R), massive and heavily wooded, rise 9,000 feet and more above the valleys. The highest peaks, projecting above timber line, seem strikingly bald beside their dark-crested neighbors. The eastern slope, cut by innumerable creeks, suggests a finely molded plaster-of-Paris relief map. The highway crosses or skirts small valleys, watered by streams from mountain springs. Along the creeks are fields, orchards, huge red barns, and small white houses.

At 12.7 *m.* is the junction with US 14 (*see Tour* 10), which unites with US 87 for 19.2 miles.

The highway winds over hills, where rich sub-bituminous coal veins were discovered near the surface by early settlers. Mining on an industrial scale began when the Chicago, Burlington & Quincy laid its tracks to Sheridan in 1892. Smoky, dusty camps, with uniform company houses and towering tipples, appear along the highway. Gray smoke, rising behind low hills, indicates other mines hidden from sight.

At 20.5 *m.* a hillside (L) emits wisps of bluish-white smoke from a burning coal vein. In this vicinity, in 1920, a miner uncovered what appeared to be half a sandstone plaque, bearing a figure of a mummy in low relief, surrounded by marks resembling Egyptian hieroglyphics. Experts say the plaque may be a fragment of an Aztec idol.

The hills spread to grassy flats, and the highway descends into tray-like Sheridan Valley, 15 miles wide and 30 miles long. Buildings here are spacious and freshly painted. Many of the ranches were started by wealthy English and Scottish families. Some of these ranchmen had come to the American wilds to hunt; others were second sons, men who had no place on the family estate; still others were remittance men, living on allowances. They often ranched on a grandiose scale, and, like European landowners, they associated ownership with manorial residences, hunting lodges, servants, dinner dress, and elaborate wine cellars. The directors sometimes lived in London, Glasgow, or New York and chose their superintendents among friends, whose ignorance of ranching equaled their own. In their eyes, hunting facilities and thoroughbred horses were more important than cattle. Deals were made by 'book count,' and millions of mythical cattle changed hands far from the range. Some ranches were small empires; the '76' outfit of Moreton Frewen's Powder River Cattle Company controlled more than 100,000 acres. Few of the big outfits survived the hard winter of 1886-7, when the average cattle loss in northern Wyoming reached 80 per cent.

One Sheridan Valley family was reputedly founded by a son of Edward VII of England. Another rancher, Oliver Wallop, returned to England to assume a title and a seat in the House of Lords, after nearly 30 years' American residence.

At 28.3 *m.* is the junction with an oil-surfaced road.

Right on this road to the VETERANS' ADMINISTRATION FACILITY No. 86, 1.6 *m.*, a psychopathic hospital (*accommodations for 500 patients*). Seventy-five buildings stand on landscaped grounds, which are tended by the patients. The older structures are buildings from Fort Mackenzie, a military outpost established in 1899 and abandoned in 1918.

SHERIDAN, 29.9 *m.* (3,745 alt., 8,536 pop.) (*see Sheridan*).

A SUGAR FACTORY (L), 31.2 *m.* (*adm. by arrangement*), uses beets grown on surrounding farm land (*see Tour 1*). The SHERIDAN FLOUR MILLS (*adm. by arrangement*) are L. at 31.8 *m.*

At 31.9 *m.* roads fork L. and R. US 87 goes straight ahead; US 14 (*see Tour 10*) branches L.

Right from the fork on a graveled road to a junction, 0.7 *m.* L. here 1.2 *m.* to the WYOMING GIRLS' SCHOOL. Primarily a school of correction, the institution also accommodates homeless girls and those with unsuitable home environments. The girls work in school gardens, receive training in home-making, and study an approved high-school course. Several enter the State university each year.

US 87 crosses a cultivated area, with farmhouses of peeled logs or of stone set in small landscaped yards.

LITTLE GOOSE CREEK, 34.4 *m.*, named for the wild geese that frequent it, is bordered by cottonwoods and green-yellow willows. The highway veers through bottomland meadows.

At 35.7 *m.* is the junction with an oil-surfaced road.

Right on this wide road up Little Goose Valley to BIG HORN, 3.5 *m.* (4,059 alt., 125 pop.). Ranchers here, many of them wealthy Easterners, have consciously preserved the Old-West atmosphere of the town—its single street, plank sidewalks, hitching posts, and general store, where residents and guests sit on apple boxes and nail kegs around the stove and swap yarns, while waiting for the mail. The Bozeman Road from the Platte to Virginia City, Montana, ran through the site in the 1860's. In 1878 O. P. Hanna, reputedly the first permanent settler, found a rude cabin and 20-horse log stable here, apparently an outlaw rendezvous. The place is said to have been used by the James gang in the middle of the 1870's.

The road approaches the mountains through a region that produces some of the finest livestock in the West. Plum and apple trees border the highway. Ranches have elaborate houses, surrounded by gardens, tennis courts, swimming pools, rifle ranges, and spacious stables for blooded ponies. The GALLATIN RANCH,

5.9 *m.*, includes a nursery with a comprehensive collection of perennials and rare bulbs.

At the GAME CHECKING STATION, 7 *m.*, State game wardens check hunters' licenses and inspect the kill. Beyond vast meadows (L) rise blueblack mountains.

The MONCREIFFE RANCH (R), 7.2 *m.*, has a polo field where local and regional teams play on Sunday afternoons in summer (*adm. usually free*). Malcolm and William Moncreiffe of Scotland came to Wyoming during the Boer War to buy horses for the British Army. After shipping about 20,000 head to Africa, they bought land along Little Goose Creek and stocked it with sheep. In 1923 William returned to England. Malcolm has sold prize-winning Rambouillet and Corriedale breeding stock throughout the United States and in several foreign countries.

The road twists upward along the steep, shaly RED GRADE, 8.5 *m.* Heavily timbered slopes sweep away to the valley, which spreads out, a gigantic patchwork, below, the green-yellow meadows inlaid with deep green and blue. The opposite slopes are marked with the brown squares of dry farms.

The road (*dangerous here in bad weather*) ends at DOME LAKE RECREATIONAL AREA, 31.2 *m.* (*cabins, boats, horses, lodge*).

US 87 runs southward along a stream bordered by willows, box elders, cottonwoods, and wild fruit trees. In this neighborhood are dairy farms with large outbuildings. Holstein, Guernsey, and Jersey cows graze in willowed pastures; haystacks dot the deep-green alfalfa fields and the lighter-green meadows. The road winds upward over grassy foothills, between whose folds flow swift streams. Old log ranch buildings appear here and there. Many draws are filled with chokecherry and wild plum, which bloom luxuriantly in spring.

BANNER, 46.6 *m.* (4,605 alt., 25 pop.), was named for the brand of a rancher, who made place for the settlement's first post office in his dining room.

Left from Banner on a graveled road (*steep, narrow, winding*) to the SITE OF THE FETTERMAN FIGHT, 2.6 *m.*, near the top of Lodge Trail Ridge, a long hogback. On the morning of December 21, 1866, a wagon train set out under guard from Fort Phil Kearny (*see below*) to bring wood from the mountains about five miles away. As the morning advanced, pickets on Pilot Hill, the fort lookout, signaled that the train was being attacked. A column of 79 soldiers and 2 civilians was formed to go to its aid. Major James Powell, an experienced Indian fighter, was assigned the command, but Brevet Lieutenant Colonel W. J. Fetterman of the 18th Cavalry, who knew little of the fighting strategy of Indians, claimed the assignment on the basis of seniority. Colonel H. B. Carrington, post commander, instructed the fiery colonel to proceed directly to the train, to keep within sight of the fort as long as possible, and not to follow the tribesmen beyond Lodge Trail Ridge. Fetterman, as did Custer, held the fighting ability of Indians in contempt. Instead of going directly to the wood train, he swung to the right, over the hogback, in pursuit of fleeing Indians. A few minutes after the column disappeared, rapid firing behind the ridge was heard. Seventy-six men under Captain Tenadore Ten Eyck hurried out, but they found the bodies of Fetterman and his entire command halfway down the ridge. The wood train reached the fort late that afternoon, unaware that there had been a major encounter.

US 87, climbing higher along pine-covered slopes, curves sharply up TUNNEL HILL, 47.5 *m.*, named for the tunnels that convey water from Piney Creek to farms beyond the hill.

At 48.8 *m.* is the junction with a foot trail.

Left on this trail to a two-story rustic log OBSERVATION TOWER, 200 *yds.*, which commands a sweeping view of Sheridan Valley.

At 48.9 *m.* on US 87 is the junction with a graveled road.

Right on this road to STORY, 0.9 *m.* (4,960 alt., 50 pop.), an alpine summer town for tourists and Sheridan residents (*saddle and pack trips into mountains*).

Left from Story on a dirt road to the SITE OF THE WAGON BOX FIGHT, 1.1 *m.* After the Fetterman disaster, wood and hay crews from Fort Phil Kearny were harried constantly, and worked outside the stockade only under heavy guard. On July 31, 1867, Major James Powell, with 51 troopers, went to Big Piney Creek, five miles from the fort, to guard a wood crew. Finding the crew divided into two camps about a mile apart, he divided his small troop accordingly. To make a barricade, he removed 16 wagon boxes from the running gears and arranged them on the ground, stopping the cracks between them with anything at hand; then he placed two wagons in front, as protection against a mounted charge. On August 2, the Indians attacked simultaneously the wood crews and the stock herders, who were looking after the haulers' horses and mules. Some of the workers and soldiers were cut off from the barricade, but most escaped to the fort. Red Cloud concentrated on the 28 soldiers and 4 civilians in the wagon boxes, who were equipped with new breech-loading Springfields and 1,000 rounds of ammunition. Accustomed to delays between volleys, he timed his assaults to catch the soldiers reloading, but found that his charges withered before the steady fire of the new guns. Red Cloud dismounted his warriors and crept as close as possible to the barricade, then charged on foot, hoping to overcome the handful of white men by sheer numbers. This also failed. Then relief arrived from the fort, and the Indians retreated.

The Sheridan Commercial Club, in 1916, placed a marker at a spot identified by a survivor as the site of the battle. Four years later the Oregon Trail Commission marked a site 0.3 mile farther north, identified by several survivors. No evidence of the struggle remains at either site.

US 87 crosses mountain meadows watered by small, swift streams and bordered by silver aspens, shimmering against deep-green pines. Some slopes are patterned with vari-colored shrubs, and, in late summer and autumn, currant and wild rose bushes are crimson in the gullies.

At 53 *m.* is the junction with a road surfaced with red gravel.

Right on this road across a cattle guard to FORT PHIL KEARNY (*open; custodian*), 0.4 *m.* In 1938 a peeled-log reproduction of an officers' quarters and a seven-foot slab stockade were erected here by the Sheridan Junior Chamber of Commerce. Ruts of the Bozeman Trail wind down the hillside from Pilot Knob.

At the close of the 'bloody year,' 1865 (*see History*), the Government prepared to send troops into the country along the Bozeman Road. Major General John Pope, commander of the Department of the Missouri, ordered two forts built north of Fort Connor (*see below*) and made Colonel H. B. Carrington commander of the mountain district, with orders to proceed from Fort Kearny, Nebraska, to garrison the new posts. When Carrington arrived at Fort Laramie, he found the Plains chiefs in council with Government envoys, who were trying to obtain tribal permission for the forts. When older chiefs favored capitulation to the whites, Red Cloud united the Brule, Ogallala, Arapaho, and northern Cheyenne under his command and, with the head Ogallala chief, Man Afraid of His Horses, embarked on the campaign that made him the foremost chief of his time.

He began by denouncing white men's bad faith in pretending to negotiate for land they had already taken by force. He accused agents and soldiers of treating Indians as if they were children, and reminded his people of the invaders' ruthless killing of game. Dissatisfied factions responded to his oratory; Red Cloud and Man Afraid of His Horses left for the north with more than 600 lodges. If white soldiers came north of Fort Connor, warned Red Cloud, they must fight. Colonel Carrington, however, had his orders and crossed the Platte with 700 soldiers and civilian workmen, with Jim Bridger as guide. Near Fort Connor, Carrington established Fort Reno, and left 250 men to relieve the garrison; then he marched northward with the remaining 450 men. Hostile scouts and warriors showed themselves, from the hour the column left Reno; and signal fires sent up puffs of smoke from the hilltops. Carrington reached Piney Creek without a major skirmish and selected a spot on a plateau between its forks as the site of Fort Phil Kearny, first called Fort Carrington. A train of 90 wagons, under heavy guard, carried logs from the Big Horn foothills; sawmill machinery began whining in the land of buffalo-skin lodges; mowing machines startled the buffalo and antelope from the meadows. As the fort neared completion, the Cheyenne chiefs Dull Knife, Two Moons, Black Horse, and Red Arm rode into camp and begged the colonel to take his troops back to Fort Reno; if he remained the Sioux would force the Cheyenne to fight. Carrington listened sympathetically, but stayed.

In August, Carrington sent Colonel N. C. Kinney with two companies to build and garrison Fort C. F. Smith, 70 miles north; then, with a greatly reduced garrison, he awaited the Sioux attack. Red Cloud waited, however, until the fall hunt was over and the tribal larders filled. On fatal December 21, 1866, the day on which Captain Ten Eyck led 76 troopers to the aid of Fetterman (*see above*), Carrington armed the orderlies, the cooks, and the prisoners from the guardhouse. When the colonel himself went out next morning to recover some of the bodies, he secretly instructed a soldier to blow up the munitions storehouse, with women and children inside, if Indians stormed the fort during his absence. That night John (Portugee) Phillips, civilian scout, volunteered to go to Fort Laramie for help. With a sack of oats and a few biscuits, he rode out into a blinding subzero snowstorm. Two nights later he reached Horseshoe Station, 195 miles from Fort Phil Kearny, and sent a message to Fort Laramie. Then, taking no chances on the frontier telegraph, he followed his message, and arrived exhausted during a Christmas night ball of the officers' club. Orders were sent at once to Lieutenant Colonel H. H. Wessels of Fort Reno to take two companies of cavalry and four of infantry to the relief of Fort Phil Kearny. By neglecting to press his advantage after the Fetterman fight, Red Cloud lost his opportunity to destroy the fort.

During six months, the Indians had made 51 hostile demonstrations; 154 white men had been killed near the fort, and 800 head of stock had been lost. A military court sat to determine 'who, if any, were to be punished for the Fetterman Massacre,' and Carrington and Ten Eyck were the scapegoats. Carrington later charged that the detailed report to General Grant was suppressed, because it contained evidence of maladministration of Indian affairs. In one of its unpredictable changes of policy, the Government abandoned its forts and gave the Powder River country back to the Sioux. Red Cloud, thereupon, concluded he had defeated the white forces. The Government's aim, however, was merely to get the tribes away from the newly completed Union Pacific Railroad. Red Cloud chose to go on a reservation, but, before leaving his home, he led a last raid against his old enemies, the Shoshone (*see Tour 5b*). In later life he made several journeys to Washington. He died on the Standing Rock Reservation in the Dakotas in 1909.

US 87 crosses Little Piney Creek and winds over low, sharply folded hills. Red buttes are on both sides of the way.

At 56.1 *m.* is the junction with a graveled road.

Left on this road across barren hills to LAKE DE SMET (*exceptional fishing and skating*), 2 *m.* The lake was named for the first white man known to have seen it, Father Pierre Jean de Smet. General P. E. Connor, on his Powder River expedition of 1865, discovered on its shore the ruins of several stone houses

apparently more than a century old. Local historians say that a monster sometimes appeared amid the mist that rises from Lake De Smet. In 1938 a group
of Sheridan sportsmen, equipped with life preservers, a shortwave radio set, a
cow for bait, Izaak Walton's book on fishing, and a pitchfork, set out to capture it. The men reported that they hooked the grim thing and pulled it up but
the depth of the murky lake had accustomed the creature to great pressure
and it exploded upon reaching the surface. They claimed to have salvaged from
the monster's stomach twelve horseshoes, the wheel of a road grader, Father
De Smet's Bible, 13 Indian scalps, a backless bathing suit, a piece of track from
the old north-south railroad, and an outboard motor.

An Indian legend tells of a Crow brave, Little Moon, who once in the long
ago asked his love, Star Dust, to meet him at the edge of the lake. While he
waited, a maiden's face, fairer than any other he had ever seen, smiled at him
through the dark waters. As he prepared to leap, Star Dust touched his arm.
Furiously he commanded her to leave him, but when he turned back to the
water the face was gone. The next morning Star Dust lay drowned on the
shore. Her father bound Little Moon to a rock and left him to watch for the
water maiden. When the wind moans over the lake, Indians say the false
warrior is calling.

Through meadows between hills on which bunch grass gives way to
purple-gray sage, US 87 drops into the Buffalo Valley. Though this
region has a few dude ranches, recognizable by their elaborate buildings, most ranches concentrate on cows and ponies, rather than on paying guests. The average cowhand dresses soberly; his is dusty, rough
work, very bad for red silk shirts and highly polished boots. Huge herds
of white-faced Herefords graze in the mountains in summer and work
toward the lower hills, as snow and thinning grass drive them down.

BUFFALO, 68.7 m. (4,645 alt., 1,749 pop.), seat of Johnson County,
is a modern ranch-country town. Main Street, bordered on both sides
by false-front frame, brick, and stone business houses, follows the winding cow trail along which the first buildings were erected. Hills roll
away from it to east and west. The town has a scent of grass and fresh
mountain air. The steel-rimmed heels of cowhands click on the concrete
sidewalks; a saddle horse stands tied to a telephone pole. The low-railed
bridge over Clear Creek is the general meeting place, where the conversation runs from technical 'cow talk' to discussions of high-school
athletics.

In 1866, Captain H. E. Palmer, once of the 11th Kansas Volunteer
Cavalry, came to the Big Horn country with four wagonloads of goods
to trade. With three half-breed interpreters, he stopped on Clear Creek
near the present site of Buffalo and erected a sod hut, 12 feet square.
For nearly a week, tribesmen ignored him; then 25 Cheyenne warriors
came in. At the chief's suggestion, a pipe of peace was smoked. As the
embers died in the bowl, the chief grunted. Blankets dropped from the
braves' shoulders, and arrows on taut bowstrings pointed at the white
men's hearts. Some of the Indians dismantled the house and returned
the sod, grass up, to its place on the prairie. The chief declared that
this was virgin buffalo ground, which the white man should not break,
so long as an Indian lived. He offered Palmer and his associates their
lives and goods if they would leave the country immediately. Palmer
went north to the Tongue River, where he traded for a while with the

Arapaho. But when the First Sioux War, or Red Cloud's War, was officially declared, the Arapaho, allies of the Sioux, confiscated his goods. Palmer was permitted to leave the country. He edited a newspaper in Idaho for several years and, later, was a fire and police commissioner of Omaha, Nebraska, and a national park commissioner.

Buffalo was founded in 1879 by cattlemen, nesters, miners, and freighters, who broke over the land in a wave from the opening of the Sioux country. The cattleman and the farmer moved in almost together. Both thought their rights were valid. But the farmers erected fences; and the fences prevented herds from ranging freely, as storms and grass and water supplies dictated. The cattleman, like the Indian before him, realized that his way of living was being challenged, and, like the Indian, he tried to do something about it. Then the nester joined forces with the rustler for a show-down against the cattleman's dominance, and serious trouble began (*see History*). The hard winter of 1886-7 killed many herds, drove some ranchers out of business, and left jobless range hands to swell the ranks of the rustlers. Buffalo became known south of the Platte as the 'rustlers' capital,' just as Cheyenne was known in the north as the 'cowmen's capital.' Settlers and cattlemen watched each other cautiously, when they met on Buffalo's boardwalks. They varied their routes to town and pulled shades carefully at night. Some who neglected these precautions were found later, hanging from a cottonwood or shot in the back. Tension mounted steadily.

In the spring of 1892, the Johnson County nesters and small ranchers prepared for an early roundup. This in effect would have nullified the stock grower's protective legislation, which set definite dates for all roundups and provided State brand inspectors to oversee branding and marking on these occasions. It also would have made ineffective the State's 'maverick law,' which made all unbranded cattle the property of the State. The big cattlemen organized a society called the Regulators and planned an expedition in military style, to settle the trouble by hanging or shooting the known rustlers and frightening their friends out of Wyoming. They hired gunmen from Texas, Idaho, and Colorado and placed a former army officer in command. On the night of April 5, a special train carrying equipment, ammunition, provisions, and 52 heavily armed Regulators started for Casper. The plan was to make a lightning march from Casper to Buffalo, seize the town, round up the rustlers, and repeat the process wherever necessary before the populace realized what was happening. Couriers brought the word to Buffalo, but the residents only shrugged their shoulders, unconvinced that the cowmen meant war.

At Casper, wagons were waiting. Telegraph wires to Buffalo and Sheridan were cut. Spies reported that Nate Champion, leader of the rustlers and grangers, and Nick Ray, another wanted man, were at the K C ranch, 50 miles south of Buffalo. The Regulators immediately went there, killed Ray and Champion (*see below*), and marched northward again.

When the news reached Buffalo, men collected on Main Street, talking excitedly. Messengers were sent to spread the alarm. Robert Foote, Buffalo's leading merchant, mounted his black horse and galloped up and down, black cape and long white beard flying in the wind, calling the citizens to arms. Then he opened his store and supplied fighting men with free guns, ammunition, and tobacco. Sheriff Red Angus swore in 100 deputies and started for the K C ranch. Settlers and ranchers from the outlying country converged on the little county seat, and a Home Defenders corps was organized, several hundred strong. Churches and schoolhouses became barracks and places of refuge for wives and children. Approaches to Buffalo were guarded.

The cattlemen never reached the town. Warned of the mobilization, they retreated to the T A ranch, 14 miles south of Buffalo. There, as the Johnson County men were about to storm their position (*see below*), they surrendered to Colonel Van Horn of Fort McKinney. Because of local feeling, the Government refused to turn the arrested cattlemen over to Johnson County authorities. They were held in Cheyenne at the expense of Johnson County and, when the county was unable to meet the cost of their lodging and subsistence, the case was dismissed. Soldiers were quartered in Buffalo until resentment cooled.

In a drug store on Main Street is the GATCHELL COLLECTION (*adm. by arrangement*), owned by Jim Gatchell, who spent years among the Blackfeet and Sioux and who speaks their languages fluently. The collection includes Indian relics and frontier firearms. The store is a rendezvous of oldtimers.

In Buffalo is the junction with US 16 (*see Tour* 8).

Section b. BUFFALO to JUNCTION WITH US 20; 122.7 *m. US* 87

Along this section of US 87 many of the scenes of the Johnson County War were enacted. The highway swings near the Hole-in-the-Wall, traverses the upper Powder River country, and crosses the Salt Creek oil field to the largest refining center in Wyoming.

South of BUFFALO, 0 *m.*, US 87 traverses wide fields and meadows. From BULL CREEK, 5.7 *m.*, an indolent stream, sharply ridged sagebrush hills stretch away (R) to an uneven horizon.

The road crosses the NORTH FORK OF CRAZY WOMAN CREEK, 12.7 *m.* Legend tells that a demented squaw once lived in a wickiup on the banks of the stream and was at length buried there. Another story is that a white trader was killed and scalped here, and that his wife became insane at the sight.

INVASION GULCH, 13.3 *m.*, a dry, shallow, boulder-bottomed streambed, sheltered Home Defenders during the siege of the T A ranch in 1892.

The old T A ranch, now the GAMMON PERCHERON RANCH (L), 13.8 *m.*, has spacious buildings and extensive corrals. When embattled cowmen retreated here during the Johnson County War, they were in such haste to get behind breastworks and into rifle pits that they lost their supply wagons to the pursuers—400 heavily armed grangers, rustlers, and small ranchers—who thereupon prepared to storm the ranch. After dark, they dug rifle pits within gunshot range and built a portable barricade of logs, mounted on the running gears of the captured wagons. From behind this 'go-devil,' they intended to toss dynamite into the cattlemen's barricade. The portable fort, shielding 40 men, was being moved into range when Colonel J. J. Van Horn, leading three troops of United States cavalry from Fort McKinney (*see Tour* 8), arrived. Fighting ceased and the cattlemen submitted to arrest.

The highway crosses T A Creek, 14.1 *m.*, and climbs dry rolling hills. An oil rig in the distance (R) marks the site of Billy Creek Oil Field, named for Billy Doyle, early settler. Several wells were prospected in this area during the oil boom of the 1920's. One well produced hot artesian water, which enterprising drillers piped to the Salt Creek Field to use in further drilling.

US 87 rises and falls over low hills, which give way to flats ahead.

The 28 RANCH (R), 17.4 *m.*, one of the largest and oldest intact cattle ranches in Wyoming, was founded in 1882 by F. G. S. Hesse, Englishman, who for several years was foreman of Moreton Frewen's vast 76 outfit. The Hesse family still owns and operates the 28.

The MIDDLE FORK OF CRAZY WOMAN CREEK, 21.6 *m.*, cuts a wandering course among the hills. Fenced meadows and hayfields appear unexpectedly. Strands of barbed wire, strung taut on miles of cedar posts, symbolize the passing of the old cattle empire.

Grass gives way to sagebrush, rabbit brush, and other desert flora. Sheep wagons stand motionless on the crests of the hills, with the wind tugging at their white canvas tops. Scattered bands of sheep move jerkily across the plain, sharply intent on their feeding. Herders with pipe and dog sit or stand near the flocks. Snow fences, anchored at the ends with stone weights, parallel the highway; and sheepherder's monuments jut upward from the hills, sometimes at range boundaries. At night, iron pyrites in the stones that litter the ground glitter like gold in the moonlight.

According to local tradition, treasure is hidden in the upper canyons of Crazy Woman Creek. In the fall of 1865, two prospectors stumbled into the stockade at Fort Reno and told how they, with five companions, had found a fabulously rich gold lode. They had built a small cabin and, in a few days, had gleaned $7,000 worth of gold. Indians, they said, killed their comrades, but they had escaped with the gold in a baking-powder can. Although they showed the gold, the commander did not believe their story and placed them under arrest. Later released, they spent the winter at Fort Laramie and, the following spring, organized an expedition of about ten men to find the lode. They were never heard of again. Official and unofficial expeditions have searched for the treasure without success.

KAYCEE, 46.8 *m.* (4,660 alt., 161 pop.), a cowman's town founded about 1900, was named for the neighboring K C Ranch (*see below*).

In the spring of 1860, a party of four missionaries, from the Iowa Synod of the German Lutheran church at St. Sebald, Iowa, came north from Deer Creek Station on the Oregon Trail (*see below*), to establish an Indian mission. Somewhere on the Powder River, about 100 miles north of Deer Creek, described in the missionary report as a site 'where the ground was level and the grass was thick and luxuriant for the tired oxen, and the soil adaptable to agriculture,' the Christian emissaries corralled their wagons and blessed the ground.

After erecting a temporary hut for shelter at night, the men broke the ground with their plow and planted corn and grain. Then they erected a sturdy log Mission Station, sunk a well, and looked about for the Crow, whom they had come to instruct. They soon found that the country was no longer 'Absaroka, the Land of the Crow'; the Sioux and Cheyenne had dislodged that less warlike tribe and had taken the land of the Big Horn and Powder for themselves.

But still the churchmen had hopes that the Crow would come down to them for instruction. 'We will see and converse with our dear Crows, which will take place very shortly, as they are to receive their annuities at Deer Creek this year and their road leads directly by our station,' they wrote. The Crow, however, did not venture down. When one of the mission party deserted, the leader grew alarmed and sent to St. Sebald for additional volunteer workers. A few days later he was slain, and the two remaining missionaries made their way back to Deer Creek. As soon as they were gone, the mission buildings were burned by the Sioux. No trace remains today, but it is believed that the mission stood not far from present Kaycee.

1. Left from Kaycee on a gravel and dirt road, to the SITE OF THE PORTUGUESE HOUSES, 11 *m.*, on the banks of the South Fork of Powder River. In 1828 a Portuguese trader, Antonio Mateo, erected several buildings here, with a 10-foot, hewn-log stockade, 200 feet square, around them. Only irregular mounds and deeply buried posts remain at the site.

The road runs northeast along Powder River to the SITE OF FORT CONNOR, 27 *m.*, and the SITE OF FORT RENO, 28 *m.* Fort Connor was founded in July 1865 by Major General P. E. Connor, as a temporary supply base for his Powder River expedition. The crude buildings stood on a mesa, rising more than 100 feet above the river and extending to white bluffs five miles west. Fort Connor was garrisoned for only a year. Then Colonel H. B. Carrington chose a more strategic site a mile up the river, near a pure spring, and built Fort Reno (named for Major General Jesse L. Reno), a log stockade with blockhouses and bastions. Designed so that the defenders' fire could sweep the surrounding plain, the new fort was never threatened. It was abandoned in 1868, when the land was returned to the Indians.

2. Right from Kaycee on a dirt road across the Red Fork of Powder River to Red Canyon, or HOLE-IN-THE-WALL, 18 *m.*, a gap washed through the Red Wall by the Middle Fork of Powder River. The wall, a jutting fault 35 miles long, runs almost straight south and then bends west. The region to the west is also known as the Hole-in-the-Wall, but it is not a basin or deep valley such as Jackson Hole or Brown's Hole.

The Red Wall country was long a hunting ground, and tributaries of the Powder and Big Horn Rivers, heading in this high, rough area, bear such names as Otter, Trout, Beartrap, and Buffalo (there are two Buffalo Creeks). In 1876, after the Custer Battle, Dull Knife and Little Wolf led the Cheyenne and Arapaho here. On the eve of November 26, General Ranald Mackenzie surrounded Dull Knife's camp on the Red Fork of the Powder. At dawn, with 1,100 troopers, he surprised the sleeping Cheyenne and drove them from their lodges. The Indians rallied in the hills and fought until mid-afternoon, but Mackenzie destroyed their camp and supplies. Almost naked, the Cheyenne made their way to the Sioux camp of Crazy Horse, 70 miles away. Men, women, and children walked through deep snow, leaving a trail of blood. In the camp, the soldiers found many articles that had belonged to Custer's men.

The Hole-in-the-Wall, near the Bozeman Road and not more than two days' hard ride from the Union Pacific, was an outlaw hideout for half a century. In its 35-mile length, there was only one eastern entrance, which a few armed men could defend easily; but on the west, trails led to Montana, Idaho, Utah, and Colorado. Members of the James gang reputedly used it, and bands such as those of Butch Cassidy, Flat Nose George Curry, and Nate Champion operated from it. In July 1897, ranchmen determined to 'work' the Red Wall country for cattle, for the first time in years. Bob Devine, foreman of the C Y outfit, was chosen to direct the roundup. He and his men met no resistance until they were well beyond the Red Wall; then as they started the roundup, several men rode toward them. At first the two groups passed each other slowly, at little more than arm's length, with guns pointed at the ground. In the fight that followed, Devine and his son were hit; one rustler was killed, another, Bob Taylor, surrendered; the others escaped. Taylor was tried in Buffalo, but was set free. The Hole-in-the-Wall was known, about 1900, as an important station on the Outlaw Trail of Butch Cassidy's 'Wild Bunch,' a trail extending from Mexico to Canada and from the Pacific to the Great Lakes. An elaborate system of hollow-tree or hole-in-a-rock post offices kept gang members in communication. Flat Nose George Curry and Harvey Logan, with their spectacular robberies and cold-blooded killings, gave the Hole its first widespread publicity. Newspapermen seized upon the name with glee and soon every fugitive was reported in Eastern papers to be heading for the Hole-in-the-Wall. When the Curry gang broke up, its members joined Cassidy's band (*see Tour 5b*). Cassidy, once George LeRoy Parker, a Mormon cowpuncher, a good-natured fellow with a ready smile, became a Western Robin Hood, a gunman who, despite his skill, was never known to have killed a man while in this country. In 1902, Cassidy sailed for South America, where, it was said, he killed himself in 1909, to avoid capture after a 12-hour battle with Bolivian cavalrymen. Since 1934, it has been rumored in Wyoming that Butch was not killed and that he had returned to his old haunts near Lander.

In the Red Wall region today, ranches sprawl along the green bottoms beside Buffalo Creek, and cattle and sheep graze on the hills.

The MIDDLE FORK OF POWDER RIVER, the southern boundary of Kaycee, is crossed at 47.2 *m.*

The SITE OF THE OLD NOLAN CABIN on the K C Ranch (R), 47.3 *m.*, is on a dry barren rise on the south bank of the Middle Fork. Here, in the one-room cabin, Nate Champion and Nick Ray were surrounded and killed by the Regulators, on an April day in 1892 (*see above*). Champion, Texan of good family and a top hand, was regarded as the most dangerous gun fighter in Wyoming.

US 87 climbs to a dry plateau. The sluggish, gray SOUTH FORK OF POWDER RIVER, 54.9 *m.*, marks the southern boundary of the Powder River cattle empire. Alkaline flats, broken by jutting crimson rocks and deep arroyos, roll away to the horizon in all directions. Sheep ranches lie lonely and desolate amid the waste. The tapering derricks of Salt Creek Dome rise ahead.

The road crosses a boundary of the SALT CREEK OIL FIELD, 76.2 *m.* (*speed limit, 25 m.p.h.*). Engines chug and chuff among the derricks, pumping oil from subterranean cavities through pipe lines that extend to Casper. Rigs and pipes are smudged with black oil; the age of a well is often roughly indicated by the quantity of oil on the derrick. Trucks loaded with casing and grease-stained workers rattle between wells. Walking beams rise and fall monotonously. At some wells the high rigs have been dismantled, and only the laboring pump remains to force the oil to storage tanks.

The Salt Creek Field was prospected in 1882; the first well was drilled in 1888. Two years later, an Eastern oil company brought in the first gusher at 1,090 feet. When chemists pronounced the oil of finest texture, other companies were attracted to the field, and by 1896 eight wells were brought in. In 1910 the Franco-Wyoming Company laid the first pipe line to the Casper refineries (*see Casper*).

The highway crosses alkaline Salt Creek and passes squat metal storage tanks and company warehouses (R).

MIDWEST, 79.5 *m.* (4,820 alt., 2,510 pop.), founded by the Midwest Oil Company, is the hub of activity in the billion-dollar Salt Creek Oil Field. The uniform company houses are well kept, with little spots of green lawn.

Left from Midwest on an unnumbered oiled highway to EDGERTON, 1.8 *m.* (6,600 alt., 269 pop.). It was settled on public land just outside the oil field in 1923, when Federal authorities began action to revoke leases of Government land.

South of Midwest, little settlements parallel the road. Sometimes, 'nitro-glycerin cars' are seen parked off the highway, large coupés with trunks behind, used by well shooters to transport their blasting paraphernalia.

U. S. PETROLEUM RESERVE NO. 3, 85.3 *m.*, known first as Irish Park and later as Teapot Dome, was claimed by various companies before 1910. When extensive development of the field began, President William H. Taft made the tract a naval reserve and closed it to private exploitation. Early in his administration President Warren G. Harding transferred the naval reserves from the Navy Department to the Department of the Interior. Later, the Government charged that Secretary of the Interior Albert B. Fall had leased the Teapot reserve secretly, and without competitive bids, in 1922, to Harry F. Sinclair's Mammoth Crude Oil Company.

One of the first wells sunk proved to be the largest gusher ever opened in Wyoming. It came in suddenly, hurling tools against the crown block and showering crude oil for several hundred yards; measurements showed a flow of 28,000 barrels a day. Eventually the well assumed a stable flow at 100 barrels a day. Between 1922 and 1927, Mammoth Company drilled 87 wells, of which 65 produced oil. In 1923, the average flow was 273 barrels a day.

After the oil lease scandals of the early 1920's, the U. S. Supreme Court invalidated the leases and restored control of naval reserves to the Navy. The improvements made by the oil company were transferred with the oil lands. Harry F. Sinclair was imprisoned for three months and fined $500. Secretary Fall received a three-year prison sentence and was fined $300,000.

US 87 crosses East Teapot Creek near TEAPOT ROCK, 94.2 *m.*, a formation of eroded Parkman sandstone, 75 feet high and 300 feet around, resembling a disfigured human hand rather than a teapot. The highway veers across naked sagebrush flats, with low pine-crested hills rising to the right. Stone faults, eroded to gargoyle forms, change in aspect and color as the perspective shifts. Sheep wagons dot the countryside. The road rises and falls sharply (*blind curves*). Bleak ranch buildings sit doubtfully on the plain, as if blown there by a desert wind. Casper Mountain, like a huge stone tortoise, rises ahead.

The highway mounts to a plateau. Below is Casper, spread out along the sluggish North Platte River. The refinery stacks, towering above the trees along the streets and parkways, seldom emit smoke, as gas is used in the furnaces. Squat, circular, white-steel storage tanks clutter the hillsides and riverbanks.

At 122.7 *m.* is the junction with US 20 (*see Tour 6a*), which unites eastward with US 87.

Section c. JUNCTION WITH US 20 to ORIN JUNCTION; 67.5 m. US 87-20.

US 87 bisects Casper, then parallels the Platte River and the Oregon Trail over dry plains. No one knows what white man first followed the Platte across Wyoming. Part of a map dated 1720, found in a French museum, shows *La Rivière Platte* coming up from the south in a horseshoe curve around the Haystack, Deer Creek, and Shirley ranges, then swinging southeast to join *La R. Platte du Sud.* There was a stigma in the name: Early travelers regarded rivers as highways; but the 'Flat River,' shallow and full of sandbars and whirlpools, was unsuited to navigation even with small boats. One explorer called it 'a broad, but dirty, uninviting stream, differing from a slough in having a swift current, often a mile wide . . . three inches of fluid running on the top of several feet of moving quicksand . . . too yellow to wash in, and too pale to paint with . . .'

South of the junction with US 20, 0 *m.*, US 87 crosses the river.

The STANDARD OIL REFINERY, 0.6 *m.*, one of the largest in Wyoming, appears to be made up of spiral stairways, steel ladders, masses of pipes of all sizes, and buildings set on cement posts. Stillmen, in oily overalls, watch gauges; pipemen work with wrenches on overhead lines.

At 1.4 *m.* is the junction with State 220 (*see Tour 11*).

CASPER, 1.8 *m.* (5,123 alt., 16,619 pop.) (*see Casper*).

US 87 passes small industrial establishments, surrounded by houses 'thrown up' during boom years. In the REPTILE HOUSE (L) (*visitors welcome*), 4 *m.*, a one-room concrete building, hatbands, belts, necklaces, and other ornaments are made from rattlesnake vertebrae and skins. Behind the shop in summer, more than 100 rattlesnakes are kept in a large concrete pit. Jess Webster, 21-year-old keeper, demonstrates to spectators the 'milking' of the snakes for venom from the sacs above the fangs. With forked sticks and wooden tongs, he goes snake hunting each spring in the rocky hills and on the plains north of Casper. The snakes are fed rats and mice. In the autumn, they are turned loose to hibernate in dens in the hills.

EVANSVILLE, 5.1 *m.* (5,200 alt., 174 pop.), is a community of refinery workers.

At 7.2 *m.* is a SODIUM SULPHATE REFINERY (R). Sodium sulphate is found in the prairies near by, in deposits, 50 to 100 feet deep, known as lakes. The refined product is shipped East for use in livestock feeds, paper, glass, and dyes.

The highway follows the North Platte River across waste lands, where high winds, in winter, sweep snow into gullies and draws, uncovering the sparse, sinewy desert plants, on which sheep subsist. In the days of the Oregon Trail, the wagon wheels of emigrants wore ruts in the powdery soil on both sides of the river, and fires blinked in an almost unbroken line from Omaha to Fort Hall.

PARKERTON, 20.7 *m.* (5,123 alt., 505 pop.), at the western boundary of the BIG MUDDY OIL FIELD, is a typical oil town of neat company houses, surrounded by green·lawns and.shrubs. The Big Muddy Field, named for the small, usually dry, tributary of the Platte that flows through it, was developed during the World-War boom. It reached maximum production in 1919, with an average of·8,000 barrels a day from 200 wells. Daily output in 1938 was about 1,500 barrels.

GLENROCK, 26.4 *m.* (5,000 alt., 819 pop.), is an attractive town, with well-built business blocks, modern residences, a refinery, and a sheltered 30-acre park, on the bank of Deer Creek. The smell of crude oil pervades the place.

East of the Deer Creek bridge, 26.7 *m.,* is a junction with a graveled road.

Left on this road to GLENROCK PARK (*play and picnic grounds*), 0.3 *m.,* which encloses the SITE OF THE DEER CREEK STATION, established in 1861 as a military post on the Oregon Trail. Until the telegraph line was moved farther south, the station was the scene of sporadic battles with Indians, bent on wrecking the line. Deer Creek is old in the history of Wyoming. In the small sheltered valley where Deer Creek joins the Platte, the Mormons built a comfortable way station in the 1850's, where their emigrant trains could lie over for a day or so and refresh their livestock on the lush grass and fine water. They abandoned their sturdy log buildings, when Colonel Albert Sidney Johnston led United States troops against their Utah Eden in 1857 (*see Tour 2C*), and 'Major' Thomas Twiss, Indian agent at Fort Laramie, promptly and without asking permission, moved his agency 100 miles up the Platte and established himself in the Mormon houses with his Ogallala bride and his ·pet bear. From his new station, which he called the Upper Platte River Agency, Twiss administered his Indian affairs until President Lincoln removed him in 1861.

The Major (all Indian agents were called 'major') was born in Switzerland of a good family, came to the United States, and was graduated with honors from West Point. After serving with distinction in the American Army, he joined the Indian Bureau and was sent as agent to Fort Laramie, regarded as one of the most important posts in the country. Twiss for years executed his office with the efficiency and foresight expected, but toward the end of his career he became a typical example of the corrupt agent. It was charged, in his later years, that 'the major's bear got more sugar than the Indians did.' After his removal for corrupt practice, Twiss moved up on the Powder River with his wife's people, and only his flowing white beard distinguished him from the Sioux, whose way of living he adopted.

Topographic engineers, led by Captain W. F. Raynolds and accompanied by Dr. F. V. Hayden, geologist, wintered at Deer Creek with Twiss in 1859. They went on to the Yellowstone country in the spring, guided by Jim Bridger. In 1933, residents of Westfield, Massachusetts, Dr. Hayden's home town, erected a monument to him in Glenrock.

Right from Glenrock Park, 5 *m.* on a foot trail to MORMON CANYON on Deer Creek. Here a party of Mormons settled in 1853, by order of Brigham Young, to raise vegetables and cattle to feed the converts bound toward Utah. The settlement flourished until travel declined in the late 1860's, when the gardeners moved on to Salt Lake Valley. Grass-grown irrigation ditches remain.

At 30.1 *m.* is the junction with oil and dirt-surfaced Boxelder Road.

Right on this road to CAMP CAREY, 8 *m.*, summer home of the Casper Council of Boy Scouts. The late Senator Robert D. Carey gave the scouts this 40-acre tract along Boxelder Creek.

The A. H. UNTHANK GRAVE (R), 31.5 *m.*, is protected by an iron-pipe enclosure and marked with the original sandstone slab. Unthank, an Indiana man traveling with a party of emigrants to the California gold fields, died and was buried here on July 2, 1850. Names of members of the party are carved in a ridge of sandstone half a mile west.

The highway winds down Boxelder Valley. Cottonwoods and willows border the stream (R); green meadows and pastures spread away to yellow prairie.

CAREYHURST, 36.6 *m.*, one of the largest ranches in Wyoming, is the estate of Senator Robert D. Carey, who served as U. S. Senator from 1931 to 1936. Its 15,000 acres of grassland, sprawling over the entire Boxelder Valley, were originally part of the C Y holdings of the senator's father, Judge Joseph M. Carey.

At 41.5 *m.* is the junction with a dirt road.

Right on this ungraded road across sheep-grazing lands, cut by deep arroyos, to AYER'S PARK, 5 *m.*, a 15-acre amphitheater inclosed by a NATURAL BRIDGE and by red cliffs, 100 feet high. The park, green with grass and cottonwoods, is always cool. Shady La Prele Creek, which heads in the mountains (R), has worn a passageway through thick stone, leaving an arch 30 feet high and 50 feet wide, large enough to admit three locomotives abreast. The arch supports several hundred tons of sandstone, directly over the small stream. Cold crystal springs flow into the creek. The park was originally part of the ranch of Alva W. Ayers, whose son, A. C. Ayers, gave it to Converse County. The county equipped it with benches, fireplaces, a water system, and other conveniences.

South of the Ayer's Park junction, the highway runs through farming country.

At 51.4 *m.* is the junction with a dirt road.

Left on this road, which follows the old Bozeman Trail over scraggy range-land, to the SITE OF FORT FETTERMAN, 6.6 *m.*, on a sagebrush plateau south of the Platte. The large adobe barn, covered with corrugated iron, and the log duplex residence, erected in the late 1860's as officers' quarters, still stand. The plateau is sheep range, and the officers' shelter is a herder's house.

Fort Fetterman was built by Major William McE. Dye in July 1867, and named for Brevet Lieutenant Colonel W. J. Fetterman (*see Tour 3a*). Red Cloud's warriors seldom rode as far south as the Platte, and for seven years the fort was not even equipped with cannon, but it was an important supply base during the later Sioux wars. After the Treaty of 1868, it was the last army outpost along the Indian border. Its garrison, little more than a warehouse crew, was charged with making both white men and Indians respect the boundary. The fort was abandoned in 1882, when the conquered Plains tribes had been confined to reservations. Cattlemen then took over Fort Fetterman and made it a hell-roaring frontier town. Barns and warehouses became business houses, barracks and officers' quarters served as residences. Ex-soldiers, cowhands, trail-hands, and others came here to blow their pay; a small graveyard, at the southeast corner of the site, holds the bones of the careless and the slow. The town declined after the founding of Casper and Douglas in 1886-8 and was eventually deserted.

The road crosses the Platte River to the SITE OF THE HOG RANCH, 7 *m.* 'Hog ranch' was a local name for a mushroom 'recreational' community that clung to military posts on the Plains, a gambling and dance resort and segregated district. The one near old Fort Fetterman, however, was established by Jack Saunders and John Lawrence in 1882, after the Government had abandoned the fort.

In 1883 Malcolm Campbell, fire-eating sheriff, came to the ranch to arrest Alfred Packer, who was later convicted of killing and eating five prospectors, with whom he had been snowbound in the high Colorado Rockies in the winter of 1874. The Hog Ranch was closed in 1886, when Jack Saunders was killed by Billy Bacon during an altercation.

The valley widens to fertile farm and ranch land. Along the creeks that head in the mountains (R) are large cattle outfits, and farms and smaller ranches cluster along the river bank (L). The highway crosses the Platte at 53.3 *m.*

DOUGLAS, 53.8 *m.* (4,815 alt., 1,917 pop.), seat of Converse County and home of the Wyoming State Fair (*usually held in September*), is on the east bank of the North Platte River, adjacent to thriving livestock and farming areas and oil fields.

Great shade trees line the straight streets of the town, which stretch away to the farms near by. Much purebred dairy stock is raised in the region, and the feeding of lambs and steers from the ranges has become an established industry.

During the 1870's and 1880's, Fort Fetterman, some eight miles northwest of the site of Douglas, was not only a garrison, but also the supply point for stockmen. When, in 1886, it was announced that the Fremont, Elkhorn & Missouri Valley Railway would extend its lines westward from Chadron, Nebraska, up the Platte River, men of foresight established themselves in Wyoming in anticipation of the coming railway. In April of that year, three tents were pitched on the banks of the Platte River, just north of the confluence with Antelope Creek. These canvas structures, housing a general merchandise store owned by C. H. King & Company, a restaurant, and a saloon, were called Tent Town. Hearing of the larger stocks of merchandise in the new tent town, the ranchmen soon began to go there to do their trading. Since distances were long and loading had to be done early in the morning, it was not uncommon for King & Company to sell $500 worth of goods before breakfast.

The first church services in Tent Town were held in a saloon in May 1886, by two theological students. The altar was a card table; the bar was partially hidden by a new wagon cover, and only a few bottles were in sight.

Tent Town soon had three streets and many businesses, including a newspaper, *Bill Barlow's Budget*. The editor of the paper, Merris Clark Barrow, who wrote under the pseudonym, 'Bill Barlow,' gained much attention with his philosophic and humorous writings. For two years Barrow was city editor of the *Laramie Boomerang* under Bill Nye.

About June 1, 1886, it was announced that the railway station and townsite would be some ten miles east of Fetterman on the opposite side of the river. Shortly afterwards, when the Pioneer Townsite Company had laid out the permanent site of Douglas, Tent Town was put on wheels and was moved, in three days, to the intersection of the Bozeman and Texas trails and the historic routes traversed by Robert Stuart, Captain Bonneville, and General Frémont. The new town was named in honor of Stephen A. Douglas.

On August 29 the first passenger train arrived, loaded with people, and the sale of lots began. The first lot sold brought $760. Erection of buildings began at once, and, for the next 60 days, hammers pounded from daylight until dark. Five brick buildings were constructed of hand-made brick; the streets were lined out in broad, orderly avenues, and trees were planted. Railroad construction crews mingled with soldiers and cowboys, and for a time there was a preponderance of the lawless element. Most of these men, however, were more fun-loving than dangerous, and the saloon brawls resulted in few killings. During the first year of its existence Douglas had 25 saloons but only 6 by the end of the year.

Among the early unruly characters, but not a killer, was George Pike. Once, it is told, he walked out of a poker game when he realized it was not straight; returning soon after, dressed as a hobo, with his cap pulled low, he held up the boss of the game and collected $2,500. Coming back in his own person, he expressed great sympathy for the man who had lost so much money. Pike was known on the range as a top hand, but one who had no scruples about appropriating to himself any unbranded critter that came handy to his lariat. Cattle outfits decided that perhaps it would be more expedient to hire the man and to pay him good wages, so that, if he persisted in his rustling practices, his immediate employer would be the beneficiary. Old-timers say that the outfits employing him never lost anything by it; this appears to be borne out by the fact that one company erected over his grave, in the Douglas Park Cemetery, an expensive tombstone inscribed as follows:

GEORGE W. PIKE

Underneath this stone in eternal rest
Sleeps the wildest one of the wayward west.
He was gambler and sport and cowboy, too,
And he led the pace in an outlaw crew.
He was sure on the trigger and staid to the end
But was never known to quit on a friend.
In the relations of death all mankind's alike
But in life there was only one George W. Pike.

In the beginning Douglas was in Albany County, but, when Converse County was created in 1887, an election was held at Douglas to determine the location of the county seat. Four towns were in the race: Douglas, Fetterman, Lusk, and Glenrock. Douglas won the election. In these early-day informal affairs, maverick votes in the election booth were as common as mavericks on the range. For the Converse County election, a Captain O'Brien was one of the judges; when the names of 69 O'Briens had been counted for votes, the Captain shouted: 'No more O'Briens today!' There were only 16 O'Briens in the county.

Until the railway was extended farther west in 1887, Douglas was a distribution point for large consignments of freight. From there, mail and passengers were carried by stage to Badger, to connect with the Colorado and Southern, and to Buffalo, Sheridan, Rock Creek and Laramie.

The region around Douglas was attractive to livestock men, because of its abundance of water and its fine native grasses. One of the oldest cattle brands in the state, the S O, was used by John Hunton, who settled on Boxelder Creek near Douglas in 1870. In the early 1880's many big outfits ran cattle in the vicinity, and, during the fall of 1886, great numbers of cattle were driven in from Texas. The range was soon very much overstocked. When the March storms of 1887 came on, there was little feed, and the cattle, being thin and poor, died by the thousands. These losses were largely responsible for the failure of many of the big outfits, and this setback to the livestock industry, plus the fact that the railway was building westward, stopped the growth of the community; from a settlement of 1,500 or more, Douglas dwindled to less than 400.

Although many large cattle ranches and sheep outfits remained in the vicinity, gradually the lands were taken up as homesteads, and fences forced the cattle kings to find more open range. Homesteading was slow, however, as the land office that controlled the North Platte Valley was in Cheyenne, about 200 miles away by wagon road. Settlers had to travel this distance to transact legal business and attend trials. With the establishment of the Federal Land Office at Douglas in 1890, filings were made immediately, and agriculture began to take the place of the extensive cattle business.

Douglas was the goal of settlers intent upon helping to open up the new 'Fetterman Country,' and speedy agricultural development brought stability to the town. Permanent buildings and fine homes gradually replaced the first rude shacks. Among the early residents were some of Wyoming's most distinguished citizens, including DeForest Richards, who served the State as the fourth governor, and Dr. A. W. Barber, acting governor during the historic Johnson County Invasion (*see Tour* 3). Barber is believed to have been the prototype of Governor Barker in Owen Wister's *The Virginian*. Robert David's *Malcolm Campbell, Sheriff* is the story of the first sheriff of Converse County, a man whose bravery and skill made him an outstanding peace officer of the West.

In 1936 Douglas celebrated its 50th anniversary with a three-day show, during which businessmen of the town displayed signs like those common in the old days. At the same time, the Wyoming Pioneer Association held its tenth annual meeting and free barbecue.

STATE FAIR GROUNDS, on E. bank of the Platte River, at the W. end of Center St., occupy several acres, including an athletic field. Besides the main exhibit hall, racing stables, and grandstands, there are poultry houses, arts and crafts buildings, 4-H club building, the Old Timer's Log Cabin, and first schoolhouse. In 1905 the State legislature made an appropriation for the State fair to be held at Douglas, and the town, by subscription, raised an equal amount of money.

The OLD TIMER'S LOG CABIN (*open to visitors during Fair week*), 28 by 42 feet, was built of logs in 1926, with funds gathered by popular subscription. The picturesque structure, set in landscaped lawn, is a memorial to pioneers of the county and State. The building, housing many relics of pioneers days, is the headquarters of the Wyoming Pioneer Association, in which each county is represented by a vice president.

Directly back of the Old Timer's Log Cabin is the PLEASANT VALLEY SCHOOLHOUSE, the first county schoolhouse erected after the school district was formed in 1886. The first library in Converse County was kept in this building. The schoolhouse was moved in 1930 to the Fair Grounds.

GEORGE WASHINGTON MEMORIAL PARK, on the east-central edge of Douglas, is beautifully landscaped and has a public swimming pool (*charge* 25¢). A two-story log house, approximately 65 by 150 feet, in dimensions, serves as a recreational center and community meeting place. The most interesting feature of the building is a fireplace made of stones, donated by the American Legion auxiliary departments from every State in the Union.

A large WOOL STOREHOUSE, on the western edge of town, provides a shelter that is convenient to shipping facilities. Sheepmen haul their wool here to be held pending sale, usually to representatives of large Eastern manufacturers.

WOODRUFF SEED PACKING PLANT, at the W. edge of the town, specializes in seed peas. An average of 65 workers are employed during the winter months.

At 53.9 *m.* is a junction with an oil-surfaced road.

Left on this road to the SITE OF THE LIGHTNING CREEK BATTLE, 22 *m.*, last Indian fight in Wyoming and the most bloody result of the misunderstandings between Indians and whites over hunting laws. In October 1903, Eagle Feather, Sioux chieftain from South Dakota, led 25 braves into Wyoming to hunt antelope. When Sheriff Billy Miller of Newcastle, with a five-man posse, attempted to arrest them, the Indians resisted. Deputy Louie Falkenburg was shot dead; Sheriff Miller and Chief Eagle Feather, Chief Black Kettle, and two other Indians were wounded fatally. Several Indians were arrested later and taken to Douglas to face charges of murder, but they were released after preliminary hearing, because the State's witnesses could identify only one of them. Interest in the case was nationwide; there were rumors of a general uprising of reservation tribes.

The country southeast of Douglas, sloping toward the Laramie River, is an excellent example of badlands topography. The plain is cut by deep ravines, which drain it within a few hours after the heaviest rain. The Laramie Mountains are blue in the distance, topped by the massive cone of Laramie Peak (10,274 alt.).

ORIN, 66.9 *m.* (4,699 alt., 50 pop.), with a post office and several filling stations and stores, is some distance to the left of the site of the original town, established when the Chicago, Burlington & Quincy met the Chicago & Northwestern here in 1900. The town was also at the junction of main highways. The old Orin railroad crossing, an engineering freak that sent automobiles across two railroads on an incline and at an angle, became notorious as a danger point, and in 1936 an overpass was built and US 87 was re-routed past Orin. The old town was abandoned; its drab, deserted buildings still stand near the railroad station.

At 67.5 *m.* is the junction with US 20 (*see Tour 6a*).

Section d.   ORIN JUNCTION to COLORADO LINE; 140 *m.*
US 87-85.

Between the North Platte and the Colorado Line, US 87 roughly parallels the Laramie Mountains. Bleak prairies alternate with sheltered ranches and reclaimed farming areas. The grassy Cheyenne Plains extend northeastward into Nebraska and southward into Colorado.

South of the junction with US 20, 0 *m.*, US 87 crosses the Platte. Cattle graze in the fertile streambank meadows. At 1 *m.* is the BRIDGER'S FERRY MARKER (R), 1,500 feet downstream from the actual ferry site. Jim Bridger established the ferry in 1864.

In GLENDO, 14 *m.* (4,718 alt., 201 pop.), a busy ranch supply town, is J. R. Wilson's collection of fossils and artifacts, one of the finest in the State.

The SITE OF HORSESHOE CREEK STATION is in a meadow (L) at 16.5 *m.* When Russell, Majors & Waddell bought the Hockaday-Liggett Stage Line in 1858 (*see Transportation*), they built additional stations, where horses could be exchanged and travelers could rest briefly. Horseshoe Station, established early in 1861, was supervised for a time by Jack Slade (*see Tour 4B*). Although the Overland

Stage route was shifted southward in 1862, the telegraph line remained, and the station continued in operation. In 1868, four settlers, Marion Thornburg, William Warrell, John R. Smith, and Bill Hill, converted it into a ranch. On the morning of March 19, about 70 Ogallala and Miniconjou Sioux, led by Crazy Horse, appeared near the place. When the white men, firing from within the stockade, killed two Indians and wounded several others, the Indians retaliated by burning the stockade, the stables, and finally the station house. The settlers retreated to a cellar and tunneled beyond the ring of dancing, shouting, howling Indians, who believed their enemies were trapped. The white men cached a few salvaged belongings under a ranch building at Twin Springs, burned the building to destroy signs of the cache, and started for Fort Laramie. On the way, three other white men joined them. Overtaken near Little Cottonwood Creek, the party sought refuge in a deep wash lined with scrub cedar, but the Indians fired the timber and smoked them out. Three were killed in trying to escape; the others barricaded themselves on a rocky prominence. Crazy Horse at length agreed to let them go, in exchange for the articles they had cached at Twin Springs.

The prairies dip to fertile valleys, watered by Bear Creek and its tributaries, Little Bear and Middle Bear. South of OASIS, 24 m., a sheltered camping spot, the highway winds sharply up pine-clad hills to a plateau. Laramie Peak, sometimes sharply outlined, sometimes partly concealed by clouds, is blue in the distance (R). Hills, with limestone outcrops, rise (L) at 27.1 m., covered with pines almost russet in color. Scorched by fire, the area is struggling to recover its growth of grass and trees. In August purple asters fringe the highway, and in autumn rabbit brush and sunflowers add a dash of yellow to the brown landscape.

At 37.2 m. is the northern junction with US 26 (see Tour 4), and at 38.7 m. is the southern junction.

Sagebrush hills give way to dry-farmed flats, where many acres lie fallow each season. Grains and cane are the principal crops.

Squat, massive, pine-blue SQUAW MOUNTAIN bulks on the horizon (R) at 42.1 m. Long ago, say the Indians, a young squaw and her papoose were caught here in a blizzard. Sitting on a large boulder, the woman held her child close to her to give it warmth, and, when the storm ended after many days, mother and child were frozen to the boulder. The woman's bowed body became the mass of rock on top of the mountain.

Descending into a low valley, US 87 crosses NORTH LARAMIE RIVER, 44.9 m. Here raccoons 'holler' in the cornfields at night, and large turtles bask in the sunshine along the river banks.

At 45.4 m. is the junction with a dirt road.

Left on this road is UVA, 1 m. (4,000 alt., 40 pop.), where Colonel W. G. Bullock, sutler's agent at Fort Laramie, started a ranch in the spring of 1871. Indians were so annoying that he moved to the Chugwater; later his holdings became part of the Duck Bar Ranch. The hamlet seems to have been named for an early brand. Near Uva chalk bluffs rise (L) above the valley. Late after-noon shadows lend depth to the folds of the cliff face and create an illusion of great height.

LARAMIE RIVER, 46.1 *m.*, which heads far south in the glacial Colorado Rockies, drains the vast Laramie Plains. Formerly a mighty and temperamental stream, it now runs almost dry in late summer. Much of its water is used to irrigate the fertile beet-growing Wheat-land Flats, which were once regarded as desert.

A sugar refinery of brick and cement is (L) near WHEATLAND, 50.9 *m.* (4,733 alt., 1,997 pop.), seat of Platte County, in the center of a prosperous farming district. Mexican beet workers in picturesque clothes mingle on the streets with conventionally dressed townspeo-ple; their ancient automobiles overflow with their sturdy offspring. Farm wagons rattle over the hard-surfaced streets, and trucks loaded with white, strong-smelling beet pulp rumble out to ranches, where the pulp is fed to livestock.

Each year in August, the Days of '49 are celebrated with a two-day rodeo and a parade. Prizes are awarded for roping, bull-dogging, wild-cow milking, and riding—and for the best beard. The Laramie Peak Stone Age Club sponsors an annual Stone Age fair, displaying flint and obsidian arrowheads and spear points, stone plows, axes, hammers, and knives; pottery; fossil fish and dinosaur remains. Lec-turers from scientific research organizations attend.

In 1885, Joseph M. Carey, territorial judge, governor of Wyoming, and United States senator, took the lead in organizing the Wyoming Development Company, with headquarters at Wheatland, to bring water to 60,000 acres of arid land on the Wheatland Flats. Settlers obtained the land free under desert entry, but were required to buy water rights, which thereupon became part of the real property. A reservoir with storage capacity of 120,000 acre-feet was built on the Laramie River about 40 miles southwest of Wheatland. A 3,000-foot tunnel conveys water through the hills from the reservoir to Blue-grass and Sybille creeks, whence it is distributed over the flats by a system of lateral canals and earth ditches, whose sides are some-times rip-rapped to prevent washing. The flood system of irrigation is used here, as throughout Wyoming. The ditch-beds are lower than the canal, and water runs into the ditches when headgates are lifted. Portable canvas dams are placed in the ditches to flood the water over the sides, and, when the area near the head of the ditch has been well flooded, the dams are moved down the ditch to unwatered areas. Each user has a certain time for 'watering,' and he gauges on his head-gate record the amount he uses. Farmers in gum boots and 'ditch riders' on horseback, with glistening shovel blades above their heads, are familiar figures in the beet and hayfields in early summer. The ditch rider's duty is to be alert for leaks in the central canals and to watch for 'water hogs,' those who leave their headgates open at night during another rancher's turn.

Left from Wheatland on a winding dirt road to the SITE OF EAGLE'S NEST STAGE STATION, 11 *m.*, at the mouth of Eagle's Nest Gap. Wagon trains on the Oregon Trail in the late 1860's and 1870's, swung south from the main road and made a wide loop drive through Eagle's Nest Gap, to avoid the difficult drive through North Platte Canyon. The route became known as the Fetterman Cut-off, since it connected Fort Laramie with Fort Fetterman. The cliffs are soft and porous, and many emigrants paused here to carve their names. Hundreds of initials and insignias are still decipherable. One date is 1842; if not faked, it must have been left by a solitary trapper, as there is no record of wagons' using the pass that early. The pass takes its name from a high eroded formation resembling an eagle's nest. Numerous birds and hornets live in the holes in the soft rock.

When the Cheyenne and Black Hills Stage Line ran north in the 1870's, a station was established here at the Gap. The pass was extremely narrow, however, and was an ideal spot for road agents, who harassed the line for the treasure that came out of the Deadwood mines.

The highway runs southward through green beet fields. Well-kept farm buildings, almost hidden among cottonwoods and boxelders, contrast with the huddled shanties of the beet workers.

At 59 *m.* is the junction with State 26, the Wheatland Cut-off.

Left on this oil-surfaced road across irrigated farmlands. Yellow roses, irises, and red poppies bloom in front yards; Russian olives, willows, and cottonwoods line the creeks and canals. Many farm families live in strange 'basement houses,' flat-topped cement structures that rise above the ground only far enough to make room for a few small windows. The owners started to build fine houses, but were able to complete only the basements.

The road climbs to a region of scattered cattle ranches. Native hay meadows spread out from small streams; rosebushes along the streams are pink with bloom in June and covered with red berries in autumn. BLUEGRASS CREEK, 15.1 *m.*, offers excellent fishing. The highway crosses and recrosses Sybille Creek, and the grade increases. The mountains and rocky hills are covered with sage and scrub pine; streambanks are heavily wooded. Fertile meadows lie between the hills, their green surface flecked with the yellow of sweet peas and the pink and white of locoweed, a plant that is injurious to livestock, chiefly horses and sheep. Ranch buildings are old and usually of logs. Meandering to avoid sandstone ledges, the highway skirts shallow canyons and descends through foothills to the Laramie Plains. Bands of sheep graze here, watched by herders and dogs. At 51.6 *m.* is the junction with US 30 (*see Tour 2*).

US 87 curves over a broken ridge, veers southeastward across high farmland, where grain and alfalfa predominate, and dips into the valleys of small streams. Cattle ranches lie L. and R. Ahead rise eroded bluffs along the Chugwater, where in spring the meadows are emerald below the beige cliffs. In autumn a haze hangs over the valley, and the leafless willows are brownish red. From the deeper valley the high, pitted bluffs resemble porous chalk. Beyond them are level grazing and dry-farming plateaus. Ranchers sometimes search out and dynamite rattlesnake dens in the cliffs.

CHUGWATER, 78.7 *m.* (5,288 alt., 286 pop.), is headquarters for one of the oldest and largest ranching outfits in the West, a firm organized in 1883 by Alexander H. Swan, English gentleman. The Swan Company, managed from London and Edinburgh, was capitalized at $3,000,000; at its peak it owned 120,000 head of cattle and controlled more than 600,000 acres of Wyoming and Nebraska range.

After the hard winter of 1886-7, it went into receivership. Reorganized in 1888, it regained some of its range, but settlers finished what the hard winter had begun. In 1924 the British owners sold out, and the last of the great foreign-owned spreads was gone. The Swan still uses its old Two Bar and Horseshoe brands.

An Indian legend explains the name Chugwater. Long before white men came West, the valley of the cliffs was the home of Wacash, powerful Mandan chieftain, and his people. One day during the fall hunt, Wacash was gored and trampled by a buffalo bull. Summoning his only son, Ahwiprie, the Dreamer, he commanded him to lead the hunt. The son merely grunted and continued to gaze at the white bluffs and dream. Growing impatient, the old chief prepared to adopt another son. But Ahwiprie summoned the braves to council and spoke of the wasted effort in ordinary hunting. He told them to ride out the next morning, surround the buffalo on the plains, and drive them over the bluffs. The plan worked. As the buffalo fell into the Indian camp, their bodies struck the stones with a chugging sound. Indians called the stream 'the water at the place where the buffalo chug'; the white settler shortened this name to 'Chugwater.'

The SITE OF THE CHEYENNE AND BLACK HILLS STAGE STATION, at the south edge of Chugwater, was the first important stage stop north of Cheyenne and was used until the Colorado & Southern Railroad was completed in 1887. It is recorded that the stage station once exchanged hands in a poker game.

The valley gives way to hills. Windmills tower above the wells on streamside ranches. Purple thistle blossoms and yellow flower of rabbit brush add color to the drab plains. The MARK HIRSIG RANCH, 95.8 *m.*, specializes in the raising of polo ponies.

At 118.7 *m.* is the junction with US 85 (*see Tour* 1), with which US 87 unites for 13.1 miles. At 122.2 *m.* the smokestacks, gables, aerials, and golden Capitol dome of Cheyenne are seen projecting above the treetops ahead.

CHEYENNE, 126.4 *m.* (6,062 alt., 17,361 pop.) (*see Cheyenne*).

At 131.8 *m.* the roads fork. US 85 runs L. to the Colorado Line (*see Tour* 1). US 87 curves R. over a grassy plateau, then swings southward between rolling meadows.

The large WARREN RANCH, 139.6 *m.*, was started in the late 1870's by Francis E. Warren (*see Cheyenne*). At 139.7 *m.* a pile of rocks and a weather-beaten marker (L) identify the grave of 'Old Blue, The Best Cowpony That ever pulled A Rope.'

Jutting rocks (L) merge into a formation known as Natural Fort, just south of the Colorado Line. In 1831, drought drove the buffalo southward into this region, and the Blackfeet and Crow of northern Wyoming followed them for the fall hunt. The tribes were unaware of each other's presence, until 160 Blackfeet rode straight into a large party of Crow. The Blackfeet, outnumbered, took refuge in the Natural Fort. The Crow had with them 20 white trappers, led by Jim

Beckwourth (*see Tour* 9), who urged them to attack. In a battle that lasted several hours, all the Blackfeet and 40 Crow were killed.

At 140 *m.* US 87 crosses the COLORADO LINE, 101 miles north of Denver.

Tour 4

(Scottsbluff, Neb.)—Torrington—Junction with US 87; US 26. Nebraska Line to Junction with US 87, 55.6 *m.*

Oil-surfaced highway.
C.B.&Q.R.R. parallels route between Nebraska Line and Guernsey.
Good accommodations.

US 26, the North Platte Valley Highway, follows the North Platte River along emigrant trails of the 1840's and 1850's, which in turn followed old Indian trails and early routes of exploration. Here, prosperous irrigated farmland produces sugar beets, artichokes, corn, wheat, and apples. Turkeys are raised in the valley, and livestock feeding is an important industry. Animals need little shelter aside from occasional windbreaks, for the winters are dry and mild.

US 26 crosses the NEBRASKA LINE, 0 *m.*, 31 miles west of Scottsbluff, Nebraska. In an alfalfa field near here is the SITE OF ROBERT STUART'S CAMP OF 1812, where Stuart and his men spent several winter months on their return from Astoria (*see History*).

The highway runs through rolling grassland; in spring and summer bright-green fields contrast with the green-gray sage-covered hills, while in autumn the riverbank cottonwoods and willows are aflame with yellows and reds.

TORRINGTON, 7.9 *m.* (4,098 alt., 1,811 pop.) (*see Tour* 1), is at a junction with US 85 (*see Tour* 1). Between Torrington and Lingle, US 26 and US 85 are one route.

At the LIVESTOCK SALES YARDS (R), 8.5 *m.*, inspectors work the herds of cattle and horses, trailed or trucked in at auction time, to make sure that brands conform to those shown on bills of sale. Up to 1,400 head of livestock are often placed on sale at one time, for consignment to Eastern feed lots or markets.

At 10.1 *m.* is the eastern boundary of the STATE EXPERIMENT FARM, which tests livestock-feeding methods. Experiments here have shown that substitution of skim milk for one-third of the meat meal, in standard growing-chicken ration, increased the rate of gain and reduced feeding costs 23 per cent; and that the use of alfalfa and cod liver oil in laying mashes produced the most eggs at the least cost. It has been proved also that beet tops are a good substitute for alfalfa in fattening feeder cattle.

As the soil here is light and sandy, alfalfa sown in the spring frequently dies soon after seeding. Tests show that spreading the seed in grain stubble during the summer keeps the tender plants moist during the hot months, when they are establishing a root system.

At 12.8 *m.* is the junction with a dirt road.

Left on this winding road across the North Platte River to a ranch gate, 1.3 *m.;* L. here 0.7 *m.* to the SITE OF THE ROCK RANCH BATTLE. In the early 1850's, a party of emigrants, with Negro slaves, stopped here at the trading post to rest. During an Indian attack, some of the slaves were killed; their masters buried them under the floor. The old post, its loopholes blocked up, still stands.

The highway runs through dry lands alternating with potato and sugar-beet farms. Russian-German and Mexican families work in the fields, planting, thinning, irrigating, pulling, or topping beets, according to season.

The TORRINGTON RIFLE CLUB (R), 14 *m.,* schedules local and statewide shooting matches.

The valley widens near LINGLE, 17.5 *m.* (4,150 alt., 415 pop.), a farmers' trading center, with the largest sugar-beet loading station in Wyoming. Here is the western junction with US 85 (*see Tour 1*).

Left from Lingle on a dirt road across the North Platte to the marked SITE OF THE GRATTAN FIGHT, 3.5 *m.* Here, on August 19, 1854, Lieutenant John Grattan of Fort Laramie, with 28 men and an interpreter, attempted to arrest an Indian accused of killing an emigrant's cow. The chief of the Indian Village refused to give up his tribesman, but offered to bring him to the fort. Grattan, determined upon the man's instant surrender, threatened to use force. 'If you shoot,' the chief replied in effect, 'all your men will be killed.' 'Fire!' commanded Grattan. The Indians returned the fire and closed in. Grattan and five of his men fell at once; others were killed while trying to get away. The next day a detachment from Fort Laramie buried the bodies in a single pit. For some time the fort was almost in a state of siege. According to Seth Ward, a trader at Sand Point, the interpreter had been intoxicated and unable to translate correctly the conversation between Grattan and the chief.

US 26 continues westward between farms on which apples and plums are grown. At 21 *m.,* across the river (L), is the SITE OF FORT BERNARD (1849), a trading post that consisted of one crudely constructed log building. According to Ware's *Emigrant Guide to California,* this post had 'accommodations far inferior to those of an ordinary stable.' At 26.3 *m.* LARAMIE PEAK comes into view ahead (L), once a landmark for emigrants.

The village of FORT LARAMIE, 28.3 *m.* (4,250 alt., 245 pop.), is at the junction with the old Fort Laramie Road (*see Tour 4A*).

OLD PETE'S CURIO SHOP displays Indian artifacts, pioneer relics, and geological specimens picked up in the vicinity.

US 26 runs through a fertile stretch of valley, with chalk bluffs R. South of the Platte (L) are pine-tipped ridges. As the road rises and dips, the view widens.

At 41.2 m. is the junction with an oiled road.

Right on this road, between pine-clad hills and red sandstone outcrops, to HARTVILLE, 5.5 m. (4,900 alt., 189 pop.), in Eureka Canyon. The spot was occupied by a populous Indian village long before white settlers came; for many years, traces of the camp could be found throughout the canyon. Rings of flat rocks outlined the positions of tepees. Scrapers, arrowheads, and stone axes were abundant, as were the grinders, with which red and brilliant yellow clays were prepared for face and body paints.

In 1881 a copper strike brought hundreds of miners and prospectors from the Black Hills into this region. Hartville came into existence as a roaring mining camp, with saloons, dance halls, and gambling houses running full swing. Punchers from neighboring ranches came to the camp for their celebrations. There was plenty of gunplay; if a man was slow on the draw, he was buried the next day, with a bartender friend conducting a brief service at the grave. The saloon keeper, who also operated a store, kept his books on a double-entry plan. If he forgot to enter a credit sale when it was made (as he often did), he charged it to several customers who had been present at the time, and thus made sure of hitting the right one. When the copper boom ended, the store, the saloon, and a lodging house remained in operation to serve the ranchmen.

In 1899 and 1900, when Eastern capital began development of the iron deposits at Sunrise and Chicago mines, there was a second boom. Tents and dug-outs sheltered a large part of the population, as there was neither time nor material for building. When the Chicago, Burlington & Quincy Railroad was being extended from Nebraska, to connect with the Colorado & Southern line running north from Cheyenne, construction gangs added their wages to the stream of money that flowed into the camp from the pockets of miners and settlers. All payments were made in gold; a $5 piece was regarded as small change. With the completion of the railroad and the centralizing of mining operations in the Sunrise Mine, the floating population vanished. Hartville became a comparatively modern town, but retained its frontier appearance.

In 1902 a gambler known as the White Swede died in Hartville, and local legend relates that three gambler companions agreed to conduct the wake. Tired of staring at one another and at the corpse, they started a poker game; after sampling a bottle of whisky, they were moved to cut the corpse in. By dawn, the dead man had won enough to pay for his burial.

At SUNRISE, 7 m. (4,900 alt., 360 pop.), are the SUNRISE MINES. A continuous concrete sidewalk runs through the canyon, with trim frame houses and little gardens scattered along it in all available spaces. Because of the steepness of the hillsides, the householders keep their automobiles in a community garage on the only large level area in town. Sunrise was established in 1903, three years after C. A. Guernsey (see below) obtained options on the mining claims in the vicinity and sold them to a Colorado firm.

Sunrise ore is mined chiefly by the milling system, in an open pit known as a glory hole. This pit is so large and deep that the Washington Monument, if placed on the lowest level, would rise only a few feet above the rim; and so wide is it that men on ladders at the far side look like pygmies. The sound of picks digging at the bottom is heard only faintly at the rim. The mine is said to contain the largest producing body of iron ore west of the great Minnesota deposits. Two hundred men work here. Production averages 500,000 tons yearly; in boom times it has exceeded 800,000. The ore is shipped to smelters at Pueblo, Colorado.

Early explorations indicated that Indians at some time had quarried here, probably to obtain pigments.

GUERNSEY, 41.4 *m.* (4,361 alt., 656 pop.), was named for Charles A. Guernsey, rancher, mining promoter, and author of *Wyoming Cowboy Days*. Beautifully situated just below the mouth of Platte River Canyon, the town is a supply base for the Sunrise mines and the adjacent limestone quarries. It lies in a region notable for the many traces of prehistoric man that have been found here, chiefly primitive implements of war and agriculture. Embedded in the concrete of an OREGON TRAIL MARKER are many relics of a more recent past—ox and mule shoes, bullets, wagon irons, and guns found on the old trail.

The LESTER ROBINSON COLLECTION, in the Guernsey Hotel, contains geological specimens, artifacts from the Spanish Diggings (*see Tour 6a*), arrowpoints from Platte County, Sioux beadwork, and pioneer relics obtained at or near Fort Laramie and along the Oregon Trail. Among these relics are yokes and hand-made wheels, bayonets, old-type guns, and a small Mason & Hamlin melodeon, which was brought to Fort Laramie by ox team and is still in good condition.

Left from Guernsey on a dirt road across the Platte to the foot of turreted chalk cliffs; then L. through a cattle guard, 2.6 *m.*, and over a field to the marked SITE OF A PONY EXPRESS STATION (1860–61), 2.7 *m.* Spurs and horseshoes are set in the concrete. The GUERNSEY RANCH (L) is the locale of the book *Wyoming Cowboy Days*.

REGISTER CLIFF (R), 3.1 *m.*, is about 650 feet south of the North Platte River. On its chalk face, thousands of travelers over the old trails cut their names; some of those who died on the way were buried near its base. About 700 inscriptions remain legible; one is dated 1842. The meadow at the foot of the cliff, which was originally called Sand Point, was the first stopping place of emigrants west of Fort Laramie. Two traders, Seth Ward and William Guerrier, kept a post here. Guerrier was killed in 1856, when a keg of powder in his wagon exploded. Ward became post sutler at Fort Laramie in 1857. Near the cliff, Jules E. Coffey operated a stage station in the 1850's; for many years a remnant of the station chimney marked the site. At the cliff's summit was an Indian burial ground.

At 41.9 *m.* is the junction with a dirt road.

Right on this road, which parallels the North Platte, past the RUINS OF A COPPER SMELTER, 1.1 *m.*, to the SITE OF FAIRBANKS, 1.3 *m.*, a busy smelter town in the 1880's. Wagon trains drawn by mules brought coke here from the railroad at Cheyenne, 110 miles away, and took metal back. All supplies had to be ferried across the river. Despite such difficulties, more than $200,000 worth of copper was smelted at Fairbanks. The place, now called Kelly's Park, is a rendezvous for fishermen and picknickers. A cabin, built early in the 1880's, still stands in the park.

US 26 crosses the NORTH PLATTE RIVER, 42 *m.*
At 42.2 *m.* is the junction with a dirt road.

Left on this road along an old streambed to WARM SPRING, 2.4 *m.*, which was known as the Emigrant's Laundry Tub, because many did their washing here. The spring has an abundant flow of water, registering 70° F. the year around. It is mentioned in many diaries kept on the Oregon Trail; the journal of the Brigham Young train described it as having 'sufficient quantity to turn a millwheel.' Lieutenant John C. Frémont camped here in 1842. For many years the spring has been a watering place for stock. A limekiln is near; the lime was probably used in purifying water.

At 42.3 *m.* is the junction with the Guernsey Lake Road (*see Tour 4B*).

At 43 *m.* is the junction with a dirt road.

Right on this road to COLD SPRING, 0.5 *m.,* an early landmark. Rifle pits on the hill above Cold Spring were probably dug for protection against Indians.

US 26 climbs to a plateau marked irregularly with weather-beaten farm buildings and doggedly spinning windmills. It runs westward toward Laramie Peak, which rises darkly against the horizon, then curves through chalk hills topped with cedars. In late summer and autumn, sunflowers line the road. The hills (L) look scalloped; deep gullies are cut at a steep slant from the almost level plateau that stretches away beyond their tops. In some places the eroded sandstone resembles gigantic mushrooms, old castles, and ships. For a short distance the road parallels a deep arroyo (R), then it emerges in hay fields.

At 54.3 *m.* US 26 branches.

Left here 1.1 *m.* to a junction with US 87 (*see Tour 3d*).

The main route of US 26 continues westward, bordered by masses of color in autumn, when purple asters mingle with yellow gumweed and rabbit brush. At 55.7 *m.* is the southern junction with US 87 (*see Tour 3d*).

Tour 4A

Fort Laramie—Fort Laramie National Monument; 3.1 *m.,* Fort Road.

Unsurfaced roadbed.

It is a rare document dealing with Western travel in the early days that does not mention Fort Laramie. Thousands upon thousands of emigrants paused here to rest themselves and their footsore stock, to buy supplies, or to wait for others to catch up with them on their way to Utah, Idaho, Oregon, or California. Forty-niners hurried through, with gold-fevered eyes fixed on the horizon. Pony Express riders stopped in a swirl of dust, exchanged horses, and were off again; telegraph operators relayed messages of triumph or tragedy; and stagecoaches, drawn by frothing horses in jangling harness, swayed through the fort entrance with mail and passengers. Soldiers outfitted here for dangerous trips into the wilderness, or returned, wounded and weary, to seek medical aid and relief from the effects of blinding blizzards or blistering sun and wind. Oxen plodded up to the fort, drawing wagons loaded with supplies or ammunition, or raced from its shadows in early morning to get the road first. The ring of hammers on anvils, where shoes for many hoofs were being made, mingled with bugle notes.

Hunting parties outfitted here; the most spectacular was that of Sir George Gore, Irish peer, who used 6 wagons, 21 carts, 12 yoke of cattle, 112 horses, 14 dogs, and 40 servants. In 1835 the missionaries Parker and Whitman, and in 1836 Whitman and Spalding and their wives rested at Fort Laramie. Frémont's exploring expedition stopped here in 1842; Brigham Young and his followers, in 1847. Gamblers, traders, prospectors, homeseekers; cowpunchers who brought in the first herds of cattle; everyone who trekked across the Plains knew Fort Laramie.

Fort Road branches south from US 26 (*see Tour* 4) at the town of FORT LARAMIE, 0 *m.*, and crosses a narrow three-span bridge over the NORTH PLATTE RIVER, 0.9 *m.* Local patriots insist that the bridge (1876) is the oldest now in use west of the Missouri. The iron for it was freighted to the crossing from Camp Carlin in 1875.

At 1.6 *m.* is the junction with a dirt road.

Right on this road to the junction with another dirt road, 0.7 *m.*, R. here 0.3 *m.* up a steep grade and down into a canyon to the GRAVE OF MARY HOMSLEY. In the spring of 1852 Benjamin Homsley, a young blacksmith, with his wife Mary and two daughters, started for Oregon. When, on June 10, Mrs. Homsley died of measles, her husband buried her body on this bleak hillside and, to mark the place, carved her name on a piece of sandstone. Then 'the oxen surged heavily against their yokes, the wheels complained, the ragged dusty canvas tops lurched as the wagons swayed in the ruts, and walking beside his oxen with bowed head, was the man who had lost heart for the trail . . .' Mary Homsley, one of many women who died on the westward trails, has come to represent them all; and on Memorial Day, 1926, citizens of Wyoming erected a monument above her grave.

The road runs through sagebrush past the Fort Laramie village cemetery (L), 1.9 *m.* At the top of a hill overlooking the fort are the RUINS OF THE POST HOSPITAL. Near a 14-foot concrete Oregon Trail marker, at 3.1 *m.*, is the entrance to FORT LARAMIE NATIONAL MONUMENT. Fort Laramie lies on a level tract within a large bend of the Laramie River, which flows by on the south and east, forming a deep V at this point. The river is named for a French-Canadian trapper, Jacques La Ramée, killed by Indians about 1820. Along the pebbled streambanks are clumps of trees and bushes, and beyond rise bare and dun-colored hills. More than a dozen buildings are set around the spacious parade ground; some are well preserved; others are somewhat decayed, with badly cracked plaster and boarded-up windows. Most are built of local materials: lumber, stone, adobe, and grout (mortar), for which the limestone was quarried and prepared by the troops themselves. One or two buildings, adorned with porches and dormer windows, resemble ordinary gabled cottages; the majority are little more than sheds, with simple slant roofs and bare walls. Four-strand barbed-wire fences surround the site; slatted wooden gates sag between heavy gateposts, braced with two-by-four scantlings against the pull of the wire.

Robert Campbell and William L. Sublette founded a trading post at this point in 1834 and called it Fort William. In 1835 they sold out to a syndicate of trappers, who shortly afterward sold to the American Fur Company. A post called Fort Platte is believed to have been built by rival trappers in 1841, about a mile and a half from Fort William and nearer the confluence of the Laramie and Platte Rivers. The owners of Fort William then enlarged the original fort and furnished it with bastions, blockhouses, and loopholes. The rebuilt structure was named Fort John for John B. Sarpy, an officer of the company.

For a time, the names Fort William and Fort John were used interchangeably for the post; then, it is said, a shipping clerk by mistake marked a box 'Fort Laramie' instead of 'Fort John on the Laramie.' Robert Campbell, who owned a supply house in St. Louis, thought the new name a good one and adopted it immediately.

When the Government, on Frémont's recommendation, bought and garrisoned Fort Laramie in 1849, it was already known as a major stopping place on the great Western trails and as the center of a mountain and plains region, hundreds of miles in extent.

In the early years, bison roamed so near the fort and in herds so large that, according to one tale, an officer one day fired a 6-pounder among them and killed 30 at one shot.

Both before and during the migration period, the fort was a rendezvous of Indians. Squaws lazed in the shade of its walls, while their almost-naked children galloped about, shooting blackbirds with arrows. The slope back of the fort quite commonly swarmed with Ogallala, whose horses and dogs wandered at will. Sometimes more than 100 lodges were outlined along a hillside. Often the young men came into the fort with their families and danced, chanted, and beat their skin drums. Green, vermilion, gray, or blue paints, wolfskins, and scarlet feathers added barbaric color to the scene. Some squaws wore dresses of white antelope skin, heavily beaded; others wore buffalo robes or blankets.

When the Indians, in their last stand against white invasion, pillaged emigrant trains, drove off stock, and killed ranchmen, the occupants of Fort Laramie were constantly alert for attack. Although 1862–5 were the worst years on the Plains as a whole, the period of greatest danger here was 1867–77, when men were pushing into the forbidden Sioux country (*see Tours* 1 *and* 3). Among the important treaties signed at, or near, the fort was the treaty of 1851, which was regarded as the cause of hostilities that terrorized the northern plains for a score of years. A peace commission, created by Congress in 1867, negotiated a year later the Sioux treaty, by which the country north of the North Platte River and east of the summit of the Big Horn Range was held to be Indian territory.

Soldiers were stationed at Fort Laramie until 1890, when the Government sold it. The State later obtained title to the property and, in 1938, transferred it to the National Park Service.

Among the stories associated with Fort Laramie is that of Ah-ho-appa, or Falling Leaf, daughter of Spotted Tail. Ah-ho-appa, quiet and aloof, often sat on a bench by the sutler's store, watching the activities around her. Major Wood, post commander, saw to it that the officer of the day wore a red silk sash and a plumed hat, when she was watching the parade ground. Ah-ho-appa particularly liked guard mount; it was said she was in love with a white soldier. Hoping to make her forget the soldier, Spotted Tail moved his tribe to the Powder River. There, Ah-ho-appa died of tuberculosis, in the autumn of 1866. Her body was brought to Fort Laramie, as she had requested, and given platform burial according to tribal custom, but with military honors. Some years later Spotted Tail removed it to the cemetery at the Rosebud Agency in South Dakota.

In the early days, the Sioux maintained a tree burial ground beyond the Laramie River east of the fort. The papoose tree, a big box elder, having a spread of 75 feet, contained at least 40 bodies of children, wrapped in buffalo skins and lashed to the branches. As the thongs rotted, the bundles fell to the ground, and buzzards and coyotes tore them open. Bones and trinkets were scattered widely under the tree.

OLD BEDLAM, the officers' club, was built in 1851 of lumber hauled by ox team from Fort Leavenworth, Kansas. This two-story structure, with porches across the front on both floors, cost $70,000, an extravagant sum at that period. In the center of a row of officers' quarters, Old Bedlam faced across the parade ground towards the river.

The ENLISTED MEN'S BARRACKS, N. of the trail marker, the largest building, is 300 feet long and has walls of lime grout more than 20 inches thick. A dance hall (124 x 34 feet) on the second floor was a place of relaxation for soldiers and cowpunchers. The building is now used by the National Park Service.

The stone GUARDHOUSE, S. of the marker, built between 1849 and 1859, has a double-barred window and a dungeon. Just north of it was the parade ground.

The SUTLER'S STORE, SW. of the marker, built of adobe in the 1830's, is probably the oldest building now standing in Wyoming. Jim Bridger once lived in it, and here, in 1868, Red Cloud signed the Sioux treaty. The store was not merely a general supply house; it was also the chief banking institution for outlying posts. Through the hands of the sutler and his clerks passed promissory notes, checks, and deposits of credit, from places as far away as Utah and Ireland.

Tour 4B

Junction with US 26—Dead Man's Gulch; 5.6 *m.*, Guernsey Lake Drive.

Dirt road, graveled in part.

With the building of Guernsey Dam and the formation of a great reservoir behind it, the naturally beautiful area around the little town of Guernsey was given the one element it lacked—a body of still water to lie among its forested hills and bluffs. Several shelter houses and picnic areas have been established at points from which may be seen, to greatest advantage, Laramie Peak in the distance or Lake Guernsey and the rocky ravines below. Romantic legend attaches particularly to Dead Man's Gulch and Slade Canyon, once supposedly the rendezvous of dangerous Jack Slade.

Guernsey Lake Drive branches north from its junction with US 26, 0 *m.*, 0.9 mile west of Guernsey (*see Tour* 4), and crosses in pine-clad hills a boundary of GUERNSEY PARK (*camp and picnic grounds; swimming, boating, fishing, hiking*).

At 1.2 *m.* the drive forks.

Left on graveled Skyline Drive along the west shore of Guernsey Lake (R). In their season, bluebells, daisies, asters, and sunflowers are scattered here among sagebrush and rabbit brush. The road winds upward between steep hills to NEWELL BAY, 2 *m.* At 2.3 *m.* is a side road; R. here 1.4 *m.* to BRIMMER POINT LOOKOUT TOWER, on the edge of a sheer cliff. Stone steps lead up from a parking space beneath the tower, which has rock walls and seats, but no top. The lake spreads out below, with plains and mountains in the background. Brimmer Point is named for George Brimmer, a Cheyenne resident whose influence helped make the area a park.

At 2.5 *m.* on Skyline Drive is the junction with a foot trail; R. here 300 *yds.* to DAVIS BAY. The pine-bordered road winds up and down hill through small draws.

At 3.7 *m.* is another foot trail from the drive; R. here 200 *yds.* to ECHO CAVE. Calls sent out across the lake from the cave come back with startling clearness.

The area around NORTH BLUFF SHELTER HOUSE, 4.2 *m.*, a sturdy stone structure in pueblo style, is an attractive summer and autumn picnic spot. The spacious first floor of the shelter has a large fireplace, grills, tables, and seats. Stone steps lead to the roof, which affords a wide view, especially impressive at night.

Guernsey Lake Drive follows (R) the base of the foothills to the PARK ADMINISTRATION BUILDING (R), 2 *m.*, and winds downhill to the SPILLWAY (L) and the POWERHOUSE (R), 2.1 *m.* It crosses GUERNSEY DAM, which was completed in 1928 by the Reclamation Service, and parallels the edge of GUERNSEY LAKE, a reservoir created to regulate the Platte River, to provide water for irrigation, and to produce power for the North Platte Valley. The stone gate in the north spillway, 50 feet square, is one of the largest of its type, and the two drum gates are unusual in dam design. The lake, which covers an area of 2,336 acres, is hedged in for the most part by high bluffs, covered with cedar and pine. Since the development of recreational possibilities began in 1933, a large-scale water carnival is held each summer, usually in August. One of the features of the 1936 program was a re-enactment of the battle between the *Monitor* and the *Merrimac.*

At *2.2 m.* on the drive is the junction with a graveled road.

Right on this road to a CCC CAMP, 0.2 *m.*, and GUERNSEY LAKE MUSEUM (*open by arrangement*), 0.3 *m.* Along the stone steps, leading (R) up the mountain side to the museum entrance, grow cactus, seedling pine, and wild geranium. The large metal arrow in the floor at the entrance points out over Lake Guernsey to Laramie Peak, 35 miles away. Sturdily built of local yellow sandstone, with tapering walls, the museum is massive in appearance. It contains two rectangular exhibition halls, set at right angles, and a library with a large stone fireplace. The museum director plans to portray, through exhibits, the whole story of the Guernsey area, from the days of its prehistoric quarries to the present. Maps, charts, and models and carefully selected photographs, specimens, and relics will be used.

From the SPOTTED TAIL PICNIC AREA, 3 *m.*, one foot trail leads to a high bluff (R); another, 50 yards to the left, to a motorboat wharf. At *3.4 m.* on the Drive is the RED CLOUD PICNIC AREA (*shelter, good water, conveniences*). The shelter, equipped with massive fireplace and stone benches, permits an exceptional view from three sides.

The road winds along shelves for a distance (*drive slowly*), then climbs steeply. Geological formations are well exposed here. Boulder-strewn FISH CANYON (R) is at *4.6 m.* Veering around an arm of the lake, the road reaches DEAD MAN'S GULCH, *5.6 m.*, and the junction with a rough trail.

Left on this trail through SLADE (SAWMILL) CANYON, in which are the SLADE CHIMNEYS, 9 *m.* The origin of the chimneys is unknown; some believe they were built by Spanish explorers. There is a persistent story that Joseph A. (Jack) Slade, for a time superintendent of the Overland Stage Line between Julesburg and Salt Lake City, was the leader of a gang in this vicinity. Slade and his men are said to have stolen stock from emigrant trains, in many instances selling it back to the owners. Men who knew Slade well say he was killed in Montana so soon after his dismissal from the stage line that it is quite unlikely he could have carried on such operations. Diligent search has not revealed the caches of gold and jewelry, plunder of bandits' raids, supposed to be hidden in the canyon.

At the time that Slade was made superintendent at the Julesburg Stage Station on the South Platte (near the site of Julesburg, Colorado), he displaced Jules Reni, a French Canadian. Reni became his bitterest enemy, and quarrels between the two were frequent. One day, Reni fired 13 buckshot into Slade, intending to kill him. Slade, though severely injured, survived and, from then on, went about threatening that he would wear one of Reni's ears as a watch charm. Sometime later, Slade received word that Reni was coming along the stage route with a gang, prepared to kill him. Slade went at once to consult the officers at Fort Laramie, who assured him that, under the circumstances, it was his right to shoot Reni on sight. He then ordered his men to capture Reni. The story goes that the man was held, securely tied, at Chausau's Ranch near Cold Spring until Slade arrived; then his captors stood him up against the wall of a corral. There Slade fired at him repeatedly, announcing before each shot exactly where it was going to hit Reni; he never missed. Between shots he invited the onlookers to drink. After Reni was dead, Slade cut off his ears and put them in his vest pocket. In spite of Slade's report to the authorities and his prompt exoneration for the killing, the story was so often reaffirmed with embellishments and again denied, there is no way of knowing the truth. After Slade left Julesburg, his violence when drunk encouraged popular acceptance of the legend of his cruelty. In 1864 he was hanged by vigilantes in Virginia City, Montana, not for any of his more vicious misdeeds, but for riding his horse into the general store.

Tour 5

South entrance of Yellowstone Park—Junction with US 187—Dubois—Lander—Rawlins—Laramie—(Fort Collins, Colo.); US 287. South entrance of Yellowstone Park to Colorado Line, 444.4 *m.*

Graded dirt, oil- and gravel-surfaced roadbed; snow blocks highway in winter between Yellowstone Park and Dubois.
Accommodations of all kinds; improved camp sites near springs and streams in forests, with long drives between.

US 287 runs diagonally across the State, a direct route between Yellowstone National Park and Denver. From timbered mountain slopes, it descends southeastward to rich, irrigated valleys, passing the Teton and Washakie National Forests and the Shoshone Indian Reservation on its way. Emerging through rounded hills to the desolation of the Great Divide Basin, it unites for 118 miles with the Lincoln Highway (US 30), then swings southward across the Laramie Plains and climbs pine-tipped foothills to the Colorado Line.

Section a. YELLOWSTONE PARK to JUNCTION WITH STATE
287; 140.7 m. US 287-89.

This section of Wyoming is characterized by the boldness and grandeur of its natural features. Between Yellowstone Park and the junction with US 187, the highway winds through dense forest. At the foot of the epic Teton uplift, it veers southeast across a landscape that seems to be set on edge, then descends eastward in long sweeps, the State's loftiest peaks always in sight.

South from SNAKE RIVER STATION, 0 *m.*, the southern ·entrance of Yellowstone Park, US 287 runs through the TETON NATIONAL FOREST. Lupine, blue aster, scarlet fireweed, paintbrush, and goldenrod grow on the hills and along winding roads; even when the slopes are rich with autumnal red and yellow, the wild flowers continue to bloom.

At 2.7 *m.* is a primitive CAMPGROUND (R). Near a small stream, 5.3 *m.*, is a PICNIC GROUND (R), with tables and rustic seats; broad low willows and richly colored flowers make it an attractive stopping place. The highway, at 6.1 *m.*, commands a full view of the jutting peaks of the TETON RANGE (*see Tour 7a*). An excellently constructed BEAVER DAM is L., 6.4 *m.*

JACKSON LAKE, with the Tetons rising in the background above dark pines, appears at 9.9 *m.* Silvery trunks of large aspens show among the evergreens (L); lower down grow long-stemmed daisies, Indian paintbrushes, dwarf willows, and huckleberries. In autumn red and brown leaves are conspicuous in the undergrowth, and reddish needles tip the pine twigs. Narrowing as it skirts the lake, the highway runs through forests, whose floors are bright with sunflowers, purple asters, and wild strawberries; across small parks; and down timbered avenues to open country, edged with patches of sage, yarrow, and asters. Jackson Lake gleams silvery through a fringe of trees (R). A primitive campground and cabin camp are near the lake.

At 22.5 *m.* is a junction with a graded road.

Left on this road to JACKSON LAKE LODGE, 0.1 *m.*

Meadows of timothy, redtop, and other tall grasses, spotted with scrub willows, line the highway. The Teton Range (R) lifts its magnificent 'three breasts,' under the blue veil of height and distance.

At 22.7 *m.* is the junction with US 187-89 (*see Tours 7 and 13*).

The timbered Continental Divide, which comes down in a southeasterly direction from Yellowstone Park, arches here toward the west to form a three-way watershed. Streams from these mountains eventually join the Columbia, Colorado, and Missouri Rivers.

PACIFIC CREEK, 26.5 *m.*, heads near the summit of the range and flows westward to join the Columbia. Atlantic Creek, which joins the Missouri system, heads in the same swamp at Two Oceans Pass, about 25 miles northeast.

Left from the Pacific Creek crossing on a graveled road to EMMA MATILDA and TWO OCEAN LAKES (*camp sites*), 3 *m.*, sister lakes of glacial origin. Emma Matilda Lake was named for his wife by William O. (Uncle Billy) Owen, who made the first public survey in the Jackson Hole area (*see Grand Teton National Park*). Two Ocean Lake, whose waters actually reach only one ocean, is drained by a branch of Pacific Creek.

From BUFFALO FORK, 41.2 *m.*, foot and bridle trails parallel Pacific Creek northward to natural parks, where cow elk and their young feed in summer, and where black bears eat the serviceberries and chokecherries that grow along mountain streams. Moose graze in swamps created by beaver dams. In the higher and more rugged country, mountain sheep browse the sparse vegetation, and grizzlies prowl among stones and rotten logs.

US 287 climbs into denser timber. Balsam and spruce show silver-blue through matchstick forest of lodgepole pine. At evening, mule deer start from open glades, where Indian paintbrush, rose of Sharon, aster, and goldenrod bloom between clumps of wheatgrass and sage. These glades once held the summer camps of the Sheep-eaters (*see Yellowstone National Park*).

At TOG-WO-TEE PASS (9,658 alt.), 60.6 *m.*, the highway becomes a narrow, winding avenue between dense pine and spruce. A Shoshone word, Tog-Wo-Tee has been translated 'Goes [or sees] from this place,' and also, 'Shoots with a spear [arrow, gun].' Captain William A. Jones of the Engineering Corps, U.S.A., reported that he named the pass in 1873 for Lance Striker, a Shoshone guide.

East of the pass, GANNETT PEAK (13,785 alt.), highest in Wyoming, shows blue in the distance (R).

At 67.7 *m.* is the junction with a graveled road.

Left on this road to large DIAMOND G RANCH, 3 *m.*, on the south shore of small BROOKS LAKE (9,060 alt.), which drains into a tributary of the Wind River. Tall pines cluster within a few feet of the water; their reflections on the still surface create an illusion of depth. Holcomb Terrace, a jutting ragged cliff several miles long, breaks the sky line to the north. In early spring, great masses of snow, softened by sun and wind, slip from this ledge and hurl rocks, trees, and shale into the valley. The booming of the avalanche, flung back and forth between mountain walls, resembles heavy cannonading.

Stockmen hold annual picnics in the Brooks Lake area, with barbecued beef, coffee, long speeches, range songs, and 'tall ones' of pioneer days.

The highway skirts the base of the rugged and inaccessible Wind River Range (R), a 100-mile uplift, holding ice fields 18 miles long, unbroken except where crags protrude. Gannett and Dinwoody glaciers, eight miles square and 500 feet deep, spread fanwise to fill a gigantic white amphitheater on the north shoulder of Gannett Peak. Beside them on the south is the Bull Lake ice field, hardest to reach of the Wind River glaciers. No highway penetrates any part of the glacial region, and the range is crossed by only eight known trails, steep and precipitous, made by migrating wapiti and mountain sheep.

John Colter swung down the Stinking Water (Shoshone River) to the northern tip of the range in 1807, in search of trapping areas. Those who followed found a bonanza in the lower streams. Lieutenant John D. Frémont penetrated the region of the peaks and ice fields in 1842, under Kit Carson's guidance, and climbed what he thought was the highest peak, where he jammed a ramrod into a crevice and unfurled the American flag. He returned to the Green River Valley to tell of his experience—and only when Henry Gannett, associate of Ferdinand Hayden, found the mountain that was later named for him, did Frémont learn that he had missed the highest peak by less than ten miles.

WIND RIVER, 81.8 *m.*, supplies water for mammoth irrigation and power projects. A northwester blows down on the region from the mountains. Some early authorities say that Indians called the river Washakeek (water shooting and dropping).

At 83.1 *m.* is the junction with a dirt road.

Right on this road to DU NOIR, 7 *m.* (8,300 alt., 350 pop.), headquarters of a tie-cutting firm that operates along Warm Springs Creek, a stream that does not freeze in winter. Three hundred or more tie hacks cut and trim ties in winter and pile or crate them along the stream banks. The drive to Riverton takes place in late spring.

At 86.1 *m.* is the junction with a foot trail.

Right on this trail, up Warm Springs Creek, to an old GEYSER, 0.5 *m.*, on a rolling sagebrush bench. The water, often used for bathing, bubbles into a large natural basin; once boiling hot, it is now only comfortably warm. Warm Springs Creek cuts a canyon through a gray cliff and passes under a natural bridge (R), visible from US 287.

Along Wind River, green slopes sweep upward to conical peaks (R). The pine-covered lower mountains and parks open into a vast ranching and recreational area (L). Forage is good here, but winter winds sometimes pile snow deeply over the lower pastures. The region was used by rustlers, who harried western Wyoming during the 1890's (*see Tour 3a and 3b*).

DUBOIS, 93.1 *m.* (6,917 alt., 177 pop.), is a community of frame and log houses on the bank of Horse Creek. Charlie Smith built a log-cabin post office here in 1886, and a carrier on snowshoes brought mail from Fort Washakie for Smith to distribute to settlers in the area. When postal authorities asked a name for the little post office, William L. Simpson, a resident of the Lander Valley, suggested Dubois, the name of a family he had known in Colorado. Later Dubois became a hunter's base (*guides*). Elk, moose, deer, and bear are killed within a short distance from the place, and the largest mountain sheep-hunting area in the State is near it on the north. The Dubois Rodeo, usually held the first week in August, is one of the larger amateur rodeos in Wyoming. The ARCHAEOLOGICAL FIELD LABORATORY, in the Dubois Public School, is used by scientists engaged in research in the adjacent Dinwoody area.

The Wind River Basin widens to broad sage flats and hills. Ranch buildings cling to the slanting lower meadows; grassy cattle lands give way to scrubby sheep range on the high slopes.

At 97.1 *m.* is the junction with a dirt road.

Right on this road, which parallels Jakey's Fork of the Wind River, to another dirt road, 0.5 *m.*; L. here 6 *m.* to deep, oblong TORREY LAKE, near a border of the Washakie National Forest. Here, rustic log buildings shoulder each other among the pines. At the top of a divide (R) is a layer of soapstone, from which Indians made pipes and pottery; fragments have been found here marked and chipped, indicating that they were tested for softness. Bits of old dishes are scattered about. In the vicinity are remnants of Indian corrals, apparently used for trapping game.

At 3 *m.* on the main dirt road is a STATE FISH HATCHERY (*open to the public*), one of the largest in Wyoming.

US 287 curves through short, shallow canyons, where deep-red rocks outcrop from the pine-fringed foothills of the Wind River Range.

At 104.7 *m.* is the junction with a dirt road.

> Right on this road to the BLUE HOLES, 0.5 *m.* and 1 *m.*, extinct geysers. Although depth gives the pools an azure hue, the water is so clear that large fish are visible far down the craters. On rugged ledges near by are pictographs. Above the upper hole is a series of CASCADES, 1.3 *m.*, where cool mineral water has formed pools in pockets of the geyser crustation. Falling from pool to pool over the terraces, it has created a fairyland of reefs, grottoes, and tiny pinnacles. Below the cascades, it disappears into a subterranean passage, emerging at the base of the ledge as a deep clear spring.

Below towering cliffs called the RED WALLS, 106.7 *m.*, the Wind River swirls around a bend. The roadbed is cut from the cliff face. The canyon widens. Beside the shaded river is a PUBLIC CAMPGROUND, 106.8 *m.*, on a grassy flat (L) dotted with aspen and cottonwood. Deep-green pines cling in scattered groups to the dull-red scarps. Slanting light on the cliffs and bluish-green water accentuates the color tones.

At 111.7 *m.* is the junction with a dirt road.

> Right on this road up Dinwoody Creek, around low hills to DINWOODY LAKES AND CAVES, 7 *m.*, in a region of stunted sage and cedar. Long, low cliffs border the three lakes, which are connected by Dinwoody Creek. Caves in their bases are nearly filled with blown dust and debris. A research project under the WPA, which began work here in 1938, has uncovered broken arrow and lance shafts, stone awls, arrowheads, bone needles, pottery, and other artifacts, in layers representing, archeologists believe, distinct culture levels. Unexplored small caves, high in the canyon, are believed to be entrances to large caverns.
> On sheer walls at the upper end of the second lake, figures and inscriptions have been chiseled, often 20 feet above any projection on which a person might stand. The figures include representations of owls, turtles, and men. One depicts a brawny man chastising a woman who lies across his knee. Another is a maiden sitting cross-legged before a snake with lifted head.

Ranches in the lower Wind River Basin are owned by Shoshone Indians. Some fields are cultivated; on others, ponies graze. Shoshone ranchers jolt along the highway in ancient motorcars or in wagons drawn by ponies. Squaws and papooses sit on the floors of the wagon boxes, the men high and immobile on the spring seats.

CROWHEART, 128 *m.* (5,700 alt., 20 pop.), is a post office near CROWHEART BUTTE (ahead L), site of a battle in 1857 between Shoshone warriors and Arapaho, Gros Ventre, and Cheyenne, who despised the Shoshone for having made peace with the white invaders. Legend says that the Shoshone chief once fought a duel on Crowheart Butte with a Crow chieftain; that he killed the Crow, cut out his heart, and ate it to augment his courage. Washakie did kill a Crow chief in personal combat; there is no evidence, however, that he ate his enemy's heart.

At 138.7 *m.* is the junction with a dirt road.

> Right on this road to BULL LAKE, 3 *m.*, which was known to the Shoshone as The Lake That Roars. Legend tells that a white buffalo bull was

once chased into it by hunters who wanted his white robe. The bull drowned; in winter, when the wind catches under the ice, lifts it slightly, and lets it drop with a grumbling moan, the Indians say the white buffalo's spirit roars in anger.

Bull Lake and Bull Lake Creek supply part of the water used by the Riverton Reclamation Project (*see Tour 12*). In 1938, a dam was built at the outlet, to enlarge the lake's storage capacity to 150,000 acre feet. The earth embankment is 3,400 feet long and 75 feet high; 500 feet wide at its base, it tapers to a 30-foot roadway along the top. The water is released through two concrete barrels 8 feet in diameter, controlled by four high-pressure gates. A spillway, capable of handling 10,000 second-feet of water, has automatic radial gates.

Winter ling fishing, through holes cut in the ice, is a favorite sport at Bull Lake. Ling, a variety of whitefish, is not classed as game fish in Wyoming. It sometimes reaches a length of 4 feet and a weight of 20 pounds. Most anglers adjudge the flesh equal in quality to that of trout.

At 140.7 *m.* is the junction with State 287 (*see Tour 12*).

Section b. JUNCTION WITH STATE 287 to LANDER; 32 m. US 287.

This section of US 287 crosses Wyoming's only Indian reserve. Merely a fragment of the extensive region set aside for the Shoshone in 1868, the roughly triangular reservation comprises 524,960 acres. The northern part, along Wind River, is a series of rolling sage flats cleft by occasional streams. Beside the creeks are little green farms and ranches. On the west, sage-covered grazing land rolls away toward the Wind River foothills. The fertile Little Wind Valley in the south and east is cultivated intensively.

Crossing the northern boundary of the reservation at the junction with State 287, 0 *m.*, US 287 traverses boulder-strewn sagebrush mesas and bleak hills. An occasional canvas-topped sheep wagon breaks the bare line of the horizon.

Along SAGE CREEK, 8.9 *m.*, log cabins and frame shacks of various designs stand half-hidden among willows. Beside each cabin is a large white tent, successor to the skin tepee, which passed out of existence with the buffalo. The family often lives in the tent, using the cabin as a storehouse. Some families live in their cabins in winter but move into the tents as soon as weather permits. Around the cabins are some shelters of upright poles and brush roofs, where the Indian likes to loll in hot weather.

FORT WASHAKIE (*pack trips into Wind River Range*), 16.1 *m.* (5,502 alt., 1,780 pop.), reservation headquarters, has a businesslike air unknown to earlier agencies. The autumn trip for supplies was once a matter of ceremony, a substitute for the fall hunt. Heavy wagons loaded with families and paraphernalia rumbled over the sagebrush flats. Tepees formed a huge circle around the agency for days or weeks, as the tribesmen visited and traded. Modern Fort Washakie is a country village, rather than a trading post. Indians wearing somber black hats come singly in motorcars or wagons, and remain only long enough to transact their business.

In the middle 1800's, when a tidal wave of white immigration pushed Indian tribes westward, Chief Washakie of the Shoshone asked for the valley of Henry's Fork of Green River, 40 miles southeast of Fort Bridger, as a reserve. After the Shoshonean uprising of 1861–2, the Government, busy with the Civil War and eager for peace in the West, set aside almost the entire Rocky Mountain and Great Plains regions for various tribes. The Shoshone were granted an area between the Wind River and Uinta Mountains, extending eastward to the Platte. No western boundary was set, and such boundaries as existed were not respected; both white men and Indians freely invaded Washakie's domain. Finally, he requested a more definite reserve where his small tribe might live safely.

The Government, wishing to reward the aging chieftain for his friendship, let him select, in 1868, an area that included the Popo Agie Valley (pronounced 'popo'sia'), regarded as a prize by Indians and white men alike. This he agreed to share with the Bannock, the firebrand among Shoshonean tribes. The Bannock apparently possessed unusual recuperative capacity. Jim Beckwourth reported them annihilated by enraged trappers in 1826; Joseph L. Meek made a similar report in 1836; in 1863 General P. E. Connor killed 250 of them at Bear River in Idaho. Agents recommended that the remnants of the tribe be quartered where Washakie might 'keep a thumb on them.' The area allotted the two tribes was nearly as large as Connecticut. The Sioux, Cheyenne, and Arapaho, however, were free to go as they chose; and, in the spring of 1869, Red Cloud's last raiding party killed 30 Shoshone warriors and stole a large band of horses. Washakie refused to settle down without military protection, and he divided his time between Fort Bridger and Salt Lake Valley until the autumn of 1872, when he was summoned to Fort Stambaugh (*see Tour 5A*) and informed that the Bannock were to be transferred to Idaho—that the whites wanted the Popo Agie Valley.

Washakie knew that the valley was too rich a prize to be held long by the Indian. Already the agency and military post had been removed from it. He decided to bargain for as much as he could get and to relinquish gracefully what would be taken from him anyway. For 601,120 acres of fertile valley land, he accepted $25,000 (in reservation improvements and goods) and the promise of protection. This time the Government kept its promise. Fifteen log and adobe buildings, including hospital, telegraph office, and storehouses, were erected at Fort Brown, near the confluence of the Little Wind River with the North Fork of the Wind. The handful of soldiers at old Camp Brown was re-enforced; a strong Indian police was organized. The Crow and Shoshone united with the bluecoats to conquer the Sioux, Cheyenne, and Arapaho; for this service, the Shoshone received the ironic reward of having to share their reservation with the Arapaho (*see Indians*).

In 1878 Fort Brown was renamed Fort Washakie. Twenty-one years later, feeling that the need for a military post no longer existed, the Government abandoned it. Washakie, more than 100 years old, had visions of painted Sioux descending on the reservation, scalping his warriors, and stealing his horses and women. At his strenuous objections, the order was revoked; Fort Washakie was not abandoned until nine years after Washakie's death (1909).

The modern Shoshone is relatively well off. His automobile varies in age and horsepower with the wealth of his farm and the family's inclination toward work, but he manages to get around in it. Of the 200,000 acres of individually owned Indian land, some 115,000 acres are heirship lands; the rest is largely in the hands of the older people. About 50,000 acres are irrigated. The Government allots Indians 40-, 80-, and 120-acre tracts, but holds title in trust; when owners are unable to farm their allotments, they are permitted to lease or sell under supervision. Some white settlers now occupy such tracts.

When the Shoshone could no longer hunt and fight, they lived at first on the Government pittance. Tilling the soil was a woman's task. Now, farm produce constitutes the major part of their diet. In 1937, members of the reservation's two livestock associations owned 4,000 cattle and 15,000 sheep. Beef, butchered for future use, is jerked (cut in strips and dried) and sometimes pounded into pemmican.

For years the Arapaho had no property of their own and seemed disinclined to work. Emulating the Shoshone, they have, however, learned to take some pride in their surroundings. Physically a fine type, they were always more warlike than the Shoshone. In arts and home life, they were a typical Plains tribe. They have no trace of the clan system, but do have the military organization common to most Plains tribes, with seven ritual societies for men and one for women. They are much given to ceremonial observances. Between 1889 and 1891 they propagated the Ghost Dance, a cult banned by the Government in the latter year. The Arapaho mix less than other tribes with white people, whom they call Tiboes (strangers). They do not intermarry with the Shoshone. The chief means of intertribal communication is the sign language.

Most reservation Indians have adopted white man's clothing, but the blanket is still a favorite garment. Some of the old people—men and women—wear their hair long, braided with yarn or strips of cloth, and smoke stone pipes. Both Shoshone and Arapaho women are skilful tanners. The Arapaho man's holiday garb is usually of buckskin, worked so thin and white it resembles satin. The seams of the tunic are marked with fringes of deer or antelope skin, and all garments are worked with beads in brilliant and intricate designs. Women's ceremonial robes are of buckskin, beaded, fringed, and hung with elk's teeth. Shoshone women paint scenes of the hunt on tanned hides, using native pigments.

The Arapaho, more than the Shoshone, cling to the tent shelter, deserting it only when someone has died in it. They cook and eat outdoors around an open fire or stone fireplace, when weather permits. Young people use modern cookery increasingly. Better housing is planned under Government auspices; a community sawmill is available, and any Indian may cut logs in reservation forests. Despite home nursing, hygiene classes, and a well-equipped hospital, pneumonia, tuberculosis, and trachoma prevail. Many Indians hesitate to accept medical care, because of their faith in medicine men, who claim supernatural ability to recognize and cure diseases.

Of the reservation's 25 supervisors, 15 are Indians. Indian-supervised elections are held, and both tribes turn out to vote. In 1937, for the first time, women voted with the men. Each tribe chose six councilors; the Arapaho elected one woman and five men. Old reservation leaders resigned, when their opposition to Federal farm programs met with ridicule and anger; among the young men who took their places is Charles Washakie, grandson of Chief Washakie. All ablebodied men work on farms or on Federal projects; they build houses, roads, telephone lines, horse trails, stock driveways, and dams; fight forest fires, police game areas, and aid in insect control. Work centers for women at Fort Washakie and Arapaho (*see Tour* 12) bring together mixed and full-blood Shoshone and Arapaho women of all ages, to make clothing and tan hides. Three mission and two Government schools instruct children of Indians and of the white personnel; for Indian students, crafts are emphasized. Although some Indians accepted Christianity and were 'washed' by the Mormons years before missions were established, most of them still respect the old gods.

The outstanding social event is the three-day sun dance (*white spectators admitted; no photographing*). The Shoshone hold theirs near Fort Washakie in late July or early August; the Arapaho, at Ethete. The dance never takes place twice on the same ground. In the old days it was the ultimate in tribal incantation; its object seems to have been to conquer certain cosmic elements and, by strong medicine, compel the thunderbird to release rain. Legend tells that it originated when a warrior wandered forth to find relief for his starving tribe. He met a deity, fasted, and learned a ritual; when it was performed, buffalo came. As years passed, the dance grew in mystic significance; it furnished a vehicle for the expression of emotion in rhythm; it knit the tribe in closer unity by renewing the ranks of the chiefs. Because Indian patriotism mounted to fervor during the ceremony, the white conquerors frowned on it. It was outlawed for a time; when revived, it was Christianized.

Weeks before the dance, the chiefs meet in solemn council to select a site for the sun lodge and to choose braves worthy of cutting the cottonwood medicine pole. Two war parties engage in sham battle for possession of the pole; it is then dried in the sun, beaten, and treated with a potion to drive out evils. A crier calls all tribesmen to help erect the sun lodge. The medicine pole is placed upright in the ground, and 12 shorter uprights are placed in a circle around it. Rafters converge at the top of the medicine pole. There is no roof, but brush is piled against the sides of the lodge for shade. An individual stall, woven of willows, is provided inside for each dancer. The medicine pole, the fetish of the thunderbird, also represents the Shoshonean conception of the white man's God; the outer poles, symbols of the Great Eagle's tailfeathers, may be understood to symbolize the twelve Apostles as well.

From the top of the medicine pole, where once a captured enemy was suspended alive, hang two bunches of red willow (for peace and tranquillity); a buffalo head (appreciation of blessings received); a beaver pelt (industry); a long braid of hair instead of the old-time scalp (sacrifice); and the tailfeathers of an eagle, one of the indispensables of Indian ceremonial. The participants, men only, fast for three days, while the women tempt them with rich foods. They wear little clothing, but their bodies are painted by medicine men; each dancer has a whistle made of the thighbone of an eagle or blue crane, which gives a shrill, piping note like that of a bird in distress. To each whistle, a fluffy white feather is held by a bead necklace. The head medicine man's slender staff bears feathers symbolic of the Great Eagle.

The dancers face the east each· day at sunrise, and, as the rays reach their bodies, the whistles wail, and drums are beaten. The medicine man chants the prayer song, which the sun's rays transmit to the Great Spirit. After an hour spent in repainting their bodies, the dancers form an arc in the sun lodge; they keep their eyes on the sun throughout the dance. At night, a big fire takes the sun's place. The women sit with the drummers outside the lodge, chanting steadily and shaking dry willows to the throbbing of the drums. The half-hypnotized dancers move forward and backward, blowing their whistles. At intervals they touch the medicine pole with their hands or with feathers, to transfer to themselves the healing power the pole takes from the sun. When exhausted, they retreat within their stalls to rest and pray and, perhaps, to see visions. The dance ceases abruptly when the Dog Star rises.

On the fourth morning, medicine men and dancers face the sun and give thanks. The dancers wash the paint from their bodies; then they may eat. The Shoshone, unlike the Arapaho, never eat dog meat; if no other meat is available, they eat vegetables.

Right from Fort Washakie on a foot trail to the old MILITARY CEMETERY, 0.3 *m.*, which contains WASHAKIE's GRAVE. The granite marker bears the dates 1804–1900, but authorities agree the chieftain was born about 1798. Legend says he was an orphan of a Shoshone mother and a Flathead father. His name is probably an adaptation of wau-sik-he (rawhide rattle). Washakie is remembered because he understood the history of his time better than many statesmen. He refused to fight white men on any provocation, and gave his tribe peace in a bloody era. For nearly 60 years, he was despot of the Shoshone; in 1869, when the Government was slow to fulfil treaty obligations, he heard young braves disputing as to what warrior should succeed him as chief. He rode eastward alone, says legend, and returned with seven Sioux scalps; hurling them on the ground before the disputants, he challenged any of them to duplicate his act. During the campaigns of 1875–6, Washakie and his warriors joined General Crook and figured in the battle of the Rosebud and the Dull Knife defeat (*see Tour 3b*). President Grant gave him a silver-mounted saddle, in token of appreciation. The chief was proud of his military record and periodically re-enlisted as a scout. Wise army officials winked at physical requirements and allowed him to continue joining the colors until his death.

In 1897 Washakie was baptized. Though partly paralyzed and blind during the last months of his life, he retained the respect of his warriors. He died February 2, 1900, troubled by the thought that he might go to the white man's heaven and be lost to his own people. He was given military burial, with rites proper to the rank of captain. In 1907, the soldiers buried in the cemetery were exhumed and reburied at Fort Leavenworth, but Washakie's bones were not disturbed.

US 287 passes brown fields. Red bluffs and sharp ridges break the sky line (R and L).

At 17.2 *m.* is the junction with a graveled road.

1. Left on this road to the GOVERNMENT SCHOOL, 0.9 *m.*, which has red pressed-brick and stucco dormitories, workshops, gymnasium, and laboratories. It is open to reservation children—white, Shoshone, and Arapaho. A HOT SPRING (*free; visitors bring own suits*) is L. at 2.2 *m.*

In ETHETE (pronounced Eth-e-tay), 5.7 *m.* (5,500 alt., 100 pop.), is Episcopal ST. MICHAEL'S MISSION for Arapaho children. Facilities include a school and a ranch. The log chapel, which combines ecclesiastical design with sturdy construction, faces west; its door is decorated with native symbols. Inside are rustic seats and unplastered walls, covered with plumes and dressed skins painted with Indian devices. The crucifix, silhouetted against the mountains through the reredos window, dominates the chapel. Each summer the minister in charge arranges separate 12-day pack trips into the Dinwoody wilderness (*see above*) for groups of 60 boys and girls.

2. Right on a dirt road to WIND RIVER, 0.7 *m.* (5,500 alt., 75 pop.), irrigation headquarters. Most of the buildings are old, covered with white clapboards. Along the west side of a circle drive is an old blockhouse, built when the reservation agency was transferred from Fort Brown in 1871. Portholes pierce the thick sandstone and adobe walls. In one corner are two jail cells, the bars rusty but intact. Beneath the floor is an old well, intended to provide a water supply in case of siege. Settlers here dug the first ditches before 1868. When the area was set aside for the Shoshone, the improvements were transferred with the land. After 1933, the Public Works Administration built two reservoirs and several canals. Washakie Reservoir stores 8,000 acre-feet; Ray Lake Reservoir, about 7,000.

The SHOSHONE MISSION BOARDING SCHOOL (1889), 2.2 *m.*, is a large brick structure, surrounded by log buildings. Bricks were made at the site; near-by forests supplied the timber. Here, Indian girls receive formal schooling up to the eighth grade, supplemented with instruction in cooking, sewing, and other household duties. This school was founded by the Reverend John Roberts, a Welshman, who reached the reservation in 1883 to do missionary work for the Episcopal Church among the Shoshone, Arapaho, and the whites. For a time he was in charge of all of the mission work within a radius of 150 miles of Fort Washakie. He established the Government School and lived there four years, before building the Shoshone Mission School. Mr. Roberts retired after 40 years of active service, and the position of warden of the school was assumed by his wife. Mr. Roberts buried the old Shoshone woman, mother of Bazil, said to have been Sacajawea. He also translated parts of the Bible into both the Shoshone and the Arapaho languages. He still (1940) officiates at weddings and

Agriculture: Industry

SHEEP RANGE

WHITEFACES

CUTTING HIGHLAND GRAIN

THRESHING BEANS, BIG HORN BASIN

HARVESTING SUGAR BEETS

BEET DUMP

Photograph by courtesy of Department of Interior

POWER TRANSMISSION LINES CROSSING THE DESERT FROM SEMINOE DAM

DOWNSTREAM FROM ALCOVA DAM

Photograph by courtesy of Department of Interior

POTATO FIELDS, SHOSHONE IRRIGATION PROJECT

RIVERTON PROJECT HOME

Photograph by courtesy of Department of the Interior

SALT CREEK OIL FIELD

OIL REFINERY, CASPER

Photograph by courtesy of Union Pacific Coal Company

MINE TIPPLE, SUPERIOR

OPEN PIT COAL MINE IN THE GILLETTE AREA

Photograph by courtesy of Wyoming Department of Commerce and Industry

Photograph by courtesy of United Air Lines

AIRLINE HANGAR AND OVERHAUL BASE, CHEYENNE

BOX CAR CONSTRUCTION, UNION PACIFIC RAILROAD

Photograph by courtesy of Union Pacific Railroad Company

burials in the families of his early parishioners. He is an authority on the ways and customs of the Indians on the Wind River Reservation.

At 2.3 *m.* is a junction with a dirt road; R. here 0.5 *m.* to WIND RIVER CEMETERY, probable burial place of Sacajawea, the 'Boat Pusher.' Many of the graves are marked with bedsteads, washboards, and other former possessions of the dead. Beside Sacajawea's grave are the grave of her nephew Bazil and a monument to her son Baptiste, who was buried at an unknown spot in the Wind River Mountains. Sacajawea, a Shoshone, was stolen in childhood by Hidatsa raiders and, when grown up, was sold as wife to Jean Baptiste Charbonneau, French-Canadian trapper at the Mandan villages along the Missouri. When Lewis and Clark spent the winter of 1804–5 there and learned that Sacajawea was familiar with the wilderness to the west, they engaged the trapper and his wife as guides and interpreters. Sacajawea carried her infant son Baptiste on her back during the 3,000-mile journey. The party met her kinsmen in the Beaverhead Valley, Montana, and Sacajawea adopted Bazil, orphan of her sister, according to Shoshone custom. From that point her story is not definitely known. It is said that Clark on his return to St. Louis, sent for the family and placed Baptiste (Pomp, the Dancer) and Toussaint, Charbonneau's child by another wife, in school. Baptiste, described by Clark as 'a beautiful and promising boy,' attracted the attention of Prince Paul of Württemberg, who took him to Europe for schooling. Sacajawea eventually left Charbonneau because of personal indignities. In Oklahoma she married a Comanche, who died in battle, leaving her with two babies. She rejoined her people in the 1840's, and died among them in April 1884. Authorities disagree about her name and burial place. She was long known as the Bird Woman, but Boat Pusher (*sac,* boat or raft; *jawe,* launcher) is a better translation. In 1812, John C. Luttig, trader for the Missouri Fur Company, recorded the death in the Dakota country of the 'wife of Charbonneau.' Charbonneau, however, had three wives.

A census record for 1877, discovered recently at Fort Washakie, lists one resident as 'Bazil's Mother.'

US 287 passes farms and cattle lands, and crosses the southern foothills that border Popo Agie Valley on the west.

LANDER, 32 *m.* (5,357 alt., 1,826 pop.), western terminus of the Chicago and Northwestern Railway and commercial center of the Popo Agie Valley, is one of the oldest communities in the State. Main Street windows feature tourists' and hunters' equipment. Tall shade trees and trim flower gardens surround pressed-brick, stucco, and frame buildings. Dudes and residents mingle on the street with Indians who wear blankets, bright dresses, and tall black hats with gay handkerchiefs dangling under the brims. Willow-fringed Popo Agie River meanders through the town, and behind it are blue-black timbered foothills, rising to snow-capped peaks on the west. At the edge of Lander is the Wind River Wilderness, which extends along the eastern slopes of the Wind River Range (*see above*) and contains thousands of lakes and tumbling streams stocked with trout. 'Where the rails end, and the trails begin' is the local slogan. The 75-mile Show Me Trip, guided by the Forest Service, is made each year, usually in August; it lasts five days, and reservations are limited to 50.

The Pioneer Days celebration (July 4) attracts riders and ropers from neighboring ranches, as well as professionals. Indians pitch tepees in a hilltop field at the eastern edge of town and contribute their buffalo dance, wolf dance, war dance, and death dance to the entertainment.

In 1856, after white renegades and Indians massacred a train of emigrants at Mountain Meadows, Utah, trouble flared between the Mormons and the gentile Government. Congress provided for a road branching northward from the established Oregon Trail, to avoid the Mormon country. Surveyors from Fort Kearny, Nebraska, spent the winter of 1857-8 in the Popo Agie Valley, two miles east of present Lander, and built the first house at what they called Camp McGraw. When plans to shift the Great Road of the White Tops (covered wagons) displeased the Shoshone, Colonel W. F. Lander was dispatched from Washington to bargain for the right-of-way, with horses, guns, ammunition, and trinkets. The road, officially the Fort Kearny, South Pass & Honey Lake Route, became known as Lander's Cut-off.

By July 1868, when new boundaries identified the Popo Agie Valley as Indian land, so many settlers had drifted in that Washakie appealed to the Government for redress. He took part of his tribe to Utah (*see above*), where he was the guest of Brigham Young for nearly two years. On June 28, 1869, Camp Augur was established. The settlers used the post sutler's store as a trading center, and a few set up residences. Shoshone unrest grew. Suddenly, the Bannock petitioned for lands in Idaho, thus offering a solution that the Government eagerly grasped. The Bannock were transferred to Idaho in 1872. Since reduction of the Shoshone reservation was then justified, according to the white man's point of view, half a million acres were lopped from the original reserve, and the Popo Agie Valley was opened to settlement.

When Fremont County, then including Park, Big Horn, and Hot Springs Counties, was created in 1884, Lander became county seat and political center of almost one-fourth of Wyoming. Soon afterward, oil and coal were found near the town. In the early 1890's, outlaws from the Hole-in-the-Wall (*see Tour 3b*) often came through, on their way to the Star Valley or Jackson Hole (*see Tours 7 and 13*); coming by way of Thermopolis, they were known as the Thermop Gang. George (Butch Cassidy) Parker frequented Lander, and 'horse ranched' somewhere in the Wind River area; discreet neighbors appeared not to notice that he sold more than he raised. Legend has it that Cassidy once cached $70,000 in the Wind River Mountains, when hard pressed by a posse, and old-timers say he returned to look for the hidden gold in 1936, 27 years after his reported death in South America.

The NOBLE HOTEL, 3rd and Main Sts., has one of the largest collections of Indian relics in the State. The walls are hung with tomahawks, war bonnets, whistles, ceremonial regalia, moccasins, bows and arrows, buffalo robes, and peace pipes. Around the spacious fireplace, old-timers tell stories of Chief Washakie, Butch Cassidy, and other figures they knew in early Lander.

The PIONEER CABIN (*open by arrangement with caretaker*), 6th and Lincoln Sts., houses a collection that includes early photographs, guns, ox yokes, and an old organ.

The SITE OF FORT AUGUR, Main St. near 3rd St., is marked with a block of native granite. The fort occupied a quadrangle 175 feet long and 125 feet wide, surrounded by a ditch. The buildings of unhewn logs, roofed with sod, were 'unsubstantial and comfortless, without floors and destitute of bunks.' Its name was changed to Camp Brown, in honor of Captain F. H. Brown, who died in the Fetterman Fight in 1866 (*see Tour 3a*); in 1871 it was moved to a spot near the confluence of the Little Wind River and the North Fork of the Wind; and in 1878 it was renamed Fort Washakie (*see above*).

Right from Lander on the graveled and dirt Sinks Road, which parallels the Popo Agie River, to a side road, 6 *m.;* L. here 1 *m.* to the UNIVERSITY OF WYOMING EXPERIMENT STATION, where new varieties of apples have been developed.

At the SINKS, 7 *m.*, on the Sinks Road, a fork of the Popo Agie River disappears into the side of a mountain and emerges in a water fall several hundred yards below. Near here, the University of Missouri maintains a summer school for geologists in a group of sturdy cabins.

At the south edge of Lander is the junction with State 320 (*see Tour 12*).

Section c. *LANDER to COLORADO LINE;* 271.7 *m.* US 287-30

Winding down along the northern and eastern edges of the Great Divide and Red Desert Basins, US 287 unites with US 30 between Rawlins and Laramie, then rises rapidly toward the Colorado Rockies.

South of LANDER, 0 *m.*, the rounded hills are patterned with grain fields.

At 9.2 *m.* is the junction with a graded dirt road, the South Pass Mail Road (*see Tour 5A*).

US 287 crosses the LITTLE POPO AGIE, 9.6 *m.*, and climbs to sage flats. DERBY DOME (R), 14.2 *m.*, is a plainly exposed, oil-bearing structure. Scrub cedar and pine dot the cliffs (L).

TWIN CREEK, 13.3 *m.*, runs through sheep country. During spring drizzles, fires sputter and flicker beside sheep wagons and crude brush shelters, erected for the protection of lambs. There is little sign of human habitation; here and there a narrow dirt road runs back into the hills from a homemade mailbox by the highway. US 287 curves along shelves and ridges to level country.

At OREGON TRAIL CROSSING (HUDSONS), 40.4 *m.*, is a filling station (R). The highway crosses SWEETWATER BRIDGE, 40.5 *m.* The river, which here threads its serpentine way through sagebrush and meadowlands, was named by William H. Ashley in 1823, after his trappers told him that the water left a pleasant taste in their mouths. Tradition tells that a pack mule fell, while crossing the stream, and spilled its load of sugar into the water.

At 40.7 *m.* is the junction with the old South Pass Road (*see Tour 5A*).

Veering away from the river across a plateau, US 287 passes occasional cabins and pole corrals. The treeless cattle ranches here are reminiscent of those whose herds covered the range in the early days.

The road edges back toward the fine hay meadows along the river (L). Through this country, many herds of cattle were trailed from Oregon to Wyoming and Nebraska in the 1880's.

At about 58 *m.* US 287 runs near the SITE OF THREE CROSSINGS, a telegraph and stage station (L) of the 1860's. It was to this station in 1860 that Bill Cody, 15-year-old Pony Express carrier, rode from Red Buttes on the Platte, 76 miles away. There he found that the rider of the 85-mile stretch to Rocky Ridge had been killed. Cody thereupon, without resting, rode to Rocky Ridge and returned to Red Buttes, with eastbound mail, on time. This 322-mile ride is the longest on the records of the Pony Express.

SPLIT ROCK (L), 69 *m.*, is a massive, cleft upthrust of igneous material. In this vicinity, Russell, Majors & Waddell erected a stage station in 1859. Deep in the Shoshone country, the station escaped the wrath of the eastern and northern tribes. But, in March 1862, the traditionally friendly Shoshone went on the warpath, striking simultaneously at every station between Platte Bridge and Bear River. Drivers, station attendants, and guards, taken completely by surprise, permitted them to capture every horse and mule belonging to the company in this area; coaches laden with passengers and freight were left standing where encountered. At President Lincoln's request, Brigham Young sent the Mormon Battalion, 300 volunteers under the command of Captain Lot Smith, to quiet the Indians.

The Shoshone killed nobody, except at Split Rock. Here they ordered a Negro, who had lived only among the Pennsylvania Dutch, to prepare a meal. When he did not understand, the Shoshone killed him and helped themselves to the larder.

At 82.2 *m.* is the junction with State 220 (*see Tour 11*).

THREE FORKS, 82.3 *m.* (6,250 alt., 5 pop.), is at the southern point of a triangle formed where the highway divides. (*Store, filling station, cabins.*)

Between the red stone ledges of MUDDY GAP, 83.5 *m.*, flow the murky waters of Muddy Creek. At 85 *m.*, pines grow along the seams of a sandstone slope (L), as though planted in a formal pattern. In summer, masses of wild roses bloom at the base of the slope.

At 85.5 *m.* is the junction with a dirt road.

Left on the road to WHISKEY GAP, 3 *m.* (6,380 alt.), and WHISKEY SPRING. When Ben Holladay shifted his stage route in the summer of 1862 (*see Transportation*), all equipment was assembled at Devil's Gate and moved southward under the protection of a troop of the 11th Ohio Volunteer Cavalry. While encamped in this canyon, some of the soldiers showed signs of intoxication. Officers found a barrel of whisky in one of the civilian wagons, knocked its head in, and poured the liquid on the ground above the spring. Soon soldiers, teamsters, roustabouts, and guides converged on the spring, with cups, canteens, buckets, camp kettles and plates. That night, in his report, the commanding officer thanked heaven, parenthetically, that the Indians did not attack.

The highway curves southward across dry gullies and wastelands to LAMONT, 93.9 *m.* (6,820 alt., 80 pop.), a post office, with store and filling station.

1. Right from Lamont on an oiled road to LOST SOLDIER OIL FIELD and BAIROIL, 4.8 *m.* (6,860 alt., 400 pop.), a company camp of neat white houses, on the outer escarpment of Buffalo Buttes (R). One of a group of soldiers from Fort Fred Steele (*see Tour 2b*) was lost on this salt-sage dome in 1880.

2. Left from Lamont on a dirt road to the MAHONEY DOME, 12 *m.*, and the FERRIS DOME, 14 *m.*, both gas producers.

Barren country stretches southward from Lamont, bordering the Great Divide Basin, an eastward continuation of the Red Desert. Patches of alkali alternate here with clumps of sage and greasewood; occasional jutting red rocks disturb the monotony of gray salt soil and greenish-gray shrubs. Winter winds sweep the snow into deep arroyos and gulches, leaving the sparse plants uncovered for sheep feed. On the far southeastern horizon, barely distinguishable from the cloudy low haze of desert skies, lift the white-tipped Medicine Bow Mountains.

RAWLINS, 128.5 *m.* (6,755 alt., 4,868 pop.) (*see Tour 2b*), is at the junction with US 30, with which US 287 unites between this point and Laramie (*see Tour 2b*).

LARAMIE, 245.6 *m.* (7,165 alt., 8,609 pop.) (*see Laramie*).

At the UNION PACIFIC FOREST PRODUCTS TREATING PLANT (R), 247.2 *m.*, timbers cut in the Medicine Bow National Forest (*see Tour 2B*) and on the headwaters of the Green River (*see Tour 9*) are treated with creosote to prevent decay. Steel cranes deposit great armloads of timbers in the vats of odorous black compound. Later, the treated material is placed in uniform piles, parallel with the railroad (R) and the highway.

At 248.4 *m.* is the junction with a graveled highway.

Left on this highway to the SITE OF FORT SANDERS, 0.2 *m.*, on Soldier Creek. Fort Sanders was established July 19, 1866, as part of the Government's program of military protection for the Overland Trail and the U.P. Railroad. Known first as Fort John Buford, for General John Buford, killed December 16, 1863, it was renamed for Brigadier General William P. Sanders, who died of wounds in November 1863. Log, frame, and stone buildings made up the quarters. The garrison did police work among the rail workers, besides protecting them from Indian attack. A newspaper, the *Frontier Index*, was printed in a boxcar on the equipment train. In the summer of 1868, General U. S. Grant, General Philip H. Sheridan, and General W. T. Sherman met at Fort Sanders to discuss gradients and curvatures with railroad officials. According to her own story, Calamity Jane was stationed here in 1871–2, as a scout, after completing a campaign with troops in Arizona. The next spring she guided a detachment to the Powder River country, where she saved the life of her commander in an engagement with Sioux and Cheyenne (*see Sheridan*).

At the large MONOLITH PORTLAND CEMENT PLANT (R), 248.7 *m.*, is the junction with a dirt road.

Left on this road (*impassable when wet*) through ranch country, in which buildings erected during the 1880's still stand. Hundreds of white-faced Herefords roam the meadows. Buck fences, set up before 1900, separate the grazing tracts. Jelm Mountain thrusts up its heavily wooded cone in the distance (R). At 9.3 *m.* is a boundary of the Hutton Lake Migratory Bird Refuge.

The WOODEN SHOE, 17.5 *m.*, a cattle ranch transformed into a dude ranch, has good examples of early log buildings, pole fences, and stone fireplaces.

Eroded rocks (L), 19 *m.*, resemble gigantic beehives. The road skirts a deep arroyo walled with fantastic figures. CHIMNEY ROCK, also known as Camel Rock, is visible in the Sand Creek area, just across the Colorado Line.

The highway crosses rolling meadows and sagelands, with ranches L. and R. Thistle, rabbit brush, lady's-slipper, phlox, larkspur, aster, and beeflower bloom here in summer.

At 255.6 *m.* is the junction with a dirt road.

Left on this road to a large STATE FISH HATCHERY (*open to the public*), 0.1 *m.*

In the distance (L) are red sandstone towers and turrets. Snows drift heavily here in winter; slat fences, anchored with large granite boulders, zigzag along the highway and the track of the Union Pacific (L). Ahead the Laramie and Medicine Bow Mountains converge, appearing to block passage southward.

TIE SIDING, 263.2 *m.* (7,753 alt., 50 pop.), is a post office on the southeastern border of the Laramie Plains. When the Union Pacific rails reached the Laramie Mountains in 1867, this heavily timbered region, lying between the prairies and the desert, was a bonanza to tie contractors. When the railroad was completed, Tie Siding became a supply center for ranches in the Red Buttes and Pole Mountain areas. In 1931 the hamlet was moved a short distance, to take advantage of travel on US 287.

US 287 winds steeply upward, curves around a hill by means of a shelf, and gains a height, 267.4 *m.*, from which an excellent view of the great Laramie Basin spreads northward.

At 271.7 *m.* the highway crosses the COLORADO LINE, 36 miles north of Fort Collins, Colorado.

Tour 5A

Junction with US 287—Atlantic City—South Pass City—South Pass—Junction with US 187; 75.2 *m.*, South Pass Mail Road.

Graded dirt road, not passable in winter and wet weather.
Limited accommodations at Atlantic City.

The South Pass Mail Road, deeply rutted when wet, climbs the southeastern slopes of the bold Wind River Range, cuts a narrow shelf along wooded mountain shoulders, then drops into the oldest mining area in Wyoming. From South Pass, it follows the grassed-over tracks of the older Oregon Trail to the junction with US 187 at Farson.

An unimproved branch route, east of South Pass, used only by sheepmen's wagons, follows the Oregon Trail through the Sweetwater Valley, passing near a number of historic sites. This route cannot be traveled by automobile on account of high road centers and unbridged arroyos.

The South Pass Mail Road stems south from US 287, 0 m., in the Little Popo Agie Valley, an area of fertile farms and ranches, and parallels the Little Popo Agie River through a red dirt canyon, between foothills that bristle with pines, then climbs sharply up to the top of the mountain.

The timber thins as the road winds downward, and hillsides are scabbed with old prospect holes. Ahead is an abandoned mining area, with crumbling sluice boxes and a few prospectors, still hoping to find again the lodes that stampeded 10,000 into the region in the 1860's.

Here and there are white-topped sheep wagons, looking like direct descendants of the prairie schooner, except that they usually stand alone. Herders' campfires blink along the route at night. Occasionally a husky voice, accompanied by a muffled guitar, rises over the drone of the wind. Some herders insist that the region is haunted—that, of the half-million trappers, traders, gold seekers, homesteaders, bluecoats, bullwhackers, guides, peddlers, fanatics, and refugees, at least a few ghosts must remain.

Some of the old mines are being reworked; others, deserted, have become dens for highland fauna.

The road drops into Atlantic Gulch and ATLANTIC CITY, 23.2 m. (7,655 alt., 30 pop.), a satellite of South Pass City (see below) during the boom of the 1870's, but now a center of mining activity. Its gray, weathered buildings are scattered on both sides of the gulch. Most of them are vacant in winter, but in summer 500 prospectors return to the region and bring Atlantic City back to life.

The town began in 1868, when miners from South Pass City found gold in Atlantic Ledge. By 1870 Atlantic City had 2,000 residents. Its boom was less spectacular than that of its neighbor city, but it lasted longer. In October 1878, Governor J. W. Hoyt reported to the Secretary of the Interior: 'South Pass is a scene of vacant dwellings, saloons, shops, and abandoned gulches . . . [but] seven mills are standing at Atlantic City and getting enough ore to keep them going.'

Left sharply from Atlantic City on the grass-grown wagon road to the SITE OF FORT STAMBAUGH, 3.5 m., a post established (1870) in Smith's Gulch on the Oregon Trail; the miners had demanded military protection, when the boundaries of the Shoshone Reservation were drawn almost adjoining the mining district. The post was named for Lieutenant George B. Stambaugh of Fort Brown (see Tour 5b) who was killed by Indians, May 10, 1870. Two infantry companies were quartered here in four large log barracks. The fort was abandoned in 1878.

The South Pass Road meanders through Atlantic Gulch, climbs sagebrush hills to a low, barren summit, then descends to SOUTH PASS

CITY, 27.2 *m.* (7,805 alt., 50 pop.), oldest mining camp in the area. Grass-grown placer ditches and rotting sluice boxes pattern the land on both banks of Big Hermit Creek. In the town, crumbling log and clapboard houses, barns, dugouts, and false-front stores, many deserted since the 1870's, shelter dusty odds and ends of furniture. The only sounds are the bleating of sheep and the spluttering hum of a gigantic dredge, as it tears up the gravel of near-by streambeds and digests it like a Martian monster, searching for the particles of yellow dust that slipped with the gravel from the miners' pans and sluice boxes.

The first gold strike was reported at South Pass in 1842, when an anonymous trapper announced that he was going East to organize a company to develop a claim at the head of the Sweetwater. On the way, the trapper was killed by Indians. Thirteen years later, prospectors took some pay dirt from the streambeds, but the values were not impressive. In 1861, the last of these men abandoned their diggings, to cut poles for Creighton's telegraph line. In 1867, a party of miners, returning disappointed from California, prospected the diggings and found rich placer gold.

There was a rush, and South Pass City, laid out in October, had a population of 700 before 'cold weather.' Carter County was created, embracing nearly a third of present Wyoming, and South Pass City was made its seat. New discoveries swelled the population. A sawmill ripped out raw lumber for hastily erected shelters. Two stage lines began operation between South Pass and the Union Pacific at Point of Rocks. Within a year South Pass City had 5 hotels, 13 saloons, 3 meat markets, 2 bakeries, a band, 4 law firms, a weekly newspaper, a gun store, several stamp mills, a shooting and bowling alley, a beer garden, and 2 doctors, who alternately attended patients and worked at their diggings.

By 1870, South Pass City boasted 4,000 inhabitants; its main street was half a mile long, and its school system was rated one of the best in Wyoming. In the spring of 1869, William H. Bright, a local citizen, introduced and championed in the territorial legislature the bill that gave women full franchise in Wyoming. In 1870, Esther Hobart Morris, who had agitated for the woman suffrage bill, became justice of the peace. Her first case was a suit against her predecessor, to gain possession of the court docket. She at length dismissed the case, deciding in favor of a 'new, clean docket.' This first woman justice boasted that she never lectured outside her home, but that she contributed regularly to *Revolution,* organ of the Woman Suffrage Society.

Life in South Pass was not all frontier chivalry and sudden wealth. With the promoters, miners, freighters, and ex-soldiers came the adventurers and bad men. Mountain Jack Alvese, Vinegar Zeriner, and 20 others ended their careers here and were carried to 'boot hill' at the edge of town. Also, until the summer of 1868, whenever the Sioux, Arapaho, and Cheyenne suffered reverses in the war along the Bozeman Trail, they compensated themselves with a raid or two on isolated South Pass City.

Speculators manipulated stocks and leases to gain control of the gold properties; stampedes to supposedly richer areas developed; rich veins played out or were lost, and the boom was over. By December 1873, the town was deserted, and the county seat was moved to Green River (*see Tour 2c*).

The road winds southward over foothills and gray ridges to SOUTH PASS, 39.4 *m.* (7,550 alt.), a long treeless valley, 25 miles wide, broken by low, flat-topped sagebrush hills and pyramidal sand dunes. Old wagon tracks are so numerous that the valley resembles an old plowed field, grassed over before the furrows were pulverized. The white cones of Wind River Mountains rise ahead. The incline on both approaches is so gradual that early travelers topped the summit, unaware that they were crossing the Continental Divide. Even Frémont, guided by Kit Carson, was in doubt about the highest point. When Whitman and Parker crossed here in 1835, Parker, not dreaming that the most mountainous country lay west of the divide, noted in his journal that 'there will be no difficulty in constructing a railroad from the Atlantic to the Pacific.'

Although Robert Stuart discovered South Pass in 1812, on his eastward journey from Astoria (*see History*), but the pass was not used by trappers until the 1820's. In 1824, Thomas Fitzpatrick, of the Rocky Mountain Fur Company, while searching for a route over which his pack trains could reach the mountain valleys, chanced upon the pass. He at once reported it to General Ashley, as it offered a wide, grassy gateway to the Green River Valley and, therefore, to Pierre's Hole, Colter's Hell, and the Three Forks of the Missouri on the north; to Bear Lake, Cache Valley, Ogden's Hole, and Great Salt Lake Valley on the south.

Although Ashley, in 1827, sent wheels through the pass—those of a four-pounder cannon drawn by four mules—it was Captain B. L. E. Bonneville who took wagons over it in 1832. By 1843 trains of wagons were rolling toward the Columbia, wearing deep tracks in the earth of South Pass. During the next two decades, possibly 300,000 persons, in covered wagons, on horseback, or pushing handcarts, crossed the pass. In the late 1850's, the stagecoach provided faster transportation, the Pony Express was inaugurated in 1860, and in 1861 Creighton built his telegraph line through the broad gateway.

Although Indian uprisings caused the shift of the freight and stage lines southward in 1862, to what became known as the Overland Trail, private trains continued using the South Pass route (after the uprisings had been put down) because of its grass and water. Wagons became fewer, however, as the Union Pacific Railroad advanced westward.

Left from South Pass on an unimproved road that follows the Old Oregon Trail down the Sweetwater River, to a wide sheep- and cattle-ranching area. Neither the road nor region has changed much since pioneers surveyed them from rocking prairie schooners. The hills and plains are, if anything, more barren; nibbling sheep have replaced the pronghorn and bison; the old wagon tracks are grass-grown near the streams and eroded more deeply on the sand dunes; willow and sagebrush, uprooted for firewood, have grown back, gnarled and sickly; mounds that marked graves have bleached and leveled; discarded washtubs and cooking utensils, which once glistened like skeletons along the road, are buried in deep dust. Winds have scattered the remains of log ranch houses and stage stations.

BURNT RANCH, 7.1 *m.*, originally South Pass Stage Station, established in 1859 by the Russell, Majors & Waddell Line, was garrisoned in 1862 with troops of the 11th Ohio Volunteer Cavalry. Indians burned the station twice. From this point, in 1856, Colonel W. F. Lander began his survey for the Lander Cutoff (*see Tour* 5). The marked CAMPSITE OF JAMES G. WILLIE'S HANDCART COMPANY (R), 16.9 *m.*, is on a bleak knoll in a bend of Rock Creek. To encourage immigration to the new Zion by Great Salt Lake, the Mormon Church had undertaken to pay part of the traveling expenses of its destitute converts from European countries. The expense for each person was only $44. In 1855–6, the immigrant fund was low, and there were not enough wagons and oxen available to transport across the plains the great number of immigrants who had responded. Handcarts, each capable of carrying a 100-pound load, were therefore made at Iowa City, the railroad terminus at that time. Several dauntless brigades started westward, pulling and pushing the heavy contrivances. The Willie Company, 500 strong, had 3 cows, a wagon, and 3 yoke of oxen for each 100 travelers; a tent for every 20, and a handcart for every 5. The company, after a late start, lost most of its cattle to Indians. Carts broke down, causing further delay. Early Wyoming blizzards found the travelers exhausted and starving, several hundred miles from Salt Lake. On October 18, they camped in deep snow on Rock Creek. Five persons died that night; the next night 15 died, and were buried in one grave. Three supply wagons that arrived from Utah on October 20 enabled the survivors to go on to Fort Bridger (*see Tour* 2C). Another handcart company, two weeks behind Willie's, suffered even more (*see Tour* 11). Of the more than 1,000 persons in the two companies, about 800 reached Salt Lake City by November.

The SITE OF ST. MARY'S STAGE STATION (L), 30.7 *m.*, also called Rocky Ridge Station because of a cliff near by, is marked with a stone tablet. The station was built in 1859 by Russell, Majors & Waddell, and when the transcontinental telegraph line was established in 1861, St. Mary's was made a depot. In May 1865, while the five-man garrison hid in an abandoned well, 150 Cheyenne and Arapaho burned the station and cut 400 yards of telegraph wire. When the ammunition in the buildings exploded, they fled. The station was rebuilt, but nothing remains except old square-cut nails, melted glass, broken pottery, and pieces of telegraph insulators.

Lieutenant John C. Frémont described the Sweetwater Valley, which he explored in the summer of 1842: 'On either side of the valley, which is four or five miles broad, the mountains rise . . . On the south side the range is timbered. On the north . . . granite masses rise abruptly from the green sward of the river, terminating in a line of broken summits. Except in the crevices of the rock, and here and there on a ledge or bench of mountain, where a few hardy pines have clustered together, these are perfectly bare and destitute of vegetation. Among these masses, where there are sometimes isolated hills and ridges, green valleys open in upon the river, which sweeps the base of these mountains for 36 miles. Everywhere is deep verdure and profusion of beautiful flowers in pleasing contrast with the sterile grandeur of the rock and bareness of the sandy plain . . . The saline efflorescences which whiten the ground, make it shine like lakes reflecting in the sun.'

At 41.3 *m.* is the junction with US 287 (*see Tour* 5).

In South Pass is the WHITMAN-SPALDING MONUMENT, commemorating the first Independence Day celebration on the west slope. When Marcus Whitman, H. H. Spalding, and their brides came West in 1836 (*see Tour* 9), they paused near Pacific Springs on July 4. With a Bible in one hand and an American flag in the other, Dr. Whitman knelt and took possession of the land to the west as a 'home of American mothers and the Church of Christ.'

West of South Pass, at 41.4 *m.*, is a junction with an unimproved dirt road.

Left on this unimproved road to PACIFIC SPRINGS, 0.5 *m.*, a favorite camp site for emigrants 'just over the hump.' The waters of the spring originate less than four miles from the Continental Divide and eventually reach the Pacific Ocean. Here is the site of a stage and pony express station of the early 1860's.

The LITTLE SANDY CROSSING, 67.6 *m.*, an emigrant camp site, also had a stage station in the 1860's. *Ware's Emigrant Guide to California* (1849) advised: 'When you cross the Dry or Little Sandy, instead of turning to the left and following the river, strike out across to the Big Sand, twelve miles. If you get to the river along through the day, camp 'til near night. From the Big Sandy to Green River, a distance of thirty-five miles, there is not a drop of water. By starting from the Sandy at the cool of the day, you can get across easily by morning.'

At FARSON, 75.2 *m.* (6,580 alt., 126 pop.), is the junction with US 187 (*see Tour* 7).

Tour 6

(Crawford, Neb.)—Lusk—Casper—Shoshoni—Greybull—Yellowstone Park (East Entrance); US 20.
Nebraska Line to Yellowstone National Park, 443.8 *m.*

Chicago & Northwestern R.R. parallels US 20 between Nebraska Line and Shoshoni; Chicago, Burlington & Quincy R.R., between Orin and Greybull.
Good accommodations at long intervals.
Oil-surfaced roadbed throughout; open all seasons. Excellent trailer route.

US 20, crossing Wyoming in three giant sweeps, traces a wide lazy Z over its northern half. The long, relatively straight eastern stretch between the Nebraska Line and Shoshoni, covers more than half the total distance. The road passes over the dry, flat Niobrara Plains, parallels the Oregon, California, and Mormon Trails through North Platte Valley, cuts northward across a plateau to Wind River Canyon and a fertile farming basin, then turns westward again across bleak sagebrush flats toward the spectacular driveway that twists along a shelf on the wall of Shoshone Canyon. Its western end is the timbered approach to Yellowstone National Park.

Section a. NEBRASKA LINE to SHOSHONI; 228.9 m. US 20-87

This section of US 20 traverses four characteristic types of Wyoming countryside: broad grassy plain, green valley, rugged mountain range, and wasteland. The plain represents the cattleman's Wyoming; the valley boasts modern industrial communities as well as agricultural areas; the mountains and wastes typify the grandeur and immensity farther west.

Northwest of the NEBRASKA LINE, 0 *m.*, 38 miles west of Crawford, Nebraska, is a basin rimmed with buttes of volcanic ash. Van Tassell Creek, 0.8 *m.*, cuts through the VAN TASSELL RANCH (R), the original owner of which was R. S. Van Tassell, one of the principal backers of the Johnson County invasion (*see Tour 3a*).

VAN TASSELL, 1.8 *m.* (4,738 alt., 99 pop.), known locally as Homesteaders' Landing, became, in the early 1900's, a supply point for settlers as far south as Torrington. Good water, obtainable by drilling to the comparatively convenient depth of 200 feet, was a determining factor in settlement here, but water for irrigation was too scanty to make intensive farming possible. For some time, nearly every half-section was occupied; today there is only one family to every four sections.

Right from Van Tassell on a dirt road to the SITE OF THE CODY-YELLOW HAND FIGHT, 20 *m.*, where Wyoming, Nebraska, and South Dakota meet. Here, at the foot of a bluff near a small cottonwood-bordered stream, Colonel W. F. (Buffalo Bill) Cody and some soldiers of the Fifth U. S. Cavalry surprised six or seven Indians one day in 1877. Cody himself confronted Yellow Hand, a Sioux chief. Both fired; Yellow Hand's horse fell dead. At almost the same instant, Cody's horse stepped into a badger hole and fell. The antagonists blazed away again, and Yellow Hand dropped with a bullet in his brain. According to one story, Cody then scalped the Indian.

US 20 runs westward between broken, fossil-bearing cliffs and through the easternmost foothills of the Rockies. The Rawhide Buttes (*see Tour 1*) are in plain view to the southwest. Windmills near the road pump water for cattle and sheep. West of NODE, 13.5 *m.* (4,937 alt., 25 pop.), a post office named for a cattle brand, hayfields spread for miles. After harvest, brown stacks stand curing in the sun. At 18.5 *m.* the highway intersects the TEXAS TRAIL, marked (1940) with one of the finest markers in the State, over which bawling longhorns were driven to the ranges of northern Wyoming and Montana in the 1870's and 1880's. John B. Kendrick, later Wyoming governor and U. S. senator (*see Sheridan*), wrote of the trip up the trail: 'I do not remember . . . seeing a wire fence between Fort Worth, Texas, and the head of the Running Water [near the present city of Lusk] . . . Danger . . . did not detract from the fascination of the trip . . . the danger from Indians and the holding of a large herd of cattle in the night [without] ray or glimmer of light . . .' The thousands of cattle that now graze here are fenced in by miles of barbed wire.

LUSK, 22.1 *m*. (5,015 alt., 1,218 pop.) (*see Tour* 1), is at the junction with US 85 (*see Tour* 1). A massive granite monument on a tiered concrete base marks GEORGE LATHROP'S GRAVE (L), 24.3 *m*. Lathrop was a driver on the Cheyenne and Black Hills Stage Line (*see Tour* 1), the route of which is now marked by two rows of white posts.

MANVILLE, 31.9 *m*. (5,245 alt., 101 pop.), and KEELINE, 39.4 *m*. (5,289 alt., 101 pop.), are trading centers for ranchers and dry farmers. String farms, producing kaffir corn, field corn, and wheat, follow the creeks that worm their way across the arid flats. Corn is usually planted in 12-foot strips, alternating with 12-foot strips of summer-fallowed land. In contour farming, which is practiced to some extent to conserve soil and moisture on the range land, the furrows are plowed, three in a group, about 40 inches apart. The groups of three furrows are located at intervals of 40 to 50 feet across the slope.

At 42.7 *m*. is a junction with an ungraded dirt road.

Left on this road (*passable only in dry weather; guide advisable*) to a crossroads, 4.1 *m.*; R. here 4 *m*. across Muddy Creek to a picnic ground. The road diminishes to a dim trail, leading to the rim of the SPANISH DIGGINGS, 11.1 *m.*, among the rugged hills, rocky gulches, and bare mesas of the Rawhide Range (*rattlesnakes numerous*). Scattered prehistoric quarries and village sites, amid outcroppings of quartzite, jasper, and agate, here cover an area of 400 square miles. Before white traders introduced metals, the tribes used the quartzite and jasper for arrow and spear heads, knives and scrapers. The soil has drifted considerably, but vegetation is scant, and little mold covers the work pits and refuse heaps. Partly filled quarries are 25 to 30 feet in diameter and 10 to 30 feet deep. Fine flakes or chips are rare, and rejected articles display only the roughest handiwork. Since finished implements of identical materials have been found in mounds in the Ohio and Mississippi Valleys, it is assumed that the rough pieces were transported down the Platte and Missouri Rivers to work sites. Stone knives, wedges, mauls, hammers, axes, grinders, and other implements are scattered over the diggings. Rough outlines of animals are found in caves; a stone cross about 90 feet long, with 16-foot arms, lies on a northern slope. From the foot of the cross, two parallel rows of cairns run northward for more than a mile. No burial places have been found, and the only signs of habitation are tepee rings. It is thought that the camps were maintained only while workmen quarried raw material. Authorities estimate the age of the quarries at 250 to 5,000 years.

Range riders in the 1880's called the area the Mexican Mine. Two ranchers, J. L. Stein and William Lauk, assuming that it had been worked by Spanish conquistadores, prospected there in the hope of finding valuable ores. Since 1893, the universities of Wyoming and Nebraska, Yale University, Amherst College, the United States National Museum, and the Field Museum have sent expeditions into the diggings.

US 20 continues through gently rolling grassland. LOST SPRING, 48.2 *m*. (4,995 alt., 65 pop.), is named for a near-by stream, which sinks into the ground and appears again at a lower level. SHAWNEE, 52.6 *m*. (5,026 alt., 75 pop.), is near producing coal mines, and drilling is carried on in the Shawnee Oil Field northwest of town.

Gray salt flats slope down to merge into green riverside meadows along the Platte. At 64 *m.* is the junction with US 87 (*see Tour 3d*), which unites with US 20 for 68.6 miles (*see Tour 3c*).

CASPER, 130.9 *m.* (5,123 alt., 16,619 pop.) (*see Casper*).

At 132.6 *m.*, US 87 goes R.; US 20 runs westward over gray flats. Deserted shacks stand here and there; the white canvas tops of sheep-herders' wagons, with large bands moving around them, break the monotony of sage and rabbit brush. The CASPER ROD AND GUN CLUB (*trapshooting*) is R. at 153.1 *m.* A typical ranch dwelling, a low house with antlers over the doorway, is L. at 156.2 *m.*

SODIUM (R), 160.2 *m.*, is a shipping point for sodium from central Wyoming lakebeds. Tom Sun, Boney Ernest, and Frank Harrington filed on the deposits and built cabins there in the early 1870's, but Indians burned them out.

When the highway, seeking a direct route, failed to run through POWDER RIVER, 167.3 *m.* (7,500 alt., 61 pop.), the little village moved away from the railroad and became a wayside settlement. The Station, once the center of town, is about 400 yards R. West of town, the highway overpasses the railroad and winds through badlands to the SOUTH FORK OF POWDER RIVER, 168.9 *m.*

At 173.6 *m.* is a turnout to the rim of DEVIL'S KITCHEN, a part of HELL'S HALF ACRE (L), 173.7 *m.*, which Natrona County main-tains as a public park. This 320-acre chasm in the flat wilderness con-tains deep caverns, crevices, and pits; towers, spires, and buttresses; and fantastic nondescript shapes carved out by wind and water from sandstone and shale. The Devil's Kitchen is the eastern part, rougher and more striking in appearance than the rest. Indians held the freak-ish depression in superstitious awe, and trappers avoided it on what they regarded as unlucky days. Foot trails now wind among the strange figures. Many fossils have been found in the vicinity.

At 179.4 *m.* is the junction with a dirt road.

Right on this road to ARMINTO, 8 *m.* (6,000 alt., 75 pop.), a ranchers' hamlet named for Manuel Armenta, who started the Jack Pot ranch close by. The Chicago, Burlington & Quincy Railroad changed the spelling. The second incorporated town in Natrona County, Arminto once hoped to rival Casper as a business center.

HILAND, 188.2 *m.* (5,998 alt., 15 pop.), is in a region notorious for violent winter storms, usually preceded by a fairly warm west wind that shifts into the east. The blizzard strikes without other warning and visibility swiftly becomes zero. Wind velocity sometimes reaches 70 to 80 miles an hour; the mercury drops 20° or 30° in a few minutes. Roads are obliterated; windshields are caked with sleet.

At 191.1 *m.* the Wind River Mountains appear far ahead. In a country of hills, flats, and sand draws is MONETA (Lat., mint, or minted money), 205.1 *m.* (5,428 alt., 20 pop.), with large shearing pens and a wool warehouse.

1. Left from Moneta on a dirt road (*impassable in wet weather*) to CASTLE GARDENS, 18 *m.*, in a valley two miles long and a half mile wide. The east-ern end of the valley gleams with white ledges and varicolored sandstone cones,

shelves, minarets, and campaniles that rise almost 100 feet. Cliff walls are covered with Indian picture writings, some of them almost perfectly preserved. The symbols are carved with greater care and skill than are evident in other Wyoming pictographs.

2. Right from Moneta on a dirt road to CAPTAIN BATES' BATTLEGROUND, 33 *m.*, near the head of Nowood Creek. In 1874, Captain Alfred Bates led a cavalry troop, accompanied by about 100 Shoshone under Chief Washakie, eastward from Fort Washakie in pursuit of Arapaho plunderers of small camps and wagon trains. On the morning of July 4, Bates found the Arapaho tents pitched near a rocky ledge; back of the camp, on a flat, the horses were picketed under guard. The Shoshone, eager to capture the horses, did not time their attack to support that of the soldiers, and the Arapaho reached the ledge, where they had the advantage. Four soldiers were killed and about 40 wounded before the Arapaho surrendered. The Indian losses were heavier.

US 20 crosses sagebrush flats and gulches and skirts irregular cliffs, paralleling SPIDER CREEK (L), which has little water in summer. Supposedly, the creek was named by early residents for a spider found in a camp on its bank. Near Shoshoni, the road emerges into a wide valley, which spreads to the Wind River Range on the west and the Owl Creek Mountains on the north.

SHOSHONI, 228.9 *m.* (4,820 alt., 263 pop.), a sheep-raising center, was established in 1905 when the Shoshone Reservation was opened for settlement (*see Tour 5b*). In early days the general store brought all its supplies by wagon from the railhead west of Casper. As storage quarters were cramped, the new stock, including such supplies as bacon and dynamite, was piled outside the store. To keep bears from rummaging among the boxes, the proprietor had to build a 16-foot stockade around the store.

At Shoshoni is the junction with State 320 (*see Tour 12*).

Section b.   SHOSHONI to GREYBULL; 107.2 *m.   US 20*

US 20 runs due north along the gray cliffs of Wind River Canyon to the Big Horn Basin, a region of thriving towns, irrigated farms, and livestock ranges. It skirts the hot springs region near Thermopolis and winds northward to the Greybull oil flats. The building of the roadbed through Wind River Canyon was a major feat of highway engineering.

North of SHOSHONI, 0 *m.*, US 20 climbs toward the Owl Creek Mountains, which form part of the southern rim of the Big Horn Basin. Sagebrush plains roll R. and L. in a series of constantly higher ridges.

BADWATER CREEK, 2.9 *m.*, usually almost dry in summer, responds quickly to heavy rains in the Big Horn foothills. Tradition says Indians named it when floodwaters from a cloudburst swept away an encampment near its mouth. In 1923, one of Badwater's rampages washed out several miles of railroad; for weeks no trains ran between the basin and Casper.

US 20 crosses a sage plateau and skirts chalk cliffs (R).

At 8.2 *m.* is a junction with the Birdseye Road.

Right on this rough dirt road up Birdseye Creek and over Birdseye Pass on Copper Mountain (7,500 alt.) to the BIRDSEYE STAGE STATION, 5 *m.*, of the

1880's and early 1890's. The false-front log station and crumbling outbuildings still stand. Sage hens and meadow larks nest near by.

The road worms down Copper Mountain and turns west along a red-rock wall that rises 1,000 to 1,500 feet, partly covered in spring and summer with bright green grass. Indian paintbrush grows here profusely; in late summer the yellow of sunflowers mingles with the red and green of the walls and grass. In the lower valley is an occasional one-room shanty, with a sheep wagon near it. Both cattle and sheep are trailed to summer range on Copper Mountain.

At 22 *m.* the road rejoins US 20, which curves between high hills and through a cut in red rocks.

At night, natural gas bubbling from an artesian well (R), 11 *m.*, glows weirdly as it burns above the water. At 13.6 *m.* the highway is pinched between the walls of WIND RIVER CANYON, a great cleft through the Owl Creek Range (*speed limit* 35 *m.p.h.*). Wild flowers grow in sheltered spots here; cold springs gush by the roadside. The Burlington R.R. parallels the highway on the opposite side of the river. At 15.3 *m.* it emerges from a tunnel, crosses the river on a steel bridge, and passes through another tunnel; a long freight train will occupy the bridge and both tunnels at the same time. At 16 *m.* black diorite cliffs, 2,000 feet high, seem to close the canyon ahead. Figures resembling monuments, castles, and pyramids overlook the river and the highway.

A strong wind always blows down Wind River Canyon. According to the Shoshone legend, a young chieftain once walked at the head of the canyon with his sweetheart. The wind plucked an eagle feather from the girl's hair and wafted it down the canyon. The feather drifted to the ground about where Thermopolis stands; there, the lovers found steam issuing from the ground. Knowing that the Great Spirit had led them, they were not afraid. They bathed in the hot, clean-smelling springs and later told their people of the good qualities of the water. The tribe moved to the spot, and its members became famous for strength and endurance. To this day, it is said, a feather released at the head of the canyon will float down to the spring.

BOYSEN DAM, 16.8 *m.*, was formerly part of a hydroelectric system for Shoshoni and Riverton. It was abandoned when the stored water flooded the railroad tunnels near by.

US 20 passes through a long tunnel, which pierces the mountain flank and emerges below jagged diorite peaks above the river. The black road twists over a bed that was blasted from basic rock; three more tunnels carry it through a sheer, rose-colored granite cliff. As the highway climbs, the canyon widens; grassy slopes dotted with cedars lie under its rock-shod rims. The vicinity is a State preserve for elk and deer.

BOB WHITE'S PLACE, 21 *m.*, a little terraced homestead on the mountainside, has buildings of local stone, with thatched roofs.

The highway follows a shelf around WIND POINT, 22.6 *m.*, where winds issue from a canyon across the river (L). At 23 *m.* is a pure cold spring. LEANING ROCK and CHIMNEY ROCK, 24.3 *m.*, are detached columns of the canyon wall, slanted against each other.

The canyon opens to the Big Horn Basin, a roughly circular ranching and farming area, more than 100 miles across. Divided by the Big Horn River, which drains something like 20,000 square miles between the Wind River and the Big Horn Canyons, the basin is enclosed by the Big Horn Mountains on the east, the Owl Creek Range on the south, the Pryors and Beartooths on the north, and the Absarokas on the west. Cloud Peak (13,165 alt.), a bald cone jutting above the irregular line of the Big Horns (R), overlooks the valley. Washakie Needles (12,495 alt.) and Frank's Peak (13,140 alt.) are like bared teeth lifted between the Owl Creek and Absaroka Ranges (L). The basin is an excellent place for the study of geology and paleontology; fossil remains found here include specimens from nearly all geologic eras.

John Colter, first white man known to have penetrated the basin, was cordially received by the Crow. Edward Rose and other trappers soon followed. The basin was officially explored by Lieutenant H. E. Maynadier, of the Raynolds-Maynadier expedition of 1859-60. Maynadier had trouble getting through Wind River Canyon; at length, he crossed the mountains to the east with empty wagons and brought his goods over on horseback. Later, he abandoned his wagons and lost his mules and instruments in the Stinking Water (Shoshone River). When John M. Bozeman proposed opening his road through the Sioux country to the Montana gold camps in the early 1860's, Jim Bridger warned against arousing the Indians (*see Tour 3a*), and offered to guide a train of miners through the Big Horn country instead. He found a swale in the mountains, thereafter known as Bridger's Saddle, less than ten miles from where Maynadier's wagons had stalled; but the route was rough and difficult. Bozeman raced Bridger to Virginia City, cutting the time by several weeks. The Bozeman Trail became the more popular road.

Maynadier reported evidences of gold in the basin, but prospectors did not take this seriously until about 1870. The Sioux were then maintaining a surly peace; Washakie had refused to settle on his reservation; troops at Fort Brown (*see Tour 5b*) and at Fort Stambaugh (*see Tour 5A*) turned all whites back. In the minds of gold seekers, the refusal to admit them to the basin confirmed the richness of its deposits. Agitation for admittance spread to Cheyenne, where the Big Horn Mining Association was organized. Mass meetings were held; by the spring of 1870, an expedition boasting 1,200 members was ready to move. The Army, however, permitted its members to proceed only upon the promise that they would not go beyond the Sweetwater. About 100 then left Cheyenne in carts and covered wagons and on horseback. On July 19, they reported that they were eight miles from Greybull River, feasting on buffalo and wild fruit. By the time a troop of cavalry from Fort Brown overtook them there, the company was disorganized; at length it left the basin, without gold.

For a time even the newspapers forgot the valley; but in 1870 the first Wyoming-finished cattle were shipped to market, and Wyoming prairies assumed a new value. Seven years later, when the Sioux land east of the Big Horns was given to the whites, cattle began to pour into the grass valleys on both sides of the range.

Charles Carter trailed the first cattle to the Big Horn Basin from Oregon in 1879; by 1883 the entire valley was stocked. Foreign capital was conspicuous; English, Scottish, and German owners controlled huge blocks of range. Sheep had an even start with cattle, but the range for both shrank, as irrigation projects attracted homesteaders. Later, oil and coal were found in profitable quantities. With the introduction of sugar beets, the rural population was increased by numbers of Mexicans, Russian-Germans, and Japanese.

Near the mouth of a cave (R), 28.4 m., which penetrates the mountain to a depth of 150 feet, a large warm spring sends wisps of steam into the air. Livestock come here to drink, and some of the water is used for irrigation.

At 30.2 m. is a junction with the Birdseye Road (see above). On a red rock wall (R), near a crossing of the Big Horn River, are INDIAN PICTOGRAPHS. Farms with cherry and apple trees and well-kept fields contrast with almost barren hills along the route.

THERMOPOLIS, 34.3 m. (4,326 alt., 2,129 pop.), a resort town on the west bank of the Big Horn River, clusters about its hot springs and baths. Brick and stone buildings, lawns and shrubbery, and landscaped parks give the town a well-groomed air. It is a trading center for a stock-raising area and for several oil fields. Citizens claim '300 days of sunshine yearly' for Thermopolis. The annual Labor Day rodeo, originally called Night Herd, attracts local and professional riders.

Settlement was begun in the 1870's near the mouth of Owl Creek, six miles from the present site of Thermopolis. Outlaws from the Hole-in-the-Wall often annoyed the community. In 1894, on election day, 50 rowdies rode in from the east and took possession of the place. They were dislodged by citizens toward evening, after a gun battle. A correspondent reported, 'Scores of men with six-shooters were seen . . . Judge Joe Magill, with knee leggings, 45 colts, and full cartridge belts, had the air of a commanding general.' When land near the hot springs was opened for settlement in 1897, the present town was founded. Dr. Julius A. Schuelke selected the name, a combination of *thermae* (Lat., hot baths, or springs) and *polis* (Gr., city). When Hot Springs County was created in 1911, Thermopolis became its seat.

1. Left from Thermopolis on a graveled and oil-surfaced highway to the OWL CREEK VALLEY, 6 m., an area of cattle ranches, alfalfa fields, and sage flats between tinted hills. Here, in 1871, J. D. Woodruff built the first house in the basin. His claim became the nucleus of the Embar Ranch, which once ran 50,000 head of cattle. Turkey raising is an important industry in the valley. One grower annually herds 3,000 birds in the foothills, where they fatten on grasshoppers and seeds.

The highway becomes a dirt road at 18 m. and winds over foothills to TIM MCCOY'S RANCH, 32 m. In his youth, McCoy was Chauncey Olcott's understudy. When his voice failed, he came West and became a cowhand. With a horse and bed-roll, he drifted to the Shoshone Reservation, lived with the Shoshone and Arapaho and learned their sign language. He enlisted in the cavalry in 1917 and became an instructor. Later, he was adjutant general of

Wyoming, but resigned to start his dude ranch. He divides his time between the ranch and his work in motion pictures.

2. Right from Thermopolis on an oil-surfaced road to HOT SPRINGS STATE PARK, 0.5 *m*. The park, one mile square, is cut almost in half by the Big Horn River. A driveway, with connecting footpaths, winds through it. In the center is MONDELL PARK, a triangle of lawn hedged with honeysuckle. WASHAKIE FOUNTAIN is a canopied monument of rough travertine slabs from local deposits. Cedar, spruce, yellow pine, wild currant, chokecherry, dogwood, and buffalo berry have been transplanted here. In early summer, the air is scented with lilacs.

BIG HORN SPRING, 25 feet across, pours out 18,600,000 gallons of water, at 135° F., every 24 hours. The blue-green water, used in the treatment of rheumatism and infantile paralysis, bubbles and boils from an unknown depth at the foot of Monument Hill and flows into large enclosed pools. Dr. Thomas Maghee, post surgeon at Camp Brown, used and tested the water in April 1875. Dr. Julius Schuelke took a sample to Paris and had it analyzed by Professor M. P. Schuetzenberger of the Collège de France, who was unable to distinguish it from Carlsbad water. Water for baths, fountains, and local irrigation leaves the pool by way of a large conduit under the surface. Since only a small quantity is used in this way, the pool constantly overflows, forming terraces lined with brilliantly colored algae. A boardwalk extends over the terraces. Ripples disturb the five-acre surface, moving toward the 50-foot fall into the Big Horn River. A suspension bridge, connecting the eastern and western halves of the park, affords an excellent view of the falls. Hot springs bubble up through the river water.

BLACK SULPHUR SPRING, north of Big Horn Spring, is slow moving and dark; attempts to measure its depth have been frustrated at 117 feet by hot-water pressure. It was the site of a bathhouse used by Chief Washakie. THE DEVIL'S PUNCHBOWL, north of Black Sulphur, once a large spring, is now an almost dry hole 60 feet deep and 300 feet across. Minerals in the water built a circular rim around it, like the curved edge of a bowl. Indians call the spot Thunder Ground, probably because the rocks give off a hollow sound when struck. TEPEE FOUNTAIN, about 24 feet high, started as an ordinary standpipe. As hot water from the spring trickled over its edge, it became coated with travertine. Now its basal diameter is about 25 feet. WHITE SULPHUR SPRING, at the north edge of the park, flows from a sulphur-coated cave.

On MONUMENT HILL, near the center of the park, invalids who have been cured of their ills have erected six large travertine monuments. Buffalo graze near by. ELK HILL (4,850 alt.), in the northwest corner of the park, covered with grass and cedars, affords pasture for a small herd of elk.

Hot Springs State Park originally was the northeast corner of the Shoshone Reservation, and each year the Indians came here to bathe and drink. When Chief Washakie sold 10 square miles of the land to the Government, which in turn gave the springs to the State, he asked that part of the water be kept free to Indians. Provision for this did not appear in the treaty of 1896, but in 1899 the Wyoming Legislature granted the old chief's wish. Today, Indians come in motorcars, or in light wagons drawn by ponies, and camp for days near the springs.

In 1925 a pageant, *The Gift of the Waters*, written in memory of the Shoshone chief, was presented at Big Horn Spring. The principal part of the program was read in the Shoshone language by Chief Dick Washakie, the old chief's son.

INSPIRATION POINT (R), 35.4 *m.*, is a parking area overlooking the park. Truck gardens on ARTOIS FLAT, 36.9 *m.*, once known as Stagner Bottoms, are irrigated from four hot-water wells sunk by oil prospectors.

The highway descends to a large free outdoor swimming pool (R), 37.2 *m.*, known as the SCOTCH PLUNGE (*bathers bring own suits*). The

OWL CREEK PUMPING PLANT (L), 38.9 *m.*, pumps water from the Big Horn River to irrigate 2,600 acres of land around LUCERNE, 41.7 *m.* (4,300 alt., 150 pop.), a hamlet named for its staple crop (alfalfa).

Right from Lucerne on a dirt road up Kirby Creek to the BLACK MOUNTAIN OIL FIELD, 25 *m.* In the 1880's, the Casper-Thermopolis stage and freight road followed this route. Outlaws from the Hole-in-the-Wall had a rendezvous on the banks of Kirby Creek.

At 44.8 *m.* on US 20 is the junction with a graveled road.

Left on this road are CROSBY, 1 *m.* (4,560 alt., 303 pop.), and GEBO, 2 *m.* (4,570 alt., 900 pop.), declining bituminous coal-mining towns. At Crosby, an uncontrolled mine fire has reduced mining activity, but near Gebo, named for an early promoter, are many small mines.

KIRBY, 47 *m.* (4,270 alt., 173 pop.), is a shipping point for the Gebo mining district.

At 51 *m.* is the junction with a dirt road.

Right on this road across railroad tracks and under the tip of a hill to the SITE OF WILLOWS STAGE STATION, 0.5 *m.* Here the Hanover Canal cuts the west bank of the Big Horn River, carrying water to the Worland district.

WINCHESTER, 52.8 *m.* (4,210 alt., 150 pop.), was named for the first postmaster, R. S. Winchester. When the railroad built through, the postmaster objected to having his name on the boxcar that served as a freight station, and the station was named Chatham. Winchester had a freight boom in 1917–18, when pipes and equipment were hauled to the Grass Creek Oil Field by 20- and 24-horse teams. From the pump station here, a pipe line carries crude oil to the Greybull refinery (*see below*).

At TIE-DOWN HILL (R), 55.1 *m.*, on the east bank of the Big Horn River, lived 'Tie-Down' Brown, so named for his agility in tying down and branding other ranchers' calves—for himself. In 1880 Brown's partner killed him with an axe, and his ghost, it was said, rode up and down the hill waiting for vengeance.

On a hill north of NEIBER, 59.2 *m.* (4,180 alt., 25 pop.), is an old SHOSHONE BURIAL GROUND, where Indian ceremonies were sometimes performed in honor of the dead.

The STATE INDUSTRIAL INSTITUTE FOR BOYS (L), 62.5 *m.*, has landscaped grounds around sturdy, red-roofed, stucco buildings. This reformatory is maintained for the custody and discipline of boys from 16 to 25. The boys print their own paper. On the 1,000-acre farm, experiments are carried on in the raising and breeding of dairy cows, horses, hogs, chickens, and sheep.

The adobe houses of Mexican beet-field workers mark the outskirts of WORLAND, 67.5 *m.* (4,061 alt., 1,481 pop.), seat of Washakie County and center of a rich farming and winter stock-feeding area. Within the town are modern houses, with good lawns and gardens. The stacks of the sugar refinery rise above it on the southeast. Worland irregularly celebrates Washakie Day, commemorating the building of the Burlington Railroad in 1906, and holds annual corn and wool shows, usually in early September.

In Worland is the junction with US 16 (*see Tour* 8). US 20 continues over cultivated fields, with badlands R. During harvest, trucks loaded with sugar beets wait in long lines at the Eccles Dump (L), 77.5 *m.*, where the beets are weighed for shipment.

MANDERSON, 87.8 *m.* (3,890 alt., 96 pop.), at the confluence of Nowood Creek and Big Horn River, was first called Alamo. A ferry was operated here.

Right from Manderson on a dirt road along Nowood Creek to the SITE OF JORDAN MILL, 3.4 *m.*, first flour mill in the basin. At 5.2 *m.* is a striking view of the southwest face of the Big Horn Mountains; Black Butte and Medicine Lodge, Shell, and Paintrock canyons are conspicuous, with Tensleep Canyon R. BONANZA, 13 *m.*, is a ghost village at the confluence of Paintrock and Nowood creeks. Here, in 1887, someone found oil flowing from a spring; a boom followed. Only a rambling log and frame building that once housed a saloon and general store remains.

HYATTVILLE, 23 *m.* (4,457 alt., 208 pop.), is a cow-town of quaint false-front and tin-roofed buildings, at the junction of Medicine Lodge and Paintrock creeks. Founded in the 1880's, it still retains much of the temper and severity of the frontier. No highway or railroad reaches it. It was known as Paintrock until 1886, when Sam W. Hyatt of Buffalo became its first postmaster. Cowboys carried the mail once a month over the Owl Creek Mountains from Fort Washakie, 175 miles southwest. When pioneers of the Big Horn Basin are guests at Hyattville's annual Old-Timers' Day (*no fixed date*), each old-timer wears a blue ribbon announcing the date of his arrival in the State.

The road drops to a valley of bean fields and skirts the SITE OF THE LUM WILLIAMS RANCH on Medicine Lodge Creek, 25.4 *m.*, where Teton Jackson, notorious rustler, was captured in 1885.

At 27.2 *m.* is the junction with another dirt road; L. here to PAINTED ROCKS, 2.5 *m.*, at the mouth of Medicine Lodge Canyon, where Indian pictographs on the face of a sandstone cliff show elk and buffalo, bristling with arrows, and medicine men wearing buffalo headdresses.

The main dirt road winds northward up the steep face of the Big Horn Range (*carry water to cool radiator*) to the PAINTROCK LAKES (*good fishing*), 39 *m.*

US 20 traces a black and silver stripe across green velvety fields of beans, sugar beets, alfalfa, and grain. The tan pressed-brick buildings of the STATE TUBERCULOSIS SANITARIUM (L), 97.8 *m.*, established in 1921, stand among pleasantly landscaped grounds.

BASIN, 88.1 *m.* (3,870 alt., 903 pop.), a farmers' town and seat of Big Horn County, has comfortable dwellings, wide streets, and a four-block civic center with courthouse, post office, library, and park. Its citizens began a tree and shrub planting campaign in 1910 and a 'lilac town' drive in 1936; now the streets and approaching highways are lined with perfumed hedges, and the shade trees are among the finest in Wyoming. Basin, with its large bean-seed treating plant, holds a yearly festival during which bean dishes of amazing variety are served free at every corner; samples of beans are exhibited with the growers' names, and prizes are awarded. The women of the vicinity have become expert in fashioning pictures and plaques from beans.

Basin City, as it was first called, came into prominence in 1896 as a candidate for the seat of Big Horn County. Otto (*see below*) was the favored contender. Then W. S. Collins, frontier attorney, moved the *Paintrock Record* to Basin City from Hyattville and renamed it the *Basin City Herald*. Joe Magill, an Embar cowboy, became its editor. The *Otto Courier* engaged Tom Dagget, tramp journalist from New York, to direct its campaign. The duel that followed is still rehearsed with relish. When Cody (*see below*) entered the race, the vote of the western part of the valley was split, and Basin won.

At 99.5 *m.* is the junction with a dirt road.

> Left on this road is OTTO, 9 *m.* (4,000 alt., 200 pop.), a town in the Greybull River country, named for Otto Franc, who founded the Pitchfork Ranch (*see below*).

The highway crosses sagebrush flats and irrigated fields, then climbs to barren benchland.

GREYBULL, 107.2 *m.* (3,788 alt., 1,806 pop.), industrial center of the Big Horn Basin, is supported largely by refineries handling oil from the Grass Creek, Elk Basin, Garland, and Byron fields. Indian pictographs on a cliff overhanging Greybull River represent a buffalo bull, with an arrow through his body. Legend relates that an old gray bull ranged along the river for years, in defiance of hunters who sought to kill him. Washington Irving called the stream the Bull River.

In Greybull is the junction with US 14 (*see Tour* 10), which unites westward with US 20.

Section c. GREYBULL to YELLOWSTONE PARK; 107.7 m.
US 20-14

Here, US 20 crosses the Emblem Bench between Greybull and Cody, burrows through sheer Shoshone Canyon to the Shoshone National Forest, then climbs the pine-dark slopes of the Absaroka Mountains to the eastern gate of Yellowstone National Park.

West of GREYBULL, 0 *m.*, the highway climbs to a sage plateau, where it is marked with mileposts for speedometer tests.

At 4.8 *m.* is the junction with US 310 (*see Tour 6A*).

The road crosses EMBLEM BENCH, a long, elevated flat that is farmed intensively. White frame dwellings and red outbuildings dot the land between fields of alfalfa, grain, and beans. First settled by Mormons and German immigrants, the area was known as Germania Bench until the World War of 1914–18. In 1893 the settlers adopted an ambitious irrigation scheme—a ditch system to cover 15,000 acres with water from the Greybull River. They had little money, however, and the work was slow. Drought in 1894 left many families without food; in discouragement, the people turned for a time to the lower lands. When the bench canal system was completed in 1907, hundreds of additional families came in.

At 20.4 *m.* on US 20 is the junction with an improved road.

Left on this road is BURLINGTON, 4 *m.* (4,300 alt., 400 pop.), a town on the Emblem Bench, named for the railroad. In early days, Burlington stores were unable to obtain enough goods to supply local demands, and settlers made annual shopping trips to Billings, Montana, and to Lander.

US 20 traverses vast scrubby sage flats and dry-land grain fields, freckled with strawstacks. The dim high outlines of the Absaroka and Carter Mountains assume body and bulk, as the road heads straight toward them.

At 51.8 *m.* is the junction with an oil-surfaced road.

Left on this road over rolling ranchlands and past sheep camps, watched by mounted herders, to MEETEETSE (Ind., place of rest or far away), 30.1 *m.* (5,797 alt., 296 pop.), on the upper Greybull River. Old false-front buildings shoulder solidly against pressed-brick structures in this old cow-town; punchers and sheepherders lounge along Main Street. In the background, the Carter Mountains are massed high. Meeteetse, the last outfitting point for the vast rugged wilderness drained by the Greybull, was one of the first settlements in the Big Horn Basin. Fragments of old boardwalks rot in front of early frame buildings, now warped and windowless. Old-Timers' Day, in July or early August, recalls the open range and the long drive.

Right from Meeteetse on a dirt road up the North Fork of the Greybull to the PITCHFORK RANCH, 18 *m.*, which has a large antelope herd. Charles Belden, one of the owners, often delivers the animals by airplane to zoos and other buyers. One shipment traveled to Germany by Zeppelin in 1936. Belden's fine photographs of Western life and landscapes are widely published.

Left from the Pitchfork Ranch on a foot trail to the GREAT ARROW, 25 *m.*, on a prominent hogback between Spring and Rush Creeks. Built of rocks, 58 feet long and 5 feet across at the head, the arrow points toward the Medicine Wheel on the western slope of the Big Horns (*see Tour 10*).

US 20 passes BECK LAKE (L), 53.6 *m.* (*crappie and bass*).

In CODY, 54.7 *m.* (5,018 alt., 1,800 pop.), on the Shoshone River, a vacation town at the western terminus of the Burlington's Frannie branch, are the headquarters of the Shoshone National Forest. Guides and dude wranglers are indistinguishable from the town's merchants and clerks, for, until deep snows end the tourist season, all wear bright silk shirts, cowhide vests, whipcords, high-heeled boots, and big hats. Visitors come in throngs. On Buffalo Bill Day (February 26), Cody celebrates, with a frontier ball and other entertainments, the anniversary of William F. Cody's birth. A Trappers' Ball, usually held in March, honors Bridger, Colter, the Sublettes, and others who trapped in the basin 50 years before settlers came. Guests appear in frontier costumes. The three-day Cody Stampede, which includes Independence Day, features prizefights, exhibitions of riding, and all modern rodeo acts. Cody is overrun by cowboys, cowgirls, cowmen, and cowwomen, all gay in fancy chaps, high heels, and fringed gauntlets. Indians in bright blankets and somber hats perform tribal dances.

The jagged Absaroka and Beartooth Mountains, west of Cody, cradle glacial lakes and support vast forests. Highways and byroads lead to guest ranches and breath-taking timber-line trails. Within a day's ride on horseback are wilderness pastures, where elk, deer, antelope, moose, and bighorn sheep graze.

The first Cody townsite was platted in the fall of 1895, near De

Maris Springs (*see below*), by George T. Beck, Horace Boal, and others. Buffalo Bill was then traveling with his Wild West Show. 'Horace and I had a talk,' Beck reported, 'and we concluded that as Cody was probably the best advertised man in the world, we might organize a company and make him president.' The company dug a canal to divert water from the South Fork of the Shoshone, and attracted homesteaders both by low rates and by the name of its president. Beck insisted that the town be moved up river to its present site, and Cody suggested his own name for the place; after some debate it was adopted. 'This did no harm to us, and it highly pleased the colonel,' said Beck. Within a year the Burlington built a branch from Frannie; when Park County was created in 1909, Cody became its seat. The first cabin, built by former Governor Frank L. Houx, is still standing.

From the beginning Cody was a true frontier town. When a missionary came to establish a church, some poker players in a saloon helped the good cause by giving him the pot. Cody was also one of the first Western towns to capitalize on its situation and atmosphere. Not many years after the Eaton brothers developed the dude ranch idea (*see Tour 10*), and before Western States started seriously to build highways, the little shacktown became a vacation center and took full advantage of its proximity to the increasingly fashionable Yellowstone Park.

The IRMA HOTEL, a rambling white frame hostelry and landmark, was built by Buffalo Bill and named for his daughter Irma Cody Garlow. In the lobby is a fireplace built of stones from many countries; on the walls are Western paintings by Remington. A cherrywood bar, intricately carved by hand, was brought from Europe by the colonel, and now serves as a lunch counter in the dining room; in the old days, its brass rail was scuffed simultaneously by the specially made boots of noblemen and the crude hobnails of freighters.

The OLD CODY HOUSE (*not open to public*), on the grounds of the Burlington Railroad station, was moved to Cody from Le Claire, Iowa. Cody was born in this house on February 26, 1846. The elder Cody started with his son for the California gold fields in 1857, but died in Kansas. Young Cody, already a skilful horseman, found work with a freighting outfit, and the next year he was on the road to Salt Lake City, with a herd of beef for Federal soldiers. On the Platte, he killed an Indian. During the Civil War, Cody served as a frontier scout for Northern armies. He acquired his nickname later, when, having contracted to supply buffalo meat for Kansas Pacific Railroad construction workers, he killed 4,280 bison in 18 months. After his frontier service ended, Cody toured America and Europe with his Wild West Show. During off-seasons, he visited old stamping grounds and guided hunting expeditions. He died in Denver in 1917.

The CODY MUSEUM (*adm. 25¢ during tourist season*), sponsored by the Buffalo Bill Memorial Association, is housed in a low, seven-room, log building, copied from the T E Ranch (*see below*). Here are displayed the showman's personal effects and other relics: boots, saddles, spurs, pistols, buffalo robes and heads, tomahawks, blankets, head-dresses, and mementos of the Wild West Show. Robert Lindneux's painting of the Cody-Yellow Hand fight (*see above*) hangs on the museum wall.

The MOLESWORTH SHOP, on the west edge of Cody, makes furniture of gnarled pine, decorated with hand-tooled leather, and sells it largely to hotels affecting a rustic atmosphere. The shop boasts a collection of rare Indian blankets.

1. Right from Cody on an oil-surfaced continuation of Main St. to the bronze equestrian STATUE OF BUFFALO BILL, 0.1 *m.* The mold was made by Mrs. Harry Payne Whitney in 1924. The horse, which stands 12 feet above the ground on a granite base, represents Smoky, the colonel's favorite, who was expressed to Mrs. Whitney's New York Studio and photographed in fast and slow motion, to assure faithfulness to the original. The Buffalo Bill figure is poised in the saddle, with Winchester held high.

2. Left from Cody on an improved road along the South Fork into dude-ranching country. Herefords are raised on the T E RANCH, 35 *m.*, which once belonged to Buffalo Bill. Cabins, barns, and corrals have been kept in their original state. The VALLEY RANCH, 43 *m.*, one of the region's old outfits and dude ranches, conducts the Valley Ranch Winter School for boys of high-school age.

3. Left from Cody on a dirt road to DE MARIS SPRINGS (*plunge and bath-house*), 3.2 *m.*, also called Needle Plunge, where warm sulphur-flavored water fizzes from the riverbank. The springs were named for Charles De Maris, who homesteaded here in 1885. Near by are tepee rings; legend tells that all tribes here laid aside their weapons to bathe and drink. A map drawn by John Colter, who passed this way in 1807, for Lewis and Clark, shows a 'boiling spring' in the vicinity.

US 20 crosses semi-arid, sage-covered hills. At 56.6 *m.* is the eastern end of SHOSHONE CANYON, the only pass through the enormous volcanic and sedimentary rocks that wall Yellowstone Park on the east. For five miles, the road threads its way around massive rocks that buttress the 1,000-foot cliffs and spires above. There are no habitations within 50 miles, except an occasional dude ranch, half-hidden among pines.

At 48.7 *m.* is a junction with a foot trail.

Left on this trail along the river's edge, then up Cedar Mountain to the mouth of SHOSHONE CAVERN (*closed, 1939*), 1 *m.* The entrance, 20 feet wide and 6 feet high, with scattered pines on either side, opens into a fracture zone that extends obliquely 2,500 feet into the mountain. The descent, by ladders, is perilous. The walls of the subterranean shaft are covered with crystal incrustations and fantastic dripstone formations, white, brown, and reddish in color. Ventilation is good. The cave, discovered by early settlers, was made a national monument in 1909, but most of it remains unexplored.

The highway, like a long black snake, creeps through tunnels and sandstone overhangs, along a blasted course up the face of the wall to the level of Shoshone Lake. In some places in the canyon, layers of sedimentary rocks range up to 700 feet in thickness; in others, the hard underlying granite core is exposed, and here the walls are less eroded, the passage narrower. The hardest rocks have been polished by erosion, but are only slightly worn away. Where the sedimentary rocks vary greatly in consistency, strange sculptured figures, like gargoyles, peer from the cliffs. At the bottom of the canyon, the river is churned to white froth over a bed of rocks.

SHOSHONE DAM (L), 61.7 m., completed in 1910 after four years' work, was built to impound water for 300,000 acres of dry land in northern Shoshone Valley. It is 328 feet high, 200 feet wide at its crest, and varies in thickness from 108 feet at the base to 10 feet at the top. From downstream, the dam resembles a white concrete wedge thrust solidly between the towering cliffs. Water cascades from the spillway (R). The reservoir covers a tract 10 miles long and 4 miles wide.

The valley west of the canyon is dotted with ranches. Old Indian trails, modernized and improved, lead into the mountains. The road crosses a boundary of the SHOSHONE NATIONAL FOREST, 79.6 m., oldest national forest in the United States, which was established in 1902 as the Yellowstone Forest Reserve. Here the slopes of the Absarokas, heavily timbered with pine, spruce, and fir, meet the dry Park County wastelands; peaks flank the road like gigantic monuments. The area is drained by tributaries of the Yellowstone River. Cattle and game animals feed on the rich summer range. The Forest Service maintains 50 campgrounds.

Grotesque rock figures along the North Fork of the Shoshone are identified by signs: Laughing Pig, Camel, Garden of the Goops, Mr. Punch, Bear, Hanging Rock, Goose, Wooden Shoe, Holy City, Ptarmigan Mountain, Devil's Elbow, Thor's Anvil, and Four Old Men on a Toboggan.

WAPITI RANGER STATION, 84.3 m., is the oldest (1903) forest ranger station in the United States.

At 96.9 m. is the junction with a trail.

Left on this trail along Fish Hawk Creek to FISH HAWK GLACIER, 10 m.

PAHASKA TEPEE, 105.5 m., a two-story log lodge for tourists, was built as the hunting lodge for Buffalo Bill. PAHASKA CAMPGROUND, 105.7 m., has free facilities.

Sylvan Pass Ranger Station, the EAST ENTRANCE TO YELLOWSTONE PARK, 107.7 m. (see Yellowstone National Park), is on the western boundary of the Shoshone National Forest.

Tour 6A

Junction with US 14-20—Lovell—Cowley—Frannie—(Billings, Montana); US 310.
Junction with US 14-20 to Montana Line, 49.6 *m.*

Oil-surfaced; open all year.
Route paralleled by Chicago, Burlington & Quincy R.R.
Accommodations in larger towns.

US 310 is a short cut between US 20 (*see Tour* 6) and US 10 in Montana. State 114 branches southwestward from it at Deaver to unite with US 14-20 at Cody (*see Tour* 6c).

US 310 branches northwest from US 14-20 (*see Tours* 10 *and* 6), 0 *m.*, at a point 4.8 miles west of Greybull, in one of the most arid and barren regions of Wyoming. For 20 miles there is no vegetation, except stunted clumps of salt sage. The wind whips fine dirt from the eroded hillsides and weathered sandstone protrudes from low ridges, like the plates on an armored dinosaur's back. In the distance (R) are high hills, broken midway by a deep canyon. The outlines of the Carter Mountains are dim in the southwest.

At 25 *m.*, the highway enters the irrigated and fertile Lovell beet-growing district, a part of the Shoshone Reclamation Project (*see Tour* 6c). The gray, alkaline desert soil contrasts with the velvet green of the beet and bean fields. Drab adobe dwellings of Mexican seasonal workers squat in field corners.

At 28.5 *m.* is the southern junction with State 14 (*see Tour* 10A), which unites with US 310 for 2.9 miles.

LOVELL, 28.7 *m.* (3,814 alt., 1,857 pop.), largest town in northwestern Wyoming and an important supply point on the Chicago, Burlington and Quincy, is a busy, attractive town of wide streets and handsome buildings. It was founded by Mormon colonists who came into the region in 1900 (*see below*), and was named for a big-scale rancher who had preceded the Mormon settlers. During the beet campaign, the population is considerably increased by sugar-factory workers.

The GREAT WESTERN SUGAR FACTORY (R), 29.5 *m.*, a group of pressed-brick buildings on landscaped grounds, was built in 1916; irrigation, begun in 1909, had previously made sugar-beet cultivation a thriving industry. During the fall campaign (harvest and refining season), the plant is the center of regional activity. Three crews keep its processing machinery grinding continuously for several months; long queues of trucks rumble between the factory and the fields. Beet pulp and tops are made into feed for hogs and cattle.

At 31.4 *m.*, near the marked site of WOODRUFF'S CAMP OF MAY 1900 (*see below*), is the northern junction with State 14 (*see Tour 10A*).

The fields ahead are flat and divided by numerous canals and ditches. Here, in early summer, women, men, and children work long hours with the crops.

COWLEY, 35 *m.* (3,976 alt., 900 pop.), built on level benchland north of Sage Creek, has its chief business establishments along the north side of Main Street. Many dwellings and public buildings are of rose-colored sandstone from neighboring quarries. Cowley was founded in 1900 by Mormon colonists from Utah and Idaho, led by Abraham O. Woodruff. Officials of the Church of Jesus Christ of Latter-day Saints encouraged migration to select farming areas, but they were skeptical of the arid Big Horn benchlands. Woodruff's colonists headed north on their own initiative. When water reached the benchlands from the Shoshone River Reclamation Project, however, and Cowley, Lovell, and other Mormon settlements began to flourish, other converts were urged to settle in the basin.

The CHURCH SQUARE, south side of Main Street, is the social center for Mormon families in the vicinity. The COMMUNITY BUILDING (1936), a large, squat peeled-log structure in the center of the block, provides recreational facilities for young people, whose Mutual Improvement Association sponsors regional contests in debating, storytelling, athletics, dramatics, and other activities. The outstanding event each year is the Gold and Green Ball (*open to the public*), usually held in January or February. The dance is different each year, and instructors are dispatched from church headquarters to the various wards to teach the music and intricate steps.

The RELIEF SOCIETY HALL is a tan-colored sandstone story-and-a-half building. Here the Relief Society Sisters, the ladies' aid of the Mormon church, formerly served dinner on 'Good Roads Day,' when every man in the community turned out to improve public roads.

At 35.4 *m.* is the junction with a dirt road.

Left on this road to the BIG HORN CANNERY, 1.2 *m.* Peas, corn, beans, and other vegetables are processed in this plant.

US 310 runs almost due west across sagebrush hills and green irrigated flats. Ahead and to the west are the northern Big Horn Basin oil fields, and the massive Big Horns thrust their cones above the foothills to the east.

DEAVER, 41.5 *m.* (4,105 alt., 85 pop.), is a ranchers' and oil workers' supply point, at the junction with State 114, an oil-surfaced highway. Its few houses are scattered over the prairie, frontier fashion.

Left from Deaver on State 114 over beet-growing land to GARLAND, 11.7 *m.* (4,247 alt., 85 pop.), a beet-growers' hamlet at the junction of State 114 with State 14 (*see Tour 10A*).

North of Deaver, ranches and small irrigated farms spot the alkaline flats.

FRANNIE, 47.4 *m.* (4,219 alt., 50 pop.), named for a settler's daughter, is a supply point for oil fields near by and a railroad junction, from which a branch runs southwest to Cody. Large trucks rumble along the highway, loaded with oil and oil-well casing.

Left from Frannie on a dirt road to the Elk Basin Oil Field, 15 *m.*

At 48.7 *m.* is the junction with a graded road.

Left on this road to the Frannie Oil Field, 1 *m.* Derricks and storage tanks rise on the slopes.

At 49.6 *m.*, where drab foothills hide the more distant mountain ranges on either side, US 310 crosses the MONTANA LINE, 74 miles south of Billings, Montana.

Tour 7

Junction with US 287—Jackson—Junction with US 189—Rock Springs; 214.6 *m.*, US 187.

Oil-surfaced and graveled; closed between Moran and Jackson in winter.
Good accommodations at long intervals.

Between northern Jackson Hole and Rock Springs, US 187 passes through strikingly diverse areas. Rugged snow-capped summits and timbered slopes are mirrored in clear lakes. Primitive areas shelter elk and other wild animals. Then the route cuts southeastward, through spectacular canyons, native meadows, and mountain parks, and crosses a desert of salt sage to connect with the Lincoln Highway.

Section a. JUNCTION WITH US 287 to JUNCTION WITH STATE 22; 34.9 m. US 187-89

From forest land along the edge of Jackson Lake, US 187 descends into Jackson Hole, a valley shouldered by spired mountain ranges.

It commands many fine views of the stately Teton Range and borders some of the finest hay lands in the State.

The highway swings southwestward from the junction with US 287, 0 m. (see Tour 5), near a border of the Teton National Forest. Against the background of pine, lowland meadows are deep green or yellow, according to the season. JACKSON LAKE (R) is the second-largest lake in Wyoming.

At 1.2 m. is the junction with a graveled road.

> Left on this road is MORAN, 0.1 m. (6,742 alt., 102 pop.), a tourist village and reclamation headquarters. In summer, a boat trip is made twice daily across Jackson Lake to the base of the Tetons. The water, generally deep and cold, is warmed at one place by a spring in the lake-bed. (Boaters, for fishing or pleasure, must report to Moran Ranger Station before embarking.)

US 187 climbs a sharp grade to the top of JACKSON LAKE DAM, 1.4 m., which impounds water for irrigation along the Snake River in Idaho.

At 2.8 m. is the junction with a dirt road.

> Right on this steep and narrow road to SIGNAL MOUNTAIN, 4 m. (7,230 alt.), from whose summit Jackson Hole is seen in panorama. The name of the mountain commemorates the search for Robert R. Hamilton, who lost his way while hunting in the vicinity. Searchers agreed that if Hamilton were found, a signal fire should be lighted on this summit. The body was found in Snake River.

The road runs southwestward through forests of pine, with silver spruce intermingled. Groves of aspen spot the sea of dark green with pastel islands. There is much dead wood, and occasional open spaces are thickly set with gray and weathered stumps. Yellow wild flowers and grass cover the forest floor. To the northeast rise the peaks of the Continental Divide, rugged and blue, yet less austere than the Tetons, which loom ahead through a haze of deep, but delicate, azure. The bases of these vast crags are robed in forest; the upper masses are sheer, frowning rock. Their summits, all just noticeably slanted in one direction, suggest the spearheads of some titanic phalanx moving into action. The road crosses a boundary of TETON NATIONAL FOREST, 5.2 m., and of JACKSON HOLE, 5.3 m.

This green and fertile valley, about 400 square miles in area, extends about 50 miles from north to south. Its width varies from 6 to 12 miles. Snake River flows southward through the valley, while smaller streams flow in from east and west, joining the Snake or emptying into Jackson Lake. High mountains bound the valley; the Continental Divide is about 30 miles away.

John Colter, probably the first white man in this region, left Manuel Lisa's fort in Montana, crossed the Big Horn Basin and Union Pass, and went up Hoback Canyon into Jackson Hole in 1807. He climbed Teton Pass, journeyed through Pierre's Hole in Idaho, and re-entered Wyoming in the Yellowstone region (see Yellowstone National Park). Andrew Henry built a fort for the Missouri Fur Company west of the Teton Range in 1810; a year later, Wilson Price Hunt left several members of his overland party to trap along the headwaters of the Snake; but not until William H. Ashley's land brigades came West in the 1820's was the region worked systematically (*see History*). Jackson Hole was named for David E. Jackson, an Ashley associate and later part-owner of the fur company. With Ashley and Jackson were the Sublettes, Jim Bridger, Kit Carson, Broken Hand Fitzpatrick, Jim Beckwourth, and others whose names are legend.

The first settlers came about 1883, but Jackson Hole long remained isolated, a convenient spot for rustlers and others who needed a hiding place. A road survey was made over Teton Pass in 1901, but the route had grades as steep as 19°. Though roads now lead into the valley from four directions, it is still sparsely settled. Ranches run to thousands of acres. Some land produces hay, grain, and potatoes, but cattle raising and dude ranching are the main industries. A few sheep are kept, although public ranges are closed to them. The struggle to keep sheep out of the valley began in 1901, when cattlemen killed 300 head on forest range near Mosquito Creek.

The foresight of sportsmen and the isolation of the country have made Jackson Hole the home of large numbers of deer, moose, and elk. Bear and mountain sheep roam the higher ranges; geese, ducks, sage hens, and grouse live on the swamps and meadows. The lakes are stocked with trout.

Summers in Jackson Hole are pleasant. Winter weather ranges from thawing temperatures to −65° F.; but, because of the altitude and the dryness of the air, only extreme temperatures are hard to bear. Tobogganing and skiing are popular sports, and, in some parts of the valley, skiing and snowshoeing are usual modes of winter travel.

At 8.8 *m.* is the junction with an oiled road.

Right on this road to the STRING LAKE ENTRANCE TO GRAND TETON NATIONAL PARK, 2.8 *m.* (*see Tour 7A*).

Glimpses may be seen of quiet water at the foot of the Tetons. The dike on Mount Moran shows up clearly, its edges straight and abrupt, like a strip of dark filling in a gigantic sandwich.

At 13 *m.* is the junction with an oiled road.

Right on this road to the JENNY LAKE ENTRANCE TO GRAND TETON NATIONAL PARK, 0.2 *m.* (*see Tour 7A*).

At JENNY LAKE STORE AND CAMPGROUND (L), 13.4 *m.*, the highway swings directly southward at the foot of the Tetons. Tall pines are scattered along the slopes, which rise rapidly toward the peaks; others crest the distant wind-swept ridges. River flats and knolls (L) are sparsely grassed.

The log CHURCH OF THE TRANSFIGURATION (L), 19.9 *m.*, built in 1914, has only one room. The grounds, set off from the surrounding flat by a buck fence, are entered through a peak-roofed gate. The window behind the altar frames a view of the Tetons.

US 187 crosses the SNAKE RIVER, 20.1 *m.*, which rises in southeastern Yellowstone Park, flows southward through Jackson Lake, and winds down through its Grand Canyon (*see Tour* 13) to Idaho. It was known to the Indians as Yam-pah-pa, for a plant that grew along its banks. French trappers who came to grief in its rapids called it *La Maudite Rivière Enragée* (the accursed mad river). It is not certain whether the stream was renamed for its twisting course or for the Shoshonean Indians, who dried and cooked the long pencil-like roots of the yam-pah-pa for food.

East of the bridge is the junction with a graded road.

Left on this road is the post-office station of GROVONT—phonetic rendering of Gros Ventre (Fr., great belly), the name of an Indian tribe, 2 *m.* The road goes southeast toward GROS VENTRE RIVER, which it parallels through a narrow steep-walled valley. Small lakes nestle in the hollows; groves of aspen patch the dark-green slopes. The Gros Ventre Mountains are the home of most of the mountain sheep of Wyoming. Many of the rugged peaks rise to nearly 12,000 feet.

A vein of coal was opened in 1890 at a spot near what is now the upper end of Slide Lake, a body of water formed a few years later by a landslide that dammed the river. Transportation difficulties prevented commercial development of the 15-foot vein, which, however, supplies fuel for local use.

OUZEL (oo-zel) FALLS, near the head of the Gros Ventre, is reached by trail from GOOSEWING RANGER STATION, 30 *m.* Snow fields around the falls, high on the eastern slope of the Continental Divide, feed the Wind River, which empties into the Missouri-Mississippi system; Indian Creek, a branch of the Gros Ventre, which empties into the Snake-Columbia system; and Green River, a tributary of the Colorado. Game trails lie between the streams, which head only a few miles apart. Ouzel Falls is named for the water ouzel, or American dipper, a slate-gray, stocky bird, five to seven inches long, which frequents the torrents that come down from the glaciers and snow fields. Although it lacks webbed feet or any apparent equipment for aquatic life, the ouzel bobs around unconcernedly on slippery rocks in the water, diving at intervals into the rapids.

Upper Gros Ventre Basin comprises half a million acres of wilderness. Between the peaks around it, knifelike ridges sketch a bold, sharp sky line. Forests alternate with high meadows and clear, icy lakes. Fierce winds drift the snow into banks of almost glacial hardness, some of which can support the weight of a horse in midsummer. The snow, as it melts, feeds innumerable springs and rills. Thousands of elk, deer, moose, and bear feed here in summer, and almost every kind of bird of the Rocky Mountain region enters the basin.

US 187 offers constantly changing views of the Teton crags, glaciers, and shadows. Cirques are clearly defined at the glacier heads, where the constant grind and pull of ice has hollowed out amphitheatral recesses in the rock wall.

At 22.5 *m.* is the junction with a graded road.

Left on this road is KELLY, 5 *m.* (6,400 alt., 30 pop.) (*ranger station, store, filling station*). In June 1925, the whole north end of Sheep Mountain (11,900 alt.) moved suddenly into and across the Gros Ventre Valley, about four miles east of Kelly. The obstructed river created Sudden Lake. On May 18, 1927, the barrier broke, and the flood destroyed several ranches, killed six persons and many animals, and left of Kelly only the church and schoolhouse.

US 187 proceeds across sage flats, where poles and tree branches are set to outline the road after heavy snow. In summer, fields of grain and hay extend (R) toward the Tetons. On the Federal refuge here (*see below*) about 10,000 elk are fed hay and cottonseed cake from trucks and bobsleds in winter. In autumn, the elk may be seen grazing near the highway.

JACKSON, 33.2 *m.* (6,209 alt., 538 pop.), seat of Teton County and supply point for hunters and ranchers, has become a kind of symbol of Jackson Hole and the West. False-front and log buildings border the grassy park that forms its center. Men and women alike dress in cowboy regalia; saddle horses are usually tied along Main Street. Jackson caters especially to summer vacationists, who visit the neighboring dude-ranching and hunting areas; prices are high, because of the short summer season. The Days of '49, chiefly a rodeo, is held annually. A local winter-sports association sponsors a carnival and dog derby. A good skating rink is maintained; near-by hills afford ski and toboggan slides.

Left from Jackson on a graded road to the U. S. BUREAU OF BIOLOGICAL SURVEY ELK AND BIRD REFUGE, 0.5 *m.*, a 24,000-acre tract of meadow and foothill land, set aside by Congress as a wild-life refuge. Elk, originally plains animals, were driven to the mountains, as the prairies and valleys were gradually fenced in for domestic animals. Unlike deer, elk have large feet and are unable to paw through ice-coated snow to uncover frozen grass.

During the severe Wyoming winter of 1908–9, about 20,000 elk in the Jackson Hole region were starving. Residents of the valley raised a fund of $1,000 to buy hay for them, and the Wyoming State Legislature appropriated $5,000 to purchase additional feed. In answer to an appeal from the Wyoming State Game Warden the U. S. Bureau of Biological Survey helped feed the big herds through the next year and in 1912 Congress set aside 1,000 acres as a winter refuge. With increased Governmental appropriations and donations from national sportsmen's organizations, the refuge was expanded to its present acreage. Hay is harvested from the meadowland in summer, and additional concentrated foods, including cottonseed cake, are provided. The refuge now accommodates an average of about 10,000 elk.

In 1921 the Elk Refuge was also made a refuge for all species of birds.

At 34.9 *m.* is the junction with State 22.

Right on this graveled road across a broad valley, with the jagged Tetons in full view (R). Haystacks, surrounded by tall pole fences, freckle the yellow and green of the valley floor. In every direction are ranch houses; some are spacious frame buildings with steep gables; others are log cabins. The road crosses the NORTH FORK OF SNAKE RIVER, 4 *m.*

WILSON, 5.7 *m.* (6,080 alt., 500 pop.), was named for 'Uncle Nick' Wilson, the first settler here, who came to Jackson Hole in 1889. Nick spent several childhood years among the Shoshone and was the hero of H. R. Driggs' *The White Indian Boy, or Uncle Nick Among the Shoshones* (1919).

In Wilson is the junction with the Grand Canyon Road (*see Tour 13*).

The grade steepens as State 22 approaches the mountains and crosses a boundary of the TETON NATIONAL FOREST, 7.5 *m.* West of LEE RANGER STATION (L), 8 *m.*, is a shelf climb. The highway ascends 2,200 feet in less than six miles; from one point near the top, seven hairpin turns are visible below. Tall blue pines border the road; luxuriant wild flowers adorn the hillsides. Colors here seem deeper than in the lower country. Purple aster, goldenrod, thimbleberry, mountain ash, daisy, fireweed, beeflower, wild rose, rabbit brush, dandelion, strawberry, Indian paintbrush, purple loco, sweet clover, Indian tobacco, Rose of Sharon, and less brilliant plants grow together in a chaos of color. The bright red and gold of frost-bitten chokeberry and aspen leaves add their richness in autumn.

At 9.9 *m.* is a commanding view of the southern floor of Jackson Hole. A sign (R) bears a greeting for the eastbound traveler: 'Howdy Stranger. Yonder is Jackson Hole.' At 12 *m.* is the summit of TETON PASS (8,429 alt.) and the boundary between TETON and TARGHEE NATIONAL FORESTS. A deserted shack (L) was once a haven for freighters. In winter, mail is carried over the pass to Jackson from Victor, the Idaho railhead, on dog sledges and on bobsleds drawn by four- and six-horse teams. The view here is one of the grandest in the West.

Teton Pass was long known as Hunt's Pass, for Wilson Price Hunt, who crossed it in 1811 (*see History*). Trappers and traders crossing between Jackson Hole and Pierre's Hole (Teton Basin) used it constantly for years. Wagons were brought over it in the late 1880's. When Negro troops sent to Jackson in 1896, during the Bannock scare, found that their horses could not pull the wagons up the steep grade, they hauled them up by hand. In 1901, Uinta County, which included Jackson Hole, appropriated $500 to build a wagon road over the pass. The survey was accomplished with a crude instrument fashioned from a walnut table leaf contributed by a settler. The road was so steep on both approaches that wagons could descend only with the aid of 'roughlocks'—large untrimmed trees chained to the wheels to prevent their turning. Even today, the drive is not suited to automobiles in less than first-class condition.

The lower slopes west of the summit are heavily timbered. Higher up are perpetual fields of snow and ice, from which streams tumble through jagged canyons. Flowers rivaling those of the eastern slope are dominated by the sturdy, delicately lavender Rose of Sharon. Ferns, turning yellow in autumn, thrive in the thick stands of fir (L). In the sunlight, the leaves of mountain ash shimmer among the dark pines and firs.

At 14.6 *m.*, near a small park, is the junction with the Coal Creek Trail; R. here to big-game country. The descent becomes gentler, and, as the pines recede, groves of aspen dapple the slopes. At 18.5 *m.*, State 22 crosses the Idaho Line, becoming Idaho 31, 5.4 miles east of Victor, Idaho.

Section b.   JUNCTION WITH STATE 22 to ROCK SPRINGS;
179.7 m.   US 187.

This section of US 187 runs southeastward through a rugged canyon to a ranching area, from which pack trails lead to the Wind River glaciers; then it crosses a hundred miles of barren sheep land and unites with US 30.

South of the junction with State 22, 0 *m.*, US 187 winds between green alfalfa fields and meadows of wild hay, broken by cottonwood groves. At 1.5 *m.*, two summits of the Tetons are in view to the north. The road crosses the southern extremity of Jackson Hole and parallels the Snake River (R) along high shelves. Lavish reds, yellows, browns, and greens are splashed over the canyon walls and floor. At a turn in the road, a peak comes into view, vividly red above, green below. This contrast of red rock against green forest continues up the canyon. Softer colors are not lacking—patches of gray sage, blue flowers, and pale green grass against the gray-white lower slopes. Some of the cliffs, ocher or slaty in color, have columnar fronts. The sparkling clear stream that flows beside the road mirrors the crags, the slopes, and the forest.

The highway turns L. at the mouth of HOBACK CANYON, 12.7 *m.*, which was named for John Hoback, Wilson P. Hunt's guide through the region in 1811. The canyon is walled with towering cliffs. The road follows narrow ledges, sometimes at the very edge of the Hoback River. Throughout the canyon are evidences of snow slides. One of these, which recurs annually, is called the Bull-of-the-Woods; in the spring this slide comes down a steep and winding gulch, jumps the river without touching the ice, is carried up the hillside beyond for several hundred yards by its own momentum, then slides back down the slope. It has the appearance of two slides meeting at the river.

At 17 *m.* is the junction with a dirt road.

Right on this road to BRYAN FLAT RANGER STATION AND CAMP MICHIGAN, 2 *m.* Camp Michigan, the oldest of its kind, is a summer school of engineering founded in 1874 by the late Professor Joseph Baker Davis and maintained by the University of Michigan and Northwestern University.

Up the Hoback River, the highway curves and twists around sheer rock barriers, past caves and slides, and along shelves. At 21.4 *m.,* a bending of strata has marked the face of a cliff (R) with an Indian war bonnet pattern.

At 24.1 *m.* is the junction with a graded road.

Left on this road to GRANITE FALLS and a Hot Spring, 3 *m.,* where the U. S. Forest Service has built a concrete swimming pool and cabins. Near by is OPEN DOOR PEAK, so named for a rock formation on its side. BATTLE MOUNTAIN, northwest of Granite Creek, is near the site of a skirmish between Jackson Hole residents and Bannock Indians in 1895.

Early treaties permitted the Indians to hunt in Jackson Hole, and, after the valley was settled, the Indians refused to relinquish this right. Threatened with arrest for game-law violations, they faced officers with Winchesters. A posse of 40 white men surprised them near Battle Mountain and started to take them to Jackson for trial. As the caravan passed along a winding path through the timber, a war whoop signaled escape. A few shots were fired as horses and riders flashed among the trees, but, except for a two-year-old child and one Indian who was killed, all the prisoners got away. When the news of the affair reached the East, a New York paper solemnly reported: ALL RESIDENTS IN JACKSON HOLE, WYOMING, MASSACRED.

Chief Race Horse, arrested again, was later freed by the district court because of Indian treaty rights. The case was carried to the State supreme court, which reversed the decision, holding that a State has jurisdiction over the game within its borders.

The canyon widens to a valley; grassy or wooded hills rise gently to the Snake and Salt River Ranges (R) and the bare, bold Gros Ventre (L). This is dude-ranch country, and guests are often seen riding near the road. At the V BAR V RANCH (R), 29.1 *m.,* is the marked site where the first Protestant sermon in Wyoming was preached on August 23, 1835, by the Reverend Samuel Parker (*see Tour* 9).

At BONDURANT, 34 *m.* (6,588 alt.), a ranch post office, formerly called the Triangle F Ranch, headquarters are maintained for highway snowplows in winter.

US 187 crosses the Hoback River and winds upward between heavily forested slopes. Near the road bloom brilliant red fireweed and blue-white aster. South of FALER GUARD STATION, 45.5 *m.,* US 187 follows THE RIM, which suddenly reveals, to the north, a breath-taking view of the lower country. The contrast between valley and highland is emphasized by the dramatic abruptness of the transition. The highway crosses a boundary of TETON NATIONAL FOREST, 47.5 *m.* The vivid green of aspen and pine and the gray of sage alternate in the landscape. An occasional cabin is set among the trees.

At 59.8 *m.* is the junction with a graded road.

Left on this road are CORA, 7 *m.*, KENDALL, 26 *m.*, and GREEN RIVER LAKES, 49 *m.*, in one of the finest recreational areas in Wyoming. (*Boating, fishing, camping, horseback riding, pack trips to lakes.*)

The highway passes ranches that were abandoned during the decline in the cattle business in the early 1930's. It runs over sage-covered hills and across flats rich with grass, shrubs, and willows. The Gros Ventre Mountains recede in blue haze to the north; the Salt River Mountains loom dimly (R); the Wind River Range rears its peaks ahead (L).

At 66.1 *m.* is the junction with a dirt road.

Right on this road to a STATE FISH HATCHERY (*open to visitors*), 2 *m.*

At 66.7 *m.* is the junction with a dirt road.

Right here to good fishing at GREEN RIVER BRIDGE, 1.3 *m.* The road winds through ranchlands to the riverbank SITE OF FORT BONNEVILLE, 3.3 (*see History*), among low willow and wild rose bushes. A granite boulder on a concrete base marks the site.

At 67.1 *m.* is the junction with US 189 (*see Tour 9*. US 187 goes east over green-gold and umber meadows and gray hills, with snow-splashed peaks ahead.

PINEDALE, 78.1 *m.* (7,175 alt., 219 pop.), seat of Sublette County, reflects the frontier in its peeled-log buildings and streets edged with pines. It is the home of the *Roundup,* said to be published farther from a railroad than any other newspaper in the United States. The first settlers came here in 1878–9, to winter their herds on rich hay from the easily watered meadows. (*Pack trips and fall big-game hunting; cabins; camping; fishing.*)

1. Left from Pinedale on a dirt road to ten-mile FREMONT LAKE, 4 *m.* The boat trip to the head of the lake reaches FREMONT and PINE CREEK CANYONS.

2. Left from Pinedale on a dirt road to HALFMOON LAKE, 9 *m.*, BOULDER LAKE, 18 *m.*, and NEWFORK LAKE, 22 *m.*

US 187 swings southward through hills and across a valley, where cattle feed in meadows dotted with haystacks. Thick streambank pines (R) fringe the route darkly. The edge of the valley is sharply marked; sagebrush crowds the richer growth.

Along the single street of BOULDER, 90 *m.* (7,903 alt., 25 pop.), are deserted log houses, without doors or windows. (*Store, gas station, auto camps; good trout fishing near by.*)

At 90.4 *m.* is the junction with a dirt road.

Left on this road to STEELE HOT SPRINGS, 5 *m.*

The road dips into East Fork Valley, a strip of green between ranges of hills. In NEW FORK, 93.2 *m.*, now nearly deserted, is a community hall still used for dancing. US 187 winds to a plateau, on which sheep and cattle graze. A wilderness of sage rolls southward, scarred with small arroyos and dry streambeds that carry torrents during heavy rains. There is no more greenery; near at hand is the dusty, light-gray of sage; farther out, the desert shows dark-gray, blue, brown, and, in the farthest distance, almost black. In some places it is tinted yellow by rabbit brush, or shot with sudden bright streaks of tan. Plainly outlined on the horizon far ahead is Pilot Butte, a pioneer landmark. The road rises and falls, crosses flat stretches, and dips between ridges topped with lonely sheepherders' monuments. Shelter shacks along the bleak stretches have saved many lives during blizzards. A boundary of the TAYLOR GRAZING AREA, 114.1 *m.*, is marked with small concrete pyramids.

The horizon to the north and east is banked with rock-tipped blue mountains, so softened by haze and distance that the farther peaks melt imperceptibly into the sky, like blue-gray clouds with patches of white among them. Salt River Range is a dim drift of blue along the western horizon. For miles the road runs between narrow strips of richly colored Russian thistles—green, red, lavender, magenta, and purple.

FARSON, 138 *m.* (6,680 alt., 126 pop.), is one of two outposts, 4.3 miles apart, in nearly 100 miles of desert between New Fork and Rock Springs. A granite monument (R) with a bronze plaque marks the SITE OF THE BRIDGER-YOUNG CONFERENCE of June 28, 1847. Here, Jim Bridger and Brigham Young met in overnight camp and conferred regarding the route westward and the possibility of sustaining a large population in the Valley of Great Salt Lake. According to legend, Bridger pessimistically offered $1,000 for the first bushel of corn grown in that valley.

Directly south of the monument is the marked SITE OF THE BIG SANDY PONY EXPRESS STATION, burned by Indians in 1862. The Sandy and the Little Sandy flow past on the west and south.

At Farson is the junction with the South Pass Road (*see Tour 5A*).

EDEN, 142.3 *m.* (6,590 alt., 256 pop.), the center of a 28,000-acre irrigation project, lies on a small fertile plateau, where extensive work is carried on by the State Agricultural Experiment Station. Near here, Horace Greeley spent the night of August 16, 1859, sleeping in a log house that was said to be the only house between Fort Bridger and Fort Laramie. Clover and alfalfa fields stretch for miles around Eden; but, where irrigation ends, the desert begins abruptly. Barns and sheds on farms and ranches are thatched securely against winds that sweep the area. Water is pumped from deep wells, with derrick-surmounted pump houses.

As the road runs out into the desert, the slatted wheel of a windmill, and shortly the ranch buildings of WELLS, 154.5 *m.*, a sheep ranch, come into view. South of Wells, as the snow drifts deeply here in winter, tall willows are set in the shoulders of the highway to indicate the route. At 166.7 *m.* a sign points to drinking water. Barren hills and alkali flats, greasewood and salt sage characterize the country ahead. In the springtime, the small ridge of hills (R) shows splashes of green within the cup-shaped depressions near the crests.

At 169.4 *m.* is the junction with an improved road.

> Left on'this road is WINTON, 4 *m.* (6,945 alt., 303 pop.), a coal-mining community.

North of Rock Springs, the valley stretches eastward to ocher-tinted mountainsides, with an occasional blue summit beyond. To the R. are washed clay and shale banks, white below but streaked with gray above. The highway crosses KILLPECKER CREEK, 178.9 *m.*

At 179 *m.* is the junction with a dirt road.

> Right on this road to the foot of the chalk bluffs, 0.2 *m.*, west of Killpecker Creek. Here is the SITE OF BLAIR'S STOCKADE and the old ROCK SPRING for which the town is named (*see Tour 2c*). Archie and Duncan Blair built a trading post here, in 1866, and furnished hungry travelers with venison steak and coffee. Becky Thomas, the station master, charged 10¢ a head for watering thirsty horses. The post was sold in the 1870's for $14, and only a few crumbling stones remain on the site. Back of it rise great rocks on which emigrants carved their names.
>
> About 200 yards south is the site of No. 6 POWDER HOUSE, where, on July 17, 1891, two men on a drunken lark fired into 1,200 kegs of blasting powder and 700 pounds of dynamite. The building disappeared, leaving a great ragged hole. Four men were killed.

Miners' houses, set against the cliffs along the highway, are built of local stone chinked with mortar from Killpecker Creek.

ROCK SPRINGS, 179.7 *m.* (6,271 alt., 8,440 pop.) (*see Tour 2c*), is at the junction with US 30 (*see Tour 2*).

Tour 7A

Junction with US 187—Grand Teton National Park Headquarters; 11.6 *m.*, Park Drive and US 187.

Oiled roadbed.
Dude ranches, cabins, camp and picnic grounds.

Park Drive branches southwest from US 187, 0 *m.* (*see Tour 7a*), at a point 31.5 miles south of Yellowstone National Park, and runs across sage flats toward the spectacular Teton uplift. Sharp, ragged cones rise abruptly above the timbered lake areas at the foot of the range; their sheerness, unrelieved by foothills, is accentuated by the flat, cobble-strewn floor of Jackson Hole. The range is tipped slightly toward the east, and the east face, exposed by uplift and erosion, is one of the steepest fault escarpments in the world. Little spires and turrets rise from the shoulders of the larger peaks; small glaciers are cradled in shaded basins and chasms. Shifting light and changing perspective throw into relief giant spearheads, Gothic towers, stone forests, and frowning battlements. Under light from the east, the massive rocks are clear-cut and austere; the glaciers and snowbanks are cold glass furrows. When the light is from the west, long pointed shadows slide across the valley floor, and each pinnacle has a silvery, sometimes a crimson, edge. Evening and morning shadows conceal the smaller crags, leaving only sharply slanting cones. Red sunset floods the canyons with vermilion; the ice fields become small pink lakes.

The jagged sky line is climaxed by ten major peaks: Grand Teton (13,766 alt.), Mount Owen (12,922 alt.), Middle Teton (12,798 alt.), Mount Moran (12,594 alt.), South Teton (12,505 alt.), Mount Teewinot (12,317 alt.), Buck Mountain (11,923 alt.), Nez Perce Mountain (11,900 alt.), Mount Wister (11,480 alt.), and Mount St. John (11,412 alt.). A barrier 40 miles long, the range stretches from Yellowstone Park to Teton Pass (*see Tour 7a*), where it joins the Snake Mountains.

As the road runs toward the pines that blanket the base of the mountains, sage gives way to fallen and dying timber. Farther ahead, the forest is green and deep. Naked peaks tower above the tree line.

At 2.8 *m.* is the String Lake entrance to GRAND TETON NATIONAL PARK, a wilderness reaching from a point on the western shore of Jackson Lake, 11 miles south of Yellowstone Park, to Rendezvous Peak, about 7 miles northwest of Jackson. The park, 27 miles long and 3 to 9 miles wide, covers 150 square miles, including the most rugged section of the majestic Teton Range. Much of its area is above timber line; the highest peaks rise 7,000 feet above the valley floor. The interior is penetrated only by bridle and foot trails.

(*Guided pack and hiking trips arranged at Park Headquarters or at Jenny Lake Station; riding or hiking alone or without first registering is absolutely prohibited. Hunting forbidden, but streams and lakes may be fished; standard licenses required. Bathing suits and towels at Leigh Lake. Campfires outside auto camps only by special permission. Pets must be kept on leash.*)

The Teton Range began its existence when a great block of the earth's rocky shell, cleanly fractured late in the era that saw the Rocky Mountain system built, was tilted upward until its eastern edge stood nearly 10,000 feet higher than the adjoining rocks. For millions of years natural forces—rain and wind, heat and cold—sculptured the uplifted block. During the Pleistocene epoch, tremendous masses of ice inched down the face of the Pre-Cambrian rocks, channeling out canyons thousands of feet deep in the softer materials and polishing the harder ones. Deploying unchecked upon the floor of the Jackson Basin, they created moraines, outwash plains, and lakes. Phelps, Taggart, Bradley, Jenny, Leigh, and other piedmont lakes, 10 to 400 feet deep, originated in this manner. A great sluggish ice field, created by the convergence of adjacent glaciers, was the beginning of Jackson Lake. At the heads of the glaciers, cirques or amphitheaters were quarried out by the wrenching and pulling action of the down-creeping ice. Where glacial action deepened the canyons below the level of tributary streams, small valleys were left hanging. From these, the milky water released by melting ice now cascades to creeks below.

Along the eastern face, core rocks of early geologic eras have been exposed by faulting, glaciation, and weathering. Inclined limestone strata, quartzite, shale, and later volcanic remnants are on the western slope. Eroded in large areas, these deposits extend for long distances under the grain fields of the Teton Basin. On this slope, 10,000 feet above sea level, are coral reefs.

Four life zones are represented in the park: Arctic-Alpine, Hudsonian, Canadian, and Transition. Shiras' moose browse in the marshes near lakes, sometimes feeding with heads completely submerged for several minutes. Mule deer and elk are seen frequently along the higher trails; white-tailed deer are glimpsed rarely. In late fall, elk move in large herds to feeding grounds in the valley. Rocky Mountain sheep graze in small bands near timber line, and black and grizzly bear inhabit the canyons (but seldom intrude on campers). Beaver dams impede every stream; mink, marten, otter, coyote, badger, fox, lynx, and weasel live deep in the forests. The inquisitive golden-mantled marmot (rockchuck), pine squirrel, ground squirrel, and chipmunk heckle the camper or hiker. All summer the cony, or little chief hare, makes hay above timber line. More than 100 species of birds have been seen in the park.

Most trees of the park are evergreens; lodgepole pine and alpine fir predominate. Lodgepole extends from the valley floor up the steep escarpments to 8,000 feet. Alpine fir extends to timber line, but is sprawling and gnarled at high levels. Whitebark pine is the timberline tree; specimens found at lower levels are usually stunted. Limber pine grows at about 7,000 feet; Douglas fir, at lower elevations; and Engelmann spruce, largest tree in the park, along creeks and moist places near lakes. Aspen, the most common deciduous tree, dapples the slopes to about 8,000 feet. Balsam poplar grows along streams at low elevations. Flowers and mountain shrubs bloom profusely from May until the frost comes in August.

The Tetons were named by French trappers who penetrated the area in the early 1800's. They first applied the name to Grand, Middle, and South Teton (*les trois Tetons:* the three breasts). Wilson Price Hunt (*see History*) had called the peaks the Pilot Knobs.

The area was trapped systematically by the Rocky Mountain and

American Fur Companies for 40 years. In 1871–2 and 1877–8, Dr. V. F. Hayden made the first official surveys of the region. Lakes, streams, and mountains in and near the park bear the names of persons in Hayden's party: Leigh, Jenny (wife of Beaver Dick), Bradley, Taggart, St. John.

The Jackson Valley was settled in the 1880's and 1890's, but the Teton Range was too rugged for ranches. It served, however, as summer grazing land. The first attempts to scale the peaks failed; not until 1898 was the Grand Teton itself conquered, but, since 1923, several parties have climbed it every year. The Teton National Park was created on February 26, 1929.

Right from the String Lake Entrance on an oil-surfaced branch of Park Drive along the east shore of STRING LAKE, a widening of Cottonwood Creek south of Leigh Lake. It was formerly known as Beaver Dick Lake, for Dick Leigh, Hayden's guide, who was known as Beaver Dick because of his toothy resemblance to that animal.

The road winds among pines, affording frequent views of the lakes and creek (L). LEIGH LAKE, seen first from a turnout at 2.1 m., is an irregular glacial lake covering 1,229 acres. Mount Moran thrusts its squarish bald head out of the timber beyond; its great black diabase dike, 125 feet wide at the base, looks like a deep crevice, a man-made stair, or the high straight molten-rock wall that it is, depending on the perspective and the slant of the sunlight. The dike is a cross-section exposure of rock, which upwelled into a fissure and solidified in Pre-Cambrian time. Similar structures, less conspicuous, occur on Grand Teton and Middle Teton. Mount Moran was named for the English painter and etcher, Thomas Moran, who came West with Hayden in 1871.

At 2.6 m. the road ends, near the northern edge of Leigh Lake.

The main Park Drive swings south from the String Lake entrance and parallels Cottonwood Creek through pines and over open sage flats. The ragged Teton profile assumes new lines, as Grand Teton recedes behind the pinnacled shoulders of Mounts Teewinot and Owen. The road is high above JENNY LAKE (R), 4.2 m. (boats available), a small circular pool, whose waters reflect the blue-green forest that grows to its edge on three sides. In the afternoon, Jenny Lake also mirrors the cathedral crags of Teewinot, Owen, and Grand Teton— deep-blue inverted spires, faintly tremulous in the shimmering water.

JENNY LAKE STATION, 5.5 m., has a natural museum, ranger station, and photographic studio. Foot and bridle trails lead to the lake. Near the museum is an open-air amphitheater, where ranger-naturalists lecture each evening on geology, wild life, and related subjects.

Right from the station on Lakes Trail, first link in the system of bridle and foot trails into the glacial back country. Lakes Trail unites with Indian Paintbrush Trail, Skyline Trail, and Death Canyon Trail, to encircle the highest peaks and largest glaciers in the range. (Trails three to four feet wide, moderate gradient, free of boulders: no smoking along trail; no short cuts; trails often blocked by early and late snows.)

Lakes Trail crosses the hummocky crest of the inner JENNY LAKE MORAINE, a typical glacial dump-ground, then goes straight toward conical Mount Teewinot (Indian, pinnacles). The battlements of Grand Teton are visible over Teewinot's shoulder.

At 0.7 m. the trail forks; L. here 6 m. to PARK HEADQUARTERS (see below),

R. along Jenny Lake's west shore line, outside the moraine. Beavers have dammed the small unnamed streams (L) between the Jenny moraine and Teewinot, creating a broad marsh. The trees are scarred where moose have rubbed their antlers to shed the velvet that nourishes them during growth. Beyond the swamp, the moraine merges with the lower Teewinot talus. Douglas and Alpine fir are encroaching on the shaly slopes; water seepage through the loose rock gives the lower area a luxuriant flora.

At 2 *m.* the trail descends to the Jenny Lake shore line. The tree-studded moraine on the north and east is clearly outlined here, revealing the lake basin, partly glacier-scooped and partly the result of morainal damming.

At 2.3 *m.* is the junction with the Cascade Canyon Trail; L. here up Cascade Creek, which is milky with glacial rock flour. Water ouzels dart from wall to wall, diving suddenly for fish. The canyon deepens, and the creek cascades between sheer rock walls several thousand feet high. Cascade Canyon is the deepest chasm in the Teton Range. The view of the Teewinot, Grand Teton, and Mount Owen summits (L) is startling.

At 0.4 *m.* is a turnout to the base of HIDDEN FALLS (7,050 alt.), where a stream plunges from a high glacial bench. Its roar rings far down the canyon. Gray granite is exposed here, with an inclusion of black schist rock and pegmatite, of white feldspar, gray glassy quartz, and black mica.

The Cascade Canyon Trail climbs sharply to the glacial bench, over a series of switchbacks. Exposures of rounded bedrock are R. At 0.9 *m.* is a broad view of Jackson Hole, nearly 1,000 feet below.

The wide TALUS WALL (L), 1.5 *m.*, was formed by frost-loosened angular boulders of gray granite and pegmatite, gray banded gneiss, and schist. Ahead, massive mountains divide the north and south forks of Cascade Canyon. The sound of water flowing beneath the talus is audible at 1.9 *m.* Here forest growth penetrates the canyon. Grand Teton goes out of sight behind Mount Owen's less spectacular crag, but the extreme top of Teewinot is in view, barren and austere. The banded structure of the summit rocks, which are pegmatite intrusions into older rock, is conspicuous. Trees at 3.2 *m.* are small, gnarled, and broken by spring snowslides.

Grand Teton's spearhead summit, highest point in the range, comes into sight over Owen's northwest shoulder at 3.4 *m.* Spruce dominates the forest. It grows large here; some trees are 13 feet in circumference. Boulders are mantled with dense buckwheat, and thimbleberry bush grows between the spired pines. Across the canyon (L) at 3.7 *m.* is the mouth of a large hanging canyon, headed by a cirque between Mount Owen and Grand Teton.

At 4.5 *m.*, where Cascade Canyon forks, is the junction (7,480 alt.) with the Skyline Trail (*see below*).

The Lakes Trail continues northeast, across distributaries of Cascade Creek at the Jenny Lake Delta. Hummocky Jenny Moraine is plastered against the mountain front (L). Slow seepage through the moraine provides moisture for the spruce and fir forest that comes down to the lake shore. The few lodgepole pines are probably remnants of the original forest.

At 4.1 *m.*, the Lakes Trail divides. One fork goes R. to Park Drive, which it parallels northward to its end; the other goes L. to unite, at 5.5 *m.*, with Indian Paintbrush Trail, skirting the base of Rockchuck Peak (11,150 alt.) on the way. String Lake (R) fills a narrow, meandering depression, possibly an old river channel, obstructed by Leigh Moraine on the north and Jenny Moraine on the south. Snowslides have carried huge boulders from the slopes of Rockchuck into the lake. The lower bay of Leigh Lake is R., at the mouth of Indian Paintbrush Canyon.

At 5.8 *m.* is a good view of Mount Moran's black diabase dike and falling glacier. The Indian Paintbrush Moraine to the south forms a rocky ridge below the lower slopes of Rockchuck Peak.

Indian Paintbrush Canyon is neither as profound nor as steep as Cascade Canyon. It contains numerous steps, or glacier levels; ascent is made from one to another over sharp switchbacks. Bedrock, rounded and polished by glacial action, forms the lower walls. Above the ice level, the rocks are rough and angular; many seem balanced precariously above the trail. The mountains' mottled appearance indicates that the older formations were broken up and enclosed in the cooling magma. The unnamed peaks at the head of the canyon are in sight at 7.8 *m*. High cascades to the south are formed, as a stream falls from the hanging valley that heads between Mounts Rockchuck and St. John.

At 9.8 *m*. is the junction with a dim trail; R. here 0.5 *m*. to HOLLY LAKE (9,469 alt.), which lies in an old cirque. The glacier that gouged out the basin was exposed on the south and melted rapidly when the climate changed. Thus, little morainal debris surrounds the lake.

The INDIAN PAINTBRUSH-CASCADE CANYON DIVIDE PLATEAU, 12.2 *m*. (10,650 alt.), is conspicuously flat in an area of deep, twisting canyons and jagged peaks. It is of the same hard granite and gneissoid rock that forms the main Teton core and peaks. From this high vantage point, it is evident that the broad basin at the head of upper Indian Paintbrush Canyon was formed by the convergence of many small glaciers. These left a jumble of mounds and ridges that form small intervening basins and steps.

The trail descends over sharp switchbacks to the CASCADE-LEIGH CANYON DIVIDE, 12.5 *m*. (10,100 alt.). Leigh Canyon (R), one of the longest in the Teton Range, can be traced a mile and a half from this point. The black streak on Mount Moran is a continuation of the diabase dike visible from the east.

The trail swings southeast into the north fork of Cascade Canyon and passes LAKE SOLITUDE, 14.4 *m*. (9,024 alt.), a rock-floored lake in a glacial cirque. Its ice field did not last long enough to build the usual moraine.

At 16.8 *m*. the forks of the canyon join, and here also is the junction with the Cascade Canyon Trail (*see above*). Down the south fork runs the Skyline Trail, which penetrates the sheerest areas of glaciers, hanging canyons, cascading streams, and jutting masses of rock in the range. The Absaroka Mountains, on the far side of Jackson Hole, are visible down the canyons. The vertical east face of TABLE MOUNTAIN (R) comes into view at 18 *m*. W. H. Jackson took the first pictures of the Tetons from this peak in 1872.

The SOUTH HEAD OF CASCADE CANYON, 21 *m*., is a maze of cliffs, talus formations, and broken ledges. The trail climbs sharply to the CASCADE-AVALANCHE CANYON DIVIDE and the LIMESTONE WALL, 22.4 *m*. (10,613 alt.). This vast barrier of Cambrian rock forms the Teton watershed. Soft, crumbling, shaly segments, falling from its perpendicular, scoop-shaped front, increase greatly the hazards of the trail below. The trail skirts the wall, crosses a divide, and drops into DEATH CANYON, 30.1 *m*., a sheer-walled, round-floored chasm formed by glacial erosion. Down its rim, the trail passes pink feldspar formations, with numerous quartz needles intruding. This formation is called 'graphic granite,' because from the end section the quartz needles resembles hieroglyphic writing. The horseshoe moraine of Phelps Lake is visible below.

From Death Canyon, the trail drops suddenly to an open brushy slope. Here mountain maple, chokecherry, buckbrush, and mountain ash grow. Below is dense blue-black forest; beyond, the open floor of Jackson Hole.

At 32.3 *m*., on the valley bottom, is the junction with the Phelps Lake Trail; L. here 1.5 *m*. to PHELPS LAKE (6,615 alt.), named by members of the Hayden survey. The main trail, here Lakes Trail, goes northeast over wooded Phelps Lake Moraine, a remnant of an old morainal system formed by a glacier that once filled most of the north end of Jackson Hole. Lodgepole here grows densely, with heavy thimbleberry undergrowth.

WISTER DRAW (L), a small valley of snow-broken trees and shrubs, is a typical snowslide area. Owen Wister once had a homestead here. On BEAVER CREEK, 37.3 *m*., the trail forks; R. here 1 *m*. to a junction with Headquarters Trail; R. on this trail 0.5 *m*. to PARK HEADQUARTERS (*see below*).

Lakes Trail swings almost due north to TAGGART LAKE, 39.1 *m*. (6,800 alt.), and BRADLEY LAKE, 40.6 *m*. (7,016 alt.), in moraine-blocked basins at the mouths of Avalanche and Garnet canyons (*good fishing*). The north slopes of both moraines are heavily timbered; the southern slopes have scattered forest and much low growth.

At the mouth of TETON GLACIER CANYON, 42.1 *m.*, is the junction with the Glacier Trail; L. here up the steep, rugged canyon to SURPRISE LAKE, 3 *m.* (9,650 alt.), AMPHITHEATER LAKE, 3.2 *m.* (9,750 alt.), and the most easily accessible glacier area in the Tetons. The bridle trail ends on a high ridge overlooking Amphitheater Lake; R. here 1 *m.* over loose broken boulders to TETON GLACIER. (*Lose as little elevation as possible; cross last high moraine where it abuts (L) against basement rock of Grand Teton's northeast ridge; do not start rocks rolling, or slide when crossing snowfields; stay away from glacier crevices.*)

Glacier Canyon was carved by water before the glacial epoch; when snow accumulated at its head faster than it could melt, the glacier was formed. Its tremendous weight, together with the wrenching action of melting and freezing, formed the cirque in which it rests. Armed with rocks frozen into its sides and floor, the glacier scoured out the lower part of the canyon and deepened, widened, and smoothed the original chasm. Erosion and deposition continue today; the high loose ridge that encloses the lower end of the glacier is still being built up.

The Lakes Trail continues northward across a treeless flat, covered with glacial debris. At 44.8 *m.* is the junction with the Jenny Lake section of Lakes Trail, 0.7 *m.* west of the Jenny Lake Museum (*see above*).

South of the JENNY LAKE ENTRANCE, 5.9 *m.*, Park Drive unites with US 187 for 4.7 miles (*see Tour 7a*). It branches R. over graveled roadbed at 10.6 *m.*, and runs straight to PARK HEADQUARTERS, 11.6 *m.*, a small cluster of peeled-log buildings under a high flagstaff.

Tour 8

(Custer, S. Dak.)—Newcastle—Gillette—Buffalo—Worland; US 16. South Dakota Line to Worland, 283.9 *m.*

Route paralleled by Chicago, Burlington & Quincy R.R. between Newcastle and Ucross; by Wyoming R.R. between Ucross and Buffalo.
Oil-surfaced between South Dakota Line and Buffalo; graveled between Buffalo and Worland. Open June 1-Oct. 1 between Buffalo and Worland; snow in winter sometimes 15 to 30 feet deep.
Accommodations limited.

US 16 crosses the Wyoming Line in a little green valley between red hills. The Black Hills of South Dakota bulk up to the east. In Weston County, northwest of Newcastle, the highway runs for 20 to 30 miles across the corner of a huge Land Utilization Project, established by the Soil Conservation Service. This project covers nearly 2,500,000 acres in four northeastern counties: Weston, Campbell, Converse, and Crook.

For more than 100 miles the road runs through a sheep and cattle range, so broad that it seems to scorn boundaries. It crosses the Belle Fourche and Powder Rivers, along whose tributaries vast herds of Texas cattle ranged in the 1880's. Here, early-day cowmen held huge roundups, branding cattle and driving them long distances to the railroad. Rich grass, abundant water, and comparatively low elevation made the territory better for cattle than the plains to the south.

Northeast of Buffalo the landscape is splashed with the luxuriant green of irrigated sugar-beet and alfalfa fields. Between Buffalo and Tensleep, the dramatic Big Horn Mountains rise suddenly a mile and a half above the rolling plain.

US 16 crosses the SOUTH DAKOTA LINE, 0 *m.*, 32 miles west of Custer, South Dakota.

Through GILLETTE CANYON, 0.1 *m.*, a stream flows between deep-cut red banks. RED BIRD CANYON, 0.5 *m.*, is a dry streambed.

The road rises and dips and rises again to open grazing country. Here, over an area 40 miles wide and 65 miles long, the white Custer Wolf ranged for nine years, killing $25,000 worth of livestock. In March 1920, the U. S. Biological Survey sent H. P. Williams into the district with instructions to 'stay after the wolf.' When Williams first saw it on April 1, two coyotes were acting as its bodyguards. The wolf seemed to tolerate them, because they warned him of danger, but never allowed them to come within 100 yards of him, or to feed from his kills until he had had his fill. Williams killed the coyotes, but spent weeks and months with traps and gun before he got the wolf. On the day the animal was killed, the telephone lines at Custer were busier than on the day the Armistice was signed at the end of the World War.

At 3.5 *m.* is a junction with a dirt road.

Left on this road to WHOOPUP CANYON, 1 *m.*, whose dry floor is paved with smooth, many-colored stone. Great gnarled gray cottonwoods border the creek bed. The soft red walls, full of caves and fissures, are almost perpendicular in places and are marked with well-preserved petroglyphs, which seem to tell the story of a hunt. The carved figures include representations of crows, wolves, and deer. Through this canyon, in the late 1870's and early 1880's, ran the Cheyenne and Black Hills Stage Line. Cowboys named the canyon for spring floods that came through 'a-whoopin'.'

The L ∧ K RANCH, 4.8 *m.*, on Stockade Beaver Creek, is the site of a stockade erected in 1875 by the geologist Walter P. Jenney and his party, who were making a mineral survey for the Government with a view to the purchase of the Black Hills from the Sioux. Miners, already in the country, assisted Jenney. The stockade was moved in 1933 to Newcastle (*see Tour* 1).

The L ∧ K· Ranch, the first 'cow ranch' in the region, is now a showplace with green fields and flocks of fine sheep. Deer also graze in the pastures.

> Right from the L ∧ K Ranch on a dirt road along Stockade Beaver Creek, an excellent trout stream. High gray and red rimrocks fence the east side of the prosperous ranching valley; spring buttercups, bluebells, lady's-slippers, daisies, and other wild flowers bloom among the boulders. Red-winged black-birds, king-fishers, and meadow larks nest along the stream. Deer, golden pheasants, and wild ducks are frequently seen.

US 16 runs westward through sagebrush to SALT CREEK, 6.4 *m.*, which joins Stockade Beaver Creek 4 miles east of Newcastle. In 1877 explorers found near this stream 70 salt springs on half an acre of ground. The following year, two evaporating furnaces were erected, each with a 4-by-10-foot pan, capacity 1,000 pounds. The salt obtained from the first large test was sold at Deadwood. Orders immediately came for more. For several years the furnaces produced both table salt and coarse stock-feeding salt. At one time, teams were put on the road to haul the salt to the silver mines at Galena, South Dakota.

The creek is now a popular bathing place. Large boulders along its course tend to check its flow and to form natural pools of clear, warm salt water.

At the SITE OF TUBB TOWN, 7.9 *m.*, in the spring of 1888, De Loss Tubbs of Custer, South Dakota, built a store as the first step in establishing a road ranch. As railroad builders and homeseekers came into the region, F. R. Curran built a saloon, setting up the bar first and then erecting a shelter around it. Tubb Town grew rapidly after that. The first city ordinance provided that strangers 'shall not pass without paying a toll sufficient to set 'em up to the bunch.' Men afoot, riders, and drivers of wagons drawn by oxen, mules, or horses all paid. The *Stockade Journal,* forerunner of the Newcastle *News-Letter Journal* appeared about September 1; the printer had only a cigar box of type. Business went on day and night, and, if the noise became annoying, the only recourse was to take a blanket and hunt some quiet place among the jack pines on the surrounding hills. Despite its boisterousness, Tubb Town was not a dangerous place; no one was ever shot there. But it did not last long. On September 10, 1889, the first lots were sold in Newcastle, two miles away. Within 48 hours, Tubb Town was deserted. Only its rock steps and foundations remain.

At the site is a junction with US 85 (*see Tour* 1). Between this point and Newcastle, US 16 and US 85 are one route.

NEWCASTLE, 10 *m.* (4,334 alt., 1,600 pop.) (*see Tour* 1), is at the western junction with US 85 (*see Tour* 1).

US 16 runs northwest into open country.

At 13.6 *m.* sandstone outcrops (R) along a hogback tipped with pines. The highway continues across prairie, broken by dry draws that run bankfull after sudden rains.

At 16.3 *m.* is the junction with a dirt road.

Right on this road to PLUM CANYON, 4 *m.* High red rimrocks at the canyon's mouth contain shallow caves marked with faint examples of Indian picture writing. In some places the canyon opens to green meadows and fields. The east side slopes from the tableland to broken, heavily forested hills. Willow, box elder, and wild plum border the creek; luxuriant cattails grow in the marshes. Near the head of the canyon, upland pastures show through vistas of birch and pine. Many gulches opening upon Plum Creek contain secluded primitive spots.

For seven miles the highway runs through sagebrush and stunted trees. Here and there stand deserted farmhouses whose paneless, uncurtained windows give them an appearance of wide-eyed, shocked surprise. The slanting walls and sagging roofs of near-by barns and sheds seem to express the weariness of some former owner's long and losing battle with drought.

OSAGE, 25.8 *m.* (4,300 alt., 500 pop.), a refinery town built along one street, lies in the center of an oil field in which many wells produce at only 300 feet.

Left from Osage on a dirt road to a FOSSIL-BEARING RIDGE, 1 *m.,* where fossilized oyster shells, clam shells, great turtle shells, and petrified fish have been found.

US 16 skirts the western edge of the Black Hills (R) through sheep-grazing country. Shacks and cabins, many of them deserted, are scattered among the pines on the foothills.

One half of UPTON, 39.1 *m.* (4,234 alt., 373 pop.), clings to the pine-clad foothills, while the other ranges out on a wind-swept sagebrush flat. Tar-paper shacks, brick stores, log, frame, and brick dwellings are intermingled. The main street begins at the railroad and climbs the pine-covered knoll into the residential district. Although a typical frontier town, Upton has modern light and street drainage systems. Cowboys clatter into town with a whoop or gather on the corners to discuss the news. Carloads of bentonite are shipped from Upton to Chicago each year, to be used in making beauty clay.

US 16 crosses IRON CREEK, 40 *m.,* near the site of a ghost town called Iron Town. From 1890 to 1892 about 500 people lived here. Most of them helped build the Chicago, Burlington & Quincy Railroad grade.

At a representative BENTONITE MILL (L), 42.5 *m.,* loads of clay from local deposits are hauled in, dried, and sacked for shipment. Smaller mills operate elsewhere in the region.

To the northeast are Devil's Tower and Missouri Buttes, visible for about 50 miles. The Tower is soon lost in the hills. Sundance Mountain seems to lean against the last slope of the Bear Lodge Mountains. Directly east, Inyan Kara lifts her pine-bonneted head to look out over Pine Ridge (*see Tour* 10).

Dry draws, deserted shacks, and farmsteads alternate across miles of hills, green with short grass in spring, burned dry by wind and sun toward fall. The gumbo lily, sego lily, yellow wild celery, sunflower, and goldenrod come and go with the seasons.

Supplies are transported largely by automobile here. Big eight-wheeler trucks rumble through, loaded with rusty oil-well casing, with a red cloth waving from the rear; other trucks are piled high with coal, potatoes, hay, logs, or grain. A streamlined roadster flashes past as a four-horse wagon, loaded with a farmer's possessions, draws up on the highway from a dusty side road. A rooster in a crate, wired high on the load, squawks half-heartedly; a roan cow plods behind the wagon, lowing at intervals or coughing at the dust.

A small OIL REFINERY, 59.1 *m.*, is L.

MOORCROFT, 59.6 *m.* (4,206 alt., 351 pop.), at the junction with US 14, is on the site of a horse ranch owned by the Miller Brothers, who named it for their English estate, Moorcroft Acres. The town began as a railway station and developed as the trade and shipping center for a large stock-raising area; it also has a grain elevator. 'Big Bill' Thompson of Chicago once punched cows here.

At the SALES RING adjoining the stockyards, livestock, farm machinery, fence posts, oil barrels, household goods, seeds, and what not are sold to the highest bidder.

Between Moorcroft and Ucross, US 16 and US 14 (*see Tour* 10) are united. Ranches here produce purebred cattle and sheep.

The BELLE FOURCHE RIVER, 61.2 *m.*, often mentioned in cow-country story and song, flows northeast into South Dakota.

The road crosses the TEXAS TRAIL, 62 *m.*, where a monument (R) commemorates the era when great herds of cattle were brought to Wyoming and Montana to replace the vanishing buffalo. The road winds westward over hilly prairies, on which sandstone outcrops alternate with sagebrush flats. In the spring, clouds of dust follow farmers' harrows, as fields are prepared for grain and alfalfa.

ROZET, 70 *m.* (4,286 alt., 50 pop.), is a rural community center, with consolidated school and recreation hall. The hall, built of a cindered, porous, black and green stone, in Spanish design, contrasts oddly with the false-front stores along the one street.

The highway runs through a broad, dry valley, crosses DRY DONKEY CREEK, 77.4 *m.*, and DONKEY CREEK, 82.4 *m.*, along whose banks there existed for several months a camp called Donkeytown, headquarters for the engineers constructing the Chicago, Burlnigton & Quincy Railroad about 1890.

At 82.5 *m.* is the junction with a dirt road.

Right on this road to the WYO-DAK COAL MINE, 0.3 *m.*, said to be the largest strip mine in the world, where a 65-foot vein has been worked since 1924. A steam clam and an electrical clam and shovel convey the coal to hoppers at the surface, by means of giant endless belts. Much of the coal is shipped to the Homestake holdings in Lead, South Dakota.

The UNIVERSTY OF WYOMING EXPERIMENT STATION (L), 86 *m.*, specializes in the development of farm and ranch shelterbelts.

GILLETTE, 87.7 *m.* (4,544 alt., 1,340 pop.), seat of Campbell County, has a flour mill and oil refinery. In the region around it are more than 30 burning coal mines, apparently ignited by lightning, by campers' fires, or by spontaneous combustion. Indians and trappers who visited the country in the early 1800's reported one deposit burning then. Some of the larger ones glow distinctly at night. Wide crevices open above the burning coal; it is said that a man on horseback once rode into one near the narrows on Little Thunder Creek, about 60 miles south of Gillette. Animals often walk into the fissures.

Soon after completion of the railroad, Gillette became the largest shipping point on the Burlington system; cattle from Buffalo, Kaycee, Sheridan, and other places were brought here. As many as 40,000 sheep and 12,000 cattle were in the yards at one time.

Local legend commemorates a bullwhacker named Daniel Boone, who hauled freight to and from Gillette. Boone had such control that he could turn a complete circle in the street with wagon, trailer, and six yoke of oxen.

The annual roundup, July 4-5, features bronco riding, roping, horse racing, Indian dancing, and other events. National Music Week activities are held here each year.

Left from Gillette on State 116, the Fiddleback Rd., to the R. B. MARQUISS BUFFALO RANCH, 35 *m.* Marquiss bought a pair of buffaloes from the herd of Scotty Phillips at Pierre, South Dakota, in 1922, and raised a herd of 28, which he later reduced to 16. In 1934 he furnished a buffalo hide for mounting to the Natural History Museum of Lausanne, Switzerland.

Turning R. just west of Gillette, US 16 runs for 20 miles or so through open, rolling country, in which deserted homestead shacks alternate with small fields. The region is barren and sparsely settled. Even the names of the streams and buttes—Rawhide, Twenty-Mile, Wildcat, Lone Tree—emphasize its remoteness and isolation.

To the northeast (R) is the Spring Creek Area, in which the Government purchased 35,452 acres of land from 48 owners. This land comprised small dry-land farms, abandoned homesteads, and tracts of range located at strategic points for water development. In addition to the privately owned land, relinquishments were obtained on 11 homesteads amounting to 5,828 acres. The total cost of all land purchased amounted to $111,000, each tract having been appraised to determine its fair value. According to reports of the Soil Conservation Service,

. . . as a result of the allocation of the purchased lands, and the private leasing of lands not purchased by the Government, the average size of operating units in the area was increased from 1,700 acres to 4,760 acres. Each operator in the area now has the use of enough land for a successful stock ranch . . . Considerable work has been done on the land to improve its usefulness for grazing. Water facilities, including stock reservoirs and spring developments, have been the outstanding improvements made. Fence lines were altered to facilitate the management of the range . . . After tearing down purchased farm buildings that were no longer of any use, the salvaged material was utilized in the construction of a small recreational center and community hall, filling a long-felt local need . . . To provide for proper conservation and management of the range, the Spring Creek Cooperative Livestock Association, consisting of the 22 stockmen remaining in the area, was formed in November 1936. This association leases all federally owned land from the Government, and all the

state-owned land and such absentee-owned lands as are not under direct management of a member of the association . . . A few residents have not accepted
the Government's offer to purchase and are continuing cash-crop operations on
relatively small units . . . Of the 27 operators whose farms were purchased and
who moved from the Spring Creek area, 5 have located on farms in eastern
Wyoming and 8 on farms in other states. Three operators have taken up non-
agricultural work, 1 of them resuming his former job as a railroad conductor.
Three more, 2 of whom are bachelors, are working as hired hands on ranches
nearby, while 2 elderly people have retired to spend their remaining days with
relatives. One man of foreign birth has returned to his native land. Another died
shortly after selling his farm. Inquiries regarding the 4 remaining families have
failed to bring information as to their present situation.

At 121.7 *m.* the road winds down into a wide valley, hedged L. and
R. by hogbacks.

SPOTTED HORSE, 125.7 *m.* (3,890 alt., 5 pop.), a post office
with store and filling station, was named for an Indian chief. West
of the post office is a corral with a stuffed horse lunging out of the
gate. Many tourists have their pictures taken atop this 'bronco.'

The highway goes through a deep cut and out over barren hills.
Pines clothe the more distant slopes (R). Bands of sheep nibble at
the thin hillside forage. As the road lifts and descends, fields and pastures appear, and the snowcapped Big Horn Mountains rise ahead.

The road crosses POWDER RIVER, 141.1 *m.* (*see Tour* 3).

At 141.3 *m.* is the junction with an oiled road.

Left on this road is ARVADA, 3.4 *m.* (3,649 alt., 100 pop.), an old town
with false-front stores, an elevator, and an artesian well, from which natural
gas flows with the water. Hardy citizens sometimes amuse visitors by igniting
the 'firewater' and drinking from the flaming mouth of the pipe. From the
Arvada vicinity came some of Wyoming's most expert cowboys. One of them,
Lib Vincent, accompanied Buffalo Bill to Europe with his Wild West Show.

The highway runs through wide stretches of grassland, in which
clumps of delicate yellow cacti bloom amid brown plains grasses. In
1938, crickets often completely covered strips of road here.

US 16 crosses CADIZ DRAW, 148.8 *m.*, and heads toward the majestic
Big Horns.

LEITER, 149.4 *m.* (4,000 alt., 50 pop.), is a settlement in the
Clear Creek Valley—a region of pastures, trees, and prosperous grain
and beet farms. In CLEARMONT, 157.7 *m.* (3,921 alt., 214 pop.),
are several houses made of large blocks of local sandstone.

The valley narrows. Its irrigated floor produces fine crops; on the
upper dry lands, deserted shacks testify to the inroads of drought.

UCROSS, 168.7 *m.* (4,085 alt., 15 pop.), a trading hamlet, bears
the name of a cattle brand. Here, at 168.9 *m.*, US 16 and US 14 (*see
Tour* 10) separate again; US 14 continues west, and US 16, the main
route, turns south. Large well-kept ranches and farms with brick
buildings indicate the productivity of this part of Clear Creek Valley.

BUFFALO, 186.9 *m.* (4,645 alt., 1,749 pop.) (*see Tour* 3a), is at
the junction with US 87 (*see Tour* 3).

At 188.7 *m.* is a junction with a graveled road.

Left on this road to the SOLDIERS AND SAILORS HOME (old Fort McKinney), 0.5 *m.*, a 1,290-acre reserve with red-brick and frame buildings. It is a home for all physically disabled veterans of wars in which the United States participated, and who have been residents of Wyoming for one year.

General Crook, in preparation for a long campaign, after his advance had been stopped by Crazy Horse at the Rosebud in 1876, ordered a series of supply depots established between his camp on Goose Creek and the base at Fort Fetterman (*see Tour 3b*). Cantonment Reno, three miles north of abandoned Fort Reno, was one of these. In the spring of 1877, the cantonment was moved from Powder River to Clear Creek and renamed Fort McKinney. Five years later, General Philip H. Sheridan, anticipating future wars with the conquered Indians, recommended that McKinney be made a permanent post. Further buildings were provided, and several troops of cavalry were sent in. When Sheridan's wars never came, the post buildings and land were transferred from the War Department to the State. For some time the fort was the headquarters of Frank Grouard, well-known scout, who had served under General Crook. Grouard was born in the Paumoto Islands, South Pacific Ocean; his father was a missionary and his mother, the daughter of a high chief of the Island of Ana. Grouard was a remarkable woodsman and, because of his appearance, was often mistaken for a Sioux. In 1903 the State legislature ordered the Soldiers and Sailors Home transferred from Cheyenne to Fort McKinney.

US 16 ascends the wooded eastern slope of the Big Horn Mountains through steep Clear Creek Canyon. At 210 *m.*, it reaches a plateau where long pine slopes, broken by meadows, sweep away in a wide V to dark hilltops. Thousands of acres of meadowland along streams make this one of the most prized grazing areas in Wyoming. The prairies and badlands of the Red Wall and Hole-in-the-Wall are glimpsed far L.

West of MUDDY RANGER STATION, 214.6 *m.*, near Muddy Creek, the climb stiffens. Timber is sparse and stunted; grass is paler, drier. Near the highway are many cold springs.

POWDER RIVER PASS, 224.4 *m.* (9,666 alt.), known also as Muddy Pass, is the highest point on US 16. Vegetation here is sickly and dry, 'fit only for sheep.' Jagged granite peaks thrust upward (R). Along the forested west slope, clear lakes (*good fishing*) glisten.

Artificial MEADOW LAKE (L), 234.4 *m.*, covering basined Tensleep Meadows, was formed in the late 1920's by the construction of a dam across East Tensleep Creek, to reduce spring high-water hazards and to store water for irrigation in Tensleep Valley. The mountains on both sides slope to the shore, with no obstructing ledges or cliffs. Often commanding a clear sweep of 800 yards, these slopes form the most popular winter-sports area in the Big Horn country. Rustic lodges stand on the lake shore; the State highway department keeps the highway from Tensleep open.

Right from Meadow Lake on a foot trail to TENSLEEP LAKES, 2 *m.*, at timber line. Fed by water from perpetual ice fields and cold mountain springs, these lakes provide good fishing.

Parks and timber stands between Meadow Lake and SQUAW CREEK, 240.7 *m.*, are favorite summer-grazing lands for blacktail deer and elk. Black bear and mountain sheep frequent the more rugged heights.

As the highway makes the steep descent, timber recedes, and the cliffs of Tensleep Canyon seem to come together and block passage ahead; massive rocks jut from the granite walls on both sides, like bastions of medieval fortresses. US 16 cuts long shelves down a steep-shouldered gorge, winding sharply to avoid the ragged edges of the walls. The cliffs, reddish-gray, dwarf the pines that rise out of the canyon or sprout surprisingly from rocks higher up.

The canyon widens and the highway descends to the level of Tensleep Creek. At 241.9 *m.* the descent becomes very steep; the road drops several hundred feet in less than a mile (*keep car in gear*). The broken pine and sagebrush country below stretches away to red cliffs on both sides. Green patches of valley floor show through the widening gap ahead.

LEIGH'S MONUMENT, 242.7 *m.*, a 600-foot precipice at the end of a scarp, was named for Gilbert Leigh, English gentleman, who was killed in a fall from the cliff on September 14, 1884. Leigh lived on a ranch near Tensleep and made frequent trips into the mountains. One day his horse returned riderless. Buzzards led searchers to his body, in a tree at the foot of the cliff.

The Tensleep ranching area opens ahead. Great herds of sheep are moving patches of white on the foothills. Heavily willowed Tensleep Creek twists irregularly across the valley.

The STATE FISH HATCHERY (*open to the public*), 246.1 *m.*, near the junction of Tensleep and Leigh Creeks (L), is the largest in Wyoming (1940). Thousands of fingerlings are raised in its 82 troughs.

At 252.9 *m.* is a junction with a dirt road.

Left on this road to the old HATFIELD RANCH, 6 *m.;* L. here on a wagon road that becomes a foot trail to INDIAN·POWWOW CAVERN, 1 *m.*, where centuries of wind and driving rain have worn a vast opening in the face of a high red cliff. In this cavern, 50 feet high at the mouth, 300 feet deep, and 900 feet wide, the Crow and Sioux met in powwow or sought shelter in bad weather on the hunt. The walls and ceiling display ancient figures and pictures—undeciphered records of tribes that used the rendezvous. The cave has unusual acoustic properties; a word spoken at the entrance can be heard clearly at the rear. Artifacts have been uncoverd in the fine sand that deeply covers the floor, probably washed there by a forgotten stream.

The footpath parallels Canyon Creek to the SINKS, 2 *m.*, where the creek disappears into a subterranean channel, to emerge half a mile below. The underground passage is high enough for a man to stand erect within it.

TENSLEEP, 254.9 *m.* (4,206 alt., 200 pop.), a short row of false-front frame and brick buildings, serves neighboring cattlemen and sheepmen and preserves much of the mood and vigor of the frontier. On the one business street, teams and solitary horsemen still dispute the right-of-way with sleek cars and pickup trucks. The name of the place is borrowed from the Indians, who reckoned time and distance in sleeps. The site was ten days' travel from Fort Laramie and the same distance from the Yellowstone Park area.

In 1882, only one rancher's cabin stood by Tensleep Creek; but, as the area on both sides of the Big Horns filled up, men crossed the

Nowood badlands to Tensleep Valley, with their cattle and sheep. During the range feud that swept Wyoming in the 1890's and early 1900's, cattlemen here, as elsewhere in the State, opposed the introduction of sheep on two counts: the ranges were already overstocked with cattle; sheep were not good for the range. Cattle, said the battle-scarred cowmen, could wander at will over the summer ranges, but sheep must be kept in concentrated herds; sheep nibbled the grass too closely, their sharp hoofs destroyed the exposed roots, and they polluted streams; cattle, nauseated by their smell, could not feed on the same range.

In 1903, several herders and camp tenders were shot by masked riders; their sheep were slaughtered or scattered to die. During the next six years, more herders were killed. Herds valued at hundreds of thousands of dollars, were dynamited or 'rimrocked'—driven over cliffs by whistling, shouting raiders. Camps were burned; vicious dogs were turned loose on the sheep.

Despite this, sheepmen prospered. In 1908, fall lamb shipments from the Big Horn Basin were valued at $2,000,000, and wool growers announced plans to expand their industry.

In the spring of 1909, Joe Emge, a cattleman who had bitterly resisted the introduction of sheep, decided to change with the times. With one Joe Allemand, he brought 5,000 sheep into the Big Horn area. Twenty armed and masked men, on the night of April 3, surrounded Allemand's camp on Spring Creek, killed the owners and a herder, and cremated the bodies in the wagons.

This brought the feud to a climax throughout the West. The National Wool Growers' Association appropriated $20,000 for prosecution of the 'Tensleep raiders'; a grand jury investigation was launched; jurors and sheriff's officers were threatened; one witness committed suicide, leaving a note that incriminated several prominent ranchers. Early in May, seven men were arrested; two turned State's evidence. When conviction became certain, influential friends intervened, and a 'deal' was made. Those arraigned pleaded guilty to lesser charges and received prison sentences ranging from three years to life. These events sobered both factions and established arbitration as the means of settling range disputes. Deadlines across which sheep may not pass, once held by rifles and six-guns, are now fixed by law.

NOWOOD CREEK, 255.4 m., named by settlers who found no fuel along its banks, marks the eastern edge of the badlands. The dull red formations to the west contrast with the green carpet of Tensleep Valley. On SIGNAL CLIFF, half a mile long and nearly 1,000 feet high, Crow scouts watched for smoke signals from lookout points in the Big Horns, and relayed to tribesmen in the basin the latest movements of enemies or buffalo.

At 258.5 m. is a junction with a dirt road.

Left on this road to CASTLE GARDENS, 4 m., an area of red spires and giant toadstools, cut from soft lava by wind and water. Many of the figures are supported precariously by thin red stems.

US 16 climbs a high ridge to SCENIC POINT, 271.3 *m.* West of vari-colored, deep-fissured wastelands, is the saucer edge of the Big Horn Basin. On clear days the Owl Creek, Wind River, and Absaroka Mountain chains, the distant western rim of the basin, are like folds of fallen blue draperies beyond the crazy quilt of green and brown fields. To the east, the slopes of the southern Big Horns are scarred by the Shell Creek, Medicine Lodge, Paintrock, and Tensleep gorges. Higher than all the rest towers the shaggy bald head of Cloud Peak (13,165 alt.), surrounded by lesser peaks, like a chieftain in council.

The highway traverses miles of painted badlands. Flat salt sage adds its haze of gray and lavender to the glaring red and orange rocks. In winter, snow fills the gullies and drifts against the weird buttes, providing moisture for sheep range.

At the foot of a long sagebrush bench, grazing land gives way to the irrigated sugar-beet country of the Big Horn Basin.

WORLAND, 283.9 *m.* (4,061 alt., 1,461 pop.) (*see Tour 6b*), is at the junction with US 20 (*see Tour* 6).

Tour 9

Junction with US 187—Kemmerer—Junction with US 30S; 135.1 *m.,* US 189.

Route used by freight trucks to Piney and Jackson ranching areas; part of main tourist route between Yellowstone Park and Salt Lake City.
Oil-surfaced or graveled roadbed, open all seasons; occasional heavy snows.
Accommodations at larger towns; shelter cabins along desert stretches.

The country traversed by US 189 is rich in early Western lore. During the trappers' rendezvous, the upper Green River Valley had a greater population of white men and Indians than it accommodates today. Almost before the hills and gullies had ceased echoing the noises of the rendezvous, they began ringing with the shouts and lusty songs of emigrants and religious zealots. The highway crosses several routes of the Oregon Trail; landmarks and monuments beside it retell parts of the familiar saga of migration to the West.

The fertile upper valley, veined with willow-fringed tributaries of the main stream, is an extensive hay-producing and cattle-ranching area. To the west, the rugged Salt and Grey's River Ranges stand blue on clear days. From meadows, the highway climbs sagebrush sand-steppes through a region that is rich in minerals and invaluable as winter sheep range.

US 189 branches southwest from US 187 (*see Tour 7b*), 0 *m.*, 1.9 miles north of Daniel, and swings almost due south through the broad Piney meadowlands. White-faced cattle graze in willowed pastures here. The road crosses the GREEN RIVER, 1 *m.*

RENDEZVOUS PARK (L), 1.7 *m.*, at the juncture of Green River and Horse Creek, was a popular site for the annual assemblage of trappers in the 1820's and 1830's (*see History*). The first gathering in the vicinity (1824), conducted by Thomas (Broken Hand) Fitzpatrick, was small, with only employees of William H. Ashley's Rocky Mountain Fur Company participating. The next year, Ashley selected a spot on Henry's Fork of the Green River and posted signs inviting all trappers to attend. After that, until the end of free trapping in the middle 1840's, the rendezvous was an annual event vital to the industry. Trappers trekked in singly, in pairs, and in groups, to swap their catch for the powder, traps, and other things they needed. Rival companies competed with gusto, and not too many scruples, for pelts already taken and for the future services of trappers. Sometimes more than 1,500 men took part in the daily activities. Trading went on briskly at fixed hours, followed usually by target shooting, wrestling, horse racing, and gambling. By day, men lounged in the shade of the cottonwood trees, while their animals fed on the rich valley grasses. At night, the air vibrated with the pounding of tom-toms, the chanting of Indians, the barking of dogs, and the singing, cursing, and laughter of white men.

The most significant gathering was that of 1835, at which Dr. Marcus Whitman and the Reverend Samuel Parker were present, on their way to Oregon to study the problem of missionary work among the Indians. The advent of piety to the roughneck concourse was a novelty, but, more important, it heralded the advance of white settlers into the West and the end of an era the Astors, Ashleys, Sublettes, Bridgers, and Beckwourths had believed unending. The trapper and trader could flourish only in the wilderness; the appearance of missionaries foreshadowed the wave of families and plows that was to transform the West. Settlement and civilization, symbolized by the substitution of the silk hat for the beaver cap, were to complete what ruthless slaughter of the fur bearers had begun—the destruction of the fur trade. But in 1835 the trade was at its zenith. Mountain men came to the rendezvous from scores of widely separated trapping areas; historians have speculated on the number of foreign states whose agents may have been present. England was striving to hold the Oregon country; other nations had not entirely abandoned the hope of obtaining American lands.

The trading, drinking, and roistering often led to violence. Boasts were made and challenges accepted. Indians performed warlike rituals for pay; trappers joined in the songs and dances of the Indians. During a lull in activities, the men made love to Indian maidens or listened to the sermons of Whitman and Parker.

The missionaries had joined Lucien Fontenelle's supply train in Missouri and arrived at the rendezvous on August 12. When Whitman removed an arrowhead that had been embedded for three years in Jim Bridger's back, the Nez Percé and Flathead were greatly impressed. Humbled by the Blackfeet, these tribes were seeking a more powerful magic, and they had already displayed keener interest in the white man's God and Book than had the white trappers. They had seen white men defeat the Blackfeet, and they supposed that the paleface medicine could make them also invulnerable. To the missionaries, their eagerness for power proved their readiness for faith. Dr. Whitman returned East with the fur train, to return the next year with assistants. Parker accompanied Jim Bridger down the Hoback, where he preached to the Indians (*see Tour 7b*). In Pierre's Hole, Bridger's party turned off, and Parker, with a small Indian escort, advanced into the canyons of the Snake on his way to Oregon.

At the rendezvous of 1836, mountain men who had seen the wonders of Colter's Hell and listened with gravity to the ornamented exploits of Bridger and Beckwourth were amazed when two white women, the wives of Dr. Whitman and the Reverend H. H. Spalding, arrived with the American Fur Company's supply caravan. They gave the women an enthusiastic welcome; and the Indians, not to be outdone, killed their fattest dogs and overwhelmed the white squaws with hospitality. The missionary party rested several days, then, with a small escort, continued its journey to Oregon. A monument, on a sagebrush knoll overlooking Rendezvous Park, now honors Mrs. Whitman and Mrs. Spalding as the first white women to pass through Wyoming.

DANIEL, 1.9 *m.* (7,192 alt., 70 pop.), a ranch-country hamlet of log and frame houses, is the supply center for the sparsely settled upper Green Valley. T. P. Daniel opened a general store here in the early 1890's; but, overshadowed by Pinedale to the east and Big Piney to the south, the place has not changed essentially since 1900. Although the first church service in Wyoming was conducted on the prairie near Daniel, the community has never supported a chapel.

US 189 follows the general course of the river down a fertile valley, occupied by large ranches. Most of the one-story houses are built of logs floated down from the mountains to the west; the outbuildings, surrounded by extensive branding corrals, are much like the dwellings.

HORSE CREEK, 2.5 *m.*, is said to have been named in 1823 by trappers, who discovered a large herd of wild horses grazing near it. The timbered slopes along upper Horse Creek supply ties for Western railroads. Lumberjacks fell the lodgepole pines for this purpose in winter, saw them to six-foot lengths, trim them with razor-sharp broadaxes, and then stack them near frozen streams. Pole ties, the most durable, are made from small trees and the tips of large trees, with only two sides surfaced; slab ties are made of larger poles, split once, with three sides surfaced; quarter ties are made of poles, split into four segments, with four surfaces finished. An experienced trimmer can leave the surfaces of a tie almost as smooth as if planed. In early summer, the timbers are floated 15 or 20 miles to the Green River, where they are boomed (held back by cables stretched across the creek mouths), until the waters are at the best height for the drive to the city of Green River (*see Tour 2c*). The boomed timbers extend upstream for miles. If they jam when the booms are removed, men with spiked boots and long pikes walk out to the middle of the stream, upon the treacherous floor of sticks, and work them loose. Dynamiting is usually avoided because of the loss incurred.

At 3.6 *m.* is the junction with a dirt road.

Left on this road to the summit of a hill, 0.3 *m.*, where the road forks; L. here 2.2 *m.*, through a cattle guard, to LA PRAIRIE DE LA MESSE, where Father Pierre Jean De Smet, on July 5, 1840, celebrated the first High Mass in Wyoming. In 1925 the Knights of Columbus erected a cruciform granite altar set in a concrete base, and Mass is celebrated annually here.

De Smet was born in Termonde, Belgium, January 31, 1801, and came to the United States in his youth as a missionary for the Society of Jesus. He worked in Kansas and Missouri, where his understanding of the Indians' problems gained him their regard. He came West in response to Flathead appeals for instruction, arriving at the rendezvous on the Green with a supply train on June 30, 1840. Each night of the rendezvous, says legend, he left the revelers and climbed to a sagebrush ridge, 500 feet above the valley, to tell his beads. A rude altar, adorned with bows and arrows and garlands of wild flowers, was erected on July 5 for the first Mass. The priest later founded missions in other parts of the West but returned to Wyoming at intervals for two decades.

Right from the monument on a dirt road to the PINCKNEY SUBLETTE GRAVE, 0.1 *m.*, marked with a pink granite boulder set in concrete. Pinckney Sublette, one of five brothers, all eminent mountain men, trapped for the Rocky Mountain Fur Company, of which William Sublette was part owner. He was reported killed in 1828, but Perry W. Jenkins, who has pieced together much historical evidence, believes that he may have 'sold out' to Peter Skene Ogden's Hudson's Bay outfit and spent some years trapping in northern Idaho and Canada. In 1897, during a St. Louis lawsuit to establish the heirs of Pinckney's brother Solomon, a grave on Fontenelle Creek, southwest of La Barge, was identified as that of Pinckney. His bones were exhumed and taken to St. Louis to establish his death. For nearly 40 years, they were shunted about in the vaults of the court clerk's office; then the court ordered them returned to Wyoming, where they were reinterred July 4, 1936, not in the original grave, but on the Prairie de la Messe, in the county that bears the family name.

US 189 climbs a plateau of gray sage and yellow-flowered rabbit brush, flecked with green meadows and cut by arroyos formed by cloudbursts. Sheep graze here. At 13.2 *m.* (R) is a formation of red sandstone, resembling a steamboat.

MARBLETON, 24.2 *m.* (6,850 alt., 15 pop.), was founded by Charles P. Budd in 1912, in opposition to D. B. Budd, his father, who had founded Big Piney in 1888. Six distinct types of log houses may be seen in the village.

When the older town definitely eclipsed Marbleton, young Budd deserted his village and moved to BIG PINEY, 25.7 *m.* (6,780 alt.,

250 pop.). On this site between the North and Middle Forks of Piney Creek, the elder Budd had wintered cattle as early as 1878. A service station has replaced the livery barn, and some of the false-front business houses are giving way to modern structures, but the community has retained many of the attributes of the frontier. Lean, hard-muscled cowhands ride dusty ponies into town on Saturday nights and invade saloons as old as the town, to be served by bartenders who never acknowledged prohibition. Buggies still come in occasionally from the back country. Ranching is the basic industry of the region, although oil and gas wells have been drilled on the prairies, and a minor boom was experienced in the late 1920's.

The Piney ranch hand is more familiar with the pitchfork and hay sweep than with the six-gun. His rustic garb differs greatly from that of the gaudy 'dude wrangler' to the north. He can rope the front leg of a dogie at 15 yards, however, or break an outlaw colt single-handed. Once a year he joins other hands on the open range to the west, to spend 16 hours a day in the saddle, sorting the bawling, milling herds according to brands or earmarks and for marketability. The job is done just as it was 50 years ago, without the aid of corrals, but with cowponies that, in their way, are as skilful as their masters. On the 75-mile drive to the railroad, as in the roundup, several ranchers handle their herds together. Then these men, whose legs were bowed by saddles before they were ten years old, ride railroad cabooses to the Omaha or Los Angeles markets, to supervise the selling of their stock and to honor tradition by indulging in a 'blowout' for themselves and their friends after the sale.

Right from Big Piney on a dirt road, which follows roughly the old Lander Cut-off, to SNYDER BASIN, 25 m., and STAR VALLEY, 60 m. (see Tour 13).

The highway crosses sage flats and meadows along the Green River. At 28.1 m. is the old RODEO GROUND (L), site of the annual Big Piney Fiesta: rodeo, barbecue, and dance. The barbecue is emphasized, because of the local boast that 'Big Piney beef is the finest in the world.' South of South Piney Creek, 28.5 m., occasional small cabins, weather-beaten and gray, blend with the sage against dull limestone cliffs in the background. Many of the cabins are deserted and falling down; some are maintained as shelter cabins. The flat, bearing only sage, sparse rabbit brush, and tough desert grass, looks worthless; a local saying is that 'squirrels must pack a lunch when they cross it.' Nevertheless, it is invaluable winter grazing ground for sheep, who are able to subsist where other domestic animals would starve.

The desert blizzard is the terror of sheepmen here; each winter, herders lose their lives in these terrific storms. The wind carries snow with punishing velocity; sheep sometimes drift many miles before it. Since the snow immediately conceals tracks, the herder is obliged to follow the flock, disregarding those that separate from it. If a camp tender is at hand, he follows with the wagon, and the herder is safe.

In large outfits, however, the tender has several camps to move with his mules, and, once he has set the herder's wagon in a particular spot, it must stand there until he makes the rounds again. When the blizzard strikes, the herder must leave his shelter and fire and follow the sheep. If the storm lasts long, both herder and herd may perish.

To the south, great red and gray buttes, many of them with flat tops, loom against the sky. Occasional deserted oil rigs recall the boom of which LA BARGE, 46.5 m. (6,820 alt., 100 pop.), was the center in the early 1920's. Optimists originally called the town Tulsa, for the Oklahoma oil city. In 1935, after the boom collapsed, they adopted the name of near-by LA BARGE CREEK, 48.7 m., which was named in 1824 by General Ashley for his friend, Joseph La Barge. More than 100,000 ties are floated down the stream each spring (see above).

At NAMES HILL (L), 52.7 m., where one of many branch trails begins a climb over broken cliffs, emigrants paused to carve their names in soft limestone. The earliest dated inscription is 1822; one of the most legible is 'James Bridger—1844.' The initials J.B. are carved on several neighboring cliffs. Southeast of the hill is the SITE OF A MORMON FERRY, 54.7 m., where a short cut to Idaho crossed Green River.

The road runs southward along river bottomlands, between fantastic buttes. At 69.3 m. it crosses SLATE CREEK.

Left from the crossing on a trail to EMIGRANT SPRINGS, 5 m., a camp site on the Sublette Cut-off to Fort Hall, Idaho. The spring was discovered by the Sublette Brothers, who traveled the route in the 1820's. The cut-off branched from the Oregon Trail below Pacific Springs and swung almost due west. Although it reduced the distance from South Pass to Bear River by 53 miles, it was unpopular because of the 30-mile waterless stretch between the Big Sandy and the Green (see Tour 5A).

The highway veers (R) away from the river over desert flats. Long, dry tree branches stand upright in the shoulders of the road at uniform distances, to mark the route when snow is deep. Shelter cabins are painted orange to make them readily visible during storms. The road runs under a trestle, 90.1 m., with mine buildings overhead, to SUSIE (6,623 alt., 110 pop.), a coal-mining camp in a canyon bridged by a gray shaft house. The Susie Mine, opened in the early 1900's, was named for Mrs. P. J. Quealy, wife of the president of the mining company. Above the highway, an electric car line (L) carries coal from the mine shaft to the Union Pacific tracks (R).

US 189 crosses HAM'S FORK OF GREEN RIVER, 92.9 m. Abandoned mine workings scar the hillside (L), bleak mementos of a period of wildcat development. A SILVER FOX FARM is R. at 93.2 m. Winding sharply downhill, the road crosses a one-line bridge over a dry streambed to FRONTIER (6,954 alt., 700 pop.), a prosperous mining community, with comfortable houses and attractive flower gardens, on the outskirts of Kemmerer. The Frontier Mine, opened in 1897, became one of the best-paying coal mines in the area. Ninety-eight men were killed here in an explosion in 1919.

The highway crosses a viaduct over the Union Pacific (Oregon Short Line) tracks and joins US 30N (*see Tour 2d*) at KEMMERER, 96 *m.* (6,940 alt., 1,884 pop.) (*see Tour 2d*). For the short distance between Kemmerer and a junction at 97.6 *m.*, US 30N unites with US 189.

·US 189 swings slightly R. across the Cumberland Flats, vast stretches of sagebrush where coal mines, active and abandoned, appear at intervals. Only rusted tin cans, rotten bits of lumber, and scrap iron remain on the SITE OF CUMBERLAND NO. 1, 110 *m.*, once a thriving mining camp. Similar rubbish (R), at 111.5 *m.*, marks the SITE OF CUMBERLAND NO. 2. Bordering LITTLE MUDDY CREEK, 114.6 *m.*, are small ranches and wild hay meadows. Cattle graze on the surrounding sage and greasewood flats. The road runs straight across a desert, where nothing breaks the monotony of the nearer landscape. In the distance are rusty buttes (L) and the pine-topped Uinta Mountains (R).

At 135.1 *m.* is the junction with US 30S (*see Tour 2C*), 18.1 miles east of the Utah Line.

Tour 10

(Spearfish, S. Dak.)—Beulah—Moorcroft—Ucross—Sheridan—Ranchester—Greybull; US 14.
South Dakota Line to Greybull, 319.1 *m.*

Oil-surfaced roadbed between South Dakota Line and Dayton; graveled between Dayton and Shell; oiled between Shell and Greybull. Section between Dayton and Shell closed during winter.
Route paralleled by C.B. & Q.R.R. between Moorcroft and Ranchester.
Accommodations in larger towns; a few tourist camps.

US 14 curves and angles erratically westward across northern Wyoming, running through pine-clad mountains between the Bear Lodge and Spearfish divisions of the Black Hills National Forest and then traversing a vast cattle and sheep country, to reach the fertile valleys of the Sheridan district; approaching the Montana Line, it intersects US 87, a route to the Custer Battlefield and Glacier National Park, ascends the Big Horns, and then drops sharply into a rich farming region. At Greybull, it unites with US 20, the Yellowstone Highway.

The Black Hills of Wyoming and South Dakota were so named by the Sioux, because, from a distance, their heavily forested sides looked deep blue or black. Thousands of buffalo and antelope once roamed the plains near by. Yellowstone Kelly, it is recorded, paid men $50 a month and 50¢ a head to kill the buffalo for their hides. To the Sioux, the Black Hills were sacred as the home of their deities. Their arrowheads, spears, grinders, and scrapers are often found among the hills. Their trails to the Big Horns followed the divides and streams much as US 14 does.

The remains of fur presses, bullboat frames, skinning knives, and flintlock guns attest the early presence of white men. Wilson P. Hunt and his Astorians traversed part of the route in 1811; many others were turned back by the Sioux. The first settlers in northeastern Wyoming came from the Dakotas to cut hay for the oxen, horses, and mules of freighters and miners in Black Hills camps, or to raise gardens and poultry for the miners themselves. Prospectors found small quantities of gold at Bear Gulch, Sand Creek, Tinton, and other sites. Then cattlemen brought herds from Texas and, despite Indian raids, established their ranches. Stock raising remains the leading industry, but dry farming, coal mining, and lumbering are also carried on.

US 14 crosses the SOUTH DAKOTA LINE, 0 *m.*, at a point 12 miles west of Spearfish, South Dakota. At the State Line is one of the low metal barriers placed throughout this district to check the spread of crickets.

MONTANA LAKE (R), 0.2 *m.*, fed by springs, was named for the Montana Expedition into the Black Hills. Some of the expedition's engineers were attacked here by Indians and forced to abandon their survey.

The highway skirts ranch lands and large meadows. The soil is red. At 1.3 *m.* is the junction with a dirt road.

Left on this road to SAND CREEK, 2 *m.*, a clear trout system, fringed with giant blue oak (said to be the only oak native to Wyoming), ironwood, and box elder. Pines form a dark-green blanket on the hillsides, which rise steeply to canyon walls of red, yellow, and gray stone. In 1939 the State bought 1,300 acres along Sand Creek, for a hunting and fishing reserve.

The road runs southwest up the canyon and through the landscaped ANNENBERG ESTATE (*no camping or loitering*), 4.6 *m.*, property of the well-known newspaper publisher. Large buildings, of peeled and varnished logs, are visible from the road.

BEULAH, 1.6 *m.* (3,510 alt., 174 pop.), a streamside trading center, was the scene of an early skirmish between the Sioux, under White Bull, and a party of emigrants from Iowa. Reinforcements from Spearfish, South Dakota, rescued the party after two nights of siege. In 1881, when a stage line was established to deliver mail to Sand Creek and the cattle ranches on the Wyoming side of the Hills, the seven families on the creek established their post office in a corner of a saloon run by two cowboys.

US 14 meanders along a heavily wooded stream bottom, where the water has cut deeply through red banks.

At 3.3 *m.* is the junction with the Rifle Pits Road.

Left here to RIFLE PITS DIVIDE, 5.5 *m.* The road climbs above the canyons to a magnificent view of wooded hills and red buttes. Just west of a little white schoolhouse, 6.5 *m.*, is the site (L) of one of the camps made by the Montana Expedition, which was so constantly harassed by members of the Crazy Horse and Gall bands that its members dug rifle pits at each camp. The road rejoins US 14 at ROCKY FORD CREEK, 10.8 *m.*, where Colonel Joseph T. Reynolds camped in 1876. Muleshoes, bridle bits, and army equipment have been found at the site.

At 8.2 *m.* is the junction with a dirt road.

Right on this road is ALADDIN, 8 *m.* (3,740 alt., 40 pop.), a thrifty prosperous Swedish community on the South Fork of Hay Creek. It is headquarters of the Bear Lodge District of the Black Hills National Forest. The principal occupations are farming and stock raising. Fossil cycads, petrified tree trunks, and footprints of small reptiles have been discovered in the vicinity. Just north of Aladdin is a triangular basin (bordered on two sides by the Belle Fourche), whose elevation of 3,125 feet is the lowest in the State. Here, in the MORRISON BEDS, are numerous reptile fossils.

The highway crosses rolling, wooded uplands, broken by deep gulches and small streams. The hillsides are bright with wild roses in summer. Southwest of SUNDANCE CREEK, 12.8 *m.*, a broad ranching valley opens out.

At 21 *m.* is the junction with State 585.

Left on this oiled road to open country, where deserted ranches alternate with prosperous holdings. At 16.5 *m.* is the Custer Junction:

1. Left here 0.7 *m.* on a dirt road to the SITE OF CUSTER'S CAMP July 22–3, 1874 (*see Tour* 1), on a branch of Inyan Kara Creek. On a hill to the east are the graves of two of Custer's men.

2. Right from the Custer Junction on a narrow road to INYAN KARA (Ind., stone-made) MOUNTAIN, 6 *m.*, at the top of which Custer carved his name in 1874. Ludlow, the geologist who accompanied Custer, said it resembled 'A lunar mountain, having a rim in the shape of a horseshoe, one and a half miles across, with an elongated peak rising sharply from the center . . . towering 170 feet above the rim and resembling a formation of basaltic columns . . . [with] a narrow spur projecting from it to the southward.' After leaving Inyan Kara, the expedition camped on Spring Creek, a tributary of Sand Creek. Since the valley there contained a great profusion of wild flowers, General Custer called it Floral Valley. In writing of the camp, one of the members of the party said: 'The entire expedition for the time revelled in the delights of the place, the soldiers festooning their hats and their horses' bridles with flowers while the expedition's band, seated on an elevated rock ledge played "Garey Owen," "The Mocking Bird," "The Blue Danube," snatches from "Il Trovatore" and other popular tunes of the day . . . The music of the band was weird and fascinating.' In 1854, Sir George Gore spent most of the summer in the vicinity of Inyan Kara, with his elaborate hunting party.

Although scientists explored the Black Hills as early as 1847, to Lieutenant G. K. Warren is due the credit for the first extended exploration. In 1857 he went north with a party from Fort Laramie, and at Inyan Kara he was strenuously opposed by Indians.

At 24.1 *m.* State 585 passes through grain and alfalfa fields, whose green cover contrasts vividly with the red topsoil. Grass-carpeted hills (L) are fringed with pines.

At 29.3 *m.* is the junction with US 85 (*see Tour* 1).

Flora and Fauna: Indians

Photograph by Charles J. Belden

CALL OF THE WILD

FURY OF THE STORM

Photograph by Charles J. Belden

ELK FEED GROUNDS, JACKSON HOLE

TABLE D'HOTE—BEARS IN YELLOWSTONE PARK

Photograph by Ned Frost

A BIG HORN

BUFFALO, YELLOWSTONE PARK

Photograph by courtesy of Haynes Inc.

WIND-TWISTED PINE

SAND LILIES

PRICKLY PEAR

YOUNGER GENERATION

Photograph by courtesy of Cheyenne Chamber of Commerce

ARAPAHO WOMEN TANNING HIDES, WIND RIVER RESERVATION

Photograph by courtesy of U. S. Indian Service

JOINT BUSINESS COUNCIL, SHOSHONE AND ARAPAHO INDIANS

LOUIS TYLER, A SHOSHONE, AND REVEREND
JOHN ROBERTS, AT SHOSHONE RESERVATION

FULLBLOOD SHOSHONE

ARAPAHO INDIAN WOMAN DISPLAYING HER HANDICRAFT

INDIAN PICTOGRAPHS, FREMONT COUNTY

SUNDANCE, 21.1 *m.* (4,750 alt., 369 pop.), seat of Crook County, is the smallest county seat in Wyoming. Stage lines with daily schedules connect it with the Chicago, Burlington & Quincy at Upton and Moorcroft. From 1888 to 1891, the mail was carried 175 miles from Sundance to Buffalo by horse cart, a six-day round trip. The town lies between Sundance Mountain and the Bear Lodge Range. Photographs of it, taken from the north, are sometimes mistaken for views of Oberammergau, the Bavarian village of the Passion Play. Before the days of extensive lumbering, Sundance was surrounded by pine forests. Coal deposits, near the town, are worked for local use.

1. Right from Sundance on a dirt road to WARREN PEAKS, 6 *m.* (6,800 alt.), a cluster of hills, grass-covered and nearly destitute of trees, the highest points in the Bear Lodge area. Devil's Tower is L; parts of Montana and South Dakota, R. Deer appear frequently near the road; flowers bloom along the slopes. The Bear Lodge country, the northwestern extremity of the Black Hills, is separated from the main range by the broad Redwater Valley.

2. Left from Sundance on a trail to SUNDANCE MOUNTAIN, 1 *m.* (5,800 alt.). It is a strenuous hike to the crest, from which the Big Horns, 180 miles to the west, are visible on clear days. The mountain was once a summer rendezvous of the Sioux, who came here to hunt, gather berries, and hold their sun dance. An old French fur trader named Moran described the sun dance thus: 'A young buck . . . would have the medicine men gather the skin on his back, run his knife through his skin, then thread a piece of rawhide through it. He would fasten the thong to a scaffold . . . let his weight on the thong and surge and swing there until the rawhide tore through his flesh . . . The other Indians would form a circle around him and . . . dance to lend him courage. If the brave managed to stand the torture until the thong tore through his skin, the medicine man would dress his wound and take him into a tepee. There he would rest and sleep . . .'

US 14 runs through a narrow cut in red, pine-clad hills and winds down into a valley, where abandoned ranch buildings, corrals, and old log cabins stand. At 37.6 *m.* is an observation tower in WONDERVIEW PARK (*cabins, filling station, store*). As the road curves up a hill, the Devil's Tower rises distinct ahead, a gray shaft against the sky. Much of the timber land near the highway is cut over, and cricket plagues also have impaired its agricultural possibilities.

At 43.3 *m.* is the junction with the Devil's Tower Road.

Right on this graveled and oil-surfaced road through pines, past neat farms, and over grassy hills to a valley, 6.1 *m.*, where the road forks; L. here to the Belle Fourche River, 6.9 *m.*, from which the road ascends to circle the base of Devil's Tower.

Exhibits in the MONUMENT HEADQUARTERS AND MUSEUM (*full-time custodian*), 9.7 *m.*, illustrate the Tower's geologic history and explain the several ascents that have been made.

The DEVIL'S TOWER, 9.8 *m.*, an extraordinary mass of gray igneous rock, is the most conspicuous geologic feature of the Black Hills region. It rises 600 feet above a rounded ridge of sedimentary rocks, which itself rises 600 feet above the Belle Fourche River. The nearly flat crest is elliptical, with a diameter varying from 60 to 100 feet. The columns forming the sides of the Tower are sharply fluted; near the top they are somewhat rounded, and near the bottom they have considerable outward flare. The fluting gives the tower the appearance of a gigantic petrified stump. Many of the columns are broken off part way up; near the top, their symmetry has been marred by erosion and irregular exfoliation. Phonolite, of which the tower is composed, is a volcanic rock, similar to granite, consisting of orthoclase, a form of feldspar, and nephelite; it is named for the ringing sound emitted when a slab is struck.

When the Black Hills uplift occurred more than 20,000,000 years ago, the upwelling lava formed a blister, or laccolith. The columns are massive prisms formed during the lava's rapid cooling. They are mostly pentagonal in cross section, but some are four- or six-sided. Their average diameter is six feet; most of them taper slightly toward the top. They exhibit remarkable precision of design. In some places the upper parts of several prisms unite to form a single fluted column. The flutings are not usually jointed, but are marked horizontally with faint ridges or swellings, especially toward the summit. In their lower quarter or third, the columns bend outward and merge rapidly into massive rock, which is only slightly columnar in structure.

The base of the Tower, about 1,700 feet in diameter, is surrounded by solid bench rock extending outward 30 or 40 feet. On the southwest face, the columns curve outward over the base, some lying almost horizontally. Talus extends high up the slopes of the bench and far out over the sedimentary rocks.

The tower was a landmark of the Sioux, who called it Mato Tipi (Bear Lodge). Near it, Sitting Bull made medicine and received, according to his nephew White Bull, the gods' assurance of victory in one of his greatest campaigns. Sioux legend tells that three maidens gathering wild flowers here were beset by bears. To escape, they climbed up on a large boulder; the gods, seeing their distress, made the rock higher. As the bears tried to climb the rock, it continued rising, until at last the bears fell and were killed. The girls braided their flowers into a rope, by means of which they reached the plain. The channels in the tower wall are the marks left by the bears' claws.

Another version of the legend is told by I-seo-o, a Kiowa scout. The Kiowa were camped on a stream far to the north, where many bears lived. One day the bears chased seven little girls, who were playing at a distance from the village. The girls jumped upon a low rock and prayed: 'Rock, take pity on us! Rock, save us!' The rock shot upward, and, when the bears jumped at it, they broke their claws and fell to the ground. The rock rose higher and higher, until the children were pushed up to the sky, where they remained. They are known to white men as the Seven Sisters, or the Pleiades.

Pioneers used the tower as a landmark during their exploration of the Northwest, and, during the wars in the Sioux and Crow country, military leaders directed their marches by its aid. It is visible in some directions for nearly 100 miles.

President Theodore Roosevelt made the 1,153-acre tower area the country's first national monument, September 24, 1906. Few persons have scaled the tower. In 1893, Bill Rogers, who lived near it, made a ladder of oak pegs, and, on July 4, in the presence of several thousand people, made the climb. The ladder reached within 400 feet of the crest; the wall above it offered natural means of ascent. Rogers's wife and several other persons climbed the rock later, but some who made the effort became dizzy or frightened and had to be rescued. To prevent attempts by unqualified climbers, the lower end of the ladder was raised to a height of 60 feet. In 1927, a 'human fly' named White safely made the ascent and return.

Every summer, usually about July 4, the pioneers of the region meet here for the Old Settlers' Picnic, which features speeches, stories of the early days, and demonstrations of bullwhip cracking by old freighters. A small rodeo is also presented every Fourth of July. Only broncos that have never been ridden are used in the bucking contests. The busters participate for the sport rather than for large purses.

In 1933 the National Park Service took under its protection a prairie-dog town within the area, to preserve for visitors a typical scene of the old West. Outside this sanctuary, efforts to eradicate the prairie dog continue.

Left (northwest) from Devil's Tower on a trail to MISSOURI BUTTES, 6 m., which provide an excellent view of the Belle Fourche River, Devil's Tower, Schoolma'am Lake, and the wooded country intervening.

US 14 curves southwest and crosses the BELLE FOURCHE (Fr., beautiful fork), 45.3 *m.*, often called by the Indians the Bear Lodge River. Because the wooded hills kept out cold winds, and because game, wild fruit, fish, pasturage, and firewood were plentiful, the Indians spent many winters along the Belle Fourche. Some of the oldest cattle brands on the range—the 4-J, the Hoe, the O-Bar-K, the Quarter-Circle-I, the T-7, and others—belonged to outfits along the Belle Fourche and Powder Rivers.

US 14 passes two tourist camps (R) and winds southwestward, paralleling the Belle Fourche. It passes CARLILE, 49.7 *m.* (4,017 alt., 50 pop.), a post office with filling station and store, and curves sharply through thick woods (*drive slowly*). At 57 *m.*, broad, burned-out flats replace the timbered slopes.

At MOORCROFT, 69.6 *m.* (4,206 alt., 400 pop.) (*see Tour* 8), is the junction with US 16. Between Moorcroft and Ucross, US 14 and US 16 coincide (*see Tour* 8).

At UCROSS, 178.9 *m.* (4,085 alt., 158 pop.) (*see Tour* 8), US 16 goes L. US 14, the main route, curves R. through Piney Creek Valley, an irrigated section of sugar-beet fields and wheatlands. Large stone and frame buildings, as well as log cabins, are common here. Between the draws along the edges of the valley, fields form irregular patterns on the hillsides.

At 191 *m.* is the junction with a graveled road.

Right on this road, which runs sharply up the side of a steep hill, to WAR-PATH LOOKOUT (*parking space available*), 0.1 *m.*, which commands a sweeping view of the Big Horns and the surrounding hills and vales. It is said to have been an Indian lookout.

The highway descends rapidly through the foothills, passes fields of corn and grain, and enters Prairie Dog Valley, a prosperous area with clear streams and wide haylands. Here purebred stock, particularly sheep, is raised. Wild roses flourish by the roadside. The observation tower near Story (*see Tour* 3) is visible (L) across the vast basin.

At 207.1 *m.* is the junction with US 87 (*see Tour* 3), which unites with US 14 for 19.2 miles.

SHERIDAN, 209.1 *m.* (3,773 alt., 8,773 pop.) (*see Sheridan*).

At 226.3 *m.* US 14 turns L. US 87 continues straight ahead (*see Tour* 3).

RANCHESTER, 226.6 *m.* (3,775 alt., 155 pop.), named by combining 'ranch' with the English term for a walled town, is a rural supply center for the Tongue River Valley. Indians named the stream for a tongue-shaped mountain to the west.

Left from Ranchester on an improved road, called US 14 Branch, to a gate, 1 *m.;* L. here 0.3 *m.* to primitive CONNOR BATTLEFIELD STATE PARK. A short circle drive winds along the Tongue River; rustic benches are set under the fine cottonwood trees and willows. A large stone marker designates the site where, on August 29, 1865, General P. E. Connor's soldiers from Fort Laramie attacked a large party of Arapaho, under Black Bear and Old David, and destroyed about 250 lodges. The fight had many features in common with that at Sand Creek in Colorado, which had taken place the previous year. Much of it was hand-to-hand. Many women and children were killed or captured. The soldiers took 600 horses, but later returned those claimed by the prisoners, who were sent back to their tribes under military escort.

US 14 runs westward along Tongue River (L) through a green valley of alfalfa fields and native hay meadows. The blue-black timbered Big Horns loom ahead.

At 232 *m.* is the junction with the Tongue River Road.

Right on this dirt road to TONGUE RIVER CANYON (*good trout fishing*). At 2.5 *m.* is a junction. The Tongue River Road keeps L. At 2.6 *m.* is the junction with a dim trail; R. here 0.5 *m.* to a NATURAL BRIDGE, which can be climbed.

At 5.5 *m.* on the Tongue River Road is a PICNIC AREA on the bank of Tongue River, and a junction with another trail; L. here 0.6 *m.* across a swinging bridge and by a zigzag trail to a CAVE in the mountainside (*guide necessary: visitors should bring heavy clothing, food, and a flashlight*). The cave was discovered about 1918, after a forest fire seared away the brush and timber near its small entrance. The walls are covered with arrows indicating passages. Tangled cords and wires, left by exploring parties, hinder progress. A waterfall about 20 feet high splashes into a room, 15 by 20 feet in extent, where the waterfall sinks among rocks in the floor and into a crevice under an overhanging ledge. Paul Wilson of Dayton, a guide, has explored the passageways to a depth of 3.3 miles.

DAYTON, 232.2 *m.* (3,926 alt., 275 pop.), a typical one-street Western town, attracted nationwide attention in 1911 by electing Susan Wissler its mayor. Mrs. Wissler was said to be the first woman mayor in the United States, but the claim has since been disputed. In Dayton are many summer homes.

At 232.7 *m.* is the junction with a graveled road.

Left on this road through a valley of fruit trees and hillside fields to the EATON RANCH, 9.5 *m.*, on Wolf Creek. The first real dude ranch in the West, it was established in 1904 by the three Eaton brothers. In 1880 Howard Eaton of Pittsburgh, Pennsylvania, started the Custer Trail Ranch in South Dakota; his brothers, Alden and Willis, joined him; and friends came from the East to visit. Some, who returned again and again, insisted on paying their way. Thus was born the idea of a ranch that would charge certain rates for its hospitality. Disposing of the Custer Trail Ranch, the Eatons bought the place on Wolf Creek (4,700 alt.). It comprises 7,000 acres along the foothills of the snow-capped Big Horns, which are laced with trails and bridle paths into primitive regions. The ranch is a miniature town, with its own post office, store, telephone system, individual houses, and hotel. Bill Eaton, a son of Alden, is in charge. Many distinguished guests return annually.

The road continues through a region of prosperous ranches and curves down a steep hill to Goose Creek Valley, where purebred cattle and sheep graze. In spring, the banks of the stream and its tributaries are abloom with chokecherries, wild plums, serviceberries, and currants.

At 15.5 *m.* is BECKTON JUNCTION; R. here across Goose Creek to the BOZEMAN TRAIL, 0.5 *m.* (*see History*). The main side road turns eastward along the creek to SHERIDAN, 25.2 *m.*, where it intersects US 87 (*see Tour 3a*).

At 232.8 *m.* on US 14 is the junction with a dirt road.

Right on this road through a gate to the KLEIBER STUDIO, 0.1 *m.* Hans Kleiber, a former forest ranger, taught himself the art of etching and won international recognition with his prints. The most famous are his pioneer etchings and the single print, *Geese Crossing Wyoming*. He works here most of the year, wielding his diamond-tipped tools or standing over his press.

US 14 veers southwestward to a 20-mile ascent of the Big Horn Mountains, by means of switchbacks and hairpin turns. At 238.9 *m.* is a view of the Tongue River Valley. On very clear days, it is possible to see the low Wolf Mountains in Montana and the Black Hills, 200 miles to the east. At 239.6 *m.*, the highway crosses the boundary of the BIG HORN NATIONAL FOREST, where woodsmen cut railroad ties, mine timbers, posts, poles, and fuel. Lodgepole pine predominates, but there is much Engelmann spruce, Douglas fir, ponderosa and limber pine, and alpine fir.

The STATE GAME CHECKING STATION, 239.7 *m.*, is open during hunting season. Big-game hunters report here, when entering or leaving the district.

The FALLEN CITY (L), 244.1 *m.*, a jumble of huge oblong boulders deposited on the hillside by a prehistoric glacier, suggests a city leveled by earthquake. An observation tower on the highest tip (7,000 alt.) of STEAMBOAT ROCK, 245.1 *m.*, a peak named for its shape, commands a view of the Big Horn forest plateau to the west and the valleys north and east.

At 245.2 *m.* is a startling view into TONGUE RIVER CANYON, where the stream has worn a gorge 2,000 feet deep in almost solid rock. The walls are nearly perpendicular, and only an occasional ledge supports a stunted pine or willow clump. The stream is a thread along the sunless bottom.

West of CUTLER PASS, 252.2 *m.* (8,550 alt.), the highway runs for miles across a level plateau at the top of the Big Horn Range, 4,000 feet above the floor of Sheridan Valley. The roadway becomes a narrow avenue through one of the heaviest timber stands in Wyoming. Occasional mountain parks are carpeted with grass and scrub willow. Indian paintbrush, gentian, harebell, and wild rose garnish the green background of pines and deep grass.

SIBLEY DAM, 253.8 *m.*, a riprapped stone and dirt structure 330 feet long and 34 feet high, is at the outlet of SIBLEY LAKE (*boating and fishing*). The lake spreads over 33 acres, when the gates are closed.

At 260.7 *m.* the road forks.

Right on a dirt road to CAMPGROUNDS (*tables and stoves*), 1 *m.*, near the junction of the North Fork and Willow Creek (*excellent fishing*). At 1.5 *m.* is the BURGESS RANGER STATION.

Here also is the junction with State 14 (*see Tour 10A*).

US 14 turns L. through rugged, steep country to SHELL CANYON, 275.7 *m.* The road is narrow and hazardous, but offers spectacular views of heavy forests, roaring waterfalls, and jagged cliffs. At the edge of the road in many places are sheer drops of hundreds of feet.

SHELL, 307.7 *m.* (4,210 alt., 50 pop.), is a farming community on Shell Creek (*good trout fishing; primitive picnic spots*). Petrified shells and occasional arrowheads are picked up along the stream. A small

MUSEUM contains fossils, Indian artifacts, and pioneer relics. Large fossils are found in hills of soft sedimentary materials (R). Shell Canyon is a V-shaped gap in the mountain range to the east.

US 14 runs through a thickly settled valley, with well-kept farm buildings, surrounded by lawns, trees, and flowering shrubs. Rows of poplars, called 'Mormon trees' because they were planted by Mormon colonists, pattern the landscape with vivid green.

At GREYBULL, 319.1 *m.* (3,788 alt., 1,806 pop.), is the junction with US 20 (*see Tour* 6).

Tour 10A

Junction with US 14—Kane—Lovell—Byron—Powell—Cody; 109.7 *m.*, State 14.

Route paralleled from Garland to Cody by Chicago, Burlington & Quincy R.R.
Oil-, gravel- and dirt-surfaced roadway, difficult in wet weather, closed in winter.

State 14, the alternate route between the Big Horn National Forest (Sheridan) and Cody, branches from US 14 on the east face of the Big Horn Mountains, scales the summit of the range in long curving sweeps, passes near to the Medicine Wheel, then drops into the Big Horn Basin and crosses its northern end to Powell and Cody.

Branching due west from US 14 (*see Tour* 10), 0 *m.*, State 14 climbs sharply through spired pine forest to the summit of the Big Horn Range near BALD MOUNTAIN, or Big Baldy (10,030 alt.), a barren, dome-like uplift that rises above the black timbered slopes. In the 1880's, Big Baldy was the center of a boom mining area, where men staked fortunes on finding a legendary lode, supposedly uncovered once by Indians. In 1892, Eastern capitalists were persuaded to install expensive machinery at Bald Mountain. The resulting whispers of a bonanza spawned a mushroom town called Fortunatus. Money circulated freely, and everyone prospered but the miners and investors. In 1937, a local company bought machinery to work a draw eight miles northwest of the old townsite.

At 23.4 *m.* is the junction with dirt road.

Right on this road to a parking area, 3 *m.*, from which a narrow, steep trail leads (R) 0.5 *m.* to the MEDICINE WHEEL (9,956 alt.), a gigantic wheel of limestone slabs and boulders, 245 feet in circumference, thought to have been built by a prehistoric race. Indians have no legends or traditions to explain its origin. The pattern and orientation imply that the builders were sun-worshipers. The hub consists of a circular stone mound about three feet high, from which 29 spokes radiate, possibly representing the days of the lunar month. Around the edge of the wheel, at different distances from the center, are six medicine tepees (so called by the Crow) to symbolize the planets. One of them is at the end of a long spoke extending beyond the perimeter; another is at the end of a short spoke, and a third is just inside the rim. The tepee on the east side differs from the others in that it is higher and nearly square, and has its openings on the outside, whereas all the other openings face the hub. The tepees were evidently shelters for the chiefs or medicine men during worship, and once there were large excavations under them. On a slab within the central structure, a bleached buffalo skull faces the rising sun. Some maintain that the medicine wheel is related to the worship of the Aztecs; others believe it dates back to a period when iron was unknown. Indians apparently understood that the wheel had some connection with worship, for they built small stone shelters on the large rocks at the edge of the Medicine Mountain and fasted there to invite visions. That the wheel was visited by great numbers of pilgrims is indicated by worn travois trails, visible for two or three miles near the site. The Forest Service has built a three-foot rock wall around the wheel, to keep livestock away.

State 14 twists and turns through canyons, crossing a boundary of the BIG HORN NATIONAL FOREST at 33 *m.* At 35.1 *m.* is the junction with a trail.

Left on this trail to FIVE SPRINGS FALLS, 0.2 *m.*, which spreads like a broad, silver ribbon in a 125-foot drop. Above the falls are several good trout holes (*camping facilities near by*).

The road zigzags down a steep grade along shelves (*keep car in gear*). A small stream foams over roadside rocks. The timber and the canyons recede, as the road runs out to benchlands and then winds down to a narrow one-way bridge over the BIG HORN RIVER, 49.9 *m.* Bleak hills (L) slope to irrigated lands, on which silos tower over neat farmsteads set with apple and plum trees.

KANE, 51.4 *m.* (3,645 alt., 45 pop.), is a lumber-shipping point on the Chicago, Burlington & Quincy Railroad.

At 60.9 *m.* is the southern junction with US 310, with which State 14 unites for 2.9 miles (*see Tour 6A*). At 63.8 *m.* US 310 goes R. State 14 curves L. through rich beet and oil country to BYRON, 68.7 *m.* (4,020 alt., 250 pop.), a busy town named for Byron Sessions, Mormon pioneer. Soon after Mormons settled here in 1900, a farmer observed gas escaping from a fence-post hole. Ignited, the gas burned several years. In 1906, a test hole was drilled, and oil sands were struck at 700 feet. The first well flowed without pumping, but the heavy head of gas made control difficult. Subsequent wells were all gas producers; and Byron now supplies gas to Cowley, Powell, and Lovell.

Continuing over farming country, State 14 joins State 114 in GARLAND, 80.3 *m.* (*see Tour 6A*). Southwest of Garland, the highway crosses more green beet-growing land.

POWELL, 85.3 *m.* (4,365 alt., 1,600 pop.), enjoys the trade of a wide farming and oil-producing region. It was planned in the late

1890's by the Department of the Interior, as headquarters for the Shoshone Reclamation Project; well-built houses line its wide, tree-bordered streets. Beans, sugar beets, sweet-clover seed, potatoes, and alfalfa are staples marketed through the Big Horn Cooperative Marketing Association. The consolidated school district here has the largest school bus system in Wyoming. Seventeen buses transport pupils from Penrose, Eaglenest, Ralston, Garland, and the Willwood Irrigation District to Powell.

> Right from Powell on a dirt road to POLECAT BENCH, 10 *m.*, southern boundary of the irrigated area. Fossils of crocodiles, turtles, and doglike animals, believed to be 60,000,000 years old, have been found here. In the lower stratum are dinosaur deposits probably twice as old.

The valley, through which State 14 winds southwestward, produces cattle, sheep, and hogs, and large crops of beans and potatoes. Trees and flowering shrubs surround the farmhouses. The Absaroka Mountains rise ahead, a vertical border of profound blue, beyond the varying greens of the nearer landscape. In the distance (R) is SHOSHONE CANYON, a great gash in the mountain wall, where water for the Powell farming area is stored (*see Tour 6c*). The highway parallels the Shoshone River along a high bench, spread with apple orchards and grain fields.

CODY, 109.7 *m.* (5,018 alt., 1,800 pop.) (*see Tour 6c*), is at the junction with US 14-20 (*see Tours 10 and 6*).

Tour 11

Casper—Alcova—Three Forks; 73.5 *m.*, State 220.

Oil-surfaced, open all season; severe blizzards in winter.
Few accommodations.

State 220, which links US 20-87 with US 287 in central Wyoming, runs southeast from Casper over prairies and desert hills, once traversed by early traders and explorers. It passes familiar landmarks on the Oregon, California, and Mormon Trails, connects with side roads to two extensive irrigation projects, and provides a short cut between Casper and points west of Cheyenne on US 30.

State 220 branches south from US 20, 0 *m.*, at Casper (*see Casper*). At 0.5 *m.* is the junction with 13th Street.

Right on 13th Street, which becomes Carey Lane, a graveled road, to FORT CASPAR PARK, 1.3 *m.* A small enclosed graveyard (L) holds several skeletons, discovered in 1938 by reconstruction workers.

FORT CASPAR (*guides*), 1.4 *m.*, was rebuilt on its original site in 1938. The low peeled-log buildings, with small square windows and gently sloping roofs, are arranged as they were in the 1860's; the old telegraph that was found in the ruins was reinstalled in the little room it occupied during the Battle of Platte Bridge in 1865. In the fort are the old-time vehicles used in the Wyoming-on-Parade celebration (*see Casper*). The rooms contain highly polished but rugged furniture, fashioned from native gnarled pine, and relics found at the fort and environs.

In 1847, Mormons set up a ferry at the crossing of the Platte here, and wagon trains continued to use it through the early 1850's. Brigham Young named nine men to remain and operate the ferryboat, which was made of two large cottonwood canoes fastened together with crosspieces and covered with slabs. John Richeau (Reshaw, Richards) had previously established a ferry seven miles below, but his rates were high and varied with the water level. Adobe station buildings were erected here in 1858; in 1859, troops were sent to the spot to protect wagons along the Oregon Trail. The same year, Louis Guinard completed the 1,000-foot Platte Bridge of cedar logs resting on stone-filled cribs. The structure cost $60,000. In 1863, a military post was established at the bridge.

When Indians undertook to stop traffic on the Oregon Trail in 1865, Platte Bridge Station became an important military objective. About 3,000 Sioux, Cheyenne, and Arapaho assembled on the hills to the north. On the morning of July 26, the major in command at the bridge ordered 21-year-old Lieutenant Caspar W. Collins, 11th Ohio Volunteer Cavalry, a casual officer who had arrived at the fort the night before, to lead 25 men to the relief of a wagon train under Sergeant Amos J. Custard, which was in peril near Willow Springs, 17 miles away (*see below*). Young Collins crossed the bridge and followed the road northwest near the foot of the bluffs. As his party reached the bench near the graveyard, Indians rose from every sand hill. Six hundred Cheyenne charged the command in front and on the left; a force of Sioux, estimated at 1,800, charged out of the ravine on the other side. Collins ordered a retreat toward the post, which left him as rear guard. The Indians were by that time massed so closely around the soldiers that both parties were afraid to shoot for fear of killing their own men; consequently the fighting was mostly hand to hand. At the bottom of the hill, Collins heard the cries of a fallen soldier. As he struggled to lift the man to the saddle, his horse became unmanageable and carried him straight into the enemy's hands. His body was found the next day, mutilated almost beyond recognition. Four others in his command were killed.

On November 21, 1865, Major General Pope ordered that Platte Bridge Station, 'be hereafter known as Fort Caspar, in honor of Lt. Caspar Collins . . . who lost his life while gallantly attacking a superior force.'

Adjoining the fort are the GROUNDS OF THE IZAAK WALTON CLUB (*picnic facilities; traps for trapshooting on the riverbank*).

State 220 passes the gateway to the C Y RANCH (R), 1.3 *m.* Here is the first ranch house in the vicinity, a small log cabin built by Judge Joseph M. Carey in 1876. The highway goes through a valley and canyon. Casper Mountain looms (L). At 5.8 *m.*, a granite marker (R), with an Oregon Trail plaque, commemorates the Red Buttes Fight, also called Custard's Fight, the site of which is (R) across the valley (*see below*).

At 10.6 *m.* is the junction with a dirt road.

Right on this road to the GOOSE EGG RANCH HOUSE, 3 *m.*, made famous by Owen Wister's *The Virginian.* The large stone house was built in 1877 by the Searight brothers, who came from Texas with 27,000 head of cattle. It was known as Goose Egg because of the Searight brand. The ranch was popular for its Saturday night dances, at one of which, according to Wister's book, playful cowboys exchanged the blankets and clothing of the infant children of some friends. The parents did not discover the trick until they were many miles on their homeward journey in the early morning.

At 4.3 *m.* the road turns R. to a gate, 10.3 *m.;* R. here 2 *m.* to the assumed SITE OF THE BATTLE OF RED BUTTES. Stones mark places designated as graves by former soldiers, who helped bury 19 men who died here July 26, 1865. Two others were killed near by. The bodies of the 19 soldiers have not been located, although many attempts have been made to find them in recent years.

Three wagons, under Sergeant Amos J. Custard, 11th Kansas Cavalry, left Sweetwater Station on July 25, to go to Platte Bridge. Though warned of the danger of Indian attack, Custard refused to make the entire trip that day, because his horses were tired. He camped for the night near Willow Spring. When Cheyenne, Sioux, Arapaho, Blackfeet, and Comanche warriors attacked, three of his men escaped by running to the river; the others sought the shelter of the wagons. Pushing piles of dirt before them for breastworks, the Indians crawled steadily nearer and at length overwhelmed the men of the train and mutilated their bodies.

The highway passes through a gap in red sandstone cliffs. The North Platte River winds through a fertile valley (R).

BESSEMER BEND, 11 *m.*, is a long sheltered valley west of the Casper Mountain foothills. A large spring west of the river furnishes abundant water for irrigation on adjacent lands. Fine crops of grain grow here, and there are several apple orchards. Near the spot where Poison Spider Creek empties into the river, Robert Stuart and six companions built a cabin on their return from Astoria, November 2, 1812; on December 13, fearing Indians who had discovered them three days earlier, they abandoned it and moved to a site near present Torrington (*see Tour* 4). Stuart described the cabin as 8 feet wide and 18 feet long, with walls 6 feet high. The whole building was covered with buffalo skins. A hole in the roof served for a chimney.

Near this spot is the SITE OF BESSEMER, a town established in the summer of 1888; optimistic citizens called it the 'Queen City of the West.' The Wyoming Improvement Company surveyed the site, platted 49 blocks of town lots, and reserved grounds 'upon which to erect the future capitol building of Wyoming.' For a time, the Casper-Bessemer stage made two trips daily. In 1889, when Natrona County was separated from Carbon County, Bessemer was a rival of Casper for county seat status (*see Casper*). Two years later, the county took over the bridge across the North Platte River, because of unpaid taxes. Bessemer was soon abandoned.

The highway, crossing sage land, borders the NATRONA COUNTY BIRD REFUGE, 18.3 *m.*, then goes south through a partly cultivated region and crosses the NORTH PLATTE RIVER, 22.5 *m.* On FREMONT'S ISLAND (L), 26.9 *m.*, Lieutenant John C. Frémont camped in 1842. State 220 strikes across an arid sagebrush plateau.

At 30.7 *m.* is the junction with a graded road.

Left on this road is ALCOVA (5,310 alt., 40 pop.), 1 *m.* (*log cabins, filling stations, café*), in a small valley surrounded by rock-ribbed hills. At the entrance to the town is a view of Alcova Dam, with water foaming over the spillway, spray rising. At one time a score of hot springs flowed from the solid rock walls of the canyon near by. In 1891, an Eastern syndicate bought the site for a resort, and plans were drawn for $250,000 worth of improvements. An analysis of the water showed that it had exceptional medicinal quality; but the settlement remained small. In 1933, a Congressional appropriation for an irrigation project gave Alcova its biggest boost in 40 years.

1. Right from Alcova on a dirt road up a hillside to the ALCOVA DAM (1938), 0.8 m. The road crosses at the base of three 63-ton gates, and runs atop the dam. The reservoir lies (R) between canyon walls; with water 170 feet above the riverbed, its capacity is 180,000 acre-feet. The dam is one of the three main features of what is called the Kendrick Project on the North Platte River; the others are a water distribution system consisting of the 100-mile Casper Canal and its laterals, and the Seminoe Dam and hydroelectric power system. The main objective of the project is reclamation and settlement of 66,000 acres of central Wyoming land. Alcova Dam diverts water into the Casper Canal through a tunnel in the reservoir rim about 1.5 miles west. The dam is about 700 feet long and 180 feet high and consists of a rolled fill section of impervious clay, riprapped on the upstream* face and backed with sand, gravel, and cobbles.

2. Right from Alcova on an unimproved road to the CASPER BOAT CLUB BOATHOUSE, 5 m.

3. Right from Alcova on a trail to the FIERY NARROWS, 7 m., in the Grand Canyon of the Platte, now commonly known as PATHFINDER CANYON. The narrows were named by Robert Stuart, who passed this place October 31, 1812. On the north rim, 500 feet above the turbulent river, are the REMAINS OF A CABIN, believed to have been a hide-out for cattle rustlers. A rock shelf, projecting 16 feet or so, forms the roof. The walls, chimney, and fireplace are built of flat stones. Cowhides probably covered the small door in cold weather. A window far up in the east wall commands a view of the east and south approaches for many miles.

4. Left from Alcova on a rough, lonely trail to the WALN MONUMENT on Monument Creek, 18 m., a slab of Pennsylvania granite eight feet high, with cross arms four and a half feet long. Inscribed on the base are the words: 'To the memory of God, and in the name of S. Morris Waln, of Philadelphia, Pa. Born July 12, 1866, murdered by his guide, July 28, 1888.' Waln, accompanied by C. H. Strong of New York City, came West early in the spring of 1888 to hunt and prospect. At Denver, they hired Thomas O'Brien as cook, guide, and teamster, and the three men evidently camped near Rock Creek, Wyoming, for a few days. About two weeks later, the bodies of Waln and Strong were found by cowboys; their identity was established by a wrist bangle, a handkerchief, bits of a letter scattered near a campfire, and other clues. O'Brien, although arrested later in Colorado and sentenced to 14 years in the penitentiary for horse stealing, was never tried for the Wyoming murders.

The main side road continues southward from Alcova, then turns almost due south to the 280-foot concrete SEMINOE DAM, 28.8 m., in a deep gorge. This dam, which cost about $5,000,000 to build, with an additional outlay of $2,150,-000 for a power plant and machinery, will impound North Platte flood waters. Part of the water will be passed through a 36,000-kilowatt power plant; 380 miles of main transmission line will carry the power to central and southeastern Wyoming, northern Colorado, and western Nebraska. The surplus water released for power purposes, above the current irrigation demand, will be stored in Pathfinder Reservoir (*see below*).

State 220 curves through hills, skirts red sandstone cliffs, passes several deserted cabins, and runs between sheer rock walls to open country. The valley (L) spreads far below.

At 36.6 m. is the junction with a dirt road.

Left on this road across sage flats, with Independence Rock in the distance southward, to a wild-life refuge, at the junction with a foot trail, 6.5 *m.;* L. here 0.2 *m.* to the PATHFINDER DAM (1909), a granite structure 218 feet high and 432 feet long at the top. Here is a startling view of sheer granite canyon walls and water foaming from spillway and tunnels. The gates periodically discharge water for a large area in eastern Wyoming and western Nebraska. An aerial tramway spans the canyon above.

The highway runs over mile after mile of rolling sage country, with glimpses of the 22,700-acre Pathfinder Reservoir (L). Antelope are numerous in this region.

At 44.9 *m.* is the junction with a dirt road.

Right on this road to the SITE OF BOTHWELL, 2 *m.,* near the banks of Horse Creek. Here, the Sweetwater Land and Improvement Company, incorporated with a capital of $300,000, planned a town. During the summer of 1889, Bothwell had a store, blacksmith shop, post office, saloon, and a newspaper, the *Sweetwater Chief.* Now, only the graves of Jim Averill and his wife, Ella (Cattle Kate Maxwell) Watson, mark the site. It is said that Kate had a homestead about a mile from Averill's saloon and store, and, when cowpunchers came to Bothwell to celebrate, Averill usually got their money, while Kate persuaded them to put her brand on several calves. Soon the fenced pasture near her cabin held a considerable herd of cattle. Ranchers, annoyed by Cattle Kate's homestead on their range, accused Kate and Averill of rustling. When the two ignored orders to leave the country, cowmen took them to Spring Creek Gulch, about five miles from Averill's saloon, and hanged them from a tree. The Casper deputy sheriff found the bodies and buried them near the saloon. Six men were accused of the hanging, but the case was dismissed. Friends of Averill and Kate asserted that no indictments were returned because of lack of witnesses; one died and two disappeared before they could testify.

INDEPENDENCE ROCK (L), 54.7 *m.,* a gray-brown granite monolith on the north bank of Sweetwater River, is 1,552 yards in circumference, 1,950 feet long, and 850 feet wide. At the south end, it is 167 feet high; at the north end, 193 feet. The mass is one of the most significant erosion remnants in the West, with remarkable striations left by early glaciation along its sides.

It is believed that the rock was named on or about Independence Day by the first white travelers to approach it. Robert Stuart saw it in 1812, and, in 1834, John K. Townsend mentioned in his diary that he camped at 'a large rounded mass of granite, about fifty feet high, called Rock Independence.' Father P. J. De Smet, in 1840, referred to the 'famous rock, Independence . . . that might be called the great registry of the desert, for on it may be read in large characters the names of several travelers who have visited the Rocky Mountains.' In 1842, Frémont described the rock thus: '. . . about 650 yards long and 40 in height. Except in a depression on the summit, where a little soil supported a scanty growth of shrubs with a solitary pine, it was entirely bare. Everywhere within six or eight feet from the ground, where the surface was sufficiently smooth, and in some places sixty or eighty feet above, the rock was inscribed with names of travelers . . . I engraved on this rock of the far West a symbol of the Christian faith . . . a large cross, which I covered with a black preparation of India rubber well calculated to resist the influence of wind and rain.'

Frémont's cross has disappeared, nevertheless. Coutant, Wyoming historian, suggests that the piece of rock on which the cross was cut may have been detached by a gunpowder explosion, which occurred on July 4, 1847, when more than 1,000 Oregon and California emigrants were gathered on the Sweetwater. When Frémont became a candidate for the presidency, the fact that he left the symbol on Independence Rock was used to influence Protestant voters against him.

In 1847, Brigham Young led the first group of Mormons past the spot; in 1855, some of his followers who had stonecutting tools conceived the idea of engraving travelers' names on the rock, at $1 to $5 a name.

A bronze plaque mounted on the rock honors the Mormon emigrants who passed in the 1840's and 1850's, on their way to the valley of Great Salt Lake. Other plaques are dedicated to Ezra Meeker, founder of the Oregon Trail Memorial Association; to Narcissa Prentiss Whitman and Eliza Hart Spalding, first white women to cross Wyoming (*see Tour 5A*); to Father De Smet, first Jesuit missionary in Wyoming; and to unknown pioneers who passed this way. A tablet commemorates Wyoming's first Masonic meeting, held on top of the rock July 4, 1862. Many of the 50,000 names inscribed in the stone have been more or less obliterated by wind and rain, but thousands remain clear. Dim wagon ruts still show where the Oregon Trail passed.

At the crossing of SWEETWATER RIVER, 55.1 *m.*, is the junction with a dirt road.

Left on this road to the SITE OF SWEETWATER STATION, 1 *m.*, a military post for the protection of emigrants. Lieutenant Caspar Collins (*see above*), who commanded the post for a time, wrote to his mother in Ohio, on June 16, 1862: 'This is the worst country for winds I ever saw. Yesterday . . . it commenced to blow, and it is blowing yet. My father and Mr. Pallady and myself went up last night to the Independence Rock, about a mile above here, right below the Devil's Gate to shoot at a mark . . . Immediately under the rock it was tolerably still, and we commenced shooting at a piece of paper about a hundred yards off . . . Mr. Pallady hit it and I went to see where it was . . . A gust of wind coming down from the mountains blew it away and it went up almost out of sight, when another blast . . . brought it back . . . Major Bridger went off this morning up in the mountains to get out of the wind. He says he is going to get in some canon and make a large fire.'

State 220 bears southwest from the bridge through flat grasslands, within sight of the river. At RUSH CREEK, 60.7 *m.*, is the junction with a dirt road.

Right on this road to DEVIL'S GATE, 0.2 *m.*, where the river turns abruptly north and passes through a ridge by way of an extraordinary chasm, 330 feet deep and only 30 feet wide at the bottom. The walls of the gorge are of gray granite, with a streak of black granite extending from bottom to top, at first glance resembling a roadway. Small immigrant trains were often ambushed by Indians here.

In 1812, the Stuart party noted the chasm, and Captain Hiram M. Chittenden, who investigated its possibilities as a dam site in 1901–2, pronounced the Devil's Gate 'one of the most notable features of its kind in the world.' There is no evidence that the opening was cut by 'erosion; rather, the rock seems to have been cleft by some convulsion of nature. East of the gorge the ridge falls away rapidly.

In the early 1860's, an 18-year-old girl, who had climbed with three other women to the top of the ridge, fell into the chasm. Her body was buried in the gorge, and this epitaph was inscribed on a board at the head of her grave:

> Here lies the body of Caroline Todd
> Whose soul has lately gone to God;
> Ere redemption was too late,
> She was redeemed at Devil's Gate.

At 62.9 *m.* is a monument to Captain Howard Martin's handcart company of 576 English emigrants, who were rescued here in November 1856 by men and wagons sent from Salt Lake City by Brigham Young. These Mormons, who had started from Iowa City on foot, pulling and pushing handcarts (*see Tour 5A*), were overtaken by severe storms when they reached the Sweetwater. Many died, but some found shelter in a stockade and mail station near Devil's Gate, and here they stored the remnants of their property for the winter; others were strung along the route in small groups for a hundred miles. Near the gate, more than 100 died in nine days and were buried in a single trench.

Turning L., away from the Sweetwater Valley, the highway crosses sage flats and barren hills.

At THREE FORKS, 73.5 *m.*, State 220 joins US 287 (*see Tour 5c*).

Tour 12

Shoshoni—Riverton—Lander; 46.7 *m.*, State 320.

C. & N. W. Ry. parallels the route.
Oil-surfaced roadbed throughout.
Accommodations in towns.

State 320, between Shoshoni and Lander, links US 20 and US 287 (*see Tours 5 and 6*). It crosses barren salt-sage prairies and curves through green valleys, with the snowy Wind River peaks ahead (R).

Branching west from US 20 at SHOSHONI, 0 *m.*, the highway crosses Wind River, 3.2 *m.*, and veers southwestward, straight toward the peaks, passing eroded cliffs and sagebrush flats.

At 3.3 *m.* is the junction with a dirt road.

Left on this road to worn INDIAN PICTOGRAPHS, 1.1 *m.*, carved in a ledge on the C. F. Andrews Ranch. Some of them appear to represent men in striped or slashed apparel, possibly early Spanish travelers. One device is a snake, or the letter S, in combination with another symbol. Legend says that the inscription was left by Spanish conquistadores 200 years ago, to direct the way to a treasure they had buried when pursued by Indians.

At 12.3 *m.*, a large irrigation ditch traces a broad green-edged furrow across the landscape. Scattered over the countryside are many types of farm buildings—log cabins, frame houses, and tarpaper shacks. Spring and summer cloudbursts have gouged out deep draws in the prairie. In summer the farms are vivid with green of beets and alfalfa. The planting of beets is completed by mid-April; cultivation begins as soon as they break through the surface; and thinning, soon thereafter. The beets are pulled and shipped to the factory in early October. Nearly every day in summer, Russian-German and Mexican laborers are seen bending over the rows, removing weeds or surplus plants.

At 20.2 *m.* is the junction with an improved road.

Left on this road to the 300-acre STATE PRISON FARM, 0.5 *m.*, where trusties from the State penitentiary have been quartered since 1931.

RIVERTON, 22.4 *m.* (4,956 alt., 1,608 pop.), is the business center of the Wind River Basin. Its new brick dwellings and business houses and large electric signs contrast with the primitive conditions on the Shoshone Reservation (*see Tour 5b*) near by.

In 1904, the site of Riverton was a part of the reservation, but, by a treaty effective March 3, 1905, the Shoshone and Arapaho relinquished their rights north of Wind River and left 1,346,320 acres of land available for white settlement. Work on an irrigation system began at once. Settlers came early in August 1906, in wagons and buckboards, on horseback and afoot; by August 15, more than 500 had arrived. Living in wagons and tents or under sheltering trees, they followed the surveyors, filing on land plots as soon as they were laid out. The reservation agent ruled that settlers could not occupy the land until the survey was completed, but the homesteaders refused to move. The agent then summoned cavalry from Fort Washakie to evict them. Early the next morning, a party of 20 men from Lander 'jumped' the abandoned claims. The original claimants called a mass meeting and marched to reclaim their plots. They pulled up and burned the jumpers' stakes and put back the original ones. The Lander party declared the first survey illegal and proposed another, but the first settlers, armed with rifles, held the ground. The jumpers appealed to the troops, but now the settlers refused to be driven out. At night they slept on their coats, near their stakes, rifles within reach. The survey was speeded up, and order was restored.

Another dispute arose over a name for the community. A committee agreed on Riverton, but the newly arrived railroad called its terminus Wadsworth. Travelers bound for Riverton detrained at Wadsworth and sometimes had difficulty in finding their destination.

For a time, Riverton's streets were little more than wagon tracks through the sage. Constant winds whipped the light topsoil to fine dust, which filled the nostrils of passers-by and filtered through windows. Wags remarked that a citizen of Riverton could be recognized by the quantity and color of dust on his clothes. The only crossing over Wind River was a ferry operated by an Indian. Water was delivered to town residents at 5¢ a pail or 25¢ a barrel; its flavor varied according to the original contents of the barrel—vinegar, oil, or whisky.

In August 1910, the State canceled the water company's unfulfilled contracts. Gaunt men loaded their families into buckboards or wagons and rumbled eastward without looking back. The proposal to 'give the land back to the Indians' became something more than a joke. Homesteaders who stayed, however, made progress. Federal funds to improve the irrigation system were obtained, and sage-lands were transformed into waving green fields of alfalfa, corn, and grain. Beet-sugar companies sent representatives to talk with the farmers. Today, the lower Wind River Basin is one of the best sugar-beet areas in the State, with nearly 40,000 acres under cultivation. Systematic planting and watering of forage crops has made the valley also an important livestock area, in which lamb feeding has been especially profitable. The area leads in the production of honey. As new ditches are completed, land units are opened for settlers, who are selected by an examining board on the basis of farming experience and capital. The cost of water per user is about $90 an acre, payable to the Government in 40 annual installments.

The weddings of the German-Russian beet workers, whose shacks stand about the green fields, follow Old-World custom. Immediately before the ceremony, which is performed at noon, the bride's brothers and sisters sing to her in the mother tongue. After the wedding meal, one of the bride's slippers is auctioned off to the men, often bringing $10 or more; then the bride and groom and four attendants do a folk dance. After the guests have danced with the bride, the cook enters with a heavy plate, which he hurls to the floor; if the plate breaks, it is a good omen for the married pair. The cook, thus holding their happiness in his hand, always tries to smash the plate to bits. In the public dance that follows, all who dance with the bride pin money to her clothing. In return, the bridegroom supplies enough wine to enable guests to toast the bride with generous frequency.

Right from Riverton on oil-surfaced State 287, paralleling Wind River, the northeastern boundary of the Shoshone Reservation. Green fields stretch away to silver-gray salt sage slopes on both sides. PILOT BUTTE POWER PLANT (R), 25.7 m., was built in 1924.

The highway crosses Wind River on a bridge over DIVERSION DAM, 34.3 m. (5,580 alt.), core of the $9,000,000 Riverton Reclamation Project, which is designed to irrigate 100,000 acres of the clay-sand soil of Wind River Basin. The 650-foot concrete dam, completed in 1923, diverts water from the river into Wyoming Canal (bottom width, 65 feet; capacity, 2,200 acre-feet), through which it reaches Pilot Butte Reservoir. From the reservoir (30,000 acre-feet) it is distributed through subcanals and ditches to 26,000 acres of fields and gardens. Improvements are added by the U. S. Bureau of Reclamation, as funds become available.

At 35.3 m. is the junction with US 287 (see Tour 5).

State 320 winds over bottomlands among willows, cottonwoods, and raspberry patches, then runs southwestward over sage flats, beside Indian lands (R), with one-room log cabins, canvas tents, and willow sun shelters.

The sturdy tan-sandstone buildings of ST. STEPHEN'S MISSION (L), 26.3 *m.*, are surrounded by flower, fruit, and vegetable gardens. The school, in charge of four Jesuit Fathers and eight Franciscan Sisters, combines the work of the eight grammar grades with vocational training. Business English and typewriting are taught, with a view to placing graduates in the Indian Service.

The mission works solely with the Arapaho, who were 'temporarily' domiciled on the Shoshone Reservation in 1876 (*see Indians*). Until 1884, this tribe without a country was forgotten in the campaign to educate Indians; then the Government opened a boarding school for its young people. Bishop O'Connor of Omaha raised funds to furnish the building and provided the teachers. Father John Jutz of Buffalo, New York, who was placed in charge, bought a pony, a saddle, and a tent, loaded his belongings on a wagon, and, accompanied by Father Moriarity of Lander, entered Arapaho country, without knowledge of his charges or of their language. In the triangle formed by the confluence of the Wind and Little Wind Rivers, he pitched his tent and set up a temporary altar, where he said Mass the next morning, with only Chief Black Coal, his two wives, and his children present. When a letter from Father Jutz to Bishop O'Connor, describing his work, appeared in a newspaper, Miss Catherine Drexel of Philadelphia gave $5,000 for an Arapaho mission.

At 29.7 *m.* is the junction with a dirt road.

Right on this road to ARAPAHOE, 0.7 *m.* (5,200 alt., 50 pop.), trading post and Arapaho sub-agency. Before 1920, more than 200,000 sheep grazed in this area, and more than 100 men were employed in caring for them. With post-war retrenchment, Arapaho became a quiet trading village. The INDIAN SCHOOL is (R) at the edge of town.

The road crosses Little Wind River, and continues to the GOVERNMENT CANNERY (*open by arrangement*), 1.1 *m.*, where Indian workers process corn, peas, beans, tomatoes, and other reservation-grown vegetables.

HUDSON, 36.7 *m.* (5,094 alt., 350 pop.), trading center for Indians and coal and oil workers, is also a cattle-shipping point. Three large coal mines have operated here since 1900.

The highway runs southwestward up the Popo Agie Valley and crosses the Little Popo Agie, affluent of the Popo Agie, which rises in the Washakie National Forest at the southeastern end of the Wind River Range. In this wide, productive valley, favorable climate and altitude permit the growing of fruits and vegetables not raised elsewhere in Wyoming. Grass grew so fast here in spring that the Shoshone knew the region as the Valley of the Push Root.

The STATE TRAINING SCHOOL (L), 45.3 *m.*, housed in 15 or more red brick buildings, surrounded by landscaped grounds and 600 acres of farm and garden, was established in 1907 as an asylum for mental defectives. The school maintains a hospital and gives its 300 students grammar-school instruction up to the sixth grade. The curriculum emphasizes manual training; cooking and sewing; wood, leather, textile, and metal handicrafts; and farming. Supplementary instruction is given in music and in Boy Scout and girls' club activities. Recreation includes basketball, dances and parties, motion pictures, fishing and hiking trips. A personnel department finds employment for eligible students.

At LANDER, 46.7 *m.* (5,357 alt., 1,826 pop.) (*see Tour 5b*), is the junction with US 287 (*see Tour 5*).

Tour 13

Wilson—Alpine—Afton—(Montpelier, Idaho); Grand Canyon Road, US 89. Wilson to Idaho Line, 108.8 *m.*

Graded, oil- and gravel-surfaced; narrow between Wilson and Alpine.
Accommodations in larger towns.

This cutoff south of Jackson Hole passes through country rivaling Yellowstone Park in natural beauty. It parallels one of Wyoming's largest rivers, through a chasm several thousand feet deep, crosses great national forests, and traverses the entire length of fertile Star Valley.

The Grand Canyon Road goes south from State 22 (US 89) in WILSON, 0 *m.* (6,080 alt., 400 pop.) (*see Tour 7a*), and crosses a meadow bottomland known as South Park. The wooded humps of the Snake Mountains (R) cast long shadows in the afternoon. Waterfowl rise from sloughs with a muffled whirring, and songbirds call from cattails and willows. Ahead, the mountains swing eastward in a wide elbow, sheltering the valley on two sides. The road winds over foothills, then descends to the Snake River, near the mouth of the Hoback. The Snake flows southward through a tapering green valley of cow and sheep ranches. At 25 *m.* the mountains close in ahead; the highway is cut from a shelf above the river, here more swiftly moving.

On BAILEY BAR (the ELBOW), 27.1 *m.*, where Bailey Creek falls from the Grey's River Range (*see below*), are old sluice boxes and placer flumes, where gold was washed in the early 1900's.

Left on a game trail up Bailey Creek to BAILEY LAKE (*excellent fly fishing*), 3 *m.*

As the canyon narrows, the walls become steeper, and the river twists toward rapids. The road climbs to the NARROWS, 36 *m.*, where the gorge, 3,000 feet deep, is less than 40 feet wide in many places. In this constricted channel, the river is lashed to white foam by the speed of its fall; its roar can be heard several miles away. John Day and two companions saw the rapids in 1811, while scouting from Hoback Canyon to see whether Hunt's Astorians could make the descent to the Columbia River by boat.

Below the rapids, the canyon widens suddenly to STAR VALLEY (6,200 avg. alt., 5,000 pop.), which is 5 to 7 miles wide and 50 miles long. Along the sides of this valley extend rugged peaks and ridges, cut by deep gorges and interspersed with broad, flat meadows. The highest summits are 6,000 feet above the Snake River; one area has a rise of 3,000 feet within a half-mile ascent. The isolated valley, watered by Salt River and its tributaries, is bounded by the Wyoming National Forest (L) and by the Caribou National Forest (R). The Wyoming National Forest embraces the Salt River Range and pastures about 4,000 elk; it also provides summer forage for about 200,000 sheep and 6,000 cattle.

Dairying is the valley's principal industry, but farming under irrigation is intensive and efficient. Alfalfa, wild hay, oats, wheat, barley, and rye are staple crops. Each farm maintains a herd of 10 to 50 dairy cows; milk is sold to five co-operative creameries, which manufacture cheese, butter, powdered milk, and casein (*see Industry, Commerce and Labor*). The nearest railroad is about 50 miles away, and the valley's 11 towns average less than 100 population. Originally, the land was divided into units that were comparatively big for intensive farming. Families have been large, however, and disposed to remain in the valley; so settlers' children have divided the family holdings, and their children in turn have subdivided the property. Many farms were thus reduced to sizes scarcely adequate for the owners' needs.

Fifty years before its first settlement, Star Valley was known to pathfinders, trappers, and mountain men. Several members of Wilson Price Hunt's Astorians worked the area as early as 1812; the names of Day, Hoback, and Smith were given to streams, lakes, mountains, and trails. From 1856 until the late 1860's, emigrants bound for Oregon passed through over the Lander Cut-off (*see Tour 5b*); but not until the region was included in Brigham Young's colonization project did actual settlement begin. More than 90 per cent of the population is still affiliated with the 12 Mormon wards of the Star Valley Stake.

Brigham Young, knowing the impiety of frontier mining camps and the demoralizing influence of easy wealth, looked askance at gold strikes and booms and decreed that his people devote their efforts to agriculture. After the 'Mormon War,' however, Federal authorities took a hand in the government of Deseret, and mining lands were opened to exploitation. As the number of converts from Europe grew larger, the Utah Eden became overcrowded; then Young, to enforce his decree that church members till the soil, sent emissaries to adjoining regions to look for suitable lands. In the late 1870's, Apostle Moses Thatcher stood on a point of vantage overlooking Star Valley and saw that it was good. 'I hereby name this valley Star Valley,' he said, 'because it is the star of all valleys.' A story of opposite import asserts that the 'star' was originally named Starved Valley, because the earliest settlers had insufficient food during their first winter there.

The Edmunds Anti-Polygamy Act of 1882, which sent the president of the Mormon Church into hiding, accelerated the migration of Mormons to Star Valley. Men with several families were effective colonizers and stable citizens in a frontier community; and Wyoming, aspiring to statehood, was concerned with expanding its population. Federal authorities, who attempted to enforce the law in the Territory, received little co-operation.

At ALPINE, 41 m. (5,600 alt., 20 pop.), a hamlet on high, arid flats, is the junction with US 89 and Idaho 29. For nearly a mile, the road follows the Idaho Line. One half of Alpine's street is in Wyoming, the other in Idaho. A bridge spanning the river at this point was built co-operatively by the two States in the early 1900's, about the time Alpine was established. Now, both States recognize the need for a new bridge, but neither has assumed the expense of the project, and each has built its highway only to the State line. The unimproved stretch is impassable in early spring and late fall.

Robert Stuart and his party camped in the vicinity of Alpine in the autumn of 1812. Trying to shake off a party of Indians that had harassed them for several hundred miles, they had left Hunt's route and entered this region. On the Snake River, near its junction with the Salt, they lost their horses to the Indians. There they burned their heavy baggage, sailed down the Snake on improvised rafts, made their way northward to Hunt's (Teton) Pass, and turned eastward on foot.

At 43 m. is the junction with the unsurfaced Grey's River Road.

Left on this Forest Service road to one of the State's most primitive areas, only recently accessible by automobile. Grey's River, whose roar at high water can be heard long distances, was originally named for John Day, the Virginian trapper who went to Astoria with Wilson Price Hunt in 1811, and set out with Robert Stuart on the return trip the next year. Before the party had progressed far up the Columbia, Day became insane and was taken back to Astoria. Later, according to some authorities, he trapped for Astor on the headwaters of the Snake and spent about eight years in the Star Valley region.

On broad, brush-covered SQUAW FLAT, 4.5 m., a Blackfoot brave was killed by a grizzly bear in the 1880's or 1890's. Local legend says that his squaw returned to his grave at the same season for many years, at first alone, then accompanied by a daughter, and at length alone once more.

At 7 m. is the junction with the Little Grey's River Road, a dirt road that becomes a pack trail; L. here 6 m. to the LITTLE GREY'S RIVER WILDERNESS, one of the most rugged regions in the West. So steep are its crags and gorges, according to the testimony of riders and sheepherders, that hawks and eagles use rough rocks in getting from place to place. In much of this area, road construction and hunting are prohibited. Elk, moose, deer, mountain sheep, black bear, and grizzly bear enjoy the wilderness undisturbed.

At 7.2 m. Grey's River Road enters a WINTER FEEDING GROUND, where several hundred elk are provided with hay and cottonseed cake, when deep snow makes foraging difficult.

The road roughly follows the river southward, skirts or traverses numerous meadows and canyons, and crosses trout streams, which fall from the towering range to the east to feed Grey's River. At 57 *m.*, it intersects the Big Piney Road, 10 miles east of US 89 (*see below*).

US 89 runs southeast, then due south through the widening valley. The RURAL ELECTRIFICATION PLANT (1938) is across the valley (R) at 45.7 *m.* Rectangular fields, surrounded by barbed-wire fences, checker the landscape. The prevalent style in farm dwelling is the Mormon box house (*see Architecture*); because of abundant timber, most buildings are frame. In many places, small, rough, one-story houses stand beside larger houses, the homes of sons or daughters who have settled after marriage to till the soil on which they were born. Because of the importance of the dairy industry, the barn often surpasses the dwelling in size and comfort. On many farms, the first family habitation has been converted into a shelter for the dairy herd, and a new residence built—the architecture unchanged. Milk is marketed in five, eight, and ten-gallon metal cans, which are placed on stands along the highway. Each morning, a milkman conveys them to the creamery; later in the day he replaces them, empty. The number of cans on the stand usually varies with the size of the farmhouse and is an accurate gauge of the farmer's prosperity.

ETNA, 51.5 *m.* (5,600 alt., 390 pop.), is a typical farming village.

US 89 continues southward among fertile farms, where livestock is abundant. Breeds are mixed on the average farm, producing roans, 'black ballies,' and 'spotted reds.' The dairy strains are somewhat heavy, the beef strains lighter than pure Hereford. Scattered among the red and white range animals are lean, angular Holstein steers, locally called 'magpies,' which have little physical beauty or commercial value. The birth of a bull in a dairy herd is regarded usually as less than fortunate, since few are of sufficiently pure strain to become sires. Many are destroyed immediately; others are allowed to develop as beef steers.

At 55.4 *m.* is the junction with a graveled road.

Right on this road is FREEDOM, 1.7 *m.* (5,556 alt., 459 pop.), the oldest settlement in Star Valley. It is on the State Line, with the west side of main street in Idaho, the east in Wyoming. In the summer of 1879, a party of Mormon immigrants entered the valley over the Crow Creek route from Bear Lake Valley, Idaho, and built the first wagon road connecting with settlements farther south. After a careful exploration, they settled here. One of the party, surveying his new domain, declared enthusiastically, 'Here we shall find freedom'—and the settlement was named accordingly. Later, when polygamists were being prosecuted by Federal authorities in Idaho, it had ample opportunity to prove its freedom was more than a name. When a road was built into that territory through Tin Cup Canyon, churchmen took advantage of it. During a Federal raid, residents on the Idaho side could step across the street into Wyoming and avoid arrest.

Freedom still profits by its location, for, because of Idaho's State liquor store system, popular beverages are cheaper on its Idaho side than in Wyoming.

THAYNE, 59.6 *m.* (5,790 alt., 380 pop.), established in 1889, was named for Henry Thayne, its first postmaster and merchant.

At 60.6 *m.* is the junction with a dirt road.

Left on this road to a SWISS CHEESE FACTORY (*open to visitors*), 1 *m.*, a small concrete building (L), in which 185-pound Swiss cheeses are made. The road swings southeast to mountains, skirts foothills, and enters a small valley.

BEDFORD, 4 *m.* (5,620 alt., 15 pop.), a prosperous farming community, was settled in the early 1880's. Surrounded on three sides by high wooded mountains, the valley is shielded from autumn and winter winds. Snow comes early and stays late, but its depth assures abundant water.

TURNERVILLE, 9.3 *m.* (6,665 alt., 20 pop.), is at the base of the mountains, in the southeast end of Bedford Valley. The forests of blue-green pines and shimmering white aspens that robe the mountains extend almost down to the settlement.

The road enters an avenue of pines, 9.6 *m.*, and climbs steeply to the top of Turnerville Hill, 12.1 *m.*, then descends through Spruce Canyon to Grover Park and Upper Star Valley. It joins US 89 at Grover, 15 *m.* (*see below*).

US 89 parallels Salt River through the NARROWS, 63 *m.*, where the hills close in to form a pass five miles long between Upper and Lower Star Valley. Small riverside farms are wedged in, wherever the pass widens a little.

At 66.5 *m.* is the junction with a graded road.

Right on this road is AUBURN, 4 *m.* (6,300 alt., 202 pop.), second settlement in Star Valley. Here, a party of Mormons erected cabins in August 1879. After one season, they moved to other parts of the valley, but the settlement was revived a few years later. Because the vacant cabins reminded some rustic Sappho of Oliver Goldsmith's *Deserted Village,* the place was named Auburn. The store here was the first in the valley.

Salt of 99.99 per cent purity is deposited along the tributaries of Stump Creek, west of Auburn. The salt fields were once held by Indian tribes, who traveled great distances for the salt, which they used for medicine, for tanning leather, for curing meats, and for flavoring foods. In the late 1860's, Emil Stump and William White established a salt works on Stump Creek, then known as Smoking Creek. The refined salt, hauled by ox team over the Lander Cut-off, was sold in Montana and Idaho mining camps for as much as 60¢ a pound. Hot springs and sulphur deposits are found throughout the area.

US 89 swings southeast along foothills that border the rich Salt River bottomlands (R).

GROVER, 69.9 *m.* (6,167 alt., 203 pop.), locally known as Denmark, for the native land of its inhabitants, is a farmers' village. Rows of tall poplars planted by early settlers border the unimproved streets. Here is the southern junction with the Turnerville Road (*see above*).

The UNIVERSITY OF WYOMING EXPERIMENT STATION, 74.2 *m.*, whose pastures and fields (R) border Afton on the north, carries on research in dairying, herd improvement, grain growing, and gardening.

At 74.4 *m.* US 89 intersects a graveled road.

1. Right on this road to the STAR VALLEY CREAMERY (*open to visitors*), 0.4 *m.* In the early 1930's, a farmers' co-operative bought the plant and equipment from the Kraft-Phenix Corporation. Under the 'co-op' management, the factory expanded production, until its requirements average 12,000,000 pounds of milk yearly. Equipment is maintained for making butter, cheese, and powdered milk.

2. Left on this road, which becomes a foot and bridle trail at 3 *m.*, to PERIODIC SPRING, 7 *m.*, in Swift Creek Canyon. The only one of its kind in America, this spring gushes ice-cold water for about 18 minutes, then remains inactive for a similar period. The water issues from a cavern at the base of a massive vertical rock.

US 89 is the main street of AFTON, 74.6 *m.* (6,134 alt., 897 pop.), business center of Star Valley, which boasts, in addition to its dairies, a chinchilla fur farm (established 1938), one of 30 such farms in the world. Public buildings in the town include three saloons, a blacksmith shop, and an airplane factory (*see Industry, Commerce and Labor*). The sandstone Tabernacle, Middle English in design, with a spire that is visible throughout the upper valley, is the center for valley-wide church functions.

Mormon immigrants surveyed the site in 1896, using only a carpenter's square, a long rope, and an almanac, and taking bearings by the North Star and the noonday sun. An official survey, years later, revealed that the plat was about five feet out of true. US 89 makes a jog on both approaches, to run straight through the town. For the preference given Afton over other valley settlements, the town owes much to Moses Thatcher: On a low moraine east of town, the apostle struck the ground with his hickory cane and foretold the erection of a temple. Since the temple is the final goal of community aspiration among Mormons, this assurance predetermined Afton's development.

Religious refugees were not alone in finding this region a convenient retreat during the 1880's. Men of vague occupations often dropped in from nowhere and disappeared again. Their coming was not always regarded as intrusion, as they spent money freely for shelter and food and financed, directly or indirectly, many early community enterprises. In 1889, Matt Warner and Tom McCarthy, members of the notorious McCarthy gang, holed up in Afton after a series of bank and mail robberies. They posed as wealthy Montana cattlemen, snowed in for the winter; legend has it that their barroom, the first in the valley, was papered with bank notes. During their stay they wooed and won two valley maidens, who remained true even after they learned their husbands' identities. Butch Cassidy (*see Tour 3b*), then serving his apprenticeship as horse thief with the McCarthy gang, was with Warner in Star Valley.

At 76.8 *m.* is the junction with a graveled road.

Right on this road is FAIRVIEW, 3.5 *m.* (6,000 alt., 50 pop.), once a prosperous freighters' outpost near the mouth of Crow Creek Canyon. Until the building of US 89 in the late 1920's, the Crow Creek Road, which connected with the railroad at Montpelier, Idaho, was the favored route into the valley. Long caravans of sleds or wagons made weekly trips over it. Fairview now functions only as a supply center for farm families in southwestern Star Valley. A gigantic ramshackle structure, once an elaborate and busy livery stable, serves as a blacksmith shop.

The UPPER STAR VALLEY SWISS CHEESE FACTORY, 76.9 *m.*, is a modern limestone and concrete plant (R), operated by a farmers' co-operative association.

OSMOND, 77 *m.* (6,450 alt., 25 pop.), a scattered farming community, named for George Osmond, first president of the Star Valley Stake, is known locally as Sweden, because of the ancestry of most of its citizens. SIGNAL HILL, a low benchlike knoll at the foot of the mountain range (L), at one time served as a lookout, from which warnings were broadcast to Mormons and other fugitives, when unannounced parties entered the valley. The hill, visible from all parts of Upper Star Valley, commands a sweeping view of Crow Creek Canyon. When the lookout spied strangers, he sent up a column of smoke; at this signal, apprehensive citizens took cover, and mothers rehearsed their children in replies to anyone inquiring about their fathers. If the newcomers proved harmless, another signal informed the patriarchs and outlaws that it was safe to come out.

SMOOT, 82.2 *m.* (6,519 alt., 50 pop.), is a farmers' village, named for former Senator Reed Smoot of Utah, an apostle of the Mormon church.

At 82.8 *m.* is the junction with a dirt road.

> Left on this road to COTTONWOOD LAKE RESORT, 7 *m.* (*cabins, camping and boating facilities, excellent fishing*).

US 89 runs south to Salt Creek Canyon. Aspen groves fleck the blue pine slopes, and, in autumn, frosted maple leaves flame in the lower places. At 86.8 *m.*, the canyon widens to a small valley, known as FOREST DELL, in which willow thickets alternate with irregular meadows. Scattered along the valley bottom are small log cabins.

At 89.2 *m.* is the junction with a dirt road.

> Left on this Forest Service road, which follows generally the old LANDER CUT-OFF (*see Tour 5b*) through Snyder Basin to BIG PINEY, 60 *m.* (*see Tour 9*), intersecting the Grey's River Road at 10 *m.* (*see above*). Along this trail, an occasional pile of boulders, a rude cross, or a rough-hewn slab marks the grave of someone who died on the way to Oregon. Old-timers tell stories of soldiers killed here by Indians; of smudged wagon irons that indicated the fate of an emigrant party; of a fruitless search for money, supposedly buried by a paymaster when his escort was attacked. Alonzo F. Brown of New Hampshire, who crossed the route later known as the Lander Cut-off in 1849, told of coming upon the burning remnants of an emigrant train, where the trail entered Star Valley. All members of the train, except a four-year-old girl, were dead; the stock had been driven off. The child's legs were broken, and apparently she had been left for dead. Brown's party dressed her wounds and took her to Oregon. Today a peaceful aspen grove marks the site of the massacre.

US 89 climbs in steep curves to the divide, 91.4 *m.* (7,630 alt.), between Fish Creek and Salt Creek, then winds down over the sage-covered hills, through summer sheep range. Every spring, thousands of sheep are driven from the ranching country of southern Lincoln County to the Salt River, Snake River, and Caribou ranges. In the fall, they are driven back to winter on the desert. At a boundary of the WYOMING NATIONAL FOREST, 98.9 *m.*, massive sage-covered hills close in. The highway threads its way between red slopes, past sandstone outcrops; then through lower, flatter country of hardy rabbit brush and sage, and over shelves to an open farming valley.

At 108.8 *m.*, where US 89 crosses the IDAHO LINE, 16 miles east of Montpelier, Idaho, is the junction with State 89 (*see Tour 2C*), 10.3 miles north of Border Junction.

Yellowstone National Park

GENERAL INFORMATION

Season: Regular season June 20 to September 12, during which time park utilities are operated. Between May 1 (when roads are usually cleared of snow) and June 20, and between September 13 and October 15, limited accommodations for motorists are available at various places in the park; campgrounds may be used, and general stores, gas stations, and picture shops are open at several points. The 3½-day motor-bus tour is started for the last time on September 9.

Administrative Offices: Executive offices of park administration and of public utilities that operate in park are at Mammoth Hot Springs, 5 m. S. of North Entrance; address, Yellowstone Park, Wyo. Persons charged with violation of regulations are tried at Headquarters, by U. S. Commissioner T. Paul Wilcox.

Admission: Automobile permit, $3; motorcycle permit, $1; house trailers, $1. Permit entitles visitor to free use of park roads and automobile campgrounds. Gateways are open 6:30 A.M. to 11:00 P.M. daily.

Railroads: Park reached by Northern Pacific Ry. and US 89 at Gardiner, Mont. (N); by Northern Pacific Ry. (busses from Bozeman, Mont.), Chicago, Milwaukee, St. Paul & Pacific R.R. (busses from Gallatin Gateway) and US 191 at Bozeman, Mont., by Union Pacific R.R., US 191, and Mont. 1 at West Yellowstone, Mont. (W); by Union Pacific R.R. (busses from Victor, Idaho) and US 89 and 287 at Snake River. (S); by Chicago, Burlington & Quincy R.R. (busses from Cody) and US 14 and 20 at Sylvan Pass (E); by Northern Pacific Ry. (busses from Red Lodge, Mont.) and Montana 32 (Red Lodge—Cooke Highway) at Silver Gate, Mont. (NE). Stop-over privileges for railroad passengers wishing to visit Yellowstone National Park as a side trip from Livingston, Billings, Bozeman, Three Forks, or Butte, Mont.; Pocatello, Idaho; Ogden or Salt Lake City, Utah; or Frannie, Wyo.

Airlines: In summer Western Air Express provides mail and passenger service by air from United Air Lines base at Salt Lake City to West Yellowstone airport, 30 m. from Old Faithful Inn. Western Air Express also schedules sight-seeing flights over park from West Yellowstone. Northwest Air Lines, in its Seattle to Chicago service, has stops at Butte, where it connects with Western Air Express to West Yellowstone, and at Billings. Wyoming Air Lines connects Cheyenne and Billings via Casper and Sheridan. Yellowstone Park Company operates busses to all points in park from entrances and from Moran and Cody, Wyo., and Bozeman and Gallatin Gateway, Mont. It also operates a few large touring cars for those desiring special trips, at additional cost; reservations for such trips must be made by correspondence with the company, Yellowstone Park, Wyo. Standard 3½-day tours of the park by bus are sold at railroad offices in connection with tickets to Gardiner, Bozeman, Gallatin Gateway, Red Lodge and West Yellowstone, Mont., and Cody, Wyo. Rate for these tours, including hotel accommodations (rooms without bath), $42.50; with lodge accommodations, $40.50 (*subject to possible revision*).

Highways and Trails: Park highways total 310 miles, of which 221 miles are oil-surfaced. Main road system, known as Grand Loop, is a rough figure 8, with approach roads branching from it. Trails total more than 900 miles. Horses can be rented at Mammoth, Old Faithful, and Canyon at 75¢ per hour, $2.50 for 4 hours, $3.50 for 8 hours. Guides are available at $1 an hour, $3 for 4 hours, or $5 for 8 hours. Specially scheduled trips are available; among them are excursions from Canyon Hotel to Cascade Lake and Seven-Mile Fishing Hole in Yellowstone Canyon, and from Old Faithful Inn to Lone Star Geyser. These trips may be made for as little as $2.50. (*All rates are subject to possible revision.*)
Footpaths to points of interest just off Grand Loop Road vary from a few feet to several hundred yards in length. (*For information on hikes in special areas see text on areas in question. Hikers should keep on solid trails, since in many places thin crust makes walking dangerous.*)

Boats: Speedboats, launches, rowboats, and fishing tackle can be rented from the Yellowstone Park Company. Launches (*fishing tackle included*), $3.50 an hour. Half-hour speedboat trips on Yellowstone Lake, $1 a person. Rod, reel, and landing net, 50¢ a day. Boat trips to Stevenson Island feature fishing and fish fries. (*All rates subject to possible revision.*)

Accommodations: Park hotels are first-class; rates range from $2.75 a day without meals, to $9 a day with meals. Hotels and lodges offer music and dancing. Employees ('savages' in Yellowstone slang) are usually university students, most of them musicians, singers, or readers. Impromptu entertainments are given each evening. (*All rates subject to possible revision.*)
Stores at all main points in the park carry complete lines of groceries, clothing, campers' supplies, souvenirs, and smokers' supplies. They are open before and after park season to serve motorists, weather permitting. Yellowstone Park Company and general stores are authorized to sell gasoline, oil, and automobile accessories. At hotels and lodges are newsstands, beauty and barber shops, and soda fountains. A natural hot-water bathing pool is maintained at Upper Geyser Basin. Rates, including suit and towel, 50¢; children between 5 and 12, 25¢.

Camping: Camping (*limited to 30 days in any one area*) is permitted on specially designated camp sites. About 15 campgrounds are supplied with water, sanitary facilities, and cooking grates. Between 25 and 30 smaller sites, scattered throughout the park, are especially attractive to persons wishing to get away from main points of concentration. Woodyards are operated, at which firewood may be bought.

SUMMARY OF ACCOMMODATIONS

Mammoth Hot Springs: Hotel, cottages, coffee shop, grill, store, garage, repair shops, filling station, free campgrounds, cafeteria, laundry, bathhouse, housekeeping cabins, and picture shop. *Norris Junction:* free campgrounds. *Madison Junction:* free campgrounds. *Old Faithful:* Old Faithful Inn, lodge, stores, filling stations, garage, repair shops, free campgrounds, housekeeping cabins, bathhouse, cafeteria, picture shop. *West Thumb:* free campgrounds, cafeteria, store, housekeeping cabins, picture shop, boats. *Lake Junction:* lodge, hotel, free campground, store, filling station, boats. *Fishing Bridge:* free campgrounds, garage, repair shops, cafeteria, picture shops, boats, housekeeping cabins, bathhouse, laundry. *Canyon Junction:* Canyon Hotel, lodge, garage, free campgrounds, store, picture shop, cafeteria, housekeeping cabins, filling station. *Tower Falls:* Store (meals served in store), filling station, Camp Roosevelt, housekeeping cabins.

Climate, Clothing, Equipment: Warm clothing should be worn, and preparation made for sudden changes of temperature, common at altitudes of 7,000 ft. Medium-weight overcoats, jackets, or sweaters should be carried; riding breeches, puttees, and strong gloves for those who wish to ride, climb, and tramp. Stout outing shoes are suitable for walking about geyser formations and terraces and for mountain use. Tinted glasses, cameras, and field or opera glasses will be found useful.

Medical Service: Physicians and a surgeon at Mammoth Hot Springs; well-equipped hospital with trained nurses; ambulance kept in readiness. Physicians attend patients at any place in park upon call. Nurses at each hotel and lodge. Rates for medical and hospital service, same as those prevailing in cities near park.

Church Services: Protestant and Catholic services every Sunday in chapel at Mammoth Hot Springs and at other points in park.

Post Office: Mammoth Hot Springs, address, Yellowstone Park, Wyo. Branch offices at Old Faithful, Lake, Fishing Bridge, Canyon, and Tower Falls. Carrier service on Grand Loop Road each day; mail forwarded upon request to any hotel, lodge, camp, or station.

Communication Service: Telegrams can be sent from hotels or lodges and are received at telegraph office in Mammoth Hotel, Mammoth Hot Springs, Yellowstone Park, Wyo. Lists of undelivered telegrams posted daily at hotels, lodges, leading ranger stations, stores, and information offices. Bell System maintains long-distance telephone service at regular rates.

Pictures: Pictures, albums, guidebooks, post cards, photographic supplies, and printing and developing service are available at picture shops in hotels and lodges and elsewhere in park. In photographing yellow bases, geysers, and distant mountains, ray filters should be used. Snapshots and movies of terraces are easily over-exposed, while close-ups of bears and buffalo are usually under-exposed.

Guide and Information Service: Ranger naturalists conduct parties at Mammoth, Norris Geyser Basin, Madison Junction, Old Faithful, West Thumb, Yellowstone Lake, Fishing Bridge, Canyon, and Camp Roosevelt, and deliver lectures, usually in the evenings. Central information bureau and park museum at Mammoth Hot Springs; branch museums at Old Faithful, Norris, Madison Junction, and Fishing Bridge. Maps and publications relating to national parks available at Mammoth, Old Faithful, and Fishing Bridge museums. Near each park entrance and each important road junction is a ranger station.

Fishing: No license required in park. Daily limit, 15 pounds (*dressed weight, with head and tails intact*); not to exceed a total of 10 fish per person, except in certain waters. Not more than one day's catch may be in possession at one time. Tackle for sale at stores, for rent at Old Faithful Inn, Canyon Hotel, Lake, Bridge Bay, and Fishing Bridge. Common fish in park are native, brook, rainbow, and Loch Leven trout and grayling. Mackinaw are found in some lakes.

Warnings and Regulations: Motorcars must be equipped with good brakes, horns, and lights. Careful driving required at all times. To facilitate traffic, motorists are advised to drive around the Grand Loop Road counter-clockwise. Beginning at Dunraven Pass, travel over Mount Washburn Road is limited to one way, south to north. Speed, 45 m.p.h. on straight open stretches for passenger cars; on grades and curves, 15 m.p.h. At average elevation of park roads (7,000 alt.), engines function better with leaner gasoline mixture. Saddle horses, pack trains, and horse-drawn vehicles have the right-of-way.
Do not write upon or injure formations, throw objects into springs or steam vents, or disturb or carry off mineral deposits, specimens, natural curiosities, etc. Destruction, injury, or disturbance of trees, flowers, birds, or animals is prohibited. Dogs and cats are permitted in park, but must be kept crated or on leash.
At camp sites, all combustible rubbish must be burned; other refuse must be placed in garbage cans provided. Wood for fuel should be taken from dead or fallen trees.

Fires should not be kindled near trees, dead wood, moss, dry leaves, or the like, but in some open space on rocks or earth. Before they are left, all embers should be smothered with earth or water.

It is unlawful and extremely dangerous to molest, feed, tease, or touch bears; persons who photograph them do so at their own risk. Food should be suspended in a box between two trees to be out of the animals' reach; it should never be left in a car.

Hunting within park prohibited. Firearms and trapping devices of all kinds must be declared at entrance and sealed. Violation of park regulations is punishable by a fine of not more than $500, or imprisonment for not more than six months, or both.

Summary of Attractions: Best display of hot springs and colored terraces at Mammoth Hot Springs. Geyser activities centered chiefly on west side of Grand Loop, between Roaring Mountain and Old Faithful. Mud volcanoes and paint pots, northeast of West Thumb; great variety of lake views between West Thumb and Lake Junction. Spectacular canyon views, just north of south entrance, between Chittenden Bridge near Canyon Junction and Tower Falls, and along the one-way loop drive around Bunsen Peak. Rugged mountain scenery along Cooke, Cody, and West Yellowstone roads. Waterfalls and attractive streams almost everywhere. Trail and hiking trips. Swimming, fishing, and motoring.

YELLOWSTONE NATIONAL PARK, the first (created by Act of Congress, March 1, 1872) and largest (3,472 sq. m.) national park and probably the most widely known, is an amazing museum of volcanic phenomena. Few regions in the world arouse more actively the sense of Nature's mystery. Here, more than 3,000 hot springs and geysers steam and spout; pots of mud bubble and boil; caverns growl and snort and hiss; a whole mountainside is murmurous with steam vents and covered with irregular columns of mist, like the smoke from hundreds of campfires. A waterfall nearly twice as high as Niagara; several great rocky canyons (one of them commonly regarded as second only to the Grand Canyon of the Colorado); hillsides tinted rainbow hues by mineral-laden waters; an island-dotted lake spread among forested mountains; a wealth of grass and shrubs and flowers; and a various and extensive wild-animal population—these are as beautiful and fascinating as the hot-water phenomena, if less startling.

The park lies for the most part in northwestern Wyoming, extending only a short distance into Montana on the north and Montana and Idaho on the west. It is a high, rugged region; the Absaroka Range crosses its northeastern corner, the Continental Divide its southwestern and south-central portions, while the Gallatin Range extends into it from the north, and the Majestic Tetons reach almost to its boundary on the south. Between the ranges at one extreme and the deep-cut valleys—nearly all of which rank as canyons—at the other, are the elevated areas officially designated as plateaus: Central Plateau, Pitchstone Plateau, Mirror Plateau, and others. It is on the Central Plateau that the best-known points of interest are found. This enclosed tableland varies in elevation from 7,000 to 8,500 feet, with an average of nearly 8,000 feet. Around it the peaks and ridges rise from 1,000 to 3,000 feet higher.

The mountains and the interior plain are made in part of materials ejected from the earth as ash and lava in an age when the region was actively volcanic. Evidence of this origin is found in the black glass of Obsidian Cliff, the gray and yellow ash of Tuff Cliff, the petrified forests, the buckled and twisted breccias of some of the mountains, and the decomposed lava walls of the canyons, as well as in the present-day activities of the region. These activities are indeed regarded as the final manifestations of a dying volcanism; but, as the subsidence of some activities is frequently balanced by the emergence of new phenomena, there is little danger that the wonders of Yellowstone will pass away entirely in any relatively near age. In some cases, cessation of activity has been caused by human interference, rather than by natural processes; soap thrown into geysers, for example, has resulted first in eruptions of extreme violence, and then in profound disturbance, or complete suppression, of eruption. There is reassurance in the fact that the National Park Service now carefully guards against such pranks.

The climate of the park takes its character from the geographic location, modified by the topographic features and the altitude. It is more humid than that of the surrounding lower country, and the extremes of heat and cold are somewhat less pronounced. Winter is long, summer very short, with snowstorms the rule as late as June and as early as September in the higher parts of the park. Ordinarily, however, there is much clear weather, with only light accumulations of snow before midwinter; the heaviest snowfalls come when winter is merging into spring. Through most of the winter, there are fine opportunities for skiing and snowshoeing. The air is crisp and invigorating, the winter scenery superb. Life zones in the park range from the Arctic or alpine, at the summit of Mount Washburn, through the Hudsonian and montane, to the transition zone at Mammoth Hot Springs.

The rain and chilly weather common in June are followed by a warm, dry season in July and August, at which season the park is at its best. The air is so clear that distance is defeated, and remote objects stand out almost as distinctly as those near at hand. The open spaces and the forest floors are bright with flowers. Mosquitoes, however, are plentiful in the lower parts of the park and have been found on even the loftiest mountain tops. As the region becomes dryer, severe electrical storms, sometimes entirely without rain, endanger the forests. In late August and September, the weather is often extremely dry, and small fires break out here and there, filling the air with a haze that deepens the blue of the mountains but makes distant objects less distinct.

The forests of the park are composed mostly of evergreens, or conifers. The most common species are lodgepole pine, limber pine, whitebark pine, alpine fir, Douglas fir, Engelmann spruce, and Rocky Mountain juniper. Lodgepole pine dominates the somewhat dry plateaus; fir and spruce, the moister ravines. Aspen or quaking asp, narrow-leaved cottonwood, red birch, and alder grow sometimes singly, scattered among the conifers, but more often in groups, usually near water. The aspens are often seen in large light-green clumps on the pine-dark slopes.

No trees are cut in the park, except as necessary in the building of roads, trails, and camps.

Yellowstone Park is in effect a great oasis. Its forest meadows have a luxuriance and a richness of color that are unknown in the arid reaches beyond its borders. Yet it has many sharp contrasts. Gray sage-covered hillsides, dry and dusty, verge abruptly on rank marshes. Barren sands and stony or powdery mineral deposits surround hot springs, whose walls are hung with velvet curtains of living matter. These curtains are made up of varieties of algae, forms that are rated low among living things, but are here endowed with a depth and delicacy of color unsurpassed in nature.

Flowers bloom in profusion throughout the park; 750 varieties have been cataloged. In many places they form a carpet of colors so closely woven that they leave no room for a path. 'They lift their heads,' wrote Chittenden (H. M. Chittenden's *Yellowstone National Park*), 'almost from under the melting drifts, and they persist in the autumn until the snow crushes them to the ground. They seem all to come at once, for their time is short . . . The most exquisite tints are found in . . . lofty and exposed situations where the conditions of growth seem most unfavorable. One of the pleasantest surprises . . . is that of finding permanent snowbanks bordered with banks of flowers so dense and rich as to paint the ground with color.' In one place, the summit of the Continental Divide is unexpectedly marked with a small lake, thickly covered with water lilies.

The pink, star-shaped, low-growing bitterroot is one of the most attractive spring blossoms, but is abundant only near Mammoth Hot Springs and in the lower areas, and only when the season is warm and early. Several species of violets bloom in sheltered spots; the big blue clusters of lungwort adorn the hills south of Mammoth Hot Springs; a half-dozen species of fragrant phlox mat the ground with white, pink, and lavender, often very close to the edges of the road.

The Wyoming State flower, the Indian paintbrush, grows almost everywhere in the park; near the mountain summits, it attains qualities of form and color that are scarcely approached by the varieties found on the lower slopes and in the valleys. Usually crimson, it ranges through every shade of pink and red. Strangely, all the brilliance of this plant is in the thickly clustered leaves, which conceal the tiny blossoms.

Other familiar park flowers are the tall magenta fireweed; the fringed gentian, with its deep-blue blossoms, which flourishes around geyser basins and in mountain meadows; the forget-me-not, delicate in form as in color; the short-lived wild flax, whose blossoms seem to reflect the sky. Wild geranium, harebell, sulphur flower or umbrella plant, windflower, columbine, calypso, buttercup, mallow, globeflower, goldenrod, sunflower, shooting star, prickly pear, primrose or rock rose, night-blooming mentzelia, and many others add their colors to roadside and forest and waterside. Thirteen species of showy Pentstemon, twelve of aster, and seven of arnica plant are scattered about the park. Even the

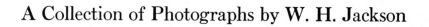

A Collection of Photographs by W. H. Jackson

These photographs, the first ever made in the Yellowstone area, were taken by Mr. W. H. Jackson (1843—), official photographer for the Hayden Survey of the Territories (1871–8).

They are reproduced through the courtesy of the U. S. Geological Survey, with the exception of the portrait of Chief Washakie, which is from the Jackson collection of photographs of North American Indians, at the Smithsonian Institution.

LOWER FALLS OF THE YELLOWSTONE

UPPER FIRE HOLE, FROM OLD FAITHFUL
(Note Geysers in Background)

MAMMOTH HOT SPRINGS, JUPITER TERRACE, LOOKING NORTH
(Superintendent N. P. Langford, center right)

OLD FAITHFUL

BAD LANDS ALONG WIND RIVER

FREMONT'S PEAK

GRAND CANYON OF THE YELLOWSTONE, FROM BRINK OF LOWER FALLS

PHOTOGRAPHING IN HIGH PLACES—SCENE IN LINCOLN COUNTY
W. H. Jackson (seated) and his Assistant, Charles Mitchell

GRAND TETON

CHIEF WASHAKIE OF THE SHOSHONE TRIBE

poisonous lupine, larkspur, and monkshood flaunt a dozen brilliant hues, from white through light blue and lavender to deepest purple.

In spring and early summer, the blossoms of wild rose, serviceberry, and other shrubs vie with the lower-growing flowers in appearance and excel them in sweetness of scent. In late summer and autumn, the frosted foliage of other shrubs, such as dogwood and Oregon grape, surpass the flowers in brilliance.

Yellowstone Park is one of the world's greatest wild-animal sanctuaries, sheltering thousands of elk, about 900 buffalo, 800 bears, and several hundred moose, deer, antelope, and mountain sheep. It is also an excellent bird preserve, in which more than 200 species live natural, undisturbed lives. Eagles and hawks swoop and soar among the crags. Wild geese and ducks frequent the park waters. Large white swans and pelicans float on the surface of Yellowstone Lake, and gulls and terns wheel and cry above it.

In the early years of the park, lax administration threatened to nullify its purpose as a game preserve. Killing of wild animals within its borders was not entirely prohibited until 1883, and the restricted license that was granted was shamefully abused. Some of the larger species were greatly reduced in numbers; a few, nearly exterminated. After protective laws were passed in 1894, elk, deer, bear and beaver rapidly increased in number; they soon learned that they had nothing to fear. It is now possible for a quiet watcher on the trails to see bear, deer, elk, antelope, moose, and even mountain sheep.

The buffalo range in the eastern section of the park, away from the main roads, and are usually seen only by travelers willing to go on foot or horseback into the region where they graze. Bears are the reverse of shy and, therefore, are seen oftener perhaps than any other park animal. They invade camps, overturn garbage cans, and occasionally frighten visitors and even damage property in their search for food; often one is seen standing or sitting near the highway, like a hitchhiker waiting for a ride.

Fossil forests are scattered over extensive areas in the northern part of the park. The two most prominent areas are in the newly acquired region on the northwest, the Gallatin Petrified Forests, and the Yellowstone-Lamar River Petrified Forests in the northeast. As the forests are not readily accessible, most visitors see only the small area, marked with a single petrified stump, near Tower Falls (*see Grand Loop Tour below*). Many of the fossilized trees are of species suited to warm, moist climates—laurel, sycamore, oak, and sequoia.

The best-known features of Yellowstone Park are, of course, the hot-water phenomena, in which it surpasses every other region in the world. Most of the 3,000 hot springs and geysers are in the western part of the park. The more prominent geysers, which in size, power, and variety of action have no equals, are confined to three basins lying near each other in the west-central part; but colored hot springs, mud volcanoes, and other strange manifestations are found in widely separated places. Around some of the hot springs, the mineral contents of the water have been deposited to form high terraces, in which lie beautifully incrusted and colored pools. The growing terraces and spreading pools often engulf and destroy fair-sized trees.

Aside from hot springs, geysers, and their intermediate forms, the chief thermal phenomena are the paint pots. They are exactly like hot springs and some geysers, except that they are pools of mud instead of water. Constantly escaping gases, or gases that accumulate for a time and then escape violently, characterize them as mud springs or mud volcanoes, respectively. Their fussy, spattering, sputtering, popping activity; their heavy sulphurous smells; and their often unpleasing forms and colors make them esthetically, though by no means scientifically, the least attractive park marvels. Small vents called fumaroles, from which steam and gas issue quietly, seldom noticed except when cold weather condenses the steam, are found all over the park.

When quiet, a geyser basin is not unlike an ordinary hot spring in appearance. The actual differences, which make it a geyser rather than a hot spring, lie in the 'plumbing' beneath the basin—the tubes or passages through which the water and gases must rise to reach the basin. Because no two geysers or hot springs have quite the same plumbing, no two are exactly alike in action. Some geysers, such as Old Faithful, play at intervals that vary only slightly. The average interval for Old Faithful is a little more than an hour; for many geysers it is less than a minute; for others, it is days, weeks, months, even years. On rare occasions, a pool that has long been believed to be a hot spring flashes into eruption and proves itself a geyser; on the other hand, a geyser may cease erupting and become a common hot spring. Not all geysers send up spectacular columns of water and vapor during eruption; not all hot springs lie quiet hour after hour or day after day. Some small geysers merely splash water a few inches or a few feet into the air; some hot springs are continually disturbed by rising gases; and some pools are intermediate forms, which never actually erupt, but stage, at fairly regular intervals, exhibitions of boiling, bubbling, and gurgling that are far more violent than those caused by the steady escape of gases from ordinary pools.

The key to the plumbing of Yellowstone geysers is the solvent action of the volcanic gas, with which the seeping underground waters of the park are impregnated. As surface water finds its way downward toward the heated lower rocks that underlie the region, it meets steam and other hot gases rising; the gases heat the water, which in turn partly absorbs them. The combination of water and gas dissolves some rocks more readily than others, and thus cavities and highly irregular passages are formed. The water that fills these passages is further heated by the gases that continue to rise from below. As the water grows hotter, it expands. If the passages provided a fairly uncomplicated tube toward the surface, the expanding water would merely 'boil over'— that is, rise and spill out of the upper end of the tube in the form of a hot spring; but, because the irregularities in the passages plus the weight of the cooler water near the surface hinder its escape, the hot water remains in the lower plumbing, growing steadily hotter. At some point in the process, the force of its expansion becomes great enough to offset the forces holding it back; the superheated water suddenly explodes into steam and literally blasts its way out. When the pressure has been relieved by eruption, the geyser subsides, and the process begins again.

In most cases, the passages become lined with silica, a substance hard enough to withstand tremendous pressures. Sometimes, this material builds the vent up to such a height that the increased weight of the water column prevents eruption; sometimes, heavy deposits within the plumbing choke off the geyser. In certain instances, geysers burst upward with such immense power that they blow away some of the rock at the surface and form craters; occasionally, too, a geyser wears out its plumbing. A geyser formed in soft material does not last long. A geyser that erupts through a built-up cone of hard matter is said to be of the nozzle type, while one erupting through a crater or open basin is of the pool type.

The first white man to behold the wonders of the Yellowstone region was doubtless John Colter, a member of the Lewis and Clark Expedition, who left the party on its return from the Pacific in 1806 and struck out into the wilderness to trap and explore. He visited the Wind River and Hoback Valleys, crossed Teton Pass and Pierre's Hole, and entered the Yellowstone country from the south in 1807. Colter must have seen Lewis and Shoshone Lakes; the three falls at the head of the Grand Canyon; and many of the hot pools, mud springs, and small geysers along his route. Apparently he did not visit the large geyser basins; yet, his account of the wonders he saw was not accepted by the public. Some merely shook their heads; others derisively called the land he described 'Colter's Hell.'

Early in the summer of 1827, a member of the Rocky Mountain Fur Company visited the Yellowstone and wrote a description of it that was published in the Philadelphia *Gazette*. The account said in part: 'The Yellow Stone has a large freshwater lake near its head . . . about 100 by 40 miles . . . and as clear as crystal. On the south border . . . are boiling springs, some of water and others of most beautiful fine clay, resembling a mush pot, and throwing particles to the immense height of from 20 to 30 feet. The clay is . . . white and . . . pink . . . The water appears fathomless, as it appears to be entirely hollow underneath. There [are] . . . places where pure sulphur is sent forth in abundance. One of our men visited one of these whilst taking his recreation . . . At an instant, the earth began a tremendous trembling, and he with difficulty made his escape, when an explosion took place resembling that of thunder. During our stay in that quarter I heard it every day.'

James (Jim) Bridger, scout and guide, is supposed to have entered the region about 1830. His stories of it were somewhat overdrawn. One day, stated Bridger, he saw an elk grazing within easy rifle range. He aimed and fired; the animal kept on grazing. The scout fired two or three more shots, with no better result. Amazed, he stealthily approached the elk, until, suddenly, he was stopped by a solid wall of glass. Upon investigation, he discovered that the glass had acted as a magnifying lens, and that the elk was actually 25 miles away.

For years the Yellowstone country, miraculous as it seemed to its rare visitors, remained unknown to people at large, except as a legendary gateway to the infernal regions, largely created by the untamed imaginations of Colter and Bridger; but, as new witnesses little by little built up the body of testimony, men of standing began to take it seriously. Captain W. F. Raynolds led an expedition toward the region, in 1859–60, but was unable to get across the snow-covered mountains. In 1863, Captain John Mullan, builder of the military wagon road from Fort Benton, Montana, to Walla Walla, Washington, mentioned the geysers in a report to the Federal Government. Captain W. W. DeLacy visited the Shoshone and Lower Geyser Basins the same year and, later, published a map showing their location. In July 1870, two prospectors, C. W. Cook and David E. Folsom, published a description of the area in the *Chicago Western Monthly*. The article attracted wide attention; before the summer was out, the official Washburn-Langford Expedition entered the region, spent a month in careful exploration, and returned with a report that electrified the Nation. Sentiment for the preservation of this land of marvels grew swiftly, and on March 1, 1872, less than two years after the publication of the Cook-Folsom article, President U. S. Grant approved the act of dedication, which set it aside 'for the benefit and enjoyment of the people,' and thereby established the first great national park. N. P. Langford, of the Washburn-Langford Expedition, became the first superintendent.

Not all the Yellowstone stories were proved true by the official report, but they continued to be told. Something about the park's air of the wonderful was (and is) powerfully stimulating to the imagination. The result is a surviving and constantly growing body of legend, ranging from relatively modest inaccuracies to such unblushing whoppers as the tale, retold by Captain Raynolds, of the petrified sagebrush that bore diamond, emerald, and ruby fruits as large as walnuts.

Development of the park proceeded steadily. Natural features were given scientific study; roads were built, and hotels erected. The Northern Pacific Railway completed a branch line to Gardiner, Montana, in 1902; the Union Pacific to West Yellowstone in 1907. Park travel became established slowly at first; up to 1895, the annual number of visitors was less than 5,000. It increased by 1904 to 13,000, a figure that was doubled the following year, only to be succeeded by a slump that lasted with only one exception through nine years. In 1915, the first automobile entered the park, and the number of visitors leaped to nearly 52,000. At the end of the World War came a tremendous increase in the park's popularity; the number of visitors reached 260,-697 in 1929, faltered during the early 1930's, and then went on toward a record of nearly a half a million.

Up to 1886, the park was governed by civilian superintendents assisted by a few scouts; then, for 30 years, troops of U. S. Cavalry were detailed to police it. Since 1916, a superintendent and rangers, appointed by the Secretary of the Interior, have administered the affairs of the park.

Originally a rectangle 62 miles long and 54 wide, the park was enlarged in 1929 and again in 1930 and 1932. Its boundaries are now irregular on the east and north, where they inclose formerly unprotected areas.

GRAND LOOP TOUR

Mammoth Hot Springs—Norris Junction—Madison Junction—West Thumb—Lake Junction—Canyon Junction—Tower Junction—Mammoth Hot Springs; 144.1 *m.*, Grand Loop Road.

Oil-surfaced roadbed throughout; open June 1–October 15. Entrance gateways open 6:30 A.M. to 11 P.M. during park season.

The Grand Loop system, the park's main highway, reaches most of the great scenic features, including the hot-spring terraces, the geysers, Yellowstone Lake, the Grand Canyon, Mount Washburn, and Dunraven Pass; those not touched by the main road itself are accessible by side trips from it. The Canyon-Norris crosscut, a narrow, slow-speed road, makes it possible to split the loop into sections, to be traveled as time affords; but to realize the full benefits of the park, it is necessary to travel the entire road. Any one of the approach roads from the north, west, south, east, or northeast can, of course, be used as the entrance to the loop or as a side tour from it, depending on the direction of travel.

The Howard Eaton Trail for horseback trips, 153 miles long, is a linking up of a former series of short trails. It follows closely the Grand Loop, touching the same points of interest; yet the trail is sufficiently distant from the road at most points to avoid contact with travelers on the loop, except at key points of interest.

MAMMOTH HOT SPRINGS, 0 *m.* (6,239 alt.), park headquarters, is a community of National Park Service and park concession workers, situated in a region of active thermal springs and terraces, a few miles south of the northern park boundary. Substantially constructed stone and frame buildings, which house park officers and their families, occupy the SITE OF FORT YELLOWSTONE, a military post used when the army had charge of the park, before the National Park Service took over the management. These buildings fringe the former parade ground, now a field of clover and native grasses.

YELLOWSTONE PARK POST OFFICE (L), a white concrete and sandstone building, was until 1928 the only post office in the park. Now six substations provide postal service at main junctions along the Grand Loop.

Due west of the post office is the junction with the Tower Falls section of the Grand Loop Road (*see below*).

The MUSEUM, a two-story, gray-sandstone building, contains collections of park flora and fauna, Indian artifacts, and much historical material. Included in the collection are: the illustrated *History of the Park Administration,* photographs of superintendents, old photographs and maps of the park, souvenirs and data from the Custer Battle area, photographs and historical material relative to Cooke City, Montana, and a drawing of old Fort Yellowstone. Plaster casts of various animal tracks on display enable the park visitor to identify such tracks along the trails. On the porch of the Museum are two old coaches: one a Deadwood coach, in which President Arthur rode on his park trip in 1883; the other an early-day Yellowstone-Western Transportation Company's stage.

The HOUSE OF HORNS, built entirely of horns and antlers by former Chief Ranger Sam T. Woodring in 1928, is opposite the Museum. The interior of the structure is about ten feet high, ten feet long, and six feet wide.

MAMMOTH HOTEL, a two-story frame building with large porch and a four-story, many-windowed wing, is the headquarters for the Yellowstone Park Company. In the lobby are a number of original oil paintings by Western artists.

The DINING ROOM AND GRILL, an oblong, frame and stucco building with French windows on the main floor and dormer windows in the second story, accommodates hotel guests and motorists.

Across a flat (L) is CAPITOL HILL, a glacial moraine. In 1879, a blockhouse on the hilltop was used as the park superintendent's office. The blockhouse was razed in 1909.

The hill on which are most of the hot springs is just southwest of the administrative and tourist village of Mammoth Hot Springs. The setting here is fantastic in the extreme. Along the sides of the hill are groups of steps or terraces, over which flow the steaming waters of hot springs, laden with minerals. Each descending step has been tinted by the algae living in the hot water, in a thousand tones of scarlet, orange, pink, yellow, and blue. So vivid are these colors that they appear to vibrate and glow in the sunlight. The direction of the flow of water is constantly changing. Where it has ceased, the terraces are pure white.

LIBERTY CAP (R), 0.4 *m.,* a conelike formation, is of harder substance than the surrounding Hot Spring deposit, owing probably to the slow rate of formation. It is made up of curved layers, with an opening in the top. The cone is 38 feet high and 20 feet in diameter at the base.

Right from Liberty Cap on the Terrace Trail, a footpath up a steep climb, to DEVIL'S THUMB, a hot spring built up vertically. Travertine is deposited in layers around the cone. Later deposits were laid down in 1881, when an attempt was made to recoat it by flooding with hot spring waters, conveyed by a trough from a higher spring.

At Devil's Thumb, the trail unites with the Old Norris Road, built about 1879 by the second superintendent of the park, Colonel P. W. Norris, to connect Mammoth Hot Springs and the Upper Geyser Basin. The Terrace Trail follows this old road to the top of the terraces. Jays and killdeer fly about, shrilling their harsh cries. Pines grow on the formation, which appears around the edges to be dry, white soil.

Yellow primroses and goldenrod fringe the path to the third terrace, where tints of bronze, pink, brown, gray, and white alternate. Dry holes lie adjacent to steaming pools, which give off a sulphurous odor. Near the fourth level are OLD PALLETTE SPRING and CLEOPATRA TERRACE.

On the top of the fourth level are BLUE SPRING and CANARY SPRING. Blue Spring completely dries up for brief periods as often as two or three times a year. In addition to the blue color of the water, yellows, wine, rust, green, and red are frequently noticeable, owing to the algae in the water. As the water dries up, the colors fade. In Canary Pool are large lilies with leaves curled up and crusted into cups. Some of these leaves resemble huge flat pastry shells filled with custard.

Opposite Mammoth Lodge is JUPITER TERRACE, said to be the largest travertine terrace in the world. Algae, which thrive on the hot and tepid waters, cover it with rich color. Other microscopic plants, known as 'diatoms,' occur singly or in colonies clinging to the sides or to the algae themselves. A famous chemist, Dr. Eugene G. Allen, says that the escape of carbon dioxide gas from the hot spring waters is the most important factor responsible for the deposition of travertine, which varies from little or nothing to more than a foot deep a year. The thin veil of water, hot and clear, courses in quick pulsations over the beaded rims of the several pools, or bowls, on each level, and down the tinted pillars until the terraces seem to live. Dr. Ferdinand V. Hayden said of the Mammoth Hot Springs: 'The wonderful transparency of the water surpasses anything of the kind I have ever seen in any other portion of the world. The sky, with the smallest cloud that flits across it, is reflected in its clear depths, and the ultramarine colors, more vivid than the sea, are greatly heightened by constant, gentle vibrations. One can look down into the clear depths and see, with perfect distinctness, the minutest ornament on the inner sides of the basins; and the exquisite beauty of the coloring and the variety of forms baffle any attempt to portray them either with pen or pencil.' Cooling and evaporation take place rapidly at the rims of the bowls, and, as the water cools and gives up its gases, it also loses its mineral content. The deposits at the edge are thus quickly made; the rims are built up until the waters are forced to seek another place to overflow. It has been estimated that, to increase the rim an inch in height, the water labors for about 60 days.

At 2.4 *m.* is the junction with an oiled loop road.

Right on this side road, called the Terrace Loop Drive, through pines to a TURNOUT, 0.2 *m.*, from which there is a fine view down into the valley towards Capitol Hill.

ORANGE SPRING MOUND, 0.6 *m.*, is probably an earlier stage of a formation much like Liberty Cap. The spring at the top of the mound is active and overflows part of the time. Elk thistles grow near by.

DEVILS KITCHEN (L), 0.8 *m.* (*now closed to visitors*), the interior of an extinct hot spring, is entered through a hole in a rock. A ladder leads into the circular pit with ridged walls, where bats cling to the ceiling. The entrance to the crater is a small log shelter house, once used as a refreshment stand. On the peeled logs of the walls, on the tables, and in every available space, names of visitors are carved.

WHITE ELEPHANT BACK TERRACE (L) is at 1 *m.*, and at 1.6 *m.*, is ANGEL TERRACE (L), a formation of very delicate travertine, resembling a huge tiered and frosted wedding cake. When the terrace is active, the coloring is one of the finest examples to be seen along the trail. When inactive, the color of the travertine is more startlingly white and its traceries finer than on any other terrace. Trees that have been killed by the overflow on the terrace will not become petrified, but will be preserved for some time by the travertine, which is building up around them.

At 1.7 *m.* is the south junction with the Grand Loop Road.

The highway climbs up out of the valley. Far below (L) is the community water works for Mammoth Hot Springs. Bunsen Peak, its sides gashed by rock slides, looms in the L. foreground. The highway ascends gradually and gains 1,000 feet in 3 miles.

At SILVER GATE, 3.7 *m.*, so named for the color of the travertine on both sides of the road, is the junction with an oiled road.

Right from this junction on a short loop through the HOODOOS, chalklike rocks, to the south junction with the Grand Loop Road, 0.1 *m.*

RHYO-TRAVERTINE GULCH is R. at 4.2 *m.*

At GOLDEN GATE, 4.7 *m.* (7,255 alt.), rhyolite walls, partly covered with yellow lichens, rise 200 to 300 feet above the highway. The Gate is an opening in the canyon, from which a spectacular view is obtained by looking back down the highway. A turnout provides ample space for parked cars. The place was originally called Kingman Pass for Dan C. Kingman, one of the early Government engineers in charge of park road construction.

RUSTIC FALLS (L), at the head of the canyon, spray 47 feet down the canyon wall.

At 5 *m.* is the junction with a dirt road.

Left on this one-way, narrow, hazardous road through high sage and pine forest around the foot of Bunsen Peak (L) (8,500 alt.).

At 1.3 *m.*, the road enters thick timber and becomes narrower as it advances. Groves of aspen fleck the mountainside (L), changing from green to red and gold as the seasons change.

At 3.3 *m.*, steep grades begin, with sharp, blind curves along the rim of MIDDLE GARDINER CANYON. This canyon (R), of great depth, beauty, and grandeur, ranks next to Grand Canyon as the most impressive in the park. A beautiful display of basalt may be seen in the canyon, and the scene across the void R. is spectacular, with far vistas over timbered canyon walls.

At 3.5 *m.* is a small turnout for parking. Here, from the guard rail R., is a view of the river and of OSPREY FALLS, very high and very beautiful in the canyon below; R. here on a dim trail into the canyon.

At 4 *m.*, the road begins a long grade with bad turns. Far down over the steep bank (R), the river threads its silver way along the valley floor. Sage, green pines, brown ripe grass, and red and gold leaves fringe the road.

Running through sagebrush, at 5.1 *m.*, the road winds down to more level ground, joining the Grand Loop Road at 6.4 *m.*, about 1.4 miles from the Museum corner at Mammoth Hot Springs.

The highway emerges on SWAN LAKE FLAT, an open park south of Golden Gate. ELECTRIC PEAK (11,155 alt.), the second highest peak in the park, is visible at the extreme R. As the highway crosses the GREAT RHYOLITE PLATEAU, four apparently united peaks loom R., DOME MOUNTAIN (showing two peaks), ANTLER PEAK, and MOUNT HOLMES. They are flanked (L) by Trilobite Point and (R) Quadrant Mountain.

SWAN LAKE (R), 5.1 *m.*, is a spring-fed lake, devoid of fish. It is the nesting place of trumpeter swans. Geologists say that it once covered the whole Swan Lake Flat, but part of the flat now supports a heavy growth of lodgepole pine.

In this vicinity are 'picket-pin' ground squirrels, pine squirrels, and chipmunks. The woodchuck, or ground hog, often suns himself near his burrow by the roadside. In autumn, he does not store up a winter's supply of provisions as the squirrel does, but hibernates for four or five months, like the bear.

At 7.9 *m.* the GALLATIN RANGE is visible far to the R.

At 8.3 *m.* is the junction with a graveled road.

Left on this road to SHEEPEATER CLIFF, 0.2 *m.*, so named by Colonel P. W. Norris, in commemoration of the only tribe of Indians known to have dwelt permanently in the park. These cliffs are the magnificent walls of the Middle Gardiner Canyon. It was upon one of the 'ancient and but recently deserted, secluded, unknown haunts' of these Indians, that Colonel Norris, 'in rapt astonishment,' stumbled one day, and was so impressed by what he saw that he gave the neighboring cliff its present name.

The CAMPGROUND (R), 8.4 *m.*, near the junction of Obsidian Creek and the Gardiner River, is open to the public.

At 10.3 *m.*, the highway enters WILLOW PARK and for some distance parallels OBSIDIAN CREEK, which winds through grassy meadows. Moose are usually seen feeding along the stream. Glimpses of the park can be seen through the thick timber that fringes the highway.

BEAVER DAM EXHIBIT, 11 *m.*, illustrates in detail the construction of beaver houses and dams, many of which are in the adjoining area. From here the Mount Holmes Lookout Station is visible (R) high against the sky line.

APOLLINARIS SPRING (L), 11.7 *m.* (7,337 alt.), spouts at the top of a short flight of stone steps. The water has a sharp, spicy taste. Across the road is a small campground, where tourists are frequently held up by bears in search of tidbits. The feeding of the bears, however, is dangerous and is prohibited by park authorities. Lush grass and thick underbrush carpet the forest floor along Obsidian Creek.

LILY PAD LAKE (L), 12.2 *m.*, is a small pond covered with yellow water lilies.

As the highway proceeds, black, glassy boulders by the roadside and in the gravel pits herald the approach to OBSIDIAN CLIFF (L), 12.6 *m.*, a mountainside of volcanic glass, black as anthracite, covered by lichens and mosses. The appearance is more like very dark granite than glass, except upon close inspection. Indians used this glassy material for arrowheads and spearheads, as well as for skinning knives. This is the cliff referred to by Jim Bridger in his elk-shooting tale (*see above*).

OBSIDIAN CLIFF EXHIBIT (R), 13 *m.*, explains the geological history of Obsidian Cliff and gives the history of the building of the Norris Road. In constructing this road, Colonel Norris broke the glassy boulders into fragments by heating them with fires and then dashing cold water on them.

A short distance beyond the exhibit, a tiny wisp of steam coming out of the ground anticipates the geysers ahead.

BEAVER DAMS, 13.6 *m.*, plainly visible, are excellent examples of the workmanship of these busy mountaineers. The pond surfaces are smooth as a mirror. Wild flowers, brilliant in color, fringe the highway. Through the pines and spruce is BEAVER LAKE, 13.7 *m.*, formerly a meadow but now a lake, backed up by a beaver dam.

At 15.5 *m.* steam rises from a small stream.

SEMI-CENTENNIAL GEYSER (R), 16.3 *m.*, was named because there was a terrific explosion at this point during the celebration of the 50th anniversary of the establishment of the Yellowstone as a national park. Rocks and boiling water were thrown 300 feet into the air.

Veering away from Obsidian Creek, the highway skirts ROARING MOUNTAIN (L), 16.7 *m.* (7,575 alt.). Under favorable conditions, a faint roaring sound caused by escaping gas from the many steaming vents of the slope is audible from the road. Dead trees stand in the yellowish-green water at the foot of the mountain. A white deposit crusts the brown rocks near by.

The water of the first TWIN LAKE, 17.1 *m.*, is emerald; of the second TWIN LAKE, 17.5 *m.*, bluish green. The lakes, which drain into the Gibbon River, are kept apart by a beaver dam and are at different levels; that of the second lake is nine feet below that of the first. As the highway winds through a lane of timber, steaming pools alternate with little red-grassed parks.

NYMPH LAKE, 19 *m.*, is a small, blue, boiling pool. Water from the lake evidently filters down on the hot underlying rocks and comes back superheated. The Nymph Lake Field Exhibit gives information concerning the fumes on the side of the mountain (L) and the boiling pools (R). FRYING PAN SPRING (R), 19.1 *m.*, gives off a pungent odor of hydrogen sulphide. The bubbling up of gases through a large number of small vents in this area creates a popping and sizzling sound, much like that of eggs in a frying pan. Tiny plants grow around the edge of the spring.

Ahead, at 19.9 *m.*, great columns of steam rise from NORRIS GEYSER BASIN, named for Philetus W. Norris, park superintendent from 1877 to 1882.

The NORRIS JUNCTION AUTOMOBILE CAMP and NORRIS RANGER STATION (a dark-brown, peeled-log building) are at the crossing of the GIBBON RIVER, 21 *m.*

At 21.3 *m.* is the junction with an oil-surfaced road.

Left on this crosscut freight road through timbered country to GRAND CANYON JUNCTION, 11 *m.* (*speed limit,* 25 *m.p.h.*) (*see below*).

There are 18 or more geysers in Norris Geyser Basin. The number varies, as some of them are short lived: the violent action of the water tears out the plumbing in the sand and clay, so that only a boiling pool or a hot spring remains.

NUPHAR LAKE, 21.8 *m.*, a cool-water pool, is above the level of the basin, but does not drain into it. Steaming CONGRESS POOL and PORCELAIN POOL, the latter a pure white formation, border the road L. and R.

NORRIS TRAILSIDE MUSEUM (L), *22 m.*, a massive structure of rhyolite boulder pillars and peeled logs, is built in two sections, with a covered runway between. Many birds, among them the finch, crossbill, flycatcher, bunting, bluebird, white-crowned sparrow, desert sparrow hawk, red-shafted flicker, mountain chickadee, gray ruffed grouse, western tanager, and killdeer, are mounted in colored dioramas. In the museum are also splendid collections of butterflies and insects.

Adjoining the museum grounds is a Parking Area (L), on the edge of which are several springs. BATHTUB SPRING, a clear, bubbling pool, is shaped like a bathtub. EMERALD SPRING, near by, is one of the most erratic in the basin; in 1923 it became very muddy, but cleared up again; in 1931 it became a powerful geyser, then subsided into a vigorously boiling spring. Near it are small pools—bubbling puddlers.

1. Left about 200 yards east of the museum on the Nature Trail (*self-guiding, 35 minutes*) through a log gate to PAINT POTS, a special type of hot springs, in which the amount of yellow and gray clay exceeds the amount of water present. Dead trees, with gnarled limbs and old stumps, outline the dirt trail, along which grow Rocky Mountain cedar or juniper, lodgepole, and limber pine. Ahead is a basin of steaming geysers.

STEAMBOAT GEYSER (L), named by the Hayden Geological Survey of 1872, because of the splashing of water in regular beats during an eruption, was renamed Fissure in 1884, by the Hague Survey. In more recent years, it has been known as New Crater. The water is dashed out of the vent, as water is churned by a steamboat wheel. Squirrels scamper along the trail, which skirts many bubbling pools. Waxy kinnikinik clusters along the ground, which sounds hollow underfoot.

On a flat, a group of geysers play at various intervals. Here FEARLESS GEYSER, a caldron of mud with a black vent, erupts several times each day to the height of a few feet. VETERAN GEYSER (R) gurgles ferociously and erupts occasionally to the height of several feet. VIXEN GEYSER, with a small cone, is very temperamental. At times it seems to have no power and then turns into a spitfire, playing in myriad crystal drops. It usually flows for 30 seconds to a height of 15 feet. A tiny MORNING GLORY POOL bubbles up L., one of many on the flat adjoining Vixen.

CORPORAL GEYSER erupts occasionally to a foot or two in height and overflows the adjacent basin during eruptions. In this vicinity, many shallow-rooted lodgepole pines have been blown over by the wind.

MONARCH GEYSER CRATER (R), inactive since 1913, at one time sent water 125 feet into the air and was the largest geyser in Norris Basin.

The main trailside path passes small FRYING PAN and others (L), which sizzle continuously from gases. Across the basin is a bright blue pool in a dangerous, thinly encrusted area.

The MINUTE GEYSER plays 15 to 20 feet in height, and its eruptions are sometimes several hours apart. The spray from it falls like strings of crystal.

Cutting back through the timber the trail leads to the Museum.

2. Right from the Museum on a footpath to the BLACK GROWLER VENT, the hottest in the park, with a temperature of 287° F. This vent roars constantly like steam escaping from a powerful engine.

VALENTINE GEYSER (L) is the highest in the basin, averaging 75 feet at 18-hour intervals. The tube in it is very unusual, in that it descends more than 60 feet without a turn. It began to erupt on St. Valentine's Day, 1907.

Hot steamy gases rise from a great depth in HURRICANE VENT. Here, where the entire area seethes and sizzles, the cracks and joints in rocks have widened, as the materials have decomposed and washed away. The pools, some bright blue, are colored by algae.

ARSENIC GEYSER, with small arsenic content in the water, erupts almost constantly, to an average height of six feet. IRIS SPRING is green and pink, while ONYX SPRING is green. The minerals in these springs are orpiment (yellow), realgar (red), and marcasite (gray and black).

WHIRLIGIG GEYSER (L), with its whirling, puffing eruptions, has been active for several years and, although small, attracts much attention. CONSTANT GEYSER sends its steam 25 feet in beadlike sprays like those of the Vixen. Although formerly regular in its eruptions, it is now far from constant. LITTLE WHIRLIGIG GEYSER is much alive. Its run-off forms a red pool.

The trail winds up a steep climb through the pines back to the Museum.

TANTALUS CREEK, 22.4 *m.*, is in an area in which the crust is very thin. From here, the geysers along the Nature Trail are plainly visible L.

MINUTE GEYSER (L), a huge steaming pool, is on the Nature Trail (*see above*).

The highway enters ELK PARK at 23.2 *m.*, a lush mountain meadow, through which meanders the GIBBON RIVER, named for General John Gibbon, an explorer. Deer and elk may be seen here in early morning or late evening.

For about a mile, the highway parallels the river (R). A heavy rock guard shields the road. Mount Holmes rises (R), with a bit of Electric Peak visible on the extreme R.

At 24.5 *m.* is a turnout from which to view GIBBON CASCADES. Purple rhyolite rises L. Directly below the road are a number of hot springs called CHOCOLATE POTS, which deposit oxide of iron—the same substance known as 'iron rust.' The more solid deposits are almost black. One cone, a miniature geyser, shoots water up out of the red river bed. The largest cone, dark brown, is on the opposite side of the river.

GIBBONS MEADOWS, 25 *m.*, is a large filled-in lake bed; R. here, 650 feet above the valley at the top of a hill, is steaming MONUMENT GEYSER.

At 25.8 *m.* is the junction with a trail.

Left on this trail to PAINTPOT HILL, 0.5 *m.*, at the foot of which are a number of brilliantly colored hot springs and pools.

Southward the road commands a splendid view of Mount Holmes (R). Sheer mountains rise L. Lilies grow along the steaming banks of the river.

At 26.4 *m.*, the highway crosses the GIBBON RIVER.

BERYL SPRING, 26.8 *m.*, a seething caldron from which rises sulphurous steam, was named for the color and mineral content of the water. For a long time, this was the hottest spring in the park. Now the temperature actually is less than boiling, 197.6° F.

Sheer walls of honeycombed rhyolite hem in the highway, as the road winds through Gibbon Canyon. The grassy river banks, in season, are yellow with sunflowers and goldenrod.

PURPLE MOUNTAIN, at 26.9 *m.*, resembles a giant's checker-board, with its cross-seams and giant cracks. IRON SPRING is L. at 29.8 *m.*

The road again crosses the river to GIBBON FALLS, 30.5 *m.*, where the river drops 84 feet from one layer of lava rock to another. The water—a wide sheet partly hidden by trees—rushes in a great torrent on one side of the falls and, on the other, sprays down ribbon-like to a great pool dammed by logs. Here is a second small fall.

For more than two miles the highway winds through an avenue of lodgepole pines with the river and meadows (L).

TUFF CLIFF FIELD EXHIBIT (R), 33.7 *m.*, explains the formation of Tuff Cliff, a mountain of volcanic ash that settled from the air. The face of the cliff is honeycombed, and the tuff, or volcanic ash, would later have been washed away entirely had it not been protected by a rhyolite cap.

The Grand Loop Road skirts the Gibbon River and emerges from the timber about 34.5 *m.*, into broad meadows, in which the Gibbon River joins the Madison River. Purple Mountain with its series of peaks is R.; in front is the wall of Madison Canyon; and on the L. is timbered National Park Mountain.

TERRACE SPRING (R), 34.6 *m.*, flows a continuous stream of hot water, bearing chemicals high in silica content, which spreads out at the nearer end of the pool. The release of gases in the water causes these chemicals to be precipitated to form terraces of siliceous sinter. Geese use this hot pool as a rendezvous in the winter.

At MADISON JUNCTION, 35.6 *m.*, is the junction with a feeder highway.

Right on this oiled road along the Madison River (L), where many fisher-men enjoy trout fishing, to open meadows.

At 2.9 *m.* is fresh drinking water piped to the roadside (R).

The highway curves sharply around the base of MOUNT JACKSON (R), 10.8 *m.*, named for W. H. Jackson, the first photographer to make pictures in Yellowstone National Park. Mr. Jackson accompanied the Hayden Survey. Opposite and across the river is Mount Haynes (L).

Willows, chokecherries, and pines fringe the river, with now and then an open meadow or a slough (L). Huge boulders in the river hold piles of drift-wood, chiefly logs. An occasional woodchuck waddles across the road. The water in the river looks green, chiefly because of crowfoot that covers the rocks. Veering away from the river, the highway runs through sagebrush hills, with vistas of high mountains (R).

The Montana-Wyoming Line, 11.9 *m.*, is in a thick stand of pines called Christmas Tree Park, about two miles east of the WEST ENTRANCE at West Yellowstone, Montana.

Adjoining Madison Junction is the MADISON JUNCTION MUSEUM, a substantially built peeled-log structure set on a high rock foundation, with a pitched roof braced by heavy timbers. At each corner is a massive rhyolite pillar. Large windows on the front (west) frame a fascinating scene of meadows and mountains, with National Park Mountain in the center. The history of the park is portrayed in this museum according to periods, from the discovery of the park by John Colter, through the development of the fur trade, the various explorations, and the creation of this national playground. Among the outstanding relics on exhibition are: an old high-wheel bicycle, used by W. O. Owen in the park in 1883; some of the first chairs made in the Yellowstone Valley, hand-hewn and with cowhide seats; photographs and maps of the Hayden Expeditions; and a California saddle, used by N. P. Langford of the Washburn-Langford Expedition. A relief map gives an excellent idea of the topography of the region.

Southward from the junction, the Grand Loop Road crosses the GIBBON RIVER, 35.7 *m.*

Ahead at 35.9 *m.* it parallels the FIREHOLE RIVER (R), whose black waters rush and roar over glacial boulders in the FIREHOLE CANYON. The name of this river dates back to 1830, when the vicinity was called by trappers 'Burnt Hole,' because of a forest fire that swept the area.

FIREHOLE FALLS, 36.7 *m.*, are rushing, thick falls. The smooth surface of the rock at the left of, and directly under, the cascade is hard, horizontally-banded rhyolite. A huge mass of volcanic rubble seems to have flowed over this underlying rhyolite. The river finds it easy to cut through the coarse breccia, but difficult to cut down through the hard rhyolite shelf. For half a mile, the river flows through a narrow gorge with sheer walls of gray, tan, umber, blue, and black. The highway curves along the river, the water roaring below. Pines protrude from the rocky cliff walls. Turrets and spires have been eroded from crumbling rock. Where the river undercuts the cliffs great boulders guard the roadway.

The canyon widens at the south end, near the FIREHOLE CASCADES, 37.9 *m.*, whose waters foam into cottony froth. Here, calm stretches with smooth grassy banks alternate with rocky channels, where the water churns into swift white riffles. Lodgepole pines grow in the rocks. High peaks are visible through vistas of pines; some are blue with forests; others are bare and yellow.

Ahead, the river narrows and the banks become steep. After running through more lightly timbered country, with thick forage on the forest floor, the highway emerges into open country, where tall elk thistles border the way.

At NEZ PERCE CREEK, 41.9 *m.*, named for the Nez Percé Indians, is the junction with a trail.

Left on this trail through Nez Perce Valley to MARY'S LAKE, 14.4 *m.*, and to HAYDEN VALLEY, 20.9 *m.* In this valley, Chief Joseph of the Nez Percé, during his historic retreat, captured and subsequently released a party of visitors, in 1877. This was several years after the creation of the park, but before there was adequate supervision of the area.

At 43.2 *m.* the Grand Loop Road approaches a steaming area called the LOWER GEYSER BASIN, the largest geyser basin in the park (approximately ten miles square), where some 680 geysers were officially counted by the Hayden Expedition in the 1870's. Many of these are now merely hot springs, although there are at least 18 active geysers (1939). Plumes of steam and sometimes pillars of water rise dazzling white against the green forest and the blue sky.

At 43.6 *m.* is a parking area (R). Adjoining the area is LEATHER POOL, so named by early explorers for its leathery exterior; R. on a foot trail to FOUNTAIN PAINT POT, a blubbering, hot, mud caldron, 40 to 60 feet in extent. This pool of bubbling, many-colored material, resembling plaster or calcimine, has a rim, four or five feet high, along two sides. Below is a great, colored, steaming basin in which pink predominates; R. here 100 yards on a footpath across a flat is FOUNTAIN GEYSER, whose deep vent is filled with greenish water. This used to be one of the best-known geysers, because of its frequent eruptions. It was one-fourth of a mile south of old Fountain Hotel. During its infrequent eruptions, typical of the 'fountain' type, it throws 75 feet of water in all directions and at all angles. On a connecting path is CLEPSYDRA GEYSER, named in 1873 because, 'like the ancient water clock of that name it marks the passage of time by the discharge of water.' This geyser has remained more or less regular through the years.

At 43.8 *m.* is the junction with a side loop road.

Left on this oiled road to STEADY GEYSER (R), 1.1 *m.,* a geyser with a lake, the largest one of its kind in such a location. R. here are BLACK WARRIOR SPRINGS, with a temperature above boiling. The superheated water rises from beneath the ledge, at the point where the bubbles are noticed.

FIREHOLE LAKE (L), 1.2 *m.,* was named for the series of gas bubbles, which rises rapidly from a vent in the bottom of the lake. From the opposite shore, these bubbles have the appearance of the flame of a Bunsen burner. The dark brown algae on the bottom and sides form a background, against which the flame can be seen. The orange color in the run-off steam is caused by plant life.

THE TURK, 1.6 *m.,* is small but quite active. The BEAD GEYSER, 1.7 *m.,* with a beaded surface around its opening, erupts irregularly to a height of 13 feet. PINK CONE, 1.8 *m.,* was named in 1878 by the Hayden Expedition for the beautiful shell-pink color of the sinter in its cone.

TANGLED CREEK, 2.1 *m.,* is a small stream with many little branches, which twist and wind through a white flat. WHITE DOME GEYSER, 2.2 *m.,* a cone of siliceous sinter, similar to the Lion and Castle (*see below*), plays to a height of 35 feet from two to three minutes. GREAT FOUNTAIN GEYSER, 2.4 *m.,* near the southeast border of Lower Geyser Basin, has an average height of 100 feet, with an interval of from 8 to 12 hours.

At 2.5 *m.* is SURPRISE POOL, a superheated pool with an overhanging rim, which acts in much the same manner as the lid of a teakettle. FIREHOLE POOL, 2.6 *m.,* seethes like a Bunsen burner with bubbling activity.

BROKEN EGG SPRING (R), 2.8 *m.,* sends up a strong sulphurous odor.

Running through thick pines, the side loop road rejoins the Grand Loop Road at 3.5 *m.,* one mile from the north junction.

At 44.9 *m.* on the Grand Loop Road is a large parking area (R).

Right from the area on a foot trail across a footbridge over the Firehole River and up a steep hill to the MIDWAY GEYSER BASIN. Here, vast steaming terraces of red, orange, pink, and other colors are fringed by pines, with blue-black mountains in the background. Plank walks make it possible to visit the most important springs and geysers in the basin. At the entrance to the area, the colors beside the drain-off stream are red, brown, tan, or orange; yet the bed where the water actually flows is only greenish-yellow. The EXCELSIOR GEYSER CRATER (L), above a cut-away bank, is enveloped in steam. The Excelsior Geyser Crater, formerly known as Hell's Half Acre, was of considerable size prior to 1878. In that year it came to life and shot 300 feet into the air. Since 1890, when last reported in eruption, it has been a great hot lake.

GRAND PRISMATIC SPRING, one of the most beautiful hot springs in the park, is a vast mound of deposited sinter, whose colors are the result of the blue water combined with the reds, browns, and other colors of algae. There is nearly every hue except violet.

Submerged plant life, in various shades of red and brown, give the blue waters of OPAL POOL (L) an opalescent appearance that justifies the name.

TURQUOISE POOL, 150 feet north of Excelsior Geyser Crater, is a silent pool about 100 feet in diameter, remarkable for its beautiful, bluish-green, translucent water. Because of their configuration and arrangement, the formations at the bottom of the pool, seen through the blue-green water and steam, look like a series of light cottony clouds. In the center, several large springs flow continually, raising foamy bubbles to the surface.

Southeastward, the Grand Loop Road runs through avenues of trees, as it parallels the Firehole River (R).

At 49.7 *m.* is the junction with a small loop road.

Right on this oil-surfaced loop road to BISCUIT BASIN PARKING AREA, 0.3 *m.;* R. here on a footpath across the Firehole River through an area of deep pools of green-blue water. On the L. are colored terraces and bleached dead trees.

SAPPHIRE POOL, which boils every 12 minutes, is an excellent example of an intermediate stage between a geyser and a hot spring. The water boils violently and overflows, but no jet of water is hurled into the air. Between violent periods is an interval of calm, when the deep pool of blue, translucent water lies still. Queer gray crustations, hundreds of small biscuitlike knobs of siliceous sinter, form a highly ornamented margin, from which the water recedes five or six inches after each eruption. Large silver globelike bubbles rise from the bottom of the pool before the overflow. The hottest point in the pool is 26 feet below the surface, where it is believed there is a reservoir. Westward along the path an unnamed vent roars (L). Near by is BLACK PEARL POOL, which bubbles continuously within its gray crust. Here and there, noisy little vents spout and splutter.

MUSTARD SPRINGS (R) resembles a great lily pad, from which water bubbles over the path. The gray deposit here, pitted with bubbles, looks like a hornet's nest. Purple asters and white yarrow fringe the trail. A little brown pool (R) bubbles vigorously. At the crest of the walk are two pools with center vents, through which water sputters. The path curves L. over a terrace of orange and gray, where many trees have been killed by the run-off. Wild strawberries grow around the roots of these trees. Birds call from the pines near by.

In SILVER GLOBE SPRING, large silver bubbles of gas rise to the surface constantly. Globular, silver-gray masses of sinter around the edge offer another explanation of the name. JEWEL GEYSER, noted by members of the Hayden Expedition, was named later for the beadlike deposit around the vent. This geyser plays with a single spout—12 to 15 feet high—at intervals of 5 to 10 minutes.

The main highway, now traversing Upper Geyser Basin, winds through pines bordered with grass, flowers, and shrubby undergrowth.

GEM POOL (R), 50.1 *m.*, has a nearly placid surface. Its setting in the pines helps to intensify the blue-green color of the water in its deep crater, where logs thrown in by early tourists show plainly. Close by, a small lily pad pool sends a narrow bronze stream across the terrace.

ARTEMISIA GEYSER (R), 50.2 *m.*, has a large central crater of blue, set off by gray-green granular sinter along the rim and sides, unlike any found elsewhere in this area. This geyser, named for the sage-colored sinter, sends a shaft of water up to 35 feet for 10 to 15 minutes every 24 hours.

MORNING GLORY POOL (R), 50.5 *m.*, is named for its symmetry and for the depth and blue color of its water. The color is due to the presence of a low form of plant life. A superstition prevails that good luck will come to those who cast something into the pool, but tokens, coins, and bits of debris thrown into the water might destroy its beauty. To avoid this, a padlocked box with a slot in it has been placed beside the pool, into which slugs and souvenirs may be deposited.

Just south of the Morning Glory Pool the highway crosses the FIRE-HOLE RIVER, 50.6 *m.* Close to the river bank is FAN GEYSER, so named for the shape of its eruptions, which occur every two or three days and average 60 feet. Its neighbor, MORTAR GEYSER, was named by F. Jay Haynes in 1883, because eruptions resembled the discharge of a light mortar cannon.

RIVERSIDE GEYSER (L), characterized by one of the most unusual cones in the area, has a beautiful eruption, lasting a half-hour, during which it throws water obliquely from the lower crater for a distance of 75 feet, at an angle over the river. After the first eight or ten minutes, there is less water and a greater quantity of steam. At the beginning of an eruption, water rises from the upper crater to five or ten feet. The period between eruptions varies from five and one-half to eight hours. Preceding an eruption, the lower crater overflows for an hour and a half or less. In SPA GEYSER (L), named for the famous mineral springs in Belgium, the water level is rarely seen twice in the same place.

Two geysers close to the roadside (L), at 50.8 *m.*, attract much attention. When ROCKET GEYSER spouts simultaneously with its neighbor, GROTTO, it throws only a 10-foot stream of water; when Grotto is quiet, Rocket sometimes throws water in jets to 70 feet. It plays at intervals of two to five hours. Grotto, discovered and named by the Washburn-Langford-Doane Expedition in 1870, is in action about half the time, its eruptions varying from 15 minutes to 8 hours in length, and rising to a height of 20 to 30 feet. Quoting from Langford's Diary: 'The Grotto was named for the singularly winding apertures penetrating the sinter surrounding it . . . Externally it presented few indications of its character as a geyser, but Private Williams . . . afterwards saw it belch forth a column of boiling water two feet in diameter to a height of fifty feet.' Opposite these geysers is CHAIN LAKE, a small pond.

MASTIFF, BIJOU, and CATFISH, just south of the Grotto and near the river bank, are closely related. Mastiff is simply an opening in the sinter. Bijou, which first was called Young Faithful, has built up a cone with several vents, the lowest of them known as CATFISH GEYSER. Usually one of these is in eruption, and just before an emptying of the near-by Giant, with considerable vigor. Seen from one angle, the surrounding beds of geyserite are white; from another, they are creamy yellow or ivory.

GIANT erupts to a greater height than any other geyser in the world today—250 feet. Eruptions last for about an hour, but only during the first 10 minutes is the maximum height reached. Three days to three months may elapse between eruptions. The irregular cone looks as if its top had been blown off by an unusually violent eruption. Water rushes and gushes in the crater.

At 51.1 m. is the junction with a side loop road.

Right on this oil-surfaced road to BLACK SAND BASIN, in which are a number of hot springs and geysers that seem to be connected. When one geyser has stopped playing, another takes its place. Even the ground is warm near the central vents. WHITE PYRAMID GEYSER CONE, an extinct hot spring from which water was flowing in 1870, has receded to a level marked by seepage, 15 feet below the top. DAISY GEYSER, a bubbling pool, one of the most famous in the park, erupts at an angle away from the road. A partial vacuum sucks water back into the tube, to be flung out again. The Daisy erupts, at intervals of 90 to 100 minutes, to an average height of 75 feet.

BRILLIANT POOL, of a blackish color, containing silica and other minerals, is sometimes considered prettier than the Morning Glory.

At 0.3 m. is PUNCH BOWL SPRING, at one time a big pool. It is shelf-built, with an open vent below.

BLACK SAND POOL, 0.5 m., has black sand at one end. Its maximum temperature is 100° F., and this extreme heat causes active boiling in the center every few minutes. The pool's deep-blue color is probably due to its great depth. The outer slopes are covered with a crust of light-brown and dark-cream-colored deposit. A warm mist blows from the pool, which runs a large stream in the flow-off.

The water in SPOUTER GEYSER, 0.9 m., is used over and over. The hot water comes out of the center of a shelf of rocks and circulates back through two openings on either side of the center; R. here on a footpath over IRON CREEK to an area of steaming pools and geysers. EMERALD POOL, with a temperature low enough for the growth of yellow algae, obtains its rich green color from its blue waters and the yellow algae. Timbers thrown into the pool years ago are now cemented to the bottom by deposits of geyserite. Tiny yellow violets grow near the pool.

SUNSET LAKE has many colors, owing to the algae: blue, bronze, gray, and red. Much steam rises from the pool.

RAINBOW GEYSER (R) changed its flow in 1938 and tore out the trail-walk. In 1935, this geyser, which had been known chiefly as a thermal spring, erupted to a height of 35 feet. Close by is GREEN SPRING, whose color varies with the temperature, which fluctuates between 170° F. and 195° F. CLIFF GEYSER, about 500 feet north of Emerald Pool, plays at one-hour intervals from 50 to 60 feet.

Near the point where the side loop road leaves Iron Creek, there are a number of small vents (R) that boil and splash noisily.

WHISTLE GEYSER (L), 1 m., which used to throw water 50 feet into the air, is now inactive but hisses vigorously. THREE SISTER SPRINGS, 1.8 m., with ten craters, seven hot springs, and three geysers, throw a spray five to ten feet high several times a day.

At 2 *m.* the loop side road joins the Grand Loop Road.

OLD FAITHFUL JUNCTION, 51.8 *m.*, is one of the most popular areas in the park, because of its nearness to the best-known geysers, its excellent accommodations, and its museum.

OLD FAITHFUL INN, built during the winter of 1903–4, is the largest native-log structure in the Rocky Mountains. Planned by R. C. Reamer of Seattle, the inn combines native woods and stone in a simple direct chalet design, well suited to the rugged landscape of the Upper Geyser Basin landscape. The great central unit, six stories high, has a steeply gabled roof, surmounted by a railed observation deck, from which searchlights play at night to illumine the mist plume òf Old Faithful Geyser. Smaller wings with gabled roofs flank the central portion. A more recent addition to the right wing is in marked contrast to the older structure, with its steep-sided, flat-crested roof and foundation levels graduated to conform to the abrupt ground slope. The roof of the wide portico that extends across the windowed lobby front is supported by eight sets of dovetailed log cribs. Within the lobby, pillars of unhewn pine carry gnarled pine staircases to the pine-balustraded balconies. The vast well of the main room extends to the roof crest. Opposite the front entrance, a towering fireplace chimney, constructed of 500 tons of rock, rises 85 feet to the roof and projects 20 feet beyond. A large clock, whose face and pendulum were hammered out at the site, is the great chimney's only fitting. Lobby appointments are of rustic design; leather and rough-finished woods have been used in the furnishings, and the light fixtures and other details are native woods, bronze, and rough-cast metal. The ceiling of the writing room adjoining the lobby is of half-finished pine slabs.

OLD FAITHFUL MUSEUM, a rustic one-story building R. across a driveway, displays numerous geologic specimens and a graphic history and explanation of the Upper Geyser Basin. An OUTDOOR HERBARIUM contains flora of the region, including wild caraway, queen's lace, wild geranium, blue-eyed grass, wild buckwheat, ladies' tresses, *Spiranthes stricta,* and orchids; Dodge's willow, the smallest of trees; lupine, low larkspur, water hemlock, monkey flower, phlox, *Galium trifidum,* or bedstraw, waterleaf, *Phacelia sericea,* balsam root, yarrow, beard-tongue, twinflower, yellow columbine, Indian paintbrush, goldenrod, sandwort, dwarf evening primrose, fireweed, gentian, monkshood, meadowsweet, smooth-leaved Labrador tea, Oregon grape, shooting star, scarlet trumpet, lichens, and mosses. Each evening during summer, ranger-naturalists lecture in an open-air AMPHITHEATER adjoining the museum.

The GEYSER SWIMMING POOL (L), almost in the center of the basin, is the largest geyser-water swimming pool in the world. Two pool sections, one for children, 20 by 50 feet, and one for adults, 50 by 150 feet, hold 280,000 gallons of naturally heated, constantly changing water from Solitary Geyser on the hillside to the northeast. The pool was built in 1924. There are 147 dressing rooms.

Log beams, lashed to thick posts by metal plates, arch over the pool. Glass sections compose most of the roof area. The front has a two-story entry and two small wings. Vertical posts, set on a rock foundation, extend a short way above the ridges of the roof levels, giving the appearance of greater height to the entry section and wing, by breaking the long horizontal lines of the gabled roofs.

OLD FAITHFUL GEYSER, east of the inn, is the only major park geyser that erupts at predictable intervals. It was named by members of the Washburn-Langford-Doane Expedition in 1870, because of its seeming regularity. Its reputation has spread as widely as the name of the park itself, and its steam plume has come to be a Yellowstone trademark.

Nature favored Old Faithful by placing it at the head of the Upper Basin, away from the other geysers that spout in the area. Low pine-covered hills on three sides make an amphitheater of the basin, in which the geyser's dead gray cone, 145 by 215 feet at the base and about 12 feet high, forms a hummocky rostrum. The tube, or crater, which seems to have originated in a rock fissure, measures about 2 x 6 feet inside.

Old Faithful plays to an average height of 140 feet at intervals averaging 65 minutes, varying on occasion from 35 to 80 minutes. Before each performance, there is a rumbling prologue that resembles the roll of distant bass drums. Steam issues from the crater in a great white cloud; water spills over, as from a pan over a hot fire. The water column mounts slowly, hissing and huffing, until it reaches a height of 120 feet or more. When the sun is right, the vapor that envelops the water reflects a hundred broken rainbows. For about four minutes the dazzling display continues; then the column sinks back, and only wisps of vapor eddy and sway above the mound until the next eruption.

'The noise is simply that of a jet of water from an ordinary hose, [but] in intensity corresponding to the greater flow,' Chittenden wrote. 'The steam, when carried laterally by a gentle breeze, unfurls itself like an enormous flag from its watery standard. The water is of crystal clearness, and the . . . drops float in the air with all manner of brilliant effects. The uniform periodicity of this geyser is its most wonderful . . . characteristic. It never fails . . . [and] varies but little.'

In each of these spectacular performances, Old Faithful hurls skyward about 15,000 gallons of water, discharging in a single day enough water to supply the needs of a small city. As the discharged water flows over the incrustation, it colors the gray geyserite brown, ivory, orange, and pastel gray, with touches of red. Since the prevailing park winds are westerly, the vapor from the geyser is usually blown toward the lodge; thus, it is better to photograph Old Faithful from the west, facing the sun when possible. Naturalists have expressed the opinion that as the area cools, probably centuries hence, the geyser may become extinct.

Left from Old Faithful on a footpath across the Firehole River to GEYSER HILL (*ranger-naturalists conduct parties several times a day*).

The GIANTESS (L) is temperamental and spleenish, sulking for six or nine months, then spewing with all the fuss and tremor of a small volcano. The eruptions, never more frequent than twice a year, come through one of three large craters. For four and a half hours, the water plays at a height of 200 feet, and the force of the upheaval shakes the inn windows, several hundred yards away, and rattles the silverware. TEAKETTLE SPRING (L), south of the Giantess Cone, boils continuously. The PUMP (R) is a little spring, pumping from a small cavern, and covering the ground with orange, red, and raw-umber incrustations.

DOUBLET POOL (L) contains bones and horns of animals that probably mistook the crust around it for ice. Snow here is melted by the heat of geyseric activity, although it often lies 77 inches deep at the inn. Grass remains green in places, and elk and deer come down to feed and bed. The temperature of the ground has been 72°, when the atmosphere was 16° below zero.

BEACH SPRING (R) has a deep central crater. EAR SPRING (L) was named because of its fancied resemblance to the Devil's ear. The four craters of the LION GROUP (L), the LION, LIONESS, BIG CUB, and LITTLE CUB, play together as many as three times a day. As their name suggests, they roar just before they erupt.

The trail crosses a wooden and concrete flume that carries water from Solitary Pool, on the mountainside, to the Swimming Pool. Concrete openings in the flume allow the steam to escape, and the water rushes and roars and then ebbs as the geyser erupts and recedes.

SPASMODIC GEYSER (L), across a small stream, is a quiet but erratic gusher that spouts through any or all of its several vents. Trees near it are brown and dying, apparently affected by the geyseric run-off. SAWMILL GEYSER, a series of bubblers in a funnel-shaped crater (R), erupts to 20 feet every three hours; the shape of the crater gives the water a twisting motion and a whirring sound, suggestive of a sawmill. Rounded siliceous sinter pebbles, in the catch-basins near the Sawmill, are known as geyser 'eggs.'

A branch walk runs R. past the BULGER SPRING, GRAND GEYSER, WAVE SPRING, BEAUTY POOL, and CHROMATIC SPRING.

The main trail crosses the Firehole on a rustic bridge to CRESTED POOL (L), formerly known as the Castle Well. The temperature and rate of overflow from Crested varies little. The bottom, 41 feet under water, is clearly visible.

TORTOISE SHELL SPRING (L), named for its varicolored incrustation, is 52 feet deep. CASTLE GEYSER (L) is said to have the largest and most imposing cone of any active geyser in the world, resembling a crumbling castle wall. It erupts only about once a day, to a height of about 75 feet, but it throws water continually to about 20 feet.

The trail ends at Old Faithful Inn.

In addition to cabin accommodations and meals, OLD FAITHFUL LODGE (L) offers the most complete recreational facilities of any lodge in the park. The main building is of stone and timber construction. Broad porches, lined with thick log pillars, face Old Faithful. The west wall of the lounge is built out a short distance from the main building wall; the four stone pillars supporting its peaked roof inclose three great plate-glass windows that frame the graceful play of the geyser. The lounge is a spacious common room furnished with a large fireplace and comfortable armchairs. The shallow vaulted ceiling is made of logs, laid across heavy beams extending the full length of the room. In the large Community Hall 'savages' and paid entertainers perform at night.

New and thoroughly remodeled cabins, all with running water, offer the best cabin accommodations in the park. The crash of a garbage-can lid at night frequently announces the approach of an ambling black bear on his prowl for food. Cabins are warmed by wood fires in small sheet-iron stoves; and, each morning at six, a 'savage' raps on the door with a huge spoon, asking, 'Do you wish a fire built this morning?' During the day and evening, informality governs tourist dress.

Southeast of OLD FAITHFUL, the Grand Loop Road runs over more geyser formations to timbered foothills.

KEPLER CASCADE (R), 53.3 *m.* (*parking space on observation platform*), is a spectacular rapid, where the Firehole River is pinched into a narrow rock channel.

At 53.4 *m.* is a junction with a graveled road.

> Right on this forest drive to LONE STAR GEYSER, 4 *m.*, in a small basin on the Firehole River. This geyser throws a thin column of water 25 feet high usually every three hours, but its habits are erratic, and sometimes it erupts every 30 minutes. Members of the Hayden party in 1871 called it the Solitary Geyser, but travelers during the 1880's changed its name.

Grand Loop Road here begins the climb to the Continental Divide. Through open parks, where the Firehole River is transformed by beaver dams into a series of small lakes and lily ponds, it winds upgrade over a course cut from sheer rock walls to the CONTINENTAL DIVIDE (8,262 alt.) at ISA LAKE and CRAIG PASS, 58.6 *m.*, named for early travelers. The highway bisects the lake.

From DELACY CREEK, 60.9 *m.*; in a bend of the mountains that form the Continental Divide, the highway climbs a pined slope to SHOSHONE POINT, 62.5 *m.* Shoshone Lake, five miles south, in an alpine setting, is visible, and beyond are the blue, pointed caps of the Tetons.

From the SECOND CROSSING of the CONTINENTAL DIVIDE, 67.3 *m.*, the descent steepens to the Yellowstone Lake Basin.

Automobile and trailer campgrounds are R. at 69.1 *m.*

THUMB JUNCTION, 69.2 *m.* (*campground, cabins, cafeteria, store, picture shop, ranger station, dock, boats and tackle*), is on West Thumb, a large oblong bay that protrudes like a misshapen thumb from Yellowstone Lake. The bay, itself larger than any other body of water in the park, is connected with the rest of the lake by a neck or strait. Dense lodgepole and spruce forest extends to the shore line on every side. Massive Colter Peak (10,500 alt.) looms blue in the southwest, across the lake.

The station and parking zone overlook a crusted, steaming area and West Thumb beyond. The buildings are rustic, with gnarled-wood decorations.

YELLOWSTONE LAKE (7,731 alt.), which spreads over 138 square miles and has a 100-mile shore line, is the largest lake in North America above 7,500 feet elevation. Its contributary streams, the upper Yellowstone River, Beaverdam Creek, Clear Creek, Columbine Creek, Bear Creek, Cub Creek, Pelican Creek, and a few unnamed streams, are small; most of the lake water comes as direct run-off from the bold Absaroka Mountains, along its east shore, and the less abrupt range that forms the Continental Divide on the south and west. Its depth

(300 feet max.) gives the surface a deep bluish hue, with delicate shades of ultramarine on cloudy days. On clear mornings, when the air is quiet, it is green and glassy, disturbed only by an occasional submerged geyser, which spouts peevishly, then recedes to a thin wisp of white steam.

The shore line is inching away from the forest, leaving a widening beach of sand and volcanic rock; the sand is studded with obsidian and trachyte pebbles, cornelians, agates, and bits of agatized wood. Inactive geyser formations, submerged near the shore, have been worn by continual washing to strange forms; early trappers and explorers mistook them for discarded pottery, stone weapons, and broken idols of an ancient race.

Lady's thumb, starwort, and other aquatic plants grow out in the deep waters. After severe storms, their uptorn stems strew the beach like kelp on the sea shore. Only two species of fish inhabit the lake, black-spotted trout and northern sucker. Other species and varieties have been kept out, in order that the two native fishes might continue unhybridized. In summer, swans, gulls, geese, brant, ducks, herons, pelicans, dippers, and sandhill cranes inhabit the small flat islands that rise high enough above the surface to grow a dense grass carpet. In the higher Lake Basin areas are eagles, hawks, crows, ospreys, prairie chickens, grouse, mocking birds, and woodpeckers.

Yellowstone Lake, in a glacier-gouged basin, once extended to the southern base of Mount Washburn, 20 miles north. Its surface was 160 feet higher than it is now, and it drained into the Snake River through Outlet Creek and Heart Lake, eventually reaching the Pacific Ocean. Washburn then formed a part of the Continental Divide. Some natural convulsion probably dammed up the southern outlet; the rising water spilled over Washburn's eastern base and began flowing northward, washing its deep gorge in the decayed lava beds. Reduced by its rapid run-off, it is now confined to an irregularly shaped basin, which, on a map, roughly resembles a hand with the fingers spread.

1. Right from Thumb Junction on the Lake Shore Trail to a GEYSER AREA, where hot pools, small geysers, and muddy 'paint pots' boil and hiss. LAKE SHORE GEYSER (R), which spews a 15-foot column of boiling water every 30 or 35 minutes, is submerged during high water. FISHING CONE (R), farther out into the lake, is a hot pool enclosed in a geyser cone that resembles a huge hornet's nest. Boiling water flows continually from this spring into the colder water of the lake. Early park visitors, who told of angling near Fishing Cone, reported that the nearness of hot and cold water simplified their camping problems. A fish pulled from the lake near the cone could be dangled in the pool and cooked, before it was removed from the line. Jim Bridger, enlarging upon this, told of a similar pool, in which all hot water rose to the top, leaving the lower water at average temperature; fish caught from this pool were cooked while they were being pulled to the surface.

BLACK POOL and KING'S GEYSER are L., in the hot pool area between the lake and the highway. Black Pool, a hot mud pot, is 60 feet deep, and its temperature is constant at 147° F.

Beyond ABYSS POOL (L), whose jade color is caused by its depth and refracted light rays, are TWIN GEYSERS (R) and MUSTARD POOL (L). Twin Geysers, also called Maggie and Jiggs, is apparently a misnomer, as they do not erupt simultaneously and, evidently, are not connected.

2. Right from Thumb Junction on the South Entrance Road, an oiled feeder highway, to LEWIS LAKE (R), 10.4 *m.*, in a heart-shaped basin, surrounded by lodgepole forest. The lake was named by early explorers for Captain Meriwether Lewis.

LEWIS RIVER, crossed at 11.8 *m.*, drains Shoshone and Lewis Lakes, then runs south to join the Snake River near the park boundary. LEWIS FALLS, where the river cascades into a deep gorge, is visible upstream from the crossing. Beavers have dammed the stream below, spreading it into ponds and pools.

At the SOUTH ENTRANCE (Snake River Station), 22.1 *m.*, is the junction with US 89-287, 31.5 miles north of Grand Teton National Park (*see Tour 7A*) and 55.9 miles north of Jackson (*see Tour 7a*).

The Grand Loop swings north, then northeast, along the West Thumb. Geysers steam along the shore, and, through the match-stick lodgepole R., Mount Sheridan's bald cone (10,250 alt.) comes into sight across the Thumb, as the road turns southwest around a point of the bay at 74.6 *m.* Trees are girded by white gummy bands, where porcupines have gnawed the bark.

DOT ISLAND is a small grassy lozenge midway between the shore and FRANK ISLAND. The latter, the largest island in the lake, was named for Frank Elliot by his brother, Henry W. Elliot, a member of Hayden's first expedition. STEVENSON ISLAND, ahead and R., was named for James Stevenson, Hayden's assistant.

A FISH HATCHERY (L), 88.5 *m.* is maintained by the United States Bureau of Fisheries. Black-spotted trout are propagated here for restocking park lakes and streams. Montana grayling, and Eastern brook, Mackinaw, rainbow, and Loch Leven trout specimens are on display. Stuffed pelicans and gulls, above the fingerling troughs, seem about to swoop down for a meal.

Commanding a gradual rise from the lake shore, the yellow and white clapboard façade of LAKE HOTEL (L), 88.7 *m.*, is in pleasant contrast to the green forest beyond. Projecting from the main wall are two two-storied, pedimented, and colonnaded porticoes. Between the porches, the lounge reaches out from the lobby in a long windowed bay. Large windows in the lounge and dining room face the panorama of the lake and hills on the far shore. White paneling has been used for trim and pillars throughout the interior. A wide stone fireplace makes the lobby a cheerful gathering place for travelers, when cold winds sweep in from the lake. Stores, a filling station, and campground adjoin.

At the BOAT DOCK (R), rowboats and motor boats may be rented by the hour or day, for fishing or trips to the islands. (*Storms on the lake are sudden and violent; do not venture too far from shore unless a seasoned boat man is along.*)

At 89.4 *m.* is the junction with a graveled road.

Left on this road to an improved automobile campground (*free*).

LAKE LODGE, 0.5 *m.* on the side road, is a large log and frame rustic building in an open park, backed by wooded hills (*cabins, meals, dancing, store, evening programs*).

At 1 *m.* is the junction with Grand Loop.

At 90.3 *m.* is the junction with the East Entrance Road.

Right on this oil-surfaced road to FISHING BRIDGE, 0.3 *m.*, a peeled-log bridge (1938) that spans Yellowstone River at its outlet from the lake. The broad outlet is a great fish thoroughfare, and the pedestrian lanes provide excellent angling points.

FISHING BRIDGE CAFETERIA and STORE are L., at 0.5 *m.* The store building is of rock and concrete, columned to resemble hewn logs. Pillars of local rock support the raftered roof. A large stone fireplace provides the only heat. Cabins adjoining the store have 'stockade' walls, formed by closely fitted upright posts.

FISHING BRIDGE MUSEUM, R. across an automobile and trailer campground, is in a one-story structure of peeled timbers and rock pillars. Horns and antlers decorate lighting fixtures inside. Typical specimens of park flora, fauna, geological formations, and Indian artifacts are displayed here. Range naturalists conduct nature walks from the museum along the lake shore, explaining geological formations and discussing the species of plant or animal life encountered.

Southeast of Fishing Bridge, the East Entrance Road skirts the lake to PELICAN CREEK, 1.7 *m.*, a small contributory stream that heads in the timbered Absarokas. It was named for the numerous pelicans that fish in its waters.

The SULPHUR HILLS (L), 3.2 *m.*, resemble large old geyser formations, studded with scrub pines. MARY BAY, 4.5 *m.*, is an open cove in Yellowstone Lake (L), named by a member of a Hayden party for his sweetheart. Shore fishing here is good on calm days. The small island R. at 6.9 *m.*, called PELICAN ROOST, is made white by hundreds of birds that come at night to remain until morning. The pelican, with its great pouched bill and short legs, is ungraceful on land, but its long wingspread (often 12 feet) makes it a powerful flyer.

At 9 *m.*, the road swings away from the lake shore and veers east through dense timber.

At 10 *m.* is the junction with a dirt road; L. here 0.7 *m.* to LAKE BUTTE, from whose top the entire Yellowstone Lake Basin is visible. The highway now goes through timber, straight toward the Absaroka Mountains. The lower slopes are blue-black with pine and spruce forest; the peaks, barren and jagged.

At TETON POINT, 15.7 *m.*, is a parking space. From here the Teton Mountains, 60 miles southwest (*see Tour 7A*), resemble great black cones.

SYLVAN LAKE, 17.6 *m.*, and LAKE ELEANOR, 19.2 *m.*, are twin alpine lakes (R) that remained when the glacier melted from the Absaroka Mountains. The dark spruce forest that grows down to their shores makes the water seem a very deep blue, almost black.

The climb steepens to SYLVAN PASS, 20 *m.* (8,557 alt.), a vast crumbling stone trough through the Absarokas. Loose talus that covered the region made the barrier formidable and treacherous to cross; even game animals swung far from Sylvan Pass when migrating. The construction of the highway here was considered a noteworthy engineering feat. For 30 miles on either side, the wilderness is primitive; the only paths are game trails, and a few Park Service or Forest Service fire trails. Grizzly bear, elk, deer, moose, mountain sheep, and numerous smaller high-altitude fauna live and die here unaware of man.

At the East Entrance Gate, 27.5 *m.*, is the junction with US 14-20 (*see Tours 10 and 6*) 53 miles west of Cody (*see Tour 6c*).

The Grand Loop Road veers north by west from Lake Junction and follows the Yellowstone River through spindling lodgepole. The Absaroka Peaks, far R., form an irregular horizon above pine-green slopes.

At YELLOWSTONE CASCADES (R), 93.4 *m.*, the river begins its descent into Hayden Valley. The water, churned to white foam as it tumbles down its broad rocky courses, contrasts sharply with the black-top boulders that protrude from the stream bed. During early-summer spawning time, black-spotted trout flash silver in the sunlight, as they climb the cascade in their migration to higher waters.

At 95.1 *m.* is a junction with a dim trail.

Right on this trail to CHIEF JOSEPH'S CROSSING, 0.5 *m.*, where the indomitable Joseph, one of the ablest military generals of his time, led his Nez Percé on their famous retreat from Idaho to Canada in 1877. General O. O. Howard, who led one of three armies in pursuit, was completely outwitted; the wily chieftain got his whole tribe, including women and children, and their camp duffel within a few miles of the Canadian border, before he was headed off by another army from the east.

At 95.2 *m.* is a turnout. MUD VOLCANO (L) is a large hot caldron with a brown mud surface that simmers and bubbles like boiling chocolate. Gas escaping from a cavern below causes the bubbling.

The DRAGON'S MOUTH, beyond Mud Volcano on a footpath, is a hot spring in the base of a small cliff. Its opening is a semicircular cavern that suggests the open jaws of a prehistoric serpent. Its muffled, continuous roaring is caused by water splashing against the wall of a subterranean cave. Unlike other hot holes in the area, its water is clear.

In BOILING MUD AREA, 95.5 *m.* (*turnout*), R. below the highway, are numerous small mud pools.

Over sagebrush hills, the Grand Loop winds to HAYDEN VALLEY, an oblong basin bounded by low pine hills. Sage borders the meadow grass along the river. Here, where the river flows slowly, moose often feed on the succulent aquatic grasses, their angular bodies often partly or completely submerged.

The valley was named for Dr. Ferdinand V. Hayden, geologist for the Geological Survey of the Territories, who conducted several expeditions and surveying parties in the Yellowstone country. It was Hayden who first mapped the Lower Geyser Basin, found a route between this basin and Yellowstone Lake, and surveyed the Yellowstone Lake shore line. Hayden's report of his 1871 expedition, the first comprehensive official report on the Yellowstone, was introduced in Congress with the bill to establish the Nation's first national park in 1872.

TROUT CREEK, 96.6 *m.*, is a crooked, slough-like stream formerly noted for its trout.

SPURGIN'S BEAVER SLIDE, a steep wooded hill (L) visible less than a mile away at 101.6 *m.*, was named for Captain W. F. Spurgin, an engineer with General Howard. Howard's troops, pursuing Chief Joseph's Nez Percé, took a short cut over Central Plateau, and encountered difficulties with their baggage train. At this point, Captain Spurgin of the 21st Infantry made the descent into Hayden Valley from the Mary Mountain area by letting his wagons down, one at a time, with ropes wound around tree trunks. The old rope burns are still visible on the spruce and lodgepole.

At OTTER CREEK, 102.3 *m.*, is the junction with a graveled road.

Left on this road to the GRAND CANYON GRIZZLY BEAR FEEDING GROUNDS, 0.4 *m.* On a raised concrete platform, from 50 to 60 black and grizzly bears are fed garbage from the Canyon Hotel and Lodge during the midsummer months. (*Open evenings; park cars in parking area and enter wire-enclosed seating area.*) The bear-feeding program serves three purposes: It concentrates bears in the Grand Canyon region in one general area, thereby keeping many of them away from the lodge, hotel, and tent and trailer campgrounds; it helps support the large bear population; and it provides an excellent bear show for visitors.

The grizzlies, larger and more favored by nature for battle than the blacks, rule the dining hall. Some grizzly varieties weigh as much as 1,000 pounds, but, in the central Rockies, they seldom weigh more than 800. Because they were bold and indifferent to men before the invention of the repeating rifle, they have fearsome fascination for most Americans today. Except when cornered or enraged, however, the grizzly is a shy, retiring fellow, and is rarely seen in the park outside the feeding ground.

Robert Ripley once pointed out that in this show the spectators are in a pen; the bears in the open. Every evening, the 'boarders' leave their shade in near-by timber and shuffle leisurely toward the supper table. Adult bears are frequently followed by one, two, three, and sometimes four furry cubs. The blacks usually sulk at the edge of the timber, until the grizzlies have supped, although occasionally an impatient black will venture close, to be driven away by a chorus of growls or a cuff from the powerful arm of an irate grizzly. Less often, an obese black champion will bluff his way to the board with threatening throat noises and hostile mien. Ranger-naturalist lectures accompany the feeding each evening.

Left from the Feeding Ground on a game trail to the SITE OF THE OTTER CREEK FIGHT, 0.7 *m.* Here, near the Otter Creek Forks, a party of ten tourists from Helena, Montana, took refuge from a small band of stragglers from Chief Joseph's retreating band on August 25, 1877. The Indians attacked the camp, and the whites fled. One, Charles Kenck, was overtaken and killed; another, Charles Stewart, was wounded and captured, but he gave his captors $260 and his gold watch and persuaded them to let him live.

Hayden Valley is pinched off by low hills at 102.6 *m.*, and the highway is crowded to the river bank. Here, the river quickens its flow toward the rapids and cataracts, where it falls more than 500 feet into Yellowstone Grand Canyon.

At 102.8 *m.* is a junction with an oiled road.

Right on this road across CHITTENDEN BRIDGE, 0.1 *m.*, to a TURNOUT, 0.3 *m.*; L. here down a steep trail to the head of UPPER YELLOWSTONE FALLS, 0.2 *m.* (*Best approach on other side of canyon, see below.*)

GRAND CANYON LODGE, 0.6 *m.*, is a large L-shaped log and shingle building near the edge of the canyon above the Lower Falls of the Yellowstone (*cabins, store, meals, cocktail lounge, dancing, beauty parlor, barber shop*). In the spacious lobby, informal programs similar to those at Old Faithful Lodge are presented each evening by the 'savages.' Dancing follows.

Left from the lodge on Uncle Tom's Trail, an improved footpath, to the foot of LOWER YELLOWSTONE FALLS, 0.5 *m.* The trail was named for an old-timer who operated a ferry across the river, before Chittenden Bridge was built in 1903. The descent into the sheer canyon is made by a series of wooden and stone steps, connected by trail.

The view of the fall from the observation platform in the bottom of the canyon is breath-taking. A wall of white water, 308 feet high, appears to fall directly out of the blue-green timber that grows down to the brink on either side of the canyon. Silver, swirling spray and a grayer, thinner mist conceal the lower third of the cataract from this point. The spray reaches the platform, more than 200 yards away; the vapor settles on the canyon walls above the brink of the fall.

The Yellowstone gorge was formed in recent geologic time, long after Central Plateau had been formed of rhyolite magma during a late volcanic era, after the glaciers had withdrawn to the higher country. For a millennium, geyseric energy sent water and vapor filtering up through the 2,000-foot rhyolite layer, gradually decomposing it and transforming it into various materials that range from rhyolite lava to soft, powdery kaolin and porcelain clays. Traces of iron and other metallic oxides add hues that range through the spectrum.

When Yellowstone Lake overflowed its northern shore, the suddenly released waters washed a deep furrow in this yielding material. The erosion continued during the succeeding centuries, and even yet the river has not reached the basement rock that underlies the volcanic rhyolite and basalt. Small geysers and hot pools still send their thin steam columns up from the sides and bottom of the gorge. The courses of the older steam vents are still marked by towers and columns and other remnants of old geyser tubes.

ARTIST POINT, 1.6 m. on the oiled road, commands an excellent view of the chasm. The canyon is nearly 1,500 feet wide at this point, and about 750 feet deep. Its colors, which change constantly with lighting and perspective, run through many shades of yellow, orange, red, purple, and brown. When the sun is high the other colors are lost in the dazzling white and sulphur-yellow glare of the friable rhyolite. The green forest border, with the blue-green ribbon of the river at the bottom of the chasm, completes a color combination rare in nature. The Lower Fall at the canyon's head resembles a great white bridal veil.

CANYON STATION, 102.3 m., has a ranger station, cafeteria, store, picture shop, service station, automobile campground, and open-air amphitheater, where evening lectures are given by naturalists.

1. Right from the Picture Shop on a foot and bridle trail to the head of the UPPER FALL OF YELLOWSTONE, 0.3 m. The Upper Fall, viewed here from two platforms, one at the head and one halfway down the side, should be visited before the Lower Fall. It is 112 feet high, and would be a major park attraction if it were not dwarfed by the Lower Fall. It is the culmination of the rapids that head near Chittenden Bridge.

The river here is crowded into a 50-foot channel; the speed of the fall, the narrow course, and the huge boulders that obstruct the passage whip the water to white foam, before it turns suddenly L. and plunges over the precipice. The ledge is apparently perpendicular, but the velocity of the fall gives the cataract a barrel-roll effect. Spray and vapor lift halfway up its arc. Its roar almost equals that of Lower Fall.

2. Right from the store on a footpath to CRYSTAL FALLS, 0.3 m., where Cascade Creek tumbles into the Yellowstone. The fall was named by members of the Washburn-Langford-Doane Expedition, and it continued to go by that name, even after most of the water was diverted from Cascade Creek for the Canyon Station water system, and the sewage from the hotel put back in the channel just above the fall. From the head of the fall, the trail continues down the side of the canyon to the OBSERVATION PLATFORM at the HEAD OF LOWER FALLS, 1 m. (see below).

At 103.6 m. is the junction with an oiled road.

Left on this narrow road to NORRIS GEYSER BASIN, 11 m. (see above).

GENERAL HOWARD'S CAMPGROUND (L), 103.7 m., is marked by a signboard. The General crossed Cascade Creek near here in 1877, while chasing Chief Joseph across the park.

CASCADE CREEK, 103.8 *m.*, is spanned by a high wooden trestle bridge, where it has cut a deep gorge through the decayed lava on its way to join the Yellowstone.

At 104.3 *m.* is a turnout.

Right here down a steep wooden stairway to the HEAD OF THE LOWER or GRAND FALL OF THE YELLOWSTONE (493 *steps; should be attempted only by persons in good health*). This close-up of a mighty river plunging more than 300 feet is awesome. Above the fall, the canyon resembles a thousand other mountain canyons; the walls slope gradually to the water, and the soil is solid enough to support pines, mountain shrubs, and high-altitude grasses. Below the fall, the canyon deepens to become the cameo-yellow abyss that is the Grand Canyon of the Yellowstone.

Here, where the gorge reaches a depth of 1,000 feet, most vegetation ceases; the yellowish-brown rock and soil formation of the walls is crumbling and disintegrating, fretted by frost and the erosion of thousands of years. At some points, the walls drop sheer for 750 feet; in other places, they slope easily at a 50-degree angle, with needles and jagged spires jutting upright from the scarp. Huge rounded hollows have been worn smooth as travertine for hundreds of feet; one talus slope is nearly 1,000 feet high.

No rapids precede the 'fall; the water flows almost lazily, until it is suddenly drawn toward the brink of the cataract. Large white moths are attracted to the fall as to a bright light, and so great is the air vacuum created by the water's drop that hundreds of these insects are drawn into the stream and hurled downward into the spray-filled chasm. Small birds that venture too close to the white sheet of falling water also perish in its trap. But the water-wise ouzels and ospreys avoid the falls and do their fishing farther up or down the stream.

At 104.4 *m.* is a junction with an oiled road.

Left on this road to the CANYON HOTEL, 0.2 *m.* (*open from late June to middle September; bar, dancing, and dining room for guests only, laundry and garage service*).

This great rambling frame building, designed by Robert C. Reamer, and completed in 1911, is set against a background of sage and pines, on the top of a sagebrush ridge. Foundation levels follow the varying slope of the hillside; but the roof, with the exception of those portions that cover the lobby and the lounge unit, maintains a single horizontal plane. Dormers break the flanks of the long roof.

The approach and entrance are by a sloping, roofed arcade that reaches out from the lobby's south front to a widened drive. The floors, walls, pillars, and low ceiling of the lobby are of fine oak and red birch. Pillars are of squared, finished birch, surmounted, at their juncture with the heavy beams, by capitals of conventionalized pine-tree design. Lobby furnishings are of wood and leather.

The lounge, entered by a broad stair leading down from the lobby, is 200 feet long and 100 feet wide. It extends out from the south front and opens on porches facing east and west. Except for the massive pillars supporting a complicated beam system, the lounge walls are almost entirely of French plate glass. The remaining wall area and ceiling are finely finished red birch; the floor is polished oak. Two rows of metal and stained-glass hanging lamps extend the full length of the ceiling; smaller lamps of similar pattern are fastened to the pillar corners.

The highway follows the edge of the canyon past LOOKOUT POINT (R), 104.8 *m.*, and GRAND VIEW (R), 105.2 *m.;* both offer breath-taking views of the deepening gorge.

At 105.3 *m.* is the junction with the Inspiration Point Road.

Right on this oiled-surface road through the lodgepole forest that borders the canyon. The irregularly shaped granite GLACIAL BOULDER (L), 0.6 *m.*, 24 feet long, 20 feet wide, and 18 feet high, was deposited by an ice sheet that covered the Central Plateau sometime after the last period of great volcanic activity. It is the only granite boulder in the Grand Canyon area, and is at least 40 miles from any place where it could have originated.

INSPIRATION POINT, 1 *m.*, at the end of the road, has an observation platform at the edge of a sheer rhyolite cliff that overhangs the canyon. Here, the gorge bends slightly to the north, and this point offers a longer view of the Grand Canyon than any other accessible point.

The Grand Loop Road turns sharply north and crosses flat forest land. The mountains here are grassy; sagebrush grows in scattered clumps. The Absaroka Mountains form a rough sky line beyond the vast forested slopes of Mirror Plateau, beyond the Yellowstone River, R.

At 108.6 *m.*, the climb steepens toward DUNRAVEN PASS, 111.3 *m.* (8,860 alt.), on the southwest shoulder of Mount Washburn (*ranger station*). The pass was named for an Earl of Dunraven, an early park traveler.

Right from the pass on a graveled road to the summit of MOUNT WASHBURN, 3.6 *m.* (10,317 alt.) (*steep, narrow road, suitable only for cars in good condition; no trailers; one-way traffic*). When visibility is good, Grand Canyon, Hayden Valley, Yellowstone Lake, and the distant Tetons can be seen south; Cook and Electric Peak to the west. The ranger-lookout, in the three-story concrete lookout station, has a telescope.

Volcanic breccias and agglomerates make up the mountain; occasional basalt dikes intrude. Trees grow on the lower slopes; the upper scarp is barren of trees, but provides pasture for mountain sheep. Often these timid animals graze near enough to the road to be photographed.

The road winds sharply downward (*be sure to take exit road, keep car in low gear*) and forks at about 5 *m.*; L. here to junction with Grand Loop, en route to Tower Falls, 7 *m.* (*see below*).

The Grand Loop winds around Washburn's massive shoulder, above Carnelian Creek, in a heavily wooded draw.

At 113.6 *m.* and 116.3 *m.*, the two exit roads from Washburn join the highway.

The road descends around a wide loop curve to ANTELOPE CREEK VALLEY, 118.3 *m.* Here buffalo graze on the sage flats below the timber, along Antelope Creek. Occasionally, they drift close enough to the mesh wire fence (R) to be seen and photographed from the road. The buffalo, part of the big herd that inhabits the eastern section of the park, are transported to Antelope Creek Valley every summer, to make them more accessible to tourists.

At 122.3 *m.* is a junction with an oiled road.

Left here to TOWER FALLS AUTO CAMP (*water, fireplaces, garage, service station*).

At the TOWER FALLS PARKING AREA, 122.6 *m.*, is a combination store, picture shop, and lunch room.

Right from the parking area on a marked foot trail to TOWER FALLS, 0.1 *m.*, a small spectacular waterfall, where Tower Creek spills 132 feet into the Yellowstone Canyon. High breccia towers, from which the creek and fall take their names, rise from the head of the fall. They resemble the pile of some medieval castle with stone palisades and ramparts, topped by spires, parapets, and broken turrets. Ice and water sculptured them from the thick layer of volcanic rock that once covered the region; their long, vertical lines exaggerate the height of the thin, columnar waterfall.

The entire Tower Falls region is an area of stone pillars, columns, and spires. From TOWER CREEK CROSSING, 122.7 *m.*, the breccia towers at the head of the fall (R) resemble broken Egyptian temple columns.

OVERHANGING CLIFF (L), a high basalt ledge, juts out more than 30 feet over the highway.

Basalt burst over the Yellowstone region a second time, in a rather insignificant volcanic era that came after the longer period of rhyolite eruption. A thin crust covered the Tower region, which in cooling formed roughly hexagonal columns, with transverse fractures and cup joints. Frost and intruding vegetable growth loosen the joints, allowing the lower segments to drop off. Overhanging Cliff was eroded in this manner, and the process still goes on. The columns crumble at the bottom and fall continually, piling their debris by the roadside. Two long basaltic columnar formations are R., separated by ancient river gravel, on the opposite side of the Yellowstone Canyon. So regular and uniform are the columns that they resemble posts in a picket stockade or bullets in a cartridge belt. Other eroded breccia pikes, spires, and columns jut from the near canyon wall (R), where the Yellowstone has cut a narrow, 1,000-foot channel through the old rhyolite.

The highway winds through an ancient glacial spillway to a drab sagebrush valley.

At 124.8 *m.* is a junction with an oiled road.

Left on this narrow road to CAMP ROOSEVELT, 0.8 *m.*, in the pines that grow along the foothills (*cabins, meals, store*). The low rustic log and frame building is surrounded by a fence made of discarded elk and deer antlers. It was built in 1906 to commemorate a camping trip of President Theodore Roosevelt and John Burroughs in Yellowstone.

At 125.1 *m.* is the junction with the Northeast Entrance (Cooke) Road.

Right on this oil and gravel-surfaced road, over sage flats to the YELLOWSTONE RIVER, 0.8 *m.*, then up a narrow shelf to rolling sage hills. Aspens and pines are scattered on the hills and in the draws.

LAMAR RIVER, 4.7 *m.*, bears the name of the Secretary of the Interior in President Cleveland's cabinet. It heads on Mirror Plateau near the eastern park boundary and flows northwest to join the Yellowstone. The highway parallels the river up shallow Lamar Valley.

SLOUGH CREEK, 6.8 *m.*, is a tributary of the Lamar. E. S. Topping, in *Chronicles of the Yellowstone* (1883), records the circumstances under which a party of prospectors named Slough Creek and Hell Roaring Creek to the west: 'Hubbel went ahead the next day for a hunt, and upon his return he was asked what kind of a stream the next creek was. "It's a hell roarer," was his reply, and Hell Roaring is its name to this day. The second day after this, he was again ahead, and, the same question being asked him, he said: "Twas but a slough." When the party came to it, they found it a rushing torrent, and, in crossing, a pack horse and his load were swept away, but the name of Slough Creek remains.'

THE BUFFALO RANCH (R), 11 *m.*, is a cluster of log cabins, sheds, and corrals (R) in a wide hay valley. On the surrounding hills and meadows, several hundred bison graze in winter. Hay crews harvest wild meadow grasses in late summer for winter feeding.

Ahead, broken grassy hills and pine ridges merge with dark barren mountains, capped with volcanic rock. There are pyramids, square platforms, and cones; their walls are terraced and deeply scored.

Here, near the head of the Absaroka Range, was the center of the volcanic activity that covered the Yellowstone area with rhyolite in an early Tertiary time. Only on the lower slopes has the lava rock pulverized enough to provide nourishment for mountain flora.

At 13.8 *m.* the highway veers northeast along Soda Butte Creek, which joins the Lamar River.

SODA BUTTE (R), an extinct geyser cone about 12 feet high, is gray and terraced, marked with scroll-shaped and circular scorings. Its white incrustations resemble caked baking soda.

At NORTHEAST ENTRANCE, 29 *m.*, in a blue spruce forest setting, are the park checking station and rest rooms. At 30 *m.* is the new community of SILVER GATE, Montana, and at 33 *m.*, the old mining town of COOKE, Montana.

TOWER FALLS RANGER STATION (L), 125.2 *m.*, is on the open valley floor, with pine-covered mountains rising behind it.

At 126.5 *m.* is a junction with an oiled road.

Left here to PETRIFIED TREE, 0.5 *m.*, on a barren slope that once was cloaked in a prehistoric forest. When the volcanoes buried the land, the heat was not intense enough to consume the trees; at least, it left many stumps standing upright. During ensuing centuries, siliceous waters percolated through the rock, destroying the fiber of the wood, and substituting its own solidifying materials, thus leaving stone images of the flora it destroyed.

Numerous stubs of such trees protruded from the hillside before souvenir hunters broke them into smaller pieces to carry away. The big stump that remains has been partially excavated and surrounded with a wrought-iron fence.

The highway climbs and dips and climbs again. Hills alternate with short canyons and wide views. The GALLATIN MOUNTAINS, at 133.6 *m.*, display a great patchwork of blue forest, gray rock, and white snow. Both the gray and the white are colored by the blue haze that hangs between them and the road.

At 135 *m.*, ELECTRIC PEAK thrusts its jagged cone above the forested hills.

The exquisite UNDINE FALLS are at 139.5 *m.*, where Lava Creek cascades down seven levels of a terraced lava formation (R). The steep slope of shale, gravel, and rubble (R), capped with a black vertical rock ledge, is Mount Everts. The Gardiner River below the road (L) is a silvery succession of foaming rapids.

In MAMMOTH HOT SPRINGS, 144.1 *m.*, the Grand Loop Drive is complete. Here also is the junction with the Gardiner (Montana) feeder road.

Right on this oil-surfaced road down a steep grade, cut from travertine and lime deposit, to the MAMMOTH AUTOMOBILE CAMP (R), an area metween 0.7 *m.* and 1.1 *m.* (*camp site, cabins, cafeteria, grocery, picture shop, rest room*).

The BOILING RIVER (R), 1.8 *m.*, enters the Gardiner River in a valley at the foot of Mount Everts. The stream does not boil, but gives off a mist of steam. It is deep and, for part of the distance to this point, flows underground.

The highway crosses the river, which here cascades between banks set with cedars, and winds southward around the base of MOUNT EVERTS (R) (7,900 alt.), named for Truman C. Everts, a member of the Washburn-Langford party, who was lost in this region for 37 days. At 2.3 *m.*, it crosses the Montana State Line and the 45th parallel, just halfway between the Equator and the North Pole.

EAGLE NEST ROCK (R), 3.8 *m.*, is a tall pinnacle rising above the edge of the canyon wall. On the rock, far out of reach, is an osprey's nest. The opposite wall of the canyon is marked with other pinnacles and with great clefts in the rock.

The Gardiner River, a tributary of the Yellowstone, is pine-fringed (R). The canyon widens to a valley at 4.3 *m.* and the road drops steeply, losing altitude at the rate of 200 feet per mile. Huge boulders on the bed of the gushing river (*good fishing*) are gray, black, brown, and red.

As the valley widens, grassy hills flank the road for about a mile. Pronghorn antelope feed in a field near by.

The road crosses the boundary of Yellowstone Park at Gardiner, Montana (5,313 alt.). The ENTRANCE, 5.4 *m.*, is roofed with a huge arch of reddish volcanic stone from a near-by outcrop. The arch was dedicated by Theodore Roosevelt, April 24, 1903, and bears the inscription: 'For the benefit and enjoyment of the people.'

PART IV

Appendices

Chronology

1743	The Verendryes and companions are first white men to sight the Big Horn Mountains in Wyoming.
1803	Louisiana Purchase (including present Wyoming) is completed.
1805	General James Wilkinson is appointed governor of region embracing Wyoming.
	Lewis and Clark employ Sacajawea as guide.
1806	John Colter comes to region (credited with being first native-born American to enter what is now Wyoming).
1807	Ezekiel Williams heads trapping party that enters Wyoming.
	John Colter is first white man to enter Tog-Wo-Tee.
1807–08	Edward Rose takes up permanent residence in Big Horn Basin (first American to do so).
1809	Many white trappers operate in what now is eastern Wyoming.
1811	Wilson Price Hunt's party, employed by John Jacob Astor, crosses Wyoming.
1812	Robert Stuart and companions returning from Astoria (it is believed) discover South Pass; build first cabin erected by whites in Wyoming.
1822	General William Ashley establishes trading post on the Yellowstone.
	Jim Bridger arrives with Ashley.
1824	Ashley party names Sweetwater River.
	South Pass is crossed by Ashley trappers, headed by Thomas Fitzpatrick and Jedediah Smith.
1825	Ashley and his men descend Green River (first white men to navigate that stream).
1826	General Ashley sells his trapping interests in Wyoming.
1827	First wheeled vehicle, a four-pounder cannon, crosses South Pass.
1828	The first of Wyoming posts, known as 'Portuguese Houses,' is established on Middle Fork of Powder River, 11 miles east of Kaycee.
1829	Smith, Jackson, and Sublette bring supplies to the rendezvous near the mouth of Popo Agie in wagons drawn by mules (first wagons ever brought to Wyoming).
1830	Kit Carson, noted scout, arrives.
1832	Captain B. L. E. Bonneville, with 110 men, 20 wagon loads of provisions, goods and ammunition, headed for Pierre's Hole,

takes first wagons through South Pass and establishes temporary fortification on tributary of Green River.

Bonneville records presence of oil in Popo Agie region of Wyoming.

1834   Fort William, later Fort John, and finally Fort Laramie, is established, first permanent trading post in Wyoming.

1835   Samuel Parker and Marcus Whitman are first missionaries to traverse Wyoming.

1836   Mrs. H. H. Spalding and Mrs. Marcus Whitman accompany their missionary husbands across Wyoming.

1838   Jim Baker joins American Fur Company; becomes noted scout and guide.

1840   Father P. J. De Smet celebrates first Mass in Wyoming on Green River.

1842   Fort Bridger established.

John C. Frémont leads an expedition to select sites for a line of military posts with a view to territorial acquisitions in the Far West.

Elijah White leads large party of missionaries and settlers across Wyoming to Oregon. Gold discovered near South Pass.

1843   Fort Bridger opened to trade.

Frémont's second expedition crosses Laramie Plains.

1845   Federal troops under Colonel Stephen W. Kearny march from Fort Leavenworth to Fort Laramie.

1846   President Polk approves an act to establish military posts along the Oregon Trail.

1847   Brigham Young leads first group of Mormons across Wyoming.

Mormons build a ferry across Platte River near Fort Caspar site.

1849   Fort Laramie is purchased by the United States for $4,000.

1851   Captain Howard Stansbury completes a reconnaissance for a railway route.

Steamboat 'El Paso' sails up the Platte River to Guernsey, first steamship on the Platte River in Wyoming.

1853   Party of Mormons form a settlement at old Fort Bridger.

1854   Grattan Massacre occurs near Fort Laramie.

1855   General W. S. Harney leads military expedition against the Sioux.

1856   Mormon 'hand-cart' exodus enters Wyoming, en route to Utah.

1857   Colonel A. S. Johnston's expedition marches across Wyoming against Mormons.

Mormons burn buildings at Fort Bridger and Fort Supply.

Camp Scott is established as winter quarters for Johnston's army. Jim Bridger leases Fort Bridger to the Government.

Lieutenant G. K. Warren explores Wyoming from Fort Laramie to the western slope of the Black Hills.

Coloniel E. V. Sumner leads troops against the Cheyenne.

1858–59   Russell, Majors, and Waddell transport more than 16,000,000 pounds of freight to Utah, passing through Wyoming on Oregon Trail.

1859 Central, Overland, California and Pike's Peak Express Company is established by Russell, Majors, and Waddell.

Fort Bridger becomes a Government military reservation.

1860 Pony Express riders cross Wyoming.

1861 Creighton completes transcontinental telegraph line across Wyoming.

1862 March. Ben Holladay takes over equipment of Russell, Majors, and Waddell.

Indians raid stage line and steal equipment.

July. Government mail route is changed from central Wyoming to southern part of State because of Indian depredations.

1863 Bozeman Road through Wyoming established.

A Mormon freights a cargo of soda to Salt Lake, the first known export of mineral from the territory.

Troops under General P. E. Connor sent to Wyoming to suppress Indians.

De Lacy prospecting expedition discovers Shoshone Lake.

1864 Indians wage war along Platte in Wyoming as a result of Sand Creek Massacre in Colorado.

1865 January 5. First proposal for temporary government for Territory of Wyoming is made by James M. Ashley, later governor of Montana Territory.

July. Platte Bridge Fight.

1866 Forts Reno and Phil Kearny are built along the Bozeman Trail. Fetterman Massacre occurs.

Fort Sanders is built on Laramie Plains.

1867 January 9. Laramie County is created by Dakota Legislature, and on December 27, Carter County.

Union Pacific builds into Wyoming.

Fort Fetterman is established.

Town of Cheyenne is founded.

Wagon Box Fight takes place in the Big Horns.

Fort D. A. Russell (now Fort F. E. Warren) is established.

Carissa lode is discovered at South Pass.

1868 Peace Commission signs treaties with Sioux, Crow, and Arapaho at Fort Laramie; with Bannock and Eastern Shoshone at Fort Bridger. Shoshone Reservation established.

July 25. Territory of Wyoming is created by Congress.

Camp Augur is established (later called Camp Brown, then changed in 1878 to Fort Washakie).

Fort Fred Steele is established.

Albany and Carter Counties are organized.

Episcopal church builds first church building in Wyoming at Cheyenne.

1869 April 15. J. A. Campbell inaugurated as first governor of Wyoming.

Cheyenne designated as territorial capital.

October 12. First territorial legislature convenes.

December 10. Act granting suffrage to women is approved (the first in United States).

Union Pacific Railway is completed across territory.

Act is passed prohibiting intermarriage of whites and Negroes.

Carter County is changed to Sweeetwater County.

Uinta County is organized.

1870   Population (U. S. Census), 9,118.

First homestead entry is perfected in the territory.

Women serve on grand and petit juries at Laramie.

Mrs. Esther M. Morris, of South Pass, is appointed first woman justice of the peace.

Washburn and Doane Expedition explores Yellowstone National Park region.

1871   Legislature passes Militia Act; three militia districts created.

1872   'Yellowstone Wonderland' is established as first national park.

State Penitentiary is built at Laramie; destroyed by fire soon after; partially rebuilt in 1873.

1873   Wyoming Stock Growers Association organizes.

1876   Cheyenne and Black Hills stage line is launched.

Custer leads expedition in northern Wyoming.

Custer Massacre occurs in Montana.

1877   Arapaho are moved to Shoshone Reservation for temporary quarters (have remained there ever since).

1879   Lotteries and games of chance are outlawed by legislation.

1880   Population, 20,789.

1883   Cheyenne completes incandescent lighting system.

1884   Fremont County is organized.

1885   Anti-Chinese 'Riot' in Rock Springs.

1886   Governor Warren approves act providing for capitol building.

Commission is appointed to build capitol and State university.

Legislature provides for construction of Institution for Deaf, Dumb and Blind at Cheyenne.

Severe winter kills thousands of cattle.

Fremont and Elkhorn Valley Railroad builds branch to Douglas called Wyoming and Central.

1887   Corner stone of capitol building is laid at Cheyenne.

September 6. University of Wyoming opens at Laramie.

Crook and Pease (Johnson) Counties are organized.

1888   400 Mormon families move into Big Horn Basin.

Wyoming National Guard is established.

Legislature appropriates funds for penitentiary at Rawlins.

Converse, Natrona, and Sheridan Counties are created.

1889   November. Wyoming adopts State constitution.

1890   Population, 62,553.

July 10. Wyoming is admitted into the Union as the forty-fourth State.

October 14. Francis E. Warren (last territorial governor) is inaugurated as governor of State.

First Wyoming congressmen are elected: Joseph M. Carey (last delegate) and Francis E. Warren, U. S. senators; Clarence D. Clark, representative-at-large.

Big Horn and Weston Counties are created.

First oil well is brought in by Pennsylvania Oil and Gas Company in the Shannon field of the Salt Creek district.

1891 President Harrison establishes Yellowstone Timber Land Reserve, first in the United States.

1892 Johnson County Cattle War.

1895 Oil refinery is built at Casper.

Dupont Powder Company begins development of soda deposits in Wyoming.

1896 Hot Springs is purchased from Shoshone Indians.

1897 First Cheyenne Frontier Day is celebrated.

1898 New penitentiary is completed at Rawlins.

Legislature enacts law taxing migratory stock from adjoining States.

1899 U.P. mail train is robbed of $60,000 in unsigned bank notes at Wilcox.

1900 Population, 92,531.

1901 Stinking Water River is renamed Shoshone by the legislature.

1903 Tom Horn is hanged in Cheyenne.

1905 Governor's Mansion is ready for occupancy.

State Fair is established at Douglas.

1906 Riverton townsite is thrown open to settlers.

First auto accident in Wyoming occurs.

Devil's Tower National Monument is established.

1909 Pathfinder Dam is completed.

Park County is organized.

1910 Population, 145,965.

Willis Van Devanter of Wyoming is appointed associate justice of the U. S. Supreme Court.

Colonel Theodore Roosevelt visits Cheyenne Frontier Days Celebration.

1911 Campbell, Goshen, Hot Springs, Lincoln, Niobrara, Platte, and Washakie Counties are organized.

1913 First automobile license in Wyoming is issued to J. M. Schwoob.

A wolf is trained to carry mail over deep snows.

1915 Workmen's Compensation Law is enacted.

1916 Non-partisan Judiciary Law is passed.

'Bill' Carlisle robs U.P. train.

Sunrise is made model town by Colorado Fuel & Iron Company.

Homestead tax exemption is increased to $2,500.

1917 Buffalo Bill dies in Denver.

State Flower and State Flag are adopted by legislature.

The State highway department is created.

Jim Baker's cabin is moved to Cheyenne.

Wyoming male citizens register for World War draft.

1918   Wyoming purchases $10,000,000 worth of Liberty bonds.
State votes for prohibition three to one.

1919   All Wyoming breweries suspend operations during national emergency.
President Wilson makes several stops in Wyoming.
'Bill' Carlisle, train bandit, escapes from penitentiary.

1920   Population, 194,531.
Transcontinental air mail planes are launched.
Night air mail flying is inaugurated across Wyoming.

1921   Great oil well roars in at the Teapot Dome.
Prize fighting is legalized in Wyoming.
Teton and Sublette Counties are organized.

1922   Union Pacific stores six months' supply of coal along tracks as a precautionary measure in strike situation.

1923   Governor William B. Ross dies in office.
Frances Warren Pershing Memorial Hospital is dedicated in Cheyenne.
99 coal miners die in explosion at Kemmerer mine.

1924   Senator Francis E. Warren obtains $3,000,000 appropriation for aid in night flying service.
State receives $1,700,000 from oil royalties, for schools.
Nellie Tayloe Ross made governor, first woman to hold such office in the United States. (In 1933 she is appointed Director of the United States Mint, first woman to hold that office.)

1925   Teapot Dome oil case is tried before Judge Kennedy at Cheyenne; decision upholds Sinclair lease.
3,500,000 pounds of honey are produced in Wyoming.
New Douglas airplane makes first flight across the State.
Gros Ventre River is dammed by huge slide.
State legislature votes ratification of the Colorado River Compact.

1926   John E. Higgins wills entire estate of $500,000 to Wyoming.
Queen Marie of Roumania visits Wyoming.

1927   Wyoming aeronautics law is passed.
Gros Ventre dam breaks and wipes out town of Kelley.

1929   Senator Francis E. Warren dies; served as U. S. senator 1890–93; 1895–1929.
Honorable Patrick J. Sullivan is appointed to fill unexpired term as U. S. Senator, on December 5.
Grand Teton National Park is established.

1930   Population, 225,565.
Fort D. A. Russell is officially renamed Fort Francis E. Warren.
6,000 people stage outdoor celebration at Independence Rock.

1931   Governor Frank Emerson dies in office.
Wyoming Air Service officials fly to Sheridan from Casper with passengers and mail.

1933   Allocation of $22,700,000 is made for Casper-Alcova Reclamation Project.
New Federal Building is completed in Cheyenne.

Senator John B. Kendrick dies in office. Hon. Joseph C. O'Mahoney, assistant U. S. postmaster general, is designated U. S. senator on December 18 for remainder of term; elected 1934 for full term ending 1941.

1934   Wyoming Air Service begins air mail route between Cheyenne, Wyoming, and Billings, Montana.

Democrats win every State elective office and majority of seats of State legislature.

1935   Lethal gas made official method of capital punishment.

A 2 per cent sales tax is put in effect.

Wyoming Democratic regime takes over entire State government for first time.

State liquor commission created; State becomes a wholesaler of intoxicating liquors, not including beer.

60-day divorce law is enacted.

December 10 is designated as Wyoming Day, commemorating Governor John A. Campbell's signing of the act granting women in Wyoming Territory the right of suffrage.

1936   Aeronautical Commission is created.

Terms of county elective officers are lengthened to 4 years.

Columbus Day, October 12, is made a public holiday by legislature.

Wyoming home for dependent children completed in Casper.

General John Pershing visits Cheyenne.

Old Cheyenne Club, landmark, is demolished.

President Franklin D. Roosevelt visits Wyoming three times during the summer.

Dr. Grace Raymond Hebard, eminent historian, dies.

Harry H. Schwartz is elected U. S. senator for term ending 1943.

1937   New Supreme Court and Library Building are dedicated.

Justice Willis Van Devanter resigns from the United States Supreme Court.

Ex-Senator Robert D. Carey dies.

Social Security and Unemployment Insurance laws are enacted.

Old Fort Laramie is purchased by Wyoming Landmark Commission.

University of Wyoming holds Semi-Centennial Celebration.

A United Airlines passenger plane crashes in Wasatch Mountains with 19 aboard.

1938   Fort Laramie is taken over by Federal Government and made 74th National Monument.

Alcova Dam is completed.

Republicans gain political control of State government by electing three out of five State officials and a majority of legislators.

Final judgment of $6,364,677, less costs of suit and all of the Government's non-treaty expenditures for the Shoshone since 1868, is granted to Shoshone Tribe in satisfaction of claims brought against Federal Government for the value of land in the Shoshone Reservation occupied by the Arapaho for 60 years. This decision clears title to 2,343,540 acres of Wyoming land; gives legal status to homes of more than 1,000 Arapaho; and brings to the Shoshone about $4,000,000.

1939   Earl Durand, 26, kills four peace officers in northern Wyoming and attracts nationwide attention as the 'Tarzan of the Tetons.'

Bibliography

GENERAL INFORMATION

Fuller, Robert P., comp. and ed. *Wonderful Wyoming, the Undeveloped Empire.* Cheyenne, 1911. 128 p., illus. (Wyoming. Department of Immigration.)

Greenburg, Dan W., comp. and ed. *Book of the Governors.* Cheyenne, 1926. 62 p., illus. (Illustrations and text describing Wyoming; prepared as souvenir for 1926 Governors' Convention in Cheyenne.)

Wyoming. Department of Commerce and Industry. *Wyoming Worth Knowing.* Casper, S. E. Boyer and Co., 1928. 32 p., illus.

————*Wonderful Wyoming.* Cheyenne, 1937. 32 p., illus. Tabloid.

DESCRIPTION AND TRAVEL

Crofutt, George A. *Transcontinental Tourists' Guide.* Chicago, The Overland Publishing Co., 1871. 3rd ed. 322 p., illus.

Johnson, Clifton. 'Wyoming Days.' (In his *Highways and Byways of the Rocky Mountains.* New York, Macmillan, 1910. p. 177–93.)

Mullan, John, comp. *Miners' and Travelers' Guide to Oregon, Washington, Idaho, Montana, Wyoming, and Colorado.* New York, W. M. Franklin, 1865. 153 p., map.

Parkman, Francis. *The Oregon Trail.* New York, Macmillan, 1930. (The Modern Reader's Series.) (First pub. as *The California and Oregon Trail,* 1849.) 369 p.

Strahorn, Mrs. Carrie Adell. *Fifteen Thousand Miles by Stage.* New York, G. P. Putnam's Sons, 1911. 673 p., illus. (Experiences during 30 years of path-finding and pioneering in the West.)

Strahorn, Robert E. *The Hand-Book of Wyoming and Guide to the Black Hills and Big Horn Regions.* Cheyenne (Chicago, Knight & Leonard, printers), 1877. 249 p., illus.

Thwaites, Reuben G., ed. *Early Western Travels, 1748–1846.* Cleveland, Arthur H. Clark Co., 1904–7. 32 vols., pl., maps. See index, Vol. 32, under Shoshone (Snake) Indians and Wyoming (State).

Tidball, Lewis C. *Geography of Wyoming.* Laramie, State School Supply, 1927. 82 p., illus.

Triggs, J. H. *A Reliable and Correct Guide to the Black Hills, Powder River, and Big Horn Gold Fields.* Omaha, Herald Printing House, 1876. 144 p., map.

Ware, Joseph E. *The Emigrants' Guide to California*. Princeton, Princeton University Press, 1932. 63 p., illus., map. Repr. from 1849 ed., with introduction and notes by John Caughey.

Wislizenus, Dr. F. A. *A Journey to the Rocky Mountains in* 1839. St. Louis, Missouri Historical Society, 1912. Tr. from the German with a biographical note by F. A. Wislizenus. 162 p., maps, 1 pl.

GEOLOGY AND PALEONTOLOGY

Bell, Howard W. 'Fossil-hunting in Wyoming.' Cosmopolitan, Jan. 1900, Vol. 28: 265–75.

Knight, Samuel H. *The Fountain and the Casper Formations of the Laramie Basin*. Laramie, University of Wyoming, 1929. 82 p., illus., maps, bibliog. (University of Wyoming Publications in Science. Geology. Vol. 1. No. 1. July 1, 1929.)

Wyoming. *Geological Survey. Bulletins*. Cheyenne, 1911–34. 25 vols. Issued under the direction of the State Geologist.

PLANT AND ANIMAL LIFE

Cary, Merritt. *Life Zone Investigations in Wyoming*. Washington, Gov. Print. Off., 1917. 95 p. (U. S. Dept. of Agriculture, Bureau of Biological Survey. North American Fauna no. 42.)

Clements, Edith Gertrude. *Flowers of Mountian and Plain*. New York, The H. W. Wilson Co., 1926. 3rd ed. 79 p., illus.

McCreary, Otto. *Wyoming Bird Life*. Minneapolis, Burgess Co., 1937. 133 p. Mimeoprint.

Nelson, Aven. *New Manual of Botany of the Central Rocky Mountains*. New York. The American Book Co., 1909. 646 p.

———*An Analytical Key to Some of the Common Flowering Plants of the Rocky Mountain Region*. New York, D. Appleton and Co., 1908. 94 p.

———*The Shrubs of Wyoming*. Laramie, 1902. 47 p. (Wyoming. Agricultural Experiment Station, Laramie. Bulletin no. 54.)

———*The Trees of Wyoming and How to Know Them*. Laramie, 1899. 110 p. (Wyoming. Agricultural Experiment Station, Laramie. Bulletin no. 40.)

NATURAL RESOURCES

Bartlett, Albert B. *The Mineral Hot Springs of Wyoming*. Cheyenne, 1926. 15 p. (The State of Wyoming. Geologist's Office. Bulletin no. 19.)

Dietz, Christian S. *The Developed and Undeveloped Mineral Resources of Wyoming*. Cheyenne, Wyoming Geological Survey (Sheridan, The Mills Co., printers), 1929. 194 p. (Bulletin XXI.)

Fisher, G. A. 'Bentonite Deposits of Wyoming.' (In U. S. Geological Survey, *Bulletin,* 1905, no. 260: 559–63.)

Follansbee, Robert. *Surface Waters of Wyoming and Their Utilization*. Washington, Govt. Print. Off., 1923. 329 p., maps. (U. S. Geological

Survey. Water Supply Paper 469.) Prepared in co-operation with the State of Wyoming.

Henderson, Charles W. 'Gold, Silver, Copper, and Lead in Wyoming.' In U. S. Bureau of Mines, *Minerals Yearbook,* 1935. p. 357–60.

Jamieson, C. E. *Mineral Resources of Wyoming and the Mining Laws of the State and of the United States.* Cheyenne, Wyo., The S. A. Bristol Co., 1911. 102 p. (Wyoming. State Geologist. Bulletin 1, Series B.)

Knight, Samuel H. *The Saline Lake Deposits of Wyoming.* 1. The Downey Lakes, Albany County, Wyoming, (Laramie) University of Wyoming, 1934. 6 numb. (Wyoming. Geological Survey. Report of Investigations No. 1) Mimeographed.

Knight, W. C. 'Gypsum Deposits in Wyoming.' (In U. S. Geological Survey. *Bulletin,* 1904, no. 223: 79–85.)

————'The Petroleum Fields of Wyoming.' *Engineering and Mining Journal,* Sept. 21, Nov. 15, 1901, Vol. 72: 348–59; 628–30. Discusses early history.

Winter, Charles E. *Four Hundred Million Acres. The Public Lands and Resources.* Laramie. Overland Pub. Co., 1932. 349 p., illus.

'Wyoming Coal Fields.' *Scientific American Supplement,* May 30, 1908. Vol. 65: 345.

ARCHAEOLOGY AND INDIANS

'Archaeological Work in Wyoming.' *Scientific American,* Dec. 14, 1907, n.s. Vol. 97: 438–9.

Coolidge, Grace. *Tepee Neighbors.* Boston, Four Seas Publishing Co., 1917. 325 p.

Dodge, Richard I., Col. *Our Wild Indians.* Hartford, Conn. A. D. Worthington and Co., 1882. 653 p.

Dorsey, George A. *An Aboriginal Quartzite Quarry in Eastern Wyoming.* Chicago, 1900. (In Field Columbian Museum. Publication 51. Anthropological Series, Vol. 11, no. 4: 233–43.)

Gilder, Robert F. 'Indian Sites Near Frederick, Wyoming.' *Records of the Past,* July 1908, Vol. 7: 179–82.

Grinnell, George Bird. *The Fighting Cheyennes.* New York, Scribner, 1915. 431 p., maps.

Hebard, Grace Raymond. *Sacajawea, A Guide and Interpreter of the Lewis and Clark Expedition, With an Account of the Travels of Toussaint Charbonneau, and of Jean Baptiste, the Expedition Papoose.* Glendale, Calif., Arthur H. Clark Co., 1933. 340 p.

————*Washakie; An Account of Indian Resistance of the Covered Wagon and Union Pacific Invasions of Their Territory.* Cleveland, Arthur H. Clark Co., 1930. 337 p.

Keith, Marshall C. *The Story of Chief Washakie, an Indian Odyssey.* Caldwell, Caxton Printers, Ltd., 1935. 218 p.

Mokler, Alfred J. *Transition of the West; Portrayal of the Indian Problem in the West and the Trials of the Pioneers Who Reclaimed This Coun-*

try from Savagery to Civilization. Chicago, R. R. Donnelly & Sons Co., 1927. 228 p.

Olden, Sarah Emilia. *Shoshone Folklore, as Discovered from the Rev. John Roberts, A Hidden Hero, On the Wind River Indian Reservation in Wyoming.* Milwaukee, Wisc., Morehouse Pub. Co., 1923. 97 p.

Renaud, Etienne B. *Archaeological Survey of Eastern Wyoming, Summer 1931.* Denver, University of Denver, Department of Anthropology, 1932. 91 p., illus.

———*The Archaeological Survey of the High Western Plains, Summer 1935.* Denver, University of Denver, Department of Anthropology, 1936. Seventh Report: Southern Wyoming and S-W. South Dakota. Part I, 21 p., 2 pl. p. 1–16 on Wyoming. Eighth Report: Pictographs and Petroglyphs of the High Western Plains. 47 p., Ch. 11, p. 9–20 on Wyoming.

HISTORY AND GOVERNMENT

Alter, J. Cecil. *James Bridger, Trapper, Frontiersman, Scout and Guide.* Salt Lake City, Shepard Book Co., 1925. 546 p., illus.

Bancroft, Hubert Howe. 'History of Wyoming.' (In his *History of the Pacific States of North America. Nevada, Colorado, and Wyoming.* 1540–1889. San Francisco, The History Co., 1890. Vol. xx: 659–806. Also pub. as Vol. xxv. of his *Works* and separately.)

Bartlett, I. S., ed. *History of Wyoming.* Chicago, S. J. Clarke Pub. Co., 1918. 3 vols.

Beard, Mrs. Frances (Birkhead), ed. *Wyoming from Territorial Days to the Present.* Chicago and New York, American Historical Society, 1933. 3 vols., 1700 p.

Bonner, T. D. *Life and Adventures of James P. Beckwourth.* New York, Harper and Brothers, 1856. 537 p. Written from his own dictation.

Brooks, Bryant B. *Memoirs of Bryant B. Brooks. Cowboy, Trapper, Lumberman, Stockman, Oilman, Banker, and Governor of Wyoming.* Glendale, Cal. Arthur H. Clark Co., 1939. 370 p., illus.

Carrington, Frances (Courtney). *My Army Life and the Fort Phil. Kearney Massacre.* Philadelphia and London, J. B. Lippincott Co., 1910. 317 p., illus., maps.

Chittenden, Hiram M. *The American Fur Trade of the Far West; A History of Pioneer Trading Posts and Early Fur Companies of the Missouri Valley and Rocky Mountains and of the Overland Commerce with Santa Fe.* New York, Rufus Rockwell Wilson, Inc., 1936. 2 vols., 1014 p., bibliog.

Chittenden, Hiram M., and Alfred T. Richardson. *Life, Letters and Travels of Father Pierre Jean De Smet.* New York, F. P. Harper, 1906. 4 vols.

Cody, Mrs. Louisa (Frederici). *Memories of Buffalo Bill,* by his wife Louisa F. Cody, in collaboration with Courtney R. Cooper. New York, D. Appleton & Co., 1919. 325 p.

Coutant, C. G. *The History of Wyoming from the Earliest Known Discoveries.* Laramie, Chaplin, Spafford & Mathison, 1899. 712 p., illus.

Coyner, David H. *The Lost Trappers; A Collection of Scenes and Events in the Rocky Mountains, with a Short Description of California; Also Some Account of the Fur Trade, Especially as Carried on About the Sources of the Waters of the Columbia, Missouri, and Yellowstone in the Rocky Mountains.* New York, Hurst & Co., 1847. 255 p.

Dale, Harrison C., ed. *The Ashley-Smith Explorations and the Discovery of a Central Route to the Pacific,* 1822–1829. Cleveland, Arthur H. Clark Co., 1918. 352 p., illus.

David, Robert B. *Malcolm Campbell, Sheriff; the Reminiscences of the Greatest Frontier Sheriff in the History of the Platte Valley, and of the Famous Johnson County Invasion of* 1892. Casper, Wyo., Wyomingana, Inc., 1932. 361 p., illus., maps.

Driggs, B. W. *History of Teton Valley.* Caldwell, Idaho, Caxton Printers, 1926. 227 p.

Frémont, John C. *Memoirs of My Life.* Chicago, Belford, Clark & Co., 1887. Vol. 1, 655 p. Journal of Five Journeys of Western Exploration.

Guernsey, Charles. *Wyoming Cowboy Days.* New York, G. P. Putnam's Sons, 1936. 288 p., illus.

Hafen, LeRoy R., and William J. Ghent. *Broken Hand, Chief of the Mountain Men.* Denver, Old West Publishing Co., 1931. 316 p. The life story of Thomas Fitzpatrick.

Hafen, LeRoy R., and Francis Marion Young. *Fort Laramie and the Pageant of the West.* Glendale, Arthur H. Clark Co., 1938. 429 p., illus.

Hebard, Grace Raymond, and E. A. Brininstool. *The Bozeman Trail; Historical Accounts of the Blazing of the Overland Routes into the Northwest, and the Fights with Red Cloud's Warriors.* Cleveland, Arthur H. Clark Co., 1922. 2 vols., illus., maps.

Hebard, Grace Raymond. *Civics, State, National and Community, for Use in Wyoming Public Schools.* San Francisco, C. F. Weber & Co., 1928. 2nd ed. 201 p.

——'The First Woman Jury.' *Journal of American History,* 1913, Vol. 7: 1293–1341.

——*The History and Government of Wyoming.* San Francisco, C. F. Weber & Co., Inc., 1919. 8th ed. 285 p.

——*Pathbreakers from River to Ocean.* Chicago, Lakeside Press, 1911. 263 p.

Horn, Tom. *The Life of Tom Horn.* Denver, for J. C. Coble by the Louthan Book Co., 1904. 317 p., illus.

Inman, Henry, and Col. William F. Cody. *The Great Salt Lake Trail.* Topeka, Crane & Co., 1913. 529 p., illus.

Irving, Washington. *Adventures of Captain Bonneville, United States Army in the Rocky Mountains and the Far West.* Philadelphia, J. B. Lippincott & Co., 1872. 288 p.

Lindsay, Charles. *Big Horn Basin.* Lincoln, University of Nebraska Press, 1932. 274 p., bibliog.

Mercer, Asa A. *The Banditti of the Plains: or the Cattleman's Invasion of Wyoming in* 1892. San Francisco, Grabhorn Press, 1935. Reprint. 136 p., illus.

Mokler, Alfred J. *History of Natrona County, Wyoming,* 1888–1922; *True Portrayals of the Yesterdays of a New County and a Typical Frontier Town of the Middle West. Fortunes and Misfortunes, Tragedies and Comedies, Struggles and Triumphs of the Pioneers.* Chicago, R. R. Donnelly & Sons Co., 1922. 477 p., map, illus.

Mumey, Nolie. *Life of Jim Baker,* 1818–1898. Denver, World Press, 1931. 234 p.

Ross, Nellie (Tayloe). 'Governor Lady; Autobiography.' *Good Housekeeping.* Vol. 85, 1927: Aug., p. 30–31; Sept., p. 36–7; Oct., p. 72–3.

Sabin, Edwin. *Kit Carson Days.* New York, Press of the Pioneers, 1935. 399 p., illus. maps.

Simonin, Louis L., 'A French Picture of Cheyenne in 1867,' in *L'Ouest des États-Unis,* Paris, 1867. Translation by W. O. Clough, *Frontier Magazine,* Missoula, March 1930, Vol. 10: 240–43.

Spring, Agnes W. *Caspar Collins.* New York, Columbia University Press, 1927. 187 p., illus. The life and exploits of an Indian fighter of the sixties.

Stone, Elizabeth Arnold. *Uinta County, Its Place in History.* Laramie, Laramie Printing Company, 1924. 276 p.

Voorhees, Luke. *Personal Recollections of Pioneer Life.* Priv. pr., 1920. 76 p.

Walker, Tacetta. *Stories of Early Days in Wyoming.* Casper, Prairie Publishing Co., 1936. 271 p.

Wyoming Historical Society. *Collections of the Wyoming Historical Society,* comp. by Robert C. Morris. Vol. 1. Cheyenne, 1897. 352 p.

———*Miscellanies,* 1919, comp. and ed. by Agnes R. Wright. Laramie, Laramie Republican Co., printers, 1919. 54 p.

Wyoming. Historical Dept. *Annals* (This periodical has been published in 10 vols. titled consecutively: *Quarterly Bulletin,* 2 vols., 1923–4; *Annals,* Vols. 3–9, 1925–34; Vols. 10–11, 1938–9; *Annals and Eighth Biennial Report,* Vol. 10, No. 1, Jan. 1938.

COLLECTED BIOGRAPHIES

Bartlett, Ichabod S., ed. *History of Wyoming.* Chicago, S. J. Clarke Publishing Co., 1918. 3 vols., 1977 p. Vols. 2 and 3 contain short biographical sketches of Wyoming residents.

Beach, Mrs. Cora May (Brown), ed. *Women of Wyoming,* Including a Short History of Some of the Early Activities of Women of Our State, Together with Biographies of Those Women Who Were Our Early Pioneers as Well as of Women Who Have Been Prominent in Public Affairs and in Civil Organizations and Service Work. Casper, Wyo. (S. E. Boyer & Co., 1927–8) 2 vols.

Beard, Frances (Birkhead). *Wyoming from Territorial Days to the Present.* Chicago and New York, The American Historical Society, Inc., 1933. 3 vols. 1700 p. Vols. 2 and 3 comprise a series of Wyoming biographies written by a staff of writers and published under the editorial supervision of Mrs. Beard.

Progressive Men of the State of Wyoming. Chicago, A. W. Bowen & Co., 1903. 965 p.

AGRICULTURE AND RANCH LIFE

Adams, Andy. *Log of a Cowboy.* Boston and New York, Houghton Mifflin Co., 1927. 324 p., illus. Experiences of a man who followed a trail herd from Texas northward.

Briggs, Harold E. 'Development and Decline of Open Range Ranching in the Northwest.' *Mississippi Valley Historical Review.* March 1934, vol. 20: 521–36.

Bronson, Edgar. *Reminiscences of a Ranchman.* Chicago, A. C. McClurg & Co., 1910. Rev. ed. 369 p.

Burt, Maxwell Struthers. *Powder River.* Illus. by Ross Santee. New York, Farrar & Rinehart, 1938. 369 p. A gentleman rancher's commentary on the Powder River and the story of Wyoming's northern range.

——*The Diary of a Dude Wrangler.* New York, London, C. Scribner's Sons, 1924. 231 p.

Canton, Frank M. *Frontier Trails.* Ed. by Edward E. Dale. Boston, Houghton Mifflin Co., 1930. 237 p., illus.

Chapman, Arthur. 'Last War on the Cattle Range.' *Outing,* Sept. 1905, vol. 46: 668–75.

Clay, John. *My Life on the Range.* Chicago, Priv. pr. by R. R. Donnelly, 1924. 365 p., 2 pl., bibliog.

Dale, Edward E. *The Range Cattle Industry.* Norman, Univ. of Oklahoma Press, 1930. 216 p.

Deming, William C. *Roosevelt in the Bunk House and Other Sketches.* Laramie, Laramie Printing Co., 1927. 2nd ed. 80 p.

Greenburg, Dan W. *Sixty Years, A Brief Review. The Cattle Industry in Wyoming; Its Organization and Present Status and Data Concerning the Wyoming Stock Growers Association.* Cheyenne, Wyo., Wyoming Stock Growers Association, 1932. 73 p.

Hultz, Fred S., and John A. Hill. *Range Beef Production in the Seventeen Western States.* New York, J. Wiley & Sons, 1930. 206 p.

McCoy, Joseph G. *Historic Sketches of the Cattle Trade of the West and Southwest.* Washington, D. C., Rare Book Shop, 1932. 427 p., illus. Repr. from the ed. of 1874.

Osgood, Ernest S. *The Day of the Cattleman.* Minneapolis, Univ. of Minnesota Press, 1929. 283 p.

U. S. Department of Agriculture, Bureau of Agricultural Economics, and Wyoming State Department of Agriculture. *Wyoming Agricultural Statistics: Wyoming Worth Knowing. No.* 12. 1937. 84 p.

(*See* annual reports and miscellaneous publications of the State Department of Agriculture, Department of Commerce and Industry, Commissioner of Labor and Statistics, Commissioner of Public Lands and Farm Loans, State Livestock and Sanitary Board, State Inspector of Mines, Public Service Commission.)

TRANSPORTATION

Bradley, Glenn. *The Story of the Pony Express.* Chicago, A. C. McClurg & Co., 1914. 175 p.

Dodge, Grenville. *How We Built the Union Pacific Railway.* Washington, Govt. Print. Off., 1910. 136 p.

Driggs, Howard R. *The Pony Express Goes Through.* New York, Frederick A. Stokes Co., 1935. 208 p., illus.

Hafen, LeRoy R. *The Overland Mail,* 1849–1869. Cleveland, A. H. Clark Co., 1926. 361 p., illus., map.

Root, Frank A., and William E. Connelley. *Overland Stage to California.* Topeka, Frank A. Root and William E. Connelley, pub., 1901. 630 p., illus., map.

Sabin, Edwin L. *Building the Pacific Railway.* Philadelphia and London, J. B. Lippincott Co., 1919. 317 p.

EDUCATION AND RELIGION

Belknap, Helen Olive. *The Church on the Changing Frontier; A Study of the Homesteader and His Church.* New York, George H. Doran Co., 1933. 143 p. (Committee on Social and Religious Surveys. Unique Studies of Rural America. 9.) 'The four counties studied in this book are Beaverhead in Montana, Sheridan in Wyoming, Union in New Mexico and Hughes in South Dakota.'

Clough, Wilson O. *A History of the University of Wyoming,* 1887–1937. Laramie, Laramie Printing Co., 1937. 199 p.

Committee on the State of the Church Missionary District of Wyoming, comp. *The Episcopal Church in Wyoming.* Denver, Smith-Brooks Printing Co., 1938. 101 p., illus.

Dale, Harrison C. *A Sketch of the History of Education in Wyoming.* Cheyenne, 1916. 39 p. (Wyoming. Department of Public Instruction. Bulletin 2.) S. A. Bristol Co., pr.

Hebard, Grace Raymond. *Teaching Wyoming History by Counties.* Cheyenne. (Wyoming. Department of Education, Bulletin no. 9, Series B.) 1926. 63 p. Rev. ed.

McGovern, Patrick A. 'History of the Diocese of Cheyenne.' *St. Louis Catholic Historical Review,* Jan. 1923, Vol. 5: 5–13.

Rennard, Robert E. 'The Development of Secondary Education in Wyoming.' 15 p., tables. (A typewritten thesis, a copy of which is in the Wyoming State Library, Cheyenne.)

Talbot, Ethelbert, Bishop. *My People of the Plains.* New York and London, Harper & Bros., 1906. 264 p.

LITERATURE AND JOURNALISM

Chaplin, W. E. 'Bill Nye in Laramie.' (In Wyoming State Historian, *2nd Biennial Report.* Laramie, 1922, p. 142–58.)

Chaplin, W. E. 'Some of the Early Newspapers in Wyoming.' (In Wyoming Historical Society. *Miscellanies.* Laramie, 1919. p. 7–24.)

Hartung, Mrs. Martin B. 'Wyoming as a Literary Field.' (In Wyoming. State Historian, *1st Biennial Report,* 1920. Laramie, 1920. p. 166–71.)

McMurtrie, Douglas C. *Pioneer Printing in Wyoming.* Cheyenne, Priv. print., 1933. 16 p.

Nye, Frank Wilson. *Bill Nye: His Own Life Story.* New York, The Century Co., 1926. 412 p., illus.

ART AND MUSIC

Shipp, E. Richard. *Intermountain Folk: Songs of Their Days and Ways.* Casper, Casper Stationery Co., 1922. 113 p.

Wills, Olive. 'Artists of Wyoming.' *Annals* of Wyoming, Oct. 1932, Vol. 9: 688–704.

SPORTS AND RECREATION

Wyoming. Fish and Game Commission. *Wyoming Wild Life.* Cheyenne. Published monthly, 1936 to date.

——Department of Commerce and Industry. *Dude Ranches of Wyoming,* 1938. Cheyenne, 1938. 34 p.

POINTS OF INTEREST

(Cheyenne Chamber of Commerce.) *Fort Francis E. Warren, Wyoming,* 1930. Cheyenne, Wyoming Labor Journal Pub. Co., printers, 1930. 67 p., maps.

Edwards, Elsa (Spear). *Trailing the Campfires.* Sheridan, Sheridan Chapter Daughters of the American Revolution, 1935. 56 p. Sketches of historic sites in northern Wyoming and southern Montana.

Ellison, Robert S. *Independence Rock, the Great Record of the Desert.* Casper, Natrona County Historical Society, 1930. 41 p.

——*Fort Bridger, Wyoming; A Brief History Comprising Jim Bridger's Old Trading Post, Fort Bridger Becomes an Army Post, Fort Bridger as a Frontier Army Post.* Casper, The Historical Landmarks Commission of Wyoming. 1931. 58 p.

(See also Reports of The Historical Landmark Commission of Wyoming, Cheyenne.)

GRAND TETON NATIONAL PARK

Fryxell, Fritiof. *The Teton Peaks and Their Ascents.* Jenny Lake, Wyoming, Crandall Studios, 1932. 105 p., illus.

U. S. National Park Service. *Grand Teton National Park, Wyoming.* Washington, Govt. Print. Off., 1939. 31 p., illus., maps. A description of the history, natural setting, recreational facilities, and administration of Grand Teton National Park.

YELLOWSTONE NATIONAL PARK

Carpenter, Frank G. *Adventures in Geyserland.* Caldwell, Idaho, Caxton Printers, Ltd. 1935. 318 p., bibliog., notes, appendices. Repr. from *The Wonders of Geyserland* (1878).

Chittenden, Hiram M. *Yellowstone National Park, Historical and Descriptive.* Rev. by Eleanor Chittenden Cress and Isabelle F. Story. Stanford University, Stanford University Press; London, H. Milford, Oxford University Press, 1933. 286 p., illus.

Corthell, Mrs. Eleanor, and Mrs. John Hill. 'Family Trek to the Yellowstone.' *Independent.* June 29, 1905, Vol. 58: 1460–67. An entertaining account of a Wyoming pioneer mother who took her family to the Yellowstone Park in a covered wagon.

Haynes, Jack Ellis. *Haynes' New Guide: The Complete Handbook of Yellowstone National Park.* St. Paul, Haynes Picture Shops, 1936. 190 p., illus.

U. S. National Park Service. *Yellowstone National Park, Wyoming.* Washington, Govt. Print. Off., 1938. 37 p., illus., maps.

Vinton, Stallo. *John Colter, Discoverer of Yellowstone Park.* New York, Edward Eberstadt, 1926. 114 p., 1 pl. An account of his explorations in 1807 and of his further adventures.

BIBLIOGRAPHY

Bovee, Gladys G. *Bibliography and Index of Wyoming Geology, 1823–1916.* Cheyenne, Wyo. S. A. Bristol Co., 1918. p. 319–446. (Wyoming State Geologist. Bulletin 17.)

Clark, Arthur H., Co. *The United States: A Catalogue of Books Relating to the History of Its Various States, Counties and Cities and Territories; Arranged Alphabetically by States, and Offered for Sale at Reasonable Prices.* Cleveland, 1928. Wyoming: p. 358–61.

Wheeler, Eva Floy. 'A Bibliography of Wyoming Writers.' Laramie, University of Wyoming, 1939. (*University of Wyoming Publications.* Vol. 6, no. 2: p. 11–37.)

Wyoming. State Library. *Catalogue of the Miscellaneous Division of the Wyoming State Library.* Ed. Mrs. Clare E. Ausherman, Cheyenne, 1932. 824 p.

——*Supplement to the Catalogue of Books of the Miscellaneous Division of the Wyoming State Library, 1932–5.* Ed. Alice Lyman. Cheyenne, Wyoming Labor Journal Publishing Co., 1935. 138 p.

Glossary

In the days of the big cattle outfits in Wyoming and Montana, many of the cowboys came from Texas, over the famous Texas Trail, with the stock that formed the foundation of most of the Montana and Wyoming herds. It was natural that the language of the cowboys of Texas and the Southwest generally should become that of the cattlemen of the Northwest. It was a distinctive vernacular, at once picturesque and pungent.

This cowboy lingo is characterized by a simplicity, strength, and directness. Living in isolated groups, visiting rarely, shy and timid as the result of long days of solitude, the cowboys developed their own manner of speech. Cowboy words, phrases, and customs ultimately became community property, and many residents of Wyoming today use cowboy diction quite naturally.

Arbuckle	Adjective applied to a cowboy, implying that the boss must have got him by mail order with Arbuckle premium stamps.
Bad one	A mean horse.
Barefooted	Unshod (horse).
Bars	Gate made by posts with holes into which or through which rails (bars) are slid.
Bed down	To lie down for the night on the bed ground.
Bed ground	The place where livestock such as sheep or cattle are held for a halt on the trail or on the range.
Bed roll	The blankets and bedding owned by each cowpuncher; they are usually rolled up with a tarpaulin around them.
Beefing	Complaining.
Bend	To turn a stampede or a general movement of animals.
Bicycling	Holding one foot down or under surcingle, while 'scratching' with the spur on the other foot, and then alternating.
Big boss	The owner of a cattle outfit. His first lieutenant is called the 'right-hand man,' sometimes 'the top screw.'
Biscuit shooter	The cook.
Biting the dust	Being thrown from a horse.

Blow (verb)	To lose a stirrup while riding. Also to let a horse stop for breath in high altitudes.
Bogged down	Trapped in a swamp or bog. Sometimes used when a person is 'swamped' with work.
Bogging them in	Holding a tight spur in the animal's belly.
Bounce (verb)	To turn animals (*see* 'bend').
Brand	To stamp with a heated iron, die, or seal.
Branding chute	Narrow lane down which animals are driven for branding or dehorning.
Branding iron	Iron used to burn brands.
Broncho, bronco	Loosely, an untamed horse.
Bronc buster or *bronc peeler*	Person who breaks horses.
Broom-tail	A wild mare.
Buck	A dollar.
Buck (verb)	To pitch, in an effort to unseat rider.
Buck strap	Strap attached to fork of saddle by which rider may hold while riding a bucking horse, to lessen jolts.
Buckaroo	Cowboy or bronc buster.
Bucking rolls	Leather-covered swells attached to saddle to make the rider's seat more secure.
Bulldog	To throw a steer by gripping the neck and horns, or sometimes the upper lip, and twist his neck until he loses his balance and falls.
Bunch quitter	An animal which strays frequently.
Bunk	Built-in bed.
Bunkhouse	The place where the cowhands live.
Bust (verb)	To throw an animal by forefeet.
Cache (verb)	To hide.
Cantle-boarding	Riding loosely and hitting the cantle or back of saddle.
Cavvy	String of horses used in ranch work such as roundups.
Cayuse	Originally an Indian pony bred by the Cayuse Indians of Eastern Oregon; hence any broncho or inferior-breed horse raised on the range. Generally speaking, cayuse has a slightly more derogatory meaning than broncho, although the words are often used interchangeably.
Chaps	Short for *Chaparejos:* leggings worn by cowboys for warmth and protection when riding in brush.
Chinook	Warm wind named from the Chinook Indian.
Choke down	To subdue an animal by choking with rope.
Chuck wagon	Kitchen on wheels that follows the roundup.
Chute	Long narrow gateway through which stock can be driven singly and held for branding, etc.

Circle horse	One selected for his stamina to cover territory in roundup.
Clodhopper	A farmer.
Coffin nails	Cigarettes.
Coffin varnish	Liquor.
Community loop	Term for extra large loop used by a few cowboys.
Conchas	Metal ornaments adorning saddles, chaps, bridles, etc.
Corral	Enclosure in which stock is confined.
Coulee	Bed of a stream, even if dry, when deep and having inclined sides.
Cowboy (cowpuncher, cowhand)	Man who cares for range cattle.
Cowpolk (cowpoke)	Cowboy.
Crow-hopping	Mild bucking.
Cut-horse	Horse used to cut out animals from a herd.
Cut out	Separate an animal or a group from the main herd.
Dally (verb)	To 'take a dally' is to circle the rope around a post (snubbing post) or saddle horn in order to hold a roped animal.
Dewlap	A strip of hide cut and left hanging under an animal's neck, for identification purposes. (*See also* 'double under-bit,' 'over-bit,' 'under-bit,' 'swallow-fork,' 'wattle.')
Dip	Strong antiseptic to kill lice or scab on cattle or sheep.
Dog-fall (verb)	To throw a steer with feet under him.
Dogie (also *doughbelly*)	Motherless calf which trails behind the herd and causes no end of trouble.
Double under-bit	Two triangular cuts in under part of animal's ear for identification purposes.
Draw	A gully or ravine.
Drift (noun, verb)	Animals 'drift' in a storm away from their regular feed grounds.
Drift fence	Fence separating different ranges.
Dry creek	A dry stream bed.
Dry-gulch (verb)	To kill a man in a gulch either by stringing him up to a tree or shooting him.
Dude	Formerly a term applied to an Eastern novice. The term is now used as the general and comradely expression of greeting to the visitor, who is soon made to feel at home and a bonafide 'pardner' on expeditions of adventure or in the everyday routine of the ranch.
Dude ranch	A ranch where vacationists are entertained.
Dudine	Feminine of dude.

Duster	A hole drilled for oil that is unproductive or 'dry.'
Fan tail	A wild horse.
Fence rider	A man employed to ride along fences and to keep them in repair.
Foot (verb)	To throw an animal by the foot.
Forefoot (verb)	To rope an animal by the front feet in order to throw it for handling.
Gather (verb)	To collect stock.
Go over the range	To die.
Grabbin' the apple	Grabbing the horn of the saddle to hang on.
Graveyard stew	Milk toast.
Greaser	A Mexican.
Grubber (*grubbing loco*)	An animal that noses about the roots of the loco weed to eat them is said to be 'grubbing loco.'
Grubstake	To furnish food for a person for a definite time, or in a certain amount, usually for a prospecting venture.
Hackamore	A halter of rawhide, braided and snug-fitting.
Hair brand	A temporary brand made by burning or picking out the hair. If skilfully done, it looks like an old brand.
Half-shot	A term applied to a person who has been drinking.
Hay cribs	Log walls without a roof enclosing hay stacks.
Hay hand	Man employed during haying season on a ranch.
Haze (verb)	To ride at the side of an obstreperous broncho in an effort to keep the horse from running into a fence or some obstruction. Term used in breaking horses.
Hazer	An assistant to keep horses from the fences.
Heel (verb)	To rope cattle by the hind feet.
High roller	A high bucker.
Hit the hay	Go to bed.
Hobbled stirrups	Stirrups tied down to surcingle to aid rider in keeping his feet in them.
Hondo	Leather or metal loop at end of lariat.
Hoof (verb)	To walk.
Hog-tie	To tie the feet of a steer or horse or calf after it has been thrown.
Hold herd	To keep the herd from drifting.
Hold-up man	Man stationed at cross-roads, on hill, or at critical points to keep herd from leaving trail.
Hoodlum wagon	A second wagon used in the roundup for carrying the extra beds and bringing wood.

Horse wrangler	Man who brings in the horses each morning from the range or out of the night herd.
Hot rocks	Biscuits.
Jinglebob	To split the ear of a steer or cow to the head, letting the pieces flap.
Jingler	Man who takes care of cavvy.
Jug handle	Slit in loose hide under animal's throat sometimes made for identification.
Juice (verb)	To milk.
Lariat	Rope (also called 'string').
Latigo	A strap for lacing saddle on.
Layout	A ranch outfit.
Lead poisoning	Term applied to describe the condition of a person who has been shot.
Line	Before the day of fences, an imaginary line separated the ranches or holdings of cattle outfits.
Line rider	Man employed to ride and repair fences. In the days of the open range, men rode an imaginary line and turned their cattle back from it.
Loco	Mad, cracklebrained.
Makin' a hand	Learning to become a full-fledged cowpuncher.
Makings	Tobacco for filling a cigarette paper.
Man-killer	A vicious horse that will kick, strike, and bite.
Martin-gale (*gills*)	A strap from bridle to surcingle, between forelegs, for control of head of horse.
Maverick	An unbranded calf or critter (derived from family name of Samuel Maverick of Texas).
Mess house	Place where cowhands eat.
Moocher	An animal, usually a pet, which hangs around dooryard and barnyard, eating anything it finds.
Moon-eyed	A horse with white, glassy eye or eyes.
Neck (verb)	To tie an unruly cow, or one with roving proclivities, to the neck of a more tractable animal.
Nester	A man who squats on land and fences it in.
Nice kitty	A skunk.
Nighthawk	Cowboy on duty at night.
Oklahoma rain	Sandstorm.
Old man (or *corporal*)	A ranch owner.
Old woman	A wife.
Open range	The range that is not fenced in.
Open winter	A mild winter with the range free of snow.
Outfit	Applied to a ranch, may mean the entire ranch organization. Also means cowboy equipment. There may be several outfits employed in different work at one ranch.

Outlaw	A horse that cannot be broken.
Over-bit	A semicircular cut in upper part of animal's ear for identification.
Pack horse	Horse trained to carry a pack.
Pack saddle	Framework especially designed for pack animals.
Pegging	Holding one horn of steer in the ground to hold him down.
Pilgrim	A newcomer.
Pinto	A spotted pony.
Poison	Liquor.
Plumb locoed	Quite crazy.
Pound leather	To ride.
Prairie lawyers	Coyotes.
Prairie schooner	Covered wagon.
Prayer book	The book of cigarette papers.
Prod pole	A short sharp stick used in handling cattle.
Pronto	At once.
Pulling leather	Holding on to saddle with the hands.
Rake	To scratch a horse with spurs, or drag the spurs along his neck, to make him buck.
Red-eyed	Mad.
Remuda	A term applied to all of the horses in a particular outfit. Sp. Exchange. *Remuda de caballos,* relay of horses.
Ride the grub line	To visit at various ranches to gain free food and lodging.
Ride herd	To ride after the cattle.
Rider	One who rides herd.
Rig	Saddle.
Right-hand man	Chief foreman of a cattle outfit.
Rodeo	A Western celebration, featuring bucking, roping, and bulldogging.
Rocky Mountain canary	A burro.
Roll in	To go to bed.
Rope horse	Animal good for roping activities.
Rope in	To take in; to trick.
Rope shy	Animal that jumps away from the rope when rider is roping.
Roundup	The gathering of the herd.
Roustabout	A man of all work about a camp.
Running iron	Ring or bar, or even piece of wire, or tool used for branding in emergency.
Rustle	To steal cattle.
Salty	Mean, applied to a horse.
Savvy (verb)	To understand.
Sawbones	A doctor.

Scratching	Scratching a horse with spurs while the animal is bucking.
Seam squirrels	Cooties.
Seeing daylight	Said of rider who bounces high in saddle, showing light between rider and saddle.
Shindig	Dance.
Skin mules	To drive mules.
Sky pilot	Preacher.
Slick	Unbranded.
Slug or *slough*	A large amount.
Slow elk	A cow that is stolen and butchered and the meat eaten or sold.
Smooth	Unshod.
Snake juice	Liquor.
Snubbing post	Post around which cowboy takes a 'dally weltie' or hitch to hold animal. Usually in a corral between center and fence.
Soft	A term applied to a horse that tires easily.
Sop	Gravy.
Sougan	Originally small blanket of thick weave, used to keep out rain or cold. With coming of tarpaulin, the word came to mean any cheap or old worn blanket used on the trail.
Sow belly	Salt pork.
Spurs	A part of equipment worn by cowboys, strapped over the boots and used to prod the pony in the side.
Squeezer or *snappin' turtle*	A chute for branding.
Steer-busting	Roping and throwing a steer.
Strays	Estray cattle.
String	Horses assigned each rider.
Sunfisher	A horse that darts from one side to another when bucking, giving the effect of switching ends.
Swallow-fork	A V-shape cut from ear for identification purposes.
Tail (verb)	To throw a calf after the rope has dragged the animal near the branding fire.
Tail-up	To pull a cow from a mudhole by the tail.
Talk turkey	To mean business.
Tarp	A tarpaulin; a large piece of canvas.
Tender	Said of a horse when he shows signs of getting saddle or harness sores or sore feet.
Tenderfoot	A newcomer. One not acquainted with cowboy habits and skills.
Ten-gallon hat	Designation of type of headgear originated by a Cheyenne merchant.

Tie-down	A strap to hold down the head of a horse that habitually carries head so high he might fall into a hole without seeing it.
Tight legging	Gripping legs tightly against horse.
Top hand	A good all-round cowhand.
Trail (verb)	To follow a herd of cattle; to drive a herd of horses on any dim path or road. To 'hit the trail' is start on a journey.
Trail boss	The boss of a herd on the trail.
Turn-out time	Time in the spring to turn cattle out to grass.
Two bits	Twenty-five cents.
Under-bit	Angular cut in under part of ear for identification purposes.
Vamoose	To move along.
W (*to put W on a horse*)	A form of hobble on a bad horse.
Wattle	A dewlap which forms a bunch instead of a string. Made for identification.
Waddy	In the fall and spring when some ranchers were short-handed, they took on anyone who was able to ride a horse and used him for a day or so; hence the word 'waddy,' derived from wadding—anything to fill in.
War bag or *poke*	Usually a canvas sack or tarpaulin used for carrying a cowboy's clothing and possessions.
Wild bunch	Horses not handled enough to be controllable.
Winter horse	A sturdy horse kept ready in winter and grained for heavy work.
Work a brand over	To change a brand.
Worked	An expression applied to calves following their mothers in a herd branded and marked with the brands of the owners; or to calves that are cut into groups either for the purpose of sale or for further identification.
Wrangler	One who herds horses.
Wrangling	Rounding up and corralling.
Yamping	Ordinary stealing.

1940
Census Figures

(The following are final figures of all incorporated cities, towns, and villages)

	Population			Population	
	1940	*1930*		*1940*	*1930*
(of 10,000 or more)			Cowley	491	526
			Dayton	240	348
Casper	17,964	16,619	Deaver	111	85
Cheyenne	22,474	17,361	Diamondville	586	812
Laramie	10,627	8,609	Dixon	94	145
Sheridan	10,529	8,536	Douglas	2,205	1,917
			Dubois	412	177
(of 2,500 to 10,000)			Edgerton	232	269
Cody	2,536	1,800	Elk Mountain	107	54
Evanston	3,605	3,075	Elmo	134	68
Green River	2,640	2,589	Encampment	331	209
Lander	2,594	1,826	Evansville	206	174
Rawlins	5,531	4,868	Fort Laramie	311	245
Riverton	2,540	1,608	Gillette	2,177	1,340
Rock Springs	9,827	8,440	Glendo	162	201
Worland	2,710	1,461	Glenrock	1,014	819
			Granger	163	135
(under 2,500)			Greybull	1,828	1,806
Afton	1,211	807	Guernsey	603	656
Albin	160	. . .	Gunn	36	2
Baggs	221	192	Hanna	1,127	. . .
Basin	1,099	903	Hartville	179	189
Big Piney	241	184	Hudson	330	328
Buffalo	2,302	1,749	Jackson	1,046	533
Burns	253	216	Kaycee	210	161
Byron	388	250	Kemmerer	2,026	1,884
Chugwater	245	286	Kirby	107	173
Clearmont	215	214	La Grange	211	. . .
Cokeville	452	431	Lingle	428	415

CITY OR TOWN (*Cont.*)

	Population 1940	Population 1930		Population 1940	Population 1930
(Under 2,500—Cont.)			Powell	1,948	1,156
			Quealy	150	. . .
Lost Cabin	34	34	Ranchester	189	155
Lost Spring	38	65	Riverside	68	34
Lovell	2,175	1,857	Rock River	349	260
Lusk	1,814	1,218	Saratoga	810	567
Lyman	378	377	Shoshoni	226	263
Manderson	130	96	South Superior	885	751
Manville	240	201	Sundance	685	369
Marbleton	43	26	Superior	1,240	1,156
Medicine Bow	338	264	Ten Sleep	345	. . .
Meeteetse	373	296	Thermopolis	2,422	2,129
Mills	379	357	Torrington	2,344	1,811
Moorcroft	387	341	Upton	545	373
Newcastle	1,962	1,201	Van Tassell	82	99
Opal	78	. . .	Wamsutter	169	. . .
Parco	604	727	Wheatland	2,110	1,997
Pavillion	176	. . .	Yoder	201	266
Pine Bluffs	771	670			
Pinedale	647	219			

Index

Absaroka, 212, 277
Academy of the Holy Child Jesus, 110
Aderville, 249
Afton, 265, 396, 397
AGRICULTURE, 98-108
  Douglas vicinity, 12; Dry Farming, 75; First settlement in State, 264; Fort Laramie, 105; Goshen Hole, 12; Platte Valley, 11; Wheatland Flats, 11, 289
Ah-ho-appa (Falling Leaf), 299
Air disaster at Silver Crown, 251
Airfields
  Bitter Creek, 243; Leroy Emergency Landing Field, 264 (see also Casper, Cheyenne, Laramie, Sheridan)
Air service, 88
Aladdin, 374
Alamo, 333
Albany County, 198, 285
Alcova, 384, 385
Alcova-Casper (Kendrick) Project, 75
Allen, R. John, Sheriff, 179
Allen, Ross, Ranch, 218
Almond Stage Station, 244
Almy, 265
Alpine, 394
American Fur Company, 61, 65, 66, 353, 368
American Livestock Association, 100
Ames, Oakes and Oliver, 85, 232
Ames Monument, 85, 205, 232
Andrews, C. F., Ranch, 388
Animals of State, 27-38
Annenberg Estate, 373
Antelope, 335
Arapahoe (trading post), 391

Arapaho Indians
  History and legends, 55-7; legal status, 78; moved to reservation, 70; 309, 310, 311
Archeological Field Laboratory, 305
ARCHEOLOGY AND INDIANS, 49-57
  Aboriginal quarries, 49; artifacts in Wind River District, 51; camp-sites, 50; expeditions for exploration, 49; game blinds, 51; the great arrow, 335; history of the Arapaho, 55-7; history of the Shoshone, 53-5, 57; Medicine wheel, 51, 52, 335, 380, 381; picture writing, 50; pottery, 51; prehistoric campsites, 262; prehistoric caves, 306; Spanish Diggings, 295, 325
Archer, 106
Archer Field Station, 230
ARCHITECTURE, 161-70
Area of State
  Land, 11; water, 11
Arlington, 234
ART, 155-60
Art shops, 157
Artists, 157
Artists Colony, 158
Armenta, Manuel, 326
Arminto, 326
Arnold, Olga (Moore), 196
Arvada, 362
Asbestos rock, 91
Ash Hollow (Neb.), 68
Ashley, James M., 72
Ashley, William H., General, 62, 63, 247, 248, 262, 264, 315, 321, 343, 367, 371
Ashley National Forest, 46
Astor, John Jacob, 61

Atlantic City, 91, 319
Auburn, 396
Averill, Jim, 386
Ayer's Natural Bridge, 16, 282; Park, 282

Badger, 285
Baggs, 242
Baggs, Maggie and George, 242
Bailey, W. F., Story of the First Transcontinental Railroad, 188
Bailey Bar, 392
Bairoil, 317
Baker, Jim, 5, 66, 165, 192, 260
Bamforth Lake, 255
Banner, 270
Bannock Indians, 70
Barber, A. W., Dr., 286
Barlow, Merris Clark (Bill), 284
Barrel Springs Station, 243
Barrett Ridge Winter Sports Area, 257
Basin, 333
Basin City Herald, 334
Bates, Captain Alfred, 327
Battle, site of, 91, 258
Battle Mountain State Game Preserve, 260
Beadle, J. H., 239
Bear City (Beartown), 84
Beaver Creek, 221
Beck, George T., 336
Beckton Junction, 378
Beckwourth, Jim, 62, 66, 291, 292, 308, 343, 368
Bedford, 396
Bedlam, at Ft. Laramie, 162, 299
Belden, Charles J., 159, 335
Benton, site of, 84, 239, 240
Bentonite clays, 45, 91, 236
Bentonite mill, 359
Bessemer Bend, 62, 384
Beulah, 373
BIBLIOGRAPHY, 449-58
Big Game country, 5
Big Game hunting, 117, 118, 245, 270
Big Hollow, 255
Big Horn (village), 211, 269
Big Horn Academy, 113
Big Horn Basin, 14; first resident, 60; 62, 96, 327, 329, 330, 335, 340, 342, 365, 366, 380
Big Horn Cannery, 340

Big Horn Co-operative Marketing Assoc., 382
Big Horn County, 333, 334
Big Horn Mining Association, 329
Big Horn National Forest, 46
Big Horn Range (see Natural Setting), 11, 12, 24, 27, 59, 60
Big Horn Spring, 331
Big Muddy Oil Field, 281
Big Piney, 368, 369, 398
Big Piney Road, 395
Big Sandy, 371
Big Sandy Pony Express Station, 349
Bill Barlow's Budget, 284
Billings (Mont.), 339, 341
Billy Creek Oil Field, 276
Birds of State, 28, 29, 30, 31, 35, 36, 37
Birdseye Pass, 327
Birdseye Road, 327
Birdseye Stage Station, 327
Bison, 47
Bitter Creek Country, 243
Black, Daniel, 248
Blackburn, Dunc, and his outlaw confederates, 223
Blackburn Hall, 142
Black Butte, 333
Black Coal, Chief, 391
Black Hills, 5, 25, 67, 70, 82, 86, 139, 144, 189, 217, 218, 219, 220, 221, 222, 294, 357, 359, 373, 379
Black Hills Gold Eagle Refinery, 219
Black Hills National Forest, 46, 71
Black Kettle, Chief, 287
Blair, Archie and Duncan, 245
Blair's Meadows, 252
Blair's Station, 245
Blair's Stockade, 350
Blue Front Theatre, The, 140, 142
Blue Holes, 306
Bonanza, 333
Bondurant, 347
Bonneville, B. L. E., Captain, 64, 92, 127, 162, 284, 321
Boomerang, The, 198, 284
Boone, Daniel, 361
Booth, Harvey, 265
Border Junction, 250, 265, 399
Bosler, 234
Bothwell, 386
Boulder, 348
Boundaries of State, 11

Boxelder Road, 282
Boy Scouts Camp, 282
Boysen Dam, 328
Bozeman, J. M., 69, 329
Bozeman Road, 69, 208, 269
Bozeman Trail, 70, 163, 271, 282, 284, 378
Bradley's Meadow, 224
Branding Iron, 203
Brands, cattle, 285, 377
Brick industry, 92
Bridger, Jim, 5, 62, 63, 64, 65, 66, 117, 263, 264, 272, 343, 349, 368, 371
Bridger's Ferry, 287
Bridger's Pass, 66, 68, 81
Bridger-Young Conference, 349
Bright, William H., 320
Brininstool, E. A., 148
Brokenhorn, John, 235
Brown, Alonzo F., 398
Brown, F. H., Captain, 315
Brown, 'Stuttering,' 223
Brown, 'Tie-Down,' 332
'Brown and Yellow,' song, 154
Bryan, 247
Bryan Flat Ranger Station, 347
Budd, Charles P., 369, 370
Budd, D. B., 369
Buffalo (town), 267, 273, 274, 275, 285, 357, 362
Buffalo Bill, 117, 139, 145, 158, 179, 212, 218, 316, 324, 335, 336, 337, 338, 362
Buffalo Bill Memorial Association, 336
Buffalo hunters, 373
Buffalo ranch, 361
Buford, 232
Buford, John, General, 317
Bull-of-the-woods slide, 347
Bullock, W. G., Colonel, 288
Burgess Ranger Station, 379
Burlington (town), 335
Burlington Railroad, 333
Burnt ranch, 322
Burntfork, 262
Burris, Dutch Charlie, 240
Byron, 381

Cache Creek, 123
Cadiz Draw, 362
Calamity Jane, 5, 139, 208, 218, 317
California Trail, 66, 67, 98, 382

Cambria, 91, 144, 219, 220
Camp Carey, 282
Camp Michigan, 347
Campbell, John A., Governor, 73, 188
Campbell, Malcolm, 283
Campbell, Robert, 62, 63, 65, 298
Campbell County, 107, 360
Canary, Martha (Calamity Jane), 208, 218, 317
Canneries, 95
Canyon Springs Station Robbery, 218
Capitol, 191, 192
Captain Bates Battle Ground, 327
Carbon (town site), 238, 240
Carbon County, 91, 92, 176, 240, 384
Cardinal's Chair, 224
Carey, Joseph M., 100, 141, 167, 175, 193, 282, 289, 383
Carey, Robert D., 100, 193, 282
Carey Act, 42, 43, 73, 105, 106
Caribou National Forest, 46
Carlile, 377
Carlisle, Bill, 233
Carrington, Frances C., 264
Carrington, H. B., Colonel, 270, 271, 272, 277
Carson, Kit, 5, 139, 304, 321, 343
Carter, Charles, 330
Carter, William A., Judge, 71, 109, 263
Carter County, 71, 320
Casement, General J. S., 83
CASPER, 173-82; 4, 70, 158, 274, 279, 280, 281, 283, 326, 327, 382, 384
Casper Boat Club Boathouse, 385
Casper Mountain, 181, 182
Casper prairie, 267
Casper Rod and Gun Club, 326
Casper-Thermopolis stage and freight road, 332
Cassidy, Butch, 123, 236, 242, 278, 314, 397
Castle Gardens, 326, 365
Castle Rock, 246
Cathedral Home, 233
Cathedral School for Boys, 111
Cats, a load to Black Hills, 222
Cattle, 101, 103, 188, 189, 199, 210, 231, 274, 285, 290, 316, 329, 330, 357, 361
Cattle Kate Watson, 386

Caves
Gothic, 221; Springs, 221; Tongue River Canyon, 378
Cement Plant (*see* Laramie), 45
Centennial, 253, 256
Central, Overland, California and Pikes Peak Express Company, 68, 81
Central Pacific Railway, 82
Chambers, William F. (Persimmons Bill), 222, 223
Champion, Nate, 274, 278
Chatham, 332
Cheese manufacturing, 108, 393
CHEYENNE, 183-94; 2, 71, 83, 84, 109, 111, 120, 139, 140, 141, 145, 152, 157, 160, 165, 166, 168, 179, 197, 217, 218, 222, 228, 231, 251, 252, 285, 291
Cheyenne and Black Hills Stage Line, 86, 87, 190, 217, 218, 221, 222, 223, 224, 234, 290, 291, 325, 357
Cheyenne & Northern Railroad, 87
Cheyenne Business College, 113
Cheyenne Club, 160
Cheyenne-Deadwood route, 190, 209, 221, 222
Cheyenne Dramatic Club, 145
Cheyenne Horticultural Field Station, 107
Cheyenne Leader, 83, 110, 185
Cheyenne Little Theatre Players, 145, 146
Cheyenne Opera House, 140
Cheyenne Pass, 251, 253
Cheyenne Plains, 11, 189, 267, 287
Chicago and Northwestern Railway, 75, 87, 177, 287, 313
Chicago, Burlington & Quincy R. R., 75, 177, 179, 207, 212, 219, 221, 251, 268, 287, 294, 326, 339, 359, 375, 381
Chimney Park, 254
Chimney Rock, 16, 318
China Mary, 266
Chinatown, 245, 246
Chinese
Dragon, 246; at Evanston, 266; Joss House, 124; Riot, 97, 245
Chinook, 15
Chittenden, Hiram M., Captain, 387
Chivington, Colonel, 69
Chromite deposits, 91

CHRONOLOGY, 441-8
Chugwater, 290
Chugwater Flats, 227
Chugwater legend, 291
Church, Harrison, 248
Church Buttes, 261
Church of the Transfiguration, 343
Civilian Conservation Corps, 46, 104
Clear Creek Canyon, 363
Clearmont, 362
Clifton, 221, 222
Climate, 15, 16, 268
Coal, 44, 71, 72, 76, 82, 92, 265
Coal Creek Canyon, 219
Coal Creek Trail, 346
Cody (town), 75, 87, 120, 158, 334, 335, 336, 337, 339, 382
Cody, William F. (Buffalo Bill), 117, 139, 145, 158, 179, 212, 218, 316, 324, 335, 336
Cody Transportation Co., 212
Cody-Yellowhand Fight, 324, 337
Coe & Carter, 250
Coffey, Jules E., 295
Cokeville, 250
Cold Spring, 296
Collins, Caspar, Lieutenant, 70, 383, 387
Collins, W. O., Colonel, 69, 237
Collins, W. S., 334
Colorado & Southern Railway, 87, 285, 291, 294
Colorado Line, 229, 242, 260, 292, 302, 315, 318
Colorado State Industrial School, 116
Colorado, Wyoming & Eastern R. R., 86
Colter, John, 60, 304, 329, 337, 342
Colter's Hell, 368
Columbia River, 393
COMMERCE, INDUSTRY AND LABOR, 90-97
Como Bluff, 19, 236
Connor, P. E., General, 69, 70, 272, 277, 308, 377
Connor Battlefield, 214
Connor Battlefield State Park, 377
CONTEMPORARY SCENE, 3-10
Continental Divide, 13, 43, 61, 229, 241, 242, 247, 303, 321, 323, 342, 344
Converse County, 283
Cook, C. W., 68

Copper mining, 92
Copperton (site of), 258, 259
Cora (post office), 348
Cottonwood Lake Resort, 398
Counties
  Albany, 198, 285; Big Horn, 314, 333; Campbell, 107, 357, 359; Carbon, 91, 96, 176, 240, 384; Carter, 71, 320; Converse, 107, 283, 285, 286, 357; Crook, 73, 107, 208, 357, 375; Fremont, 96, 314; Goshen, 226, 227; Hot Springs, 314, 330; Johnson, 73, 96, 208, 267, 273; Lincoln, 398; Natrona, 164, 173, 384; Park, 96, 314, 338; Platte, 289; Sheridan, 73, 96, 211; Sublette, 348; Teton, 96, 345; Uinta, 266; Washakie, 332; Weston, 73, 107, 357
Coutant, C. G., 387
Cowboy
  Customs, 122; expressions (see Glossary), 459-66; songs, 147-51
Cow Country, 189
Cowley, 96, 340
Cox Ranch, 251
Coyote Springs, 238
Crazy Horse, 207, 288, 363
Creeks
  Alum, 221; Antelope, 283; Atlantic, 303; Bailey, 392; Badwater, 327; Bear, 228, 288; Big Hermit, 320; Billy, 276; Bitter, 243, 245, 246; Bluegrass, 290; Boxelder, 285; Buffalo, 278; Bull, 275, 307; Canyon, 364; Chugwater, 288, 290; Clear, 273; Crazy Woman, 276; Crow, 251; Deer, 277, 281, 282; Dinwoody, 306; Donkey, 360; Dry Donkey, 360; Fish, 398; Fontenelle, 369; Goose, 363, 378; Granite, 347; Haggarty, 259; Horse, 228, 305, 367, 368, 386; Horse Thief, 244; Indian, 221; Inyan Kara, 374; Iron, 359; Killpecker, 350; Kirby, 332; La Barge, 371; Lance, 224; Little Bear, 288; Little Cottonwood, 288; Little Goose, 269; Little Horse, 228; Little Muddy, 372; Little Piney, 272; Little Thunder, 361;

Lodgepole, 228, 253; Medicine Lodge, 333; Middle Bear, 288; Middle Crow, 252; Middle Fork of Crazy Woman, 276; Monument, 385; Mosquito, 343; Muddy, 242, 316, 363; North Fork of Crazy Woman, 275; No Wood, 333, 365; Old Woman, 222; Owl, 330; Pacific, 303; Paintrock, 333; Piney, 270, 370; Plum, 359; Poison Spider, 384; Rawhide, 224, 322; Rock, 234, 235, 322; Rocky Ford, 374; Rush, 335, 387; Sage, 307; Salt, 220, 358, 398; Sand, 373; Slate, 371; Smoking, 396; Soldier, 317; Spider, 327; Spring, 335; Squaw, 363; Stockade Beaver, 218, 357, 358; Stump, 396; Sundance, 374; T A, 276; Teapot, 280; Tensleep, 364; Twin, 315; Van Tassell, 324; Warm Springs, 305; Whoopup, 222; Willow, 264, 379; Wolf, 378; Woods, 254
Creighton, Edward, 68
Creighton's Telegraph line, 320, 321
Crook, General, 71, 312, 363
Crook County, 73, 102, 107, 144, 208, 375
Crosby, 332
Crow Creek Canyon, 397, 398
Crow Creek Hill, 232
Crowheart (post office), 306
Crowheart Butte, 306
Cumberland Flats, 372
Cummins, John, 254
Cummins City (site of), 91, 254
Curran, F. R., 358
Currie, Flat Nose George, 236, 278
Custard, Amos J., Sergeant, 383, 384
Custard's Fight, 383
Custer, George A., General, 71, 218
Custer Battlefield route, 372
Custer Wolf, 357
Custer's Camp, 374
Customs, in State, 123, 124
Cutler Pass, 379
C Y Ranch, 282, 383

Dad (post office), 241
Daggett, Tom, 334
Dairying, 96, 108
Dairy products, manufacture of, 76

Dakota Legislature, 71, 186, 198
Dakota Territory, 72
Dale Creek Bridge, 231
Dams
    Alcova, 384, 385; Diversion, 390;
    Jackson Lake, 342; Pathfinder,
    386; Seminoe, 77, 385; Sho-
    shone, 338; Sibley, 379
Dana, 238
Daniel, 368
Daniel, T. P., 368
Day, John, 393, 394
David, Robert, 286
Dayton, 211, 378
Dead Man's Gulch, 300, 301
Deadwood (S. Dak.), 129, 218, 222,
    290
Deadwood Dick, 218
Deaver, 339, 340, 341
Deer Creek Station, 68, 70, 105, 277,
    281
Delaware Indians (see Natural Set-
    ting), 11
De Maris Springs, 335, 336, 337
Den of the Forty Liars, 202
Denver Pacific, 84
Derby Dome, 315
De Smet, Pierre Jean, Father, 66,
    208, 273, 369, 386, 387
Devil's Gate, 16, 316, 387, 388
Devil's Kitchen, 326
Devil's Playground, 16
Devil's Tower, 12, 16, 77, 359, 375,
    376
Diamond G Ranch, 304
Diamond hoax, 243
Diamond Ranch, 234
Diamondville, 248, 249
Dillon, 258, 259
Dillon, Millica, 259
Dillon Doublejack, 259
Dinosaurs, 19
Dinwoody Area, 305
Dinwoody Caves, 306
Dixon, 260
Doane-Rambler, 258, 259
Dodge, Grenville M., General, 82, 83,
    185, 193, 231
Dome Lake Recreational Area, 270
Douglas, 283, 284, 285, 286, 287
Douglas, Stephen A., 284
Downey, June Etta, 196

Downey, Sheridan, 203
Downey, Stephen W., Colonel, 112,
    202, 203, 256
Downs, Peter J., 143
Doyle, Billy, 276
Driggs, H. R., 345
Dubois, 305
Dubois, William A., 168
Dude Ranch, Eaton's, 214, 378
Dude Ranching, 77, 96, 118
Dull Knife, 71, 207, 277, 278, 312
Du Noir, 305
Durbin, Mrs. Thomas, 222
Dust Bowl region, 227
Dye, William McE., Major, 283

Eadsville, 91, 182
Eagle Feather, 287
Eagle's Nest Stage Station, 290
Eaton, Alden, 378
Eaton, Howard, 378
Eaton Ranch, 378
Eden, 349
Edgerton, 279
Edison, Thomas A., 259
Edmonds Anti-Polygamy Act, 394
EDUCATION, 109-16
    School lands and funds, 7
Eleventh Ohio Volunteer Cavalry, 69,
    237, 316, 322
Elk Basin Oil Field, 341
Elk feeding, 345, 394
Elk herds, 32
Elk Mountain (town), 237, 238
El Paso, steamboat, 89
Embar Ranch, 330
Emblem Bench, 334
Emerson, Willis George, 258
Emigrant Springs, 371
Emigrant's Laundry Tub, 295
Encampment, 91, 258
Encampment District, 238
Epsom Salt Beds, 237
Equal Suffrage, 6, 7, 72, 77
Ernest, Boney, 326
Ethete, 310, 312
Etna, 395
Eureka Canyon, 294
Evanston, 93, 111, 124, 141, 143, 145,
    265, 266
Evanston Dramatic Club, 145
Evansville, 281

Expeditions
Connor, 69, 70, 272; Custer, 218; De Lacy, 67; Draper, 259; Folsom, Cook & Peterson, 68; Frémont, 67; Harney, 68; Hayden, 68; Kearny, 67; Montana, 373, 374; Powder River, 82; Raynolds, 67, 282, 329; Raynolds-Maynadier, 329; Spanish Diggings, 325; Stansbury, 67, 81, 265; Warren, 67, 374; Washburn & Doane, 68

Fairbanks, 91, 295
Fairview, 397
Faler Guård Station, 347
Falkenburg, Louie, Deputy, 287
Fallen City, The, 379
Farming, 106, 107, 108
Farson, 323, 349
FAUNA (see Natural Setting), 27-38
Game preserves, 47, 48
Federal Art Project, 158
Ferris Field, 317
Ferris-Haggarty mine, 258
Fetterman (town), 283, 285
Fetterman, W. J., Brevet Lieutenant Colonel, 270, 283
Fetterman Country, 285
Fetterman Cut-Off, 290
Fetterman Fight, 214, 270, 272, 315
Fetterman Massacre, 70
Fiddleback Road, 361
Fiery Narrows, 385
Fish Canyon, 301
Fish Hawk Glacier, 338
Fishes, 37-8
Fishing in winter for ling, 307
Fitzpatrick, Thomas (Brokenhand), 61, 62, 63, 64, 321, 343, 367
Five Springs Falls, 381
Fletcher, Chris, 139, 140
Fletcher Family, 235
FLORA (see Natural Setting), 21-7
Flour, milling of, 76, 92
Flying V Ranch, 219
Folk Customs, 207, 390
FOLKLORE AND FOLKWAYS, 122-6
Folk tales, 222, 291
Folsom, David E., 68
Fontenelle, Lucien, 368
Foreigners in cattle business, 268, 269

Forest Dell, 398
Forests
Trees of the State, 24-6; Yellowstone Forest Reserve, 75
Fort Bridger (village), 262
Fort Caspar Park, 383
Fort Francis E. Warren, 193-4, 251
Fort Kearny, South Pass & Honey Lake Route, 314
FORT LARAMIE, 296-9; 293
Fort Laramie (village), 293
FORT LARAMIE NATIONAL MONUMENT, 296-9
Fort Laramie Road, 293
Fort Warren Maneuver Reservation, 251, 252
Forts
(Camp) Augur, 71, 314, 315; (Camp) Brown (Augur), 71, 308, 309, 315, 319, 329; Bernard, 293; Bonneville, 64, 162, 348; Bridger, 65, 66, 67, 68, 70, 71, 80, 90, 93, 105, 109, 162, 261, 263, 264, 308; John Buford, 197, 317; (Camp) Carlin, 188, 297; Carrington, 272; Caspar, 383; Connor, 271, 272, 277; Fetterman, 70, 235, 282, 283, 284, 290, 363; Hall (Idaho), 80; Halleck, 237; John, 65, 298; Laramie, 64, 65, 67, 69, 70, 80, 90, 104, 105, 109, 160, 162, 163, 217, 218, 222, 271, 276, 281, 288, 290, 293, 298, 302, 374; Leavenworth (Kan.), 68; Mackenzie, 214, 269; McGraw, 314; McKinney, 275, 276, 363; Phil Kearny, 214, 270, 271; Platte, 298; Reno, 70, 272, 276, 277, 363; D. A. Russell, 70, 83, 185, 188, 193; Sanders, 70, 83, 188, 197, 205, 317; Scott, 264; C. F. Smith (Mont.), 272; Camp Stambaugh, 71, 308, 319; Fred Steele, 70, 83, 238, 239, 317; Supply, 65, 105, 264; (Camp) Walbach, 253; Francis E. Warren, 70, 185, 193-4, 251; Washakie, 305, 307, 308, 309, 310, 311, 312, 313, 315, 327, 331, 389; William, 65, 298
Fortunatus area, 91, 380
Fossil (town), 249

Fossils
  Beds, 223; Como Bluff, 236; Fish
    Beds, 21, 249; Fossil-bearing
    Ridge, 359; four-toed horse, 21;
    mammalian vertebrates, 20;
    Morrison beds, 374; Polecat
    bench, 382; triceratops, 223
Foxpark, 254, 255
Fraeb, Henry, 64, 260
Franc, Otto, 334
Franco-Wyoming Company, 279
Frannie, 341
Frannie Oil Field, 341
Frapp, Henry (Fraeb), 260
Freedom, 395
Frémont, John C., Lieutenant, 67,
    128, 162, 239, 284, 295, 298, 304,
    321, 384, 386, 387
Fremont Canyon, 348
Fremont County, 314
Fremont, Elkhorn & Missouri Valley
    R. R., 283
Fremont's Cross, 386, 387
Fremont's Island, 384
French Creek (S. Dak.), 218
Frewen, Moreton, 269
Frontier, 371
Frontier Days Celebration, 1, 120,
    184, 185
Frontier Index, 198, 317
Frontier Park (see Cheyenne), 192
Fur farming, 108
Fur Traders, 260, 262
Fur Trading, 60, 62, 63, 64, 66, 90

Gallatin Ranch, 269, 270
Game Sanctuaries, 32
Gammon Percheron Ranch, 275
Gannett, Henry, 304
Gannett Peak, 12
Garland, 341, 381
Gas, 44, 45
Gatchell, Jim, 275
Gebo, 332
Geological Surveys and investigations,
    16
GEOLOGY AND PALEONTOL-
    OGY (see Natural Setting), 16-
    21
German immigrants, 334
German-Russian beet workers, 390
Germania Bench, 334
Gervais, Baptiste, 64

Ghost Light Area, 221
Ghost Towns
  Aderville, 249; Almy, 265; Battle,
    258; Benton, 239; Bessemer,
    384; Bonanza, 333; Bothwell,
    386; Bryan, 247; Cambria, 219,
    220; Carbon, 238; Copperton,
    258, 259; Cumberland, No. 1 and
    No. 2, 372; Cummins, 254; Dil-
    lon, 258, 259; Doane-Rambler,
    258-9; Fairbanks, 295; Fortu-
    natus, 380; Hecla, 252; Iron
    Town, 359; Platinum City, 256;
    Rock Creek, 235; Rudefeha, 258,
    260; Tubb, 358
Gift of the Waters, The, 331
Gillette, 360, 361
Gillette Canyon, 357
Gilmer, 223
Glaciers, 21, 304
Glendo, 287
Glenrock, 281, 282, 285
GLOSSARY, 459-66
'Go Slow, Dogies, Slow,' song, 148
Gold Discoveries
  Bald Mountain, 380; Black Hills,
    217, 218, 373; California, 66, 79;
    Encampment, 91, 256; South
    Pass, 319; in Wyoming, 90, 276
Gollings, E. W., 159
Goose Egg Ranch, 164, 383, 384
Goosewing Ranger Station, 344
Gore, George, Sir, 297
Gosché, trapper, 228
Goshen County, 226, 227
Goshen Hole, 14, 228
Goshen Hole Project, 227
Gothic Cave, 221
Governor's Mansion, 193
Government Trail, 79
Grand Canyon of the Platte, 385
Grand Canyon Road, 345, 392
Grand Teton National Park, 77, 79,
    303, 343, 351-5
Granger, 248
Granite Canyon, 232
Granite Falls, 347
Grant, U. S., General, 317
Grass Creek Oil Field, 332
Grattan, 68, 293
Grazing, 104, 107
Great Arrow, 335
Great Divide Basin, 39, 315, 317

Great Plains, 11
Great Salt Lake Valley, 67
Great Western Sugar Factory, 339
Greeley, Horace, 349
Green River, 62, 64, 65, 127
Green River (city), 84, 246, 261
Green River Basin, 14, 20, 62
Greybull, 332, 334, 339, 380
Grey's River Road, 394, 398
Gros Ventre Basin, 344
Grouard, Frank, 363
Grover, 396
Grover Park, 396
Grovont (post office), 344
Guernsey, 160, 295
Guernsey, C. A., 294, 295
Guernsey Dam, 300, 301
Guernsey Lake Drive, 300
Guernsey Lake Museum, 168
Guernsey Lake Road, 296
Guernsey Park, 300
Guernsey Ranch, 295
Guerrier, William, 295
Guinard, Louis, 383

Haggarty, Ed, 258
Hahn, Mary Bridger, 263
Hall, Robert, 157
Halleck, H. W., Major General, 237
Hamilton, Robert R., 342
Hanging of Jim Averill and Cattle
    Kate, 386
Hanna, 237, 261
Hanna, O. P., 269
Hanover Canal, 332
Happy Jack Road, 231, 233, 251, 252,
    253
Happy Jack Winter Sports Area, 253
Harney, William S., General, 68
Harney National Forest, 46
Harrington, Frank, 326
Harris, Moses, 62
Hartville, 123, 124, 139, 148, 150, 294
'Hartville Rag,' song, 150
Harvard (University) Fossil Beds,
    227
Hat Creek Station, 221, 222, 223
Hatfield Ranch, 364
Hawk Springs, 227
Hayden, F. V., Dr., 16, 158, 159, 282,
    304, 353
Hayford, J. H., 200

Hebard, Grace Raymond, Dr., 128,
    196, 201, 202
Hecla, 252
Hell-on-Wheels (see Cheyenne), 186,
    197
Hell's Half Acre, 326
Henderson Museum, 221
Henry, Andrew, 342
Henry, of Missouri Fur Company, 61
Henry's Fork, rendezvous on, 63
'Heritage,' song, 153
Hesse, F. G. S., 276
Hickok, Wild Bill, 5, 139, 196, 218
Highways, 75, 76
Hiland, 326
Hirsig Ranch, 291
Historic Markers, 160
HISTORY, 58-89
    Air service, establishment of, 76;
        emigration across State, 65;
        emigration over trails, 66, 67;
        expedition, Bonneville's, 64; ex-
        pedition crosses State, Wilson
        Price Hunt's, 61; expedition
        journeys through South Pass and
        crosses State, Robert Stuart's,
        61, 62; explorations, 59, 60, 67,
        68; fur companies, organization
        of, 61; fur trade, decline of, 66;
        fur trading, beginning of, 60;
        highways, development of, 75,
        76; homesteading era, 73, 74;
        Indian troubles, 68, 69, 70, 71;
        Johnson County Cattle War, 74;
        livestock industry, growth of, 72,
        73, 74; mail service established,
        68; militia activities, 77; mining
        communities, development of,
        71; missionaries, 64, 65; Mor-
        mon migration, 66; ownership,
        early, 58; Oregon Trail, begin-
        ning of, 62; pathbreakers, 66;
        population, marked increase in,
        74; railways, extension of, 75,
        81, 82; settlement, first, 66;
        settlers, influx of, 75; sheep on
        the ranges, 74; territorial juris-
        diction, 59; trading post at Fort
        Laramie, first, 65; trading posts,
        63; transportation developments,
        history of, 79-89; transportation
        problems, 74, 75; trappers, first
        rendezvous of, 62; trapping

HISTORY (Cont.)
methods revolutionized, 62; vehicles, first, 63, 64; Yellowstone National Park, discovery of, 60
Hitchcock, Wilbur, 168
Hoback, John, 61, 346
Hoback Canyon, 342, 346, 393
Hockaday, John M., 68, 80
Hockaday-Liggett Stage Line, 287
Hog Ranch Site, 283
Hole-in-the-Wall, 100, 277, 278, 314, 330, 363
Holladay, Ben, 81, 244, 316
Holliday Opera House, 142
Hollingsworth, Happy Jack, 251
Holly Sugar Facory, 214, 226
'Home in the West,' song, 151, 152
Homesteading, 39, 210, 285, 390
Homsley, Mary, Grave of, 297
Honey, 107, 108
Hook, H. M., first mayor of Cheyenne, 185
Horn, Tom, 74, 190, 191, 234, 242
Horse Shoe Creek Station, 68, 287
Horses, 101
Horticulture, 107; Cheyenne Field Station, 194
Hot Springs, 16, 258
Hot Springs County, 330
Hot Springs State Park, 331
Houx, Frank L., Governor, 336
Hoyt, John W., Governor, 112, 113, 319
Hudson, 391
Hudson's Bay Company, 63
Hudson's Ranch, 315
Hugus, J. H., 239
Hunt, Wilson Price, 61, 127, 342, 346, 352, 393, 394
Hunt's Pass, 346
Hunton, John, 5, 152, 285
Hutton Lake Migratory Bird Refuge, 317
Hyatt, Sam W., 333
Hyattville, 333
Hydroelectric power plants, Government-financed, 43, 44
Hynds, Harry P., 157

Idaho Line, 247, 250, 346, 394, 399
Independence (Mo.), 80
Independence Rock, 16, 386
Indian Pow-Wow Cavern, **364**

INDIANS (*see* Archeology and Indians), 52-7
Arapaho, 55-7; art, 155, 156; attacks, 234, 235, 287, 316, 322, 398; Bannock, 314; Bannock and Shoshone, 250, 308; battles, 69, 70, 270, 271, 272, 277, 278, 287, 291, 293, 327, 347, 377, 388; in Big Horn area, 267; ceremonials, 310, 311; Cheyenne, 207, 273; Crow, 207; depredations, 71, 80; near Ft. Laramie, 298; at Ft. Steele, 239; in Popo Agie Valley, 308, 309; lands, 391; legal status, 78; legends, 299, 328; music, 147; peace commission, 186, 298; population, 52; raids, 320; at rendezvous, 63; scares, 211; Second Sioux War, 208; Sheep Eaters, 54; Shoshone, 53-55, 57, 78, 250, 266, 306, 307, 308; Shoshone Reservation, 57; treaties, 70, 298; tribes in State, 52; Utes at Milk River, 239
Industry, 1, 72, 76
INDUSTRY, COMMERCE AND LABOR, 90-97
Ingleside, 231
Inland Air Lines, 88
Inspiration Point, 331
Interstate Canal, 225
Invasion Gulch, 275
Invasion of cattlemen, 274, 275
Irma Hotel, 336
Iron, 45, 92
Iron Town, 359
Irrigation, 39, 42, 43, 73, 75, 105, 106
Irving, Washington, 334
Ivinson Home, 233
Ivinson School, 202
Izaak Walton Club, 383

Jackson, 345
Jackson, David E., 63, 64, 343
Jackson, Teton, 123, 333
Jackson, W. H., 159
Jackson Hole, 5, 14, 24, 32, 62, 67, 102, 123, 148, 149, 151, 303, 341, 342, 343, 345, 346, 347, 392
Jackson Lake Lodge, 303
Jameses, The, 123, 196, 209
Jay Em, 224
Jelm (post office), 254

Jenkins, Perry W., 369
Jenney, Walter P., 217, 357
Jenney's Stockade, 220
Jenny Lake Entrance to Grand Teton National Park, 343, 356
Jenny Lake Station, 353
Jireh College, 113
'Joe Garner's Trail Herd,' 149, 150
Johnson County, 66, 73, 208, 267, 273
Johnson County Cattle War, 74, 274, 275, 286, 324
Johnston, Albert Sidney, Colonel, 281
Johnston's Army, 65, 80
Jones, Grant, 259
Jones, William A., 304
Jordan Mill, 333
Joss House, 124, 125, 266
Julesburg (Colo.), 70, 301, 302
Jungles, 253
Jutz, John, Father, 391

Kane, 381
Kaycee, 276, 277
K C Ranch, 276, 278
Kearny, Stephen W., General, 67
Keeline, 325
Kelly, 344
Kemmerer, 249, 250, 371, 372
Kemmerer, Mahlon S., 249
Kendall, 348
Kendrick, John B., 100, 213, 324
Kendrick Park, 213
Kendrick Project, 75, 385
Keystone, 254
Keystone mines, 91
King, Clarence, 16
King Brothers Sheep Co., 103, 204, 234
Kirby, 332
Kiwanis Spring, 233
Kleiber, Hans, 160, 378
Knight, S. H., Dr., 44
Kutz, Tilford, 250
Kuykendall, Judge, 109

L A K Ranch, 357, 358
La Barge, Joseph, 369, 371
Labor, 96, 97
LABOR, COMMERCE, AND IN-DUSTRY, 90-97
Lakes
    Bailey, 392; Bamforth, 255; Battle, 258; Beck, 335; Boulder,
348; Brooklyn, 257; Brooks, 304; Bull, 43, 306, 307; Cooper, 234; Crystal, 252; De Smet, 66, 272, 273; Dinwoody, 306; Emma Matilda, 303; Fremont, 348; Green River, 348; Guernsey, 43, 123, 300, 301; Halfmoon, 348; Hattie, 254; Jackson, 43, 303, 341, 342, 344; Jenny, 353; Leigh, 353; Marie, 257; Meadow, 363; Mirror, 257; Montana, 373; New-fork, 348; Paintrock, 333; Shoshone, 67, 337; Sibley, 379; Slide, 344; Sudden, 344; Sweetwater, 219; Tensleep, 363; Torrey, 305; Two Ocean, 303
Lamont, 316, 317
Lance Creek Oil Field, 223
Lance Striker, 304
Land Laws, 75
Land offices, 285
Land Utilization Project, 356
Lander, 15, 158, 313, 314, 315, 388, 389, 392
Lander, W. F., Colonel, 314, 322
Lander's Cut-Off, 314, 322, 370, 393, 396, 398
Langrishe, Jack, 218
La Prairie de la Messe, 369
La Ramee (La Ramie), Jacques, 196, 297
LARAMIE, 195-205; 84, 92, 111, 140, 141, 142, 143, 152, 153, 233, 234, 251, 253, 254, 255, 285, 315, 317
Laramie-Centennial-Rambler Stage Line, 255
Laramie, North Park & Western R. R., 253
Laramie Peak District, 236
Laramie Plains, 11, 67, 81, 195, 233, 253, 288, 290, 302, 318
Laramie Republican, 198
Laramie Sentinel, 198, 200
Lathrop's Grave, George, 325
Latter-day Saints, 113
Lead (S. Dak.), 218
Lee Ranger Station, 345
Legends
    Ah-ho-appa or Falling Leaf, 299; of Bull Lake, 306; Crowheart Butte, 306; Devil's Tower, 376; Greybull River, 334; Wind River Canyon, 328

Leigh, Beaver Dick, 353
Leigh's Monument, 364
Leiter, 362
Lewis and Clark Expedition, 60, 313, 337
Library law, 77
Liggett, William, 68, 80
Lightning Creek Battle, 287
Limestone Fossil Beds, 223
Lincoln, Abraham, President, 316
Lincoln County, 398
Lincoln Highway, 76, 229, 247, 302, 341
Lindneux, Robert, 337
Lingle, 226, 293
Lisa, Manuel, 61, 342
LITERATURE, 127-36
Little America, 261
Little Grey's River Wilderness, 394
Little Sandy Crossing, 323
Livestock Industry, 8, 13, 39, 66, 71, 72, 74, 77, 99, 100, 101, 102, 103, 104, 188, 189, 199, 200, 210, 285
Logan, Ernest A., 157
Lonetree Canyon, 227
Lost Mines: Cabin, Dutchman, Shovel, Soldier, 123
Lost Soldier Oil Field, 317
Lost Spring, 325
Loucks, J. D., 209, 211, 214
Lovell, 91, 339, 340
Lower Star Valley, 396
Lucerne, 332
Lusk, 223, 224, 285, 325
Lyman, 262
Lyman area, 248

Mackenzie, 71
Mackenzie, Ranald, General, 277, 278
Mackinnon, Hugh, 152
Magill, Joe, 334
Magnesium Sulphate Deposit, 236
Mahoney Dome, 317
Mail lines of Hockaday and Liggett, 68
Mail routes, 80, 81
Majors, Alexander, 80
Malcolm Campbell, Sheriff, 286
Man-Afraid-of-His-Horses, 207, 271, 272
Mandel, Harry, 209, 214
Manderson, 333
Mannerchor Hall, 142
Mansfield. 222

Manufactures, 96
Manville, 325
Marbleton, 369
Marquardt, William, 142
Marquiss Buffalo Ranch, 361
Martin, Howard, Captain, 388
Martin's Handcart Company, 388
Mason, Jim, 209, 214
Masonic Meeting, 387
Mass, first in State, 66
Mateo, Antonio, 63, 161, 277
Mato Tipi, 376
May, Boone, 223
Maynadier, H. E., Lieutenant, 329
McCall, Jack, 196
McCarthy gang of outlaws, 397
McCoy, Tim, 330
McFadden, 234
McLaughlin, 222
Meat-packing plant, 95
Medicine Bow (town), 235, 237
Medicine Bow National Forest, 46
Medicine Bow Peak Lookout Tower, 257
Medicine Lodge Canyon, 333, 366
Medicine Shows, 144
Medicine Wheel, 51, 52, 335, 380, 381
Meek, Joseph L., 308
Meeker, Ezra, 387
Meeker, Nathan C., Agent, 239
Meeteetse, 335
Menea, Frank, 157
Meriden, 228
Metz family murdered, 222
Mexican beet workers, 225
Mexican Mine (Spanish Diggings), 325
Migratory Bird Refuge, 205, 255
Military training in high schools, 116
Militia districts, 77
Miller, Billy, Sheriff, 287
Minerals, 44-6, 200
Mining, 71, 76, 90, 91
Missionaries, 64, 65, 276, 277, 297, 321, 367, 368
Missouri Buttes, 359, 376
Missouri Fur Company, 61, 342
Molesworth, Tom, 157
Molesworth Shop, 337
Moncreiffe Ranch, 270
Mondell, Frank W., 167, 219, 221
Mondell Park, 331
Moneta, 326

Monolith Portland Cement Plant, 205, 317
Montana Line, 208, 267, 268, 339, 341, 372
Montpelier (Idaho), 397, 399
Moonlight, Thomas, Governor, 211
Moorcroft, 360, 375, 377
Moran, 342
Moran, Thomas, 158
Moriarty, Father, 391
Mormon
  Battalion, 316; Camp Site, 261; Canyon, 105, 282; Colonists in Big Horn Basin, 339, 340; Customs, 340; Ferry, 371; Handcart Company, 322; Trail, 226, 323, 382; Wall, 263
Mormons, 65, 66, 79, 105, 125, 126, 153, 163, 262, 264, 265, 281, 334, 381, 387, 393, 394, 395, 397
Morris, Esther Hobart, 72, 320
Morrison beds, 374
Morrissey Road, 221
Mountain Home, 255
Mountain Meadows Massacre (Utah), 314
Mountains
  Absaroka, 12, 21, 24, 27, 111, 118, 329, 334, 335, 338, 366, 382; Bald, 380; Battle, 260, 347; Bear Lodge, 359, 375; Beartooth, 335; Big Horns, 17, 27, 91, 118, 206, 220, 267, 268, 330, 335, 340, 357, 363, 364, 366, 372, 379, 380; Caribou, 398; Carter, 335, 339; Casper, 91, 181-2, 280, 383, 384; Cedar, 337; Centennial, 233, 255; Copper, 327, 328; Corner, 233, 255; Deer Creek, 280; Elk, 233; Grand Teton, 353; Grey's River Range, 366, 392; Gros Ventre, 12, 14, 24, 344, 347, 348; Haystack, 280; Inyan Kara, 359, 374; Jelm, 233, 254, 317; Laramie, 17, 82, 118, 185, 197, 204, 230, 234, 251, 252, 287; Medicine Bow, 13, 14, 17, 27, 91, 118, 233, 257, 317, 318; Never Summer Range (Colo.), 232; Owen, 353; Owl Creek, 14, 327, 333, 366; Pine Ridge, 359; Pisgah, 219; Pole, 232; Rabbit Ear Peaks (Colo.), 232; Rattlesnake, 13; Salt River Range, 24, 347, 348, 393, 398; Seminoe, 13, 92; Sheep, 233, 255; Shirley, 280; Sierra Madre, 12, 14, 17, 257, 258, 259; Signal, 342; Snake, 347, 392, 398; Snake River Range, 24; Snowy Range, 27; Squaw, 288; Sundance, 359, 375; Teewinot, 353; Teton, 12, 24, 27, 303; Uinta, 247, 248, 372; Warren Peaks, 375; Wind River Range, 12, 13, 17, 24, 27, 90, 127, 304, 305, 306, 307, 313, 314, 318, 321, 325, 327, 329, 348, 366, 391; Wolf (Mont.), 379; Wyoming ranges, 24
Mud Springs Ranch (Neb.), 70
Muddy Gap, 316
Muddy Pass, 363
Muddy Ranger Station, 363
Mule Creek Oil Field, 219, 222
Murphy, John, 71
Murrin, Luke, 188
Museums
  The Casino, 219; Creation at Como Bluff, 236; Cody, 336, 337; Devil's Tower, 375; Ft. Bridger, 263; Fossil, 249; Lester Robinson collection at Guernsey, 295; Guernsey Lake, 168, 301; Hutton's Museum (Green River), 246; Jenney Stockade, 220; Lyman High School, 262; Lusk, 224; Noble Hotel (Lander), 314; Old Pete's Curiosity Shop (Ft. Laramie), 294; Shell, 379; State Historical Department, 191; J. R. Wilson collection (Glendo), 287
MUSIC, 147-54
Musical organizations in State, 152, 153
My Army Life and the Fort Phil Kearney Massacre, 264

Name of State, 11
Names Hill, 371
Narrows, 393, 396
National Forests
  In State, 103; Big Horn, 214, 379, 380, 381; Black Hills, 46, 71, 372, 374; Caribou, 393; Medicine Bow, 205, 232, 252, 254, 255, 256,

National Forests (Cont.)
257, 260, 317; Shoshone, 334, 335, 338; Targhee, 346; Teton, 302, 303, 342, 345, 346, 348; Washakie, 302, 305, 391; Wyoming, 12, 393, 398; Yellowstone Forest Reserve, 75, 338
National Monuments
Devil's Tower, 375, 376; Shoshone Cavern, 337
National Parks
Grand Teton, 351-5; Yellowstone, 399-437
National Wool Growers Association, 365
Natrona County, 91, 164, 384
Natural Bridge, 282
Natural Bridge and Cave, 16
Natural Fort (Colo.), 291
NATURAL RESOURCES (*see* Natural Setting), 38-48
NATURAL SETTING, 11-48
Nebraska Line, 230, 292, 323, 324
Neiber, 332
Nesker, artist, 160
Newcastle, 144, 158, 220, 357, 358
Newcastle News-Letter Journal, 358
New Fork (village), 349
Newspapers
Basin City Herald, 334; *Bill Barlow's Budget,* 284; *Cheyenne Leader,* 83, 110, 185; *Dillon Doublejack,* 259; *Frontier Index,* 198, 317; *Laramie Boomerang,* 198, 284; *Laramie Sentinel,* 198, 200; *Newcastle News-Letter Journal,* 358; *Otto Courier,* 334; *Paintrock Record,* 334; *Pinedale Roundup,* 348; *Republican,* 198; *Sheridan News,* 207, 209; *Sheridan Press,* 207, 209; *Stockade Journal,* 358; *Sweetwater Chief,* 386
Nickel, Willie, 74
Niobrara Plains, 323
Node, 324
North Platte Valley Highway, 292
Nye, Edgar Wilson (Bill), 129, 130, 141, 142, 165, 196, 198, 200, 201, 202, 284

Oasis, 288
Observation Point, 220

Observation Tower, 271
O'Connor, Bishop, 391
Oil development, 76, 95
Oil fields, 94, 276, 278, 279, 281, 315, 317, 332, 334, 341, 359
'Old Cowman's Appeal,' song, 148
Old Man's Face, 246
Old Pine Tree, 232
Olson, Ted, 196
Opal, 248
Oregon emigration, 79
Oregon Short Line, 86, 248, 250
Oregon Trail, 62, 66, 67, 72, 80, 98, 104, 151, 160, 163, 226, 227, 230, 248, 263, 277, 280, 281, 287, 295, 314, 316, 319, 321, 323, 366, 371, 382, 383
Oregon Trail Crossing, 315
Orin, 287
Orin Junction, 287
Osage, 359
Osmond, 398
Osmond, George, 398
Otto, 334
Otto Courier, 334
Outlaws
In Black Hills, 222, 223; in Hole-in-the-Wall, 278; on Kirby Creek, 332
Ouzel Falls, 344
Overland Route, 81, 163, 234, 237, 243, 244, 255
Overland Stage Company, 91, 190
Overland Stage Route, 69, 230, 245, 246, 287, 288, 301, 316
Overland Trail, 196, 234, 255, 257, 317, 321
Owen, William O., 303

Packer, Alfred, 283
Pacific Fur Company, 61
Pacific Springs, 322, 323, 371
Pacific Springs Station, 69
Pahaska Tepee, 338
Painted Rocks, 333
Paintrock Canyon, 333
Paintrock Lakes, 333
Paintrock Record, 334
Palisades, 246
Palmer, H. E., Captain, 273, 274
Panic of 1873, 73
Parco, 238, 239
Park County, 96, 338

Park-to-Park Highway, 76
Parker, George Le Roy (Butch Cassidy), 278, 314
Parker, Samuel, Reverend, 64, 65, 321, 347, 367, 368
Parkerton, 281
Parkman, 268
Parrot, Big Nose George, 123, 209, 240
Pathfinder Canyon, 385
Pathfinder Dam, 75, 225, 386
Pathfinder Reservoir, 385, 386
Peace Commission, 70
Peaks
   Bridger, 259; Cloud, 12, 329, 366; Fanny's, 220; Frank's, 329; Gannett, 12, 304; Laramie, 220, 233, 287, 288, 293, 296, 301; Open Door, 347; Pilot Knob, 233; Ragged Top, 232
Pendray, G. Edward, 196
Pennsylvania Oil and Gas Co., 176
Penney, J. C., 249
Periodic Spring, 397
Pershing, John J. (Black Jack), Captain, 193
Persimmons Bill, 222, 223
Pease County, 208
Peterson, William, 68
Petrified Forest, 16, 237
Petroglyphs, 50, 306, 357
Petroleum, 44, 45, 92, 93, 94, 176-9
Phillips, John (Portugee), 272
Phosphates, 45
Pictographs, 50, 327, 334, 388
Pierre's Hole (Idaho), 342, 346, 368
Pike, George W., 284, 285
Piker Springs, 241
Pilot Butte Power Plant, 390
Pilot Butte Reservoir, 390
Pine Bluffs, 230
Pine Creek Canyon, 348
Pinedale, 348, 368
Pinedale Roundup, 348
'Pitch, You Old Piebally, Pitch,' 148
Pitchfork Ranch, 334, 335
Plaster mills, 92
Platinum City, 256
Platte Bridge, 175, 316
Platte Bridge Station, 68; fight at, 70, 383, 384
Platte County, 92, 289
Platte River Canyon, 295

Platte River Crossing, 261
Plum Canyon, 359
Point of Rocks, 244, 247, 320
Pole Mountain Game Refuge, 251, 252
Polecat Bench, 382
Pony Express, 68, 81, 245, 248, 261, 295, 316, 321, 349
Population of Wyoming, 85
Porter, Frederick H., 168, 169
Portland cement, 92
Portuguese Houses, 63, 90, 161, 277
Potash beds, 91
Powder River, 267, 268, 272, 277, 278, 281, 317, 326
Powder River (village), 326
Powder River Cattle Co., 269
Powder River Pass, 363
Powell, 92, 381, 382
Prairie Store, 218, 219
Prehistoric Camp Site, 262
Price, Tom, 222
Prince Paul, 313
Producers' and Refiners' Corporation, 179
'Promised Land,' 151
Protestant sermon, first in State, 347
Pulpit Rock, 246

Quealy, P. J., 249

Race Horse, Chief, 347
Racial Groups, 6
Rambler, 259
Rambler Mines, 91
Ranch life, 104, 118, 119, 234, 268, 269
Ranchester, 377
Rawhide Buttes, 224, 324
Rawlins, 111, 217, 240, 241, 242, 315, 317
Rawlins, John A., General, 240
Ray, Nick, 274, 278
Raynolds, W. F., Captain, 282
Raynolds-Maynadier Expedition, 329
Reclamation Projects, 43
Recreation, 7, 8
Red Bird Canyon, 357
Red Bird Store, 222
Red Butte, 219
Red Buttes, 16, 316
Red Buttes Fight, 383, 384

Red Cloud, 53, 71, 180, 188, 207, 271, 272, 283, 299, 308
Red Cloud Picnic Area, 301
Red Desert, 39, 243, 250, 315, 317
Red Grade Road, 270
Red Wall Area, 278, 363
Red Walls, 306
Register Cliff, 16, 295
Renaud, E. B., Dr., 156, 262
Rendezvous, 62, 63, 64, 262, 366
Rendezvous Park, 367, 368
Reni, Jules, 301, 302
Reno, Jess L., Major General, 277
Reptile House, 280
Reptiles, 29, 31
Reservoirs, 43, 312
Reshaw, John, 383
Reynolds, Charlie, 218
Reynolds, Joseph T., Colonel, 374
Richards, De Forest, 286
Richeau, John, 383
Richey, Anna, 249
Rifle Pits Divide, 374
Rim, The, 347
Rivers
  Bear, 42, 69, 105, 250, 265, 316; Bear Lodge, 377; Belle Fourche, 11, 12, 13, 357, 360, 374, 375, 377; Big Horn, 13, 42, 67, 75, 87, 329, 331, 333, 381; Big Sandy, 323; Black's Fork, 248, 261, 263, 264; Buffalo Fork, 304; Cheyenne, 12, 222; Colorado, 13; Columbia, 13; Encampment, 258; Green, 13, 42, 62, 64, 66, 95, 246, 247, 248, 261, 308, 317, 323, 371; Greybull, 329, 334; Grey's, 394, 395; Gros Ventre, 344; Ham's Fork, 248, 249, 371; Henry's Fork, 308, 367; Hoback, 24, 61, 347, 368, 392; Horse Creek, 63; Jakey's Fork, 305; Laramie, 13, 65, 95, 105, 195, 196, 197, 226, 234, 254, 287, 289; Laramie's Fork, 64, 65; Little Laramie, 256; Little Popo Agie, 315, 319, 391; Little Snake, 260; Little Wind, 307, 308, 315, 391; North Fork of Greybull, 335; North Fork of Little Laramie, 256; Niobrara, 223; North Fork of Shoshone, 338; North Fork of Snake, 345; North Fork of Wind, 308, 315; North Laramie, 288; North Platte, 13, 42, 65, 109, 196, 222, 226, 238, 239, 257, 267, 281, 287, 292, 297, 384, 385; Medicine Bow, 236, 237; Missouri, 13; Platte, 13, 89, 217, 280, 281, 282, 283, 294, 325; Popo Agie, 313, 315, 391; Powder, 12, 42, 63, 67, 69, 70, 71, 82, 104, 206, 217, 223, 267, 272, 277, 278, 299, 357, 362; Salt, 393, 396; Seeds-ke-dee-agie, 247; Shoshone, 13, 335; Smith's Fork, 250; Snake, 13, 67, 342, 343, 346, 392, 393, 394; South Fork of Powder River, 326; Spanish, 62, 247; Stinking Water (Shoshone), 304, 329; Sweetwater, 13, 62, 67, 321, 386, 387; Thomas Fork of Bear River, 265; Tongue, 42, 273, 378; Wind, 13, 95, 304, 305, 306, 307, 344, 388, 389, 390, 391; Yellowstone, 13, 62, 338
Riverside, 255, 258, 260
Riverton, 158, 389, 390
Riverton Reclamation Project, 307
Robber's Roost, 221, 223
Roberts, John, Reverend, 116, 312, 313
Robertson, John (Uncle Jack Robinson), 161, 263
Robinson, Lewis, 65, 264
Rock Creek (station), 235, 285
Rock Creek Crossing, 234
Rock Ranch Battle, 293
Rock River (town), 234, 235
Rock Spring, 350
Rock Springs, 97, 124, 158, 166, 245, 246, 341, 350
Rocky Mountain Fur Company, 63, 64, 321, 367, 369
Rocky Mountain Herbarium, 22, 204
Rocky Point, 244
Rocky Ridge Station (St. Mary's), 68, 316, 322
Rodeos, 3, 119, 120
Roosevelt, Theodore, President, 376
Root, Helen, Mrs., bill poster, 143
Root's Opera House, 143
Rose, Edward, first resident in Big Horn Basin, 60, 329
Rosebud Agency, 299
Ross, Horatio N., 218

Ross, Nellie Tayloe, Governor, 7
Rozet, 360
Rudefeha, 258, 260
Running Water Stage Station, 224
Rural Electrification Plant, 395
Russell, David A., General, 193
Russell, Majors, and Waddell, 80, 287, 316, 322
Russell, William H., 80
Russian-German beet workers, 225

Sacajawea, guide and interpreter with Lewis and Clark, 60, 312, 313
Sage, 250
Saint John's Parochial School, 110
Saint Joseph's Orphanage, 226
Saint Mary's Cathedral (see Cheyenne), 191
Saint Mary's School, 110
Saint Mary's Stage Station (Rocky Ridge), 322
Saint Matthew's Cathedral, 202
Saint Michael's Mission, 312
Saint Stephen's Mission, 391
Sales Ring, 360
Salt Creek Canyon, 219, 398
Salt Creek field, 76, 93, 94, 176, 177, 267, 278, 279
Salt Lake City, 80
Salt Lake Trail, 80
Salt River Range, 14
Salt works, 396
Sand Creek Area, 117, 205, 318
Sand Creek Massacre in Colorado, 69
Sand Creek Station, 68
Sand Point, 295
Sanders, William P., Brigadier, 317
Saratoga, 255, 258, 260
Saratoga & Encampment R. R., 86
Saratoga and Encampment Valley, 14
Saratoga Hot Springs State Reserve, 258
Sarpy, John B., 298
Saulsbury, 223
School laws, 109, 110, 111, 113, 114, 115
Seal of Wyoming, State, 6; territorial, 77
Seminoe Dam, 77
Sermon, first Protestant, 65
Sessions, Byron, 381
Shannon Field, 93
Shawnee, 325

Sheep, 74, 102, 103, 104, 200, 241, 242, 330
Sheep-cattle feud, 365
Sheep Eater Indians, 54, 413
Sheepherder's Monuments, 236
Sheep Mountain Game Refuge, 205
Shell (village), 379
Shell Canyon, 333, 366, 379
Shell Creek School, 111
SHERIDAN, 206-14; 14, 91, 92, 120, 158, 268, 269, 285, 377, 378
Sheridan, Philip H., General, 209, 317, 363
Sheridan County, 73, 96, 211
Sheridan Inn, 212
Sheridan News, 207, 209
Sheridan Press, 207, 209
Sherman, W. T., General, 317
Sherman Hill, 82, 197, 231, 232, 252
Shirley Basin, 14, 15
Shoshone Canyon, 334, 337, 382
Shoshone Cavern, 337
Shoshone Dam, 338
Shoshone Indians, 53-7; 70, 78, 309, 310, 311, 332
Shoshone Mission Boarding School, 312
Shoshone National Forest, 46
Shoshone National Monument, 16, 337
Shoshone Reclamation Project, 75, 339, 340, 382
Shoshone Reservation, 70, 302, 307, 308, 319, 330, 389, 390, 391
Shoshoni (town), 323, 327, 388
Sibley Dam, 379
Signal Cliff, 365
Signal Hill in Star Valley, 398
Silver Cliff Mines, 224
Silver Crown Hills, 251
Silver Fox farm, 225, 228, 371
Simpson, William L., 305
Sinks, The, 16, 315, 364
Sitting Bull, 71, 217
Slade, Jack, 123, 237, 287, 300, 301, 302
Slade Chimneys, 302
Slade's Canyon, 123, 300, 301
Smoot, 398
Smoot, Reed, Senator, 398
Smith, Charlie, 305
Smith, Jedediah S., 63, 64
Smith, Lot, Captain, 316

Smith, 'Soapy,' 144
Snake River Station, 303
Snowy Range Natural Area, 256
Snowy Range Road, 253
Snowy Range Winter Sports Area, 256
Snyder Basin, 370, 398
Soda deposits, 91
Sodium, 326
Sodium Phosphate Refinery, 281
Soil (*see* Natural Resources), 38-41
Soil conservation, 39, 40, 41
Soil Conservation Service, 357, 361
Soldier Creek, 218
Soldiers' and Sailors' Home, 363
Somber Hill Lookout, 254
Songs
    Cowboy, 148-52; State, 154; University of Wyoming, 154
South Bend Stage Station, 248
South Dakota Line, 357, 373
South Pass, 13, 61, 65, 72, 319, 321, 323, 371
South Pass City, 7, 72, 319, 320
South Pass District, 90, 244
South Pass Mail Road, 315, 318, 319
South Pass Stage Station, 68, 322
Spade, Earl Mark, 157
Spalding, H. H., Reverend, 65, 368
Spanish-American War, 77
Spanish Diggings (*see* Archeology and Indians), 49, 50, 295, 325
Spanish River, 62
Split Rock, 316
SPORTS AND RECREATION, 117-21
Spotted Horse (post office), 362
Spotted Tail, 299
Springcreek Area, 361, 362
Springcreek Co-operative Livestock Assoc., 361
Spring Creek Gulch, 386
Spruce Canyon, 396
Squaw Flat, 394
Squaw Mountain legend, 288
Stagelines of Hockaday and Liggett, 68
Stambaugh, George B., Lieutenant, 319
Standard Oil Refinery, 178, 179, 280
Stansbury, Howard, Captain, 81, 265
Star Valley, 14, 108, 370, 392, 393, 394, 395, 396, 397, 398
Star Valley Creamery, 396

Star Valley Stake, 393, 398
State Department of Public Instruction, 114
State Fair Grounds, 286
State Fish Hatcheries, 305, 318, 348, 364
State Game Checking Station, 379
State Industrial Institute for Boys, 332
State Library, 191
State Prison Farm, 389
State Seal, 6
State Training School, 391, 392
State Tuberculosis Sanitarium, 333
Steamboat Rock, 379
Steele Hot Springs, 348
Stimson, Joseph, 159
Stockade Beaver Creek, 218
Stockade Beaver Recreation Camp, 219
Stockade Journal, 358
Stone Age Fair, 289
Story, 271
String Lake Entrance to Grand Teton National Park, 343
Stuart, Robert, 61, 62, 127, 161, 174, 284, 292, 321, 384, 386, 394
Stump, Emil, 396
Sublette, John, 237
Sublette, Milton, 64, 343
Sublette, William, 61, 62, 63, 64, 65, 298, 343
Sublette County, 348
Sublette Cut-Off, 371
Sublette Grave, Pinckney, 369
Sugar Beets, 76, 91, 92, 225, 226, 339
Summit Tavern, 232, 233
Sumner, E. V., Colonel, 68
Sun, Tom, 326
Sun Dance, 310, 311, 375
Sundance (town), 375
Sunrise (town), 294
Sunrise mines, 92, 294
Superior, 244
Supreme Court Building (*see* Cheyenne), 191
Swan, Alexander H., 290
Swan Company, 290, 291
'Sweden' in Star Valley, 398
Sweetwater Bridge, 68, 315
Sweetwater Chief, 386
Sweetwater County, 71

Sweetwater Land and Improvement Co., 386
Sweetwater mining communities, 85, 247, 264
Sweetwater Station, 387
Swift Creek Canyon, 397
Swiss Cheese Factory, 396
Sword Bearer, 211

T A Ranch, 275
Table Rock Station, 243
Targhee National Forest, 46
Taylor Grazing Area Marker, 349
T E Ranch, 336, 337
Teapot Dome, 12, 94, 279
Teapot Rock, 280
Telegraph line, 68
Telephone Canyon, 233
Ten Eyck, Captain, 270, 272
Tensleep, 357, 364
Tensleep Canyon, 364, 366
Tensleep Meadows, 363
Tensleep Raid, 365
Tent Town, 283, 284
Teton Basin, 346
Teton County, 345
Teton Forest Game Sanctuary, 32
Teton Jackson, 333
Teton National Forest, 46
Teton Pass, 61, 342, 343, 346, 394
Teton Range, 46, 61, 303, 342, 346, 351, 352
Texas Trail, 72, 284, 324, 360
Thatcher, Moses, Apostle, 394, 397
Thayer Junction, 244
Thayne, 395
Thayne, Henry, 395
THEATER, THE, 121, 137-46
Thermopolis, 75, 314, 330
Three Crossings Station, 68, 316
Three Forks, 316, 388
Thornburg, Thomas F., Major, 239
Tie-Down Hill, 332
Tie Plant (Laramie), 205
Tie Siding, 318
Timber, 95
Tin Cup Canyon, 395
Tog-Wo-Tee Pass, 304
Tollgate Rock, 246
Tongue River Canyon, 378, 379
Tongue River Road, 378
Torrington, 92, 158, 226, 227, 292, 324, 384

Torrington Rifle Club, 293
TOURS in State, 217-399
Towle, Frank, 223
Townsend, John K., 386
Trading posts, 63
Treaties
    Fort Bridger, 70; Ft. Laramie, 71
Trail End, 213
Trails, 79, 80, 192, 196, 226, 261, 280
Train robbery at Wilcox, 235
TRANSPORTATION, 75, 79-89
Trapshooting, 121
Trees for shelter belts, 228, 229
Triangle F Ranch, 347
Tubb Town, 358
Tubbs, De Loss, 358
Tulsa, 371
Turkey raising, 107
Tunnel Hill, 270
Turnerville, 396
12th Nite Dramatic Club, 145, 146
Twenty-Eight Ranch, The, 276
Twin Springs, 288
Twiss, Thomas, Major, 281, 282
Two Oceans Pass, 303

Ucross, 360, 362, 377
Uinta County, 266
'Undeveloped West,' 239
Union Pacific Coal Co., 92
Union Pacific Railway, 65, 67, 71, 73, 81, 82, 83, 84, 85, 86, 88, 109, 111, 115, 124, 159, 189, 190, 197, 231, 232, 234, 235, 237, 238, 244, 246, 247, 248, 252, 257, 258, 264, 265, 272, 317, 318, 319, 321
Union Pass, 342
United Air Lines, 88, 255
U. S. Bureau of Biological Survey, 104, 255, 345, 357
U. S. Bureau of Reclamation, 42, 43, 44; Projects: Alcova-Casper, 12, Kendrick, 385, Riverton, 307, 390, Shoshone, 339
U. S. Forest Service Nursery, 233
U. S. Geological Survey, 158
U. S. Horticultural Field Station (Cheyenne), 194
U. S. Petroleum Reserve No. 3, 279
U. S. Soil Conservation Service, 227
University of Missouri Geological Camp, 315

University of Wyoming, 3, 22, 75, 103, 113, 120, 145, 153, 154, 158, 195, 196, 202, 203, 204, 205, 256
University of Wyoming Experiment Stations, 254, 349
  Afton, 396; Archer, 230; Gillette, 360; Lander, 315; Lyman, 262; Torrington, 292, 293
Unthank Grave, A. H., 282
Upper Crossing Station, 68
Upper Platte Agency, 281
Upper Platte Valley, 14, 25
Upper Star Valley, 396, 397, 398
Upton, 359, 375
Utah Line, 265, 266, 372
Uva, 288

Valleys
  Bear River, 15, 250, 265; Bedford, 396; Boxelder, 282; Buffalo, 273; Centennial, 255; Clear Creek, 362; East Fork, 349; Eden, 15; Floral, 374; Goose Creek, 378; Green River, 304, 366; Lander, 107, 305; Little Goose, 269; Little Popo Agie, 319; Little Snake, 242, 260; Little Wind River, 307; North Platte, 75, 107, 285, 301, 323; Owl Creek, 330; Piney Creek, 377; Platte, 67; Popo Agie, 308, 313, 314, 391; Prairie Dog, 377; Push Root, 391; Redwater, 375; Salt Lake, 79, 246, 263, 264, 282, 308, 349; Saratoga-Encampment, 238, 257, 260; Sheridan, 14, 107, 206, 207, 208, 267, 268, 269, 271, 379; Shoshone, 338; Snake River, 15; Star, 108, 314, 370, 392; Sweetwater, 71, 319, 322, 388; Tensleep, 363, 365; Tongue River, 377, 379; Upper Green River, 162; Wind River, 15, 70
Valley Ranch, 337
Valley School for Boys, 111
Van Horn, J. J., Colonel, 275, 276
Van Tassell (village), 324
Van Tassell, R. S., 324
Van Tassell Ranch, 324
Vasquez, Louis, 65, 263, 264
Vaux, Richard, Reverend, 109
V Bar V Ranch, 347

Vedauwoo Glen, 16, 145, 205, 232, 252
Verendrye's Expedition, 59, 60
Veterans Administration Facilities, 214, 231, 269
Virginia City (Mont.), 269
Virginian, The, 236, 286, 383
Virginian Hotel, The, 236
Vocational education program, 114

Wadsworth, 389
Wagon Box Fight, 70, 271
Walcott, 238, 258
Wallop, Oliver, 269
Waln Monument, 385
Wamsutter, 243
Wapiti Ranger Station, 338
Ward, Seth, 295
Ware's 'Emigrant Guide to California,' 323
Warm Spring, 295
Warner, Matt, 397
Warpath Lookout, 377
Warren, Francis E., Senator, 100, 141, 193
Warren, G. K., Lieutenant, 374
Warren Livestock Co., 228, 291
Wasatch National Forest, 46
Washakie, Charles, 310
Washakie, Chief, 57, 70, 266, 306, 308, 309, 310, 311, 312, 314, 327, 331
Washakie, Dick, 331
Washakie County, 332
Washakie Day, 332
Washakie Fountain, 331
Washakie National Forest, 46
Water (see Natural Resources), 41-4
  Average precipitation, 41, 42; priority of water rights, 42; water entries, 42
Water Carnival, 301
Water Rights, 42, 105
Watson, Ella (Cattle Kate), 386
Wells, 349, 350
Wells Fargo Company, 244
Wergeland, Agnes M., 196, 201
Wessels, H. H., Lieutenant Colonel, 272
Weston County, 73, 107, 163, 356
Wheat, at World's Fair, 105
Wheatland, 91, 92, 289, 290

Wheatland Cut-Off, 290
Wheatland Flats, 289
Whiskey Gap, 316
White, Elijah, 248
White Indian Boy, or Uncle Nick Among the Shoshones, The, 345
White Swede's Story, 294
White's Oil Springs, 93
White Women, first in State, 65
Whitman, Marcus, Dr., 64, 65, 297, 321, 367, 368
Whitman, Narcissa Prentiss, 368, 387
Whitman-Spalding Monument, 322
Whitney, Harry Payne, Mrs., 337
Whoopup Canyon, 357
Wilcox, 235
Wild Life (*see* Natural Resources), 46-8
Williams, Ezekiel, party of trappers, 60
Williams, Lum, Ranch, 333
Willie's Handcart Company, 322
Willow Springs, 383, 384
Willows Stage Station, 332
Wilson (village), 345, 392
Wilson, J. R., 287
Wilson, 'Uncle Nick,' 345
Winchester, 332
Wind River
    Agency, 264; Area, 5, 305, 389, 390; Canyon, 323, 328, 329; Cemetery, 313; Glaciers, 346; Project, 75; Reservation, 235; village, 312; Wilderness, 313
Wind velocity in State, 268
Winter, Charles E., 258
Winter School for Boys, 337
Winter Sports, 119, 253, 256, 257
Winton, 350
Wissler, Susan, Mrs., 378
Wister, Owen, 236, 286, 383, 384
Women
    First white women in State, 322, 368; equal rights of, 320; jury duty of, 198, 200; woman mayor, 378
Wonderview Park, 375
Wood, Thomas McKinley, 157
Wooden Shoe Ranch, 317
Woodruff, Abraham O., 340
Woodruff, J. D., 330
Woodruff, Wilford, 174

Woodruff Seed Packing Plant, 286
Woodruff's Camp, 340
Woods Landing, 254
Woodson, Judge Samuel H., 80
Workmen's Compensation legislation, 96, 97
Worland, 91, 332, 366
World War, 77
Wyo-Dak Coal Mine, 360
Wyoming Academy of Arts, Sciences and Letters, 113
Wyoming Artists Association, 157
Wyoming Central Railway Company, 87
Wyoming Collegiate Institute, 113
Wyoming Cowboy Days, 295
Wyoming-Dakota Boundary Line, 208
Wyoming Eagle, 189
Wyoming Game and Fish Department, 46, 47
Wyoming Girls' Industrial Institute, 214
Wyoming Girls' School, 269
Wyoming Hereford Ranch, 231
Wyoming Improvement Co., 384
Wyoming Industrial Institute, 116
Wyoming Institute, 110
Wyoming Labor Journal, 97
Wyoming National Forest, 46
Wyoming National Guard, 77
WYOMING: Its Natural Setting, 11-48
    Admitted to Union, 6, 72, 77, 86; Name, 11; State song, 154
Wyoming School Journal, 113
'Wyoming,' song, 154
Wyoming State Historical Museum, 156
Wyoming State Penitentiary, 241, 254
Wyoming State Training School, 116
Wyoming *State Tribune-Leader,* 189
Wyoming Stock Growers Association, 99, 100, 189, 190
Wyoming *Stockman-Farmer,* 189
Wyoming Wool Growers Association, 103

Yankton (S. Dak.), 186
Yellow Hand, 324, 337
Yellowstone Forest Reserve, 75, 338
Yellowstone Highway, 76
Yellowstone Kelly, 373

YELLOWSTONE NATIONAL
    PARK, 399-437; 7, 12, 25, 26,
    38, 47, 54, 60, 61, 66, 67, 68, 77,
    79, 87, 115, 168, 302, 323, 334,
    337, 338, 342, 364, 392
Yellowstone Plateau, 21, 24

Yellowstone Timber Land Reserve,
    39
Young, Brigham, 65, 105, 174, 261,
    263, 295, 297, 314, 316, 349, 387,
    388, 393
Zimmerman, John, 223